BY STEPPE, DESERT, AND OCEAN

By Steppe, Desert, and Ocean
The Birth of Eurasia

BARRY CUNLIFFE

OXFORD
UNIVERSITY PRESS

OXFORD
UNIVERSITY PRESS

Great Clarendon Street, Oxford OX2 6DP,
United Kingdom

Oxford University Press is a department of the University of Oxford.
It furthers the University's objective of excellence in research, scholarship,
and education by publishing worldwide. Oxford is a registered trade mark of
Oxford University Press in the UK and in certain other countries

© Barry Cunliffe 2015

The moral rights of the author have been asserted

First Edition published in 2015

Impression: 1

All rights reserved. No part of this publication may be reproduced, stored in a
retrieval system, or transmitted, in any form or by any means, without the prior
permission in writing of Oxford University Press, or as expressly permitted
by law, by licence or under terms agreed with the appropriate reprographics
rights organization. Enquiries concerning reproduction outside the scope of
the above should be sent to the Rights Department, Oxford University Press, at
the address above

You must not circulate this work in any other form
and you must impose this same condition on any acquirer

Published in the United States of America by Oxford University Press
198 Madison Avenue, New York, NY 10016, United States of America

British Library Cataloguing in Publication Data
Data available

Library of Congress Control Number: 2014948240

ISBN 978–0–19–968917–0

Typeset by Sparks—www.sparkspublishing.com
Printed in Great Britain by Bell & Bain Ltd., Glasgow

*For Maggie and Stewart
who taught me about horses*

PREFACE

Many years ago I was expounding at length on some topic to my young son, who sat patiently for a while and then said, 'Yes, dad, but how does it connect?' That one question has been with me ever since. Whatever may capture our imagination—the beauty of a Song bowl, the behaviour of wild horses on the steppe coming down to drink in the evening, the statue of the mathematician al-Khwarizmi in Khiva, or the name of a Viking scratched in runic script on a balustrade in the Hagia Sophia—put them in context, embedded in a web of connectivity, and they become infinitely more fascinating and take on entirely new meanings. History is far more than a series of events and the biographies of big names; it is the subtle interweaving of human actions spread over vast landscapes and through deep time creating a dense fabric, every thread of which has significance. The wonder of it all lies in how interconnected everything is.

This book is an attempt to explore the two big themes, connectivity and mobility, as they developed throughout Eurasia from early prehistory, binding the world into a single system by the fourteenth century AD. It is the story of the energizing relationship between sedentary states, like China, the Near East, and, later, Europe, with the pastoral nomads of the steppe, whose huge homeland spread from Mongolia to Hungary, and with the maritime communities living around the ocean fringes. The steppe, the deserts, and the oceans created the connective tissue through which people, commodities, and ideas flowed.

To cover the whole of Eurasia throughout its formative first ten thousand years is something of a challenge. I am fully aware that every paragraph in this book could easily be expanded to a chapter. The task has been to be rigorously selective, to focus on the dynamics that seem important to the understanding of the narrative rather than to be lured into attractive sidelines. Thus, the impact of climate change is a recurring theme, while Alexander the Great's adventures in Asia are given only brief mention—too brief, I suspect, for some. All I can plead is that selection is a personal matter. I learnt about it early in life. As a very young archaeologist in the 1960s I had to give a lecture on one of my excavations to an august audience in Oxford. It was an unnerving experience. Afterwards my mentor, the doyen of Roman studies Sir Ian Richmond, came up to me. Sensing my discomfort, he put his hand on my shoulder and said, 'That was good . . . (pause) . . . it wasn't so much what you put in as what you left out.' I can only hope that this time I have also got the balance about right.

The narrative relies heavily on archaeological evidence, much of which has only become available since 1990, and upon historical sources. I have used DNA evidence sparingly, not because there is any doubt about its usefulness, but because there is still much to learn about how to use it. Only when much more genetic data has become available and we have come to appreciate its nuances will it become a major contributor to the debate. More surprising to some readers will be the absence of any reference to speculations about language. This omission is deliberate since I want the archaeological and historical sources to stand on their own and not be constrained by circular arguments dominated by linguistic theories as has so often happened. When the archaeological evidence has had time to demonstrate its strengths, then the debate can begin afresh.

I have always been interested in landscape, but writing this book has made me even more aware of the crucial impact of geography on human perception and behaviour. This is one of the reasons why so many maps are included to help us visualize the environments and spaces with which people had to engage. The maps and photographs are an aid, but nothing can replace the experience of being there. I have had many memorable experiences researching this book: crossing the Taklamakan desert in a sandstorm, arriving at Palmyra on the edge of the Syrian desert bowed by the intense loneliness of the place, looking east to the endless sand across which the camel trains brought exotic goods to satiate the Roman desire for luxuries, or riding on a summer afternoon across the Mongolian steppe, the horse scuffing up the heady smell of the herbs, aware only of the peace, calm, and oneness of it all. To be there is to understand. I can only hope that this book will encourage at least some of its readers to explore a few of the places mentioned, the better to appreciate the people whose lives these landscapes have shaped.

Barry Cunliffe
Oxford
October 2014

CONTENTS

1	The Land and the People	1
2	The Domestication of Eurasia, 10,000–5000 BC	35
3	Horses and Copper: The Centrality of the Steppe, 5000–2500 BC	71
4	The Opening of the Eurasian Steppe, 2500–1600 BC	111
5	Nomads and Empires: The First Confrontations, 1600–600 BC	151
6	Learning from Each Other: Interaction along the Interface, 600–250 BC	203
7	The Continent Connected, 250 BC–AD 250	253
8	The Age of Perpetual War, AD 250–650	295
9	The Beginning of a New World Order, AD 650–840	341
10	The Disintegration of Empires, AD 840–1150	381
11	The Steppe Triumphant, AD 1150–1300	415
12	Looking Back, Looking Forwards	451

A Guide to Further Reading	473
Illustration Sources	507
Index	513

I

THE LAND AND THE PEOPLE

This is the story of people and the landscapes in which they lived—the actors and the stage—a story created largely without the benefit of a script and pieced together from fragments of disparate evidence brought to light by a formidable range of specialists. It is a narrative set in Eurasia covering some ten thousand years of human endeavour.

If we begin with the proposition that 'history' is the result of human action constrained and empowered by environment, then it follows that we need to understand something of the human animal and the imperatives hard-wired into the beast's genetics, and we need to comprehend the landscape in all its ever-changing variety.

All living matter is governed by two desires: to feed itself and to reproduce its species. Humans share these desires but are more complex beings, differing from all other species in their intense acquisitiveness. This innate desire to acquire manifests itself in two forms: the passion to take ownership of commodities and the need to gather knowledge and information—to know. It is this inquisitiveness that has, over the millennia, drawn humans to explore every ecological niche on earth and to occupy most of them. It is, arguably, the one instinct that separates us from the rest of the animal kingdom.

To want to know what is 'beyond' is a natural human response. It must have been one of the prime incentives that drove the Lapita people to explore and settle the Pacific islands in the late second millennium BC, travelling across 6,500 kilometres of open ocean. It also lay behind Greek journeys into the Atlantic so vividly brought to mind by the third-century BC Greek writer Eratosthenes, who described how one could, in theory, sail from Iberia along the parallel to reach India. Strabo, who quoted him, reflected that 'Those who have tried to circumnavigate the ocean and then turned back say that the voyage beyond the limit reached was prevented not through opposition or any constraint but through destitution and loneliness, the sea nevertheless permitting further passage' (Strabo, *Geography* 1.1.8).

How many adventurers set out on the journey and how many returned? This sense of the ever-fascinating 'beyond' is brilliantly captured in classical Chinese painting with its successive horizons, each becoming paler with distance, enticing the viewer further into the landscape.

Inquisitiveness leading to travel may satisfy personal curiosity, but in many societies a voyage endowed the adventurer with renown. To return after a long journey with esoteric knowledge or exotic goods set the traveller apart: he held a power that other men did not, and story-telling about distant parts became an art. This was the very stuff of the heroic societies reflected in the works of Homer. When the unknown traveller Telemachus and his entourage arrived at the palace of Nestor, he was accepted, bathed, and fed without question, and only when the rules of hospitality had been observed could Nestor ask: 'Who are you, sirs? From what part have you sailed over the highways of the sea? Is yours a trading venture; or are you cruising the main on chance, like roving pirates who risk their lives to ruin other people?' (*Odyssey* 3.67).

Another incentive to travel was to acquire rare raw materials, the ownership of which gave enhanced status, partly for the inherent qualities of the goods and partly because they came from the world 'beyond'. Mesopotamian societies were passionate about the deep, rich blue of lapis lazuli quarried in the mountains of Afghanistan and the blood-red carnelian from India, while for the Chinese it was the subtle greens of jade from the fringes of the Taklamakan desert and elsewhere that made the stone desirable from the Neolithic period to the present day. Other commodities that feature large in our story include copper, horses, silks, and spices, all of which were rare, difficult to access, and therefore even more desirable. The essence of the matter was brilliantly summed up by the French historian Fernand Braudel when he wrote: 'So we find that our sea was, from the very dawn of its protohistory, a witness to those imbalances productive of change which would set the rhythm of its entire life' (*The Mediterranean in the Ancient World* (1998), 58–9). Braudel was writing specifically about the Mediterranean, but he was reflecting on the fact that resources worldwide are very unevenly distributed and their redistribution sets up pervading rhythms that can reverberate across time. Recognizing these rhythms, usually characterized under the mundane terms 'trade' and 'exchange', is a crucial part of the work of an archaeologist.

Prime Movers

A huge variety of factors drive social and economic development, but two in particular are rightly given prominence by archaeologists: demography and climate change.

All life forms have an innate compulsion to reproduce, and were they to do so unrestrained their populations would grow exponentially. It is only the environment they inhabit that imposes constraint because of its finite holding capacity. The relationship of human communities to the holding capacity of their territory is a highly complex matter and one difficult to approach archaeologically, but certain generalizations can be offered. If the population rises to unsustainable levels, there are various technological and social mechanisms that can be introduced. New methods of food production could be developed. For example, the cultivation of cereals and the domestication of animals could, in ideal circumstances, lead to greater and more assured yields. At a later stage productivity could be increased by intensification, such as by irrigation of the kind introduced in the valleys of the Tigris and Euphrates and the Yangtze. Animals could also be selectively bred to become more efficient meat or milk producers, and new methods of herding, using horses, could open up new pastures.

There are also social mechanisms available to relieve population pressure. Birth rate could be reduced by taboos of various kinds like advancing the age acceptable for marriage or, in extreme cases, requiring the sacrifice of the firstborn. Senilicide—removing the unproductive elderly—is another effective method for lessening the pressure on food resources. So, too, is warfare, which appears to be endemic to most societies and, if kept at a moderate level, can help to redress imbalances caused by a growing population. Equally common is outward migration, which may take many forms. At a modest level it may be little more than the social expectation that young men will move away from the home territory to establish new enclaves beyond. Mechanisms of this kind could account for the speed with which the practice of farming spread through the European peninsula in the sixth and fifth millennia. Similar imperatives lay behind the sending out of colonial expeditions by the Greek and Phoenician city states in the first half of the first millennium BC. Population pressure is said by the Roman author Livy to have been the reason why tens of thousands of Celts moved from a west central European homeland to the Italian peninsula and to the Carpathian basin and beyond in the fifth and fourth centuries BC. Population pressures may well have been one of the causal factors behind the westward advances of many steppe populations, from the Scythians in the eighth to the sixth century BC to the Mongols in the thirteenth century AD. These are issues to which we shall return.

The other 'prime mover' that undoubtedly had a significant effect on human mobility was climatic change. The overall picture is of a gradual improvement of the climate from the end of the Last Glacial Maximum about 13,000 BC until 7000 BC, when the climate began to approximate to what it is today, but there was a final last return of icy conditions in the Younger Dryas phase, 10,800–9600 BC, which rendered many environments, already peopled, difficult for human occupation. Many writers see this as a crucial factor in forcing some communities to experiment with modes of food production, leading to the development of settled farming economies. But even after 7000 BC, when the world climate reached a degree of stability, there were fluctuations of sufficient magnitude to affect the more marginal regions, triggering the need for social and economic readjustments. This is particularly noticeable in the steppe.

While demographic and climatic factors might singly affect social systems causing local readjustments, occurring together they had the potential to exacerbate change on a regional or continental scale. Understanding the narratives of history then requires an understanding of the intricate dynamics between geography, climate, and human agency.

The Land of Eurasia

The stage is vast: Eurasia, the largest of the continents, created over millions of years from the splitting and collision of plates of the earth's crust. These slabs of hardened rock, tens of kilometres thick, float on the viscous mantel of the earth's core and are constantly being moved by convection currents from below. Some of the plates float apart, creating the ocean deeps; others are forced together, pushing up mountain chains. In the beginning there was one land-mass: Pangaea. Later, in the Jurassic period (201–145 million years ago), it broke into two, Laurasia and Gondwanaland, and then fragmented further. Laurasia split into the African plate, the Arabian plate, the Indo-Australian plate, and the Eurasian plate. And it is here that our story begins as these plates moved in relation to each other, their collisions creating the great mountain chain that forms the backbone of the continent from the Pyrenees to the Himalayas. Fragments of the old Tethys Ocean were captured between, eventually to become the Mediterranean, the Black Sea, the Caspian Sea, the Aral Sea, and the Red Sea. It is plate tectonics that have created the predominantly east–west grain of

THE LAND AND THE PEOPLE

1.1 Eurasia. The physical character of the continent showing the area covered in this book

Eurasia—an accident that has given the continent its very special characteristics, facilitating movement along the latitudes.

Eurasia spans the globe from the tropics to the tundra (c.10°–c.70° north) but the vegetational zones, in part conditioned by latitude, are dependent on a number of other factors. Altitude is one, but more important is proximity to, or distance from, the oceans. The oceans—the Atlantic, the Indian Ocean, and the Pacific—have an

THE LAND AND THE PEOPLE

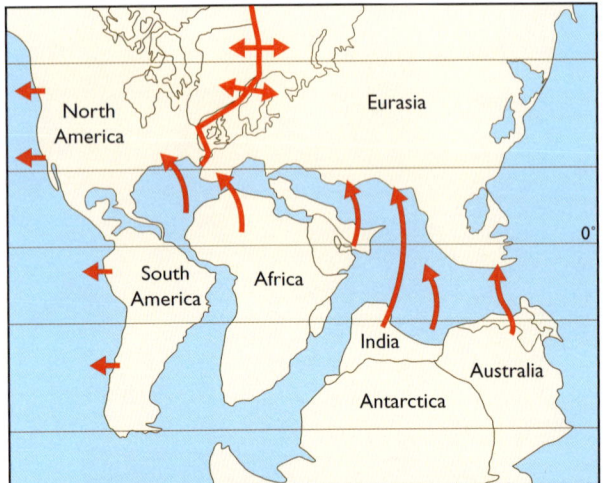

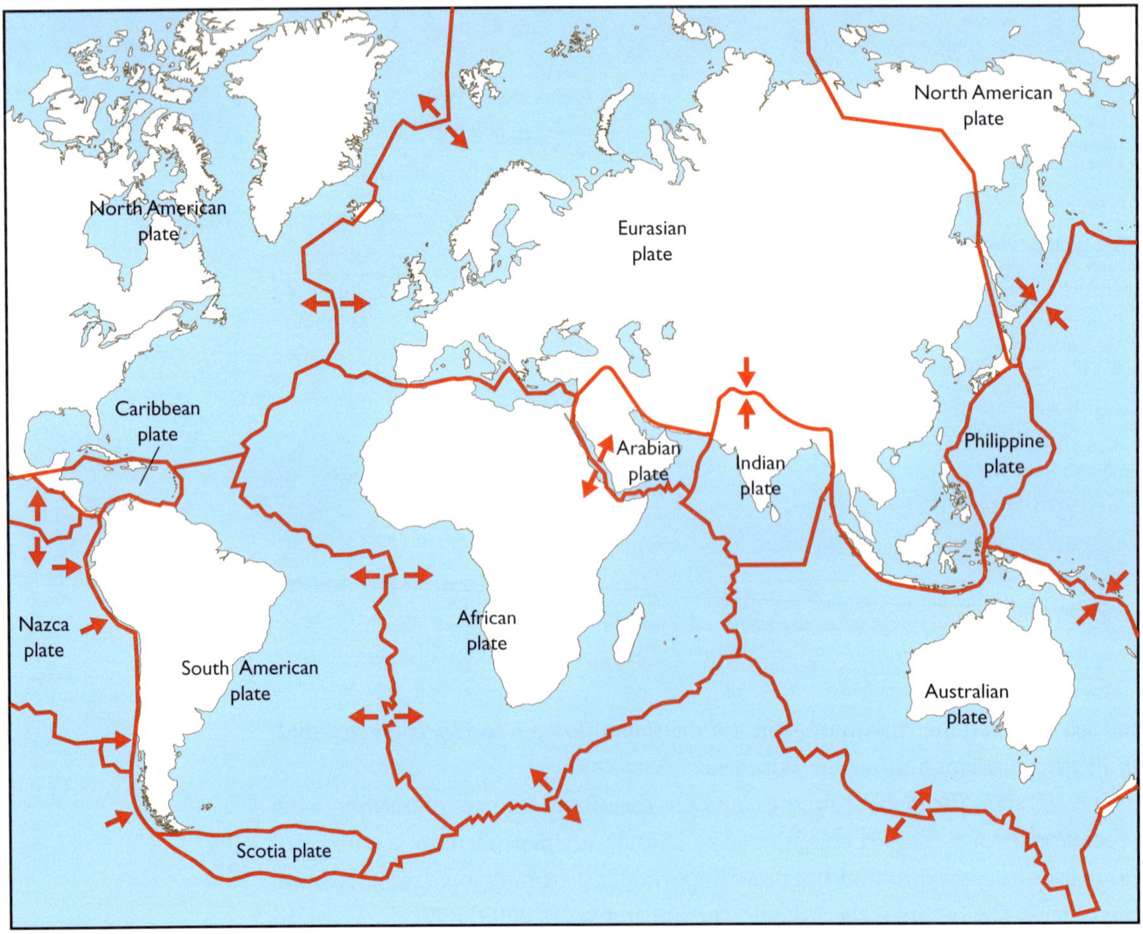

1.2 Plate tectonics. The maps show the movement of the plates of the earth's crust which have given rise to the mountain ranges of Eurasia shown in Figure 1.1. The upper map shows the break-up of the continent of Pangaea at some time in the mid-Cretaceous period, when the North American plate was beginning to move away from Eurasia to create the Atlantic Ocean and the African–Arabian and Indo-Australian plates were beginning to converge on Eurasia. The lower map shows the earth's plates and the direction of movement today

ameliorating effect on climate, moderating extremes of temperature. In Atlantic Europe the temperature range is usually between −5 and +20 °C, while on the same latitude in eastern Central Asia the range can be from −40 to +50 °C. While oceanic climates are congenial to humans, continental climates can be extremely hostile. There are, of course, many other factors that affect human settlement and activity. The valleys of the great rivers tend to provide favourable conditions for humans to settle and to farm, encouraging population growth, leading to the coming together of communities in larger configurations to form towns. The classic examples are the Nile, the Tigris, and the Euphrates, the Amu Darya, the Indus, the Yellow River, and the Yangtze, all of which have nurtured precocious human developments often referred to as civilizations. In contrast there is the steppe, a vast expanse of unmitigated grassland conducive to nomadism in its various forms. As the nineteenth-century German traveller J. G. Kohl so memorably wrote, the steppe is a land 'whose whole law is movement, whose soil abhors deep rooted plants, favouring instead mobile cattle breeding, whose winds carry everything before them far and wide and whose flatness invites everything to cross it in haste'.

In making these broad generalizations we might be verging on the dangerous ground of geographical determinism—anathema to some archaeologists—but the inescapable truth is that different ecological niches encourage different human responses. The landscape both constrains and empowers.

Humanity clings to its geography, but geography is a fickle support. It may be altered by anthropogenic factors like the Soviet-imposed irrigation of cotton fields in Uzbekistan, leading to the catastrophic silting of the Aral Sea. But natural shifts in the climate can also have long-term effects. About 3300–3100 BC, for example, when the climate of Central Asia became significantly colder and drier and steppe grassland expanded, animals had to be moved over greater distances, encouraging a new form of pastoralism identified archaeologically as the Yamnaya culture. Later, between 2500 and 2000 BC, when aridity reached a peak and forest retreated and marshlands dwindled on the steppe fringes, fortified settlements appeared for the first time, reflecting, perhaps, the need for communities to exert firmer control over vital winter forage. In the middle of the ninth century BC a decline in solar activity caused an abrupt climate shift in Central Asia, resulting in increased humidity. This in turn led to an increase in biomass on the steppe, creating a much greater holding capacity, encouraging a more nomadic form of pastoralism. It is probably no coincidence that it was at just this time that we see a sudden development of predatory nomadism across the steppe. Much later another period of abundant rainfall between AD 1211 and 1230, shown in the tree-rings of Siberian pine, may have produced conditions conducive to the sudden advance of the Mongols. In marginal areas where environmental constraints are limiting, even minor changes in climate can have a major effect on human activity. In Mongolia in 2008–9 a period of drought followed by an unusually cruel winter (a *dzud*) killed eight million animals, devastating the livelihood of pastoralists and driving large numbers to abandon the land for the city.

The delicate and complex interrelationship of humans and their environment lies at the very core of history. The remarkable achievements of humanity in Eurasia, in the period from the sixth millennium BC to the thirteenth century AD, may, in significant measure, be the result of the acquisitive (and inquisitive) nature of the human animal—the imperatives hard-wired into our genetics—but to lose sight of the significance of the ever-changing geographical theatre in which the drama took place would be greatly to diminish our ability to understand these crucial millennia of world history.

So it is to the physical character of Eurasia that we must first turn.

The Mountain Skeleton

The backbone of Eurasia was created by the collision of three of the earth's plates, the African, Arabian, and Indo-Australian plates, with the Eurasian plate. Their impacting edges forced up ridges of mountains, but the jostling of the plates was complex, the resulting rucking of the crust giving rise to discrete ranges diverging and converging one with another. In the heart of it all are the Pamir, a great knot of mountains known as 'the roof of the world', rising to heights of 7,500 metres and making up much of the present countries of Tajikistan and Kyrgyzstan. From the Pamir other mountain ranges radiate like the spokes of a wheel. To the south-east are the Karakoram Mountains and the Himalayas, merging with the huge plateau of Tibet, all more than 4,000 metres in height, and gradually dying out in narrow ranges that thrust to the south through southern China into Myanmar (Burma) and Thailand. Running north-east from the Pamir is the Tian Shan range, which, with the detached Altai Mountains of southern Siberia, merge into the uplands of Mongolia. To the west of the Pamir the mountains of Zeravshan push into the deserts of Uzbekistan, while the Hindu Kush extends to the south-west to become the plateau of Iran, continuous with which are the mountains of Anatolia lying beyond, fringed in the north by the high ridges of the Elburz Mountains and the Caucasus. Further to the west still, in peninsular Europe, the ranges continue with the Balkan Mountains and the Carpathians, terminating in the confused contortions of the Alps.

The mountain ranges could be formidable barriers constraining communication, but with determination routes could be found through them when there was need.

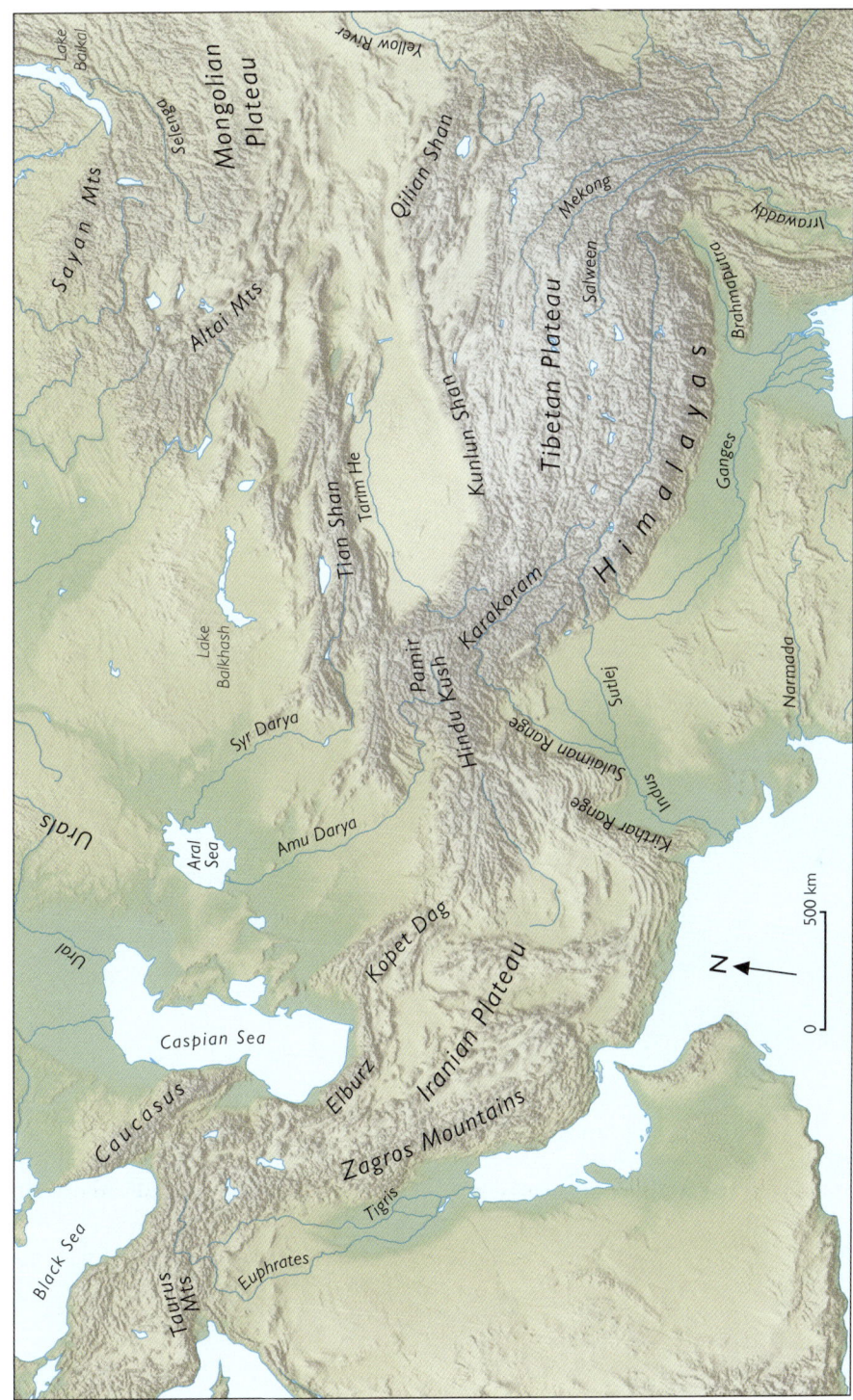

1.3 The mountains of central Eurasia. The Pamir 'knot' lies at the convergence of mountain chains caused by the collision of the earth's plates

THE LAND AND THE PEOPLE

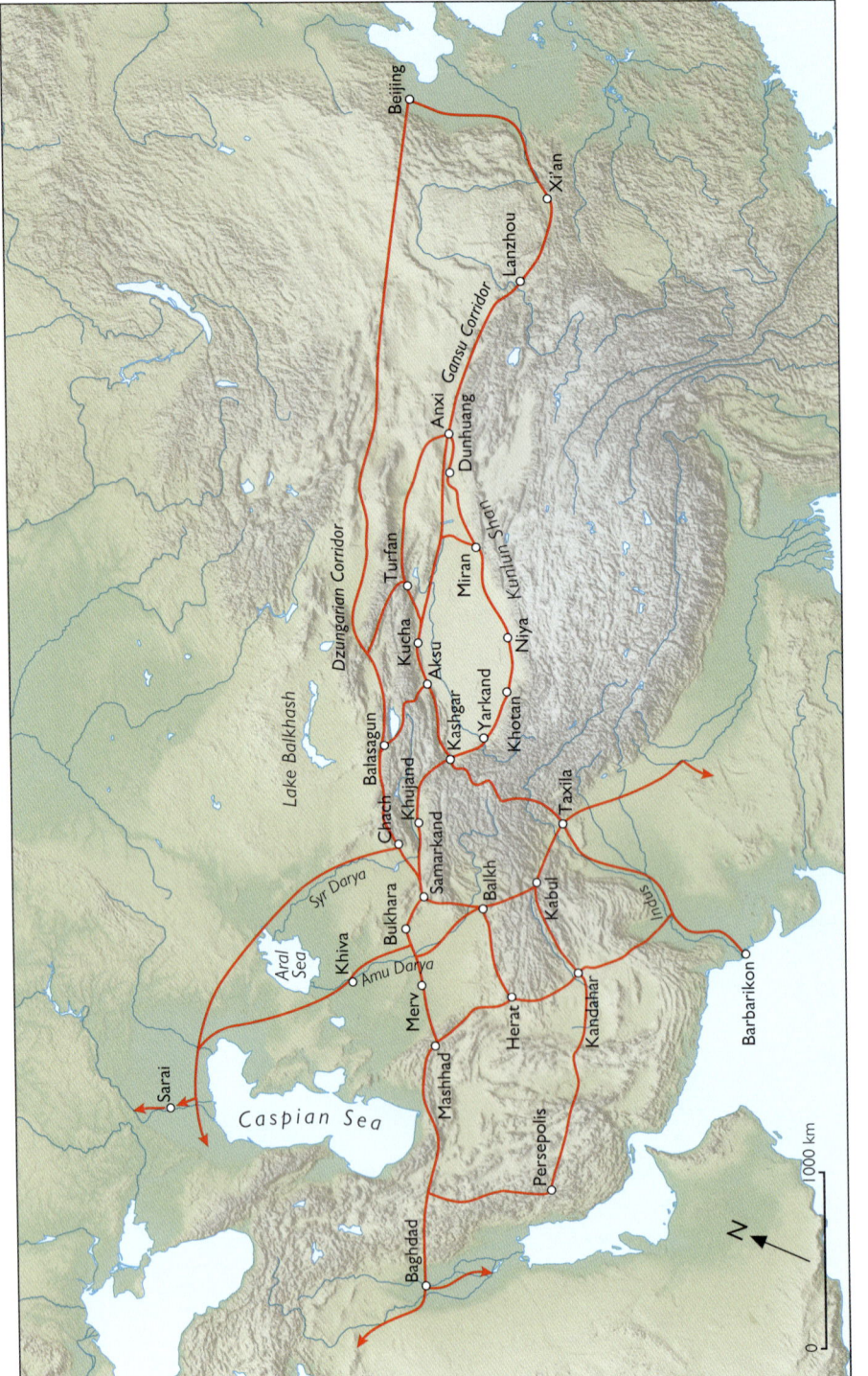

1.4 The principal routes across Central Asia negotiating the mountains and the deserts

The 'silk roads' are the most dramatic demonstration of this, so named by the German geographer Ferdinand von Richthofen in the nineteenth century to describe the network of routes taken by traders carrying goods between China and the west, particularly in the period from the second century BC to the thirteenth century AD. Some of the routes outflanked the mountains of Central Asia, passing along the north side of the Tian Shan. Others, following the edges of the Taklamakan desert, arrived at Kashgar before confronting the formidable Pamir, where the shortest route through the barrier led to the head of the Ferghana valley, thence to Samarkand and beyond. Another, more arduous track snaked through the mountains to Balkh (Bactra), where the desert roads to the west could be picked up. Such were the rewards of trade that men were willing to face the rigours and dangers of the journey. Yet the going was not all bad: passes could be found leading through lush upland pastures. The account of Marco Polo's journey through the Hindu Kush and the Pamir implies that the route was positively idyllic:

> And when he came to this high place he found a plain between two mountains with a lake from which flowed a very fine river. Here is the best pasturage in the world; for a lean beast grows fat here in ten days. Wild game of every sort abounds. There are great quantities of wild sheep of huge size.

The Karakoram Mountains were rather differently viewed by a fifth-century Chinese monk, who describes venomous dragons that spit out poisonous winds and cause snow showers and storms of sand and gravel: 'not one in ten thousand of those who encounter these dangers escapes with his life'. Perhaps not all travellers' tales can be relied upon. While the mountains are usually seen as a barrier through which to pass, Marco Polo's account is a reminder that the valleys and upland pastures offered suitable environments for pastoralists. Those living there may have had quite a different cognitive geography, seeing the great mountain chain, from the Hindu Kush through the Pamir and the Tian Shan to the Altai and Sayan, as an upland corridor providing highland routes across the centre of Asia.

The Steppe Corridor

If the mountain ranges created barriers to easy communication between east and west, the great steppe corridor provided a remarkable uninterrupted route running almost the entire length of Eurasia between latitudes 40° and 55° north. Beginning in the Great Hungarian Plain the steppe extended, unbroken, to Manchuria, a distance of some 9,000 kilometres. The vastness of this ecozone called for rapid movement.

1.5 A Kirghiz caravan crossing the Pamir mountains, here at an altitude of 4,000 metres

This was the land of the horse rider, of the pastoralist tending his flocks and herds, and, later, of the warrior horde.

The steppe may be defined as an open grassland dominated by drought-resistant and frost-tolerant perennial herbaceous species enlivened in the spring by the flowers of bulbous plants. J. G. Kohl gives a vivid impression of a spring journey:

> a mile of mullein and another half of melilot, then an expanse of swaying milkweed, a thousand million nodding heads, then sage and lavender for the duration of an afternoon doze, then tulips as far as the eye can see, a bed of mignonette two miles across, whole valleys of caraway and curled mint, endless hills covered in resurrection plant and six days' journey with nothing but dried up grass.

In many areas, particularly in the west, the grasslands are cut by rivers, usually north–south flowing, creating wooded valleys. The areas of woodland and rich valley pastures were once more extensive, but climatic changes, particularly between the

THE LAND AND THE PEOPLE

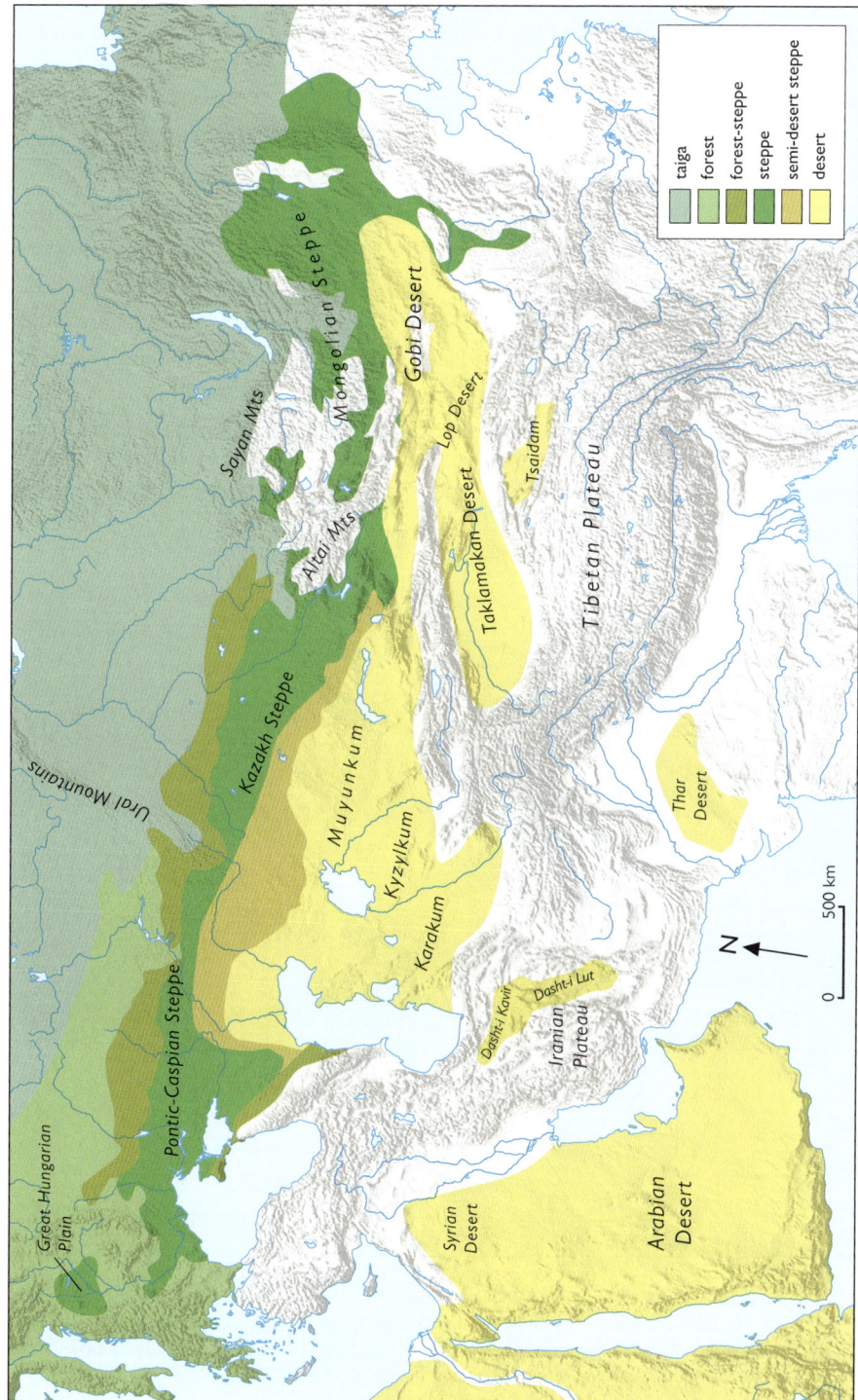

1.6 East–west communication across Eurasia was greatly facilitated by the way in which the principal ecological zones were largely determined by latitude. The desert zone favoured the camel as a means of transport while the steppe zone to the north was dominated by the horse. It was possible to travel between Europe and China by staying within a single ecological zone, crossing occasional mountain ridges

late fourth and later third millennia, introducing cooler and more arid conditions, led to the contraction of woodland and meadows and the expansion of the ubiquitous grassland.

The great swath of steppe may be variously divided, but most simply it falls into two broad zones, the western steppe and the eastern steppe, separated by the confusion of the Altai Mountains, where, for a few hundred kilometres, the grassland corridor becomes fragmented by the mountain ridges. The western steppe consists of one huge region 5,000 kilometres long and from 300 to 1,000 kilometres wide, divided into three by constricting mountains. At its western extremity, within the arc of the Carpathians, lies the Great Hungarian Plain, an isolated area of grassland often the last refuge of nomads migrating from the east. Then, beyond the Iron Gates, where the Danube cuts through the Carpathians, the steppe begins again in the valley of the

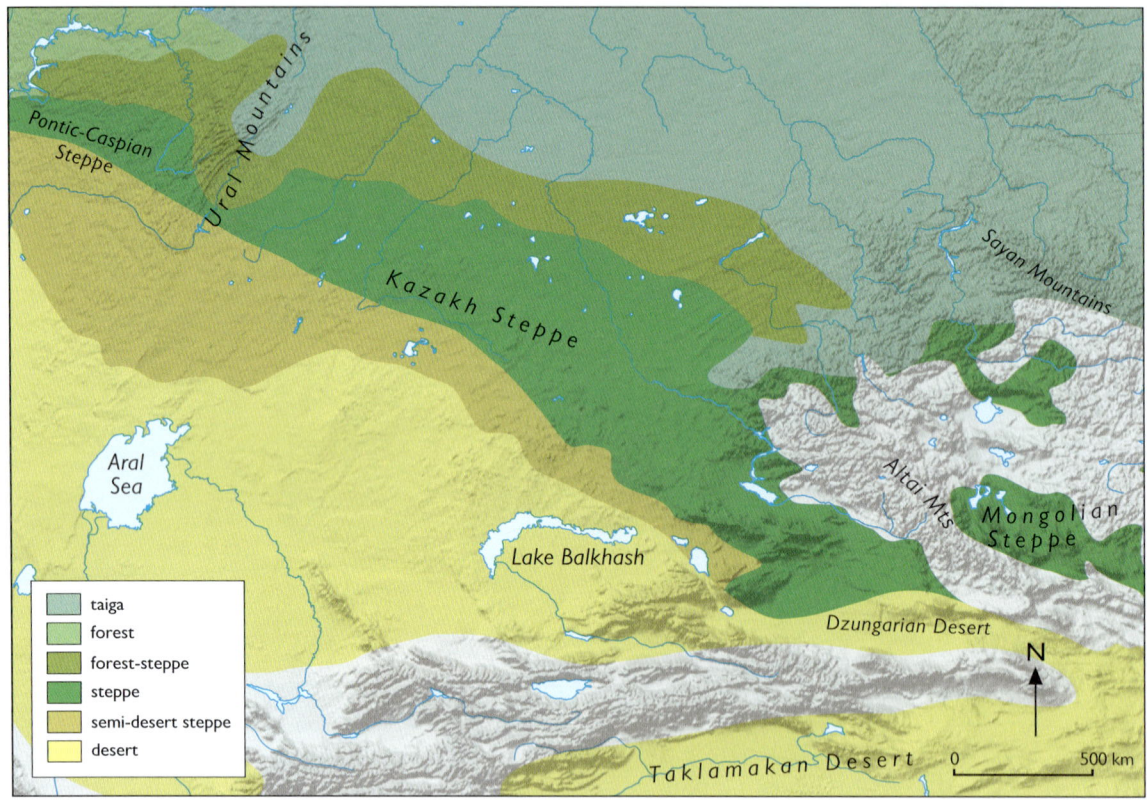

1.7 The steppe corridor of Central Asia ran continuously from the Great Hungarian Plain to China interrupted only by the southern end of the Ural mountain range and the confusion of the Altai-Sayan mountains. Neither constriction would have posed a problem for a horse rider. The entire journey from Europe to China could have been accomplished on horseback within a year

THE LAND AND THE PEOPLE

1.8 The undulating steppe of Mongolia to the east of Ulan Bator. Grassland stretching to the horizon interrupted only by shallow, fast-flowing rivers. A simple open world of blue sky and green grass where the horseman is master

lower Danube and extends eastwards to the Urals, where the southern extremity of the mountain range constricts the corridor. This vast expanse, the Pontic-Caspian steppe, is dissected by great rivers, the Danube, Dniester, Dnieper, Don, and Volga. East of the Urals and as far as the Altai is the Kazakh steppe, a huge region relieved only by the tributaries of the north-flowing river Irtysh.

East of the Altai Mountains the eastern steppe, often called the Mongolian steppe, is higher and fragmented by mountain ranges. It extends eastwards to the Greater Xing'an Mountains with corridors leading southwards to the valley of the Yellow River almost to the doors of Xi'an.

The western and eastern steppe differ in many respects, most notably in climate. The western steppe enjoys a continental climate, with very hot summers and extremely cold winters. Spring lasts from late April to June: autumn is shorter, with snowstorms beginning in October. Oceanic weather coming in from the Atlantic affects the western part of the region, mitigating the extremes of temperature and introducing more rain. As a result the steppe of Hungary, Romania, and Ukraine is richer and more welcoming than areas further east. The eastern steppe is altogether a harsher environment, the colder temperatures and lower rainfall leading to a comparatively poor quality of grassland except where mountain streams bring some relief. This difference in quality of habitat from the demanding east to the lush west—the 'steppe gradient' as it is sometimes called—offers a strong incentive for nomadic peoples to move west. It may well be one of the reasons why there has been a constant flow of population from east to west from the time of the Yamnaya culture in the mid-third millennium BC to the Mongols in the thirteenth century AD. But there were, no doubt, many other factors in play: complex cultural movements over long periods of time are seldom monocausal.

The steppe is an overpowering environment, an endless world without relief where the only response is to keep moving. It cannot have failed to have had a deep impact on those whose lives were spent there. Later writers who have travelled the steppe are almost unanimous in their view that the grassland was, above all, a monotonous place. This is nowhere better explored than in a short story by Anton Chekhov:

> the dew evaporated, the air grew stagnant, and the disillusioned steppe began to wear its jaded July aspect. The grass drooped, everything living was hushed. The sun-baked hills, brownish-green and lilac in the distance, with their quiet shadowy tones, the plain with the misty distance and, arched above them, the sky, which seems terribly deep and transparent in the steppes where there are no woods or high hills, seemed now endless, petrified with dreariness . . . The music of the grass was hushed, the petrels had flown away, the partridges were out of sight, rooks hovered idly over the withered grass; they were all alike and made the steppe even more monotonous.
>
> (The Steppe)

And yet on a spring day the smell of the wormwood and the other herbs, stirred by the hooves of the horse and the shimmering lakes of brightly coloured flowers, lift the spirit. And in the autumn the sudden contrasts between the 'senseless, angry, howling wind' (Chekhov) and the periods of utter silence, broken only by the sound of the migrating cranes, are awe-inspiring. It is not too fanciful to suggest that the peoples of the steppe were emotionally conditioned by their landscape, and it is only in this context that they can be understood.

To the north the western steppe merges through a zone of forest-steppe to the dense coniferous forest beyond. The forest-steppe is an amalgam of small woodlands dominated by oak, ash, linden, and hornbeam, and meadows supporting a varied fauna. Its many resources, not least the ready availability of timber, make it a congenial place for settlement. To the south the steppe proper gives way to a semi-desert-steppe bordering on the open desert. For the eastern steppe the borders are more sharply drawn. To the north the steppe ends on the low slopes of the mountains or quickly gives way to the taiga of larch and pine. To the south, where it is not contained within a fringe of mountains, it confronts the edge of the sandy desert. The steppe could be an unrelenting place and a disaster for those who misjudged it. In the winter of 1839 General Petrovsky set off from Orenburg, in modern Kazakhstan, with a force of five thousand troops, both Russian and Cossack, supported by ten thousand camels on a 1,600-kilometre trek across the steppe and the Kyzylkum desert to capture the oasis town of Khiva. He chose to travel in winter to avoid the intense summer heat, but in the event the exceptional cold of that particular winter proved even worse. After three months in the field he turned back, eventually reaching Orenburg in May. A thousand men and 8,500 camels had died.

Petrovsky had to cross not only steppe but also semi-desert and was wise to include camels, but for those restricted to the steppe the prime means of transport was the horse, whose natural environment this was. The true horse, *Equus caballus*, was found throughout the steppe zone and was probably first domesticated in the Pontic steppe region in the late fifth millennium (see Chapter 5). Its great advantage was that it could forage for itself even when the ground was covered by snow, it was fast where needs be, and it had the endurance to carry a rider for distances of 50 kilometres a day. For pastoralists herding flocks on the open grassland the horse enables a single man to manage much larger flocks over greater distances. It is no exaggeration to suggest that the man–horse partnership has empowered humans, increasing out of all proportion their creative, and destructive, powers.

The Deserts

The band of deserts that run discontinuously across Eurasia, sandwiched between the steppe and the mountain backbone, create frightening barriers, and yet over the millennia ways have been found around and, less often, across them. There are three large desert regions: the Gobi desert south of the Mongolian steppe, the Taklamakan desert in the Tarim basin between the Tibetan plateau and the Tian Shan range, and the desert region of Uzbekistan and Turkmenistan between the Pamir and the Caspian Sea. Beyond the Caspian, to the west, the impact of the rain-laden winds from the Atlantic has been sufficient to prevent desertification in these latitudes.

The deserts differ in character. The Gobi desert, occupying southern Mongolia and northern China, covers a massive area more than 1,600 by 800 kilometres. It is composed largely of sandy gravel with rock outcrops, but sand dunes, sometimes of spectacular size, occur in places. It is one of the harshest places in the world, with summer temperatures rising to +50 °C and winter temperatures falling to below −40 °C. Fierce winds add to the discomfort. In the thirteenth century the Franciscan traveller John of Plano Carpini summed it up by saying, 'not one hundredth part of the

THE LAND AND THE PEOPLE

1.9 The Gobi desert in southern Mongolia. This region is known as the Flaming Cliffs and is famous for its prolific dinosaur fossils

1.10 The constraints of geography are well shown by this satellite photograph taken from above the Gobi desert looking southwest to the Qilian Shan and the Tibetan plateau beyond. The only land route from the Chinese plains to the caravan routes around the Taklamakan desert and beyond was along the narrow Gansu Corridor lying between the Gobi and the mountains

land is fertile, nor can it bear fruit unless it be irrigated with running water'. He was not exaggerating. Several caravan routes crossed the desert. The most favoured way, from Xi'an to the west, was the Gansu Corridor, a narrow zone between the desert edge and the Qilian Mountains, fringing the northern edge of the Tibetan plateau. This was the route dominated by the famous Jade Gate erected in the Han period, at which time it was the most western extremity of the Chinese empire. Once through the gate the traveller made for Dunhuang.

Westwards from Dunhuang lie the Taklamakan and Lop deserts, essentially the western extension of the Gobi desert, lying in the Tarim basin almost enclosed by mountain ranges, the Tian Shan to the north, the Pamir to the west, and the Kunlun Shan to the south, fringing the Tibetan plateau. The temperatures are less extreme than the Gobi, but few would venture to cross it, a fact reflected in the name, which means 'He who goes in does not come out'. There are, however, well-travelled routes around the northern and southern extremities of the desert, hugging the foot of the mountains, where

THE LAND AND THE PEOPLE

1.11 The Tarim Depression, in Xinjiang province in China, is surrounded by mountains on three sides. It is occupied by the Taklamakan desert, a desert of drifting sand-dunes. Between the desert and the mountains is a string of oases watered by streams coming from the mountains. These were settled from the Bronze Age and were used by travellers moving from east to west around the desert

the mountain streams feed a succession of oases. There have been significant variations in the availability of water through time. Much water, not least the river Tarim, coming from the Tian Shan, flows into the depression, but that which doesn't evaporate sinks deep into the ground and the wind, blowing the loose surface sediments, constantly changes the configuration of the land. Oasis settlements along the southern route, known to have been thriving in the fourth century AD, had long been abandoned by the seventh century, when the Chinese monk Xuanzang made a perilous progress, going five days without finding water.

To the west of the Pamir lies a desert of a different kind, extending as far west as the Caspian Sea, lying between the Kopet Dag mountains to the south and the steppe to the north. Two major rivers flow across it from the Pamir, both originally draining into the Aral Sea: the Amu Darya (Oxus) and the Syr Darya (Jaxartes). To the south the region is called the Karakum ('Black Sand') desert; between the rivers lies the Kyzylkum ('Red Sand') desert; and to the north of the Syr Darya is the Muyunkum desert. All three are comparatively level tracts of scrub-covered sand and gravel, barren and unfriendly, but the main river valleys, well watered with lush oases at intervals, were flanked by settlements creating the natural routes from east to west.

1.12 The Amu Darya (or Oxus) flows from the Pamir mountains across the deserts of Uzbekistan towards the Aral Sea. The volume of water has been much reduced in recent times by irrigation systems introduced under Soviet rule to cultivate cotton. Originally the river was substantial and created a fertile swath across the desert

Just as the horse evolved as an animal adapted to the steppe and was domesticated by the steppe dweller as the prime means of locomotion, so, in the deserts of Central Asia, the Bactrian camel became the beast of burden. The wild Bactrian camel (*Camelus ferus*) still survives in the wilder parts of the Gobi and Taklamakan deserts, and was originally found across Central Asia as far as Iran. But it is its domesticated descendant *Camelus bactrianus* that is the now familiar beast. Where and when domestication took place is a matter of debate, but the most likely location is the southern fringes of the Karakum desert in the middle of the third millennium BC.

The Bactrian camel is a magnificent example of biological adaptation, a creature honed to the harsh desert conditions, able to contend with extremes of temperature from −40 to +40 °C. In winter, protected by a thick woolly coat, it can eat snow and live off the fat stored in its two humps, while in the summer it can go without water for months and, when the frequent sandstorms descend, can seal its nostrils with flaps of skin. Its widely splayed and tough-soled feet enable it to cross sandy or rocky deserts with ease. This remarkable, resilient beast has the added advantage of being able to carry loads of up to 250 kilograms over distances of 40–50 kilometres per day.

THE LAND AND THE PEOPLE

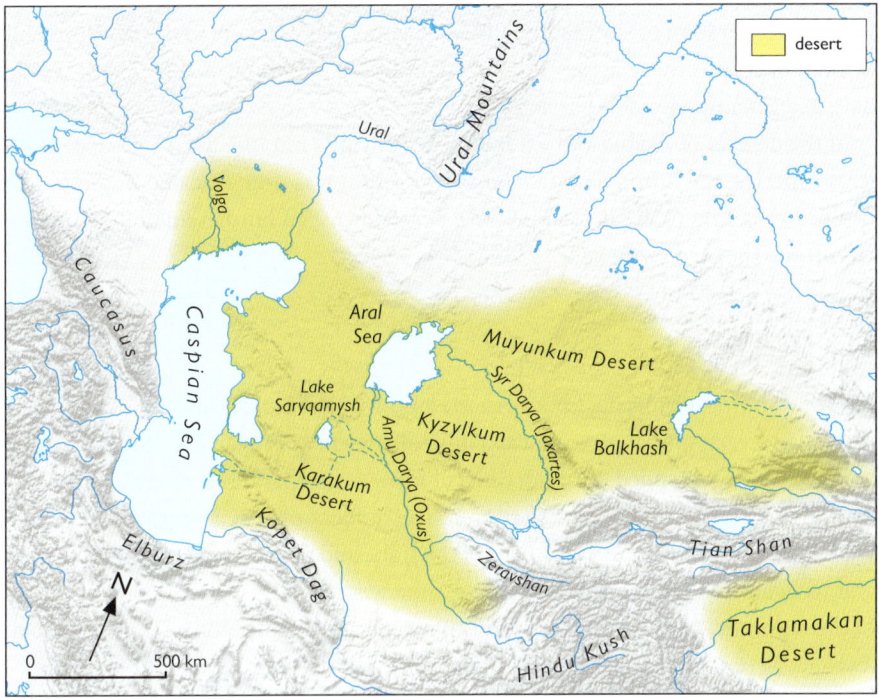

1.13 The deserts of central Asia. All the principal rivers flow from the surrounding mountains into landlocked seas and lakes, where the water evaporates

1.14 Domesticated Bactrian camels ranging free in the Gobi desert in Mongolia. The beasts are very well adapted to the extremes of climate of these regions and can carry heavy loads through harsh environments

It is no exaggeration to say that the Bactrian camel was essential to the development of human connectivity across the Eurasian deserts. Without it the deserts would have been an impenetrable barrier.

In the deserts of Arabia and extending northwards into the Syrian deserts, a different species, the dromedary (*Camelus dromedarius*) was domesticated in the fourth or third millennium BC. It became the essential beast of burden linking the Indian Ocean and the Mediterranean.

The Ocean

The long and varied interface between the land-mass of Eurasia and the ocean to the south was a very special place. It was a liminal zone between land and sea, and those who lived along it tended, through time, to form very separate communities distinct from their inland neighbours. They were the holders of special knowledge, of the winds and tides and of the movement of the stars, and they had skills as boatbuilders and navigators. Even more impressively, they were prepared to challenge the gods of the ocean in their quest for esoteric knowledge and exotic commodities. Coastal dwellers were a people apart.

For most of the time, journeys made on the ocean are likely to have been short-haul, the ship's master working only in the waters of which he had acquired a good cognitive geography; long journeys out of sight of land would have been rare. But the Romans' desire for spices from the east changed all this when, from the first century BC, trading ships set out in increasing numbers from the Red Sea ports to India and beyond.

The one great ocean is made up of a number of interconnected seas, each with its own special character. The Arabian Sea linked the coasts of India, Persia, Arabia, and East Africa and, through the Persian Gulf and the Red Sea, was linked to the Near East and the Mediterranean. The Bay of Bengal was a separate entity, with access, through the Strait of Malacca, to the South China Sea, protected from the Pacific by a chain of islands. Further to the north, beyond the Taiwan Strait, lay the East China Sea and the Yellow Sea, safe inland waters serving the many ports of China.

Each one of these seas developed its own specific range of sea-going vessels. This is particularly well exemplified by the situation in the fourteenth century when the large lateen-rigged boats spearheading the Islamic trade with India and Indonesia met the fast, light sampans and prahus of Malaya, Myanmar (Burma), and the Indonesian islands and the stately lumbering Chinese junks with their sails made of fan-shaped bamboo mats and their enormous size. At the time of the Mongol empire these vessels might be found tied up alongside each other in many an Indonesian port. Behind these three basic shipbuilding traditions lay a bewildering variety of individually named vessel types recorded in historical times. Such variety is likely to be as old as boatbuilding itself.

For the most part, the vessels will have kept to their familiar spheres of operation, but there must also have been more enquiring souls who set out on voyages of discovery. One such was the Chinese admiral Zheng He, who in 1405 sailed from the estuary of the Yangtze with a fleet of sixty-three ocean-going junks carrying twenty-eight thousand men. In a series of seven voyages between 1405 and 1433 he visited the Indonesian islands, India, Hormuz on the Persian Gulf, and Jeddah on the Red Sea, and sailed down the east coast of Africa, his adventures recorded in *Triumphant Visions of the Boundless Ocean*, written by Ma Huan, who travelled with him. It was a remarkable enterprise by any standards, not least in demonstrating the ease with which the ocean could be used to cover huge distances by those daring and skilled enough. Towards the end of his life he reflected on these matters:

> We have travelled more than one hundred thousand miles and have beheld in the ocean huge waves like mountains sky high, and we have set eyes on barbarian regions far away hidden in a blue transparency of light vapours, while our sails, loftily unfurled like clouds day and night, continued on their course as rapidly as a star, traversing those savage waves as if we were treading a public thoroughfare . . .
>
> (Tablet erected at Fujian in 1432)

One of the unifying factors known to all who sailed the Indian Ocean was the predictable cyclic weather pattern determined by zones of high and low pressure, alternating between the Eurasian land-mass and the equator. These generated a weather pattern dominated by the monsoon wind. Between April and August the low pressure over the Himalayas drew in air from the south, creating the south-east trade winds, which, once they had crossed the equator, picked up water to become the south-west monsoons, bringing heavy rains with them. In the second half of the year, between December and March, the high-pressure zone now over Central Asia gave rise to the north-east monsoon as the winds blew towards the equator. This annual, and entirely predictable, pattern would have been well known to sailors far back in time; it controlled the timing and duration of their journeys and gave them some reassurance of a successful voyage and a safe return.

The traditional wisdoms of Indian Ocean navigation, learnt over generations by experience, were eventually codified by a Greek merchant in the first century AD in a sailing guide known as *The Periplus of the Erythrean Sea*, which offered guidance for maritime traders making the journey from the Red Sea ports to India. The compiler

THE LAND AND THE PEOPLE

of the *Periplus* acknowledged his fellow sailor Hippalus as 'the pilot who by observing the location of the ports and the condition of the sea, first discovered how to lay his course straight across the ocean'. But Hippalus will have been just one voice in the transmission of the hard-learned sea lore. Before this crucial knowledge reached the west, trading vessels leaving the Red Sea would take the long coastwise course north-eastwards along the Arabian coast and across the Gulf of Oman to the Indus, and thence down the long west coast of the Indian peninsula. Knowledge of the monsoons meant that a far more direct route could be taken across the open ocean, cutting the travel time and greatly reducing the risk of piracy. By setting out from the Red Sea in July at the time of the south-west monsoons, and keeping the ship's head well off wind, south India could be reached in forty days. Alternatively, if the wind was kept on the quarter, it would have been possible to reach the Indus mouth on a near-direct course.

Intimate knowledge of this kind would have existed for every tract of the sea along the ocean face of Eurasia and would have been passed from one ship's master to

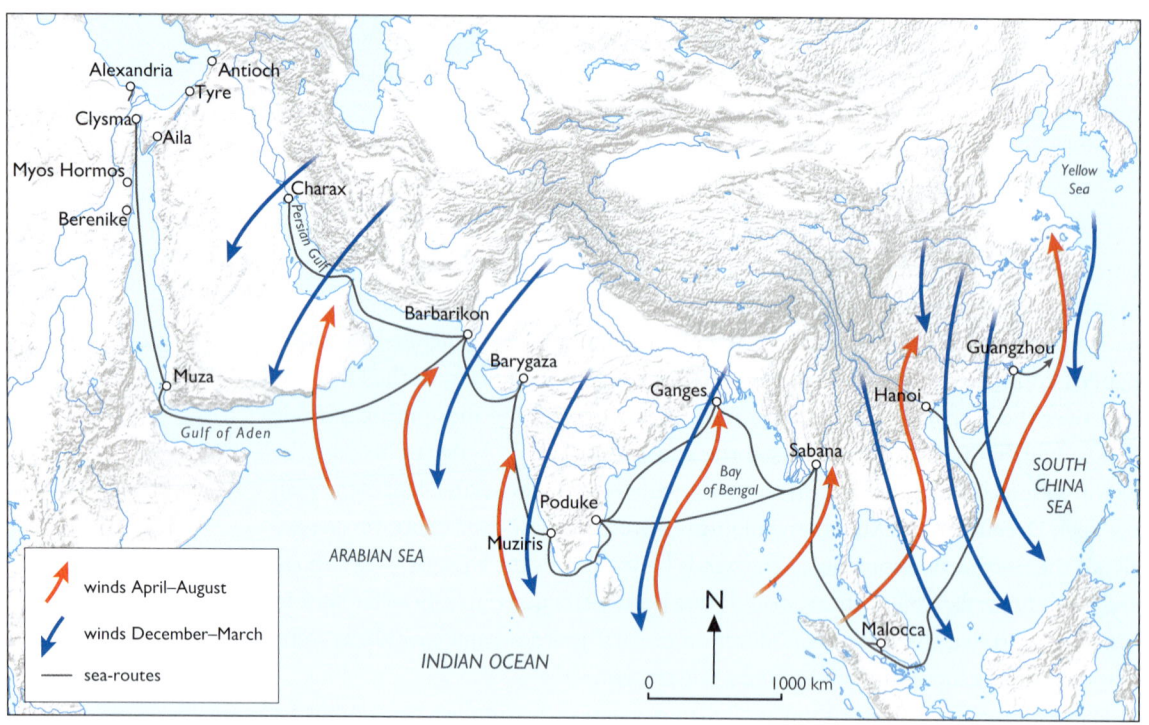

1.15 The Indian Ocean and South China Sea provided maritime routes between the east and the west. The map shows the main ports and the monsoon winds which conditioned sailing times and routes

another in a rich fabric of oral tradition. Just as the horseman on the steppe would have carried in his mind a cognitive map of the endless pastures, and the camel driver of the desert knew the safest routes between the oases, so did the navigator hold in his memory the behaviour of the winds, the crucial sea marks, and the host of other detail so essential to a safe return.

Intensifying Connectivity

The steppe, the deserts, and the ocean in their different ways facilitated movement. Along a network of traditional routes raw materials and ideas could be transmitted over great distances, even though, for much of the time, people probably moved only on limited journeys and in small numbers. There may also have been long periods when some communities lived in comparative isolation. This loose and intermittent connectivity was probably the norm over considerable periods of time, creating an underlying rhythm of being. From time to time that rhythm was disturbed, sometimes by internal, sometimes external, imperatives. The rapid and large-scale movement of Huns and, later, Mongols resulted from internal social pressures, but the demands of external peoples also had their effects. The Chinese passion for jade, the Parthian need for war elephants, and the insatiable Roman demand for luxuries such as spices and silks, all had an impact on the connectivity that linked east and west. With the growth of Europe as a centre of consumption, trade through Eurasia and the Indian Ocean intensified until, from the fifteenth century, we can begin to talk of globalization as Europe, the Islamic world, and China became inextricably bound up in a single network of complex interactions.

Regions of Precocious Development

Within the great mass of the Eurasian continent there are two regions where precocious economic and social development led to the rapid emergence of complex societies, specialized communities that may be regarded as the earliest manifestations of that ambiguous term 'civilization'. One lay in South West Asia, in what is often referred to as the Near East, the other in eastern Asia, in what is now northern China. Why the communities in these two regions should have become increasingly complex, moving rapidly along the trajectory that took them from simple foraging to organized food production and urban living, is, in large part, the result of geography. It was simply that both regions showed great geographical diversity and significant climatic variation over limited distances. This offered a range of different ecologies for exploitation. Here we shall sketch out these physical characteristics, leaving until later a consideration of the remarkable social developments springing from the interaction between these human-friendly ecozones and their inventive inhabitants.

The South West Asian Homeland

South West Asia is a zone enclosed by seas, mountains, and deserts: the Mediterranean, Aegean, Black Sea, Caspian Sea, Persian Gulf, and Red Sea, the mountains of the Caucasus and the Iranian plateau, and the deserts of Syria and Arabia. In simple terms it is a land between the mountain ranges and the desert washed by oceans. But other factors combine to give the region its special character. Most important is its proximity to the Mediterranean, a long corridor serving to draw eastwards the cool, moist air from the Atlantic that ameliorates the climate of the Levantine coast and falls as rain on the arc of mountains running from the Taurus of southern Anatolia to the Zagros on the edge of the Iranian plateau. The surface run-off from the rainfall eventually collects in the two great rivers the Tigris and the Euphrates, which flow through the desert creating the fertile plains of Mesopotamia. The less impressive mountains along the eastern Mediterranean fringe rising to the Jebel Lubnān and Jebel Ash Sharqi of Lebanon and Syria also capture moisture from the Atlantic air stream, channelling it into the rivers Orontes and Jordan, which flow in different directions in a long north–south trench, a continuation of the Rift Valley, created by plate tectonics. These accidents of geography coalesce to produce an unusual juxtaposition of environments sweeping in a tight arc from the head of the Red Sea to the head of the Persian Gulf.

This favoured zone has long been known as the Fertile Crescent, its attractions to human communities lying not only in the comparative fertility of the soil and equable climate but also in the close proximity of many discrete ecozones, each offering a contrasting range of resources and thus different opportunities for exploitation. On the western arm of the arc one could pass from the Mediterranean littoral zone through wooded mountains and valleys to the desert fringe in a trek of merely 150 kilometres, while on the eastern arm it was only 200 kilometres from the crest of the Zagros Mountains down across the hilly flanks to the alluvial plain of the Tigris. The variety of different ecological niches for the human inhabitants to explore was endless.

In the Holocene period, following the last ice age, the fauna and flora of the region began to stabilize. The hilly flanks of the Fertile Crescent became the habitat for a range of wild grasses, among them strains of emmer wheat, einkorn wheat, and barley, while wild sheep and goats spread even more extensively across the

Iranian plateau and much of Anatolia. Wild aurochs, the ancestor of domesticated cattle, were restricted to the Iranian plateau but roamed westwards as far as the Zagros Mountains. Thus, by about 10,000 BC, human foraging groups were sharing a landscape with the plants and animals they were soon to learn to cultivate and domesticate.

There were other advantages too. Obsidian, a black volcanic glass favoured for making sharp-edged tools, was readily available from sources in eastern and central Anatolia and was widely distributed through networks of gift exchange, as were desirable shells from the Mediterranean and the Red Sea. The perennial rivers of Mesopotamia also provided easy routes of communication. These factors conspired to encourage the development of social networks linking the disparate human communities.

This small corner of South West Asia, jammed between the tectonic plates of Eurasia, Africa, and Arabia, was, then, a region of extraordinary variety and potential, and, as we shall see later, was soon to witness the first crucial transition from foraging to settled food production, which set in train a series of spectacular developments.

Broadening the focus, the Fertile Crescent can be seen to be the core to a series of peripheries. The most spectacular is the Nile valley, a long, narrow strip of fertile alluvium winding its way across a vast desert, created and sustained by tropical rainfall falling deep in Africa. Here another accident of nature created a lush environment for human development, but one always constrained by the engulfing desert and therefore limited in its impact.

To the east of the Zagros Mountains extends the upland plateau of Iran, which continues through what is now southern Afghanistan and western Pakistan to end at the Kirthar and Sulaiman mountains, beyond which the land falls dramatically to the Indus valley. This upland plateau can reasonably be regarded as a periphery to the early developments in the Fertile Crescent and Mesopotamia since it was, in the first instance, a recipient of cultural influences from the west. It was soon to develop distinctive cultures of its own and in later times to become the hub of mega-states. The contrast with the Nile valley periphery could not be greater, the one isolated and enclosed by desert, the other open on all sides to cultural stimulation from neighbouring zones, becoming more central as trading connectivity intensified.

To the east of the Iranian plateau lies the Indus valley. The Indus and its major tributaries rise in the Karakoram range and flow southwards into the Arabian Sea across a wide flood-plain delimited on the west by the Kirthar and Sulaiman ranges and on the east by the Thar desert. From an early date the communities of the Indus valley were in contact with those of the Fertile Crescent and Mesopotamia. Overland routes across the Iranian plateau no doubt developed, but the sea passage through the Persian Gulf, the Gulf of Oman, and the Arabian Sea would have been the fastest and safest route. The valley itself also provided a major axis of communication between Central Asia and the Indian subcontinent, the only major obstacle being the Hindu Kush, which had to be negotiated via Balkh, Kabul, and the Khyber Pass. It was by way of the Indus valley that Alexander chose to make his exit following his brief exploration of Central Asia.

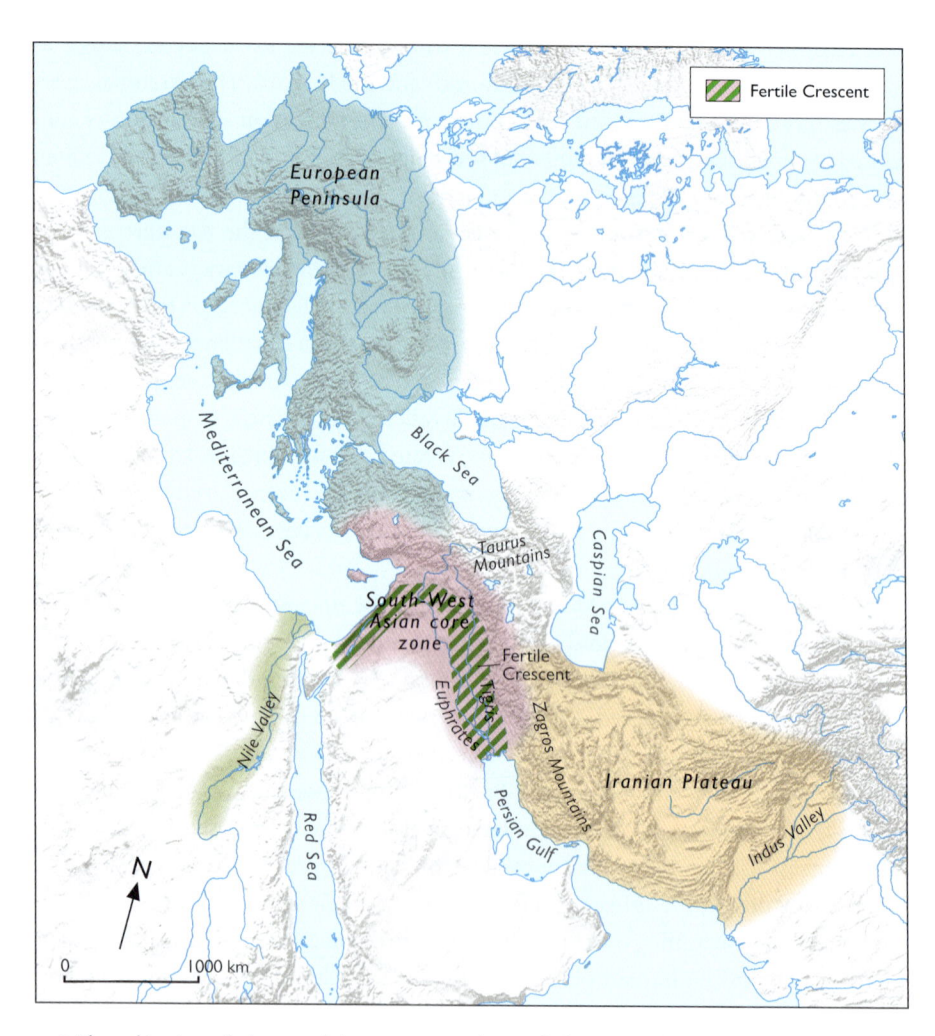

1.16 The cultivation of plants and domestication of animals began in the hilly flanks of the Fertile Crescent in South West Asia and soon expanded to a larger core zone. From here the practice of food production quickly spread into new ecological zones, the Iranian plateau, the Indus valley, the Nile valley, and Europe, becoming well established in these areas by the fifth millennium BC

The final periphery to be considered is Anatolia and peninsular Europe extending westwards to the Atlantic. It is a temperate zone enjoying an Atlantic climate and, but for the higher mountain ranges, it was covered by broad-leafed deciduous forests merging into the coniferous forests of the north and the distinctive Mediterranean flora fringing the sea to the south. It was a region of gentle gradations rather than sharp contrasts, providing a palimpsest of different environments for human occupation rich in a wide variety of resources. The reasons why Europe was a late developer compared with the South West Asian core are several, but it is tempting to suggest that the principal cause lay in its comparative lushness and extensive uniformity. When, soon after 11,000 BC, Eurasia suffered a significant deterioration in climate known as the Younger Dryas phase, the foraging communities of the European peninsula simply had to retreat further to the south to continue their traditional lifestyles: there was little incentive to improvise. In the Fertile Crescent of South West Asia, where there was nowhere to retreat to, the only strategy was to adapt. That adaptation led quickly to the development of food-producing economies. Other complex processes were also at work in South West Asia, but a fuller discussion of this must wait for a later chapter.

A vivid illustration of the impact of South West Asian productive innovations on the rest of Eurasia is shown by the extent to which the cultivation of wheat had been adopted by about 3000 BC. All the regions peripheral to the Fertile Crescent core were now cultivating the grain as a staple. The map of the spread of farming from the South West Asian core reflects the level of connectivity that now linked the core and its peripheries. Over time different centres of power and innovation developed and moved within this broader zone, but after the middle of the first millennium BC power became evenly balanced between the empires of the Iranian plateau and those of Europe. The old South West Asian core was now an interface between them and was often fought over. This broad geographical divide is evident in the confrontation between the Romans and Parthians in the second century AD, and by the struggle between Christian Europe and the Islamic east in the latter half of the first millennium AD.

The East Asian Homeland

The chains of mountains and upland plateaux, thrust up in the Tertiary period as the Indo-Australian plate collided with the Eurasian plate creating the Himalayas and the vast Tibetan plateau, faded out to the east in a series of north–south mountain ridges, giving a grain-like structure to the countries we now know as Myanmar, Thailand, Laos, and Vietnam. To the east, between the Tibetan plateau and the Pacific Ocean,

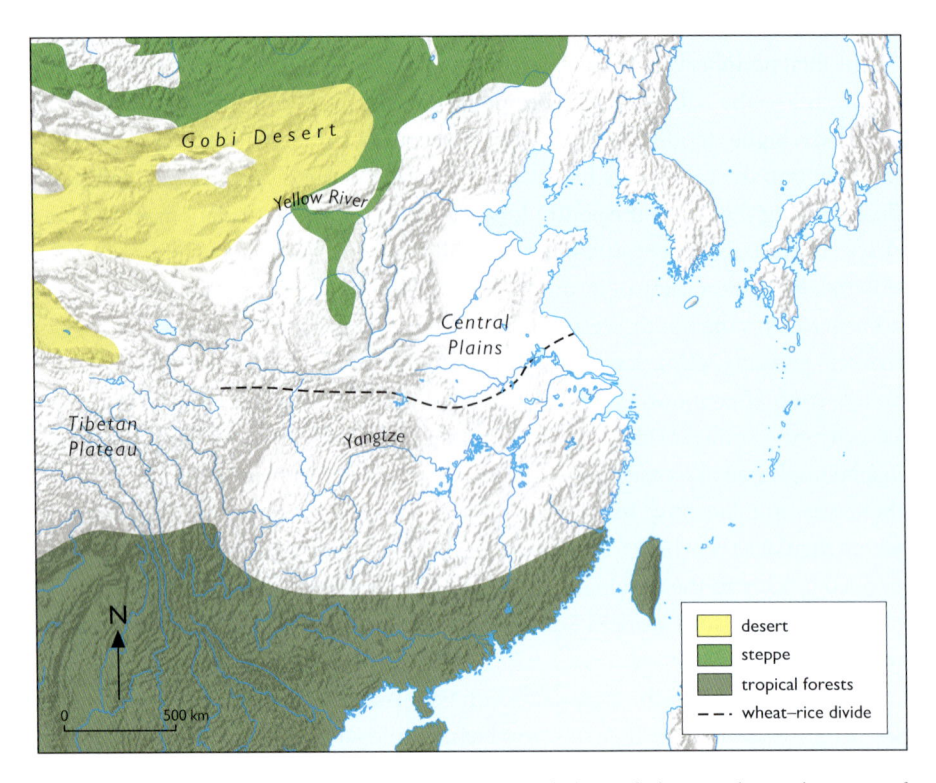

1.17 Agriculture in South East Asia originated in the Central Plains of China. In the northern part of this region millet, and later wheat, were the predominant crops, while in the southern part rice was the main staple. Unlike South West Asia, surrounded by ecological zones conducive to agriculture which soon took up food production, South East Asia was encircled by ecozones uncongenial to crop growing: steppe, desert, mountain plateaux, and dense tropical forests

lies the comparatively low-lying heartland of China, for the most part gentle rolling country crossed by two long, snaking rivers, the Yellow River to the north and the Yangtze to the south.

China is a land apart, a rich, warm, temperate environment isolated by the mountains of the Tibetan plateau to the west, the deserts of the Inner Mongolian Plateau to the north, and the tropical rainforests to the south. Its long maritime interface looks out on the Pacific, here divided into two conjoined seas: the South China Sea and the East China Sea (with its northerly part known as the Yellow Sea), protected by island chains.

China's isolation needs to be stressed. Unlike the South West Asian core, which communicates easily with its peripheries, China's natural routes to the outside world were far more limited. The South China Sea provided access to the Indonesian islands and, through the Strait of Malacca, to the Indian Ocean beyond for the adventurous, but the inland interface was more daunting. There were really only two routes leading into Central Asia. One was the narrow Gansu Corridor running between the Qilian Mountains, on the northern edge of the Tibetan plateau, and the Gobi desert. This led through the Jade Gate Pass to the desert edge roads extending around the Taklamakan. The other followed the narrow band of steppe running northwards from the Yellow River around the Gobi desert to the Mongolian steppe, and ultimately to the Altai Mountains and the Kazakh steppe beyond. The two routes played very different roles in the history of China. The steppe route was most likely the way by which western influences reached China, bringing knowledge of copper and bronze technology, and it was from the steppe that China learnt of the power of the horse and the chariot and came face to face with northern horsemen intent on raid and conquest. The Gansu Corridor, on the other hand, was the route used by traders and by the Chinese armies when, in the Tang period, territorial expansion to the west was an imperial imperative. It may, however, have been the route by which a knowledge of wheat cultivation reached China from the west, along with domesticated sheep much earlier, in the middle of the third millennium.

China's physical exposure to the ocean greatly affects its climate. In the summer it is subjected to monsoon winds blowing northwards from the South China and East China seas. In the winter the monsoon winds blow in the opposite direction from Mongolia and Manchuria. This has a significant effect on rainfall. Much of the southern part of the country has in excess of 1,300 millimetres of rain per year, while the north has less than 700 millimetres. The warm, wet south, well-watered by the Yangtze and its many tributaries, provides ideal conditions for the growth of rice, while the drier, cooler north is better suited to cereals such as wheat and millet. Another characteristic of the north is that much of the lower-lying area is blanketed with a thick layer of loess, a wind-blown yellow earth, or with loess mixed with alluvium transported by the Yellow River, which runs through the region. The loess provides a rich growing environment ideal for cereal crops. The northern limit of the loess was a significant ecological boundary that, for a long period, marked the limit of sedentary Chinese culture. It was formalized by the Great Wall, which reached its final form in the Ming period, between the fourteenth and sixteenth centuries AD, and was designed to protect Chinese lands from the nomads to the north.

The East Asian core was, then, an isolated and distinctive region climatically well suited to human settlement. In the period following the cold episode known as the Younger Dryas (c.10,800–c.9600 BC) temperate conditions returned to the northern loess lands of the Yellow River catchment. Trees spread to areas that had previously been open steppe, and a range of wild grasses, already present before the Younger Dryas, began to flourish, among them green foxtail millet, which was being harvested by foragers as early as 8000 BC. The region was also well supplied with wild animals, including deer, horse, cattle, sheep, and pigs. It was a resource-rich environment providing all the opportunities needed for communities to settle down and become farmers.

In the middle reaches of the Yangtze the climatic conditions were rather different. It was a landscape of lakes with high rainfall exceeding 1,000 millimetres per year and hot humid summers. In such conditions wild rice, which needs a marshy habitat to survive, can flourish. There is evidence that the plant was being collected and processed by foraging communities well before 6000 BC and was already a significant component of the diet. By 6000 BC rice was being cultivated and soon became the main staple in the region.

The East Asian core, by virtue of a variety of factors, notably its relative isolation, distinctive resource-rich ecological zones, and equable climate, provided the optimum conditions for the development of settled economies founded on the cultivation of millet and rice and the domestication of a range of animals. Cultivation led to the establishment of settled communities and the eventual development of state societies. The processes evident in East Asia are similar to those observed in the South West Asian core but with differences. The causes may have been broadly the same in the two regions—rapid climatic change impacting on demographic pressures—but the cultivates adopted were different, as were the trajectories of social and economic change. These are matters to be explored further in the next chapter.

Geography Matters

Sufficient will have been said to show that the geography of Eurasia offered widely varying opportunities to the human communities who chose to inhabit its diverse ecological niches: micro-environments created by the interaction between solid geology and climate. There were specially favoured ecozones like the Fertile Crescent and the valleys of the Yangtze and Yellow rivers, where inventive humans were drawn to settle and to create complex societies from an early date, and harsh environments like the Taklamakan and Gobi deserts, which were largely avoided. But there are many intermediate zones—the vast steppe, the upland plateaux, and the forested European peninsula—where people could develop different socio-economic strategies to deal with the constraints and opportunities of their chosen habitat. But if the dynamics of population growth or climate variation became of sufficient magnitude, these systems would have to change. Such adjustments created a restlessness, sometimes building into a tumult of movement. When the archaeological and textual evidence is good enough, we are able to recognize reflections of this and to build them into a narrative history.

Finally, connectivity. Given the propensity of humans to be acquisitive, there will always be mobility. The geography of Eurasia facilitates this, providing swaths of open grassland, oceans, strings of oases, river valleys, and mountain passes for people, commodities, and ideas to move through. So it is that rhythms of movement are created and networks of interaction come into existence. There is a tendency for these networks to link up over time, giving rise to what some economists have called world systems. In the chapters to follow we shall explore these connectivities and attempt to understand the people who created them.

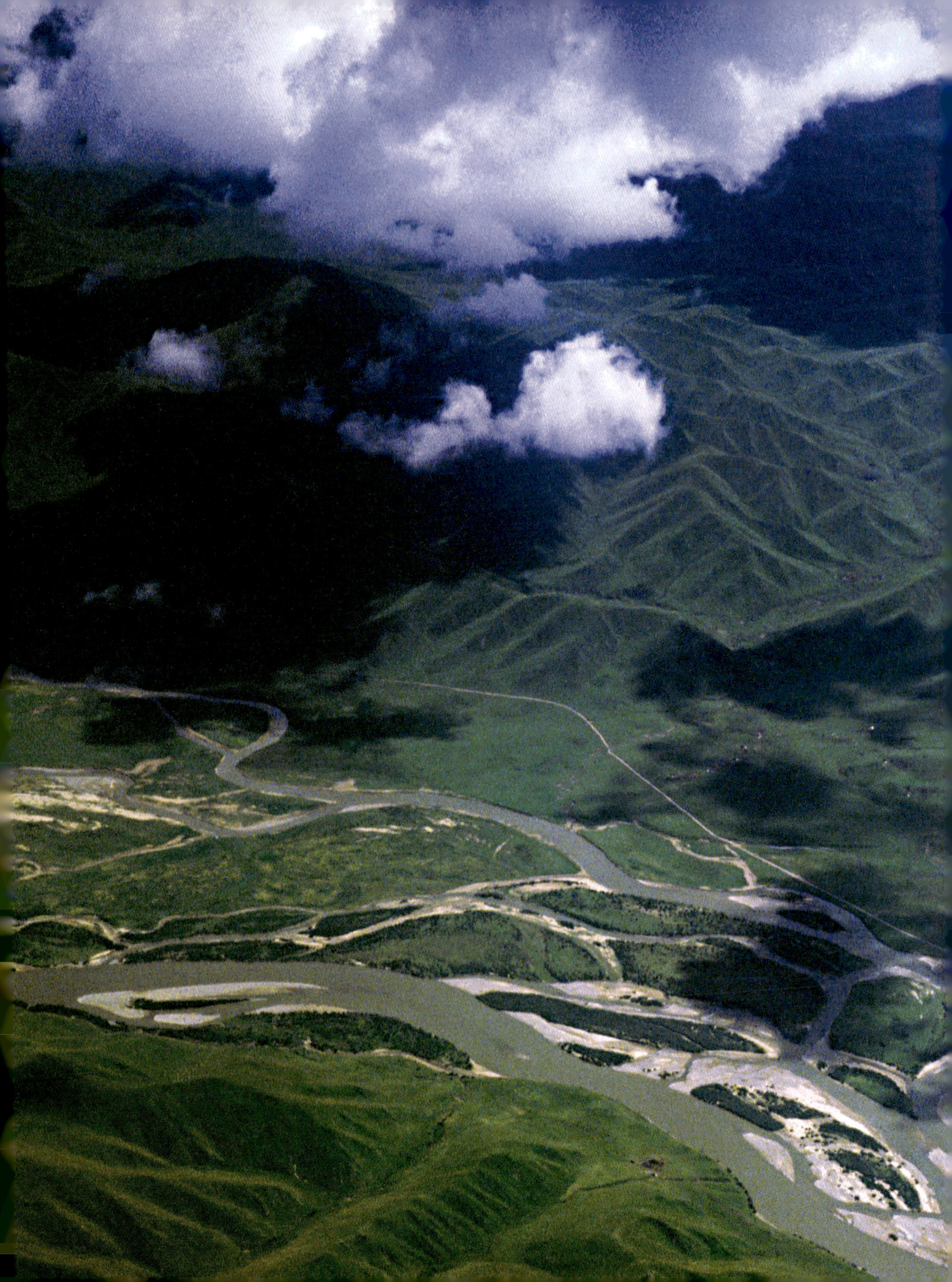

2

THE DOMESTICATION OF EURASIA,
10,000–5000 BC

THE transformation from the hunter-gatherer way of life to economies based on agricultural production was a crucial stage in the development of society. It happened independently in various parts of the world, on all continents, involving a variety of plant cultivates and animal domesticates. In Eurasia, where food-producing regimes were first to develop, the processes leading to full agriculture can be traced in two widely separated regions: South West Asia, in the hilly flanks of the Fertile Crescent; and East Asia, in the valleys of the Yellow River and the Yangtze. By 6000 BC fully fledged farming communities had been established in these two precocious regions, and within the next millennium agriculture had spread widely across the continent.

It used to be thought that agricultural practices developed rapidly in South West Asia, and indeed the transition was for a long time referred to as the Neolithic revolution, but more recent work has shown that the change from hunting and gathering to full food production was long-drawn-out. While different societies progressed in different ways, and there were some reverses, the general trajectory is tolerably clear.

The first step came about when hunter-gatherer communities moved from opportunist collecting regimes to a more controlled foraging. This would have involved deliberate interventions, for example, by making clearances in woodland to encourage prey animals to congregate to eat the new, young vegetation, and by clearing unwanted plants to allow stands of useful wild grasses to flourish, always making sure that sufficient was left to reseed. Such practices would have led to less mobility with a more extended use of favoured base camps. This closer interaction between humans and plants and animals was the first crucial stage in the process leading to domestication, that is, the selection, intentional or unintentional, of certain genetic varieties in preference to others. A wild grass with a tough rachis that holds the grains to the stalk, rather than allowing them to scatter easily, is more likely to be selected by humans and thus will be given preference over other varieties, which might be deliberately uprooted and disposed of before seeding. Similarly, in hunting animals, those that were more docile because of their genetic make-up may have been treated preferentially. By actions of this kind human foraging communities became a significant force in the selection that led to the dominance of specific genotypes. This was the beginning of domestication.

It was a small step from the nurturing of preferred plants to cultivation involving the collection of seed for resowing. Cultivation takes with it changes in material culture and behaviour: special storage facilities for the seed grain need to be constructed and plots of land prepared, while sowing and harvesting take on a greater prominence. There is also a tendency for communities to become more sedentary, to remain close to their crops, which now demand a greater expenditure of labour and have to be protected from animal predators, not least from other humans.

The herding of animals was also a natural development arising from the processes of domestication that selected more docile, human-dependent beasts. Flocks and herds could be controlled and moved between pastures under human protection, while culling and castration could be deliberately directed to select for particular characteristics, thus improving the quality of the stock.

Communities that begin to cultivate and to herd inevitably change as more complex mechanisms have to be introduced to deal with both the division of labour that is demanded and the beneficial integration of the two modes of production. Humans are now committed to a close symbiotic relationship with their animals and plants, and this inevitably drives change, perhaps the most significant being when the domesticates and cultivates are moved out of their traditional ecological niches into new environments. When the communities of the Zagros Mountains colonized the alluvial plains of Mesopotamia, methods of irrigation were developed to cope with the increased aridity of the climate. Similarly, when the cultivation of rice was extended from the marshes of the middle Yangtze to the drier loess lands of the Yellow River, the creation of irrigated paddy fields was essential for the crops to flourish. This enhanced relationship between humans and their plants and animals constitutes the practice of agriculture.

While it is possible to generalize in this way about the trajectory from hunting and gathering to agriculture, many disparate factors were in play that affected the pace and direction of the change both over time and between regions. The transition took place against the background of near-continuous climatic change as the world moved from the Last Glacial Maximum, ending about 18,000 BC, to the more stable conditions of the present, beginning about 6000 BC. The magnitude of the climatic change had a direct effect on the environment in which the human communities sought to live and, at least in part, may have helped to drive the transformation leading to full agriculture. But factors embedded in the human genes will have played a part. The gregarious nature of the human species and its predilection for reproduction led, inevitably, to a growth in population and the emergence of larger social groups. These imperatives within human society, played out against a changing climate, created the tense dynamic that nurtured the transition to settled agriculture.

The Changing Environment of the Fertile Crescent

The period of recovery from the end of the Last Glacial Maximum, about 18,000 BC, to the beginning of the Early Holocene, about 7500 BC, saw the zone of forest and dense woodland established around the Mediterranean coastal zone of the Levant and southern Anatolia gradually expand eastwards across the hills of the Levant and deep inland along the hilly flanks of southern Anatolia to the northern part of the Zagros Mountains. At its advancing edge the dense forests gave way to a more open woodland of oak and terebinth interspersed with grassy areas that gradually became more extensive and were dominated by stands of wild wheats and ryes. Beyond lay steppe merging into desert. Between 10,800 and 9600 BC the advance was halted and put into a sharp reverse when cold conditions briefly returned during the Younger Dryas. The forests and woodlands died back to such an extent that even in the coastal zones only a thin scattering of trees remained. Elsewhere, much of the area once forested became an extensive tract of wild cereals and legumes with only occasional areas of woodland. After 9600 BC, when the cold period came to an end, the climatic change was put in reverse and the forest zone and the lighter wooded and grassy zones peripheral to it became quickly re-established.

It was against this background of an often fast-changing climate leading to widespread environmental change that the indigenous hunter-gatherers began to adapt their lifestyles, embarking on their long progress to sedentary farming. To what extent the social and economic changes were directly driven by climatic readjustment is a matter for debate and requires much more fieldwork. All that can safely be said is that the Younger Dryas created ecological conditions that were conducive to the domestication of animals and crops and facilitated the social changes that had begun in the region much earlier.

New Strategies for Subsistence

Much archaeological effort has been expended in researching the cultural sequences in the Fertile Crescent, and the principal stages of development are now reliably established, though there are variations from place to place within the zone. Culturally, the long period from 18,000 to 9600 BC is referred to as the Epipalaeolithic, which can be divided into an early and a late phase around the date 12,000 BC. In the Levant the Late Epipalaeolithic is called the Natufian culture after a type site excavated in 1928 in Wadi el-Natuf, now in northern Israel. The Epipalaeolithic (and with it the Natufian) ends with the end of the Younger Dryas about 9600 BC. Then follows the Aceramic Neolithic (c.9600–c.6900 BC), by which time farming practices are evident but, as the name implies, pottery is not yet being made. The Aceramic Neolithic is generally divided into an early and a late phase around the date 8800 BC. In the Levant a different terminology is used, dividing the Aceramic Neolithic (here called the Pre-Pottery Neolithic) into an A and B phase. With the introduction of pottery about 6900 BC the full Neolithic begins. Terminologies of this kind provide the essential framework within which the archaeological evidence can be displayed and analysed.

In the early part of the Epipalaeolithic, as the climate began to improve after the Last Glacial Maximum, changes in hunting strategies become evident, reflected in both the tool-kits now in use and the animal bone debris recovered from settlement sites. While large herd animals like gazelle continued to be hunted, far more effort was now spent in hunting and trapping smaller animals such as fox, hare, birds, fish, and reptiles. The change led to greater sedentism, with a tendency for more time to be spent at the base camp, and this may well have contributed to the increase in population that can now be recognized: estimates suggest that some Epipalaeolithic settlements were now between five and ten times larger than before. Concomitant with the rise in population went the need for greater productivity and the imperative to build up food stores for the winter, particularly of wild cereals and pulses, which grew in abundance and could be gathered in the summer months.

A classic site reflecting the tendencies to sedentism is Neve David on the edge of the coastal plain in northern Israel. Its large extent, of some 1,000 square metres, and thick depth of occupation deposit (over 1 metre) implies that the camp was occupied by a large community over a long period of time. The discovery of grindstones, of black basalt brought from some distance away, shows not only that the inhabitants were grinding wild cereals with hard seed-cases, but that they were exchanging goods with other communities. Yet not all settlements of this period were large. In other, more challenging environments, in south Jordan and the Negev, seasonal occupation of smaller sites suggests a more transhumant pattern with communities

THE DOMESTICATION OF EURASIA

moving into the highlands to gather fruits and nuts in the summer months. Different regions offering different ecozones called for a variety of responses.

The Late Epipalaeolithic saw an intensification of many of the trends noted earlier with the appearance of larger, more sedentary settlements and a greater emphasis on the collection, processing, and storage of wild crops. This was facilitated by the die-back of the forest during the colder Younger Dryas interlude, which allowed

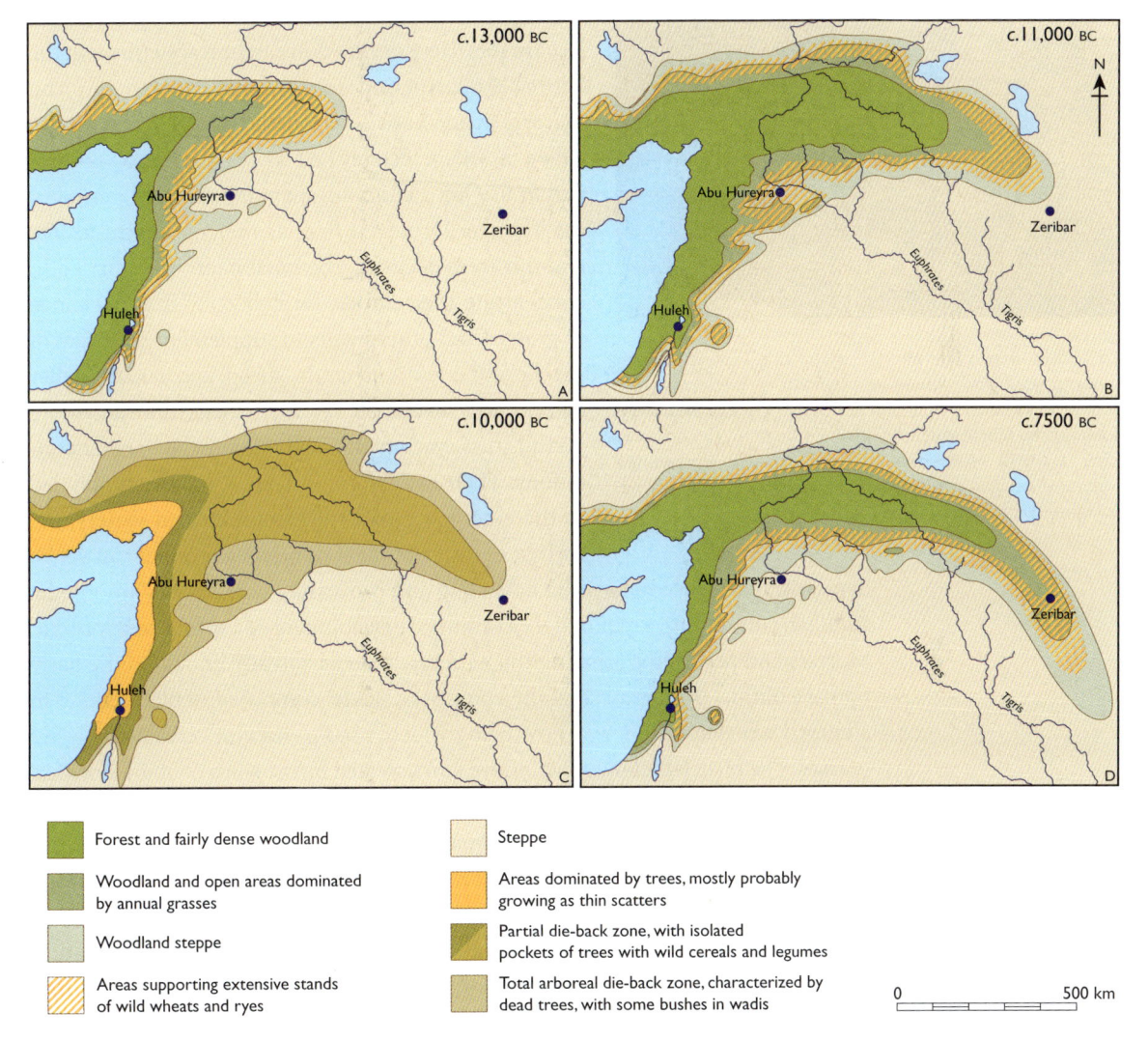

2.1 The four maps of South West Asia chart the change of vegetation from the end of the last Ice Age, c.1300 BC, to the beginning of conditions similar to today, c.7500 BC. The Younger Dryas 'die-back', c.10,000 BC, created conditions that forced human societies to develop new economic strategies intensifying the pace of change leading to a full food-producing economy

extensive areas of wild grass to flourish. In the Levant and northern Syria, where the distinctive Natufian culture developed, villages of varying sizes, some of up to two to three hundred people, have been found. Some settlements, like Eynan (or Ain Mallaha) in north-eastern Israel, consisted of circular houses, replaced from time to time as the village developed, interspersed with storage pits. Here occupation can be traced through the entire Natufian period from 12,000 to 9600 BC. At Abu Hureyra in northern Syria, on the flank of the Euphrates valley, a village established about 11,000 BC continued in use until 9600 BC, spanning the cold period of the Younger Dryas. At first, as the cold began to bite and nut trees declined, the inhabitants were forced to concentrate their efforts on collecting a wider range of grasses and other plants to supplement their diet of gazelle and a few wild cattle, sheep, and ass. A further deterioration in climate saw them focus more and more on the grass rye, which could tolerate the harsher conditions. Their careful cultivation of rye eventually led to the emergence of a fully domesticated variety, the earliest example of plant domestication that can yet be demonstrated. The emphasis on collecting and processing wild grasses among the Natufian communities required the continued development of a specialized tool-kit. Mortars and pestles for grinding the wild cereal seeds (already known in the Early Epipalaeolithic) proliferate, and the composite sickle, composed of bladelets set in a curved wooden frame, was now being widely used to harvest cereals and other grasses. The bladelets show a distinctive gloss created by the silica contained within the grass stems.

2.2 A deep trench dug into the occupation deposits at Abu Hureyra, sited on a limestone promontory overlooking the flood-plains of the Euphrates in northern Syria, exposed house floors of the Epipalaeolithic settlement dug into the bedrock. After a metre of deposits had accumulated, representing continued occupation, a rectangular mud-brick house of the Aceramic Neolithic period was built

With a more settled form of economy and larger agglomerations of people living together in one place, social behaviour begins to develop greater complexity. Individuals display their identity through personal ornaments, which family groups or lineages carefully bury with their dead, usually within the settlement. There is also evidence for inter-community interaction in the form of traded commodities such as obsidian from central and eastern Anatolia and sea-shells from the Mediterranean and the Red Sea. Exotics of this kind will have passed in cycles of gift exchange from one community to the next, strengthening the networks of social harmony at a time when population growth threatened to create tensions.

While the Natufian culture of the Levant and northern Syria is now comparatively well known, the evidence for Late Epipalaeolithic settlement in the Zagros Mountains of Iraq and Iran is somewhat thinner, but, that said, a number of sites have been explored showing that developments in this broad region reflect those in the Natufian area, with an increasing diversification in hunting, the collection and storage of wild cereals, and the appearance of larger, more long-lived settlements. However, against these inter-regional similarities local differences develop as each community learns to respond to the opportunities offered by the ecozone in which it lives. One notable variation was noted at the village of Zawi Chemi Shanidar in north-east Iraq. Here wild sheep were being extensively exploited. The high percentage of young animal bones found in the refuse deposits may be an indication that flock management was such that the animals may be regarded as being formally domesticated.

The varied social and economic changes that intensified during the cold downturn of the Younger Dryas brought the communities of the hilly flanks to the threshold of agriculture. As the climate began to ameliorate in the three millennia after 9600 BC, agricultural practices became established and widespread.

2.3 A Natufian sickle handle made of bone found in a cave on Mount Carmel in Israel. Struck stone blades, possibly of obsidian, would have been set in the shaft, now missing. The animal carving may have been of ritual significance

The Beginnings of Agriculture

Population growth, already evident in the Epipalaeolithic period, became an increasingly important dynamic throughout the Aceramic Neolithic. This is reflected in both the number of new sites established and their size, some being larger than preceding settlements by a factor of ten. It is as though, once the constraints of the cold period had been removed, the innate desire to reproduce, now unconstrained, took over and drove social development to new heights of complexity. Subsistence strategies were forced to keep pace with the needs of fast-expanding communities.

The careful cultivation of select plants had already begun in the Late Epipalaeolithic times. Now, focusing on plants naturally occurring in the hilly flanks zone—einkorn wheat, barley, rye, and pulses, including, in particular, chickpea—more inten-

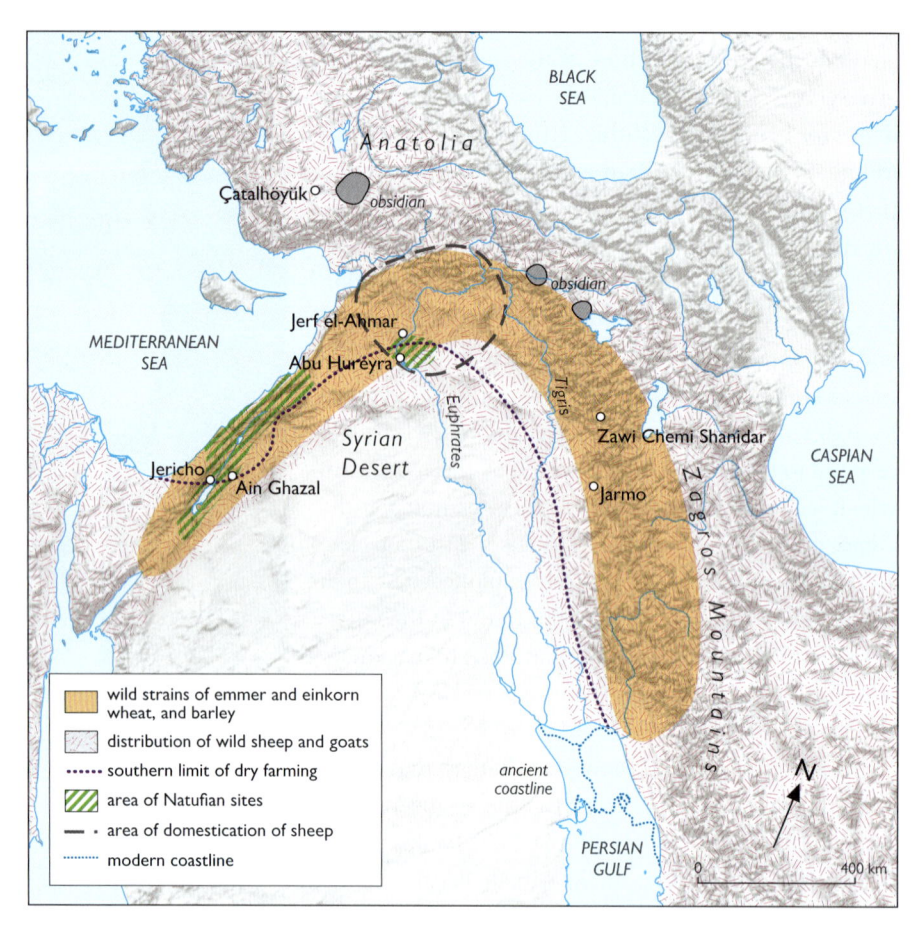

2.4 Agriculture began on the Fertile Crescent and the adjacent hilly flanks where wild sheep, goats, and cattle roamed, and wild emmer and einkorn wheat and barley grew. The domestication and cultivation of specific species took place in discrete areas but soon spread throughout the zone. Desire for rare raw materials, like obsidian, encouraged contact and exchange

sive cultivation led to domestication as selection for favoured genetic variants was increasingly practised. It is thought likely that the genetic changes leading to the domestication of species took place at one time and in one location. Barley seems to have evolved in the southern Levant, while einkorn wheat was probably first domesticated in south-east Anatolia. Once the new strains had emerged, the seed grain was distributed widely through the social networks.

The increasing importance of the cultivation of morphologically wild plants in the Early Aceramic period is well demonstrated by the sequence of deposits, covering the period 9500–8000 BC, excavated at the settlement of Jerf el-Ahmar in the Euphrates valley in northern Syria. The principal wild cereals gathered were barley and rye with small quantities of einkorn. In the later levels cereals and pulses had increased at the expense of other gathered plants, and the percentage of einkorn had also grown. The processing of the grain required the use of quernstones, of which four hundred were discovered. Judging by the distribution and density of querns throughout the settlement, it is evident that some rooms within houses were set aside for cereal processing, and one communal building seems to have been devoted to storage. That storage was practised on a large scale is indicated by extensive evidence of rodent activity. Taken together, the data derived from Jerf el-Ahmar shows not only that the collection of wild cereals and pulses was crucial to the substance strategy, but also that it intensified over the five centuries during which the site was occupied.

Throughout the Fertile Crescent the favoured domesticates were sheep, goats, cattle, and pigs. On present evidence the earliest domesticated sheep appear to have emerged in south-east Anatolia and northern Syria, while the goat is more likely to have been domesticated in western Iran. The first domesticated cattle were probably Anatolian, while domesticated pigs first appeared in Lebanon or southern Syria. Once the fully domesticated species had emerged, the animals would quickly be distributed through complex networks of social exchange in the same way as were the seeds of the cultivated cereals. So it was that by about 7000 BC most of the communities around the Fertile Crescent shared the same range of domesticated plants and animals.

The population surge that characterized the Aceramic Neolithic led to the creation of some exceptionally large settlements supporting communities several thousand strong, places like Jericho in the Jordan valley and Çatalhöyük on the Konya Plain in central Anatolia. Jericho extended over some 2.5 hectares. Clearly such sites, with their controlled planning and elaborate architecture, implied an increasing degree of social complexity. Some of the settlements, notably those in south-east Turkey, had elaborate communal structures quite different from the surrounding domestic houses. The most spectacular of those so far known have been excavations at Göbekli Tepe, where a series of subterranean buildings, mostly circular in plan, have been uncovered. Monoliths carved with elaborate decoration were set into the walls, while free-standing monoliths with cross-beams at the top were placed within the buildings, standing 5 metres in height and similarly carved. These remarkable structures, which would have absorbed a huge amount of societies' surplus energy, reflect the significant degree of coercive power now at work. At some sites like Çatalhöyük the communal structures were elaborately painted with figurative and geometric designs, while at Ain Ghazal, near Amman in Jordan, some of the non-domestic buildings contained half-size human figurines made of plaster. Taken together this remarkable display of human creativity reflects the size and comparative economic stability of the Aceramic Neolithic communities; it is also symbolic of their fast-

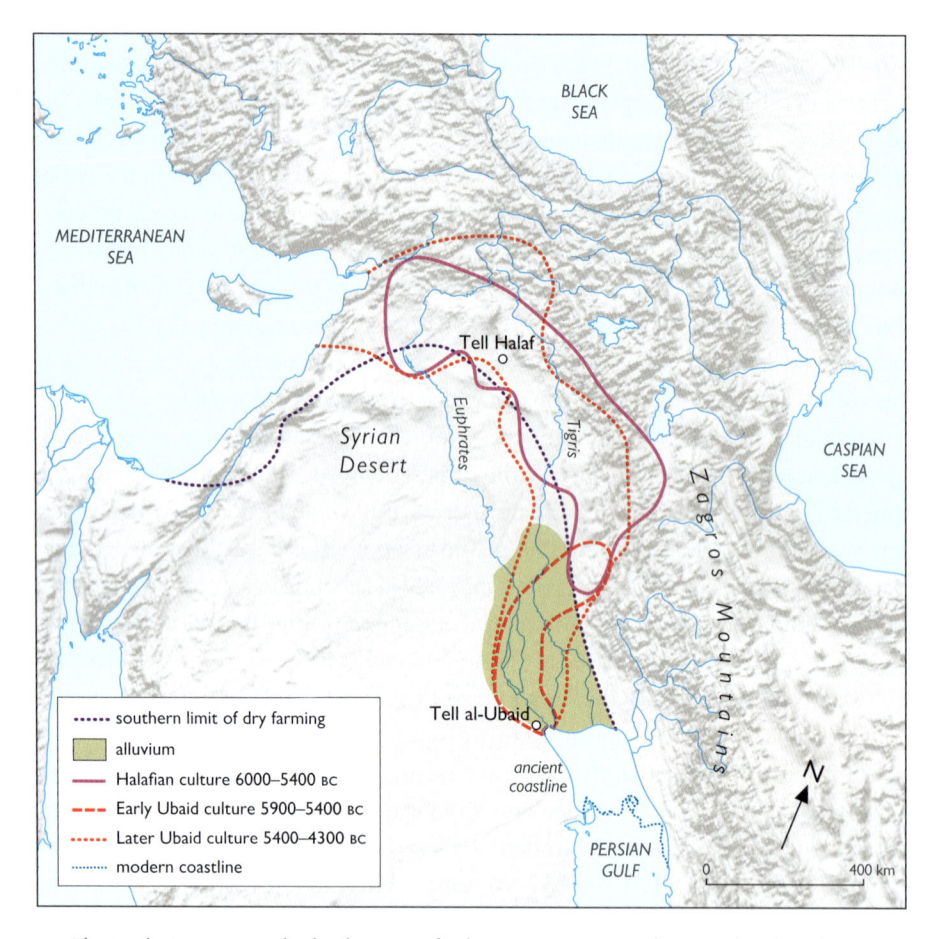

2.5 The Fertile Crescent saw the development of sedentary communities sharing cultural attributes over wide areas, first the Halafian and later the Ubaid cultures. It was during the Ubaid that communities moved out of their original ecological niche and into the alluvial land of the Tigris and Euphrates valley. It was here that the first cities developed

growing complexity and their need to engage in communal activities to enhance societies' coherence.

The various social and economic developments sketched out above were under way throughout the Aceramic Neolithic period, but the pace of change escalated during that time, reaching a peak in the late phase (c.8800–c.6900 BC). It was almost as though the changes, once in progress, had a momentum of their own. By the end of the period distinct signs of stress can be discerned. At Ain Ghazal the need to support a large population occupying a site of some 10–14 hectares began to create environmental problems. Tree clearance for fuel and building, the intensive herding of goats, and the continuous tilling of the land led to soil degradation and erosion to such an extent

2.6 Excavations in progress at the Pre-Pottery Neolithic A site of Göbekli Tepe in south-eastern Turkey dating to the late tenth century BC. The site is remarkable for its sophisticated architecture and stone carving, which show not only a highly developed ritual life but a society producing sufficient surplus food to support non-productive activities

2.7 One of two central pillars in enclosure D at Göbekli Tepe depicting a clothed anthropomorphic figure

that the large population could no longer be sustained. In the event some groups appear to have moved off to the steppe and semi-arid lands towards the desert edge, there to take up semi-nomadic herding, while a much smaller population remained, relocating to the head of a nearby spring. Elsewhere, Jericho was abandoned, and at Çatalhöyük the population melted away a few centuries later, about 6200 BC.

A dislocation in settlement patterns can be recognized across the entire region at the end of the Aceramic Neolithic or soon after. The most likely reason is that over-exploitation of the land and the plant and animal resources to support the burgeoning population so degraded the environment that, in the ensuing crisis, in many areas people were forced to relocate in much smaller groups and to adopt new food-producing strategies. The situation may have been exacerbated by the onset of a more arid climate.

Relocation and a New Stability, 6900–5400 BC

The collapse of the systems that supported the large, complex settlements of the Late Aceramic Neolithic was dramatic and widespread. In the aftermath smaller settlements came into being, sometimes colonizing new ecological niches like the Amuq basin west of Aleppo, or the semi-arid lands that had previously been avoided. Such moves required readjustments to the economic strategies. On the northern and eastern arc of the Fertile Crescent relocation is even more evident, with a move from the hilly flanks and the intermontane valleys to the rolling hills below and to the eastern edge of the alluvial plain of Mesopotamia.

By 6000 BC new communities were all well established in this dry farming zone, and some had moved beyond into areas of low rainfall around the fringes of the river plains, where, by developing systems of irrigation canals, water from the great rivers of Mesopotamia could be used to make the rich alluvial soils fertile. This was a major breakthrough and meant that crops could be grown in areas outside their natural ecozones. Another important development was the use of cattle as draft animals to pull the ards used to till the deep valley soils. The early phase of this development is called the Halaf period (c.6000–c.5400 BC) after the site of Tell Halaf in northern Syria. Settlements of the period, reflecting a broadly similar culture, are found in an arc stretching from Iran, through northern Iraq and northern Syria, to the Levant and northwards into Turkey. They are characterized by a distinctive painted pottery, some at least coming from specialized production centres, implying a high degree of connectivity linking communities over a very considerable area. For the most part, settlements were little more than small villages, but a few were larger, the largest reaching about 15 hectares.

It was soon after the beginning of the Halaf period, about 5900 BC, that people moved down in some numbers onto the plains of Upper Mesopotamia to establish

2.8 The Halafian culture is characterized by its highly accomplished painted pottery. The two examples shown here are from Arpachiyah in northern Iraq and date to 5500–5000 BC

permanent farming communities based on irrigation agriculture. The distinctive culture that developed along the lower Tigris and Euphrates in the sixth and fifth millennia was called Ubaid, after Tell el-Ubaid in southern Iraq, and lay at the beginning of the spectacular achievements leading to the first cities and to the world's first civilization.

Moving the plant cultivates and animal domesticates out of the comparatively harsh environments in which they had originated and transplanting them into a new ecological niche of enhanced fertility greatly increased yields, sufficient to support growing populations. More important was the fact that the annual floods, bringing down fresh alluvium to fertilize the land, enabled agricultural intensification to be sustainable. But one dynamic had changed. Irrigation was a communal effort requiring close cooperation and the establishment of agreements covering extensive tracts of land. Thus, there was now a need for communities to work in harmony. This, together with productivity allowing populations to increase, was a principal driver leading to the emergence of the complex societies we call civilizations.

Out of South West Asia

Cultivation, domestication, and the development of agriculture took place in a comparatively restricted but ecologically favoured zone of South West Asia in the period from about 10,000 to 6000 BC. But even before the end of that period the practice of agriculture, along with the crops and animals that sustained it, was being transferred

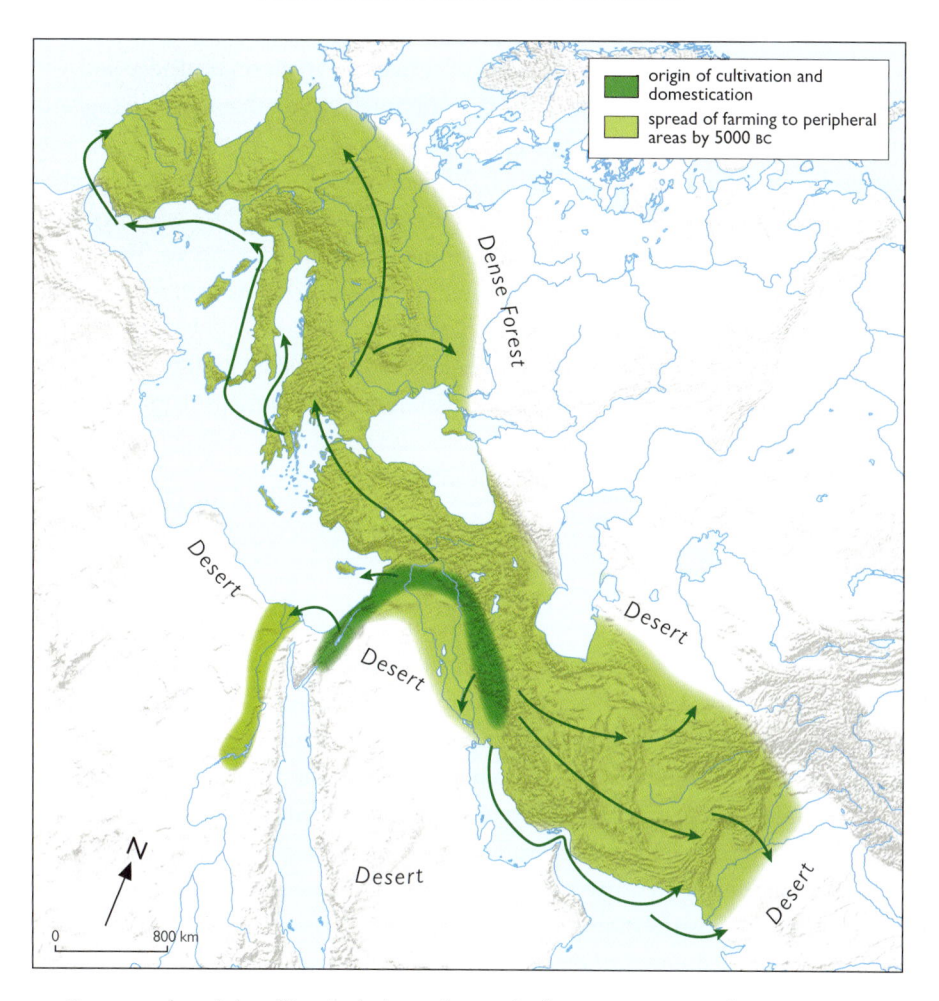

2.9 By 5000 BC knowledge of farming had spread to much of western Eurasia into favourable ecological zones bounded only by the surrounding deserts, dense forest, and the Atlantic Ocean

into peripheral areas, to the Nile valley, to Baluchistan and the Indus valley, and to the east Mediterranean islands and Europe. Eventually, from the Iranian plateau and from eastern Europe the practices of agriculture were transmitted to Central Asia. The rapidity of the spread was remarkable, with much of this huge periphery having made the transition from hunting and gathering by 5000 BC. This raises many questions about why food production was considered a superior strategy to foraging and about the cultural mechanisms by which the new ideas spread. There are no simple answers since in each region the balance of factors would have been different, but lying behind it all are two simple drivers: the tendency for populations to increase in size, and the mobility inherent in human societies driven by an innate curiosity.

The fact that the development and spread of agricultural regimes coincided with the Younger Dryas cold downturn and the climatic amelioration that followed suggests that this is also likely to have been a significant factor.

The domesticates that spread through the peripheries to become the staples in all these disparate regions—wheat, barley, sheep, goats, cattle, and pigs—were first bred in the Fertile Crescent and its hilly flanks from indigenous wild species. The spread of agriculture would initially have required the transportation of seed grain and of flocks and herds, often over considerable distances and across obstacles such as deserts and the sea. In other words, the spread of food-producing strategies did not come about as a casual drift but by a succession of deliberate acts requiring much effort and the transfer not only of the domesticates but of the knowledge and technical skills needed to maintain them in alien environments.

To the Nile Valley

The Nile valley and the deltaic region at its mouth shared many of the characteristics of Mesopotamia, not least the ready availability of water and the Nile flood, which each year brought volumes of alluvium from the African interior to replenish fertility. The differences lay in the fact that the Nile was constrained by desert on all sides, whereas to the north and east Mesopotamia gave way to the productive hilly flanks of the mountains, where the principal domesticates were bred. That said, the fringes of the Sahara, in southern Egypt, were sufficiently benign to support groups of foragers, who by about 7000 BC were harvesting wild fruits and grasses, including sorghum, and had developed a close relationship with herds of wild cattle. This might be regarded as an early form of domestication since, without human help, the beasts would probably have been unable to survive in the marginal environment. If it is accepted that the cattle were fully domesticated, then these Saharan communities were the first in Africa to set out on the road to food production. Small clusters of herders, like those living at Nabta Playa in the eastern Sahara, were well established, with a stable system of seasonal settlements, and by 5000 BC were enhancing their productivity by herding domesticated sheep and goats introduced along the Nile valley from South West Asia.

The introduction of the full range of domesticated species—emmer, barley, flax, sheep, goats, cattle, and pigs—to the Nile delta and the Fayum Depression took place about 5000 BC and there can be little doubt that the practice of agriculture, as well as the domesticates, came from the southern Levant either via the coastal strip or by sea. In the rich Nile valley, between 4500 and 3000 BC, communities flourished and the population grew, creating a stable basis for the emergence of the Egyptian dynastic state about 3100 BC. The actual process by which agriculture reached the Nile delta

To Baluchistan and the Indus

Beyond the Zagros Mountains to the east lie the uplands of the Indo-Iranian plateau fringed along its eastern limit by mountain ranges before the land falls dramatically to the valley of the Indus. At the eastern end of the plateau are the uplands of Baluchistan, now western Pakistan, and it is here that, by the middle of the seventh millennium, small farming communities had established themselves. The most extensively excavated to date is the village of Mehrgarh, sited near the mouth of the Bolan Pass. Occupation began about 6500 BC and lasted into the third millennium. In the earliest, Aceramic phase, the economy was based on the cultivation of wheat and barley and the hunting of deer, gazelle, and zebu cattle, but after about 6000 BC, by which time pottery was being made, the indigenous zebu show a significant decrease in size, which is consistent with the suggestion that they were now being domesticated.

How was it that knowledge of crop cultivation and a sufficient quantity of seed was transported over the Iranian plateau, a distance of some 2,000 kilometres, so soon after agriculture began in the hilly flanks zone? While it is possible that a trek was made across the plateau, an alternative would be to suppose that transmission was by sea. The idea is not so far-fetched, as we shall see later in discussing Europe, and we know that by the late sixth and fifth millennia a regular maritime trading network existed linking southern Mesopotamia with communities scattered along the entire southern coast of the Persian Gulf. One of the port settlements of this period in Kuwait has produced a clay model of a reed-bundle boat and a ceramic disc painted to depict a vessel with a bipod mast, implying that the sail was already in use. If regular sea voyages were being made at the end of the sixth millennium, it is quite conceivable that small boats were already plying the coastal route a millennium or so earlier. These hypothetical early beginnings

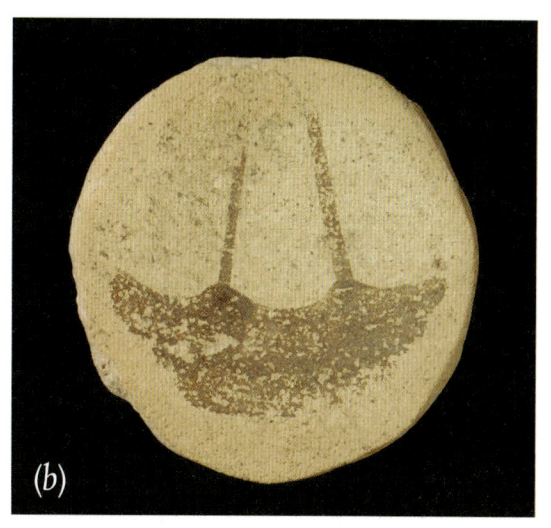

2.10 Ceramic finds from the early Ubaid period site of al-Sabiyah, Kuwait, indicate the kinds of boat available at the time: (*a*) a ceramic model of a reed boat; (*b*) a pottery disc painted with a two-masted vessel. No actual boats of this early date have yet been found

and the developed maritime network of the sixth millennium may mark the initial stages of the complex patterns of maritime connectivity that were soon to link the lands around the Indian Ocean. The possibility that the first Baluchistan farmers and their seed crops arrived by coast-hopping ships is a question that must be left unresolved at least until the coastal zone of Iran is explored in more detail.

Once established on the plateau, it was only a matter of time before farming communities moved down to colonize the Indus flood-plain. The earliest stages of this process are not well known, but settlements were established by the fourth millennium and flourished in the fertile, well-watered environment. By 3200 BC the first planned cities were beginning to develop as a prelude to what was to become the Indus civilization.

The transmission of agricultural technology to the two great river valleys of the Nile and the Indus around the fifth millennium allowed a population to grow, generating an increasing social complexity that eventually, about 3000 BC, led to the emergence of state systems. The fertility of the valley environments seems to have been the major factor in allowing these precocious developments. But the valleys were also the focuses for trading networks—the natural channels through which commodities flowed—and the elite commanding them could benefit from the traffic. The Nile valley, the Indus valley, and Mesopotamia were soon to become major centres of innovation and power, but with very different histories.

To the Fringes of the Deserts of Central Asia

By the end of the seventh millennium communities practising agriculture had settled at the foot of the Kopet Dag, the mountain range that formed the northern limit of the Iranian plateau, on the edge of the Karakum desert. A number of Neolithic tell sites of this period are known, the most extensively examined being Jeitun in modern Turkmenistan, not far from Ashgabat. The settlement was comparatively small, 0.7 hectares in area, and composed of some thirty rectangular mud-brick houses dating to 6300–5000 BC. While hunting was practised, the principal source of protein came from domesticated sheep and goats kept for their meat and milk. Barley and einkorn wheat, together with a small quantity of emmer wheat, were grown. The successful introduction of the South West Asian package of domesticates into an alien desert-edge environment where water supply was uncertain may well have required some small-scale embanking and ditching to make sure that the run-off from the mountains kept the land adequately irrigated.

Similarities between the painted pottery found at Jeitun and that in use in Iraqi Kurdistan hints at the possible origin for the pioneer desert-edge communities. If

2.11 Excavations at the Neolithic settlement of Jeitun in Turkmenistan exposed several square mud-brick houses set within yards. Each house had an oven in the centre of one side with a raised platform between it and the door. The earliest phase of the settlement dates to 6000 BC

knowledge of agriculture was brought from this region, then the route is likely to have been through northern Iran, skirting the edge of deserts that made up much of the Iranian plateau. This easterly movement was probably part of the general exodus from the Zagros foothills, which saw agricultural communities establish themselves in Baluchistan and, eventually, the Indus valley.

By Sea to the Islands and to Europe

The spread of agriculture along the length of the Mediterranean Sea and through the long peninsula of Europe was largely accomplished by 5000 BC, leaving only

Britain, Ireland, and Scandinavia to be incorporated over the next thousand years. The process can be divided into three quite separate episodes. The first covers the period from about 11,000 BC to 7000 BC and involves sea-going communities in the east Mediterranean and the Aegean. The second and third episodes are concurrent, spanning the period 7000–5000 BC: one sees the spread of agriculture by sea along the length of the Mediterranean and out into the Atlantic, extending from the Greek peninsula to Portugal; the other involves the transmission of agricultural practices overland through the centre of Europe, starting again from Greece, and ending in north-western France and the Channel Islands.

There is increasing evidence to show that the Epipalaeolithic foragers of southern Anatolia and the Greek mainland were, from 11,000 BC, taking to the sea and developing ever-extending patterns of mobility in search of both food and raw materials. The most dramatic evidence comes from the Franchthi Cave on the Gulf of Argos in the Peloponnese. Here a long-established community was exploiting a wide range of food sources, including red deer, wild ass, wild cattle and pig, shell-fish and wild oats, pistachio and almond. But they were also extending their foraging patterns by taking to the open sea to catch tuna, probably off the east coast of northern Greece. How wide their maritime expeditions ranged it is difficult to say, but they certainly embraced the island of Milos, 100 nautical miles to the south-west, from where they obtained obsidian to make tools. Nothing is known of their boats, but most likely they were made of skins around a light wooden frame, though the alternative, that they were constructed from bundles of reeds, is possible. Further evidence of sea travel comes from Cyprus, from the cave of Aetokremnos at Akrotiri on the south coast, where hunter-gatherers came together to feast off pygmy hippopotamus about 10,500 BC. The cave was probably the seasonal camp of hunters who sailed from the Anatolian mainland.

Why people should choose to face the rigours of sea travel at this time is a matter of debate. It could be that increasing populations, facilitated by improving weather conditions, encouraged communities to develop new food sources and to look for new ecological niches to settle, but there is no evidence that societies were under stress at the time. An alternative is that with greater abundance of food becoming available as the climate got warmer there was more leisure to explore, allowing the inquisitive side of the human psyche fuller rein. The discovery of new commodities, like obsidian, would have been an added incentive to mobility. No doubt there were local factors too: major changes are usually the result of multiple causes.

The return of the cold conditions of the Younger Dryas downturn about 10,800 BC may have intensified maritime mobility as communities struggled with ecological change. In the late tenth century foragers moved to Cyprus from the mainland and established settlements. One of these, at Agia Varvara on the low hills in the centre of the island, was occupied from the late tenth to the mid-ninth century. Culturally it shared many characteristics with the Early Aceramic settlements of the adjacent mainland. No cereals were identified, but bones of pig were plentiful. Since pigs did not occur naturally on the island, they must have been introduced by the new settlers, but whether semi-wild or domesticated is unclear.

By the Late Aceramic period, from the mid-ninth to the seventh century, the number of settlements had increased, and at several sites in the south of the island, notably Shillourokambos and Mylouthkia, the full range of domesticates is represented: sheep, goats, cattle, and pigs, as well as cereals and pulses. One interesting curiosity is the presence of fallow deer, which were presumably allowed to run wild and were hunted. Fallow deer were not a native of Cyprus and must have been introduced by humans. The progressive settlement of Cyprus during the period of the Younger Dryas (10,800–9600 BC), which involved the transhipping of breeding populations of domestic animals as well as the seed grain needed to sustain the pioneer communities, was a significant event, but it was only a prelude to a more widespread westerly colonization that was to follow.

The next stage was the settlement of Crete about 7000 BC by farmers bringing with them domesticated sheep or goats, pigs, and cattle, as well as a supply of bread wheat seeds. Their journey from Asia Minor, possibly from the vicinity of the Knidos peninsula, took them via Rhodes, Karpathos, and Kasos, a journey of over 100 nautical miles. That the settlement which they established on the hill, now occupied by the Palace of Knossos, was successful is shown by the considerable thickness of occupation deposits that subsequently developed. Setting up a successful farming community on a distant island is no mean achievement. It required reconnaissance, and perhaps a phase of seasonal occupation, before the arduous task of transporting a sufficient number of domesticated animals and making provision for their care could begin. Comparative studies have suggested that the minimum number of humans needed to set up a community that could sustain itself by interbreeding was about forty. Once it was established, new immigrants could join the pioneers and links with the homeland could be maintained.

During the period 7500–6000 BC the westward movement of communities from southern Asia Minor continued as large numbers crossed the Aegean to settle in eastern Greece from the southern Peloponnese to the Plain of Thessaly. To begin with the culture was aceramic, but after about 6500 BC pottery came into general use. The scale of the settlement was considerable: already thirty village settlements have been identified and many more remain to be discovered. Some were large and could have accommodated two to three hundred people. In eastern Thessaly, where the density of settlement is greatest, there is one village for every 10 square kilometres. The pioneers introduced the full Neolithic 'package': domesticated animals, barley, and emmer and einkorn wheat. They also brought a range of technological skills, pottery making, the art of moulding clay into figurines, the ability to grind stone to make implements, and knowledge of spinning and weaving using flax. While there can be no doubt that the culture of these early farming communities, well established in Greece by 6000 BC, derived from Asia Minor, nowhere in Greece can a pioneer Asian culture be identified: there are always subtle differences. This can best be explained by the dynamics of immigration. At such a time old social ties and traditional values are loosened, strangers with different cultural preferences come together, and an entirely new landscape has to be tamed. All was in flux, and when eventually the pioneer communities became established, they expressed their new identities in new ways. Nor should we forget that the indigenous population, sparse though it may have been, will have contributed not only its genes but also its values and skills to the mix through intermarriage.

The outward movement of populations from the Levant and Asia Minor, which began in earnest in the mid-ninth millennium, reached a peak in the early seventh millennium, and saw the establishment of farming communities on the large islands of Cyprus and Crete and on the mainland of Greece, was part of complex processes driven by many factors including population growth, climatic change, and environmental degradation brought about by the over-exploitation of the fragile homeland ecologies. The westward movement involved the extensive use of the sea, and, as we have seen, it is possible that the sea was also the route used by the pioneer groups who introduced agriculture into the Nile delta region and to Baluchistan. Mastery of the oceans, skills first learnt by the Epipalaeolithic hunter-gatherers, enabled the Neolithic diaspora to begin. It also continued to play a crucial role.

Across the European Peninsula

The spread of the Neolithic economy throughout the European peninsula began about 6000 BC and had, by 5000 BC, reached the Atlantic seaboard, covering a distance of about 2,700 kilometres. One axis of advance lay through the temperate forests in the centre of the peninsula, utilizing the corridors created by the Danube and other great rivers like the Rhine and the Seine. The second line of advance was by sea along the northern shores of the Mediterranean, taking in the islands of Sicily, Sardinia, and Corsica, and extending through the Strait of Gibraltar to the Atlantic coasts of Portugal.

The overland route began with pioneer farmers and spread northwards across Bulgaria through the valleys of the Vardar and the Morava to the lower Danube valley and, from there, along the middle Danube into the Carpathian basin. The move out of the Aegean zone and into the forested heartland of Europe introduced agricultural

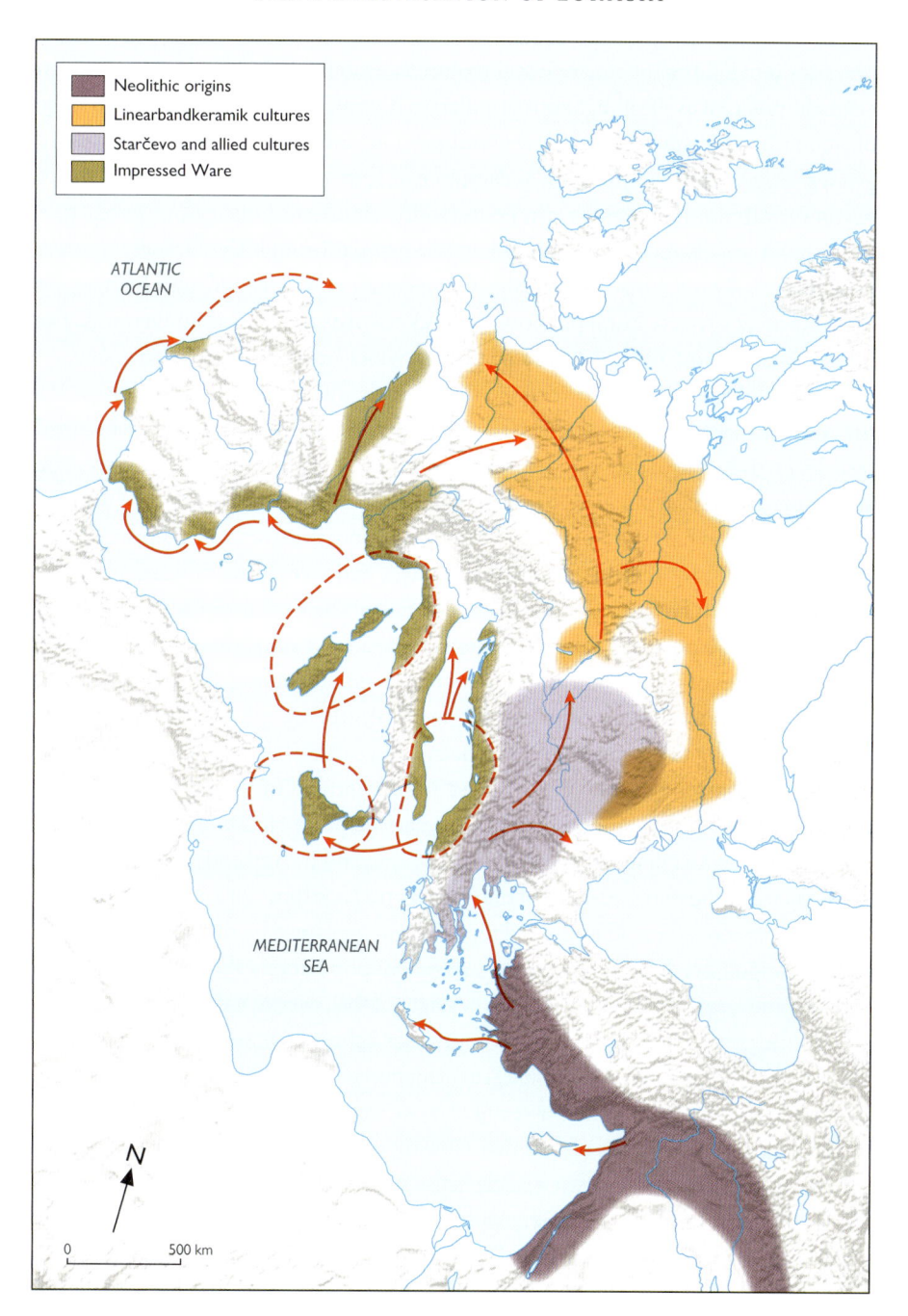

2.12 The spread of farming practice from the Fertile Crescent to the Atlantic was rapid. It began about 7000 BC and was accomplished within two thousand years. Two main lines of advance can be traced, one via the rivers flowing through the centre of Europe, the other via the Mediterranean

practices into a different ecozone and required a number of cultural adaptations to be made, not least as the indigenous population became assimilated. This initial stage of Neolithization was completed by about 5500 BC and gave rise to several regional groups variously named after type sites, Starčevo, Körös, and Criş, but showing much in common. It was from this base in Transdanubia (modern Hungary and Serbia) that a new wave of advance began extending westwards through the temperate forest zone, eventually reaching the English Channel coast and spreading into Brittany by about 5000 BC. This cultural phenomenon is known as the Linearbandkeramik, the name of a dominant form of decorated pottery widely used throughout the zone.

The second axis of advance, through the Mediterranean, began about 6000 BC on the Adriatic coast of Greece and had reached Portugal by 5500 BC. It is characterized by a distinctive style of decorated pottery known as Cardial, or Impressed, Ware. The spread of agricultural practices by sea led to the establishment of a series of discrete coastal enclaves where the new methods of food production were taken up and developed. Eventually, by about 5000 BC, the enclaves had coalesced and variants of the South West Asian farming package, modified to suit the local ecologies, were found around the entire northern side of the Mediterranean and along the Atlantic coasts.

Within a brief one thousand years two of Europe's major zones, the Mediterranean and the Temperate Forest zone, had changed from being the preserve of hunter-gatherers to being the land of farmers reliant upon cattle, sheep, goats, and pigs, and cultivated wheats and barley that had been domesticated in the hilly flanks of the Fertile Crescent. It took another thousand years before agriculture was adopted in the Netherlands and had begun to spread to Britain and Ireland and to Scandinavia.

The speed of the initial advance of the farming package through Europe is a remarkable phenomenon. It could be argued that it is best explained by the rapid acceptance of the new food-producing strategies by indigenous populations. But while this may be true in some areas, particularly in the later stages of the process, it does not adequately explain the considerable cultural similarities that appear over very large areas at the time of the initial advances. The simplest explanation is that the pioneering groups were drawn by social imperatives to move, and to move west—not unlike, perhaps, the nineteenth-century colonization of America. How this worked within the social system we can only guess, but if each newly established settlement required young sons to move away from the home base into unexploited territory, then an energy would have been generated that could well have resulted in rapid advances of the kind recognizable in the archaeological evidence. This could apply to the movements both through the heart of the European peninsula and along its Mediterranean fringe. The environmental factors that drove people to move out of southern Asia Minor and the Levant may have set up systems in society that invested status on those who were the most mobile.

Into the Steppe

To the east of the Carpathian mountain arc lay the Pontic-Caspian steppe, on the south limited by the Black Sea, the Caspian Sea, and the Caucasus Mountains running between them, and on the north by the forest-steppe zone, an area of light tree cover interspersed with open meadows soon giving way, as one progressed north, to dense forests. The eastern limit of the Pontic-Caspian steppe is marked by the southern extension of the Ural Mountains, which approaches the north end of the Caspian Sea, narrowing the steppe corridor at this point. After the Last Glacial Maximum the Caspian had been much larger, called by geologists the Khvalyn Sea. By 9000 BC it had grown to such an extent that it overflowed and poured through the Manych Depression into the Sea of Azov and thence to the Black Sea. A thousand years later the waters had receded towards the present shores, leaving an extensive surrounding plain of salty clay known as the North Caspian Depression. This unfriendly ecozone, together with the lower reaches of the Ural River flowing through it, helped to separate the Pontic-Caspian steppe from the Kazakh steppe to the east.

Between the Carpathian Mountains and the Urals the vast expanse of steppe, and its northern fringe of forest-steppe, was sliced into separate regions by a series of great rivers flowing southwards from the forest zone to the seas. These rivers were significant obstacles and tended to form the boundaries of social groups. It was eastwards across these divides that knowledge of agriculture spread in the sixth and fifth millennia.

The first farming settlements to encroach eastwards through the Carpathian Mountains about 5800 BC belonged to the Criş culture, which had developed within the Carpathian arc as a result of the first pioneer movements out of Greece. Once through the high mountains, the Criş farmers established settlements on the piedmont and then moved down into the valleys of the Siret and Prut within the forest-steppe zone. They carried with them the full range of cultivated plants: barley, a range of wheat, and pulses. They also introduced domesticated cattle and pigs, which flourished in the woodland environment. Sheep, though present, were not common.

While the evidence for the new farming settlements is clear enough, what the phenomenon means in terms of actual population movement is less certain. It could be argued that we are seeing simply the acculturation of local foragers eager to accept new ways of life. On the other hand, the adoption of the whole Neolithic cultural package over a short period of time would argue that at least some pioneer farmers from across the Carpathians were involved in the transformation. A few hundred years later, between 5500 and 5200 BC, new cultural influences from the Linearbandkeramik

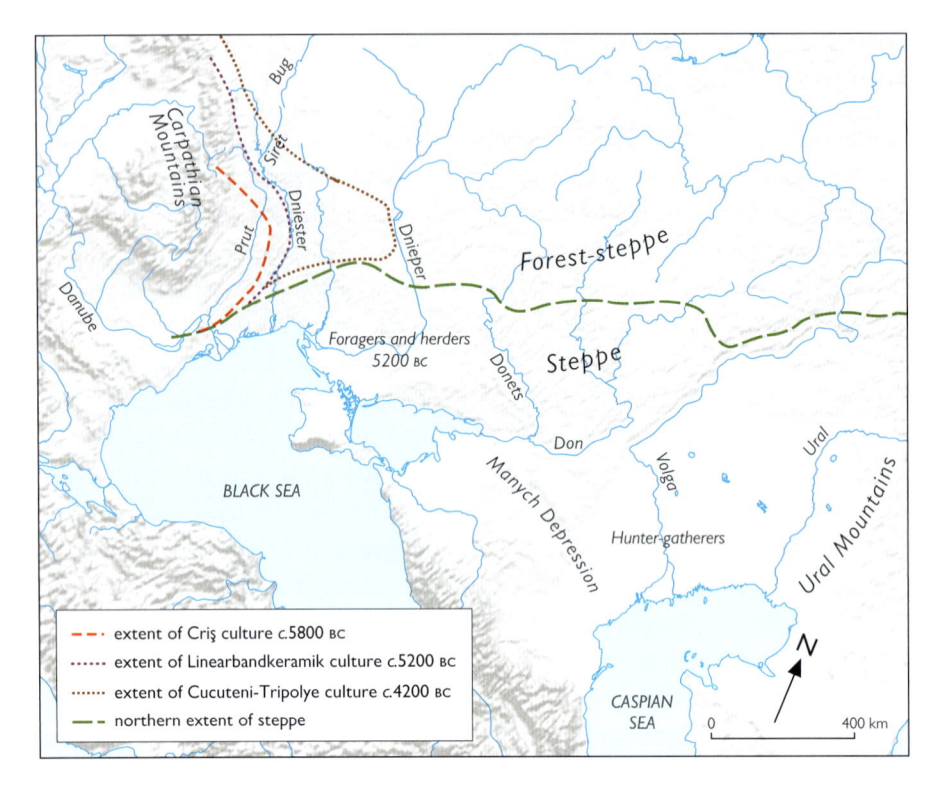

2.13 The spread of farming practices from eastern Europe to the Pontic steppe took place during the sixth and fifth millennia. Two processes were involved: the migration of farming communities from the east and the acculturation of the foraging and herding groups who were already well established there

region of southern Poland appear in the area, suggesting that another wave of farmers were moving in to augment the communities already established there.

All this time the river Dniester formed a boundary between the farmers and foragers. Beyond, to the east, in the valley of the river Bug, the foragers, whose traditional livelihood was based on fishing and hunting the red deer, roe deer, and wild boar flourishing in the forest-steppe, began to adopt domesticates from their farming neighbours. Cattle and pig were now being herded, and einkorn, emmer, and spelt wheat were grown, but hunted game still accounted for between 65 and 80 per cent of the meat eaten. These people were still strictly foragers but were prepared to accept some modification in lifestyle introduced to them through social contacts and intermarriage.

The Dniester valley 'frontier' remained until about 5200 BC, when new cultural developments among the agricultural communities, characterized by archaeologists as the Cucuteni-Tripolye culture, initiated the rapid advance of farming villages to the east beyond the Dniester and into the valley of the Bug. This new cultural complex lasted for two thousand years on the interface between peninsular Europe and the steppe. Beyond, in the valleys of the Dnieper and the Donets, the foraging groups began to herd domestic cattle, pigs, sheep, and goats, the numbers of domesticated animals varying from 30 to 75 per cent. Herding was under way in the Dniester valley by about 5200 BC and from here spread eastwards to the Volga–Ural steppe, arriving there about 4700 BC. The growing importance of herds to the steppe societies is shown by the use of animal sacrifices in human burials. At the cemetery of Khvalynsk, in the middle of the Volga region, 158 human burials were accompanied by fifty-two sheep or goats, twenty-three cattle, and eleven horses (it is not known if the horses were wild or domesticated). The sacrifice of valuable domestic animals is an indication of both the value of the animal and the close relationships that had now developed between humans and their flocks and herds. Less can be said of the extent to which grain cultivation was adopted. Low levels of wheat, barley, and millet are recorded in the Dnieper valley sites, but beyond there, cereals are hardly known until after 4200 BC.

What stands out in a study of the relationship between the full agricultural communities of eastern Europe and the foragers of the steppe and forest-steppe zone is the resilience of indigenous traditions. In peninsular Europe the new farming practices were quickly adopted, while in the east, beyond the Dniester and later the Dnieper frontiers, indigenous practices persisted. There were no doubt many reasons for this. The energy of the pioneer farmers seems to have been directed towards the west, into the more congenial wooded zones of temperate and Mediterranean Europe. One wonders, too, how much a fascination for following the setting sun may have been a factor in the westerly colonization. The farmers who looked east confronted a very different landscape, one of steppe inhabited by foragers already well adapted to the open landscape and whose livelihood was based on fishing and the hunting of deer and horses. It was much less inviting to farmers. The hunters soon adopted domesticated cattle, sheep, and pigs to become herders, but stark differences persisted. The steppe retained its identity.

The East Asian Cradle

In eastern Asia settled agriculture developed in the period between 8000 and 6000 BC in two separate regions, the valleys of the Yellow River and the Yangtze, based on the cultivation of two very different crops, millet and rice. Domestication of crops and animals in the two valleys was quite independent of the parallel processes taking place at much the same time in South West Asia. They were related only in so far as that in both regions hunter-gatherers were responding to the fast-changing environmental conditions following the end of the Last Glacial Maximum.

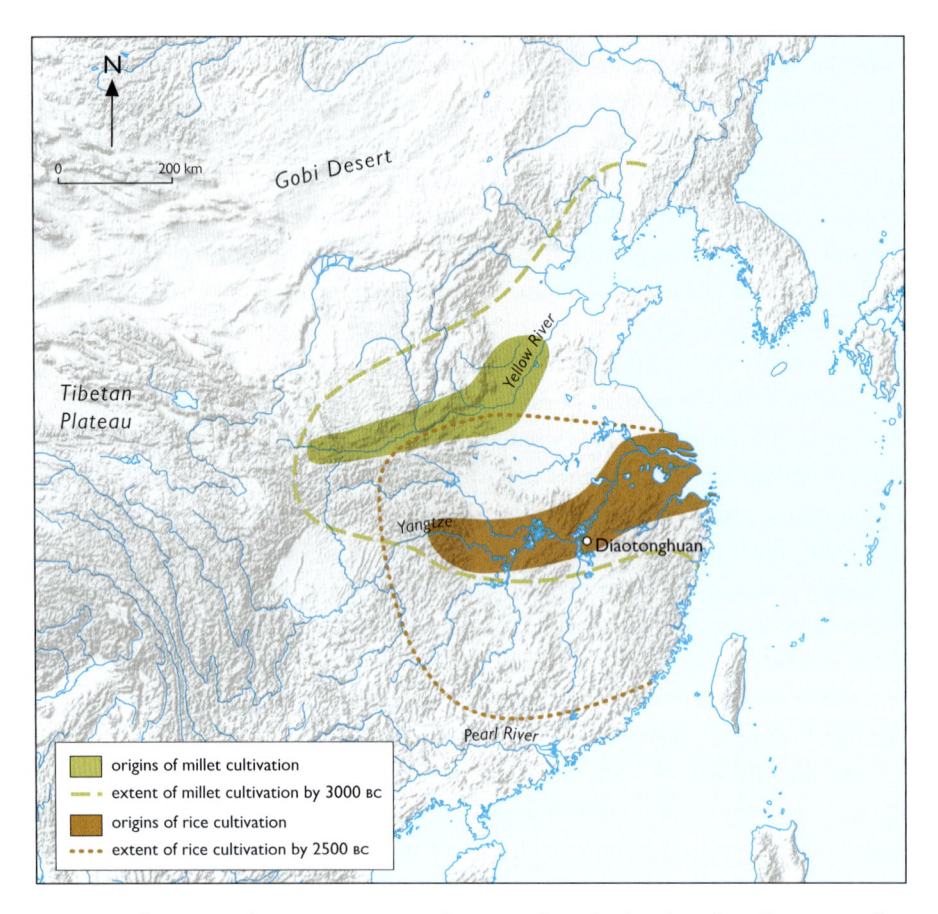

2.14 In South East Asia there were two areas where agriculture developed. In the Yellow River valley millet was the main crop, while in the Yangtze valley the conditions were ideal for rice cultivation. By the third millennium the cultivation of the two crops had spread well beyond their areas of origin

The two cereals that became the staple crops required very different growing conditions and in their wild states occupied quite separate environments. Wild rice (*Oryza rufipogon*) requires warm, wet conditions. It is essentially a marsh plant that needs to grow in standing water. In its natural state it will only grow where there is more than 1,000 millimetres of rain a year and where the summer temperatures needed for ripening are in excess of 16 °C. These conditions prevailed in parts of South East Asia and by 13,000 BC, with the climatic amelioration following the Last Glacial Maximum, had extended northwards to embrace the valley of the Yangtze.

Two different species of millet were eventually cultivated: broomcorn, or common, millet (*Panicum miliaceum*) and foxtail millet (*Setaria italica*). The wild ancestor of broomcorn millet has not been definitively identified, but weedy forms are widespread across Central Asia from Mongolia to the Caspian basin. The wild ancestor of foxtail millet was even more widespread, extending into Europe, but was not a native of the Fertile Crescent zone. Both millets grew wild on the loess soils of the Yellow River catchment, and it was in this region that they were first cultivated.

The Origins of Rice Cultivation in the Yangtze Valley

By 13,000 BC the Yangtze valley lay within the zone in which rice could grow naturally. Later, in the warmer conditions following the Younger Dryas, domesticated rice is found as far north as the valley of the Huai. The middle reaches of the Yangtze, where the river flowed through a lake-filled lowland and the deltaic region towards the river mouth, provided ideal conditions for wild rice to flourish, and it was here that cultivation began.

Several deeply stratified cave sites overlooking the middle reaches of the valley have provided the crucial evidence for the increasing importance of wild rice to the diet of the foragers and the gradual transition from the wild (*O. rufipogon*) to the domesticated (*O. sativa*) variety. One of the most informative sequences comes from the cave at Diaotonghuan, where the accumulated deposits span the period from 12,000 to 6000 BC. The first wild rice appeared about 11,000 BC as the temperature became warm enough for it to begin to grow in quantities worth gathering. The site lay on the very limit of rice viability and with the onset of the Younger Dryas cold spell wild rice became rare. With the return of warmer conditions, between 9000 BC and 8000 BC, the collection of wild rice picked up again, but now cultivated strains began to appear alongside the wild. Thereafter the cultivated form increased rapidly in proportion until, by 6000 BC, it was entirely dominant. Given this informative sequence, it is tempting to suggest that stress placed on the growth of wild rice, here at its very limit of viability, by the Younger Dryas cold downturn encouraged the foragers who had become dependent on it to begin to manipulate the plant in a way that led to the selection of the more robust domesticated forms. In parallel with the transition from wild to cultivated rice other significant changes can be traced. The bones of wild pig and chicken are found in the lower layers, but by 6000 BC both appear to have become domesticated. The appearance of pottery in the ninth millennium is a further indication that by now the community was becoming increasingly sedentary.

The story charted in the thick deposits in the Diaotonghuan cave, and supported by other sites in the neighbourhood, provides a convincing narrative of the transition from foraging to full-scale food production in the mid Yangtze valley. In the absence of other archaeological evidence to the contrary, it suggests that rice cultivation may have begun here. But this need not rule out other possibilities. Recent genetic work on rice has suggested that the actual focus of domestication may have been in the valley of the Pearl River in southern China, but there is as yet no archaeological evidence to support this.

After about 7000 BC permanent villages began to be established on the hills and plains around the lakes of the middle Yangtze. Rice was now the staple crop, but other water plants, such as edible lotus and water caltrops, were also being collected to augment the diet, and pigs and chicken were being reared. This stable subsistence base allowed for the population to increase, requiring social systems to become more complex. As a result distinct regional cultures began to appear.

Knowledge of rice cultivation spread outwards from the Yangtze valley. By the mid-third millennium it had reached north-westwards into the Yellow River valley and southwards into Vietnam and Thailand. By 2000 BC rice had been adopted by farming communities in Korea, who, for two millennia, had been cultivating millet. The highly successful foragers of the Japanese islands eventually took up rice cultivation, but not until 300 BC. In the Ganges valley rice cultivation is known from the second millennium. It has been argued that the Indian variety (*O. indica*) developed indigenously from the wild variety, but recent genetic work has shown that it evolved about 2000 BC from strains that were originally cultivated much earlier in the Yangtze.

The Origins of Millet Cultivation in the Yellow River Region

The Yellow River region of northern China is drier and colder than the Yangtze valley. It is, for the most part, an area of rolling loess lowlands. Following the end of the Last Glacial Maximum the regions would have been largely open steppe dotted with a few coniferous trees, supporting herds of wild horse, deer, gazelle, and rhinoceros together with some more limited flocks of wild sheep. With the warming of the climate, briefly reversed by the Younger Dryas episode, the vegetation gradually changed to an open woodland of deciduous trees interspersed with areas of herbaceous plants and grasses, well watered by the run-off from the glaciers of the Asian interior. It was here that the wild precursors of domestic millet, both foxtail and broomcorn, flourished. Broomcorn millet was more resistant to drought and could occupy niches less suited to foxtail millet. Before 8000 BC foragers living in the valley of the Fen River were hunting gazelle and cutting wild foxtail millet with stone sickles and grinding it to make flour to supplement their diet, but elsewhere, on the more open steppe, where gazelle, deer, horse, and cattle were being hunted, there is little evidence for the collection of wild grasses.

2.15 The Yellow River, seen here in north-west China, meanders its way across northern China from its source in the Tibetan plateau. It carries a heavy load of loessic sediment (hence the yellow colour) which is deposited in the middle and lower reaches, creating a fertile flood-plain

Cultivation of millet probably began in the foothills of the mountains forming the western fringe of the North China Plain in the period between 8000 BC and 6000 BC, leading to the emergence of sedentary villages on the plain and in the Wei valley. Some were large. At Cishan, on the Nanming River, occupation covered an area of 8 hectares and the site probably supported a population of several hundred. The villages were characterized by semi-subterranean houses and numerous pits for storing grain (over three hundred at Cishan): the dead were inhumed in cemeteries nearby. Cultivated broomcorn millet was now the staple crop but was augmented by rape, wild huckleberry seeds, and nuts. Fields were cultivated with stone spades and the crop harvested with stone or shell sickles and ground with mortars and pestles. The protein component of the diet came from domesticated pigs and chickens augmented by fishing and the hunting of deer and wild pig. Other domestic crafts, consistent with a sedentary style of settlement, were spinning, weaving, and potting. Thus, by 6000 BC the tentative steps leading to a full agricultural economy had been taken. Communities were now firmly established in their own territories and were sufficiently stable to be able to support a rising population.

The consolidation of Neolithic culture that followed in the Yellow River regions saw settlements increase in number and size. Social stratification is evident in the quality of the grave goods accompanying the dead. In parallel with this there was a

THE DOMESTICATION OF EURASIA

development in craft skills. Specialist jade workers and potters can now be identified, and the potter's wheel was invented in the late fourth millennium. The increasing population and the growing complexity of society led to distinctive regional cultures identified principally through their traditions of potting. By 3000 BC the stage was set for the emergence of state systems.

The parallel development of agricultural systems in the Yangtze and Yellow river valleys, relying on different staple crops but the same domesticated animals, raises a number of interesting questions. Did one region have precedence over the other and was there creative interaction between them, or were the gradual steps towards the domestication of plants and animals taken in isolation and only later, when societies had become more populous and complex, did networks begin to link them? There are no easy answers, and on the evidence currently available it is simplest to explain the phenomenon as the natural response of two groups of people, living in areas of different resource, to the climatic changes that encouraged them to become more sedentary and to begin to exercise a greater control over their food staples. It was geography that determined what grasses were available to them.

2.16 The excavation of part of the early Neolithic settlement of Xinglongwa in north-east China. The close-packed rectangular houses were laid out in rows with storage pits both inside and outside the houses. Occasional human burials were found beneath house floors. The settlement dates to 6200–5200 BC and vividly demonstrates the high degree of social organization already under way by this early date

The Steppe Corridor: Some Possibilities

The apparently wide distribution of domesticated millet by about 5000 BC is at first sight puzzling. It is concentrated in northern and central China, where, as we have seen, there is evidence that it was domesticated from wild strains but has also been claimed to have been found in eastern and central Europe by this time. Since wild foxtail millet is found in both regions and the tract in between, and wild broomcorn millet is certainly known as far west as the Caspian Sea, there remains a possibility that domestication may have taken place in both China and Europe independently. However, a recent reassessment of millet grains from early contexts in Europe using radiocarbon dating methods has shown that all the samples tested are more recent than originally thought, dating to no earlier than the mid-second millennium. If this proves to be the case for all the claimed 'early' occurrences in Europe, then the simplest explanation would be that there was only one focus of domestication, in China, and that cultivated millet was introduced in the west much later, probably along the steppe corridor. In this context the site of Begash in eastern Kazakhstan is of some relevance. Here cultivated broomcorn millet has been found in contexts dating to 2500–2000 BC. Begash probably lay on the route along which commodities and knowledge were being exchanged between east and west.

The reality of east–west exchange is supported by another discovery: Begash has yielded a significant quantity of wheat. Wheat has also been found in China at four sites dating variously between 2600 BC and 1700 BC. Since wild wheat is not found outside South West Asia, the Kazakh and Chinese examples must have come from the wheat-growing areas of the west. This would suggest that by the latter part of the third millennium wheat was being transported through the Central Asian steppe to China. Begash occupies a crucial position on an east–west route leading through the Dzhungar Mountains, while one of the Chinese sites where wheat has been found, Xiashanping, is sited on the Gansu Corridor, the main entry point to China from the west. Where the imported wheat originated is uncertain. The nearest sources, on the southern fringe of the Karakum desert or the northern extremities of the Indus valley, are unlikely because of the formidable desert and mountain barrier in between. A far more plausible route would have been from the Pontic steppe by way of the steppe corridor. The domesticated millet, found along the steppe route, could be another reflection of east–west exchange. It is not yet clear what the status of cereals was in the steppe zone, but the excavation of Begash suggests that since here they were used in burial rituals, they are more likely to have been a rare and valuable commodity than a staple crop in everyday consumption.

THE DOMESTICATION OF EURASIA

Finally, what of the origin of the domesticated animals found on early sites in China? Dogs and pigs had been domesticated locally by 7000 BC and it is possible that chickens were domesticated not long after, but such evidence as there is suggests that domesticated sheep, goats, cattle, and horses may not have appeared in China before the latter half of the third millennium. These grazing beasts, which often coexist in pastoral economies, are most likely to have been introduced into northern China from the steppe. The other principal domesticates, zeba cattle and water buffalo, arrived from the south-west but probably not until as late as the Han dynasty.

While it must be admitted that the evidence is at present somewhat sparse, it does point to the intriguing possibility that, as early as the third millennium, the steppe was already serving as a corridor for the transmission of cultural commodities and ideas. We shall see later the crucial role the steppe was to play in the spread first of copper technology and later of domesticated horses from the west to the east.

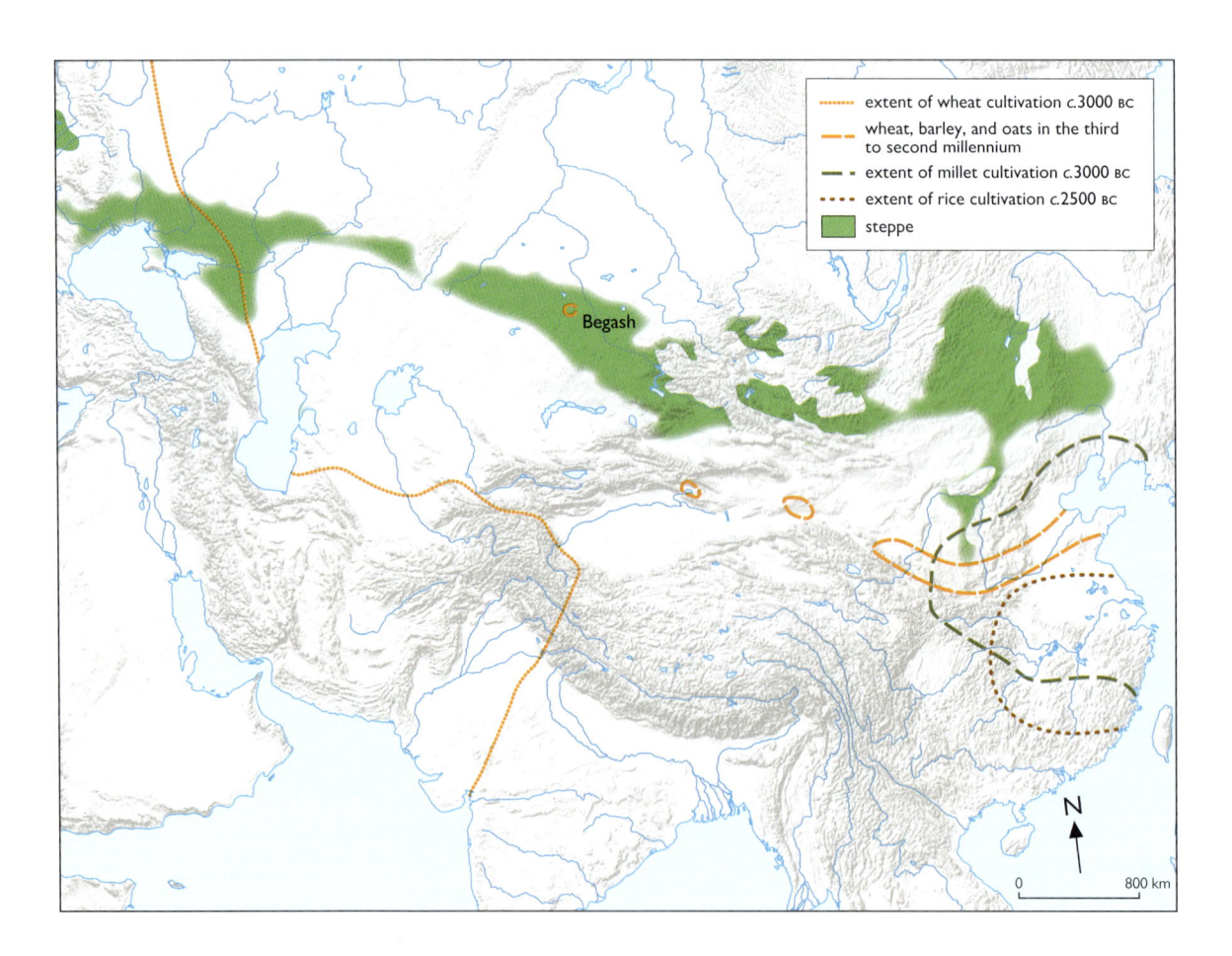

2.17 Wheat was the principal crop of South West Asia, while millet and rice predominated in South East Asia. Towards the end of the third millennium, wheat, barley, and oats were introduced into South East Asia from the west, either via the steppe route or through the Pamir mountains. This is the first recognizable long-distance transfer between east and west

Retrospect

Until about 10,000 BC Eurasia was occupied by a palimpsest of hunter-gatherer communities, all with subsistence strategies carefully geared to the ecological niches in which they lived and all striving, in their different ways, to cope with pressures created by the changing climate and by population growth. Some, occupying particularly favoured environments in the hilly flanks of the Fertile Crescent and the valleys of the Yellow River and the Yangtze, were able to give stability to their food-gathering pursuits by bringing selected grasses into cultivation and by domesticating some of the animals they had previously hunted. Once these new productive systems were in place, a more sedentary way of life could evolve, leading to the creation of large permanent settlements and an increasingly complex social system. Where natural resources were prolific and large surpluses could be generated and stored, state systems, or 'civilizations', could result as they did in Mesopotamia, in the valleys of the Nile, the Amu Darya (Oxus), and the Indus, and in China.

The agricultural package originating in the hilly flanks of the Fertile Crescent spread rapidly to Egypt and Europe, and across the Iranian plateau to the Amu Darya and Indus valleys. That which evolved in China had a less immediate geographical impact. The difference is likely to have been due to a number of interacting variables. In the rather fragile environment of South West Asia overproduction exacerbated by population growth led to environmental degradation, encouraging communities to move away from their homelands in search of new territories. The number of people on the move may have been comparatively small and may have affected only the immediately peripheral lands, but once the movement had begun, knowledge of agriculture spread far and wide, covering a vast territory from the Atlantic to the Indus valley and from the southern deserts to the coniferous forests and the western steppe.

China was altogether different. The river catchments of the Yellow River and the Yangtze were rich and varied enough to sustain a growing population. The loess soils were easily cleared and highly fertile, while the irrigated rice fields maintained their fertility through flooding. As a result the population grew steadily without crisis. Geography also constrained outward expansion. To the north and west lay mountains interspersed with deserts and steppe, while to the south the lightly wooded landscapes quickly gave way to tropical jungle, into which agricultural practices were slow to spread: China was a tightly contained world.

By 4000 BC the two agricultural zones, east and west, were still worlds apart, separated by formidable mountains and deserts. Only the steppe offered an easy passage between them.

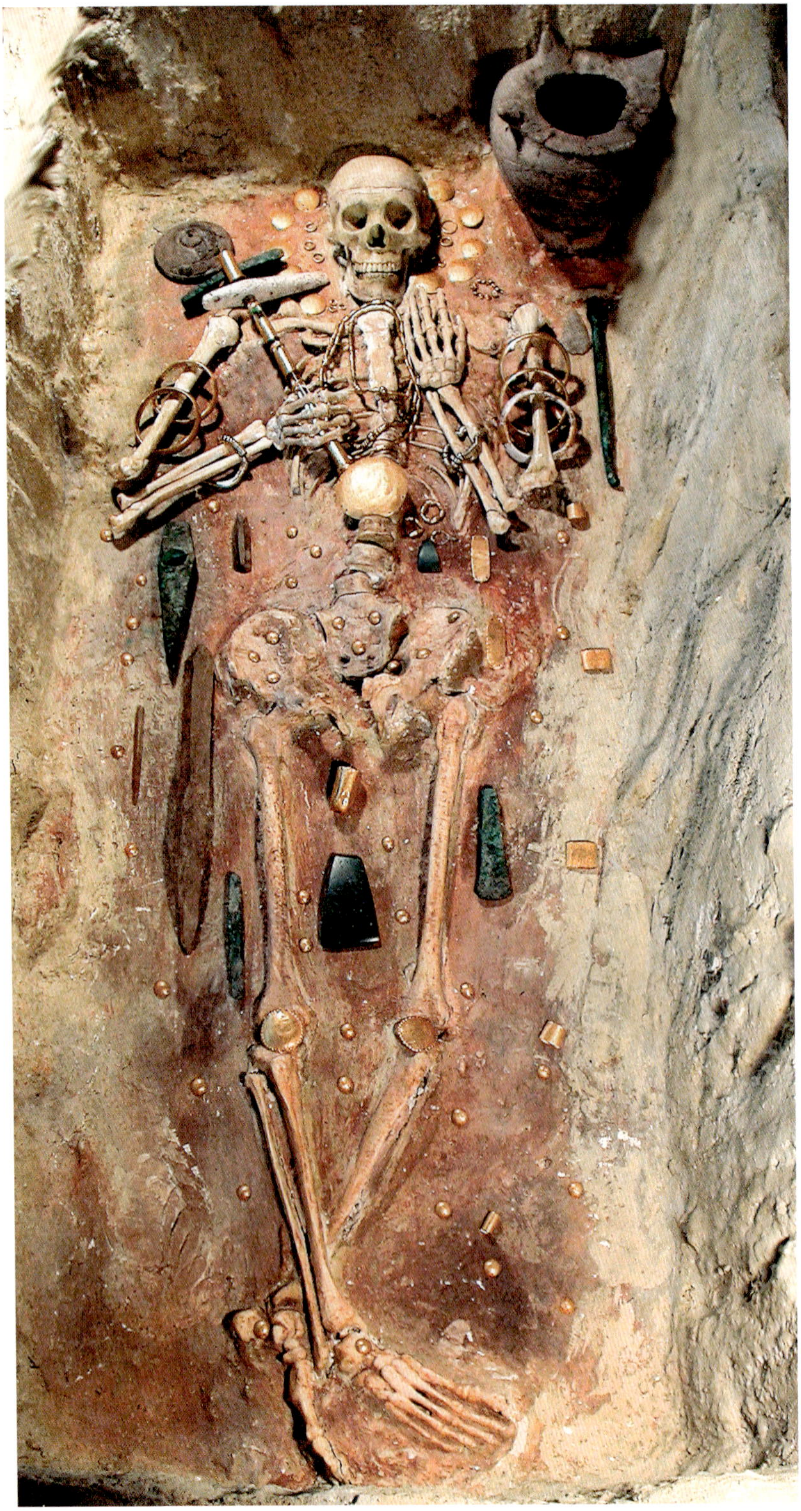

3

HORSES AND COPPER

THE CENTRALITY OF
THE STEPPE, 5000–2500 BC

Starting out on horseback from the Great Hungarian Plain in early spring and never leaving the steppe it would be possible for a rider to reach Mongolia before winter had set in. On his progress from the wide Pontic-Caspian steppe to the Kazakh steppe the traveller would have passed around the southern extremity of the Urals in the narrow corridor flanked by the desert to the south, and to reach the Mongolian steppe would have meant negotiating the upland plains through the Altai Mountains or using the Dzungarian Corridor to the south, but all the time the rider would have been confronted by the familiar, monotonous grassland except when crossing the rivers, fast-flowing in their wooded, marshy flood-plains. Our traveller would have set out in oceans of spring flowers, have spent the scorching days of high summer crossing the parched Kazakh grasslands, and would have reached Mongolia just in time to enjoy the sudden flush of new autumn growth before the intense cold of winter gripped the land. The steppe is the most remarkable natural corridor in the world. It is here that the first horses were domesticated and ridden, where mobile pastoralism first emerged, where the fast two-wheeled chariot was invented, and where riders first learnt to work together as cavalry with world-shattering effect.

The steppe was not a static environment: it was subject to fluctuations in climate which had a direct effect on the human communities living there. Between 6000 and

4000 BC, known as the Atlantic period, the climate of the earth reached its warmest. Temperatures peaked in the centuries after 5200 BC, causing the steppe grasslands to expand and the forests in the river valleys to contract. Then, about 4200 BC, temperatures declined rapidly, heralding a period known as the Piora Oscillation, which lasted until 3800 BC, when temperatures were at their coldest for two thousand years. Traditional crops struggled to grow and the great rivers flooded, causing massive erosion in the fertile flood-plains, while the intense cold of the winters would have made it more difficult to keep cattle and sheep alive. Although temperatures recovered after 3800 BC, there were further minor fluctuations in the period to follow. The most far-reaching was a change to much drier and cooler conditions between 3500 and 3000 BC. For the steppe dweller this meant that to feed and water flocks and herds, animals had to be moved over much greater distances. All these changes, as we shall see, had significant effects on the lifestyles of the steppe communities and drove changes, sometimes of great social import.

Herders and Farmers on the Pontic-Caspian Steppe, 5200–4500 BC

Until the late sixth millennium the Dniester valley had formed a cultural frontier between the sedentary farming communities to the west and the foragers to the east, who had begun to herd domesticated cattle and pigs and to grow some wheat. By about 5200 BC an advance of the farmers eastwards into the valley of the Bug brought the foragers in the Dnieper and Donets region into direct contact with the farmers, from whom they began to acquire domesticated animals, cattle, pigs, and some sheep and goats to augment their diets. It was from here over the next five hundred years that herding spread across the steppe to reach the river Ural.

The shift from foraging to herding across the Pontic-Caspian steppe initiated major economic, social, and cultural changes, but the region was vast, and there were many different local responses to the availability of domesticates. Domesticated animals as a percentage of the total meat bones found at settlements can vary between 30 and 75 per cent, and the composition of flock and herds can show significant differences between sites, with sheep sometimes reaching as high as 50 per cent of the domesticates. The wild animals favoured in the hunt were horses, red deer, roe deer, wild pig, and beaver, the last no doubt more attractive for its pelt than for its meat. Differences in animal bone assemblages may well reflect real differences in food-producing strategies, but there is always the possibility that they were caused by the way in which rubbish was disposed of and the vagaries of archaeological recovery.

The growing importance of domesticated animals to the lives of the herder-forager is well demonstrated by their association with burial rituals. The classical site is the cemetery at Khvalynsk on the west bank of the middle Volga, which dates to the period 4700–3900 BC. Here twenty-two of the 158 human burials were associated with sacrifices of sheep or goats, cattle, and horses. The animals were presumably slaughtered at the time of the burial to provide meat for the funeral feasts and their bones subsequently deposited in the latter stages of the *rite de passage* of death. It is here that we find for the first time 'head and hide' burials, a practice that was to become widespread throughout the steppe region. Only the skull and the bones of the lower parts of the legs are deposited, the implication being that the animal was butchered in such a way as to leave the head and legs intact, held together by the hide. Draped over a framework it could give the impression of a complete standing beast. Just such constructions were still being set up by shamans in Siberia in the late nineteenth century.

Herders invariably develop close relationships with their beasts through spending long hours with them. In addition to providing an appropriate sacrifice for the burial of a person of status, sheep and cattle can provide meat, milk, and blood for the diet, as well as a range of secondary products including hide, wool, horn, bone, sinew, and dung. Meat would rarely have been taken from domestic stock other than for funerals or other occasions when feasting was called for. Milk was a vital commodity and would have made cattle more valuable to the community than sheep or goats, whose yield was lower. Humans are naturally lactose-intolerant but the mutation favouring tolerance occurs sporadically in populations. Recent genetic research has shown that this mutation quickly became dominant in the steppe region west of the Urals in the period 4600–2800 BC. Clearly, in an area where milk was available as a supplement to diet, natural selection would have worked in favour of those able to digest milk. Once this genetic change was under way, milk production would have become increasingly important to herders, who now needed to spend less time supplementing the diet by hunting. But a decline in fresh meat would have brought its own dietary problems since the body needs salt. The deficiency could, however, have been overcome by bleeding the livestock from time to time and drinking the blood.

The maintenance of flocks and herds, and the increasing dependence on domesticated, as opposed to wild, animals created a system in which a social hierarchy could emerge among the herders with status reflected by herd size. The loan or gift of animals could also create ties of patronage and clientage. Such a hierarchical system is amply demonstrated by sacrifices accompanying funerary rites, as at Khvalynsk and at cemeteries such as Mariupol in the Dnieper valley, where the elite were buried with boar's tusk plaques, thousands of strung shell beads, imported items of exotic polished stone, and ornaments of copper and gold. The same range of items is found in elite burials throughout the Pontic-Caspian steppe at the time. The exotics would have been acquired by gift exchange networks from far-flung sources. Shell beads came from the Aegean, copper from the Balkans, and rare stone like jet, rock crystal, and porphyry from the Caucasus. The increasing quantity of rare materials in circulation implies not only that the steppe communities had networks of connectivity stretching into Europe and South West Asia, but that they produced desirable surpluses that could be used in reciprocal exchange. What these surpluses could have been at this stage is a matter of speculation. Animal furs from the forest-steppe is one likely possibility, but so, too, are wool and horses for riding.

Whence Came Woolly Sheep?

Sheep and goats, as we saw in the previous chapter, were domesticated in South West Asia, probably in the region of eastern Anatolia and northern Syria between 8000 and 7500 BC, and were part of the agricultural package that was transmitted to Greece and the Balkans during the pioneering movements in the seventh millennium. From there the herding of domesticated sheep and goats was gradually taken up by foraging communities in the Pontic-Caspian steppe during the sixth and fifth millennia and became an essential part of the herder economy. In their wild and early domesticated state sheep were essentially hairy animals with short wool growing between the hair to provide warmth in winter and shed before summer. Once the flocks had been transferred by humans from their natural habitat into more alien and colder climates, it is likely that natural selection began to favour the beasts that grew more abundant winter wool.

The earliest use of wool, acquired when it was shed or by plucking the animals, would have been to make felt by beating the short fibres together. But as natural selection began to favour longer and longer wool fibres, the plucked wool could begin to be spun and the resulting yarn woven into fabrics. The most likely scenario, then, is that woolly sheep evolved on the Pontic-Caspian steppe as a response to the colder steppe winters and that it was here that felt working, and later the spinning and weaving of wool, first developed. There is little direct evidence that can be called to support this, but at the cemetery of Khvalynsk (4700–3900 BC) the large number of sheep sacrificed in the funerary rituals were all mature, suggesting that they came from flocks reared for wool or milk (or both), while at Svobodnoe, a settlement in North Caucasus (4300–3700 BC), sheep were the dominant domestic animal, five times more common than goat, the preference hinting at an emphasis on wool.

Surplus wool, in bales or as fabrics, would have made a valuable item for exchange, but so, too, would the woolly sheep themselves. At the end of the fourth millennium

3.1 Sheep surviving the Mongolian winter. Selective breeding of sheep on the cold steppe, far from their natural habitat, favoured beasts that grew thick wool to augment their normal hairy coat to protect them from extreme cold

there is evidence suggestive of wool production in Hungary and in the Late Uruk culture of the Near East. It is tempting to see these innovations as the direct result of the trade in woolly sheep bred on the distant icy steppe.

The Horse

Another highly desirable product of the steppe was the horse trained for riding. Complex questions still surround the origins of the domesticated horse and the beginning of horse riding, and there has been much lively debate of late. But although there are matters still in contention, a broad agreement has been reached on a number of the important issues.

The true horse (*Equus caballus*) is one of several equids found in Eurasia. In the Near East the native equid was the onager (*E. hemionus*), which was found in Syria, Iraq, Iran, and Central Asia, and the ass (*E. asinus*), occurring mainly in the Levant and in Egypt. Onagers were not easy to domesticate, but asses were more compliant and became the major beast of burden throughout the region. In the steppe zone the onager is found on hunter-gatherer sites in the Caspian Depression, while the *E. hydruntinus*, a small gracile creature, roamed the North Pontic steppe. The true horse is found throughout the steppe region and is thought to have evolved in Manchuria or Mongolia and spread westwards across the steppe and into Europe, where small herds survived the Last Glacial Maximum.

The open grassland of the steppe was the natural habitat for the horse. In the wild, horses run in herds comprising a single stallion and a number of mares with their young. The stallion fights off other males as long as he is able and guards the flanks and rear of his harem, while the lead mare controls the wanderings of the herd. The young stallions are turned away from the parent herd at the age of about 2 or 3 and form bachelor bands, which tend to occupy the periphery of the main herd ready to acquire their own harems when the occasion arises. The horse is particularly well suited to the steppe since it lives on grass. It is also well adapted to the winter snow and ice, having learned to hoof it out of the way to reach the grass beneath.

The large herds roaming the steppe provided a valuable meat source for hunter-gatherers: at some camps more than 40 per cent of the animal bones recovered were of horse. It was during this long hunter-gatherer interaction with the horse that humans learnt the nature of the beast. The later introduction of domesticated cattle and sheep and goats served only to emphasize the superiority of the horse and, in particular, its ability to survive the snow. Cattle and sheep, with no natural instinct

3.2 Przewalski's horses, a wild breed originally native to Mongolia. Part of a small harem herd seen here roaming free in the Hustai National Park in central Mongolia, August 2013

to kick away snow, and with noses too soft to push it aside, had to be provided with winter fodder or they would starve. Thus, once communities had taken up herding of imported domesticates, it was a natural step to turn to the domestication of the indigenous horse. How domestication began, we can only guess. The simplest way would have been to select a herd, kill the stallion, and capture the lead mare and the rest would follow. For the herd to reproduce, it would have been necessary to select a young docile stallion or capture one from one of the bachelor bands.

There can be little doubt that horse domestication originated on the Pontic-Caspian steppe, in areas where communities habitually hunted horses, at some time in the fifth or fourth millennia BC. The funerary deposits of horse carcasses found alongside those of cattle and sheep in contexts dating to between 4600 and 4200 BC may suggest that domestication was already under way by then in the middle Volga region: similar ritual deposits covering the same date range are found on other sites between the rivers Volga and Ural. There is also an increase in horse symbolism at the time in the form of carved bone and stone images. None of this need prove domestication, but it is highly suggestive of an increasingly close relationship between humans and horses. Once the early steps towards domestication had been taken, instead of running wild over the plains the domesticated beasts could now be kept close to the settlement, their legs hobbled so that they would not range too far while grazing. The great advantage to the human community was that the horses could feed themselves even in deep winter. As an assured winter meat supply, they required little maintenance.

Having domesticated the horse, most likely during the fifth millennium, the next crucial step for the herding community was to isolate the more docile beasts and to learn to ride them. Horse riding offered many advantages for both foragers and herders. It would have been very much easier to hunt wild horses and other animals on horseback than on foot, and for a herdsman the increased range and speed of being on horseback offered great advantages. On foot a man and a good dog could herd two hundred sheep; on horseback with his dog he could look after five hundred and cover distances of 50–60 kilometres a day. The enterprising youngsters who first dared each other to jump on the backs of wild horses started a revolution.

Where and when horse riding began is a matter that has been hotly debated in recent years. Much of the discussion has focused around the interpretation of deposits of horse bone found at settlement sites. There are two broad approaches. One is to look for variations in skeletal morphology that might indicate domestication or riding. The other is to consider the composition of the horse population represented by the bone deposits, especially the age range and ratio of male to female, to see if it better reflects hunting or domestication. For both approaches a large sample is needed so that the figures can be statistically tested for probability.

The site that, to date, has offered the largest sample of horse bones of the appropriate period is Botai in the forest-steppe region of northern Kazakhstan to the east of the river Ishim. Botai is a large settlement of about three hundred sunken-floored houses extending over an area of some 15 hectares dating to the period 3700–3000 BC. Excavations over a fifteen-year period have produced 10 tons of animal bone, of which 99.9 per cent is of horse. The remaining 0.1 per cent were wild animals including aurochs, a range of deer, wild boar, and bear. Clearly the community was dependent on the horse for its sustenance, and this was typical of other sites in the catchments of the rivers Ishim and Tobol, to the east of the Urals, where horse bone is never less than 65 per cent of the total.

A number of scholars have worked on the horse bones from Botai and have come up with varying interpretations. Some have regarded the horses as entirely wild, the result of highly specialist hunting strategies. Others have argued that some at least were domesticated. The arguments in favour of a domesticated component are now strong. They rest on two observations: the discovery of dung deposits within the settlement, and the analysis of the cooking pots, which shows that lipids (fats), which had penetrated the pottery fabric, were from milk. The implication is that horses were probably stabled close to the settlement and were being regularly milked. Another argument in favour of some of the horses being domesticated is that some complete carcasses were found within the site. It is more likely that they were domestic beasts killed on the spot than wild animals killed on the open steppe and dragged entire to the settlement. On this evidence we can, then, fairly accept that the Botai community herded some domesticated horses even though an unknown percentage of the horse bones found will have come from animals hunted in the wild.

Given that the finds from Botai imply a very close relationship between humans and horses, it is reasonable to ask if there is any evidence to suggest that some horses were now being ridden. Various analytical methods have been applied, mostly with ambiguous results, but one, based on patterns of tooth wear, is promising. The theory is that for a horse to be ridden it must have worn a bridle with a bit across the mouth. At this early stage the bit would have been made of an organic material such as twisted raw hide or possibly even wood. The bit, held in the mouth, would have worked against the vertical surfaces of the premolars and the horse might also have grasped the bit between its premolars. In both cases wear patterns would result, the former causing a wear facet, the latter, in the case of a hard bit, causing damage to the occlusal enamel. Extensive experimental work with young horses has led to the suggestion that a wear facet of 3 millimetres or more is likely to represent the use of the

HORSES AND COPPER

bit and therefore riding. At Botai 26 per cent of the teeth examined had wear facets of this magnitude. At another contemporary site 12 per cent of the sample had wear facets. It is reasonable, therefore, to conclude that some of the horses at Botai and neighbouring sites were being ridden.

One other observation in favour of riding comes from the composition of the horse population represented at Botai. The analysis shows that the proportion of males to females is about 1:1 and that all ages are present. This would suggest that stallions with harem bands and bachelor stallion bands were being swept up together for the kill. This could only have been done by hunters themselves on horseback.

Taken together, then, the evidence from Botai suggests a community of foragers probably heavily dependent upon the hunting of wild horses but with a small herd of domesticated horses which they rode and milked. Where, exactly, horse riding began it is difficult yet to say. The probability is that the skills were first learnt somewhere to the west, on

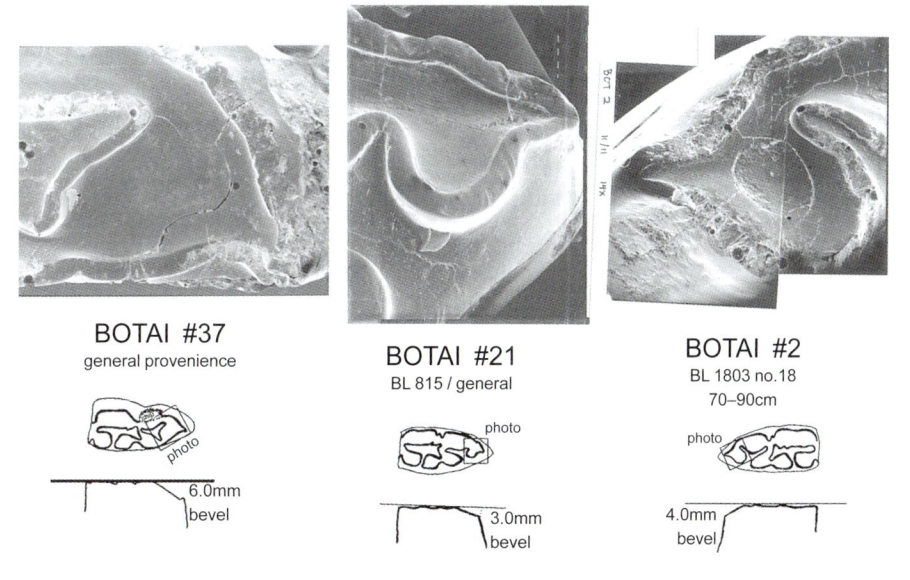

3.3 Excavations in progress at Botai in north-central Kazakhstan on a large deposit of horse bones dating to 3700–3000 BC. The horse-bone middens left by the horse hunters and herders at Botai provided a sample large enough for detailed statistical analysis into the origin of horse riding

3.4 Premolar horse teeth from Botai showing bevels of between 3 and 6 millimetres on the front edges of the teeth caused by wear from bits. Experimental work with modern horses has shown that bevels of this magnitude can result from the use of rope or leather bits

79

the Pontic-Caspian steppe, where people were used to managing domesticated sheep and cattle. Once the horse had been domesticated, the need to manage the herd is likely to have led quickly to riding; indeed, domestication and riding may have developed concurrently. It was from this area that the horse hunters of Botai in the north Kazakh forest-steppe may have acquired their domesticated horses and with them the skills of riding.

If we accept that the domestication of the horse, and horse riding, began in the Pontic-Caspian steppe, perhaps towards the end of the fifth millennium, its spread to peripheral regions was rapid. Horse riding had reached beyond the Urals to change the life of the foragers of the Botai region by the middle of the fourth millennium, and a century or two later horses were to be found in significant numbers in the foothills of Transcaucasia and in eastern Europe as far west as Bavaria. Here large herds, probably of steppe origin, were kept alongside herds of smaller indigenous horses. The trained horse capable of being ridden was of considerable value, and as an object of exchange it must have been much in demand. This is a theme to which we shall return.

The Steppe Interface with Europe, 4300–3500 BC

The settled agricultural villages of Moldavia and Ukraine, known in the archaeological literature as the Cucuteni-Tripolye culture, began in the fifth millennium in the piedmont of the Carpathians and by 3500 BC had spread through the forest and the forest-steppe zone to the Dnieper, by which time some of the 'villages' had grown to gigantic proportions of up to 400 hectares, supporting populations of several thousand. Success was based on a well-established system of agricultural production. The range of cereals grown included emmer, einkorn, bread wheat, and barley, together with pulses and, in lesser quantities, millet and buckwheat. Sheep, goats, cattle, and pigs played an important part with cattle being dominant in most areas. Traction was provided by yoked oxen, shown in a clay model to be pulling a sledge, and oxen were most likely used to draw the heavy ard for ploughing the extensive fields needed to support such a large population. In short, the farming communities were thoroughly entrenched in their now familiar environment and had learnt to maximize productivity to support their ever-increasing numbers. Trading networks linked the Cucuteni-Tripolye farmers with the herders of the steppe. Exports from the farming block included stone implements, items of copper derived from the Balkans, and decorated pottery, most of which ended up as offerings in the graves of the herders. In return the farmers will have received wool and domesticated horses.

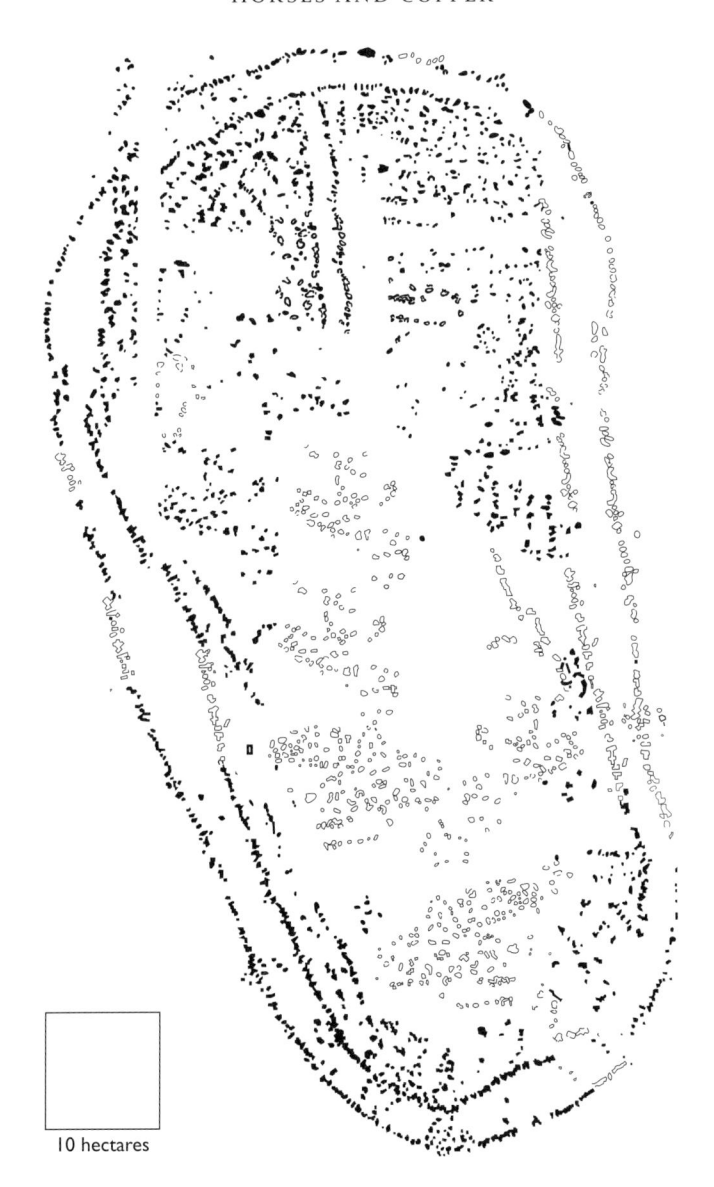

3.5 Plan of the 'megasite' of Talljanky (Ukraine) south-west of the river Dnieper. The settlement belongs to the Tripolye culture. The hundreds of houses, some of them arranged in concentric rows to provide defence, cover an area of over 400 hectares

The apparent stability of the Cucuteni-Tripolye villages throughout the late fifth and early fourth millennia contrasted with the fate of the neighbouring farming communities who had settled in the Lower Danube and northern Balkans and had developed permanent villages that had grown into high tells through repeated rebuilding

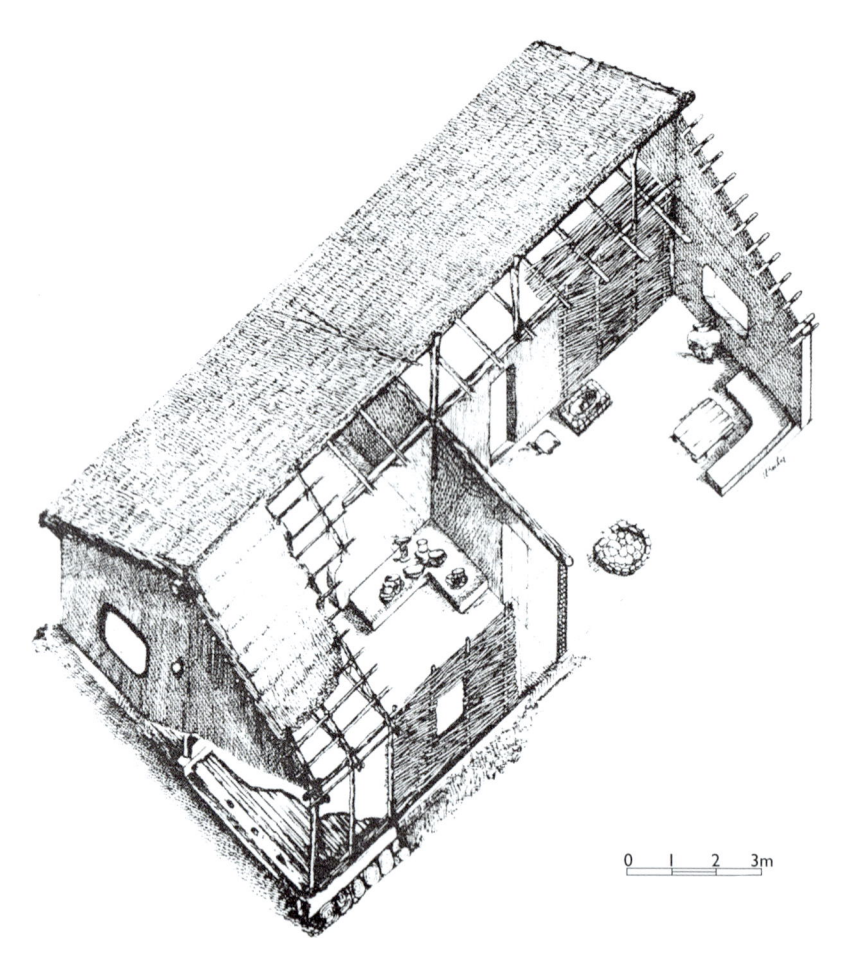

3.6 Reconstruction of a house of the Cucuteni period found at Tirpeşti in Moldavia

on the same site over a long period of stable occupation. Sometime between 4200 and 3900 BC these communities suffered a crisis that brought the long tradition of stable farming and the advanced bronze industry to a sudden end. Six hundred tell settlements were abandoned, many having been destroyed by fire, the surviving villagers dispersing into scattered, short-lived settlements. Crop growing declined and there was now a greater emphasis on sheep rearing.

The cause of the crisis has been widely debated. One popular speculation is that it was due to marauding nomadic herdsmen from the steppe, but there is little convincing evidence for this. The prime cause is far more likely to have been the sudden change in climate, beginning about 4200 BC, known as the Piora Oscillation. Its effect can be traced through the pollen record, which shows that the weather in the region became suddenly colder, with the result that trees failed to regenerate and the landscape became more open. This led to soil degeneration and flash flooding, which would have had a devastating effect on productivity. Natural events of this magnitude would have destabilized the established economy, and with it the social system, causing both to collapse. In such circumstances one can envisage heightened aggression leading to warfare, soon undermining social cohesion and forcing the surviving population to disperse. Some such scenario offers a more coherent explanation for the spectacular collapse of the old farming culture than destruction by incoming nomads. However explained, it was a major event in European prehistory, bringing nearly two millennia of cultural development to an end.

3.7 An elaborately painted vessel of the Cucuteni culture found in a pit in the settlement of Truşeşti, Botoşani, Romania. The vessel came from a level belonging to Cucuteni A3, which dates to 4200–4050 BC

Throughout the crisis of 4200–3900 BC the Cucuteni-Tripolye farmers continued to flourish in their forest-steppe homeland. It was now that the huge settlements, mega-towns as they are sometimes called, developed, some of them showing defensive features, particularly in the way that the houses were arranged close together in concentric circles forming barriers to easy penetration. The implication is that now society was coming under stress through either internal pressures or external threat. Signs of the collapse of the system began about 3500 BC, and within two centuries the mega-towns had been destroyed or abandoned and the long-established farming culture was at an end. Mobile pastoral herders from the steppe had now begun to build their funerary kurgans (burial mounds) on the hills where once the towns had been.

During much of the seven hundred years or so from 4200 BC to 3500 BC, when the flourishing farming systems of Europe came to an end, the pastoral herders of the steppe were also being forced to respond to the climatic downturn, which brought increasingly severe winters until the climate began to ameliorate after 3800 BC. One result of the cold spell would have been to place a greater reliance on herds of domesticated horses since, as we have seen, horses are far better able to deal with the snow of long winters: they are in effect a self-sustaining meat supply requiring far less maintenance than sheep or cattle.

The cold climate may also have encouraged some herders to move through the steppe zone, between the Black Sea shore and the Cucuteni-Tripolye farmers of the

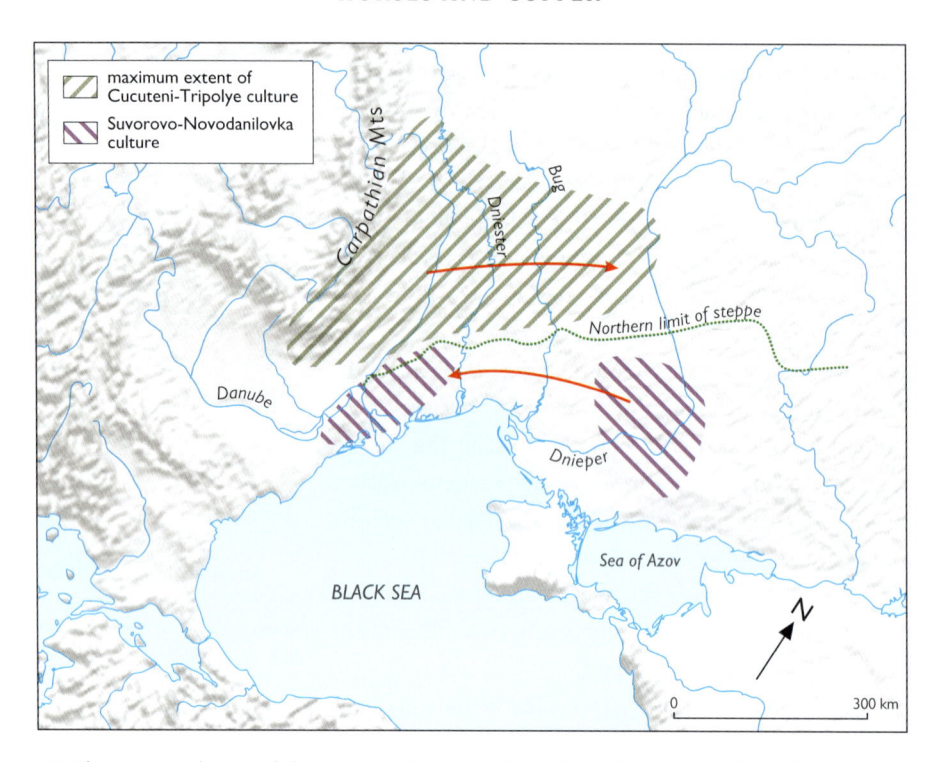

3.8 The eastern advance of the agricultural communities of the Cucuteni-Tripolye culture through the forest-steppe and the western advance of the pastoral Suvorovo-Novodanilovka culture across the Pontic steppe reflect how different ecologies accommodated different population pressures

forest-steppe, into the lusher and warmer pastures of the Danube delta region. The evidence for this is comparatively slight, but the local settlements seem now to have been abandoned and a number of kurgan burials of steppe type are found, some of them containing stone mace-heads, shaped like horse's heads, buried with the dead. The appearance of these new elements has been taken to suggest the incursion of a group of pastoral herders, referred to as the Suvorovo culture, coming from the Dnieper valley region about 4200 BC. While some archaeologists would argue that the evidence could be explained as the local population assimilating aspects of steppe culture, on balance it is simpler to see the Suvorovo phenomenon as a limited incursion of steppe communities migrating into Europe. If so, it was the first of many such episodes.

The Caucasian Barrier

While the interface between the herders of the steppe and the farmers of Europe showed a degree of flexibility, largely because one landscape elided into another, the divide between the steppe and the fast-developing farming communities of Anatolia and Mesopotamia was stark: the Great Caucasus Mountains, a precipitous snow-capped range rising to between 4,000 and 5,000 metres, with few passes allowing access from north to south. Anyone wishing to make such a journey would have had to skirt the eastern end of the range between the mountains and the Caspian Sea using the coastal strip, which narrows at Derbent to a few kilometres. Coming from the south they would have followed the Black Sea coast westwards, cutting through

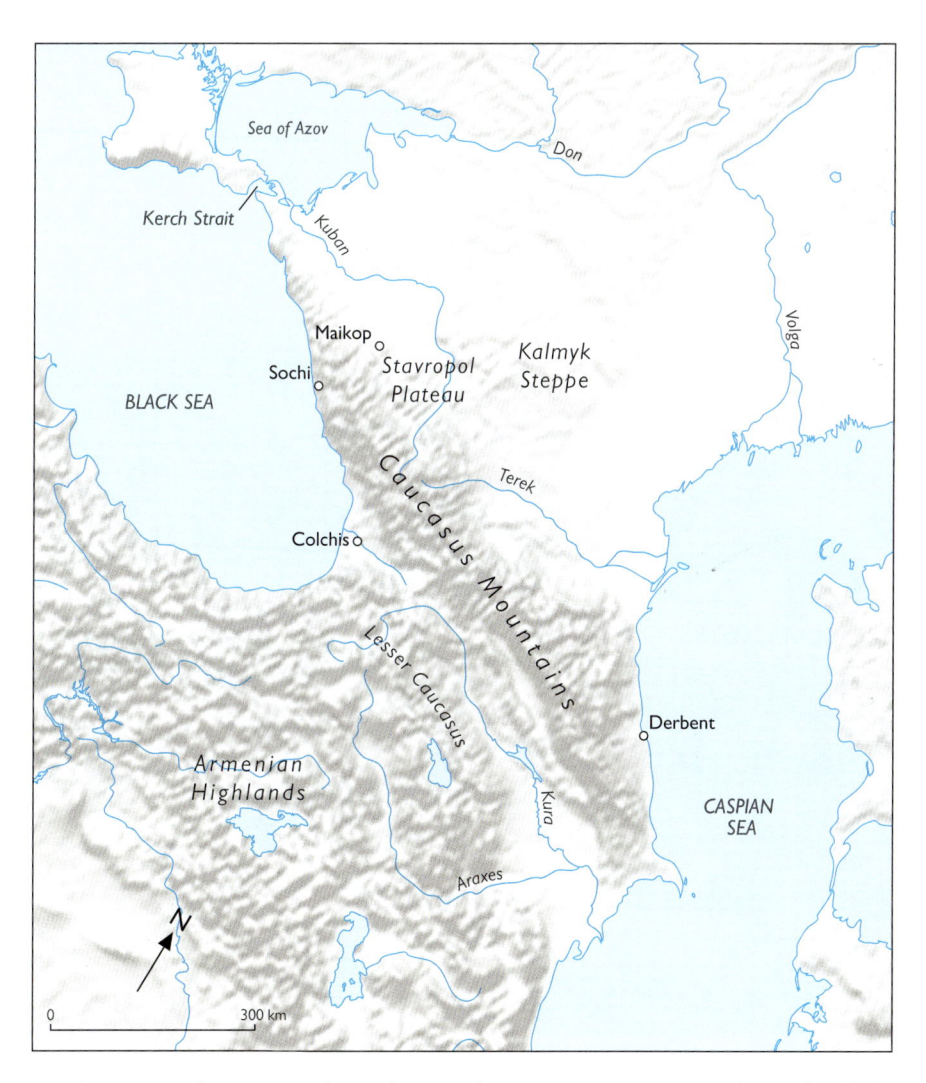

3.9 The Caucasus form a major barrier between the Pontic-Caspian steppe to the north and the Anatolian plateau to the south

3.10 The Caucasus, running between the Black Sea and the Caspian Sea, were difficult to cross, but routes could be found around the two ends of the massif using the narrow coastal plains

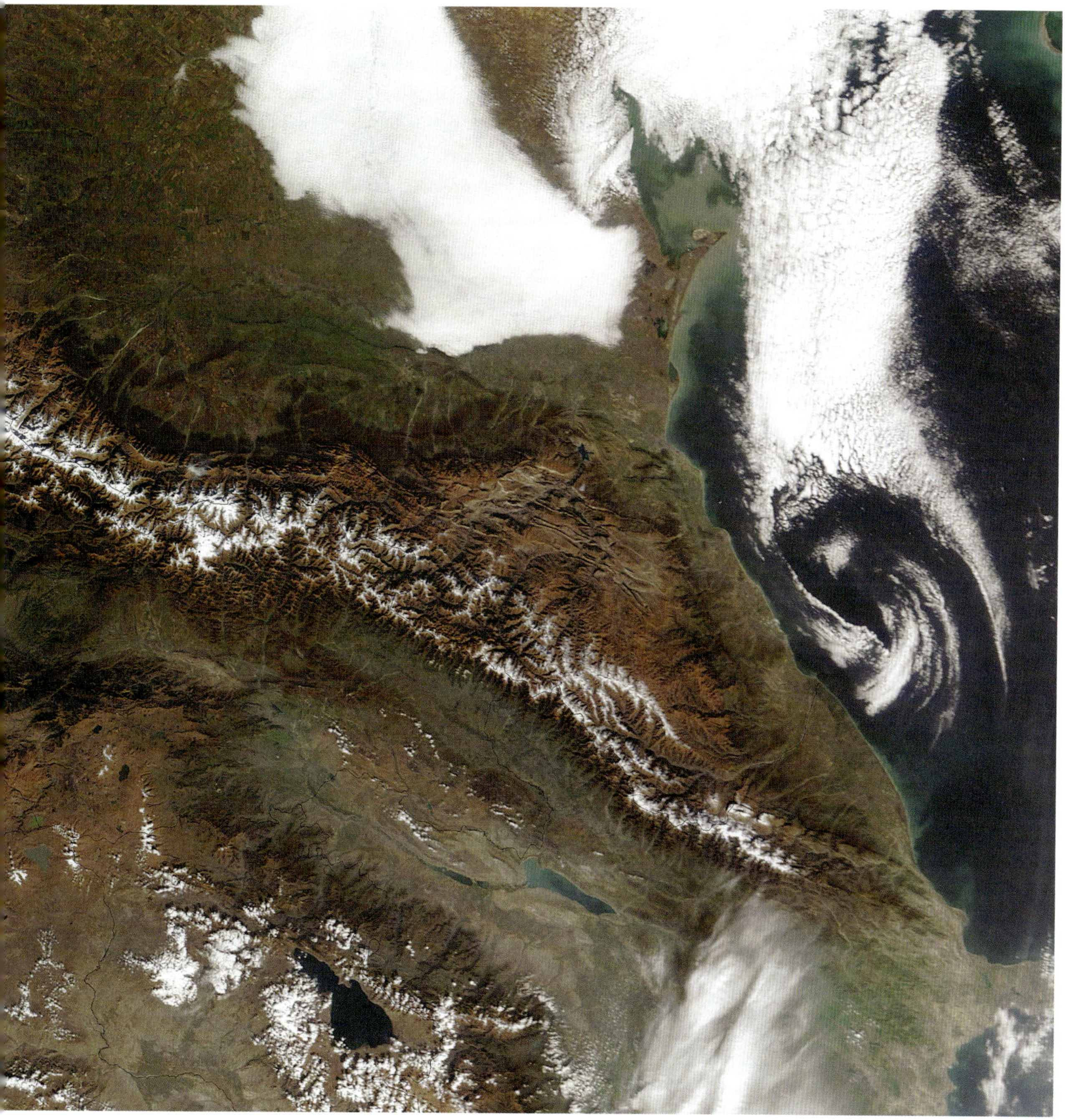

the mountains behind the modern resort of Sochi, or would have gone even further west towards the Kerch Strait, where the dying range is far less formidable.

To the south of the Great Caucasus range lie two plains separated by a piedmont, the Colchidean Plain drained by the river Rioni flowing to the Black Sea and the much larger Kura Lowland Plain, through which runs the river Kura emptying into the Caspian Sea. The Kura is joined in its lower reaches by the river Araxes, which rises far to the west in the highlands of eastern Anatolia. This great plain was densely settled from the second half of the fourth millennia by a distinctive culture referred to as the Kura-Araxes or Early Transcaucasian culture. South of the Kura Lowland plain the mountains rise again to become the Lesser Caucasus, marking the north-eastern edge of the extensive Armenian Highlands, through which the Araxes carves its sinuous valley. This whole area, the lowlands, valleys, and mountains, is conveniently referred to as Transcaucasia.

North of the Great Caucasian ridge the land falls rapidly to an extensive piedmont, the Stavropol plateau, giving way to the east to the plains of the river Terek, flowing to the Caspian Sea, and west to the plain of the river Kuban, which drains into the Aral Sea. The two plains and the plateau between them create the relatively narrow North Caucasian zone, of some 200–300 kilometres between the Great Caucasus range and the open grassy steppe to the north.

The Caucasian interface, between the herders of the steppe and the farmers of the Anatolian plateau and the lands beyond, was comparatively narrow, even if the mountain range appeared to be impenetrable. To the east of the Caspian Sea the geomorphology is altogether different. Here the Kopet Dag mountains and the Hindu Kush continue the ridge of the Caucasus, forming a northern extremity of the vast upland plateau of Iran. The northern foothills of the mountains and the steppe are separated by the deserts of Karakum and Kyzylkum, creating a wide barrier of an entirely different kind to north–south interactions.

Standing back from the details of what is to follow we may summarize the big picture by saying that the earliest contacts between the developing city states of the south and the steppe to the north were established through the Causacus in the period 3700–3000 BC using the narrowest zone of transition. It was not until much later that the complex of north–south networks threading across the Central Asian deserts came into existence. These trans-desert interactions are the subject of the next chapter.

The Late Uruk Expansion

The communities of farmers who had settled between the Tigris and the Euphrates in southern Mesopotamia in the fifth millennium underwent a series of major changes in the fourth millennium leading to the emergence of complex city life. This is known as the Uruk period after the city which features large in the social revolution now under way. At the beginning of the fourth millennium there was a sudden increase in population recognizable in the rapid growth of established settlements and the appearance of many new sites. While this change may, in significant part, have been the result of a natural demographic surge, it may have been exacerbated by incoming semi-nomadic people gravitating towards the successful and productive villages of the settled farmers. In the north of the region, central Babylonia, people lived in a dense scatter of settlements of 30–50 hectares. In southern Babylonia the settlements were less dense, but one site, Uruk, located not far from what was then the head of the Persian Gulf, began to grow. By the Late Uruk period (3500–3100 BC) the population of the southern zone had increased, with Uruk itself now exceeding 100 hectares. Surrounded by secondary centres, it had become a true city.

What caused this growth it is not possible to say with certainty. It may simply be that the highly favoured environment with its wide range of different ecological niches removed the constraint of the holding capacity of the land and allowed an exponential growth of the population. The land in southern Babylonia was particularly productive. The irrigated fields could produce an abundance of cereals and orchard fruits. Between were areas of grassland where the sheep and goats could roam, while the extensive marshlands were highly productive of fish and birds as well as offering an ideal habitat for water buffalo. It is generally assumed that most of the people at this time were involved in agriculture and would have travelled daily to the fields, but specializations were beginning to appear and the need to maintain the increasingly sophisticated irrigation systems would have required a coercive authority empowered to get people to work together for the communal good. Add to this the growing number of specialists who were now at work, potters, weavers, metalworkers, serving the burgeoning population, then it is no surprise that society had begun to develop systems for storing agrarian surpluses and for redistributing them to people providing specialist goods and services. Such social complexity required specialist, non-productive administrators to oversee the efficient working of the system upon which the stability of the society now depended. The growth of great temples as the focus of city life, providing oversight and protection for the city's vital production, suggests that power now lay in the hands of a theocracy headed by a priest-king. One of the sure signs of the increasing social complexity was the appearance of cylinder seals—small cylinders, usually of stone, carved with images—which could be rolled onto the soft clay of tablets, or sealings, to denote ownership, either by the individual or by the state. Seal cutting was a highly specialized craft but was only one of a new range of artisan skills that were contributing towards wholly new art styles which, at a monumental level, were reflected in reliefs, statues, and vast temple buildings.

Increasing specialization brought about major changes in society, including a hierarchic structure first glimpsed in a contemporary text, the 'Standard List of Professions', which appeared at the end of the Uruk period. It details various offices such as 'leader of the city' and 'great one of the cattle pen', as well as listing a series of specialist craftsmen, cooks, and gardeners. By this time the complexity of life was such that writing had been invented, in an early form of what was later to become cuneiform, to maintain the records so essential for the efficient running of the state. If we accept that specialist craftsmen, a social hierarchy, administrators, monumental architecture, measuring systems, and writing, all concentrated in central places but still dependent upon the labours of agrarian workers, are the essential ingredients of 'civilized' urban societies, then the rise of Uruk in the fourth millennium marks the birth of the earliest civilization in the world.

The kind of social system that underlay the success of Uruk was one dependent not only on local productivity but also on a constant supply of commodities from beyond the region. The most obvious were building stone and timber for its monumental buildings. Copper was also essential for tools and weapons, as well as for personal decorations. But with a growing hierarchy came the need for the elite individuals to be able to distinguish themselves from lesser men and women by proclaiming their status through displays of gold, silver, and precious stones like lapis lazuli, turquoise, chlorite, and carnelian, all of which had to be brought in from territories well outside Babylonia. Thus, with the growth of social complexity came an even more urgent need to secure an ever-increasing flow of rare commodities.

It is probably within this context that the influence of Uruk began to spread well outside the home territory. This 'Uruk expansion' began about 3700 BC and intensified after 3400 BC. Exactly what form the expansion took is a matter of debate. While it is possible that distant towns were taken by force by agents of the Uruk state, a more likely explanation is that colonies of Uruk traders were established in these outposts, in towns like Susa, on the plain below the Zagros Mountains, Tepe Sialk and Tepe Hissar on the Iranian plateau, where they could control commodities coming in from the east, and Hacinebi and Arslan Tepe in the upper Euphrates valley, where copper from the rich local sources could be acquired and it was possible to tap into the supplies of gold and silver coming from the Caucasus. A sharp rise in the number of sheep, reared on the rich pastures of Arslan Tepe at this time, might indicate that wool was now among the commodities desired by the elite of Uruk. The Uruk presence in these distant places is usually indicated by the appearance of cultural attributes from the Uruk homeland, most frequently by imported pottery. But at Susa tablets and tokens with proto-cuneiform writing point to record-keeping traders, while at Tell Brak in northern Syria a monumental temple built in Uruk style suggests a more substantial presence requiring the involvement of southern architects.

The Uruk expansion was a remarkable phenomenon reflecting the development of trading networks organized by specialists who established themselves in distant centres the better to command the efficient passage of the rare commodities necessary to sustain the Uruk state. Whereas before desirable materials passed through many hands controlled by differing social conventions along the line, now trading outposts were charged with gathering what was required and transporting it directly to the centre. It was the beginning of a new commercial order.

The Uruk expansion, which had begun about 3700 BC, came to an abrupt end about 3100 BC. At Uruk the great temple was levelled and new buildings constructed on the site, but the city continued, and other settlements in the area grew as the rural population moved in from the countryside. Clearly there was a social upheaval of some kind, though whether it was caused by internal systems collapse or by external aggression is unclear. At any event the long-distance trading networks so characteristic of Uruk's power and influence simply came to an end, at least for the time being.

Uruk and the Maikop Elite, 3700–3100 BC

To the north of the Great Caucasian ridge, in North Caucasus, lived communities of herders rearing sheep for wool and milk, pigs, and some cattle, and hunting a variety of wild game. By the end of the fifth millennium they were fortifying their villages, suggesting that the area was coming under stress possibly caused by the climatic downturn.

Things changed radically about 3700 BC, when the elite of the region began to acquire a range of luxury goods used to adorn their burials. The most impressive of these elite tombs, and the first to be excavated, in 1897, was Maikop, sited on a tributary of the river Kuban. Beneath a massive kurgan, 100 metres in diameter and 11 metres high, was a timber-built grave chamber divided into three compartments, one for the chieftain, the others each occupied by a female, presumably wives or concu-

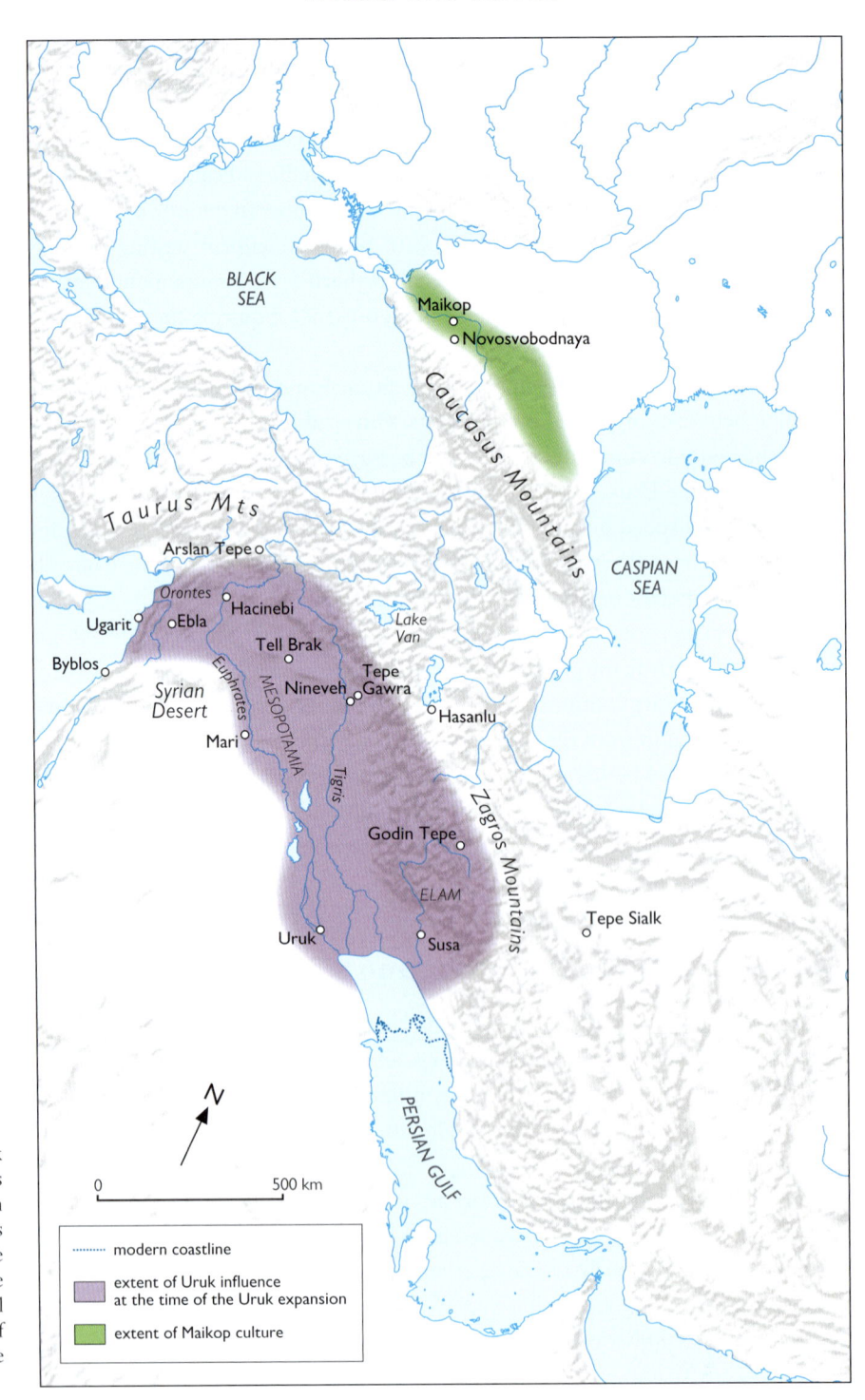

3.11 The expansion of Uruk trading interests northwards across Anatolia and through the Caucasus was a stimulus to the development of the rich Maikop culture, whose rulers were able to control exchanges in a variety of goods between the steppe and Mesopotamia

bines who had been sacrificed to be with their dead master. The man was accompanied by an astonishing array of grave goods including wheel-made pottery, bronze cauldrons, gold and silver cups, copper alloy tools and weapons, and silver-encased staves topped with cast models of long-horned bulls, two in gold and two in silver. He was buried in a tunic adorned with lion and bull reliefs and he wore a necklace of gold, turquoise, and carnelian beads, and a diadem of golden rosettes. The Maikop chieftain was buried sometime between 3700 and 3400 BC and is one—admittedly the most spectacular—of between 150 and 250 elite burials found in the North Caucasus belonging to what is known as the Maikop culture, which began about 3700 BC and lasted to 3000 BC (the later part of the Maikop culture, after 3400 BC, is named after the burial site of Novosvobodnaya).

That the rich Maikop culture is exactly contemporary with the Uruk expansion suggests that the two were linked. Exotic materials found in the North Caucasian graves are likely to have been acquired through the Uruk trade networks, turquoise from Tajikistan, lapis lazuli from Afghanistan, and carnelian and cotton fabrics from India, while much of the copper alloy used for tools and weapons in the region was probably imported from the arsenic-rich copper area of Transcaucasia and the arsenic- and nickel-rich areas of eastern Anatolia. Other close links with the Uruk region include an imported cylinder seal found in an early Maikop grave and the tunic of the Maikop chieftain with its decoration of appliqué lions and bulls. Although the garment was probably made in the North Caucasus, the symbolism is taken directly from the elite world of Uruk.

3.12 Cylinder seal of the Early Dynastic period (2600–2800 BC) from Nuzi in Mesopotamia depicting a ritual or mythological scene. The seals were used for bureaucratic control under the authority of the temple

HORSES AND COPPER

The quantity of exotic southern goods available to the North Caucasian elite implies that Uruk trading networks had established contact with the region. The earliest links probably used the western route along the northern shore of the Black Sea, but by the later period the eastern route along the Caspian littoral was the more favoured. Among the desirable commodities that the region could offer, gold and silver from the upper Kuban river probably featured large. There were also good copper sources in the area. Another resource may have been long-fibred wool provided in bales and woven into fabrics. Woollen fabrics as well as linen and cotton have been found in Late Maikop graves, and animal bone evidence shows that among some communities large flocks of sheep were kept most probably for their wool and milk. Whether or not riding horses were traded south in any number at this stage is difficult to say. The horse certainly features in Maikop iconography. A short-maned, thick-necked horse is carefully depicted on one of the silver cups from Maikop, and a frieze of horses surrounding a human figure was painted on a stone slab inset in the wall of a tomb at Klandy. Among animal bone assemblages horses are present but never numerous, a fact which suggests that they were probably used for riding rather than as food. It is possible, then, that those directing the Uruk trading networks encountered riding horses for the first time in the Caucasus. There is, however, little evidence to suggest that horses were an item of regular exchange with Uruk until after 3300 BC, when horses are to be found in Mesopotamia in some number.

The Northern Caucasian communities, by virtue of their geographical position and their control of rich metal resources, were able to benefit from trade with the Uruk world, allowing their elites to build power structures based on their command of rare exotic materials. So long as the flow from the south continued, hierarchies could be maintained by the top men who controlled the trade, establishing their patronage by making gifts to those subservient to them. This kind of

3.13 Two of the objects found in the elite burial of Maikop in the Kuban region of southern Russia dating to the mid-fourth millennium BC. The bull is one of several in gold and silver which decorated the tops of silver poles, which may have held up a fabric canopy. The silver vessel bears an accurate rendition of a steppe horse not unlike the wild Przewalski's horses shown in Figure 3.2.

socio-economic structure is called a prestige goods system. Its stability rests on the continuous supply of exotic materials: if this were to stop, the system would collapse. This is just what happened to the Maikop culture when, about 3100 BC, the Uruk trading networks suddenly contracted. Rich burials and evidence of wealth differential disappear and the communities of the North Caucasus became absorbed in the developments that now began to embrace the whole of the Pontic-Caspian region.

Back to the Steppe: The Yamnaya Complex, 3300–2800 BC

After 3800 BC the climate began to improve, and by the middle of the millennium the shift to drier and warmer conditions made the Pontic-Caspian steppe a far more comfortable place for pastoralists to live. Herds grew in size and, with this, movement across ever-larger territories became the normal way of life. The cultural adaptation that resulted over the vast Pontic-Caspian steppe, embracing a large number of disparate communities, is referred to as the Yamnaya complex, the name in Russian meaning 'pit grave', referring to the common mode of burial. The distinctive characteristics of the Yamnaya complex crystallized out in the Don–Volga region about 3300 BC and quickly spread throughout the Pontic-Caspian steppe, later, about 2800 BC, extending to the rich black soils of the typical steppe landscape along the lower Danube and into the Great Hungarian Plain. It is about this time, in the Pontic-Caspian homeland, that some cultural diversity can be distinguished. In the Don–Kuban region these later developments are known as the Catacomb culture, while in

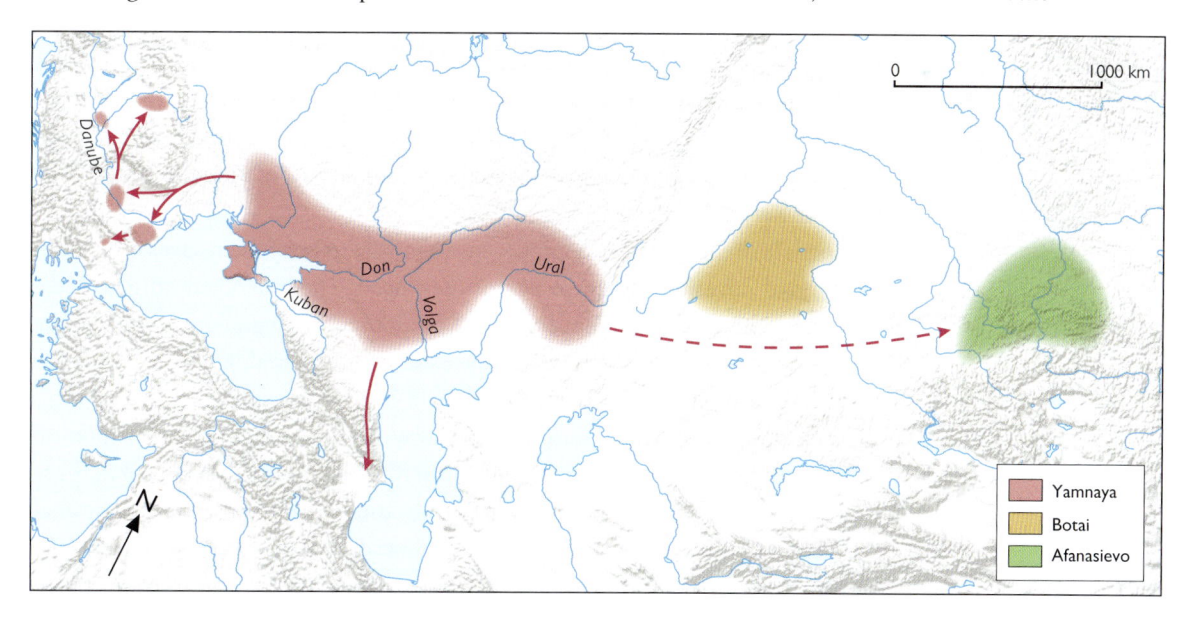

3.14 Some of the main archaeologically defined cultures of the steppe in the third millennium BC. The Yamnaya culture spread westwards into the Great Hungarian Plain and it is thought that the Afanasievo culture may have originated from Yamnaya pastoralists making a heroic trek across the Kazakh steppe to the Altai-Sayan mountains, passing the territory occupied by the Botai horse hunters

the Volga–Ural region they are referred to as the Poltavka culture. These later manifestations of the Yamnaya complex continued until about 2200 BC.

The basis of the Yamnaya lifestyle was to be on the move, to follow the large flocks and herds, the essential mobility being provided by horseback riding and ox-drawn wagons. The rider on the horse could herd the beasts, trade with other riders in pre-arranged locations, and, where this was felt to be economically desirable or socially necessary, he could raid. The wagon, trundling along behind, was the home on wheels providing shelter and transport for the women, children, and the elderly. The two modes of transport meant that the entire community could always be on the move. But movement would have been within a defined territory and was guided by the seasons. Winter would have been spent in the valleys among the valley bottom pastures, where the animals could feed and shelter and where a supply of timber, so crucial for repairing the wagons, was on hand. It was here that their cemeteries of kurgans were mostly located. Then, in the spring and summer, the entire community would move out onto the open steppe with their flocks and herds working the grasslands over a 50-kilometre radius or more.

But there were regional differences. East of the Don the communities seem to have been entirely pastoral, relying predominantly on sheep and goats but with some cattle and a few horses. Cereals were absent, but seeds of goosefoot (*Chenopodium*) and tubers were collected to add variety to the diet of milk and occasional mutton. The low-starch diet is reflected in the lack of caries in human teeth. West of the Don the families seem to have been rather less mobile and did not penetrate so far into the deep steppe. They were also more reliant on cattle, while sheep amounted to only a third of the livestock. Pigs were also kept and some cereals were grown. This implies that settlements were maintained in the valleys, where the pigs would thrive in the woodlands and crops could be cared for. Even so, the flocks and herds were so large that they had to be kept moving, requiring a substantial part of the community to be on the move with them.

The people of the Yamnaya complex have left little trace of themselves other than their kurgans covering the grave pits of their dead. The individual kurgans were not family cemeteries since few contained more than three graves and not all the dead were buried in this way. One detailed survey in the middle Volga region has shown that a kurgan was built every five years or so, suggesting that the majority of the dead were disposed of in some other way, quite possibly by excarnation on the open steppe. Where evidence is available in the Volga valley, 80 per cent of those buried beneath kurgans were male. The implication here would seem to be that only selected elite were afforded monumental burials and that the elite were usually men. The male–female differentiation was not as great in the western regions, and

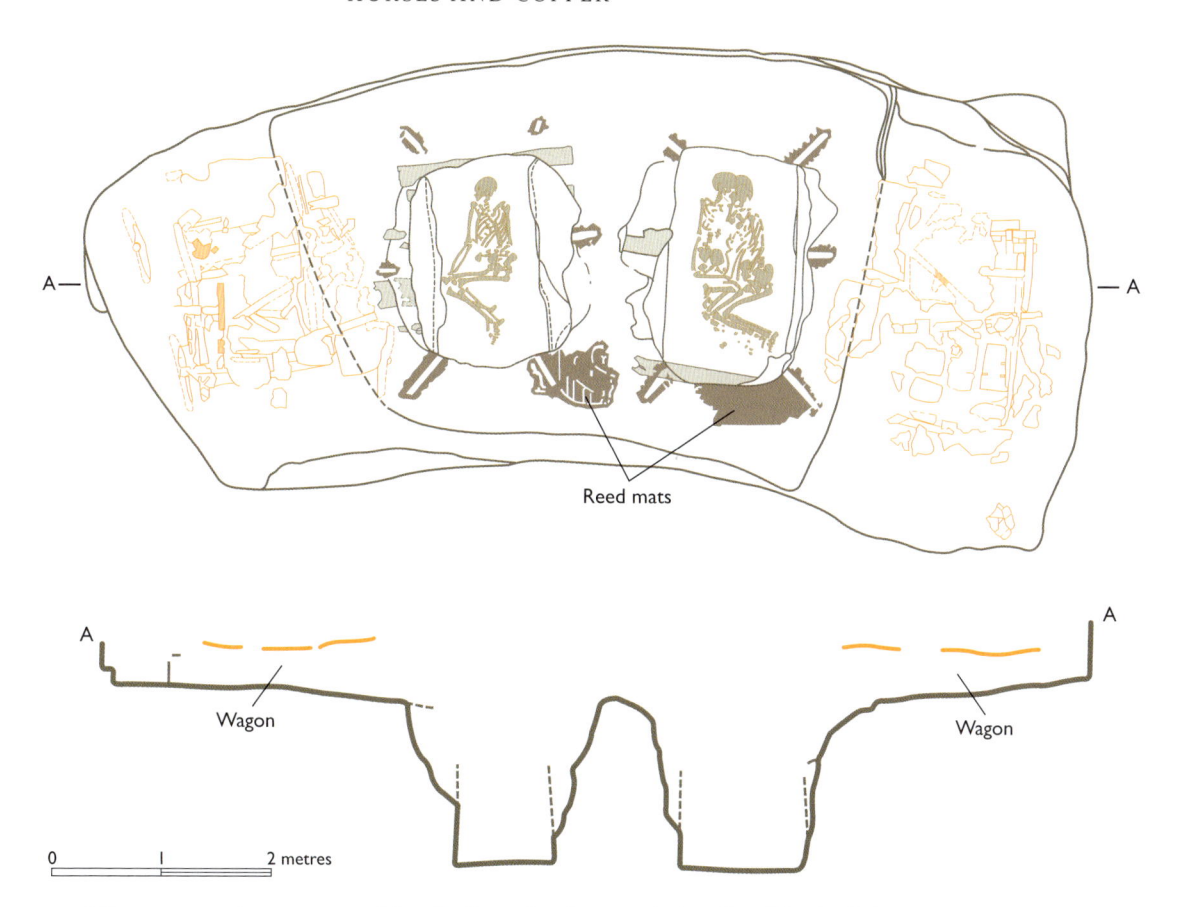

3.15 A Yamnaya grave (kurgan 2, grave 15) found at Ostanni on the steppe in the valley of the river Kuban. Two individuals were buried in deep grave pits with their four-wheeled wagons placed on either side

in the south, between the Sea of Azov and the Caspian, the ratio was more or less even. Clearly there was social variability across the steppe regions. In a number of the graves the dead were accompanied by wagons, usually dismantled, with the parts placed around the grave. Another item, sometimes found either in or near the grave pit, was a reed mat painted with red, white, and black stripes, sewn onto a backing of felt. These mats probably formed the covers for the wagons. We shall consider the vehicles in more detail below.

The elite who were buried beneath the kurgans were probably, for the most part, the leaders of the lineages, but other notable people were also honoured. A grave excavated at Pershin in the middle Ural river region contained a two-piece mould to cast a single-bladed copper axe. Other smiths' graves of this period have been found in the Dnieper valley and in the middle Volga. Analysis of the metal used for making copper items shows that local sources in the Ural valley and the North Caucasus were being regularly exploited. Copper items made by craftsmen attached to the mobile lineages will have been exchanged between groups, creating networks of reciprocity that helped to maintain the social equilibrium.

About 3100 BC Yamnaya groups began to move westwards along the steppe zone fringing the Black Sea into the valley of the lower Danube and from there along the Danube into the Great Hungarian Plain. The migration probably took place over several centuries and involved disparate groups of steppe pastoralists choosing territories to settle on the way. The most adventurous reached as far as the plain between the rivers Tisza and Mureș, some 1,300 kilometres from the Pontic homeland. What drove the migrants is unknown, but their route took them to the westernmost part of the steppe corridor to its limit in the Great Hungarian Plain. Perhaps they were simply curious to trace their world to its extremity. Their pioneering had established the route which generations of steppe people would follow over the next four thousand years.

Covered Wagons

The four-wheeled vehicle that gave the Yamnaya pastoralists their ability to lead herds deep into the steppe uplands facilitated the crucial change from sedentary to mobile pastoralism, a mode of existence that quickly spread across much of Eurasia. But where the wheeled vehicle was first developed is far from clear. Before 3500 BC they are unknown, but within three centuries the technology is found in peninsular Europe, Turkey, the steppe, and Mesopotamia. The earliest wheeled vehicle so far recorded is a depiction of a four-wheeled structure scratched on a pot from Bronocice in southern Poland dating from 3500–3350 BC. A clay model of a high-sided cart from Budakalász in Hungary dates to 3300–3100 BC, while another clay model from Arslan Tepe in Turkey is ascribed to the period 3400–3100 BC. The temple of Eanna at Uruk in Mesopotamia produced a clay tablet dating to 3300–3100 BC with pictographs that appear to depict four-wheeled vehicles. The earliest wagons so far known from the steppe are from Ostanni, on the river Kuban, and Bal'ki, on the lower Dnieper, radiocarbon-dated to between about 3000 and 2900. Parallel tracks found beneath a barrow at Flintbek in Germany dated to about 3600 BC are the only hint of anything earlier than 3500 BC, but the tracks could as well have been made by a sled as by a wheeled vehicle. What the currently available evidence shows is that, wherever the first wheeled vehicle was made, the invention was quickly taken up with enthusiasm over a remarkably wide area. While the balance of evidence is very marginally

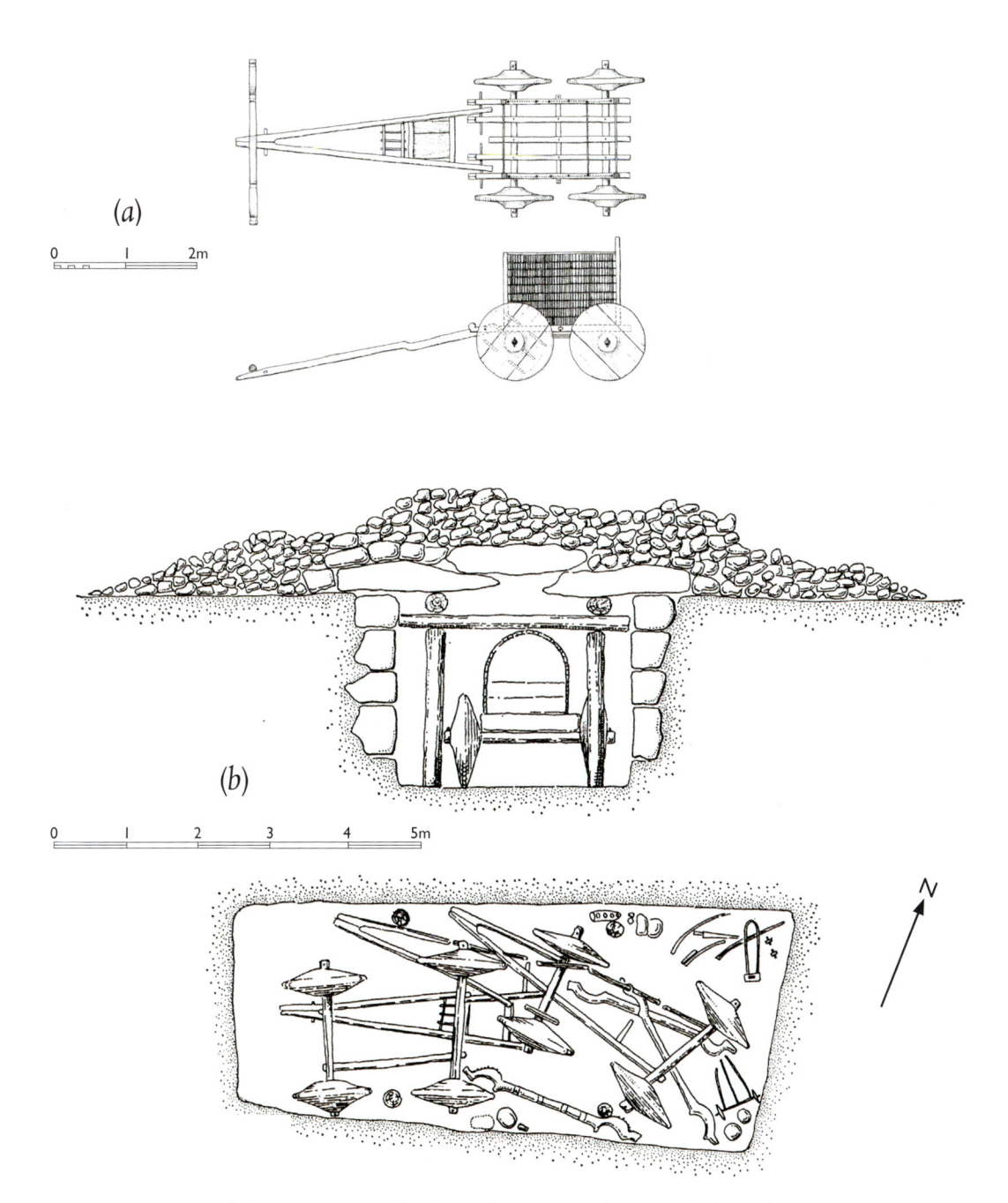

3.16 The cemetery at Lchashen, Armenia, produced several well-preserved wagons which were buried with the dead. (*a*) shows the reconstruction of the vehicle from grave 11 complete with its wickerwork cover. (*b*) shows two wagons from grave 2 in a stone-lined grave pit beneath a stone mound

3.17 Excavation in progress on a wagon burial at Trialeti, Georgia, third millennium BC

in favour of a European origin, it could be argued that the need of steppe herders to move their livestock over increasingly large distances could have been the stimulus for the invention of wheeled vehicles, and where better than on the open grasslands of the Pontic-Caspian region? New discoveries are needed before the issue can be resolved.

Wagons found in graves in the Pontic-Caspian steppe are particularly numerous. About 2,600 are now known, dating to the period between 3000 and 2200 BC. Many are fragmentary, but some found in the Kuban region, north of the Caucasus, are sufficiently well preserved to show how they were constructed. The bed of the vehicle was built of timber, sometimes cross-braced to provide strength and resilience. It was usually about 1 metre wide and 2.5 metres long with a box seat at the front for the driver. Below were two fixed axles upon which the wheels rotated, the wheels being of solid construction, made of two or three thick planks joined by dowelling. A pole, or two poles forming an A-frame, was fixed to the bed of the wagon to take the yoke for harnessing the pair of oxen. The light superstructure of the vehicle supported covers made from felt, onto which reeds were sewn and painted in bright colours. These simple but striking contraptions trundling across the steppe in a caravan carried everything that the community needed, their felt tents and utensils, their food, and those who were not able to ride horses. First seen in the later fourth millennium, they offer a timeless vision of mobile pastoralists whose lives were entirely dependent on the well-being of their flocks and herds.

Across the Kazakh Steppe

We have seen that by the second half of the fourth millennium the horse hunters of Botai had acquired domesticated horses to ride. This is the first instance of domesticated animals being found to the east of the Ural Mountains, and the impetus will have come from the Pontic-Caspian steppe either through networks of exchange or as a result of the eastwards movement of new settlers. Further to the east, in the region of the Altai Mountains, a distinctive pastoral economy known to archaeologists as the Afanasievo culture developed after about 2900 BC. The Altai lie at the eastern extremity of the Kazakh steppe some 2,000 kilometres west of the Urals and separate the Kazakh steppe from the steppe uplands of Mongolia. The Altai comprise a series of mountain ridges rising to over 4,000 metres with pines covering the lower slopes and extensive tracts of open steppe, interspersed with lakes, extending across the intermontane plateaux. The varied ecozones provide favourable environments for upland pastoralists and were already occupied by indigenous foragers before pastoralism was introduced. The new economic strategy involved the husbandry of domestic sheep, cattle, and horses. At Balyktyul, a settlement from which reliable statistics are available, sheep and goats accounted for 61 per cent of the animals present, with cattle at 12 per cent and horses, 8 per cent, but wild animals were always present, showing that hunting continued to play a significant role.

The route by which the practice of pastoralism reached this remote area, and indeed the mechanisms of its transmission, are far from clear. One possibility is that the mountain corridor from the Hindu Kush to the Altai was the main axis of spread, but the more favoured explanation is that pastoralism was introduced from the west and owed its origin to the Yamnaya culture. In support of this it is pointed out that the western practice of burying the dead, inhumed in pits under a kurgan, was part of the new pastoral lifestyle. That said, the steps by which western-style pastoralism was introduced into the Altai are not well understood. Some archaeologists would argue for a gradual diffusion of the domesticated animals eastwards through networks of social interaction, while others believe that the evidence can best be explained by an actual movement of bands of pastoralists coming from a homeland somewhere in the Ural river region and passing the length of the Kazakh steppe, a distance of 2,000 kilometres, to pastures fresh in the Altai. Once established, they argue, changes evident in the material culture of the Afanasievo communities show that contact was maintained with the Yamnaya region. Some support for the migration hypothesis has recently come from a genetic study of ten male skeletons from the Afanasievo cemetery of Krasnoyarsk. Nine of them possess the R1a1 Y-chromosome, strongly suggesting that their ancestry lay in the western part of Eurasia.

If this interpretation of the Afanasievo culture is correct, a pleasing symmetry seems to emerge. The Pontic-Caspian steppe was the centre where, in the second half of the fourth millennium, a highly distinctive style of mobile pastoralism first developed. This mobility led to expansion outwards from the centre, always following the steppe corridor. One group of migrants moved westwards, reaching the Great Hungarian Plain, where the encircling European forests brought them to a halt. The other group travelled eastwards across the Kazakh steppe until they reached the lush valleys and plateau pastures of the Altai. It was from here, centuries later, that the practice of mobile pastoralism was to spread further eastwards to the steppe region of Mongolia.

Into Transcaucasia, 3000–2500 BC

To complete the story we must look briefly at Transcaucasia in the period following the end of the Uruk expansion and the demise of the Maikop culture. The Great Caucasus range continued to form an impenetrable barrier, but the narrow route around the eastern end of the mountains along the Caspian littoral lay open and in the first half of the third millennium cattle herders with their cumbersome ox-carts began to travel south to find new pastures in Transcaucasia. Here they introduced their traditional burial rites of grave pits covered by massive kurgans up to 100 metres in diameter, the dead often accompanied by four-wheeled wagons and less often by gold, silver, and bronze artefacts. Sometimes sacrificed attendants were buried with their leader. This southerly movement of the herders seems to have taken place over a long period of time, and once in the new land the incomers adapted to the ways of the indigenous population. In this way the steppe way of life became assimilated in a land where agriculture was already well established.

Coloured Stones and Glittering Copper

Foragers and herders have plenty of time to observe and to explore their environment, whether waiting patiently for the game to make an approach in a wooded glade or sitting for long hours guarding the flock grazing on the mountainside. Unusual coloured stones, bright blue pebbles of azurite or the vivid green of malachite, would attract attention. These would be stones to collect and to treasure. An Epipalaeolithic forager sitting in the Shanidar Cave in northern Iraq dropped a malachite bead which had been carefully perforated to wear. Sometimes the bright green pebbles turned out to be malleable native copper that was just weathered on the surface. These could be hammered cold and turned into strips and sheets, which could be formed into small tools, like fish-hooks and awls, or simply into ornaments to adorn the body, hair, or clothes. It was in this way that curious humans first became familiar with the properties of copper and the attraction of its brightly coloured ores. This awareness became embedded in the culture of the early farmers of the Fertile Crescent and spread with them through Asia Minor and into Greece and the Balkans in the seventh millennium.

The next stage in the story is far more difficult to comprehend. At some date and in some place or places experiments were conducted that led to the production of metallic copper from its ores. This must have involved the grinding of azurite or malachite to a fine powder, mixing the ore with charcoal, and heating it in the reducing atmosphere of a kiln to a temperature of between 1,000 and 1,200 °C. If conditions were right, some of the ore would be reduced to copper, which would appear as prills of metal on the surface of the fused mix. On cooling, the slag could be broken up and the metal collected together. The process sounds comparatively simple, but the mental agility of the person who first smelted copper ores must have been remarkable. What set him or her off on this path of exploration we can only speculate. It might be that native copper, if heated sufficiently (to 1,083 °C), was seen to melt, introducing the thought that the green oxide coating if found in lumps would also melt. It might be that someone noted that heated galena, an unusually heavy, black, shiny ore, could be made to produce metallic lead at comparatively low temperatures and the experiment was tried on other attractive stones. Another possibility, which seems more likely, is that people were experimenting with colour, perhaps in the context of making painted pottery fired in kilns. Crushed copper ores change colour when heated. Exploring this phenomenon in pottery kilns, where both heat and charcoal were in ready supply, might have led to the accidental smelting of the ore—a stunning discovery for the first person to observe it.

Where, then, was copper first smelted? It would need to be somewhere where copper ores were reasonably plentiful and where pyrotechnical skills in pottery making were already well advanced. At the time when the first smelted copper was beginning to appear, this could have included the Fertile Crescent, the Iranian plateau, Asia Minor, and the Balkans. In all these areas there is evidence of early smelting. At Çatalhöyük, in Central Asia Minor, crucibles have been found in seventh-millennium contexts, though it is unclear whether they were used for smelting copper ore or simply melting native copper. Smelting is, however, attested at about 5000 BC at Tal-i Iblis in south-eastern Iran and at about the same time at Belovode in Serbia. Thereafter, from the early fifth millennium, it becomes increasingly common throughout the entire region. Given the fragility of the evidence it is difficult to say at present where smelting began, but in view of the near-contemporaneity of the early occurrences the most reasonable assumption is that there was only one place of origin and that knowledge of the process, established in the latter half of the sixth millennium, spread rapidly among those communities who were already familiar with native copper and its colourful ores. There is, however, no need to suppose that the discovery was made in the Near East; it could well have been made in the Balkans, where copper ore is plentiful and where, as we shall see, a precocious copper industry was very soon to develop.

Once the smelting of copper ores had been mastered, a series of technological advances quickly followed. In south-eastern Anatolia molten copper was being poured into moulds to make axes and chisels in the early fifth millennium, while in the Levant, towards the end of the millennium, copper was being cast using the lost-wax method. This technique involved making a beeswax model of the desired item and covering it with a clay outer coating leaving vents so that, when it was heated to bake the clay, the wax melted and could be poured off. Molten copper could then be introduced into the void. If the intention was to make a hollow or socketed item, wax could be moulded around a clay core.

The other skill soon to be acquired was the process of alloying, designed to change the qualities of the metal, making it harder and more easy to work and changing its colour. The earliest alloys were probably the result of chance, depending on the composition of the ores, but by the mid-fourth millennium copper–arsenic and copper–antimony alloys were being deliberately created, and by the end of the millennium copper–tin alloy (bronze) made its first appearance. What is astonishing about early copper metallurgy is the rapidity with which the basic knowledge of extraction spread and the intensity of experimentation involved, which led to a complete mastery of the material within a very short time span. While copper was useful and decorative, and had value as an elite commodity, it must also have been seen to be endowed with magic qualities: it was a solid that could flow and become solid again, and in doing so could change its form. Those who could control the metal were the guardians of that magic.

The Carpathian–Balkan Achievement

The Carpathian region and the northern part of the Balkans are rich in copper deposits, and for a comparatively short period, from about 5400 to 3800 BC, the area became a precocious producer of copper goods, weapons, tools, and ornaments used for elite exchange throughout the region. Metal analysis suggests that about ten sources produced most of the raw copper used. Of these, two have been examined in detail, one at Ai Bunar in central Bulgaria, the other at Rudna Glava in north-eastern Serbia. The Rudna Glava mine produced malachite ore of the type found on the Serbian site of Belovode, together with smelting slags, in contexts dated to about 5400 BC, the earliest in the Balkans. The Ai Bunar mines were in an area highly populated

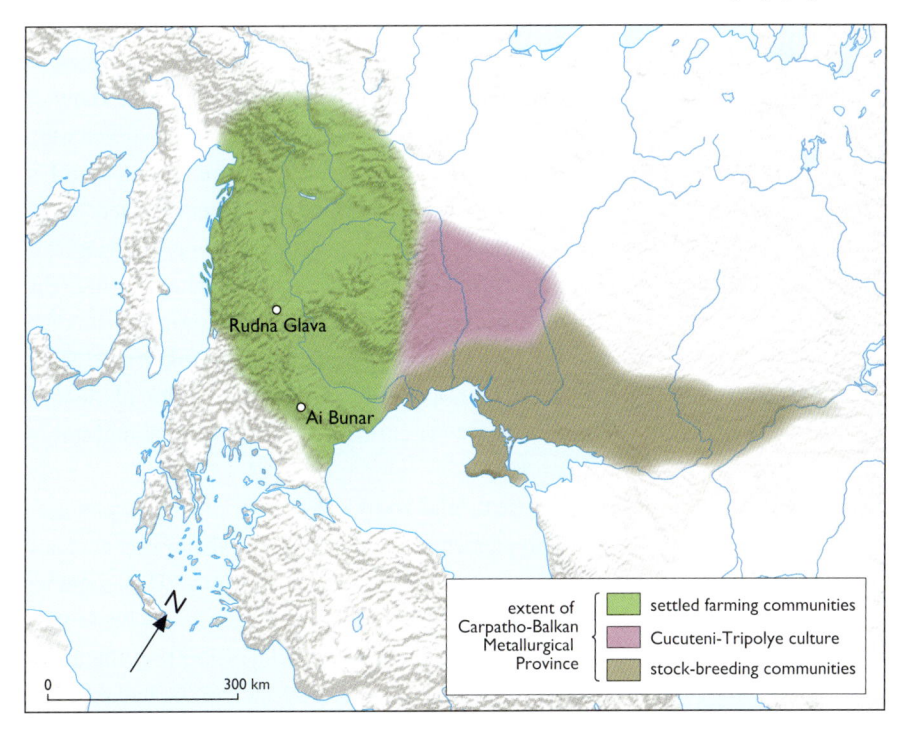

3.18 The extent of the Carpatho-Balkan Metallurgical Province. Copper alloy artefacts of types which originated in the Balkans spread eastwards with the Cucuteni-Tripolye culture and were taken up by the pastoral communities of the Pontic steppe

at the time. Here the veins of malachite ore were dug out of the limestone and marl leaving trenches 3–10 metres wide and up to 20 metres deep, running for as much as 80 metres. Estimates suggest that the mines produced between 2,000 and 3,000 tons of ore, which could have yielded some 500 tons of copper. From the old mine workings pottery from the period 4800–4300 BC was recovered, but objects made from Ai Bunar copper found at a nearby tell settlement occurred in contexts dated to about 5000 BC, suggesting that mining operations may have begun a few centuries earlier.

The total output from all the Balkan mines known to have been in production during the fifth millennium was colossal. It was mostly used to make axes, chisels, armlets, beads, and other ornaments for the human body. Most impressive were elegant shaft-hole axes cast in two- or three-piece moulds. They were designed to be visually pleasing but were also functional. Many of those found in graves showed no sign of wear and were present as symbols of status, but similar axes found at the Ai Bunar mine had clearly been heavily used. Some idea of the scale of the output of copper during this period is given by the statistic that the total weight of the items that have been found to date, mostly belonging to the period 4500–3800 BC, is 4,700 kilograms. Since they can represent only a very small fraction of the total output, the sheer enormity of the production becomes apparent.

The scale and technical quality of the Carpathian–Balkan copper industry totally overshadows that of any other contemporary production centre. This, together with the late sixth-millennium date for its beginning, gives strong support to the suggestion that the art of copper smelting was first perfected in the Balkans. The region can also claim to be the first to produce gold, beginning in the mid-fifth millennium, five hundred years or more before the earliest gold objects appear in

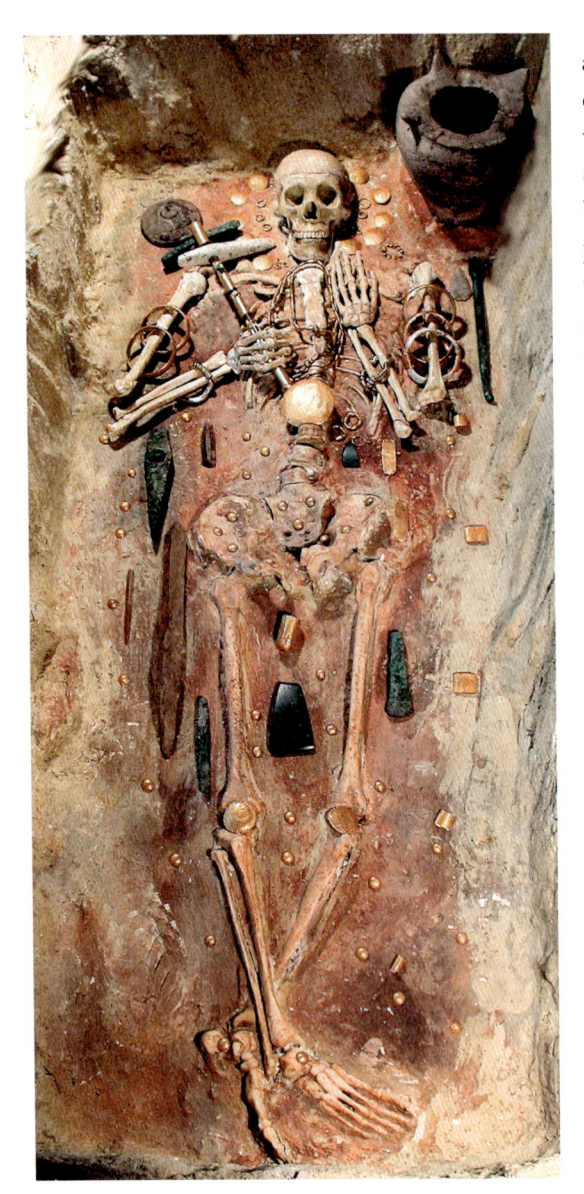

3.19 An elite warrior from a cemetery excavated at Varna, Bulgaria, on the coast of the Black Sea, dating to about 4000 BC. The grave is unusually rich and includes copper alloy tools and weapons as well as nearly a thousand individual items of gold

the Near East. Analysis suggests that the earliest gold comes from several sources, most of which are likely to have been in eastern and southern Bulgaria.

The wealth of the region is most vividly displayed at the cemetery site of Varna in Bulgaria on the Black Sea coast. Here some 280 graves have been excavated, of which eighteen were especially richly furnished with copper and gold items, one producing nearly a thousand gold objects, mostly beads, rings, bracelets, and decorations for clothes. In all, some 6 kilograms of gold were recovered from the Varna cemetery alone. The spectacular metal production of the Carpathian and Balkan region, and the complex social system that underpinned it, came to an end in the period of turmoil erupting at the close of the fifth millennium. Although copper continued to circulate, it was on a much-reduced scale, and the technological skills needed to cast the magnificent shaft-hole axes in complex moulds were all but forgotten.

The Adoption of Copper Technology throughout the Steppe

By the time of the demise of the Carpathian–Balkan copper industry a taste for copper and knowledge of the relevant technologies had spread among the Cucuteni-Tripolye farmers of the forest-steppe and across the open steppe to the Volga. A few of the artefacts made in the Balkans passed eastwards through the exchange networks, but the principal items of trade was probably copper in the form of ingots which local craftsmen later fashioned into simple tools, weapons, and ornaments. The use of Balkan metal over this vast area, and similarities in the style of artefacts, have encouraged archaeologists to refer to the whole region, from the Carpathians to the Volga, as the Carpatho-Balkan Metallurgical Province.

During the fourth millennium, with the rise of the Maikop elites, new copper sources became available in Transcaucasia, where rich supplies of two distinctive copper alloys were exploited: a copper–arsenic alloy and a copper–arsenic–nickel alloy. Both were traded across the Caucasus range to the North Caucasus and were used extensively in the Maikop period burials. In all probability the Maikop chieftains grew rich as middlemen overseeing the trade in bronze to the steppe.

By the beginning of the third millennium, by which time the mobile pastoralists of the Yamnaya complex had spread through most of the Pontic-Caspian steppe, rich copper ores mined at Kargaly in the Orenburg region of the southern Urals were being exploited to provide for almost all of the Volga–Ural region. Local coppersmiths were now accomplished enough to cast complex items like sleeved single-bladed axes and tanged daggers for their patrons. It was from the Pontic-Caspian steppe homeland that knowledge of copper production was to spread throughout the entire steppe zone over the next two millennia. Soon after the middle of the fourth millennium copper technology was introduced to the Altai region by the mobile pastoralists of the Afanasievo culture. Here the newcomers discovered ample supplies of copper ore, which they were soon to develop to become one of the principal sources fuelling the burgeoning copper industry of the steppe and forest-steppe during the Middle and Late Bronze Age.

Perspective

This chapter has focused on three conjoined regions, the Near East, eastern Europe, and the Pontic-Caspian steppe, with the discussion restricted largely to the two and a half millennia from about 5000 to about 2500 BC—a small fragment of Eurasia and a brief interlude of time, and yet the range and import of human inventiveness displayed here was astonishing. In the Near East, in Lower Mesopotamia, exponential growth in population led to the development of a complex urban-based society complete with monumental architecture and systems of writing and measurement. In eastern Europe, in the Carpathians and the Balkans, copper was produced and cast on an industrial scale, gold was extracted for the first time, and potters made vessels of exquisite quality. While on the Pontic-Caspian steppe herders domesticated the horse and learned to ride, they developed the ox-drawn cart (and may even have invented it) and bred long-wool sheep, providing wool for manufacture into cloth. Each of the three regions had a different subsistence base: irrigation agriculture in Mesopotamia, dry agriculture in eastern Europe, and pastoralism on the steppe, all made their unique contribution. Major social changes also took place. In Mesopotamia urban life—the first urban system in the world—had begun. In eastern Europe a catastrophic social collapse had left the area still a village society, while in the steppe, foraging animal herders had developed a system of mobile pastoralism which, in its many variants, perfectly suited the restricted steppe environment.

Although the three broad regions were still largely self-contained, networks of connectivity had begun to be established, particularly between the urban consumers of Mesopotamia and the productive Caucasus and the steppe beyond. This was the beginning of organized trade systems that were to spread and intensify over the next millennium.

In eastern Eurasia, at this time, agricultural communities in China were developing in isolation. The population was growing; settlements were becoming larger and craft skills more refined, though copper smelting was unknown. Social hierarchies were also becoming more complex. But compared with western Eurasia, the east had not yet begun to surge forward: it was more of a conserving society than one prone to innovate. Perhaps it was its enclosure by mountains, deserts, and jungles that limited its horizons. In contrast, in western Eurasia the three innovative regions, without inhibiting boundaries, were already demonstrating curiosity to explore the beyond and a desire to share in the discourses of others.

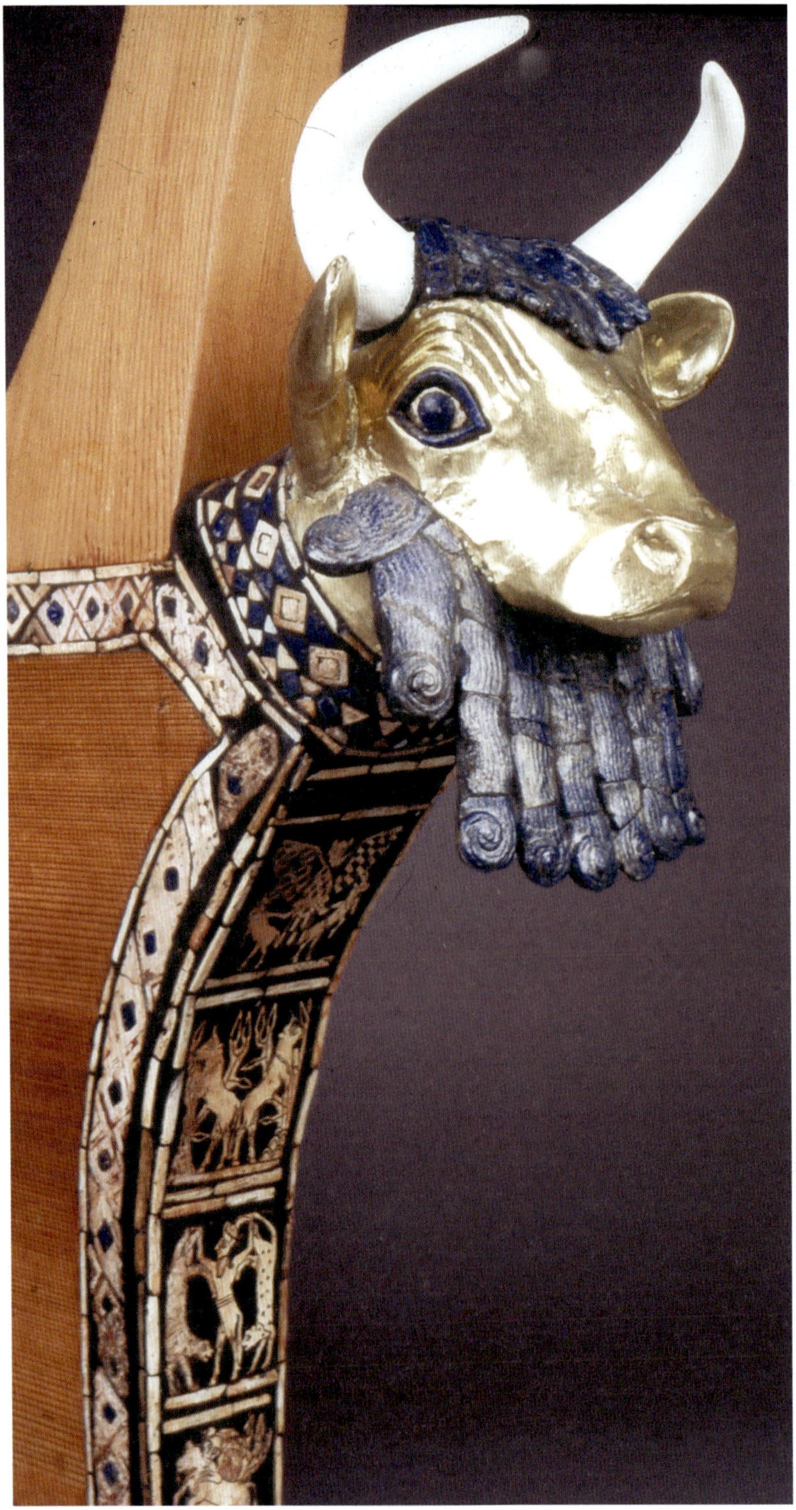

4

THE OPENING OF THE EURASIAN STEPPE,
2500–1600 BC

THE thousand-year period from the middle of the third millennium to the middle of the second millennium saw Eurasia, for the first time, drawn together by a network of connectivity that was to characterize the continent for the rest of history. There were two prime movers behind the imperatives for network building: the demand for commodities by the consuming politics of the 'civilized' world and the innate rhythms of mobility that empowered the lives of the steppe pastoralists.

The farming-based urban societies in the Near East, stretching from the Levant coast of the Mediterranean to the Indus valley, provided a cauldron of creative ferment where polities could grow into states ruled by kings, alliances could be formed and broken, and where warfare was endemic for much of the time, held in check by political and economic agreements but periodically breaking out into wholesale carnage and destruction. Complex societies of this kind consumed labour and commodities on a huge scale, for their grandiose building schemes, to support the lifestyles of the non-productive elite, and to underpin the military activities of the state. Slaves and raw materials were always in demand, and that demand ensured that trading networks were ever expanding and the flow of materials ever increasing. New routes developed, bringing turquoise and tin from Central Asia, lapis lazuli and gold from Afghanistan, carnelian from India, and the all-important copper from anywhere that

4.1 A number of early states developed in South West Asia. Maritime movements along the Persian Gulf, the Gulf of Oman, and the Arabian Sea provided the connectivity that kept the states in communication with each other and facilitated the exchange of goods

could produce it. Much of the trade was overland by mule, donkey, and camel, but an active maritime trade now began, linking territories from the head of the Persian Gulf to the coasts of Arabia and to India.

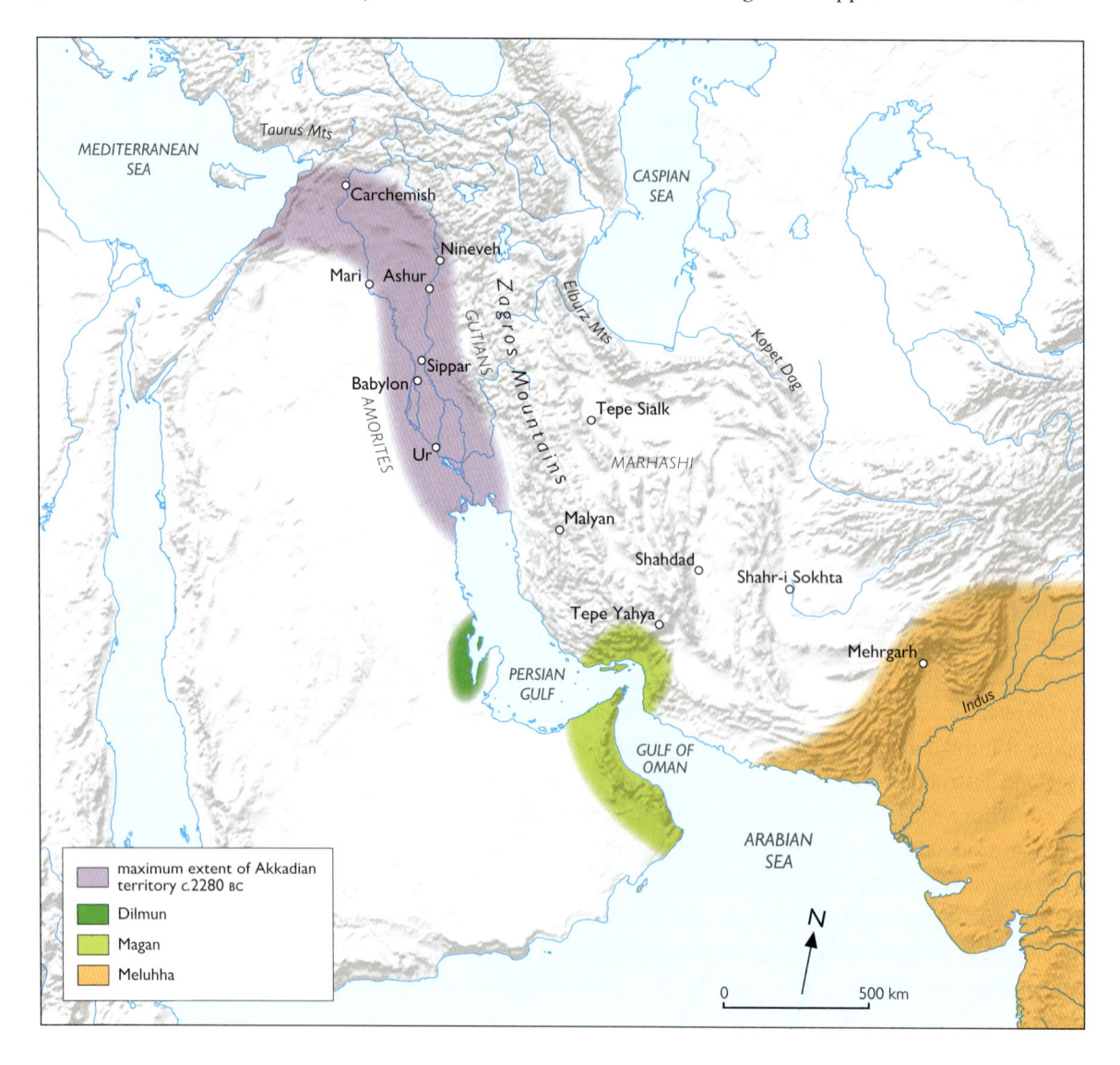

Meanwhile, in the steppe a no less significant process was under way with the intensification of systems of mobile herding, setting in train one of the most dramatic transitions that the zone had ever experienced. Regional networks were established, creating a remarkable degree of interconnectedness. Mobile herding spread eastwards beyond the Altai Mountains into the Mongolian steppe, while herders, learning the benefits of irrigation agriculture, broadened their activities to the deserts of Central Asia and across the Tian Shan range into the Tarim basin. In Central Asia new networks linked the herders with the oasis towns of Bactria and Margiana and to the polities on the Iranian plateau and beyond, while in the Tarim basin new settlers from the western steppe soon established contact along the Gansu Corridor with the communities of the Central Plains of China. In this way western crops, wheat and barley, and western domesticated animals, sheep, goats, and cattle, together perhaps with the technology of copper metallurgy, were introduced to China. A final link was forged in the middle of the second millennium with the opening of a steppe route between Mongolia and China.

The connectivity of Eurasia in the second millennium is in no better way demonstrated than by the spread of the fast spoke-wheeled chariot, an invention of mobile steppe herders living on the eastern flank of the Urals. The earliest chariots appeared here about 2100 BC. By the nineteenth century chariots had been adopted throughout the Near East. By the seventeenth century they were known in the Mycenaean world in Greece, and by the twelfth century, if not before, they had been introduced into Shang China. With the chariot spread the domesticated horse, trained for riding and for powering the chariots. The horse and the chariot, themselves the very essence of mobility, are symbolic of the new connectivity that now embraced the whole of Eurasia.

Mesopotamia, 2900–1600 BC

In the third and early second millennium the communities of Mesopotamia, and increasingly the lands around, were caught up in the energizing turmoil of rapid social and economic change. While the details do not concern us, and we should in no way fall into the familiar trap of suggesting that events in the Near East determined change elsewhere, the simple fact that this comparatively small region became a rabid consumer of a very wide range of commodities sourced from beyond its borders cannot have failed to have a dramatic effect on the neighbouring communities. In short, the demand for luxury items by successive elites created a huge market, which could only be satisfied by ever-expanding trading networks spreading deep into the surrounding regions. In this way the enormous quantities of gold, silver, copper, tin, lapis lazuli, turquoise, carnelian, fabrics, rare woods, fragrances, and all the other things that kings and courtiers needed to satisfy their aspirations and to maintain the unstable hierarchic structure, were drawn into the centre. The volume of raw materials on the move was massive. One text from Ur dating to about 1800 BC refers to a single shipment of copper weighing 20 tons.

The thousand years or so that concern us in this chapter saw a steady growth in the complexity of the state and a constant fluctuation between the centralization and the dispersal of power. During the Early Dynastic period, from 2900 to 2350 BC, a number of scattered polities existed in a degree of harmony. Then followed political centralization, first under the rulers of Akkad and later under Ur, but with the fall of Ur in 2004 BC power was again dissipated between innumerable city states and alliances until about 1800 BC, when a succession of powerful military leaders began to create large territorial states. Comparative stability lasted for nearly two centuries, but in 1590 BC the whole edifice collapsed into what has been called a dark age. Throughout this time the differing polities of the Near East, whether centralized or dispersed, exerted increasing influence on the territories about them.

The demise of Uruk domination about 3100 BC saw the emergence of a number of city states in Babylonia, about thirty-five in all, evenly spread across the landscape. Each city was surrounded by a home territory about 30 kilometres across, within which its irrigated land lay and where the farms of the citizens were scattered. Between these agricultural territories was uninhabited steppe, ideal for running flocks and herds. As populations grew and more land needed to be taken into cultivation, border conflicts became inevitable, sometimes resulting in warfare. It was the need to elect war leaders to manage these issues that eventually led to the establishment of dynastic rule, with the power of the king now being passed on to sons or brothers. The city temple remained the prominent building, alongside the palace, and continued to perform the central functions of collecting agricultural surpluses, through tax and tithe, and redistributing them to the wider community. Over time some towns became strong, their kings claiming authority over neighbouring cities through force of arms or by negotiation and treaty.

The Babylonian city states were bounded by the desert to the south-west but were otherwise surrounded by populous and productive regions. To the south lay the Persian Gulf and the state of Dilmun, most likely with Bahrain as its centre, commanding the rich copper mines of Oman. Maritime trade throughout the western coasts of the Gulf was brisk, as is shown by the quantity of Mesopotamian pottery found along the coastal region, and through Dilmun would have come a constant supply of other desirables like rare woods, incense, pearls, gold, and perhaps slaves. From the Gulf, ships would have sailed along the Makran coast of the Arabian Sea to the Indus valley, whence came textiles and precious stones. Several port sites belonging to the Indus valley civilization grew up along this coastline, and materials from the Indus are found widely scattered along the southern and western shores of the Gulf. Another of the foreign states with which the Mesopotamians were trading was Magan (now Oman and the United Arab Emirates) between the Persian Gulf and the

Gulf of Oman, where the seas narrow. Magan not only commanded the east–west maritime routes but was well suited to trade south-westwards along the Arabian peninsula.

On its eastern side Babylonia was separated from the Iranian plateau and the lands beyond by the Zagros Mountains, but on the lower slopes lay the powerful city of Susa, later to become the focus of the state of Elam. Lowland Susa and the upland city of Malyan controlled overland routes to the east, from where the desirable lapis lazuli and turquoise and the increasingly important tin came. Susa itself lay close to supplies of bitumen, an important adhesive in the ancient world. Finally, to the north, using the valleys of the Tigris and Euphrates, it was possible to reach eastern Anatolia and the Mediterranean—regions which could supply a wide range of goods, principally copper, silver, and obsidian.

For the city states of Babylonia control of the maritime trade was not difficult, but the eastern and northern routes required careful diplomatic relationships to be developed and maintained. Alliances had to be formed and nurtured, and when this proved difficult, military intervention naturally followed.

The increasing wealth that could be accumulated during the Early Dynastic period is vividly demonstrated by the sumptuous Royal Tombs of Ur, dating to about 2500 BC, in which huge quantities of gold, silver, shell, lapis lazuli, and other rare materials were buried with the dead. The social imperative requiring that such wealth be placed in the ground, thus taking it out of circulation, created a demand on a scale that could only be met by a constant inflow of new material.

The last of the centuries of the third millennium saw the rise and fall of two centralized states, the first led by the city of Akkad between 2334 and 2218 BC, the second by the city of Ur from 2112 to 2004 BC. Both in turn exercised full control over the cities of southern Mesopotamia, and both extended their influence to cover large parts of the Near East. The Akkadian kings seem to have consolidated their control over the polities of the Persian Gulf by undertaking a series of raids, but the expeditions appear to have been more to ensure the constant supply of materials through monopoly agreements than to create overseas colonies. To the east, however, Susa was brought more directly under Akkadian control, though it retained a degree of self-government. To the north, in Syria, a more direct policy was adopted. Military garrisons were established in some of the major towns, including Tell Brak, while others seem simply to have agreed to facilitate trade with the Akkad. The spread of Akkadian hegemony is indicated by the extent to which its script was used. The fact that the king added to his title 'of the four corners [of the world]' is an unambiguous expression of his sense of dominion.

Internal dissent among the towns of Babylonia and threats from without eventually brought the Akkadian state to an end. Among the external enemies now named are the Marhashi of the Iranian plateau, the Gutians of the Zagros Mountains, and the semi-nomadic Amorites of northern Syria. The cohesion of each of these groups was probably enhanced by their having to oppose the advance of the Akkadians. In the end the Akkadian state overreached itself and collapse came quickly, leaving the region to fragment into a number of self-contained city states.

About 2100 BC the rulers of Ur rose to dominance and, in a brief period of a century or so, regained some of the territorial power of their predecessors. The period, referred to as the Third Dynasty of Ur or Ur III, is one of the best recorded of any in ancient history, with tens of thousands of contemporary documents available to challenge the historian. The Ur kings concentrated their attention on taking firm control of the eastern region between the river Tigris and the Zagros Mountains. Here they installed administrators who were responsible for collecting tribute in the form of a tithe of the region's cattle, sheep, and goats, which were transported on the hoof back to Babylonia. In the north and west the trading networks were maintained through a series of diplomatic agreements with the principal cities, and much the same policy seems to have been in operation in the Persian Gulf. One of the commodities found in quantity in Babylonia for the first time in Ur III was the horse, used primarily for riding but also for cross-breeding with other equids to create beasts like the mule, an ass–horse hybrid better suited to pulling wagons or carrying loads. The horses would originally have come from the steppe either via the eastern Caucasus and east Anatolia or, more likely at this stage, across western Iran. Other raw materials flowed into the state's coffers along the traditional routes much as before but in ever-increasing quantity. The systems of supply were now stretched to the full.

4.2 The royal burials of Ur in Mesopotamia, dating to the twenty-first century BC, contained exotic goods brought in from distant countries. The queen's lyre shown here is ornamented with a bull's head in gold and with lapis lazuli brought from Afghanistan

The end came quickly. Threats from the Elamites to the east of the Tigris and from the semi-nomadic Amorites, exacerbated by internal unrest, greatly weakened the state, and in 2004 BC an alliance of the Elamites and the Shimashki of the Zagros Mountains defeated and captured the last of the Ur III kings.

With the centralizing power of Ur now broken, the Near East reverted once more to a palimpsest of city states vying with each other for power, making alliances and breaking them. Between 1800 and 1600 BC territorial states re-emerged first in Upper Mesopotamia and later, under King Hammurabi (reigned 1765–60 BC), once again in Babylon. The period of comparative stability and prosperity was not long to last. In 1595 BC a Hittite army from Anatolia marched down the Euphrates and sacked the city of Babylon, bringing dynastic rule to an end. The system of city states that had managed to maintain themselves for a millennium or more, throughout the vicissitudes of dynastic change and the rise and fall of territorial states, was now in disarray. Some had been destroyed, others abandoned. Productivity and the level of economic activity faltered and trade declined to a trickle. With the collapse of administrative systems, writing all but disappeared. Without texts the region entered a dark age lasting for a century.

Across the Iranian Plateau

The Iranian plateau stretches from the Zagros Mountains, flanking the eastern edge of the Tigris and Euphrates valleys, to the Toba Kakar range, beyond which lies the Indus valley. To the south it is bounded by the Persian Gulf and the Arabian Sea and to the north by the Hindu Kush, the Kopet Dag, and the Elburz Mountains, looking out on the vastness of the Karakum desert and the Caspian Sea. It is an area of great diversity, of mountain ridges, upland plains, and great salt deserts, mostly between 1,000 and 2,000 metres above sea-level, producing copper, some tin, and precious stones. In terms of modern geopolitics the plateau includes Iran, Afghanistan, and western Pakistan.

By the fifth millennium food-producing economies had spread throughout the whole region, reaching the Indus valley and the desert fringe. Settled communities had been established, and many of them continued to develop over the next millennium, though few have been excavated on any scale. Among those that have been examined, Tepe Yahya in Kerman province of Iran had, by the late fourth millennium BC, grown to become a large town. Social complexity led to the development of a writing system known as proto-Elamite, based on a pictographic script and now used as far afield as Godin Tepe in the north, Susa on the edge of the Tigris plain, and Shahr-i Sokhta close to the Afghan border in the east. There can be little doubt that by this time the larger towns of the region were acting as the centres of city states in the manner of those in Mesopotamia. These secondary states, as they are sometimes

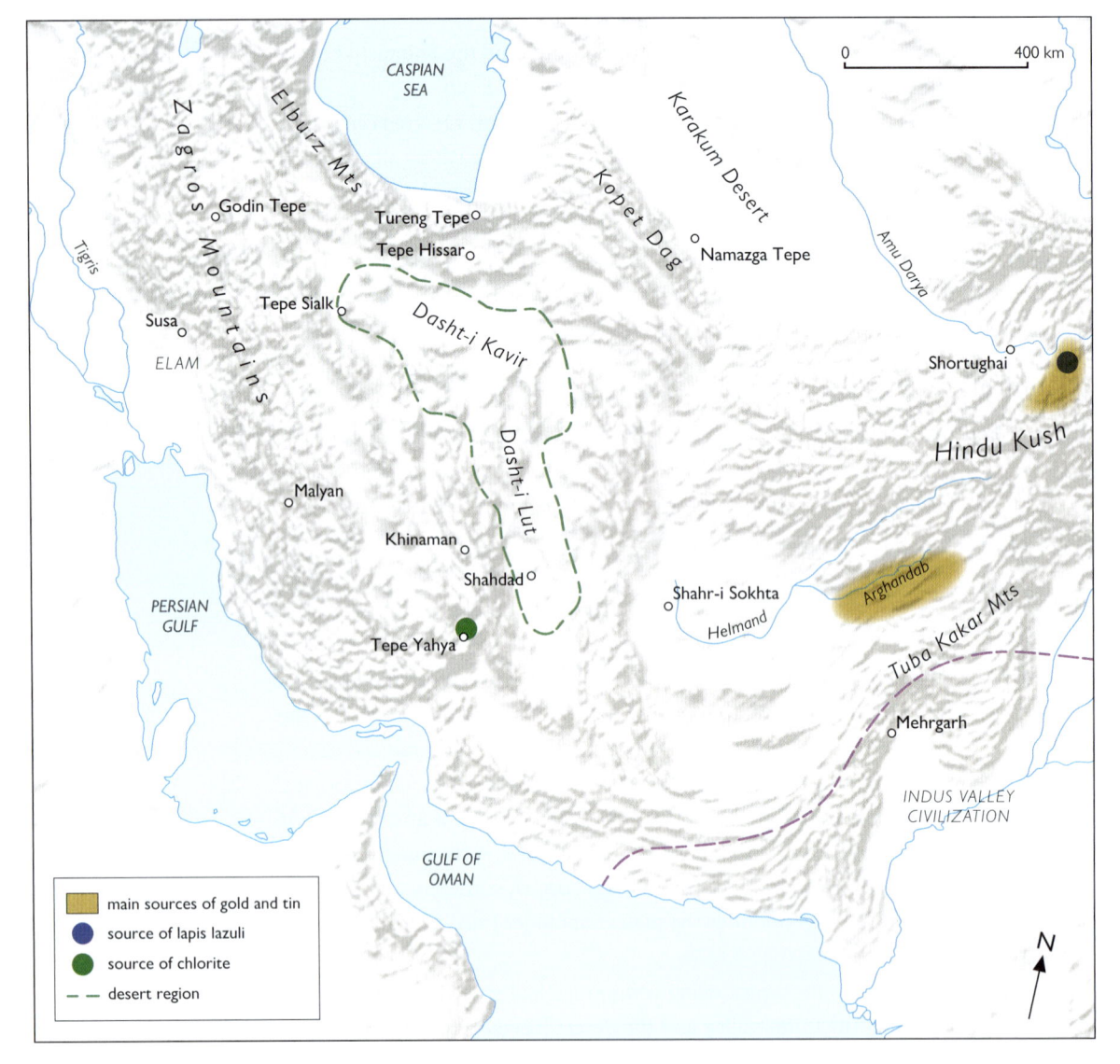

4.3 The resource-rich Iranian plateau was soon drawn into the exchange networks of the maritime and riverine states, leading to the development of towns strategically sited on the main routes

called, would have had complex histories like those of Mesopotamia, dominated by conflicts and alliances, but we know little of this until the western confederacy of Elam emerges as a significant force with Susa as one of its leading cities. In the second half of the third millennium lowland Elam came within the ambit of the Akkadians and later the Ur III dynasty, but, as we have seen, it was instrumental in the collapse of

Ur III about 2000 BC. After this Elam grew to become an independent state of power and influence.

The cities of the plateau owed their well-being to their ability to control the raw materials increasingly in demand in Mesopotamia. By the late fourth millennium there is evidence of long-distance trade at Godin Tepe, a town lying towards the northern end of the Zagros Mountains, such that it has been referred to as a merchant colony. Most of the other major settlements show some evidence for trade or manufacture. At Tepe Yahya locally occurring chlorite, a soft, greenish-grey stone, was brought to the town from local mines in the late third millennium, there to be carved into vessels that were widely traded to Mesopotamia, the Persian Gulf, and Bactria.

4.4 Cylindrical container carved from a soft stone (chlorite) depicting a religious scene. The central figure is probably a god who had power over the beasts. The vessel, dating to the late third millennium BC, most likely came from Bactria

Another commodity much in demand in the ancient world was the deep-blue lapis lazuli, a very rare semi-precious stone coming from only one major source near Sar-i Sang in the Kokcha valley in Afghanistan. Raw blocks of lapis were transported to the town of Shahr-i Sokhta on the Afghan–Iranian border, where they were worked into beads and other items for onward transport. The craft workers at the town also fashioned other exotic stones, including turquoise from Nishapur, in Khorason province, and chlorite. When the Babylonian texts talk of Marhashi and Aratta, distant, almost mythical places from where were obtained rare stone, exotic animals, and plants and metals, they may well have been referring to cities like Tepe Yahya, Shahr-i Sokhta, and Shahdad in the southeast of Iran.

The other widely traded materials were metals—copper, tin, silver, and gold—all of which were consumed in huge quantities in Mesopotamia. Copper was found fairly extensively across the Iranian plateau and, alloyed with arsenic, was used to make a wide variety of artefacts, most spectacularly the intricately cast ceremonial axes of the type found at Khinaman and Shahdad in Kerman province, manufactured about 2000 BC. The richest source of metals lies in Afghanistan: copper is found throughout the country, gold occurs over a con-

4.5 Bronze ceremonial axe from the cemetery at Khinaman, near Kerman, Iran, dating to about 2000 BC

siderable area north-east of Kandahar and in the extreme north-east, and there is silver in the mountains near Bamiyan and in the Wakhan valley. The silver mines were still productive when Marco Polo visited the area in the late thirteenth century. It is probably these Afghan sources that provided much of the gold and silver consumed by the Mesopotamian elite.

The other metal that became of increasing importance was tin. From about 3000 BC it was used for alloying with copper to provide a metal better suited to the manufacture of tools and weapons. Tin occurs in its oxide form as cassiterite, a distinctively heavy mineral which can be mined or panned from alluvial deposits. Tin is rarely found in western Eurasia but is reasonably prolific in Afghanistan between Sistan and Herat in the west and to the north-east of Kandahar. These sources must have supplied much of the Near East. One text mentions a gift of 410 kilograms of tin in 1770 BC.

The prodigious mineral wealth of Afghanistan may, at least in part, account for the prosperous urban culture that had developed in south-eastern Iran by 2000 BC concentrated in the cities of Shahr-i Sokhta, Shahdad, Tepe Yahya, and Khinaman. The region occupied a central position between resource-rich Afghanistan and the consuming states of Elam and Mesopotamia beyond: it also lay comparatively close to the Makran coast of the Arabian Sea, which had now become a part of the Indus valley domain. Meanwhile, to the north, at a series of oases in the Karakum desert, newly founded towns were beginning to provide lucrative markets as well as offering networks linking to the steppe cultures of the north. South-east Iran had become a highly favoured region by virtue of its centrality.

The Indus Valley

By the fourth millennium BC Neolithic farming communities occupying the uplands of Baluchistan at the eastern end of the Iranian plateau had successfully colonized the Indus valley, and by the third millennium their successors were building fortified settlements. It was from these early roots, known as the Early Harappan period, that the Indus (or Harappan) civilization emerged about 2600 BC. In its mature phase the integrated culture was focused around at least five urban sites, 80–200 hectares in size, of which Harappa and Mohenjo-Daro are the best known, and more than thirty smaller settlements of 20 hectares or less. Between these centres the rural population lived in many thousands of smaller villages.

For much of the time the food-producing economy was based on wheat, barley, pulses, and fruit, which would have been introduced from the west together with sheep and goats. Zebu cattle and water buffalo were domesticated locally, and cotton

THE OPENING OF THE EURASIAN STEPPE

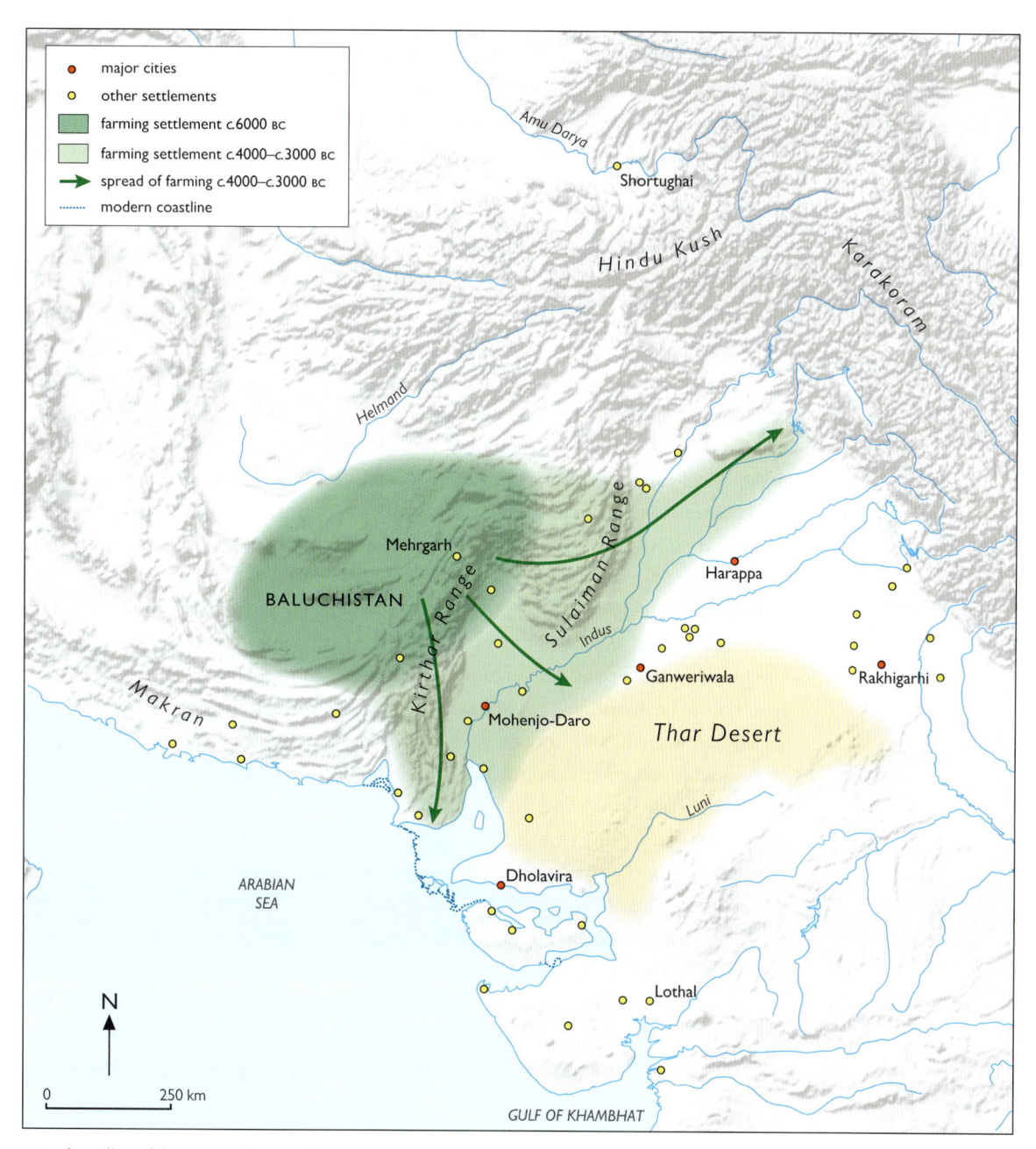

4.6 The valley of the river Indus saw the development of an urban state known archaeologically as the Indus, or Harappan, civilization. It was dominated by five major cities spaced at intervals of about 300 kilometres with smaller towns between

was also probably an indigenous addition to the economy. Towards the end of the period, about 2000 BC, sorghum and millet were introduced from Africa as the result of maritime contact possibly by way of Oman, while rice was brought in from south-west Asia, most likely via the Ganges valley. The majority of the population lived on the flood-plains, where systems of irrigation could be organized to facilitate crop growing.

While the fertile, well-watered plains provided ideal conditions for agriculture, they were poor in other resources. Since building stone was rarely accessible, mud-bricks were widely used, and even at the city of Dholavira, where local sandstone was available, stonework was interspersed with mud-brick. Other commodities were obtained through trade. From the long coastline, from the Makran in the west to the Gulf of Khambhat in the south-east, marine shells could be collected for making ornaments. At the head of the gulf a small trading port was established at Lothal, where local carnelian and agate were collected for making into beads; ivory could be acquired from the inland valleys and gold was imported from the south. Traders depended on Afghanistan and the Iranian plateau for other metals. Far to the north a distant inland trading post was established at Shortughai, in the valley of the Amu Darya, close to supplies of copper and to the lapis lazuli mines at Sar-i Sang. The Indus cities, then, were well integrated into the systems of connectivity that bound the Iranian plateau and its surrounding regions tightly together and enabled raw materials to be distributed over distances of up to 3,000 kilometres.

The Indus civilization began to disintegrate about 1900 BC: several of the cities were abandoned and the population dispersed into smaller settlements, the trading networks broke down, and the script, designed for complex record keeping, ceased to be used. Many causes for the collapse have been suggested, including flooding and the changing of the river courses, deforestation, and increased salination. It has also been suggested that the introduction of rice and millet from the Ganges valley may have encouraged a general migration of population to new lands in the east. Another contributing factor may have been the general breakdown of long-distance trade affecting much of the Near East at this time. Whatever the defining local causes, the social changes in the Indus valley are best seen as part of a much broader regional phenomenon affecting many areas in the early centuries of the second millennium.

The Desert Cities of Western Central Asia

Between the great knot of the Pamir and Tian Shan mountains and the Caspian Sea lies a vast expanse of desert, the Karakum and Kyzylkum deserts, bounded to the south by the Kopet Dag mountains and the Hindu Kush and merging, to the north,

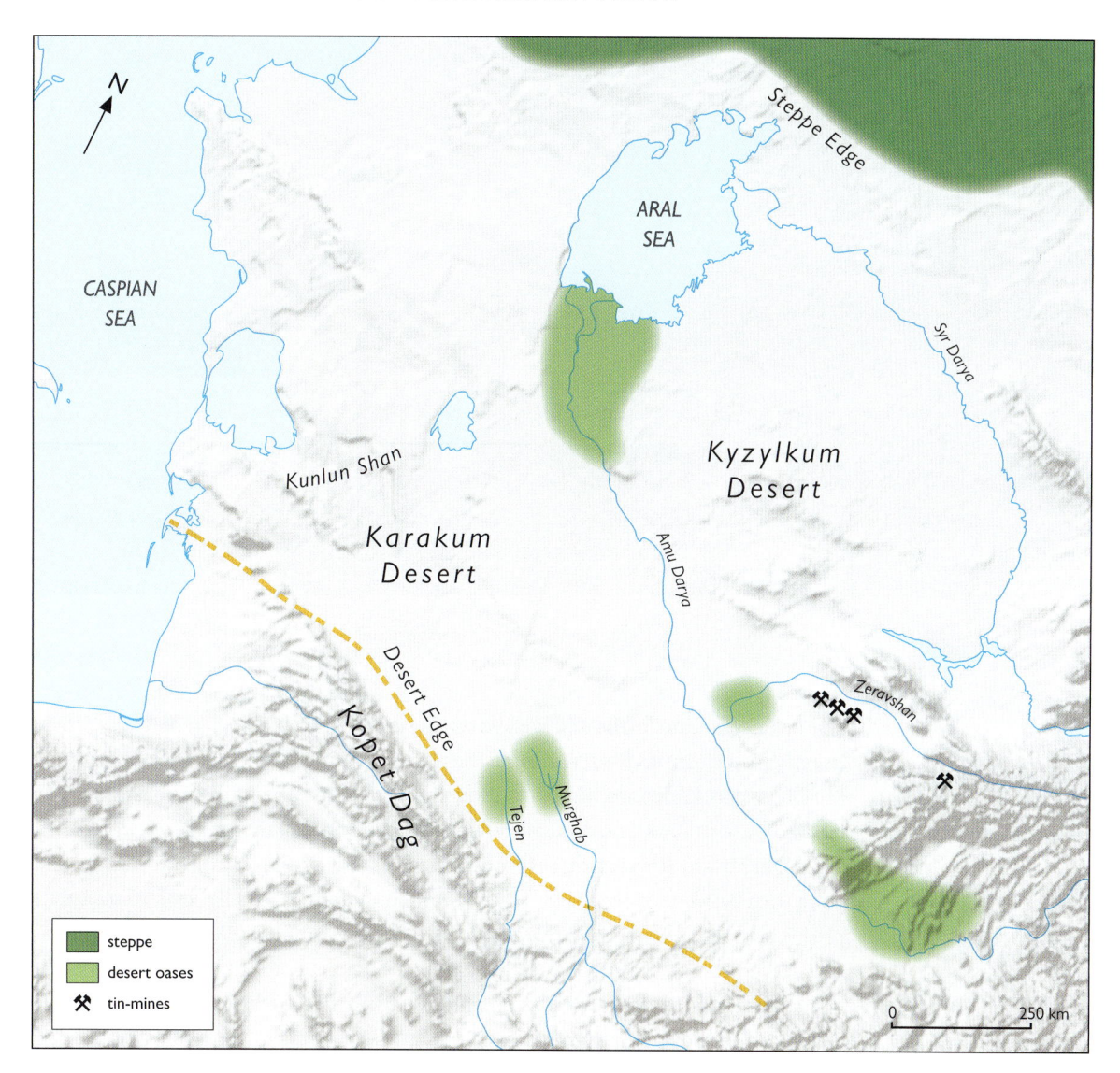

4.7 To the north of the Iranian plateau, in what is now Turkmenistan and Uzbekistan, food-producing economies developed in the desert oases of the region. These communities soon established contacts with the steppe pastoralists to the north

with the open steppe of Kazakhstan. Rivers flow into the desert from the mountain fringe. The two largest, the Amu Darya (or Oxus) and the Syr Darya (or Jaxartes), coming from the high Pamir, originally reached the Aral Sea, with a branch of the Amu Darya flowing into the Caspian, while the Murghab and Tejen, rising in the Hindu Kush, dissipate their waters in deltas along the southern edge of the desert.

4.8 The Amu Darya (or Oxus) flowing through the Kyzylkum desert in central Asia

The deltaic fans are fertile and well watered, supporting oases congenial for settlers. In early historic times the territory of the western zone of oases, focused on the river Murghab, was known as Margiana (now in Turkmenistan), while the eastern zone, north of the Hindu Kush, was called Bactria (now Uzbekistan, Tajikistan, and northern Afghanistan). It was in these favoured regions that a series of cities developed and flourished between 2100 and 1800 BC. The phenomenon is usually referred to, rather prosaically, as the Bactria Margiana Archaeological Complex (BMAC); others prefer to use the more evocative 'Oxus civilization' to describe it. But, however named, it was a remarkable brief flowering of a highly distinctive complex society brilliantly adapted to the oasis environment.

Already by the sixth millennium BC farming communities had moved from the Iranian plateau to settle on the narrow piedmont zone (the *atak*) skirting the Kopet Dag range, bringing with them domesticated sheep, goats, and cattle, and cultivated wheat and barley. The settlement of the deltaic fans and oases further out in the desert may have begun in the following millennia with farming people moving north to explore the opportunities of these special ecological niches. If so, evidence of the early stages of this colonization will be buried deep in the constantly accumulating alluvium and little is yet known of them. But soon after the middle of the third millennium communities from the Iranian plateau began to move through the Kopet

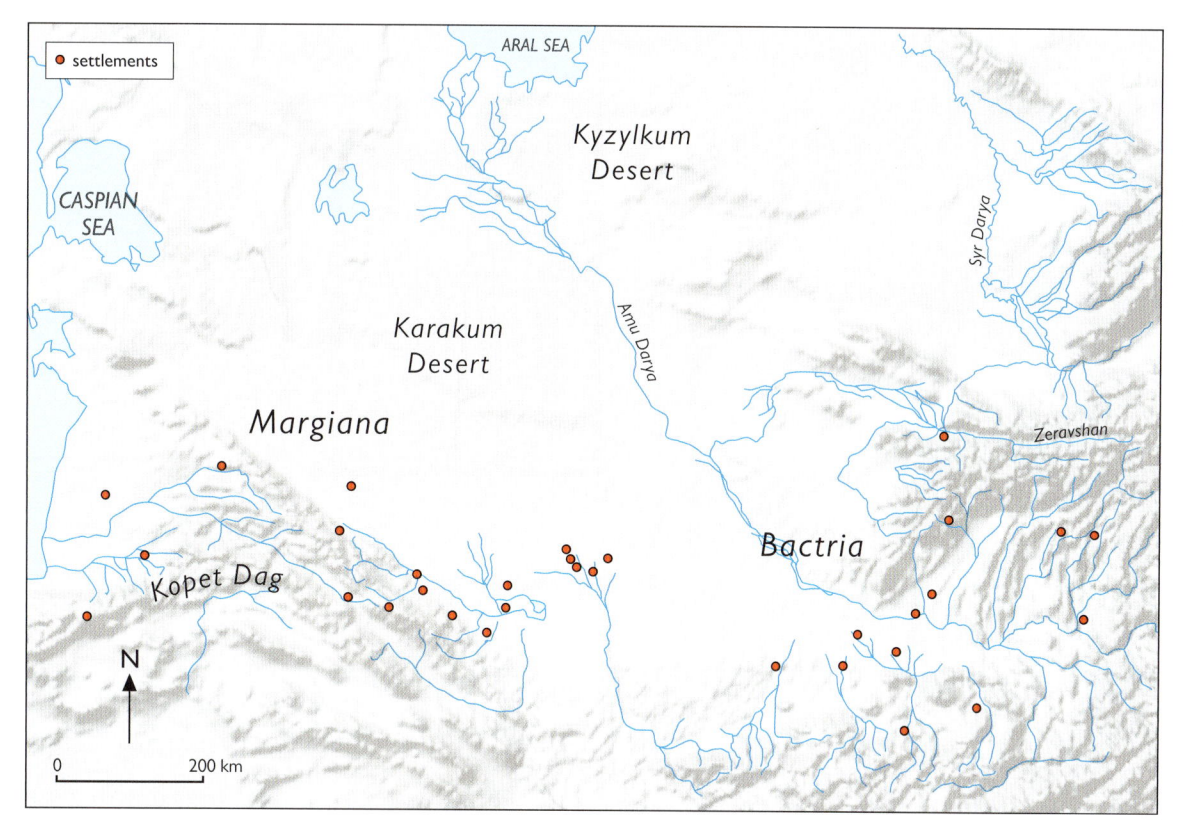

4.9 The desert oases around the southern fringe of the Karakum desert developed an urban-based culture which some archaeologists call the Oxus civilization; others prefer the more prosaic title the Bactria–Margiana Archaeological Complex

Dag, adding to the population already settled on the piedmont and spreading out onto the desert deltas.

The pioneer settlers would have found the deltaic areas covered with *tugai* thickets, dense scrub interspersed with poplar and tamarisk, and around these zones would have been salt-marshes supporting reeds and other salt-tolerant plants giving way to dunes with groves of saxaul. Wild animals included gazelle, wild boar, onager, and hare, as well as a variety of rodents and reptiles. The first settlers had to clear the *tugai* and dig drainage canals before the land was fit to grow crops. Careful analysis of the plant and animal remains from the settlement of Gonur-depe show that the pioneers had introduced barley, the most important cereal, together with various types of wheat and pulses, including peas, lentils, and chickpeas. The presence of grapes, apples, and plums implies that the tending of orchards played a significant part in the food-producing economy. Sheep and goats were by far the most impor-

THE OPENING OF THE EURASIAN STEPPE

Togolok 21

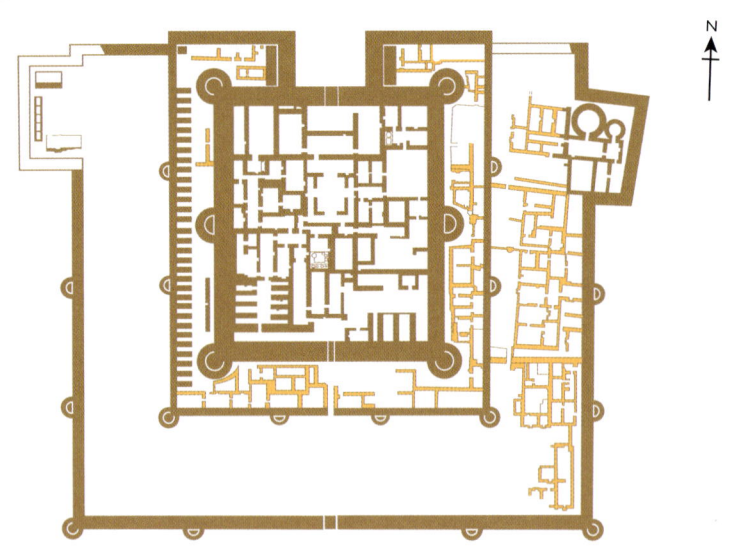

Gonur-depe South

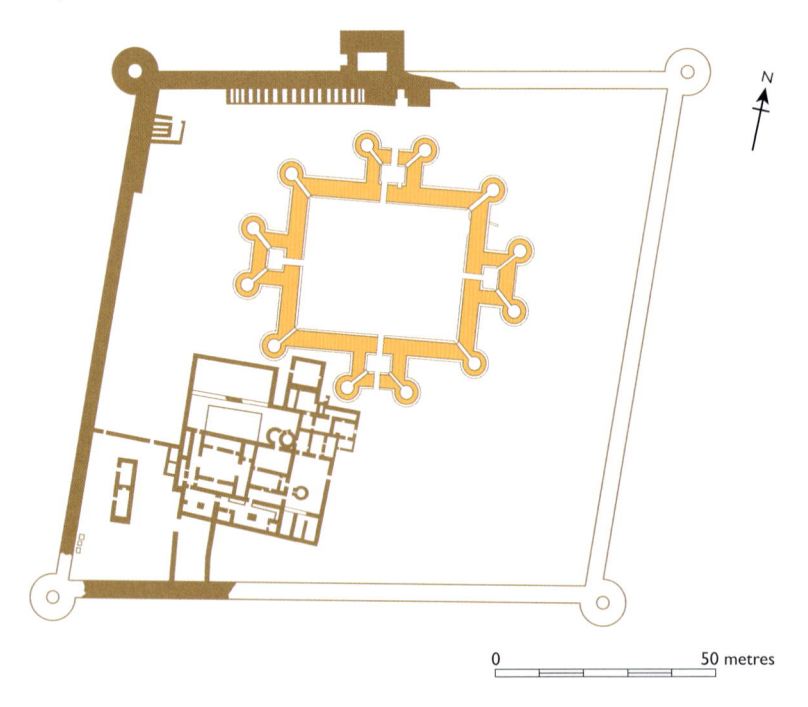

4.10 Togolok and Gonur-depe South, both in Turkmenistan, are typical of the large urban sites that developed during the BMAC period. The architecture was designed for defence but also to impress

tant domesticates, the high percentage of bones of old animals recovered from the rubbish deposits suggesting that they were kept mainly for their milk and wool and were eaten only when they were at the end of their productive life. Domesticated cattle were also reared but in much smaller numbers. Regular fresh meat would have come from hunting wild boar, gazelle, and onager. The farmers who chose to settle at the desert deltas and oases had to bring with them all their domesticated animals and cultivated plants from the south, and to establish them they had to clear the untamed land, drain it when necessary, and set up systems of irrigation. That they were well practised in these arts led to the rapid development of a complex society focused on a number of towns.

The colonization of the Murghab deltas took place about 2100 BC. What drove the colonists is unknown, but it may have been any or all of the usual factors: population growth, climatic changes, and warfare in their southern homeland. The initial settlement phase was followed by a more developed phase (c.2000–c.1800 BC), during which time the building of walled towns spread to Bactria. These settlements varied in size, with the largest covering nearly 100 hectares, but defensive architecture was used for sites of very different status, from populous cities to the strongholds of local warlords barely half a hectare in extent. A strict rectangularity of plan was widely favoured, with the brick-built walls strengthened with corner towers, and with bastions spaced regularly between them along the faces of the walls. In some cases, multiple lines of defences were provided, with the innermost serving as the citadel–palace while the outer enclosed spaces protected shrines and the close-packed houses of the farmers, artisans, and traders. The order and rigidity of the overall plans imply a high degree of centralized control and the ability of the elite to demand services from a subservient population.

Something of the power of the elite is displayed in a royal cemetery found close to the citadel–palace complex at Gonur-depe North. In one brick-lined grave pit, a four-wheeled wagon thought to have been a sacrificial offering associated with a royal burial was found, its wheels made of planks bound with bronze tyres. Within the pit were the remains of two camels, a dog, and a foal that had been decapitated. There were also the bodies of ten adult humans who appear to have been sacrificed and thrown in. Nearby rooms contained a range of valuable funerary gifts including fragments of mosaics with carpet designs, a silver cosmetic flask, and other ornaments of gold, silver, and turquoise. Another grave pit contained a four-wheeled wagon of similar type, which had been dismantled before burial.

The craft skills practised in the oasis towns were considerable. Metalsmiths had mastered the art of the lost-wax technique and were able to make an impressive variety of artefacts, most spectacularly the crested shaft-holed axes with curved blades

4.11 The royal burial at Gonur-depe North, Turkmenistan. Two human skeletons and the bones of two horses can be seen. The wheels of the four-wheeled vehicle were rimmed with copper alloy sheet

sometimes ornamented with animals much like the axes found in the urban centres of south-east Iran. In the first phase copper was used, sometimes unalloyed and sometimes alloyed with arsenic or lead, but after about 2000 BC bronze (a copper–tin alloy) began to be preferred. The tin probably came from the Zeravshan region (see below). Stoneworkers were also active, using steatite and alabaster, both of which had to be imported from the piedmont of the Kopet Dag. The stone was used to make dishes and bowls of various kinds, often decorated with geometric designs and sometimes with animals and trees. Also characteristic were stylized human figures depicted in sitting positions. The bodies were made of dark steatite, while the heads and hands were separately made from white alabaster or limestone. Steatite and alabaster were also used by seal cutters, who made both circular and cylindrical seals. Some of the pottery was found to be stamped by seals, suggesting that the seals were used as a control in production.

The creation of these highly distinctive items took place in the towns, and from the creatures depicted—snakes, scorpions, camels, and desert plants—it is clear that the artisans were responding to their desert environment. But the ultimate inspiration for the craft skills, and indeed the architecture, came from the south, from Elam,

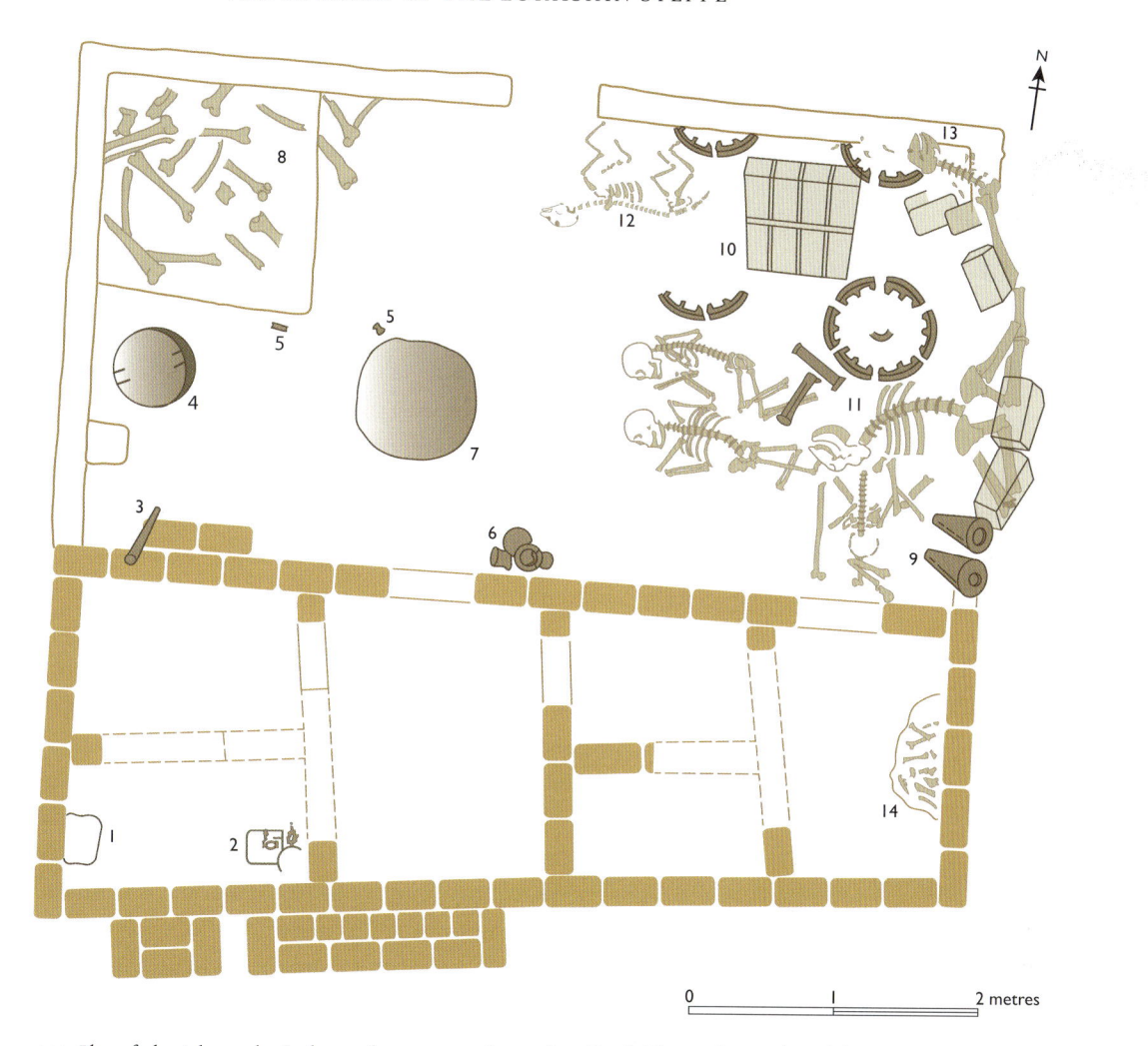

4.12 Plan of a burial complex in the royal cemetery at Gonur-depe North. The two human burials lie next to a four-wheeled vehicle (10). The disturbed skeleton of a young horse lies nearby (13). Other animals include a dog (12) and two camels (8 and 11). Grave goods lie scattered about in the burial chamber. The disarticulated remains of four humans (14) were found in one of the rooms

south-eastern Iran, and the Indus valley. It was with these regions that the BMAC towns continued to maintain contacts throughout. This is manifest in direct imports like a Harappan seal found at Gonur-depe North and from the quantities of sea-shells from the Mediterranean and the Indian Ocean used by bead-makers. The rare raw materials such as gold, silver, ivory, lapis lazuli, turquoise, steatite, and alabaster were all imported from outside the region. Items manufactured in the BMAC towns have been found in the south at Mehrgarh in Baluchistan and in the Persian Gulf from

THE OPENING OF THE EURASIAN STEPPE

Oman to Kuwait. The spectacular cast crested axes found in south-eastern and central Iran may also have been a product of the oasis towns, but this has not yet been proved. Taken together there is ample evidence to show that the towns of BMAC remained in close contact with an arc of the civilized world stretching from Mesopotamia to the Indus.

It is difficult to say for certain what other commodities, apart from value-added manufactured goods, were exchanged with the south. Wool was produced in quantity locally and may have been exported in its raw state or made into fabrics or rugs, while copper from the Urals and tin from the Zeravshan region are likely to have been traded through the BMAC towns. Another product of the north, soon to become much in demand in the civilized south, was the horse. Horse imagery is found on some BMAC artefacts, and, as we have seen, a foal was discovered in one of the elite burial complexes. We shall return to the significance of the horse later.

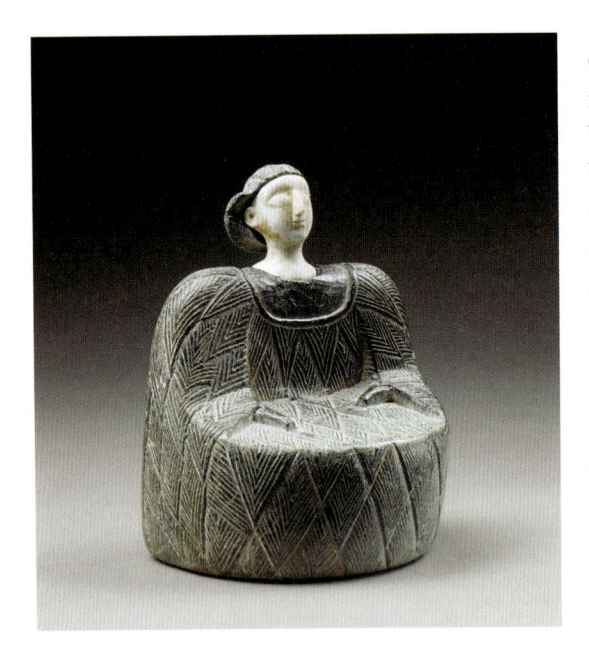

4.13 A 'Bactrian Princess' carved from black steatite with an inset alabaster head. The exact find spot of the figurine is unknown, but it probably comes from the Bactria Margiana Archaeological Complex of Turkmenistan dating to about 2000 BC

Sometime around 1800 BC the centralizing systems underlying the flourishing of the BMAC towns broke down, resulting in collapse and fragmentation. One of the causal factors may have been the effect of the arrival of increasing numbers of pastoral nomads from the steppe (pp. 138–41), but we should not overlook the bigger picture. The fall of Ur III about 2000 BC signalled the beginning of a period of rapid change in Mesopotamia eventually culminating about 1600 BC in the collapse of the once-thriving states that had extended from the Persian Gulf to the Mediterranean. What emerged was a new world that looked far more to the Mediterranean than to the east. It was during this period that the old state of Elam and the thriving polities of south-eastern Iran and the Indus valley lost impetus and fragmented. It is not surprising that the BMAC towns on the northern fringe of the civilized arc should also have suffered as the established networks of interaction withered and fragmented.

Chariot Warriors on the Steppe: The Sintashta Culture

We left the story of the Pontic-Caspian steppe with the mobile pastoralists of the Yamnaya and Catacomb cultures firmly established by the early centuries of the third millennium. Between 2800 and 2600 BC pastoral communities began moving eastwards, around the southern end of the Urals into the steppe zone between the rivers Ural and Tobol, and from about 2500 BC mobile herders were exploring the Kazakh steppe, some groups spreading southwards into the deserts of Central Asia. It was about this time that other groups were moving northwards into the forest-steppe, penetrating as far as the river Belaya and the upper Volga, there merging with the local indigenous foragers. This northern group of pioneer pastoralists is referred to as the Abashevo culture. They were accomplished copper workers, using ores from mines in different parts of the southern Urals to make tools and weapons, including cast shaft-hole axes and spearheads. They also worked more limited quantities of silver to make personal ornaments.

Miners of the Abashevo culture eventually moved eastwards, to settle between the rivers Ural and Tobol, where there were arsenic-rich copper ores to be had and where herders from the south had already settled a century or two earlier. It was from these antecedents that the remarkable Sintashta culture was to emerge about 2100 BC.

The Sintashta culture is the name given to copper-working pastoralists who lived in fortified villages, more than twenty of which are now known along the eastern slopes of the southern Urals within an area of some 400 kilometres by 150 kilometres. Some fortifications are known in earlier periods, but nothing on this scale had ever been seen on the steppe. So unusual is this regional phenomenon that Kazakh archaeologists have referred to the area as 'the country of towns', though 'towns' is rather an exaggeration for what were really large villages. The type site of Sintashta was once a circular enclosure defended by a V-profiled ditch and timber-laced earthen walls with a tall timber-built gate tower overlooking the entrance. A little more than half the enclosure has been eroded by river action, but the remaining part shows a highly regulated layout with rectangular, slightly trapezoidal, houses tucked tightly together, side by side, around the periphery. Thirty-one houses survive, but originally there would have been between fifty and sixty. Arkaim, another settlement to have been extensively excavated, is also a circular defended enclosure with houses arranged peripherally, but in this case in two concentric circles. The central circle probably represents the original settlement, to which a partial outer enclosure was added and later further enlarged. Altogether the enclosures protected about fifty houses. The other fortified villages conform to the general pattern but vary slightly in shape from circular to sub-rectangular.

Many of the houses in Sintashta, Arkaim, and the other partially excavated settlement of Ust'ye contained evidence of copper working in the form of smelting furnaces and slag. Arsenical copper was used and was cast in complex moulds to make shaft-hole axes and spears and in open moulds to make rod-shaped ingots weighing between 50 and 130 grams, presumably for trade and export. The metal came from the south Ural mines, which must now have been being worked on an intensive scale. At one of

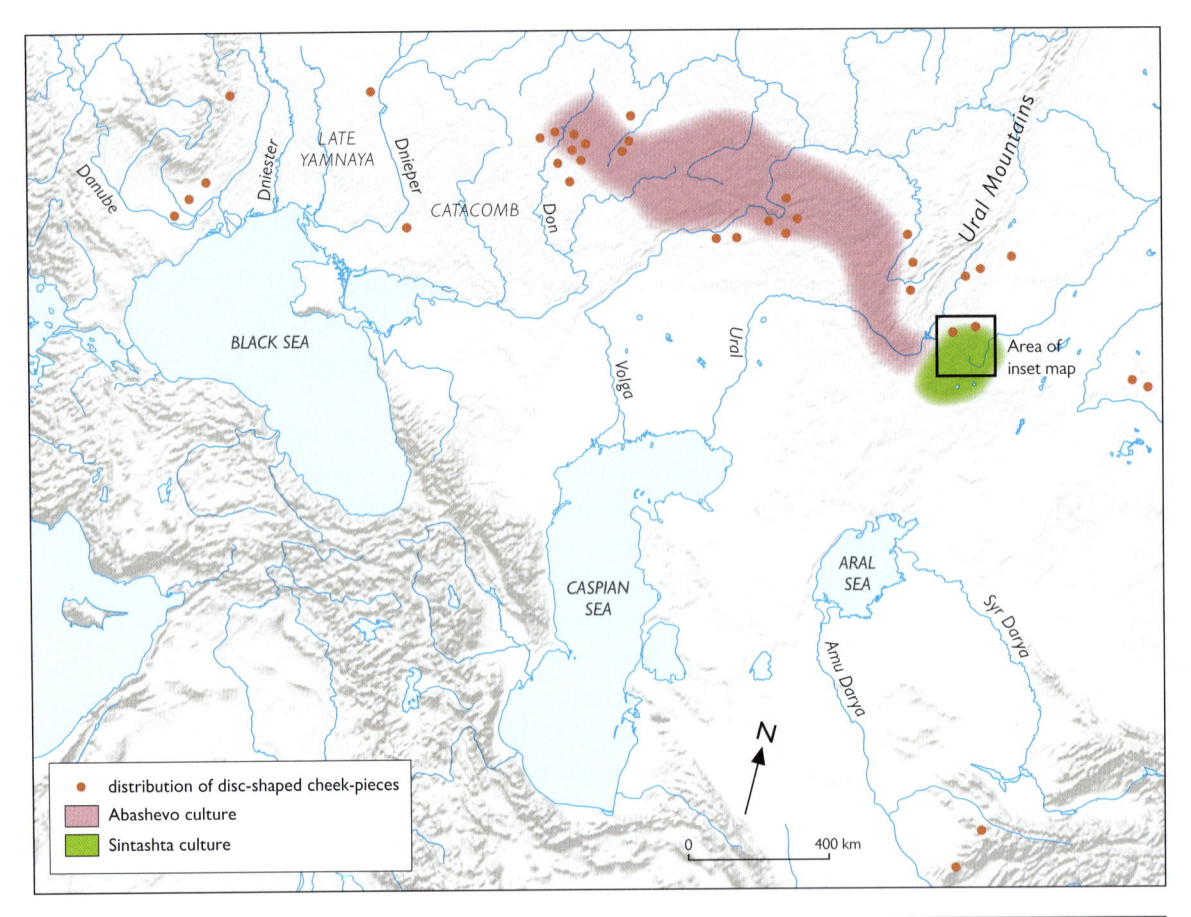

4.14 The large map shows the distribution of various cultural groups occupying the steppe in the third millennium BC. The red spots indicate finds of disc-shaped cheek-pieces from horse harnesses. The smaller map shows the distribution of settlements of the Sintashta culture

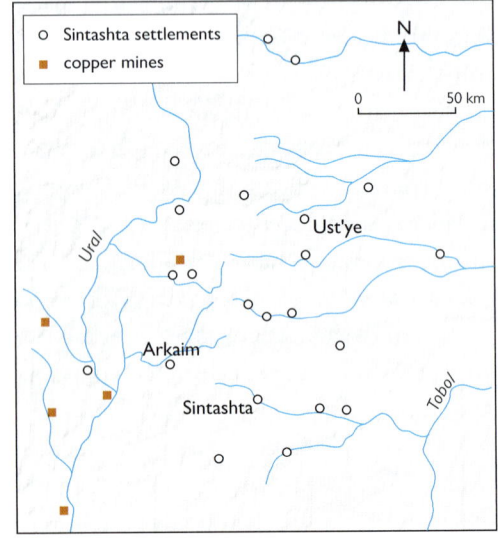

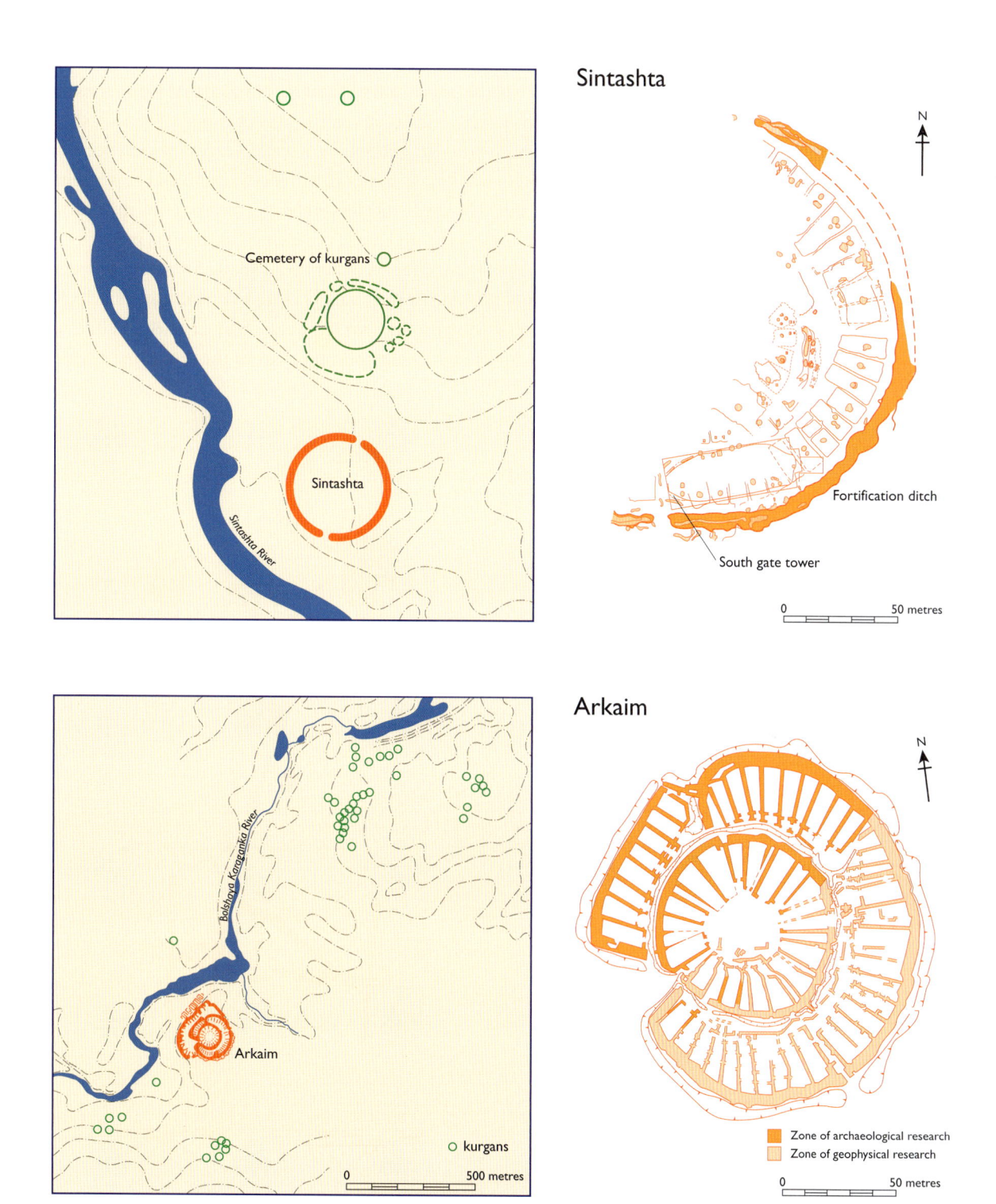

4.15 The location and details of the settlements of Sintashta and Arkaim, two of the most thoroughly excavated of the habitation sites of the Sintashta culture

THE OPENING OF THE EURASIAN STEPPE

4.16 Plans of two typical vehicle burials of the Sintashta culture. The humans were placed in the centre. The two horses used to pull the chariot are represented only by their skulls and lower leg-bones, which may have been held together by the hide when the carcass was removed for feasting

the mines, Vorovskaya Yamu in the upper Ural valley, it is estimated that 6,000 tons of ore was extracted, which would have yielded about 150 tons of copper. The Sintashta communities seem to have been producing copper on a scale in excess of local needs.

The economy of the villages was largely pastoral, with between 60 and 75 per cent of the animals being cattle, mainly a small hornless breed which were good milk producers. Sheep and goats were also kept, and horses amounted to about 15 per cent of the livestock, a number that suggests they were kept principally for riding or traction. Most of the settlements are sited in river valleys close to marshy areas, which would have provided essential winter fodder for the herds. Some millet and barley was grown, but judging from the good state of human teeth the diet cannot have been starch-rich.

Sintashta Grave 30

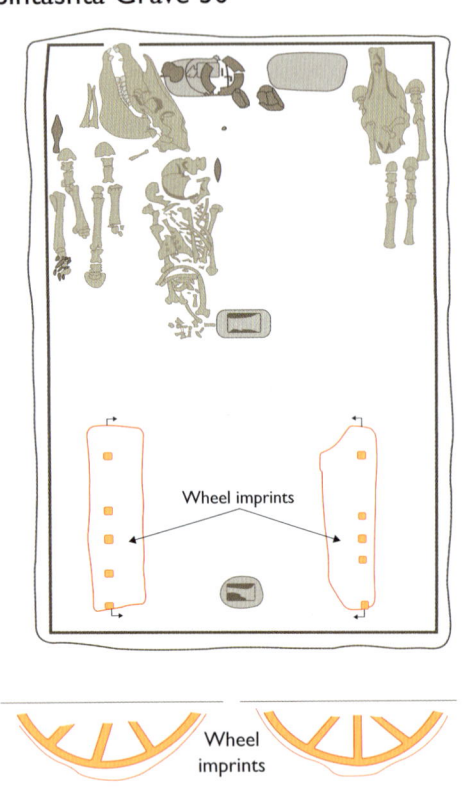

Krivoe Ozero

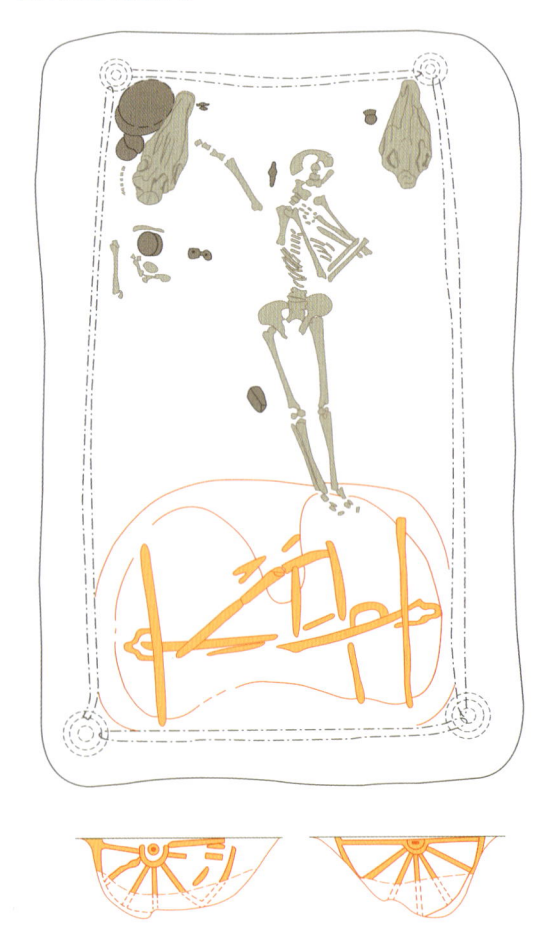

134

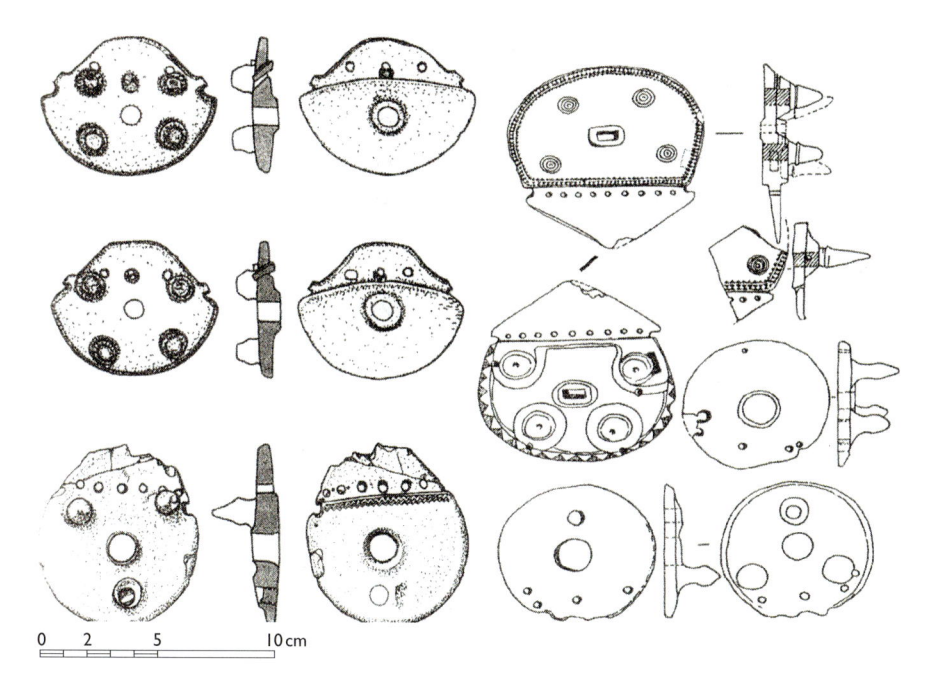

4.17 Typical cheek-pieces from horse-gear in the Sintashta period. The pointed protrusions, placed against the horse's cheek, made the animal acutely responsive to the charioteer's instructions

One of the notable features of the settlements is the lack of evidence for social differences: all the houses are very similar. But the cemeteries tell a different story, implying that there were variations in status. The cemeteries, usually covered by low kurgans, are found in the immediate vicinity of the settlements. Five are known close to Sintashta. One of these was a massive kurgan 85 metres in diameter and 4.5 metres high with the central grave robbed in antiquity. Pre-dating it was a cemetery of forty grave pits. The graves were variously furnished with tools and weapons and a few small items of gold and silver. Seven of them contained complete chariots, and in several, horses had been sacrificed, up to eight in one grave. The scale of animal sacrifice implies that the burial rites involved feasting on a considerable scale. One deposit, on the edge of the Sintashta cemetery, included the heads and hooves of six horses, four cows, and two rams with the bones neatly arranged around an upturned pot. It is estimated that this would have provided 2,700 kilograms of meat, enough to offer a substantial meal to three thousand people. Even the smaller numbers of sacrificed animals accompanying some of the other burials would have fed several hundred mourners. The evidence from the cemeteries leaves little doubt that the occasion of the funeral allowed the lineages of the dead to demonstrate their status through their ability to control resources. The larger the feast, and the more valuable the grave

4.18 Sacrificial complex 1 from the Sintashta cemetery. In a shallow pit the heads and hooves of six horses, four cattle, and two rams were carefully laid out around an upended pot. The 6,000 pounds of meat produced by this sacrifice could have provided a satisfying feast for three thousand mourners

goods, the higher their social standing. If status was reflected by the size of the family herd, there would have been no need to express it in the size or style of the house.

A burial accompanied by a chariot and the two trained horses that pulled it must have been one of a significant person. So far twenty-one chariots are known from nine different cemeteries. The usual arrangement was for the chariot to be buried intact with its wheels sunk in pits so the floor of the vehicle could rest on the bottom of the grave pit. The heads and hooves of the two horses were laid to the side and the human body was placed between them. Weapons, including knives, axes, spears, and flint projectile points, often accompanied the dead. The projectile points vary in size: some may have been for javelins, others for arrows.

The most remarkable part of the panoply was the chariot. An invention highly suited to the open steppe, they appear here for the first time about 2100 BC and are the earliest chariots known in the world. The vehicle was essentially a light platform between 1.2 and 1.6 metres wide, with some kind of side and front rail, carried on a pair of spoked wheels 1–1.2 metres in diameter. A pole, joined to the vehicle and projecting forwards, provided the means of attaching the two horses. In all cases, probably they would have been yoked, but no trace of yoke has survived. The horses were bridled with bits attached to two disc-shaped cheek-pieces of antler or bone fitted with sharp studs projecting inwards towards the horses' cheeks. Such an arrangement would have made the horses highly receptive to a pull on the reins ordering them to turn. The chariot and horse team represents a considerable investment in skill and time. The carpentry of the vehicle, especially its spoked wheels, required the input of experienced specialists, while the training of a horse team able to work together at speed needed the patient attention of someone with a deep knowledge of horses. How the chariots were used in life we can only guess. It has generally been assumed that they were designed for warfare, but other possibilities should be considered. They could have been used for display, or friendly competition, or for hunting: there is no need to see the chariot as primarily a weapon of warfare. Chariots were, above all, a means of expressing status. To be able to maintain a chariot and a team of horses, to drive it skilfully, and to fire arrows or throw javelins accurately from the moving vehicle would have endowed the charioteer with an exalted status. They are certainly symbolic of a highly competitive society, but not one necessarily engaged in perpetual warfare. That said, there is some evidence of hostile activity in the century before the advent of the Sintashta culture. A mass grave found at Pepkino on the river Sura, dating to about 2200 BC, contained the bodies of twenty-eight young men, some decapitated and dismembered, others with extensive axe wounds. Episodes of violence were evidently a part of life.

If the appearance of fortified settlements and chariots is a reflection of increased competition and the insecurity that that brings, it is necessary to consider the possible causes. One may be that climate change was causing upset to the local environment. After about 2500 BC cooler and more arid conditions began to set in, with the coldest and driest period falling between 2200 and 2000 BC. Forests declined, while steppe and desert expanded and winters became colder. Such conditions will have affected steppe herders, particularly those to the east of the Urals, where conditions were colder than in the west. Control of the river valleys with their marshes and pastures became crucial to survival. It is easy to see how, in the competitive struggle for resources, communities may have become more defensive and more aggressive.

The chariot was a creation born of competition and one that required a close familiarity with horses. All the evidence available at present argues that it was an invention of the Sintashta culture, but such was the wonder of it that it was quickly taken up by many distant cultures. Outside the steppe the earliest appearance of horse-drawn spoke-wheeled chariots is in the Near East, depicted on seals from Karum Kanesh, an Assyrian colony in central Anatolia dated to about 1900 BC. Earlier than this, solid-wheeled battle wagons drawn by ass–onager hybrids harnessed with lip- or nose-rings were known, but the light horse-drawn chariot was something quite new and quickly replaced the slower, more cumbersome devices. Rock carvings of chariots in the Altai Mountains dated to about 1650 BC mark the easterly progression. After these early dispersals the chariot was widely adopted in the Near East and across Europe, and finally, about 1200 BC, it reached China.

The Sintashta culture came into being about 2100 BC on the eastern slopes of the Urals and by 1750 BC had spread eastwards along the Kazakh steppe (where its later phases are called the Petrovka culture). It was therefore broadly contemporary with urban farmers of the BMAC 1,700 kilometres away to the south across the desert. The Sintashta communities, with their productivity in trained horses and copper and their inventiveness, had much to offer to the oasis towns, which were managing their complex social systems in a resource-poor environment. Inevitably contacts began to open up across the deserts. It was in this way that the idea of the chariot spread into the civilized world, accompanied by valuable horses and supplies of copper.

Across the Deserts of Central Asia

The great swath of desert between the steppe zone and the southern oases, through which flowed the Amu Darya and Syr Darya, was for a long while the home of hunter-gatherers who had learned to make pottery and to eke out an existence by fishing the rivers and the Aral Sea. The colonization of the oases by farming communities coming from the Iranian plateau added a new dynamic to the southern desert zone as the settlers began to use it for pasturing their flocks, developing a system of transhumance that saw the livestock driven from the oasis at certain times of the year, travelling distances of up to 250 kilometres into the desert zone to find suitable pasture. The restrictions of the oasis environment demanded the development of this kind of mobile pastoralism to provide essential support for the crop-growing regions. On their transhumant journeys the shepherds and goatherds of the oases met with indigenous hunter-gatherers. This led to a degree of acculturation and the creation of social networks throughout the southern desert zone.

At the northern end of the deserts similar processes were at work as the steppe herders, used to mobility, began to make increasing use of the desert, seeking out seasonal pastures and establishing relationships with indigenous foragers. The two rivers were essential to the colonization of the desert regions by mobile pastoralists. Both provided water and offered assured relief in the desert wastes. They were the fixed points that would encourage the herds from north and south to gravitate towards them. It was in this way that, by the end of the third millennium, pastoralism had spread throughout the desert zone and networks linking north and south had come into being.

To trace the networks and to assess the strength of contacts archaeologists have to rely largely on the distribution of artefacts, mainly pottery. The coarse, hand-made pots used by the pastoralists of the steppe were very different from the fine, wheel-made vessels of the oasis farmers. These were often inscribed with zigzag designs and usually had the marks of woven fabric on the inside surface, suggesting that the vessels may have been made over a fabric-covered form. The appearance of vessels of this kind in the southern oasis towns is taken to imply direct contact with people from the steppe. A few sherds were found at Gonur-depe North from about the same time as the foal was buried in the elite grave (c.2000 BC), and a century or two later a rather larger assemblage of steppe pottery was deposited at the stronghold of Togolok 21, another of the BMAC settlements. But steppe pottery is only ever recovered in relatively small quantities, implying limited trading activity: it cannot be taken as evidence of large-scale migration or invasion.

By what routes the steppe entrepreneurs reached the southern towns it is difficult to say with any degree of certainty, but logic suggests that they would have chosen an eastern route, perhaps along the middle course of the Syr Darya and then across the mountain ridge of the Zeravshan. Steppe pottery has been found at the town of Sarazm, not far from the important medieval caravan city of Samarkand, and less than 30 kilometres down-river at Tugai was a settlement, dating to about 1900 BC, producing a comparatively large quantity of steppe pottery together with extensive evidence of copper smelting. Tugai may have been a base used by steppe traders or even a permanent settlement of northern entrepreneurs.

There are other indications that the Zeravshan valley may have been in direct contact with the steppe. A grave found at Zardchakhalif, close to Sarazm, was provided with two sets of horse-gear of Sintashta type, two bar bits and four circular bone cheek-pieces, as well as a bronze pin with a horse cast at the terminal. While it is likely that the individual buried there was a local, he may well have been the proud owner of a pair of chariot horses, and perhaps even a chariot, imported from the steppe, acquired perhaps as a diplomatic gift or by trade. Another attraction of the Zeravshan region was the presence of tin ore found in some quantity in the mountain range immediately south of the river. So far fieldwork has brought to light four separate mining sites, one about 10 kilometres east of Samarkand, the other three clustering at about the same distance west of the city. The mineworks date to the period 1900–1300 BC and are associated with the pottery of steppe type. Taken together, then, the evidence would seem to suggest that settlers from the steppe had settled in the Zeravshan valley sometime about 2000 BC attracted by the rich metal resources and the prospects of trading with the towns of Bactria to the south and Margiana across the Amu Darya to the west.

The breakdown of central organization among the BMAC towns about 1800 BC and the localization that followed, with each oasis developing its own stylistic traditions, coincides with the development of agro-pastoral villages occupying an arc between the highlands south of the Zeravshan and the delta of the Amu Darya close

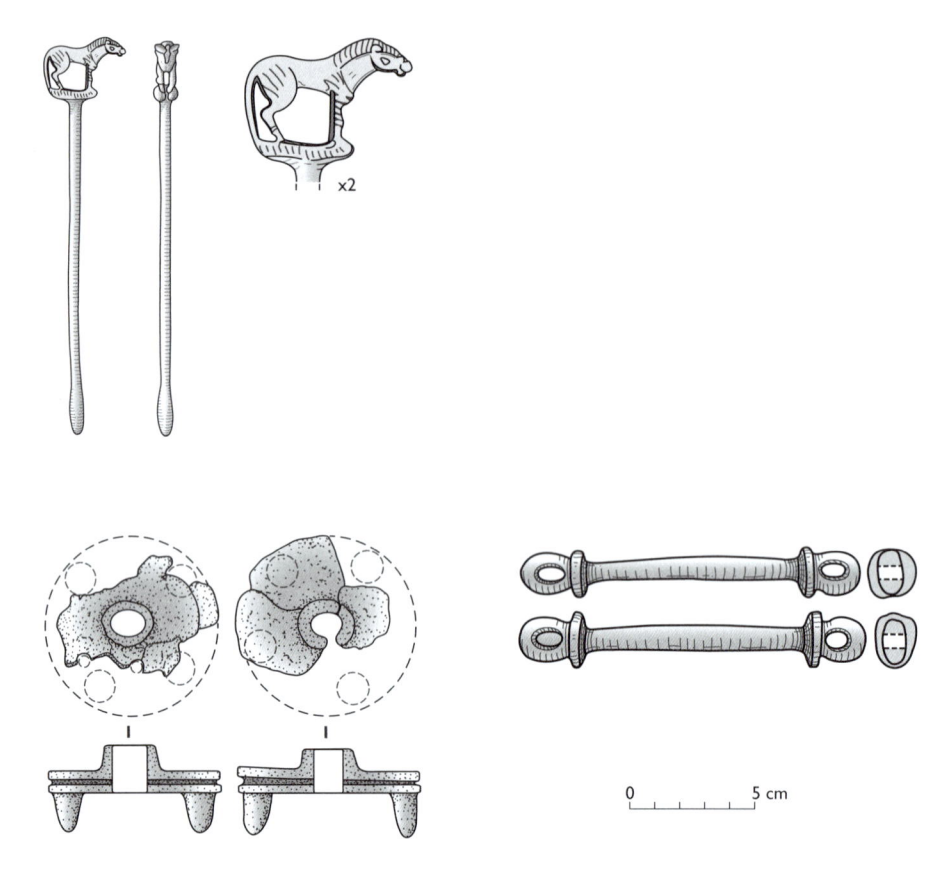

4.19 Horse-gear of Sintashta type and a pin decorated with a steppe horse from a burial at Zardchakhalif near Penjikent, Tajikistan. The burial is well outside the area of the Sintashsta culture and the find of horse-gear may indicate the long-distance exchange of horses

to the Aral Sea. These settlements were rooted in the pastoral tradition of the steppe, as their pottery indicates, but they had adopted irrigation agriculture. The simplest interpretation would be to suppose that they reflected the southern limit of steppe penetration, where the steppe communities assimilated local systems of production and settled down to adapt to the new environment in which they found themselves. From about 1800 BC they formed the interface between the steppe and the urbanized polities to the south.

The contact that developed between the steppe and the urban world of the Near East during the period 2100–1800 BC created an entirely new network of connectivity allowing commodities and ideas to flow north–south between the two very different worlds. The contribution from the north, from the Sintashta–Petrovka zone, included horses for riding and for pulling chariots, together with the technology of chariot building. It is during the Ur III period in Mesopotamia that horses appear in some numbers and men riding horses are depicted on seal stones. Horses are also mentioned in treaties between Ur and Elam. By the eighteenth century BC the horse had become so integrated into Mesopotamian culture that in elite etiquette a king could be rebuked for riding a horse rather than being transported in a chariot. The number of horses driven from their breeding grounds on the steppe across the Central Asian deserts to the Iranian plateau and beyond must have been enormous. And with them would probably have been carried copper from the mines of the Urals. Indeed, the opening up of the southern markets may have been the impetus for the Sintashta communities to increase their production. A little later the steppe miners working in the Zeravshan region added tin to the exports—a metal ten times more valuable than silver.

What did the steppe communities acquire in exchange? Here the archaeological record is almost mute. A piece of lead wire, a lapis bead, and a Bactrian handled mirror—all that has so far been recorded—is poor return. There must have been something more. A hint is given by the appearance of a stepped-pyramid motif on Sintashta pottery at this time. It is a pattern that would have been common on textiles and reed matting, and it was from media of this kind that the local potters may have gained their inspiration. Bright, multicoloured weaves used for carpets, wall hangings, or for clothing from the south would have been welcome imports; so, too, would spices and fragrances obtainable from the coasts of the Arabian peninsula via the towns of the Iranian plateau. No archaeological trace of any of this survives, but it may have been exotic southern luxuries of this kind that persuaded the Sintashta communities to part with their copper ingots and their horses.

The north–south connectivity was now in place. The temporary breakdown of centralizing states from Mesopotamia to the Indus valley in the early second millennium saw a lessening of the demand for distant goods, but, once established, the networks remained in place to be reinvigorated when the need arose. The steppe cultures and the Near Eastern states now had a common interface stretching from the Pamir mountains to the Black Sea.

The Western Steppe in the Early Second Millennium

The early second millennium provides a convenient point in the narrative to take a broad view of what was happening on the steppe between the Danube and the Altai Mountains. This huge swath of grassland is divided into two by the constriction caused by the southern end of the Ural mountain chain where it approaches the Caspian Sea. To the west of the Urals lies the Pontic-Caspian steppe extending to the

Great Hungarian Plain, while to the east is the Kazakh steppe unhindered as far as the Altai. The two zones have different cultural histories. In the Pontic-Caspian steppe we saw the gradual evolution of a broadly similar culture of mobile pastoralism called Yamnaya in its earliest manifestation and the Catacomb culture in its later stages. To the east of the Urals the picture is more complex, with the Sintashta–Petrovka herders, characterized by their fortified settlements and chariots, spreading from the eastern flanks of the Urals westwards, and the Afanasievo pastoralists and their successors occupying the western fringes of the Altai. This broad divide between east and west continued to hold good during the Late Bronze Age, beginning about 1800 BC. On the Pontic-Caspian steppe local developments led to what is known as the Srubnaya (or Timber Grave) culture (which will feature in the next chapter), while over the whole of the Kazakh steppe there emerged the Andronovo culture.

The 'Andronovo culture' is a convenient way of referring to the various communities sharing a broadly similar culture that occupied the Kazakh steppe in the period 1800–1200 BC. It represents the consolidation of disparate groups whose livelihood was based on the herding of cattle and sheep, with some recourse to small-scale crop growing, who chose to decorate their pottery in similar ways and to use bronze tools and weapons of broadly similar kinds. They lived in permanent settlements of ten to forty houses in communities of fifty to two hundred and fifty. There were variations in pastoral practices reflecting differences in the local environment. Thus, in the north, towards the forest-steppe, cattle predominated, while in the more open grasslands of central Kazakhstan sheep and goats made up nearly half the livestock, with horses and cattle each providing a quarter. It was Andronovo communities that we saw moving southwards into the desert zone and adopting irrigation agriculture in favourable places like the delta of the Amu Darya and the Zeravshan region. Some communities specialized in copper mining, which was now carried out on an industrial scale, and it was Andronovo miners who began to exploit the tin ores of the Zeravshan range to enable them to produce standard tin bronze. The pastoral nature of the economy and the trade in bronze maintained a degree of social connectivity throughout the Kazakh steppe and adjacent regions. We shall see in the next section that people sharing this broad Andronovo culture were responsible for introducing copper working and pastoralism to the east.

Broadly contemporary with the early stages of the Andronovo development a group of hunter-fishers living in the forest zone between the middle Irtysh and upper Ob' rivers, in the western foothills of the Altai, created a vibrant bronze industry, which displayed exceptional metallurgical skills including a mastery of lost-wax casting. They worked with tin bronze and made distinctive axes, spears, and daggers, which were distributed over astonishing distances, westwards through the forest and

THE OPENING OF THE EURASIAN STEPPE

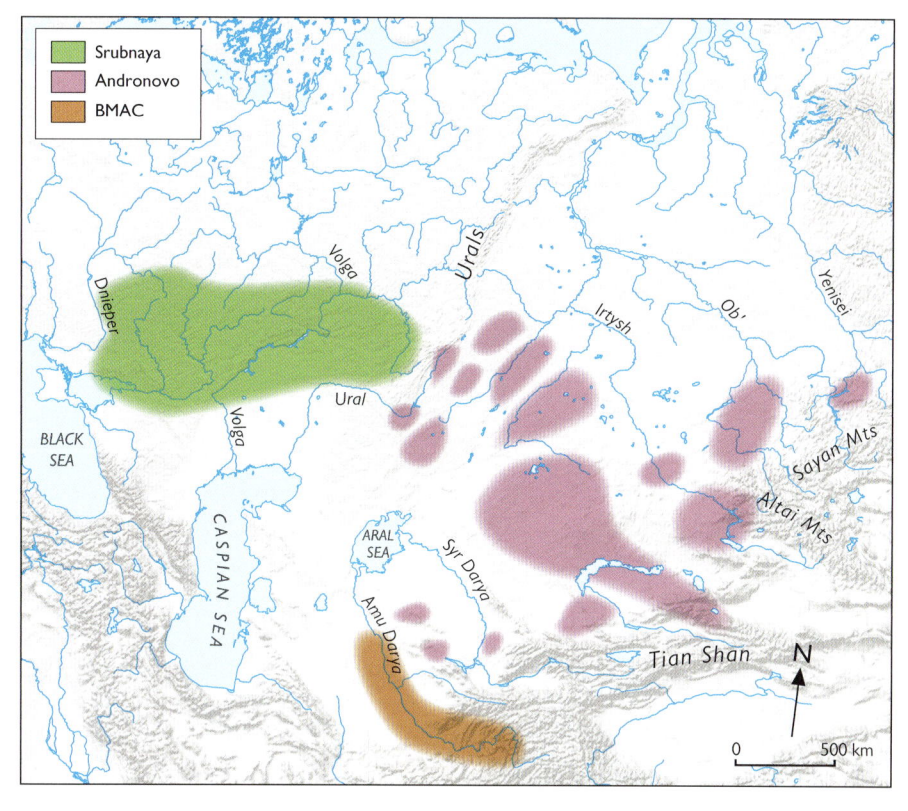

4.20 Distribution of the principal Late Bronze Age cultural complexes in Central Asia in relation to BMAC

forest-steppe zone as far as the Carpathian basin and eastwards to the fringes of the evolving Chinese state. The production is referred to as the Seima-Turbino complex after two type sites where characteristic implements have been found. The Seima-Turbino phenomenon is not easy to explain. It represents not the spread of a culture through migration but rather the rapid dissemination of high-quality artefacts among the elites of the hunter-gatherer groups occupying the forest zone. The distribution is a reminder that the networks of connectivity binding the foragers were at least as effective as those of the steppe pastoralists. After its initial development Seima-Turbino production merged with the Andronovo culture.

From the Altai to the Tarim Basin

Eastwards from the steppe of Kazakhstan the grassland gives way to a more complex landscape of mountain chains and desert basins which hamper easy movement. But the east–west grain of the land offers some routes for those who wish to pass

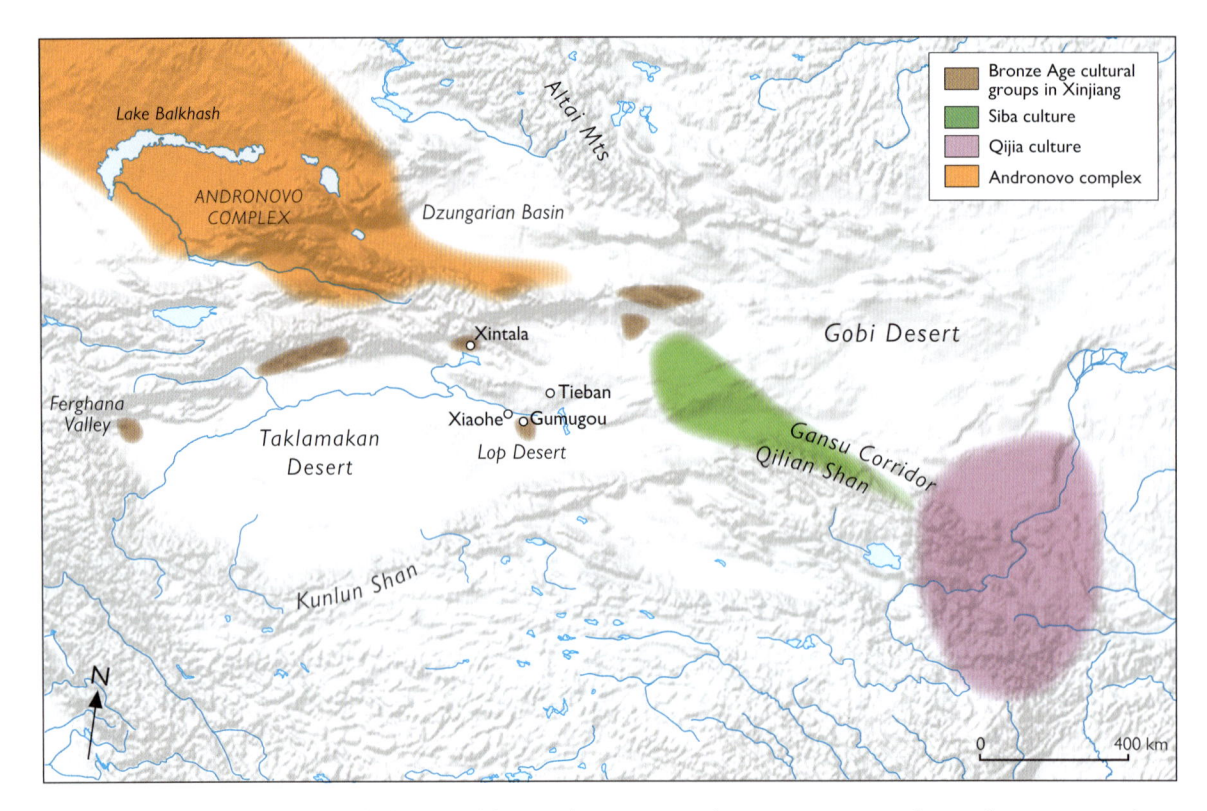

4.21 The location of the main bronze-using cultures in eastern Central Asia. The communities lying around the north edge of the Taklamakan desert were intermediaries in the spread of bronze technology to the Siba and Qijia cultures of the Gansu Corridor leading to the plains of China

through. Two great mountain ranges, the Altai and the Tian Shan, create formidable, but not impassable, barriers. Between them is the Dzungarian Depression, an uninviting desert region, while south of the Tian Shan, in the great Tarim basin, lie even more extensive deserts, the Taklamakan and the Lop desert, which merge eastwards into the Gobi. This confusion of stark landscapes constitutes Xinjiang, the westernmost region of modern China. Desert wastes and mountain heights are no place for humans, but where one gives way to the other there are more inviting environments, well watered with streams coming from the mountains. It was into these favoured niches in the late third millennium that herders growing some crops began to move, coming from the north and the west, bringing them to within easy reach of the Gansu Corridor, beyond which lay the plains of China.

The movement of people through Dzungaria and into the Tarim basin to settle in the oases along the desert flanks was of crucial importance to the establishment of connectivity between western Central Asia and China. The area is remote, and scientific excavations have been few, but gradually the picture is coming into focus. There is now clear evidence from cemeteries along the northern foothills of the Tian Shan that the area was settled by pastoralists from the west, bringing with them herding practices, pottery, and bronze technology characteristic of the Andronovo culture, and it was from this region that people moved south through the Tian Shan to settle in the southern foothills facing the Taklamakan desert. At the cemetery of Xintala typical Andronovo bronzes and pottery have been found, but in contexts with painted pottery and jade characteristic of the culture of the indigenous people already established around this northern edge of the Tarim basin. Where this indigenous culture came from is a matter of debate, but one suggestion is that it may have been introduced from the west, from Tajikistan or from the Ferghana valley by way of passes through the northern ranges of the Pamir. That the mountain passes were in operation at this time is shown by the discovery of Chinese jade in graves in the Ferghana valley. If this interpretation is correct, then the population living around the Tarim basin in the second millennium may have been of mixed ancestry, some arriving from the west, from Ferghana, while others made their way south through the Tian Shan.

Archaeologists and physical anthropologists are in broad agreement that migrants from the north, from the western Altai, formed a major part of the Tarim basin population. The human skeletal remains recovered from the cemeteries are predominantly Caucasoid and must have come ultimately from the western steppe zone. Detailed work at one of the cemeteries in the Lop desert, dating from 2000–1800 BC, claims to be able to identify the earliest skeletons as being of Afanasievo type, while the later conform to the Andronovo type. This is to some extent supported by the analysis of the copper alloys used to make items buried with the dead: the earliest finds are pure copper characteristic of the Afanasievo culture, while the later items are tin bronzes similar to Andronovo alloys. Taken together, this evidence suggests a movement of Late Afanasievo pastoralists southwards towards the Tian Shan in the later part of the third millennium with their descend-

4.22 The naturally mummified body of a woman dating to 2000–1800 BC from Loulan in the Lop desert, Xinjiang, China. Physically she is of European type, suggesting that at least some of the population of the Tarim Depression originally came from the west. Her clothing is well preserved, including the feather attached to her hood

ants crossing the mountains about 2000 BC to establish themselves at the northern oases of the Tarim basin. Once there, they maintained links with the north, leading to a trade in Andronovo metalwork and quite possibly further influxes of Andronovo pastoralists from the north.

Recent DNA work on the Tarim burials has offered further support for the hypothesis. Twenty bodies from the cemetery of Xiaohe were tested. All of the Y-chromosome DNA, which represents the male line, came from 'European' populations, while the mitochondrial DNA, from the female line, was a mixture of 'European' and 'southern Siberian'. This is interpreted to be the result of movement of Europeans before 2000 BC from the western steppe into the Altai region, where they interbred with local foragers before moving south into the Tarim basin. Although there are limitations to the interpretation of DNA analyses, especially when only a small number of samples are involved, the results do conform to interpretations based on the archaeological and skeletal data.

In summary, then, there is strong support for the view that the communities who colonized the Tarim oases in, or a little before, 2000 BC came from the north across the Tian Shan, bringing with them a pastoral economy and some cultivated grain. But we must also allow that some element of the population may have already arrived from the west across the Pamir.

The Tarim basin populations, occupying the oases fringing the north side of the Taklamakan and Lop deserts, are well known from their spectacular cemeteries, where a combination of local factors, the hyper-arid climate, the intensely cold winters with temperatures as low as −40 °C, and the high salinity of the soil, create an environment hostile to the bacteria that cause decay. The result is that organic materials including wood, cloth, leather, plant remains, and the human bodies themselves have survived in an astonishingly well-preserved state, offering a wealth of detail about clothing and other elements of material culture that is normally seldom preserved.

One of the most ancient of the burials, found at Tieban on the north edge of the Lop desert and dating to 2000–1800 BC, was of a woman aged about 45. She was wrapped in a woven woollen blanket and wore leather boots and a pointed felt hat with a feather in it. Accompanying her was a basket made of tamarisk and grass containing wheat, and on her chest were placed twigs of ephedra (*Ephedra sinica*), a stimulant with anti-inflammatory properties. Another cemetery of the same date was examined at Gumugou, close to Lop Nor. Here, forty-two burials were found, which, like the woman from Tieban, were wrapped in blankets and wore hats and boots. The bodies were placed on the natural saline sand with plank coffers built around them

4.23 The Xiaohe cemetery in the Lop desert, Xinjiang, China, owes the remarkable preservation of its coffins and their markers to the arid, salty desert conditions. In all, the cemetery comprised some 330 burials. It dates to about 2000–1600 BC

and were covered with sheep- and goatskins. Grave goods included baskets of wheat, ephedra twigs, small bronze items, and jade beads.

The Tarim basin communities who lived at the oases along the northern fringe of the deserts, so vividly brought to life by these remarkable discoveries, practised a form of irrigation agriculture allowing them to grow wheat and barley and to raise sheep, goats, cattle, and horses, as well as Bactrian camels. They also made tools and weapons by casting copper and bronze. One of the easternmost oasis settlements, at Gumugou, was barely 600 kilometres from the Gansu Corridor, which, over the millennia, has served as the major route between the west and China. The question that must be asked is, what part did this ancient route play in transmitting western technologies and domesticates to the fast-developing polities of China?

The Gansu Corridor

The Gansu (or Hexi) Corridor runs from the upper reaches of the Yellow River to the Tarim basin, a distance of about 800 kilometres, between the Qilian mountain range and the southern edge of the Gobi desert. It is the only route westwards from China, running between the two hostile environments of the deserts of Mongolia and the upland plateau of Tibet, which together conspire to isolate lowland China from the rest of Eurasia. Along the corridor lie a string of oases fed by mountain rivers, providing friendly environments suitable for settlement and for travellers.

In the late third and early second millennium the crucial corridor zone was occupied by two communities distinguished by archaeologists on the basis of their material culture. At the eastern end of the corridor, and extending into upper reaches of the Yellow River, was the Qijia culture, dating to 2200–1600 BC, while the western end of the corridor was the home of the Siba culture, which developed a few hundred years later and flourished during the period 1900–1500 BC. It was through the communities represented by these two archaeologically defined cultures that contacts between China and the west would have taken place.

It has already been suggested (pp. 67–8) that this was the route along which the western domesticates, wheat, barley, cattle, sheep, and goats, were introduced into China in the third millennium. Indeed, the site of Donghuishan, close to the western end of the corridor, produced wheat and barley in contexts dating to between 3000 and 2500 BC, and the flow of knowledge and commodities, including domesticates, plants and animals, must have been continuous. By the later stage of the Qijia culture, about 1900–1600 BC, there were sedentary settlements supported by well-established agricultural regimes based on the growing of millet, barley, and wheat and the domestication of cattle, pigs, chickens, sheep, and horses. Of these only millet, pigs, and chickens had been domesticated locally in China. The rest must have been introduced from the west via the Tarim basin.

The question of the origin of copper metallurgy in China is more complex. In the first half of the second millennium China's Central Plains were the home of a flourishing copper-using society known archaeologically as the Erlitou culture (1900–1500 BC). The distinctive and original production of the Erlitou coppersmiths included bells, dagger axes, and plaques with inset turquoise, as well as metal vessels cast in multi-piece moulds, predecessors of the astounding cast bronze vessels that were later to characterize the Shang dynasty. Original though the Erlitou copper industry was, it is possible to recognize influences from the Andronovo culture of the steppe. Steppe influence is also clearly evident in the copper metallurgy of the Tarim basin and the Gansu Corridor. Thus, while it is apparent that the spectacular bronze industry of the Central Plains was largely the result of indigenous Chinese inspiration, it remains a strong possibility that knowledge of copper working was first introduced into the region from the steppe, possibly along the Gansu Corridor. More work is needed to clarify the processes of transmission.

Whatever the outcome of the debate, the Gansu Corridor was an important route of communication between China and the Tarim basin and the Eurasian steppe beyond. Western domesticated crops and animals, as well as knowledge of copper metallurgy, flowed eastwards into the northern frontier zone of China, while the techniques for making well-fired painted pottery spread west from China to be taken up by the Tarim communities. No doubt other commodities were exchanged in both directions. One was certainly jade, for which the Chinese had an insatiable desire. One source, at Hetian near Khotan on the southern edge of the Taklamakan desert, provided quantities of the jade used to decorate the tomb of Fuhao at the Late Shang capital of Yinxu dated to 1200 BC.

After the middle of the second millennium the settlements along the Gansu Corridor show a marked change: large settlements disappeared altogether, there was an increased reliance on animal husbandry, and the bronze industry was in decline. Clearly society was in a state of crisis. The most likely cause for this was that after 1500 BC a major climatic downturn set in, with conditions becoming much colder and drier, making life in the marginal ecozones far more difficult to sustain. It was about this time that the northern frontier zone of China began to develop contacts through a new northern route to the Mongolian steppe. The Mongolian steppe had first been introduced to a horse-riding pastoral nomad economy soon after 3500 BC by the eastward spread of the Afanasievo culture. By the middle of the third millennium mobile pastoralism had reached all parts of the easternmost steppe zone together with the use of wheeled vehicles and, a little later, chariots. Although no actual chariots have yet been excavated in Mongolia, they are depicted on many rock carvings. Sometime after 2300 BC the Andronovo metalworking tradition spread to the region, bringing with it the highly distinctive animal art of the eastern steppe.

The development of a steppe route between China and Mongolia after the middle of the second millennium provided a new channel for aspects of steppe culture to reach China, first the animal art of the bronze worker, and, later, chariots which, with their trained horse teams, were introduced into China's Central Plains, making a significant contribution to the culture of the Shang dynasty. The opening up of the steppe route to China forged the last link in the chain of connectivity that ran through the very centre of Eurasia.

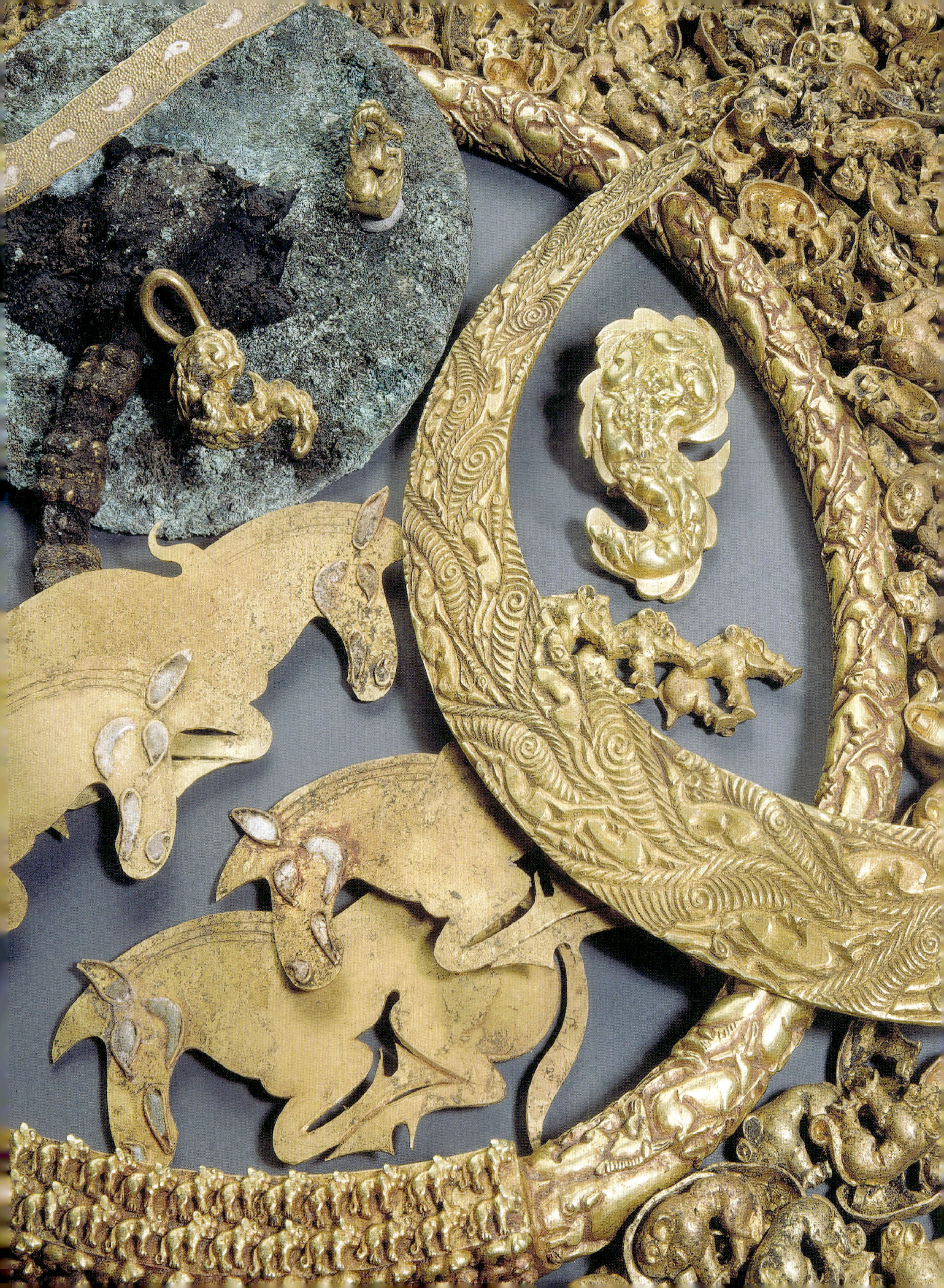

5

NOMADS AND EMPIRES

THE FIRST CONFRONTATIONS, 1600–600 BC

In this chapter we trace three broad narratives: the development of states in the Near East culminating in the emergence of the Assyrian empire, the parallel development of states in the Central Plains of China during the Shang and Zhou periods, and the spectacular rise of predatory nomadism throughout the entire length of the steppe. All three trajectories are essentially continuations of earlier developments within the different regions. What runs as a leitmotif through the narrative of this thousand years is the impact that steppe culture continued to have on its sedentary neighbours. The horse-drawn spoke-wheeled chariot, invented in the Ural region at the end of the third millennium, had already, by 1600 BC, been taken up throughout the Near East and featured as an essential component of the military machine. In China its acceptance by the Late Shang rulers came a little later, about 1200 BC. Here the chariot fast became the emblem of elite status in burial rituals. The transfer of horse-and-chariot technology must have involved, at least in its initial stages, the movement of specialists from the steppe to the Near East and to China. Contacts were maintained through the exchange networks, but a combination of factors, climatic change among them, leading to development of a more extreme form of mobile pastoralism around the tenth and ninth centuries, brought a more direct form of confrontation when steppe pastoralists began to raid the sedentary states in the eighth century.

Steppe culture of the first millennium BC, and the mobility that it engendered, created a highly fluid situation difficult to untangle from the archaeological evidence alone. But the similarity of burial rite, fighting panoply, and animal art style—a package frequently referred to as 'the Scythian triad'—across the entire steppe region speaks of a high level of transmission both of belief and value systems and of people. This chapter deals with the formative phase of Scythian culture. Its spectacular later developments will be considered in the next chapter.

Band of Brothers: The Great Powers in the Near East, 1500–1200 BC

In the late nineteenth century an archive of 350 letters, written in cuneiform script on clay tablets, was found at Amarna, the capital of Egypt under the pharaoh Akhenaten. Most of them were written in Babylonian, the diplomatic language of the day, and they represented the correspondence between the Egyptian ruler and the heads of other states, Babylonia, Assyria, Mitanni, Hatti, Alashiya (now Cyprus), and Arzawa, and his vassals in Syria-Palestine. The Amarna letters, covering the brief period 1365–1335 BC, paint a picture in vivid detail of the way in which rulers of the Near Eastern states maintained a delicate equilibrium in their relations one with another. Other archives found at Hattusa, the capital of Hatti (the state of the Hittite New Kingdom in Anatolia), Ugarit, and in smaller numbers at other palaces throughout the Near East show that communication between the great kings and between the kings and their vassals was carried on at an intensive level. Lack of communication was seen as a potential threat and a lax correspondent would be chided into response.

The letters provide an insight into the changing political geography. There were two zones of real power. Egypt constituted one, while the other was made up of Elam, Babylonia, Assyria, Mitanni, and Hatti, all of roughly equal status. On the western fringe of this group were the peripheral states of Arzawa in south-western Asia Minor, Alashiya, and the archaeologically named Mycenae (probably Ahhiyawa), occupying the lands and islands of the east Mediterranean. Between the two big power blocks lay Syria-Palestine, a palimpsest of small city states—Jerusalem, Damascus, Aleppo, Byblos, Ugarit, and others—ruled by minor kings who were small players in the power politics of the time. They allied themselves to the great kings, changing allegiances from time to time, and in the diplomatic correspondence were usually referred to as servants. This Levantine border zone provided the arena in which Egypt contested power with the Mitanni and the Hatti, a contest exacerbated by petty jealousies between the small city states.

NOMADS AND EMPIRES

The correspondence between the great kings provides a fascinating insight into the social and economic organization of the time. King wrote directly to king, the one always addressing the other as 'brother'. The essence of the message was on reaffirming the equality of the relationship through reciprocity. Familial relations were maintained by giving princesses as wives to fellow kings, and sumptuous gifts

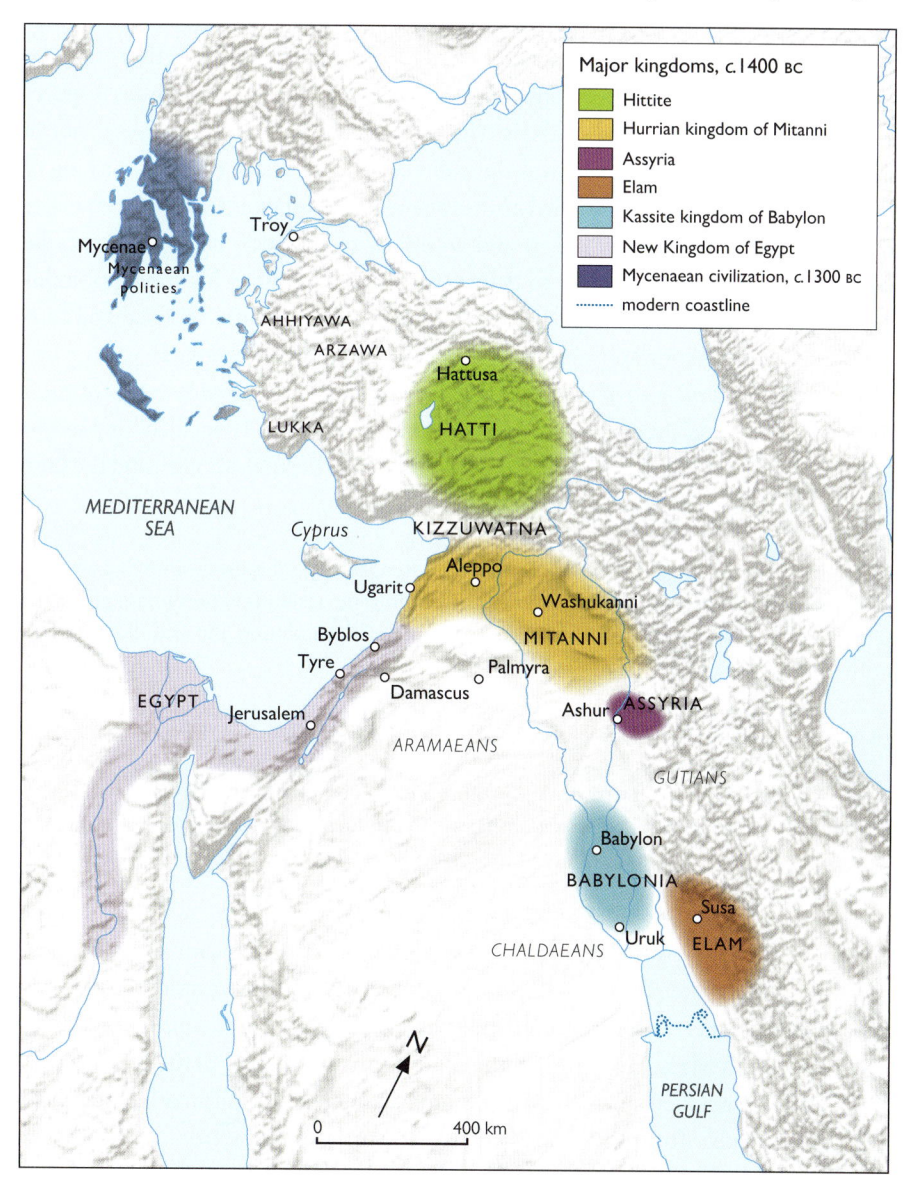

5.1 The centres of power in South West Asia in the late second millennium BC

exchanged hands on a regular basis. It was not unlike the customs in place between the European monarchies in the nineteenth century AD. It could be argued that what we are seeing is a form of competitive aggression carefully structured to maintain a degree of equilibrium and thus to avoid large-scale and destructive hostility. All the time that letters were exchanged and equal status was acknowledged through appropriate gifts, the continued prosperity of each partner could be assured. But since warfare was endemic, aggressive tendencies had to be channelled into actions that did not threaten the overall system: small-scale shows of power such as border disputes and the picking off of a rival's vassals. This was the warfare of readjustment, not of annihilation. Only occasionally was there direct confrontation, as when the king of Hatti and the Egyptian pharaoh led armies against each other at Qadesh in 1274. The Egyptian pharaoh, Rameses II, lost and withdrew to southern Palestine, where he established a fortified boundary to define the northern limit of his sphere of influence. It was a substantial engagement with armies of forty to fifty thousand on each side, but hostilities soon subsided and the status quo was little changed.

The diplomatic niceties of gift exchange were essential to the maintenance of equilibrium, no more so than when a new king came to power and expected his peers to acknowledge him. An exchange between Hattusili III, the king of Hatti, and the king of Assyria makes the point explicitly:

> When I assumed kingship you did not send a messenger to me. It is the custom that when kings assume kingship, the kings, his equivalent in rank, send him appropriate gifts of greeting, clothing befitting kingship, and fine oil for his anointing. But you did not do this today.

In another letter between two kings, Hattusili II replies to the Assyrian king:

> as for the iron which you wrote to me about, good iron is not available... That it is a bad time for producing iron I have written. They will produce good iron but as yet they will not have finished. When they have finished I shall send it to you. Today I am dispatching an iron dagger blade to you.

These exchanges are revealing in many ways. The first is a complaint about the proprieties not being met; the second seems to be an excuse for not responding to a specific request. Together they indicate something of the range of valuable commodities on offer: from Assyria, 'clothing befitting kingship' is a reminder of the massive production of fine woollen fabrics in Mesopotamia, while the 'fine oil' may be fragrances coming ultimately from the Arabian coasts. From Hatti came iron, rare and very much valued at the time when iron-producing technology may have been a monopoly of the Anatolian state.

5.2 The city of Qadesh on the river Orontes in Syria was a strategic location in the conflict between the Egyptians and the Hittites. It was captured by Seti I after his defeat of the Hittite army but was only briefly held. Later, in 1274 BC, his son Rameses II made an attempt to regain the city but failed and retreated. The scene, which shows Seti I riding to victory at Qadesh, is engraved on the wall of the Great Hypostyle Court at Karnak in Egypt

A wide range of other commodities were constantly being given by the great kings to each other: gold from Nubia via the Egyptians, lapis lazuli and tin from Central Asia via Elam, copper from Alashiya, where rich supplies were to be had, and amber from the Baltic region, acquired by the Mycenaean kings and passed on to their eastern neighbours. The quantity of rare raw materials on the move, essential to maintain the political status quo, must have been enormous. This will have required enhanced structures of supply and networks extending deep into the peripheries, with specialist traders making a living by collecting and conveying the materials. Kings receiving gifts from their peers no doubt maintained internal practices of redistribution by making gifts to their clients among the lesser elite.

A dramatic example of the scale and complexity of the exchange systems then in operation is provided by a shipwreck found off the southern coast of Anatolia at Uluburun. The vessel sank about 1300 BC while on a journey that would have taken it anti-clockwise around the eastern Mediterranean probably from Cyprus to the Aegean, then south to the coast of North Africa, along to the Nile delta, and northwards up the coast of the Levant. It sank when driven onto a dangerous lee shore with a full cargo including 10 tons of copper in 354 oxhide-shaped ingots, 1 ton of tin, 150 Canaanite jars, some probably containing wine, 175 blue glass ingots from Syria, ten large Cypriot pots for transporting smaller pottery vessels, African black wood from Egypt, as well as ivory, hippopotamus teeth, and tortoise-shells. In addition, there was jewellery, a few weapons including two Mycenaean swords, and a pan balance with sets of weights. It was an astonishing find of immense value in displaying the sheer scale and range of a single trading mission. But what it represents is open to debate. While it could be a single tribute sent from one king to another, a more likely explanation is that it was a merchant venture, the owner bartering at each port of call to increase the value of the cargo and siphoning off the surpluses accrued for investment in land-based enterprises. Whatever the economic context, it shows something of the range and scale of the trading systems now operating to satisfy the huge demands of the great kings. It also implies the existence of a skilled mercantile class.

This kind of prestige goods economy carried with it the seeds of its own destruction. Rare raw materials and manpower were invested in the state structure and in the increasingly lavish lifestyles of the elite. The kings and their entourages lived separate lives in elaborate palaces dominating the royal cities, like Hattusa, Babylon, and Akhetaten, surrounded by their palace dependants. The grandiose building programmes, the armies of servants, and the demands of the system for gift giving on an ever-increasing scale had to be paid for by the efforts of the notionally free working population living in the lesser cities and in the countryside around. The non-productive consuming centre left the masses increasingly impoverished. The demands of the state were so great that people seem to have left the land and to have become migrants to such an extent that a manpower shortage ensued. The seriousness of the problem is reflected in repeated demands by the kings that refugees be returned to them. These internal problems weakened the stability of the state and, combined with external threats, were sufficient to bring the whole delicate edifice down.

Over the three hundred years or so when the great kings prevailed, there were shifts in power. While Elam, Babylon, and Egypt retained much of their territorial integrity, Assyria and Hatti grew to such an extent that Mitanni disappeared as an independent kingdom and the upper Euphrates became the border between the two rival powers. Hatti also extended its influence westwards to take over most of central and southern Asia Minor, and, after the battle of Qadesh, assumed control of the small kingdoms of Syria-Palestine as far south as the Dead Sea. The details of these encounters and the names of the kings who engaged in them are chronicled in the many texts that survive and allow the story to be teased out in some detail. What is significant for our narrative is that for the centuries from 1500 to 1200 BC the Near East for the first time functioned as an integrated international system stretching from the Nubian desert to the Black Sea and from the Aegean to the Iranian plateau.

5.3 The excavation of copper oxhide ingots from the shipwreck of *c.*1300 BC found at Uluburun off the south coast of Turkey near the town of Kaş

The Collapse of the Regional Kingdoms, 1200–900 BC

The system of equal brothers fell apart during the course of the twelfth century partly as the result of internal factors—instabilities brought about by the social inequalities—and partly by a variety of external events, particularly the increased mobility of populations in the peripheral areas. While different local circumstances mitigated the effects of these pressures, the overall result was that the unified system that had maintained the unstable equilibrium disintegrated, leaving a very different political geography at the end of the period of upheaval.

The most dramatically affected regions lay in the west. The kingdom of Hatti in Anatolia completely collapsed. It may be that famine had something to do with it since the import of large quantities of grain is mentioned in some of the texts; but there was violence too. The royal fort at Hattusa was burned down and the city was abandoned. The collapse of central government allowed the Syrian vassal cities to become independent, but several in the coastal region were destroyed. The royal correspondence is alive with stories of raiders coming from the sea. The exchange between the king of Alashiya (Cyprus) and the king of the coastal city of Ugarit is particularly revealing. The Cypriot ruler writes:

> You have written to me that enemy shipping has been sighted at sea. Well now, even if it is true that enemy ships have been sighted, be firm. Indeed then, what of your troops, your chariots, where are they stationed? Are they stationed close at hand or are they not? Who presses you behind the enemy? Fortify your towns, bring the troops and the chariots into them, and wait for the enemy with feet firm.

In the reply, found in the ashes of Ugarit and probably never sent, the stark desperation speaks clearly:

> The enemy ships are already here. They have set fire to my towns and have done great damage in the country. Did you not know that all my troops were stationed in Hatti country and my ships are still stationed in Lycia and have not yet returned? So that the country is abandoned to itself . . . There are seven enemy ships that have come and done great damage.

References to raiders from the sea pervade the Egyptian sources. In 1224 the Nile delta had been attacked by Libyans moving in from western deserts. The threat was contained, but it was a frightening reminder that Egypt was vulnerable. Then, in 1186, a greater threat appeared: 'The foreign countries . . . made a conspiracy in their islands. All at once the lands were on the move, scattered in war. No country could stand before these arms.' The event is depicted in a lively scene carved on the wall of the Great Temple at Medinet Habu in Thebes, in which the pharaoh Rameses III is shown smiting the aggressors who had arrived by ship, the different ethnic groups among the invaders being identified by their different weapons and armour. There are some difficulties in reconciling the various texts, and it may be that events have been conflated, but that there were attacks on the Nile delta and the Levantine coast there can be no doubt. In the event, Egypt, by virtue of its protective deserts, survived, but the cities of Syria and Palestine fared less well. Some were destroyed, and new people, most notably the Philistines, arrived to settle.

5.4 The well-defended main gate of the city of Ugarit (Ras Shamra), which flourished as a trading port on the Mediterranean coast of the Levant (now Syria) in the late second millennium BC. It was destroyed in the upheavals of about 1200 BC

Who the 'sea people' mentioned in the Egyptian texts were has been the subject of constant discussion. Some may have come from the Aegean, seeking new opportunities in the wake of the break-up of the Mycenaean network of kingdoms. Others may have come from the coasts and islands of Asia Minor. The overall result was that the sea-routes were disrupted and people were on the move in large numbers, causing widespread disruptions. But not all was destruction. Many of the old cities survived and the entire kingdom of Alashiya, whose power was based on controlling the rich copper resources of Cyprus, remained strong, a strength enhanced by receiving and integrating refugees from the Greek-speaking Mycenaean world.

The eastern kingdoms of Assyria, Babylonia, and Elam continued to work together, largely unaffected by the upheavals in the west, but they had their own problems. Most debilitating were the internal tensions caused by the lavish lifestyles of the elite and the increasing indebtedness of the poor. Those who could no longer bear the burden simply fled to join the *habiru*, outcasts living outside the control of governments. The result was that the rural infrastructures collapsed, the urban centres decreased in size, and there was reversion to a semi-nomadic way of life, exacerbated, in the lower Tigris and the lower Euphrates, by changes in drainage patterns and increasing salination.

Another factor of some importance was the rise in power of nomadic peoples living on the desert fringes. The most dominant were the Aramaeans, who began raiding in the eleventh century and by the ninth century had settled large territories in the Tigris valley. Another nomadic group, the Chaldaeans, settled in the Euphrates valley. The ethnic mix was enhanced still further by the appearance of nomadic Arabs, who gradually infiltrated from the south, bringing with them their domesticated camels, an innovation that allowed the deserts and desert oases to be integrated into a more expansive mode of nomadism.

If the twelfth century had been a time of violent upheaval that saw the fragmentation of the old international system of interdependent kingdoms, the eleventh and tenth centuries were a time of readjustment. The old polities of Egypt, Assyria, Babylonia, and Elam still maintained a degree of internal cohesion, Egypt in grand isolation, the other three in a state of constant conflict. Out of this mêlée would arise the world's first empire.

The Assyrian Empire: Its Rise and Fall, 900–612 BC

The story of the Assyrian empire is usually told in terms of a series of spectacular military exploits carried out by great kings like Ashurnasirpal, Sargon II, Sennacherib, and Ashurbanipal, names made famous through inscriptions and texts discovered in the excavations of Assyrian palaces from the 1840s onwards and reflected in stories told in the Old Testament. Here we are more concerned with the general impact of the Assyrian adventure on the bigger narrative. The story falls into three parts. The first, the period from about 900 to 823 BC, saw the re-creation and consolidation of the territorial state. Then followed a period of stasis marked by internal dissent and rebellions from 823 to 745 BC. After this a succession of strong kings began to extend Assyrian dominance across the entire Near East, conquering Elam in the east and Egypt as far south as Thebes, and extending northwards into the centre of Anatolia. By 640 BC Assyria was at the height of its powers, but problems of succession and the simple fact that the empire was too vast to be governed by a centralized power began to tell. With the internal polity of Babylon beginning to flex its muscles and external attack from the Medes in the east and the Cimmerians and Scythians from the north, the edifice of empire began to collapse. The end came in 612 BC, when the capital, Nineveh, was attacked by a confederation of enemies and sacked.

The Assyrian empire was quite different from anything that had gone before. It was a single militaristic state that maintained itself by feeding off the energy and the spoils of constant expansionist warfare. After the mid-eighth century conquered states were incorporated as provinces ruled through a centralized bureaucracy. What drove

NOMADS AND EMPIRES

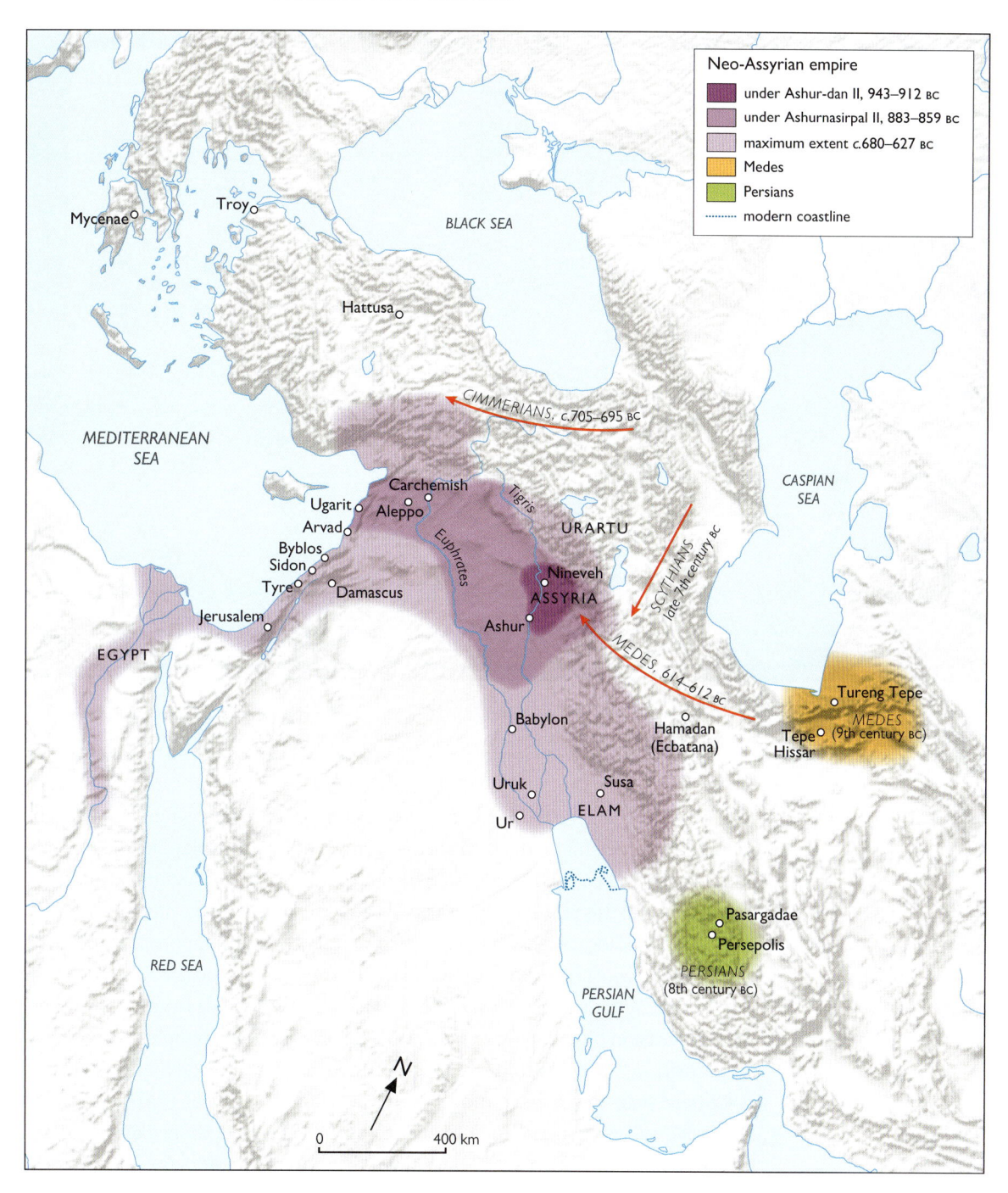

5.5 The growth of the Assyrian empire showing the direction of the threats which came from their northern and eastern neighbours

5.6 Relief from the palace of Ashurnasirpal II (reigned 883–859 BC) at Nimrud, Khorsabad, Iraq. Hunting scenes such as in this example proclaim the status and skills of the Assyrian kings, skills that kept them in practice for war

the relentless expansion is difficult to say, but the social structure, which expected the king to be a successful military leader, had a significant part to play. So, too, did religious ideology. The kings believed they were required by the god Ashur to expand the domain, though this may have been a justification rather than a driving force.

A more pressing cause for expansion was the need to support the edifice of empire with a constant inflow of raw materials and manpower. The Assyrian kings were builders on an unprecedented scale. They moved capitals from time to time, on each occasion building their vast complexes of palaces and temples anew. When Ashurnasirpal II decided to move from Ashur to Kalhu, the building programme took fifteen years to complete and involved enclosing a city site of 360 hectares with a defensive wall 8 kilometres long. To inaugurate his palaces, he invited 69,574 guests: 'for ten days I gave them food, I gave them drink, I had them bathed, I had them anointed. I did honour to them and sent them back to their lands in peace and joy.' This was conspicuous consumption on a grand scale.

After serving as capital for 150 years Kalhu was replaced by an entirely new capital of comparable style and magnificence built by Sargon II at Dur-Sharrukin. This lasted for only his lifetime and was abandoned when his successor, Sennacherib, decided to refurbish the old city of Nineveh as his capital, extending it to 750 hectares. Social expectations demanded that each king invest heavily in grandiose building projects, all predicated on the spoils of war. In this way a vicious circle was created. Wealth and human energy were consumed on a scale never before seen, and to supply it the king had to conquer ever more distant lands.

One consequence of all this was the need to assemble huge labour forces by deporting conquered populations to where they were needed in the empire to produce food, to mine and quarry, and to build. The displacements took place on a grand scale. In one case Samaria in Israel was all but depopulated when its people were moved to the eastern borders of the empire, giving rise to the story of the lost tribes of Israel. By deportation and resettlement, not only were the needs of the consumer-driven economy managed, but ethnic concentrations of potential enemies were dispersed across the empire. It is estimated that, in all, about four and a half million people were deported in massive demographic readjustments.

Assyria was above all a militaristic state: it ruled by terror, or, as one writer has put it, by 'calculated frightfulness'. In the later Assyrian empire, by which time a standing army had been created, the force numbered hundreds of thousands and was composed of specialist units drawn from all parts of the empire and maintained by a state bureaucracy. The tactics of conquest were simple and effective. When a new territory was being engaged, the smaller towns and villages were picked off first and any that resisted were severely punished, the farm land was devastated, the population slaughtered or tortured, and the results left for all to see. A few examples of this kind were often sufficient to persuade the populations of the larger cities to force their leaders to capitulate. A reputation for unmitigated terror was a highly effective weapon.

While the demands of the elite for basic commodities and manpower could be met within the ever-expanding boundaries of the empire, the more exotic commodities needed to support elite life—gold, silver, gemstones, fine fabrics, carpets, perfumes, and the like—had to be imported from beyond the frontiers through trading networks manipulated by specialists, people like the Phoenician merchants living in the port cities on the Levant coast and the caravan traders who were able to cross the deserts to work the Red Sea and the Persian Gulf. Others will have facilitated the inflow of goods from across the Iranian plateau and around the Caucasus. Something of the quantity of rare materials and the quality of the workmanship invested in them is shown by the spectacular finds made in the abandoned palaces and the rarely surviving graves. While quantification is difficult, the impression given is that consumption was on an unparalleled scale. There can be little doubt that the trading networks, extending deep into the peripheries, were invigorated as never before.

Maritime Systems in the West, 1000–600 BC

The Mediterranean and the seas beyond had long been bound by maritime networks facilitating communication between coastal communities. For the most part journeys would have been kept short, the ships' masters preferring to stick to familiar coastal waters, but more enterprising long-distance ventures would not have been unknown. The rise of the great powers in the Near East after the middle of the second millennium and the increasing demand for commodities encouraged more adventurous journeys. Already, by the fourteenth century, Mycenaean traders were beginning to explore the central Mediterranean, making stops in Sicily, southern Italy, and Sardinia. Their primary interests were probably metals, but they were also able to get hold of the much-desired Baltic amber now reaching Italy via middlemen in the Po valley.

With the collapse of the Mycenaean city states in the twelfth century, the initiative for maritime exploration passed to Cyprus (Alashiya). To what extent this was the result of Mycenaeans settling on the island is unclear. Cyprus was already involved in local trading ventures in the east Mediterranean, and it may be that the Mycenaean settlers brought with them knowledge of the riches to be had in the west. At any event, from the twelfth to the tenth century Cypriot merchants were active in the Tyrrhenian Sea, engaging particularly with the islands of Sicily and Sardinia, where many imports from Cyprus have been found. What the attraction of Sardinia was is uncertain. It can hardly have been copper, which Cyprus produced itself in quantity, but it may have been iron, which was now becoming a sought-after commodity in the Near East. High-quality iron ore was also available from nearby Etruria. Thus it was that the central Mediterranean became a trading periphery of the Near East, first through the activity of Mycenaean ships' masters and later through that of their Cypriot successors.

In the eleventh century BC a new force, the Phoenicians, began to make themselves felt. Phoenicia is the coastal strip of the Levant, extending northwards from Mount Carmel and blessed by a series of fine harbour cities—Tyre, Sidon, Byblos, and others—each a self-governing entity engaged primarily in trade. The narrowness of the coastal zone, backed by mountains, provided little hinterland or opportunity for expansion. The population, therefore, was forced to look outward to the ocean for its livelihood. Thus, the Phoenician cities occupied an interface between the consuming states and empires of the Near East and the opportunities offered by the massively productive Mediterranean. Inevitably they became traders.

NOMADS AND EMPIRES

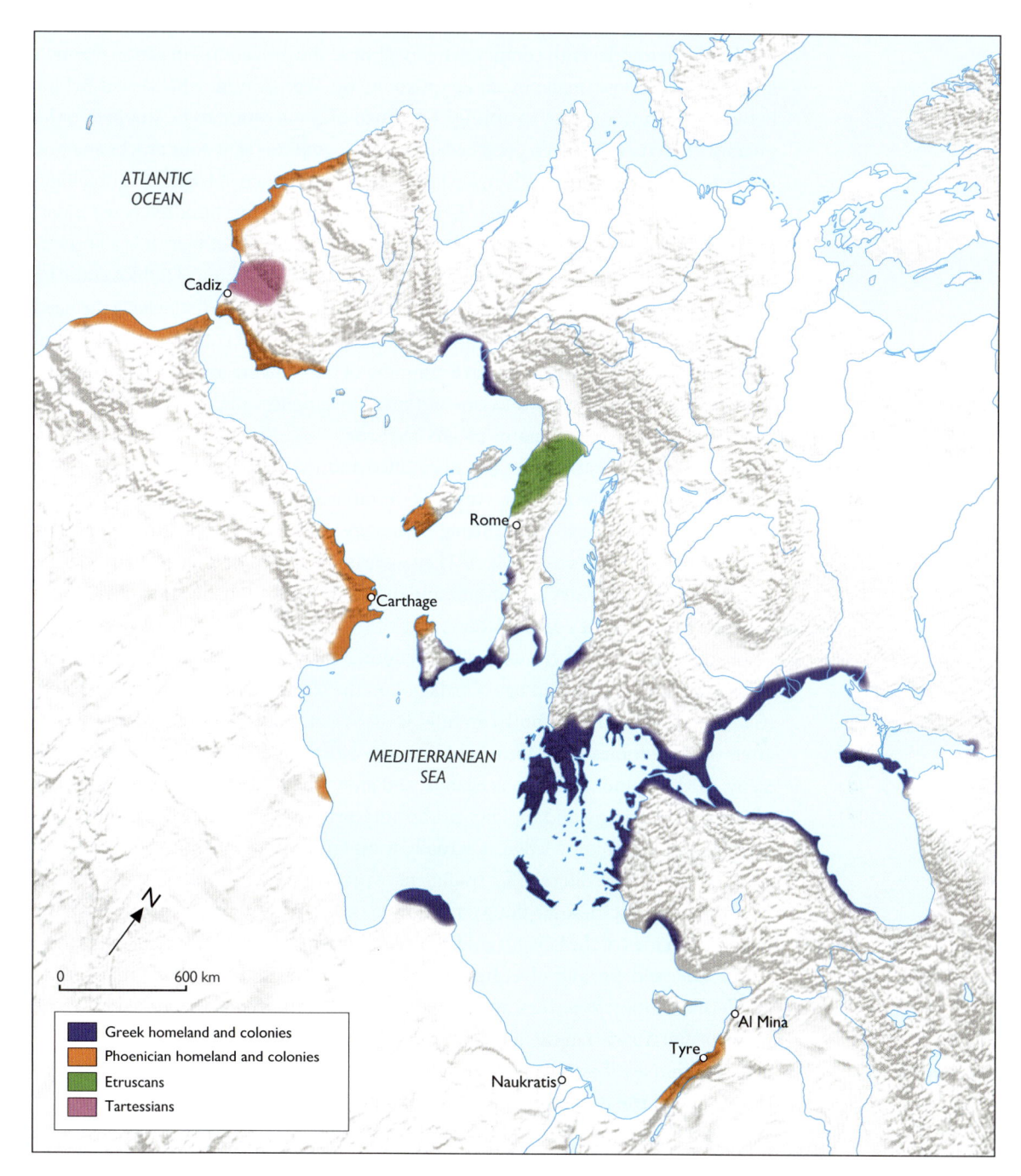

5.7 Between 900 and 500 BC Greek and Phoenician cities began to extend their influence by setting up maritime trading networks and establishing colonies. The Greeks' sphere of influence included southern Italy and Sicily, Cyrenaica, southern France, and the Black Sea, while the Phoenicians concentrated on North Africa with parts of Sicily and Sardinia, together with coastal areas of Iberia and Morocco

Already, in the eleventh century, we can glimpse the procedures in action through an account of a visit made by an Egyptian envoy, Wen-Amon, who visited Byblos between 1075 and 1060 BC to arrange for a load of cedar-wood to be shipped to the pharaoh. In return for seven great cedar logs, the Egyptians sent 'four crocks and one *kak-men* of gold, five jugs of silver, ten garments of royal linen, ten *kherd* of good linen from Upper Egypt, five hundred rolls of finished papyrus, five hundred cows' hides, five hundred ropes, twenty bags of lentils, and thirty baskets of fish'. It is a particularly interesting exchange. The array of goods acquired by the king of Byblos could be used in the imperial estates or sold on to other distributors. The list reflects the need of the maritime communities for mundane commodities that could not be produced locally. The rolls of papyrus are also a reminder of the growing importance of literacy and record keeping. Byblos was one of the main suppliers of papyrus to the Greek world; indeed, in Greek its name means 'papyrus'.

The Phoenician cities grew in importance and by the tenth century they were actively engaged with Cyprus, eventually establishing a colony at the old port of Kition. It may well have been through contacts with Cyprus that the Phoenicians learnt of the sea-routes to the west. They were quick to exploit this new knowledge, first establishing colonies on Sardinia and then sailing through the Strait of Gibraltar to explore the Atlantic coasts of Iberia and Morocco, where trading links were forged before the end of the ninth century. To strengthen their hold on the region major port cities were founded at Carthage (Carthago) on the North African coast and at Cadiz (Gadir) in southern Iberia, both carefully sited to command major sea passages. Soon after, other colonies were founded along the North and West African coasts, on Sicily, Sardinia, and the Balearic Islands, and along the southern and western coasts of Iberia. The energy and rapidity of the enterprise is astonishing. While it piggy-backed on Cypriot knowledge, it actually went far beyond, integrating the Atlantic seaboard and the Mediterranean trading networks for the first time.

The products of these far-flung parts flowed through the maritime networks to the Phoenician cities of the Levant: gold, ivory, and ostrich eggshell from north-western Africa, and gold, tin, and silver from western Iberia. No doubt there was much more beside: fine fabrics, dyes, furs, and probably slaves. Exotic materials worked on by the renowned craftsmen in the Phoenician ports were passed, with value added, to the courts of the Near Eastern elites. The quantity and quality of the ivory work found in the palaces of the Assyrian kings reflects something of the sheer volume of activity generated by elite demand.

The Greeks were relative latecomers to Mediterranean commerce. Emerging from a 'dark age' following the breakdown of the Mycenaean world took some time, but by the tenth century BC the elite living on the island of Euboea were already benefiting

5.8 Section from a wall relief found in the palace of the Assyrian king Sargon II (reigned 722–705 BC) of Khorsabad, Iraq. The vessels towing logs along a river are Phoenician. They are known as hippoi from the horse-headed prow

from trade with the Near East. One male cremation at the site of Lefkandi was buried in an urn of Cypriot origin, while the female accompanying him wore an antique gold necklace and pendant of Babylonian origin. By the ninth century trade between Euboea, Cyprus, and the Levant had developed apace, documented in the archaeological record by the distribution of distinctive pottery types (skyphoi), painted with pendent semicircles probably made in Euboea. Exactly who the carriers were, however, remains unclear. It could be that it was the entrepreneurial Phoenicians who were managing the exchange, but in all probability it was the Euboeans themselves who were beginning to explore the possibilities of overseas commerce. Early in the eighth century they were active in the central Mediterranean, and about 770 BC they established a colony at Pithekoussai on the island of Ischia in the Bay of Naples. It was the beginning of a phase of overseas activity, soon engaged in by many of the developing Greek city states, that saw much of southern Italy and Sicily settled by communities of colonizers in the eighth and seventh centuries.

The Greek traders also established regular contacts with the Near Eastern polities through two trading enclaves, one in the Nile delta at Naukratis on the Canopic branch of the Nile, 80 kilometres from the sea, the other at Al Mina on the coast of the Levant. Naukratis was founded about 630 BC, but Al Mina began earlier as a Euboean enterprise and continued in active operation until about 600 BC. The two ports provided Greek traders with access to the massive markets of the east.

A separate Greek enterprise, largely masterminded by the city of Miletus on the Aegean coast of Asia Minor, was the colonization of the Black Sea, which began in the middle of the eighth century and proceeded over the next two hundred years, by which time the sea was ringed by thriving Greek port cities. The Sea of Azov had also been penetrated. One colony, Tanis, established at the mouth of the river Don, was recognized at the time as being at the extremity of the civilized world. The importance of the Black Sea colonies, from the point of view of our narrative, is that many of them occupied the territory of the Scythians, providing a direct interface between the steppe pastoralists and Greek Mediterranean civilization. It introduces a new theme, to which we shall return.

The Red Sea and the Persian Gulf, 1500–600 BC

The integration of the southern tip of the Arabian peninsula and the Horn of Africa into the trading networks serving the Near Eastern states came about over time as maritime routes along the Red Sea developed, linking the Arabian ports of Qana, Aden, Ocelis, and Muza to Berenike and other ports on the Egyptian shore of the Red Sea, from where caravan routes led across the eastern desert to the Nile valley. Connectivity increased when, towards the end of the second millennium, the desert Arabs domesticated the Arabian camel, making the overland route direct to the Levant and Mesopotamia feasible for the first time.

Modern Yemen, at the south-western tip of the Arabian peninsula, known as Saba (or Sheba) in the Near Eastern world, was renowned for its exotic wealth. Assyrian texts report the arrival of caravans bringing a range of commodities including iron

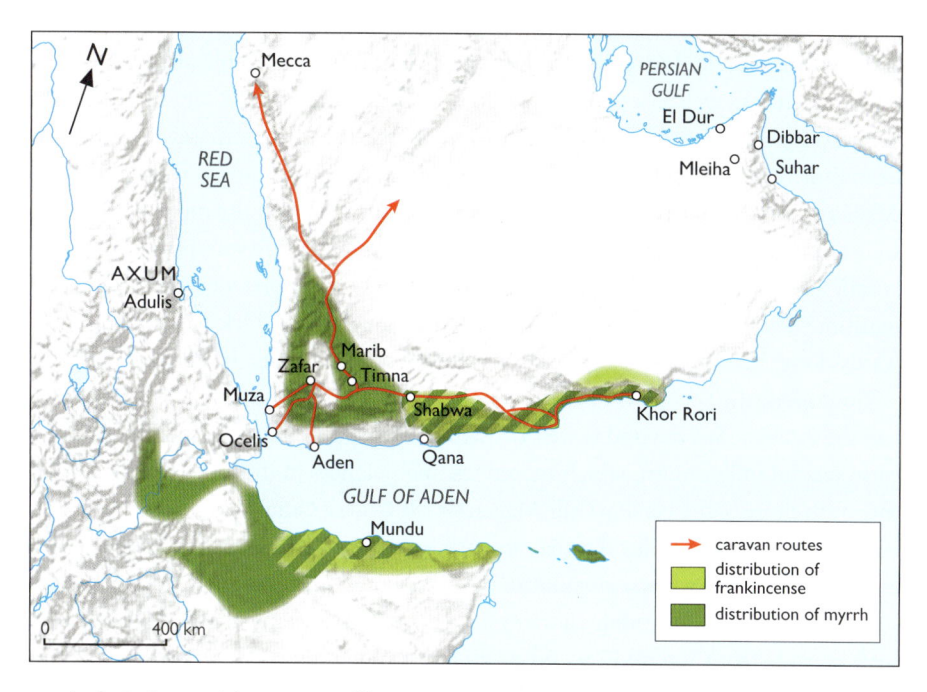

5.9 As the Red Sea and the Persian Gulf became increasingly used by maritime traders in the second and first millennia BC, coastal port cities began to grow in importance, introducing local products such as frankincense and myrrh into the trading network

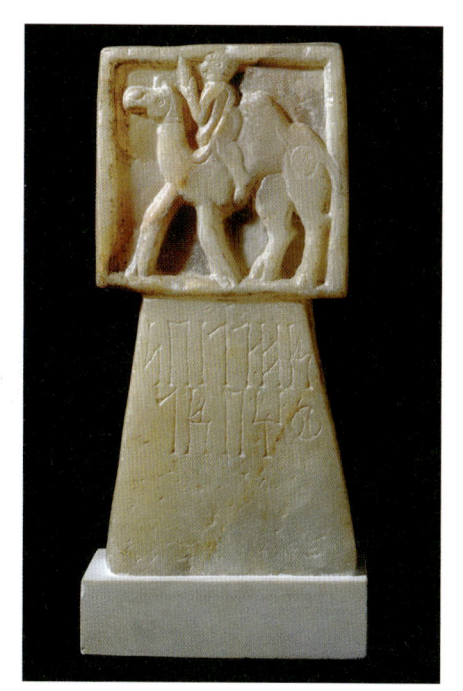

5.10 An incense burner from Shabwa in southern Arabia dating to the third century AD. Camels, with single humps, were domesticated in the Arabian peninsula by the beginning of the first millennium BC and were extensively used for riding and carrying goods, opening up new desert routes

and the much-desired incense, frankincense, and myrrh. The Bible also reports the gift of incense as well as a precious cargo of gold and other items sent by the queen of Sheba to King Solomon. Frankincense and myrrh are both aromatic resins tapped from thorny trees found only on the hills of Yemen and Oman and across the Gulf of Aden in northern Somalia. Among the other commodities on the move at this time were elephant ivory and copper: both were found in quantity in a warehouse excavated at Sabr near Aden dating to the twelfth century BC. The gulf ports were part of broader maritime networks stretching southwards down the coast of Africa and north-westwards along the Arabian coast to link with the networks serving the Persian Gulf.

Trade along the Persian Gulf and through the Strait of Hormuz to the Gulf of Oman and the Arabian Sea beyond is well attested in Mesopotamian texts of the third and early second millennium, which record trading partners in the lands of Dilmun on the south shore of the Persian Gulf, Magan on the Gulf of Oman, and Meluhha, which is probably the Indus valley. Textiles and other consumer durables were shipped out, and in return the Near Eastern polities received wood, stone, copper, ivory, precious stones, and animals, including monkeys and dogs. There seems to have been a downturn in trade from the mid-second to mid-first millennium. Meluhha is no longer mentioned in the texts after about 2000 BC, and trade with Magan seems to have ceased soon after. What this means in real terms is unclear. It may simply be that all trade was now articulated through Dilmun, whose entrepreneurs served as middlemen jealously guarding their monopoly with partners beyond the Strait of Hormuz.

Medes and Persians on the Iranian Plateau, 1400–600 BC

The situation on the Iranian plateau in the late second and early first millennia is not yet well understood. This is largely the result of a paucity of sound archaeological data, but the situation is further confused by having to try to accommodate tenuous theories about the spread of Indo-European language groups. It is commonly argued that as the Iranian language is Indo-European it must have been introduced either from the north-west—from beyond the Caucasus (or, as some would argue, from Anatolia)—or from the north-east across the deserts of Central Asia. Much of the debate focuses around trying to match these theories to the archaeological evidence in a way that is also consistent with what little textual evidence survives. While this is a legitimate approach, the hard evidence is such that few firm conclusions can be reached.

The earliest mention of the peoples of western Iran are to be found in an Assyrian text of 835 BC which refers to Medes and Parsua (Persians), the Medes living in the territory of Hamadan, in the vicinity of modern Isfahan, the Persians occupying the territory of Fars to the south. Since both peoples were Iranian speakers, the questions

NOMADS AND EMPIRES

that are commonly asked are, when did they arrive and from where? Both questions are based on the unproved assumption that they were not an indigenous population who had simply acquired an Indo-European language.

The archaeological evidence derived from the excavation of settlement sites and cemeteries in western Iran points to a major cultural change taking place about 1400 BC, when a new type of grey burnished pottery came into use and burials began to be placed in regular cemeteries rather than scattered within the settlement itself. These changes, it is argued, represent the influx of new people. The best match for the pottery is to be found in Late Bronze Age sites dating back to the third millennium BC, sites like Tepe Hissar and Tureng Tepe, clustering around the south-eastern corner of the Caspian Sea. This could be taken to imply that new people began to arrive in western Iran after 1400 BC from the Central Asian deserts flanking the eastern side of

5.11 Part of a gold belt said to be from Ziwiye, Iran, dating to the eighth–seventh century BC. The repoussé decoration depicts recumbent stags and goats linked by lions' heads. The portrayal of the stags is highly reminiscent of nomadic art

the Caspian Sea, but the interpretation is at best tenuous and in the present state of knowledge it would be wrong to reject other explanations. It is by no means impossible that the Medes, by virtue of their central location, were subject to cultural influences from several directions, from Central Asian deserts, from the Trans-Caucasian steppe, and from the Anatolian plateau. Complex movements of people on a small scale over an extended period of time could have helped to mould the culture of the Medes and the Persians by the time they were identified as discrete peoples in the Assyrian texts: there is no need to call up massive migrations. The discovery of gold plaques at Ziwiye in Kurdistan decorated in repoussé with recumbent stags and goats closely comparable to the Scytho-Siberian animal style of the eighth and seventh centuries is clear evidence of continuing influence from south Russia.

In the second half of the eighth century the Assyrian kings campaigned against the Medes, and in the opening decades of the seventh century the latter are represented as vassals to the Assyrians, for whom they provided mercenaries. What had probably been a loose confederation of tribes gradually gelled into a centralized polity, growing in strength as it came together under a single king. By 612 BC, in alliance with the Babylonians and Scythians, the Medes were strong enough to attack Assyria and to sack the principal cities of Nineveh and Nimrud, bringing the Assyrian empire to its knees. What followed is part of a later narrative.

China and the Early States, 1700–481 BC

Early state development in China can be approached in two different ways. The first, the traditional approach, is through the historical records; the second is by focusing on the archaeological evidence, a resource that has grown much richer in recent years as the result of an increasing number of large-scale excavations. The two approaches offer different insights and, in theory at least, they should complement each other.

The period that concerns us here is traditionally divided into the Shang period, beginning about 1700 BC and lasting to 1046 BC, and the Zhou period, which is further divided into the Western Zhou (1046–771 BC) and the Eastern Zhou (771–221 BC). The Eastern Zhou is divided again into the Spring and Autumn period (770–481 BC) and the Warring States period (480–221 BC). This simple historical classification provides a convenient nomenclature of familiar names far easier to remember than the plethora of archaeological cultures and subdivisions, and provides a starting point for the discussion.

In the historical tradition the Shang dynasty is said to have followed the Xia dynasty, supposedly the first of China's dynasties. The Shang developed on the Central Plains in the eastern part of Henan province and the south-west part of Hebi province. The

Shang state was rigorously hierarchical and was dominated by a ruling house, the Zi, whose various lineages constituted the elite with one pre-eminent lineage providing the ruling household. In the early centuries the capital was moved from place to place, but by the Late Shang (about 1200 BC) the city of Anyang ('Great City of Shang') became the permanent capital and residence of the royal court. Other members of the Zi, who served as princes and generals, lived in towns scattered throughout the territory, where they helped to maintain the authority of the state. In the territories beyond this central core were smaller, semi-autonomous polities (*hou*), which owed allegiance to the Shang. Over the centuries the state became increasingly centralized and bureaucratic with separate departments set up to run the administration. The *hou* became provinces administered by the centre, and the king began to be considered a god. The Shang maintained a large army composed of archers, who were driven about in war chariots, supported by foot-soldiers drawn from the rural population.

The evolution of the early state in China during the Xia and Shang dynasties can be traced in the archaeological record and is characterized by two cultural sequences named after the sites of Erlitou and Erlingang. Erlitou is a city over 300 hectares in extent sited in the valley of the river Yiluo, a tributary of the Yellow River. Occupation began about 1900 BC and ended about 1500 BC, thus covering the Xia dynasty and the transition to the Early Shang. The sequence of four major levels shows a complexity of activities and a rise in population reaching to between twenty and thirty thousand by 1600 BC. The ruler lived in a palace set within a colonnaded courtyard, and by this date craftsmen in the city were making a range of elaborate bronze vessels, by multi-piece casting, which served as symbols of political, religious, and economic power. There were also other high-quality manufactures such as fine white ceramics made from kaolin, providing another symbol of elite status.

In addition to the capital, a number of secondary centres were established to control and maintain supplies of essential resources such as food, timber, metals, salt, and kaolin. Dongxiafeng, for example, was sited close to the Hedong Salt Lake and the copper mines in the bend of the Yellow River, while the city of Panlongcheng was built on the middle Yangtze to control supplies of copper, tin, and lead from mines in the Yangtze valley.

The last phase of occupation at Erlitou (1600–1500 BC) showed the city in rapid decline. This coincided with the establishment of a new capital at Zhengzhou, 150 kilometres to the east. Zhengzhou soon grew to massive proportions. The inner walled city containing the palaces was 300 hectares in extent. There was also an outer walled area, and, in all, occupation spread over some 2,500 hectares. The shift of the urban focus from Erlitou to Zhengzhou probably reflects the beginning of the Shang dynasty, establishing itself by moving away from the traditional capital of the Xia.

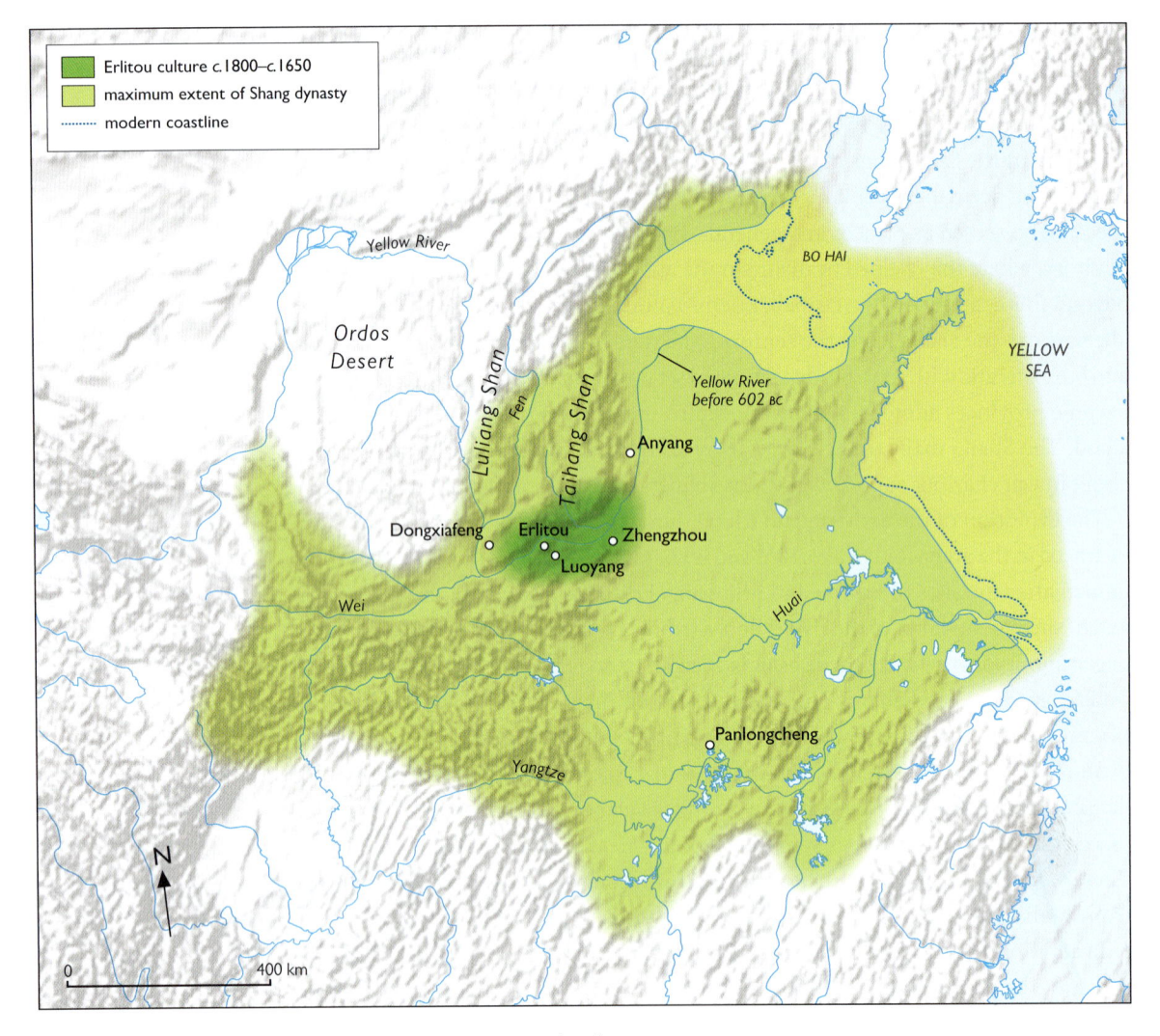

5.12 China during the late second millennium

Zhengzhou remained the capital of the Early Shang dynasty for two hundred years, during which time the scale of industrial production grew to enormous proportions. Several bronze foundries have been found around the central city, producing a variety of artefacts from simple domestic items to weapons and horse-gear and the elaborate bronze vessels used in elite ceremonies. There were also pottery kilns and bone-working establishments.

5.13 (*opposite*) Two cities of Shang dynasty China

174

Yanshi Shang City

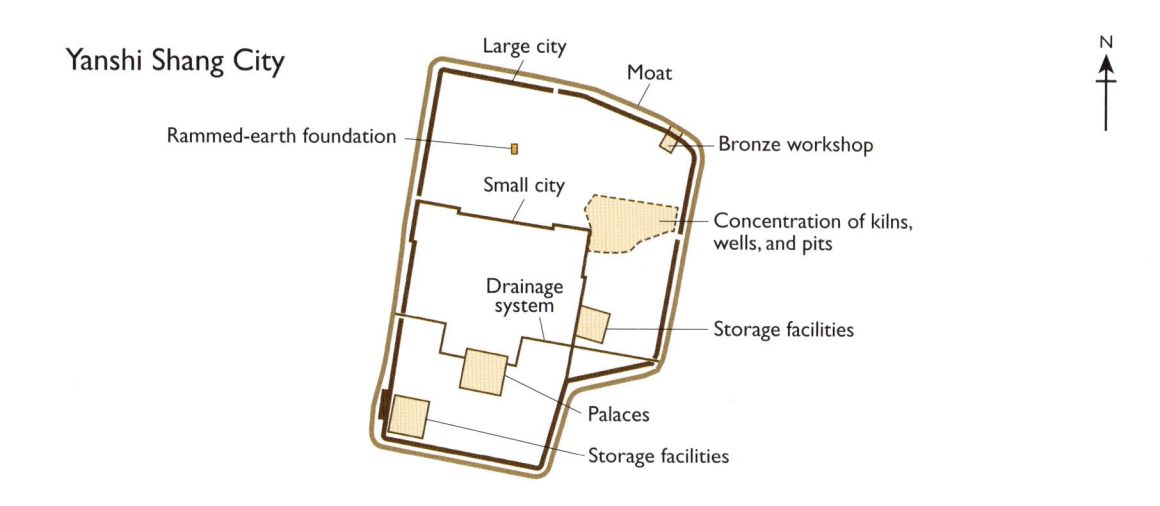

- Large city
- Moat
- Rammed-earth foundation
- Bronze workshop
- Small city
- Concentration of kilns, wells, and pits
- Drainage system
- Storage facilities
- Palaces
- Storage facilities

Zhengzhou Shang City

- Inner city wall
- Palaces
- Xionger
- Outer city wall
- Moat

○ Bronze hoard
▲ Bronze foundry
■ Bronze workshop
● Pottery workshop
▫ Cemetery
▨ Residential area

0 500 1,000 metres

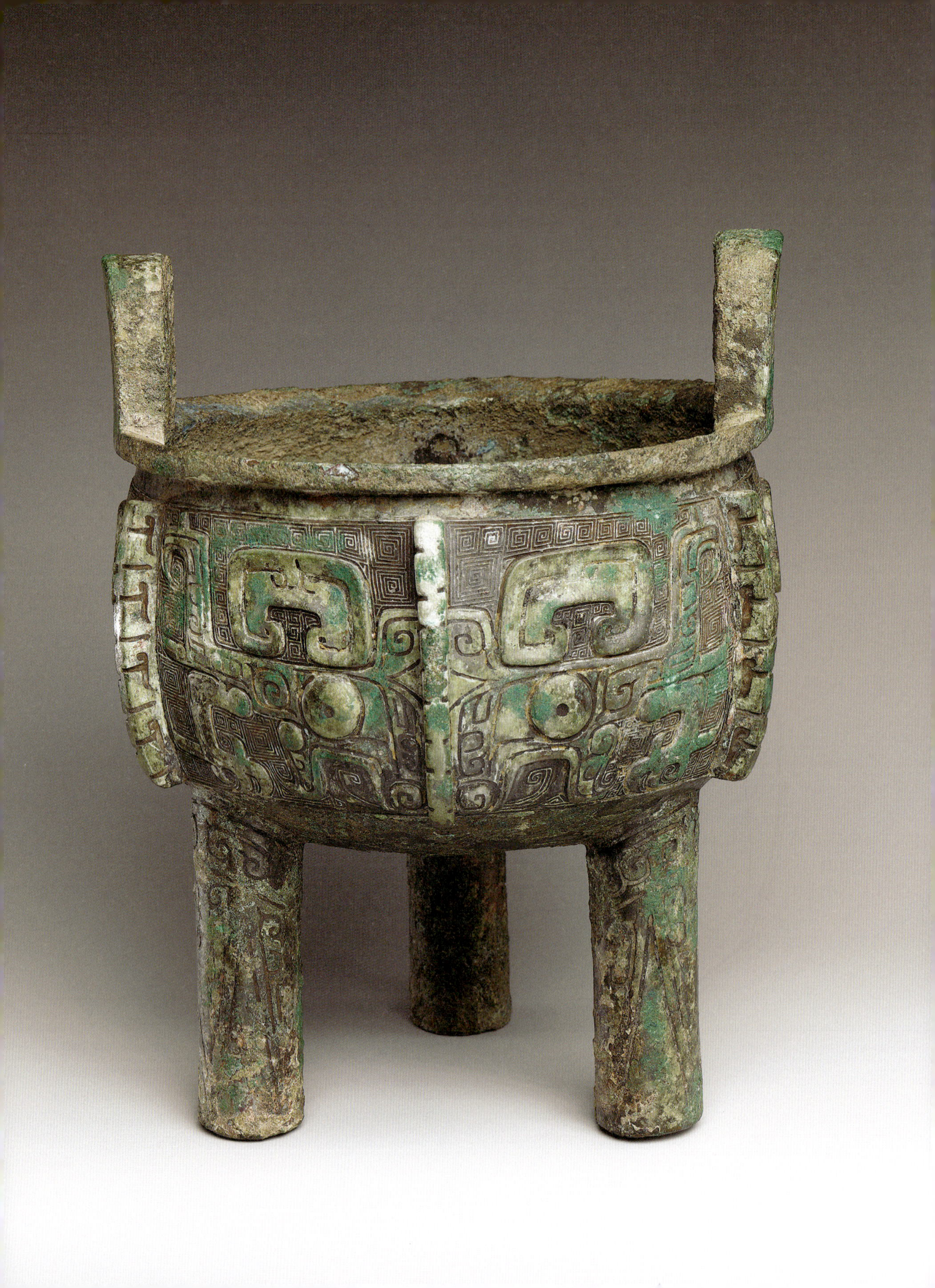

The Early Shang period saw an extension of state territory. There was a move north-eastwards along the river Ji to the sea coast to include Bohai Bay, where salt could be produced more easily than from the Salt Lake. An expansion also took place along the upper and lower Yangtze valley and to the south of the Yangtze along the river Gan to establish firmer control of the rich metal resources of the regions. Other territories embraced by the expansion yielded jade, turquoise, ivory, turtle-shells, and cowries: the control of commodities was now a central concern for the Shang state.

Towards the end of the fifteenth century Zhengzhou went into a rapid decline: the craft workshops ceased production, the palaces were abandoned, and burials were found dug into the city walls. The implication is that the old order had broken down. This correlates well with the historical record, which talks of a period of chaos in 1435 BC during a contested succession. The event is used to divide the Early Shang period from the Middle Shang. Until this point the state had been ever expanding. Population increases, combined with the inevitable tensions caused by a rigorous class stratification, upon which the redistribution of wealth depended, drove the expansion. Surplus population from the centre was sent to the peripheries of the state, creating new wealth, which could be redistributed across the network. But herein lay the problem: it was the mushroom ring effect, with the core dying as the peripheries expanded. This would explain why Zhengzhou declined into insignificance, its position being taken during the Middle Shang period by Huanbei on the eastern periphery. The eastwards shift of the centre was completed in the Late Shang period, beginning around 1200 BC, with the creation of a new capital city at Anyang.

The rise of the regional centres saw another change. The new regional elites were able to control the flow of raw materials and to use this power to build local power structures based on redistribution. This is most evident in the production of the elaborate bronze vessels, the redistribution of which, through carefully regulated cycles of gift giving, was used to maintain the class structure. Originally these vessels were produced only in the palace workshops, leaving the kings with the power to distribute them as personal gifts. Decentralization in the Middle Shang period saw the regional centres begin to manufacture their own. In this way patronage and power passed to the peripheral elites. Once under way, decentralization escalated.

In 1046 BC Wu, king of the Zhou, led his people and their allies in an attack on the Shang, his avowed intention being to end what he saw as the corruption of the Shang rulers. The Zhou were one of the peripheral groups who occupied the Wei

5.14 (*opposite*) Ritual tripod (ding) of the Shang dynasty *c.*1300 BC. Vessels of this kind were given as elite gifts, reflecting the status of the owner. They are the masterpieces of highly skilled bronze-smiths proficient in casting with two-piece moulds

NOMADS AND EMPIRES

river valley on the western fringe of the Shang state. Classical literary sources imply that the Zhou had originally lived on the northern steppe before moving to the Wei valley and that they were originally pastoralist before settling in the valley, but by the time they were strong enough to contest the power of the Shang rulers they had already absorbed much of Shang culture. Within a few decades of their initial success, they decided to found a new eastern administrative centre at Luoyang, well within Shang territory. Members of the ruling family were also sent eastwards to establish new regional centres, the better to take firm control of the conquered territory. The new regime was robust and for about two centuries was able to maintain

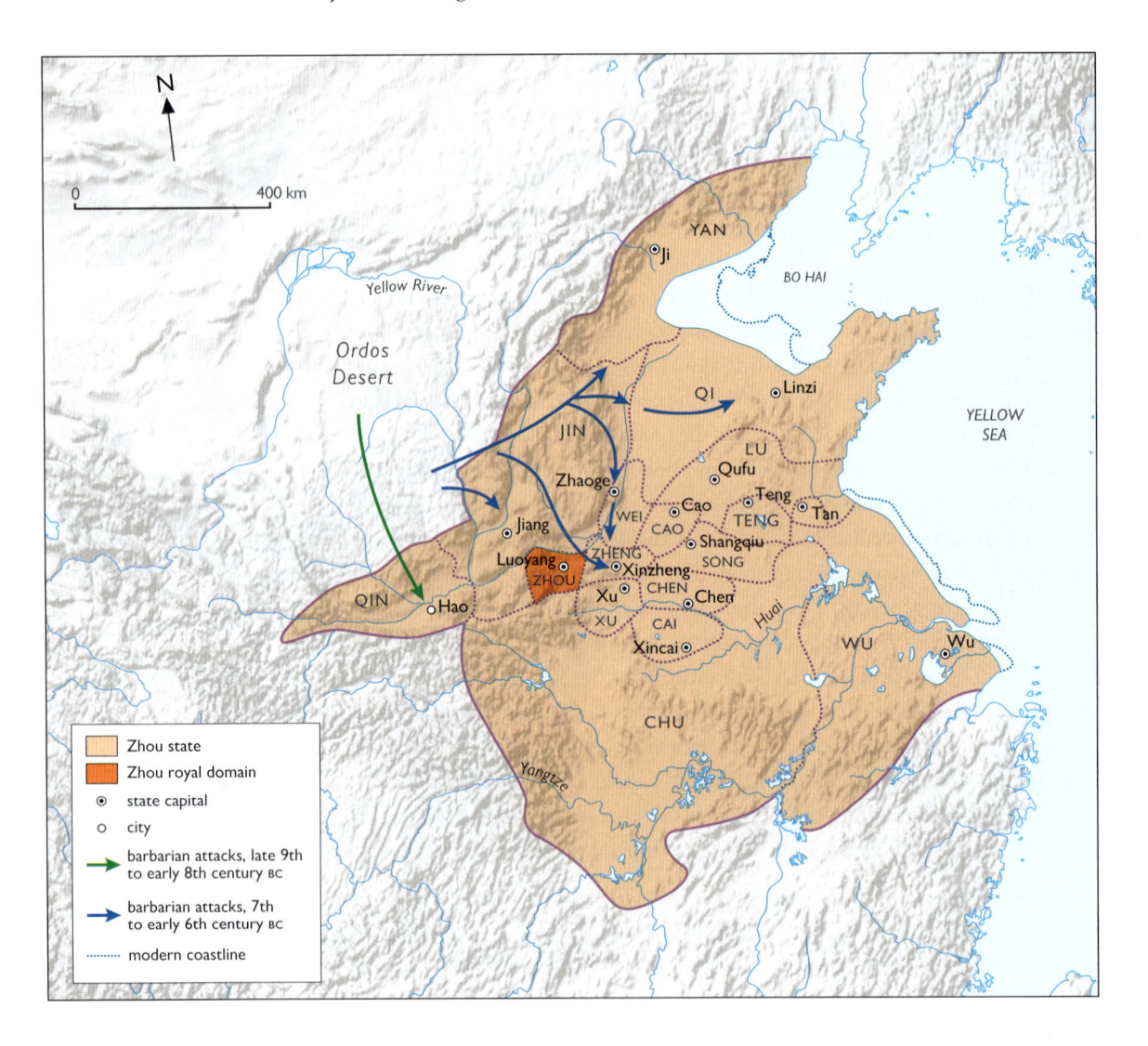

5.15 China during the Zhou dynasty (770–481 BC) showing the constituent states and directions of attack by northern nomads

comparative peace: it was a time presented by later texts as a golden age of tolerance and culture when the kings held real power. In economic terms it seems that the early Zhou rulers managed to restrain the decentralizing tendencies within the system, at least for a while.

This period, known as the Western Zhou, came to an end in 771 BC when the western capital was attacked by north-western steppe nomads, forcing the elite of the Wei river valley to move eastwards to establish a new capital at Zhengzhou, initiating the period known as the Eastern Zhou. But the new court lacked the strength to hold the larger state together. The vassal states, now spread over a vast territory, were fast developing a sense of independence. While they were prepared to afford notional recognition to the Eastern Zhou court, they each began to act as separate polities or states in their own right. This transitional period, from 770–481 BC, is known as the Spring and Autumn period, named after a chronicle recording the events of the time. It was a time of rapidly changing alliances as each polity struggled to retain power. The result was that the old core zone crumbled, while four peripheral powers rose to dominance, vying with each other for overall power: the Jin in present-day Shanxi, the Qi in Shandong, the Qin in the Wei river valley, and the Chu occupying the middle Yangtze river valley and beyond. Out of this power struggle, known as the Warring States period (480–221 BC), the Qin were eventually to emerge as the leaders of a new empire.

Chinese Chariots

One of the most spectacular aspects of the Late Shang and Zhou periods, brought to light by excavation over the last fifty years or so, are the chariot burials of the elite. One of the earliest of these, found at Qiaobei in the Fen river valley, dating to 1200 BC, serves to illustrate the rite in its simplest form. The chariots were found on entry ramps leading down to the tomb. The vehicles and their horses were arranged as they would have been in real life with the body of the charioteer laid out in front. On the floor of the vehicles were placed a number of items including arrowheads, rattle terminals, whip tops, and a bronze bow-shaped object of a kind frequently found in chariot burials, which is thought to be a fitting either for attaching a bow to the belt of the driver or, more likely, to be strapped to the body for helping to control the reins while keeping the hands free. Since chariots and horses are unknown in China before they suddenly appeared in the Late Shang period but are found in Central Asia in the Sintashta culture as early as 2100 BC, there can be little doubt that the chariot, the trained horse teams, and the accessory fittings for the charioteer must have been

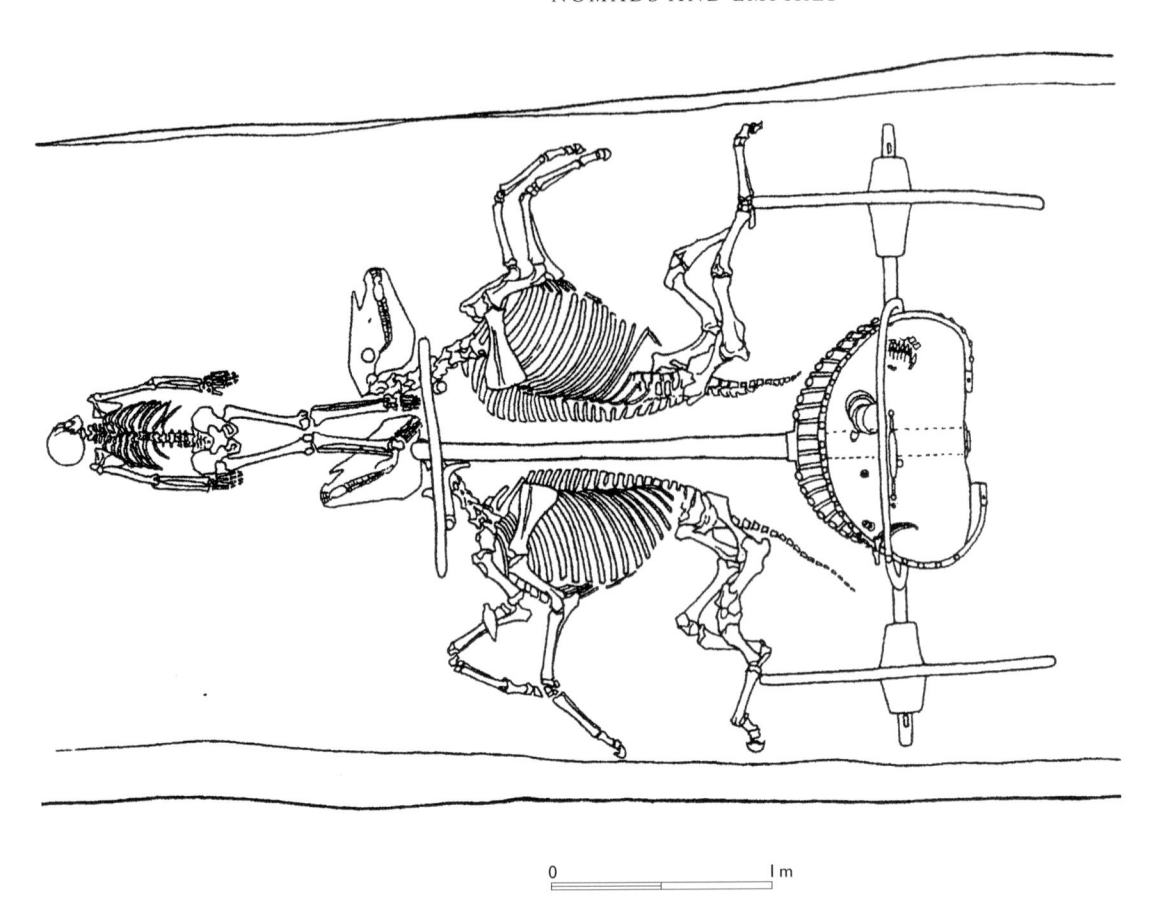

5.16 Late Shang chariot burial found in tomb M1 at Qiaobei, Shanxi, dating to 1200 BC

introduced into China from the steppe about 1200 BC or a little before. The process of transmission will be considered in more detail later (pp. 199–201). In China charioteering was rapidly accepted and integrated into elite culture. The Late Shang vehicles and their fittings may have been modified to suit Chinese taste, but so novel was the innovation that vehicle builders and horse trainers must have been brought in from the steppe to teach local craftsmen, at least in the first instance, and it may be that steppe specialists continued to contribute their skills, especially in providing and training the teams of horses.

In the Early Zhou period, in the eleventh and tenth centuries, chariots increased in popularity, and it was at this time that the four-horse chariot was introduced from the steppe. It required even greater skills in its management since, while the central pair of horses were yoked in the usual way, the outer horses were attached by neck collars to the yoke-bar and by withers collars to the underside of the chariot box. The four-horse teams and their chariots were usually provided with much richer fittings of bronze, suggesting that a vehicle pulled by four horses was of exalted status. Some sense of the grandeur of these vehicles can be appreciated from an inscription found on a bronze vessel, the Mao Gong Ding, which notes the deeds of a Western Zhou king at the end of the ninth century and includes the following description:

> I confer on you . . . a golden chariot, with a decorated cover on the handrail; a front-rail and breast trappings of soft leather, painted scarlet, for the horses; a canopy of tiger skin, with a reddish brown lining; yoke-bar bindings and axle couplings of painted leather; bronze jingle bells for the yoke-bar; a draught-pole rear-end fitting and brake fittings, bound with leather and painted gilt; a gilt bow-press and a fish-skin quiver; a team of four horses, with bits and bridles, bronze frontlets, and gilt girth straps; a scarlet banner with two bells.

The horse-drawn chariot was a powerful new symbol of elite authority in the Late Shang period. Chariots performed many functions. Most practical would have been in warfare and in hunting, both aristocratic pursuits. They were also used in the parade to proclaim the status of the rider, and (fortunately for archaeologists) in the rituals associated with death and burial.

In the Late Shang period chariots were usually placed high on the sloping ramps leading down to the burial pits, after the pits had been largely filled, as if to guard the approach to the tombs, but by the Western Zhou period the practice had become more complex. Now the chariots were deposited in two different ways, either buried with horses in horse-and-chariot pits beside the graves or dismantled and buried on the tomb ramps at a late stage in the funeral process. At the cemetery of the Jin ruling family at Beizhao, Shanxi, nine generations of rulers and their consorts and relatives were buried over a period extending from the tenth to the eighth century BC. Here the horse-and-chariot pits were usually larger than the main burial chambers, the largest containing 107 horses and forty-eight chariots. Conspicuous consumption on this scale was facilitated by the fact that the Jin occupied a territory close to the steppe, in easy reach of a constant supply of horses. The burial of dismantled chariots within tombs involved a different ritual associated with the final sealing of the tomb at the end of the *rite de passage* of death.

Chariot burials continued through the Spring and Autumn period as a symbol of power and of legitimacy to rule, not only in traditional Zhou regions but in the newly established states of the Qin in the west and the Chu in the south, and were still widespread during the Warring States period. The longevity of the horse-drawn chariot, introduced about 1200 BC and remaining dominant as both a practical means of

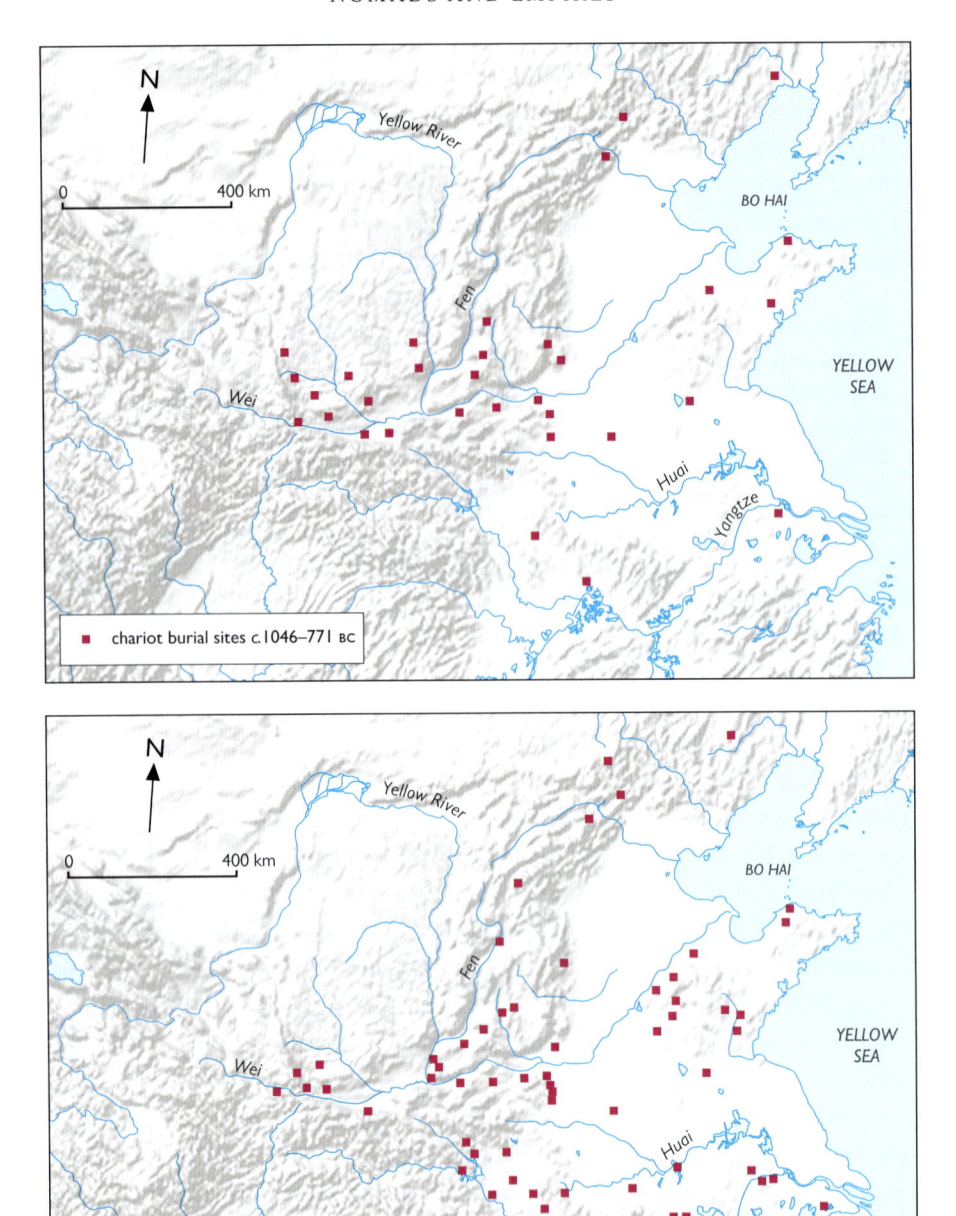

5.17 The distribution of chariot burials in China. Upper map: Western Zhou period (c.1046–771 BC). Lower map: Spring and Autumn period (770–481 BC)

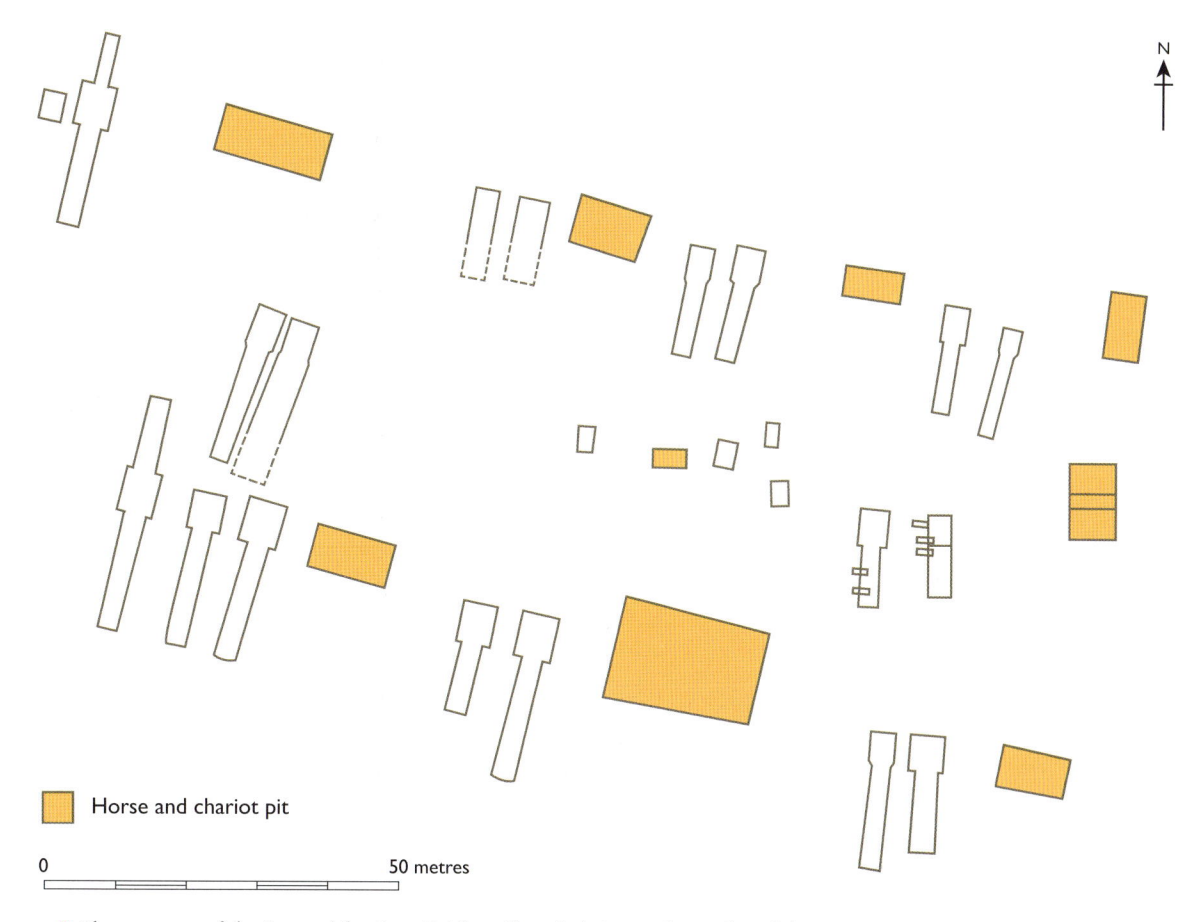

5.18 The cemetery of the Jin royal family at Beizhao, Shanxi, dating to the tenth–eighth century BC. The chariots and horses were buried in pits separate from the burial chambers of the elite, which were reached by long sloping ramps

warfare and a symbol of authority over a period of a thousand years, is remarkable. At the very least it hints at a close awareness of steppe culture and its values by the Shang and Zhou elite, even though tensions between the Chinese of the plains and the steppe nomads were very real. Perhaps the Zhou could never forget their distant steppe heritage.

The Steppe Corridor

The middle centuries of the second millennium, from 1800 to 1200 BC, saw the emergence of a broadly similar Late Bronze Age culture across a great swath of the

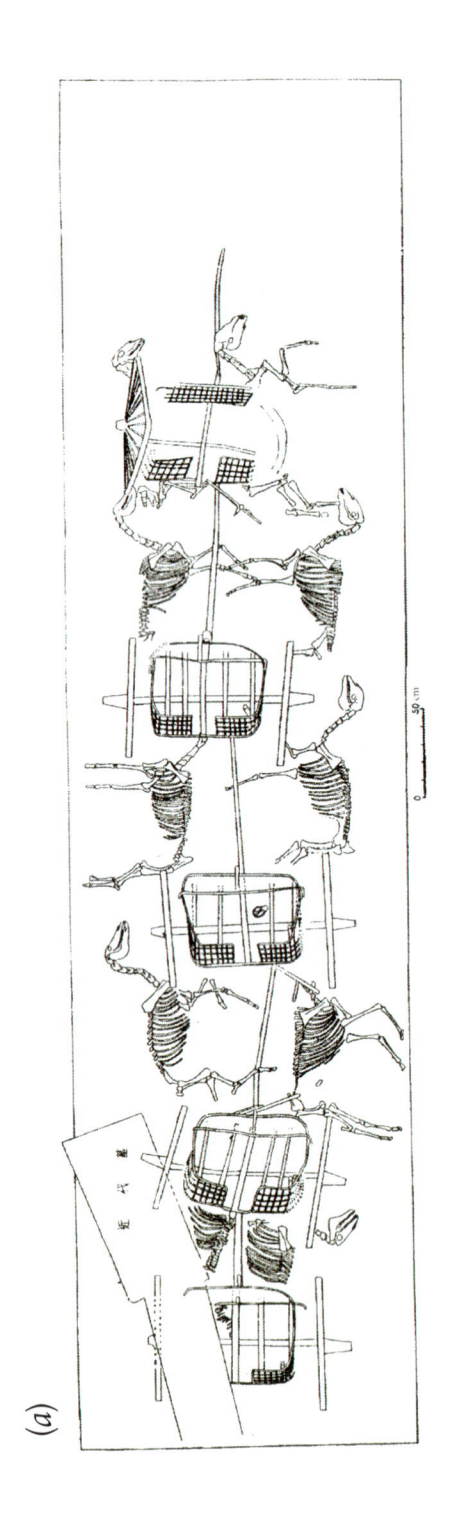

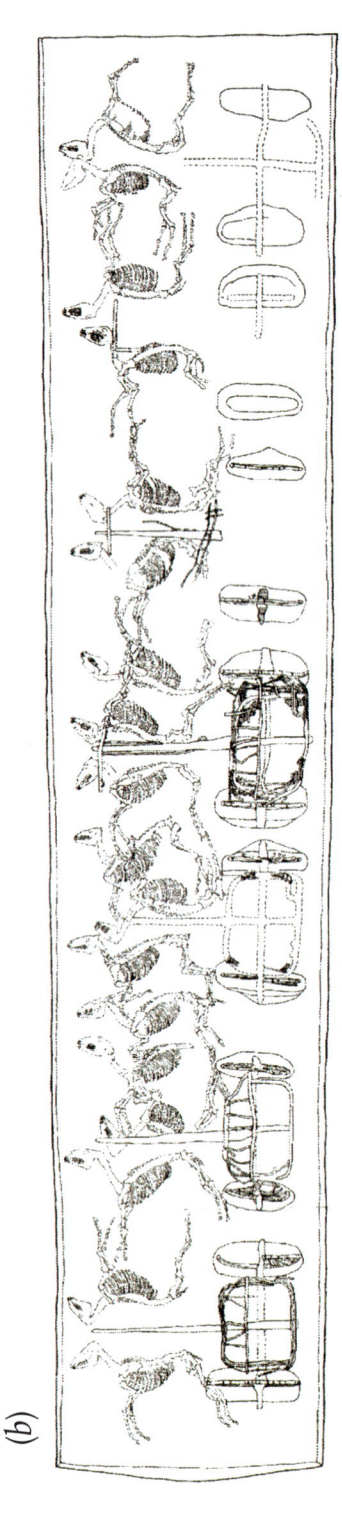

5.19 Burial pits containing only horses and chariots (a) Sanmenxia, Henan, eighth century BC; (b) Luogang, Yicheng, Henan, fourth century BC

5.20 One of the horse and chariot pits from the cemetery of Zheng-Han Gucheng at Xinzheng, Henan, Late Spring and Autumn period, sixth–fifth century BC

steppe from the Dnieper valley in the Pontic region to the Altai Mountains. Although there were many local differences—and regional sequences and local culture names abound in the archaeological literature—it is possible to divide the region into two cultural zones: the Srubnaya culture in the western steppe, west of the river Ural, and the Andronovo cultural complex extending eastwards from the river across the eastern steppe.

The Srubnaya culture is characterized by hundreds of small hamlets and villages scattered across the steppe, representing a return to a more settled lifestyle after the mobility of the Yamnaya period. It is a process that can be traced back to the last centuries of the third millennium and may have resulted from a change of climate bringing cooler and more arid conditions. Such a change probably encouraged the population to settle so as to be better able to control the winter pastures. Settlements were usually of family or extended family size and probably commanded pastures no further than 10–15 kilometres from the home base where the cattle, sheep, and horses could graze. Agriculture was not widely practised, especially east of the Don, but wild seeds, particularly *Chenopodium* (goosefoot), were collected to augment the diet.

The Andronovo archaeological complex of the eastern steppe, spread over a much larger region, was far more varied, but here, too, permanent settlement was the defining characteristic with hamlets and villages of up to two hundred people. Animal herding was dominant, but the composition of the flocks and herds varied from region to region. Agriculture was practised, but on a relatively small scale.

Throughout the entire region copper alloys were widely used. In the Srubnaya zone a vast mining centre had developed at Kargaly in the south Urals, and there were smaller copper mines in southern Samara. In the Andronovo zone copper was supplied largely from two mining centres, one at Uspensky in central Kazakhstan, the other in the southern Ulutan hills. Easy access to tin from the Zeravshan meant that most Andronovo metals were usually tin bronzes.

The very broad similarity of culture over a vast area of steppe, forest-steppe, and semi-desert during the Late Bronze Age was the result of many interacting factors: an increase in population bringing people into more regular contact, a degree of mobility conditioned by a pastoral economy, and complex networks of connectivity allowing copper and copper products to be distributed far and wide. These factors created a zone of cultural interactivity allowing ideas, belief systems, and behaviour patterns to be shared across the western and eastern steppe to a degree never before seen.

It is widely agreed that the change in climate was a prime cause of culture change in the steppe zone during the period from about 1200 to 700 BC. Overall the change was from a sub-boreal to a sub-Atlantic climate, but the stages were complex and would have affected different regions in different ways. However, as a generalization one can say that there were two broad stages to the overall direction of change. In the first, from the twelfth to the tenth century, humidity increased while the overall temperature decreased, while in the ninth and eighth centuries the humidity continued to increase while the temperature became significantly warmer. To understand the social effects of these changes we must consider the key regions in turn.

The Altai-Sayan region

The Altai-Sayan region is an upland area of complex geomorphology lying between the Kazakh steppe to the west and the Mongolian steppe to the east. In terms of modern geopolitics it sits astride southern Siberia and western Mongolia. The vegetation is conditioned largely by altitude. Much of the uplands and the mountain chains are covered with Alpine forests, but the lower plateaux, and in particular the river valleys, range from forest-steppe to more open grassy steppe. Culturally the

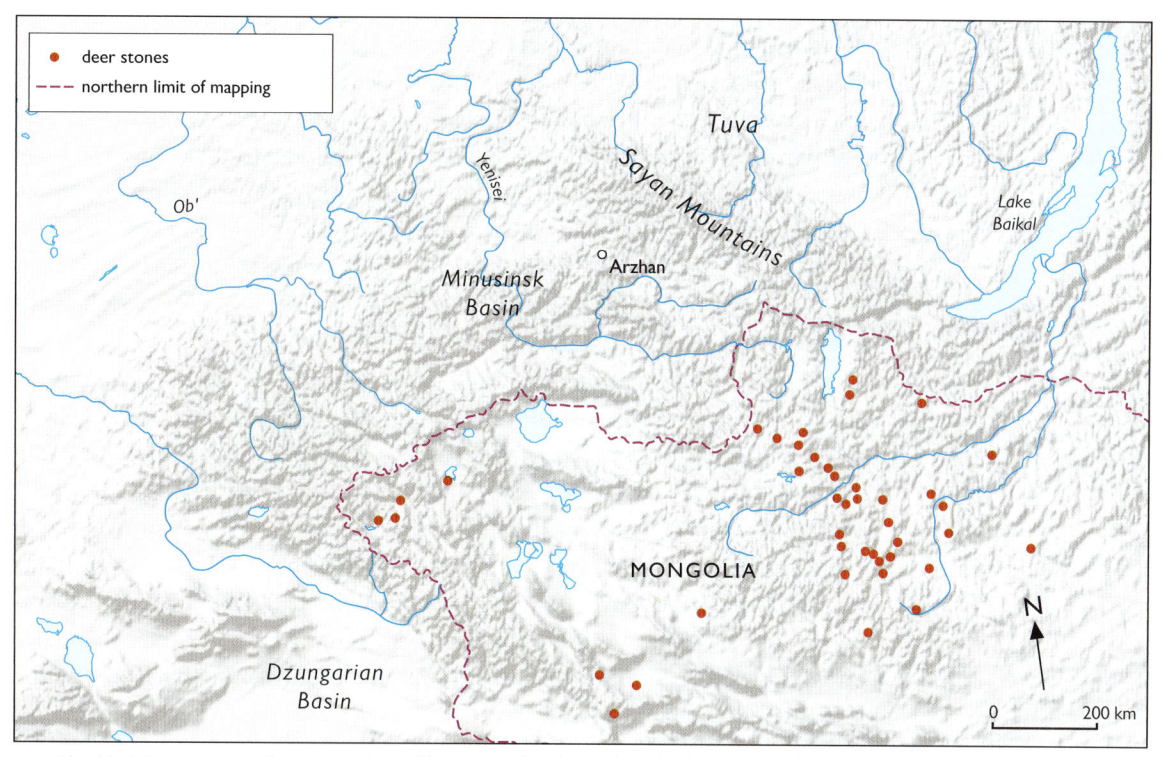

5.21 The Altai-Sayan region. The distribution of deer stones has been plotted only for Mongolia. Others are known in Siberia to the north

region can be divided into three zones: the Minusinsk basin, through which runs the river Yenisei, the Tuva region, and the western Mongolian steppe.

The best known of the regions is the Minusinsk basin, an isolated area of steppe surrounded by forested mountains. Here archaeologists have distinguished two phases in the cultural development of the indigenous community: the Karasuk culture, which arose from Andronovo origins about 1400 BC, and the subsequent Tagar culture, covering the period about 900–200 BC. The Karasuk phase coincided with the transition to a more humid and cooler climate leading to the spread of steppe at the expense of forest, and it is during this time that we can detect major changes in lifestyle from the relatively settled economy of the Andronovo stage to a more nomadic form of pastoralism, with segments of the communities beginning to use the high pasture of the mountainsides and the intermontane valleys. Larger flocks and herds were now managed and the horse became increasingly important for transport and riding. To facilitate this, metal cheek-pieces and bits were now introduced for the first time. Alongside these changes the population increased dramatically, one estimate suggesting that it may have multiplied by a factor of ten by the end of the Karasuk phase. This was probably largely the result of internal factors, but there may have been some inflow of people from the west. Another change, which becomes evident in the burial record, was the recognition of a male elite. The body was now usually accompanied by sacrificed animals together with copper alloy tools and weapons, including distinctive knives with the ends of the handles decorated with animal heads. Knives of this kind were to become popular across the Mongolian steppe and in China, where they were adopted by the Late Shang elites along with horse-drawn chariots.

In the ninth century climatic warming continued apace, leading to an improvement in, and expansion of, pasture. The much greater carrying capacity encouraged a further move towards a more pastoral economy. This heralded the beginning of the Tagar culture, which developed directly from the Karasuk phase. Many of the trends already under way now intensified. In the cemeteries elite burials are more frequently found, characterized by the size and elaboration of the burial mounds and the range of grave goods buried with the bodies, now placed in the timber-lined tomb chambers. One burial mound, at Bolshoy Salbyksky, was covered by a pyramidal mound 11 metres high, enclosed within a rectangular wall built of slabs, some of which weighed 50 tons apiece. The burial pit had been robbed and only a bronze knife and fragments of gold foil survived. A structure of this grandeur, involving immense labour, was meant to impress the observer with the power of the dead man and his lineage.

Grave goods were now more numerous and elaborate, reflecting a highly developed bronze-casting technology. They included the basic weapons, short daggers, shaft-hole battle-axes, and bronze arrowheads, together with bronze horse harness comprising bronze bits and cheek-pieces and decorative fittings for the harness straps. The frequent occurrence of horse-gear and the large number of petroglyphs depicting horses leaves little doubt that horse riding was now a socially important pursuit. Other grave goods include elaborate cast bronze cauldrons and various kinds of disc-shaped mirrors, some with handles decorated with animals.

While the items themselves are impressive, redolent of an assured culture firm in its traditions and beliefs and served by craftsmen of considerable skill and inventiveness, it is the emerging animal art style that particularly excites. The style is usually referred to as Scytho-Siberian and here, in the Tagar culture of the ninth and eighth centuries, we see its beginnings. Innovative castings depict a range of animals: deer, horses, boars, goats, preying felines, and fabulous griffins. Those not imagined are all carefully observed by a people who lived daily in the presence of animals: the horned goat standing, four feet together, on an eminence, and the resting horse with head in repose. But most characteristic are the stags, some with legs folded beneath them suggesting rest and antlers flowing wave-like along their backs, others leaping through the air. It was to become an image emblematic of Scytho-Siberian art across the length of the steppe from Mongolia to the Great Hungarian Plain.

The origin of this potent stag imagery lies in the Bronze Age culture of Mongolia's northern steppe and the southern Sayan foothills in the period 1300–700 BC. Here stag images are frequently found carved on tall standing stones, the famous deer stones, associated with a distinctive type of field monument known as khirigsuur mounds. The mounds are complex burial structures serving as the focus of ceremonies involving feasting and horse sacrifice. What part the deer stones played in these beliefs and rituals is uncertain, but some are clearly meant to represent human figures with belts and weapons, including swords, bows, daggers, and axes. The flying stags, so characteristic of many, may represent protective emblems carried by the warrior perhaps as tattoos, or may in some way be associated with the journey through life to the afterworld. The potency of the symbol is clearly evident in the later Pazyryk graves from the Altai (p. 238), where one of the dead elite was found to be heavily tattooed with a spirited representation of a flying stag. In the Mongolian steppe the deer stones represented the warrior. That human burials are rarely found here suggests that bodies may not have been buried but were disposed of in some other way, quite possibly by excarnation.

In the Tuva region of southern Siberia, by contrast, the elite were afforded elaborate burials, the best known of which come from a cemetery in Arzhan in the lush valley of the river Uyuk. Two tombs are of particular importance: Arzhan 1, dating to the ninth to early eighth century, and Arzhan 2, which dates to the late seventh century. Arzhan 1 comprised a burial pit and an elaborate surrounding log-built structure buried beneath a circular platform of stone boulders 100 metres in diameter and 3–4 metres high: it represents a colossal input of labour. A deer stone once stood on the platform. The central grave pit had been robbed, but sufficient remained to show that there were two bodies, a king and his consort, elaborately equipped with furs, gold, and turquoise ornaments and weapons including daggers, a battle-axe, and bronze arrowheads, a range of

5.22 Deer stone from Ushkin Uver, Hövsgöl Aimag, Mongolia, Late Bronze Age. The horizontal band towards the bottom represents the belt of the warrior who is commemorated. His weapons are depicted above and below the belt

horse harness, and a pair of bronze finials from poles or staves, topped with mountain rams typical of the Scytho-Siberian animal style. Around the central burial, in the compartments formed by the timber structure, were found the bodies of fifteen attendants who had presumably been killed for the occasion, and more than 160 saddled and bridled horses, all stallions and geldings, prime riding beasts, their decorated tack suggesting that they had been brought in from considerable distances, from the Minusinsk basin, the Altai, Kazakhstan, and Mongolia, quite possibly as tribute from neighbouring elites to honour the dead king and his lineage. The final stages of the funeral ceremony culminated in a vast feast, when hundreds of animals—cattle, sheep, goats, and horses—were slaughtered. It is estimated that three hundred horses were killed on this occasion. The feasting detritus was carefully buried beneath hundreds of small stone mounds around the great kurgan.

Arzhan 1 is a remarkable discovery, displaying something of the grandeur and elaboration of nomadic warrior society in the Altai-Sayan region around 800 BC. It is, above all, a monument to the mobility of the times when members of tribes from hundreds of kilometres away would come with gifts to the funeral of a great man to take part in the ceremonies that marked his passing. A burial of this kind would have been an occasion for social bonding, when alliances were agreed and treaties made, when those attending would compete for status through the quality of their gifts to the dead, and when the values and beliefs of the steppe community were reaffirmed. Arzhan 1 is the earliest known example of the type of complex burial ritual that was to become widespread across the whole of the steppe, typifying the culture of the predatory steppe nomad, with its emphasis on great leaders, the power of horse riders skilled with the bow, and with beliefs symbolized by the Scytho-Siberian style of animal art.

The second burial excavated in the Arzhan cemetery, Arzhan 2, dating to the late seventh century, was completely undisturbed. The principal burial of a man and a woman lay at the bottom of a rectangular timber-lined burial chamber. Both were dressed in garments sewn with gold plaques, mostly depicting predatory beasts. They wore headdresses covered with gold plaques representing horses, stags, and panthers. Other embellishments included a massive gold torc, a golden pectoral, and beads and pendants of gold, turquoise, and amber. Among the grave goods were a bronze mirror, leather vessels containing grain, a bow and a quiver of arrows, an iron short-sword, knives, and a battle-axe. It was an astonishing ensemble of riches, vividly demonstrating the continuing prominence of the Tuva region in the nomadic culture of the steppe.

5.23 (*Opposite*) Plan and section of the late ninth-century warrior's tomb (tomb 1) at Arzhan, Tuva, Siberia. The elite warrior and his consort were buried in the central timber-built chamber. Sacrificed horses were buried within the surrounding log-built structure

0 50 m

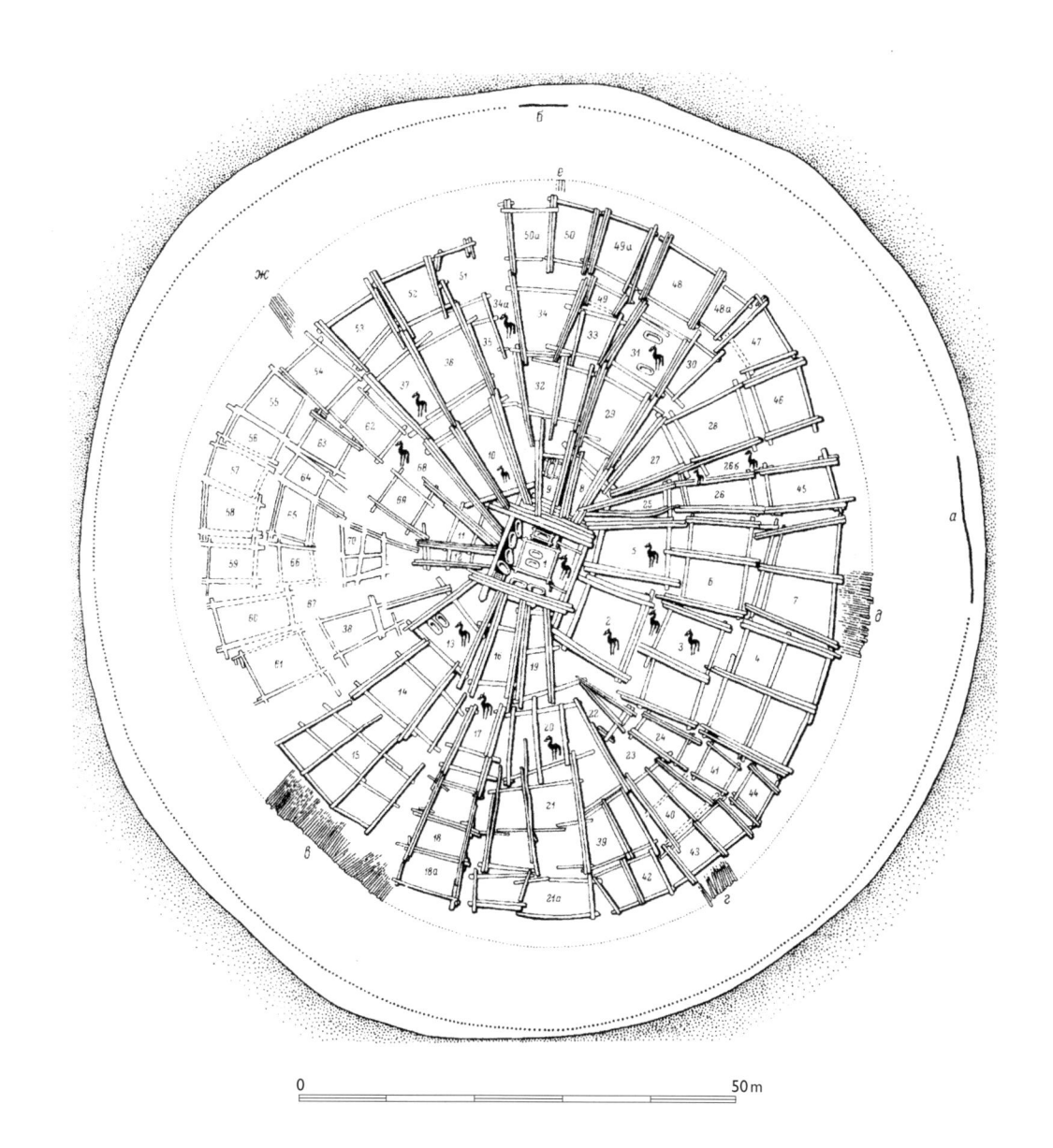

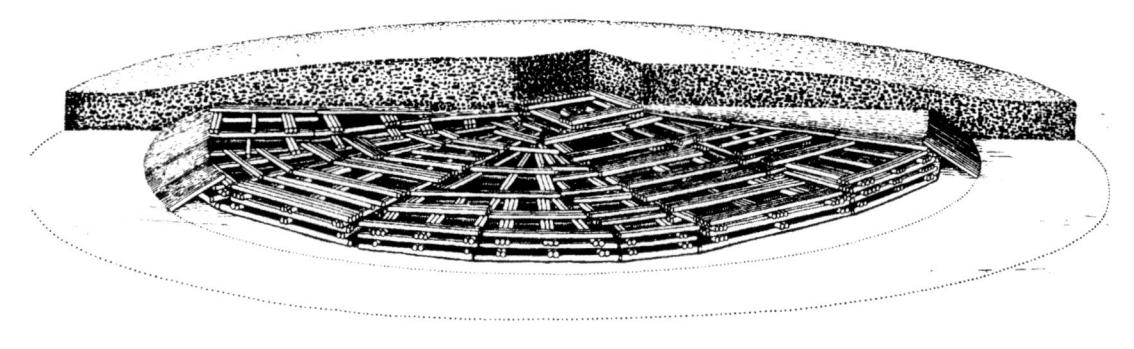

The discoveries at Arzhan and the recent archaeological work in the Minusinsk basin and on the Mongolian steppe have completely revolutionized our understanding of steppe culture in the early first millennium BC. Previously it was dominated by the archaeology of the Scythians, who lived in the Pontic steppe region and were described by the Greek historian Herodotus in the late sixth century. The discoveries in the Altai-Sayan region suggest that the origin and spread of the kind of predatory nomadism of which the Pontic Scythians are an example is a far more complex process than originally believed and had its roots in the eastern steppe region. This is an issue to which we shall return (pp. 196–8).

The Nomads of the Pontic-Caspian Steppe

We have already seen that in the latter part of the second millennium BC the Pontic-Caspian steppe was occupied by pastoral communities settled in hundreds of small farmsteads or hamlets to the east of the river Dnieper. These are referred to as the Srubnaya culture, while similar settlements to the west of the river are known as the Sabatinovka culture, but really there is little significant difference. The climatic changes that were affecting the whole of Eurasia in the twelfth and eleventh centuries BC began to give rise to more arid conditions in the Pontic steppe region. These changes, combined perhaps with the over-exploitation of traditional pastures, led to a change in economic strategies with a greater emphasis now being placed on semi-nomadic and nomadic pastoralism and a marked decline in permanent settlements. This phase is known archaeologically as the Belozerka culture. In some areas, particularly the steppe between the Dnieper and Dniester, the surviving inhabitants seem to have taken up a nomadic lifestyle dependent upon cattle herding, while those occupying more favourable niches, in the Dnieper valley and in the coastal region and the Danube delta area, remained more dependent on crop growing. It was between the two rivers that nomadic pastoralists known to Homer and Herodotus as Cimmerians are thought to have arisen.

Homer tells us little about the Cimmerians, saying only that the ships of the Greek heroes in the Black Sea were drawn to 'the frontiers of the world, where fog-bound

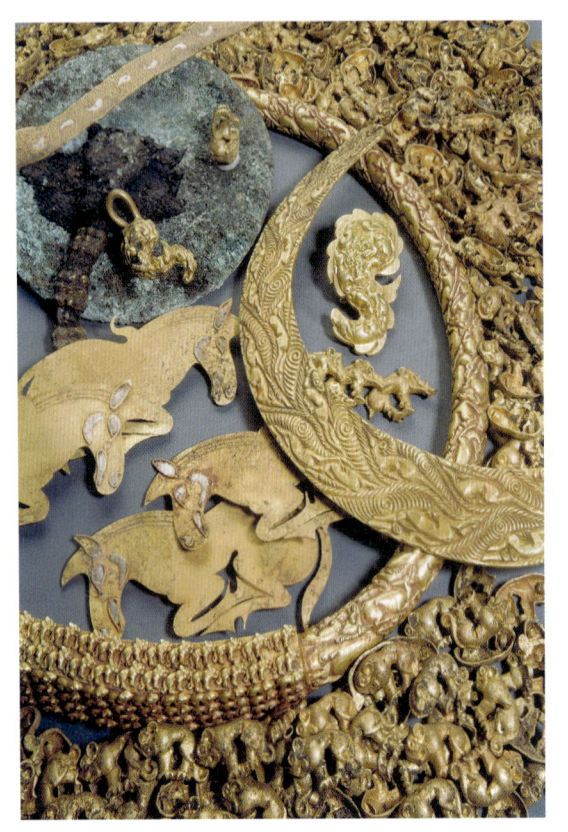

5.24 Burial 2 of Arzhan, Tuva, was completely undisturbed when excavated in 2000–1. It produced an array of gold decorative work, much of it once sewn onto fabrics worn by the deceased. The burial dates to the second half of the seventh century BC

Cimmerians live in the City of Perpetual Mist'. But Herodotus, writing in the fifth century, is a little more informative. He learnt from his informants that the land formerly occupied by the Cimmerians was now held by the Scythians, who had arrived from somewhere to the east of the Volga. There had been dissent among the Cimmerians, leading to internal conflict, and some had migrated, leaving an empty land for the Scythians to occupy (*Histories* 4.11). Some of the migrating Cimmerians had moved southwards, following the coast of the Black Sea, into Asia Minor.

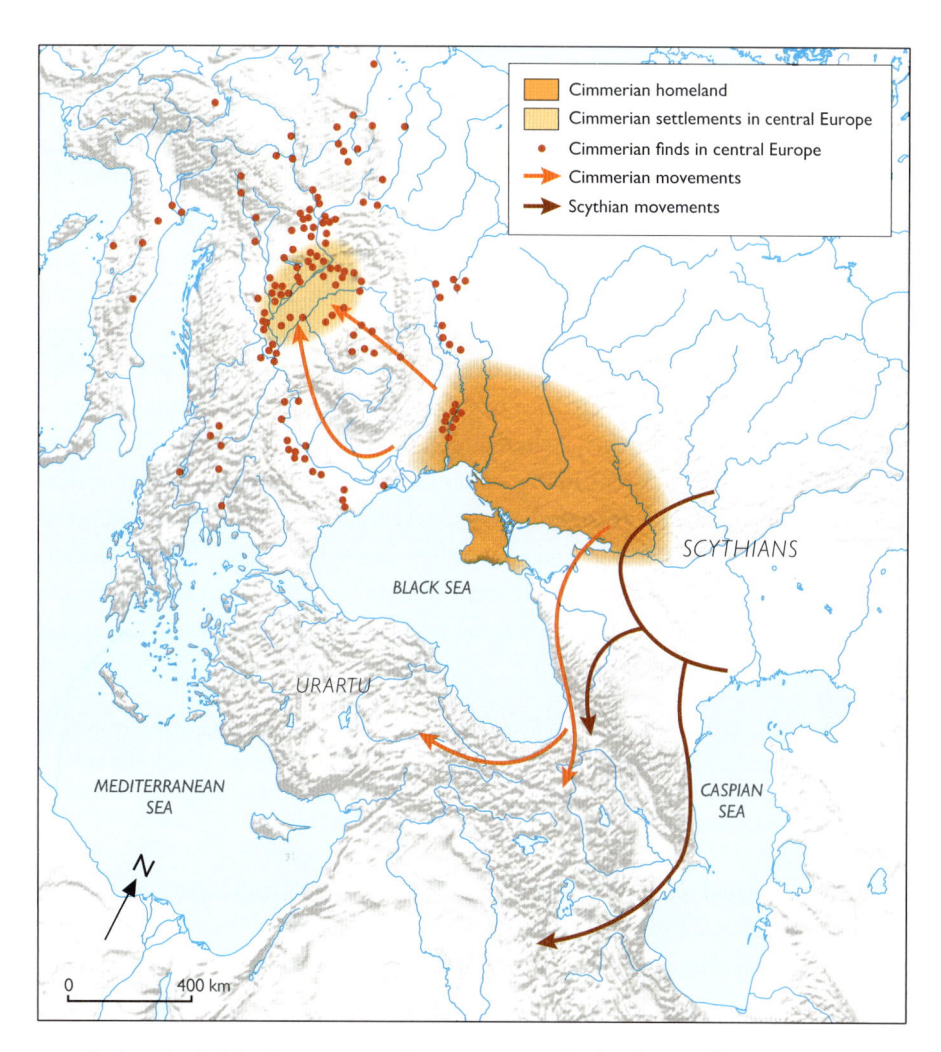

5.25 The homeland of the Cimmerians on the Pontic steppe. The distribution of Cimmerian-style finds in central Europe (mainly horse-gear) indicate the extent of Cimmerian influence on the west through raiding and trading

The archaeological evidence shows that these events took place over time between the tenth and eight centuries with the people moving into more congenial ecological niches. Some moved to the Dnieper forest-steppe zone, some to the Crimean peninsula, and others to the North Caucasus. There was also a westerly movement into Europe through the Carpathians and along the lower Danube valley into the Great Hungarian Plain. The settlers in Hungary are easily recognizable through their material culture (here known as the Mezőcsát culture). The burials were always inhumed, in contrast to the indigenous cremations, and were often accompanied by animal offerings and bronze horse-gear. No doubt these pioneers, still maintaining contacts with the Pontic steppe, were responsible for importing riding horses from the steppe to trade with their European neighbours. The distribution of distinctive Cimmerian-style horse-gear in eastern and northern Europe is an indication of the extent to which the steppe horses were drawn into the European sphere.

The Cimmerian horsemen who moved south-eastwards along the Black Sea coast and from there into Anatolia reappear in Assyrian sources as the Gimirrai, serving as mercenaries fighting in the wars between the Assyrians and the kingdom of Urartu, whose capital, Tushpa, was on Lake Van. The first mention of Gimirrai is in the reign of Sargon II (721–705 BC) when his son Sennacherib records in a letter dated 707 BC that the king of Urartu has been defeated in battle by the Gimirrai. Nothing more is heard of this until 677 BC when Ashurhaddon claimed to have killed a Cimmerian king and decimated his troops in the west, now Cilicia. Cimmerian threats against Cilicia continued, and in the 650s Lydia was attacked. It was finally overcome in 652 BC when the capital, Sardis, was taken and the king, Gyges, was killed. The Cimmerians also make an appearance in the Old Testament as the 'children of Gomar', one of the northern tribes sent by God to punish the people of Israel. The prophet Jeremiah conjures up the terrifying threat:

> I [the Lord] am bringing up a distant nation against you ... Their quivers are like an open grave ... Look, an army is coming from the land of the north ... They are armed with bow and spear, they are cruel and show no mercy. They sound like the roaring seas as they ride on their horses.

From these isolated scraps it is clear that mobile bands of Cimmerians were active in Anatolia from the end of the eighth century and maintained their ethnic identity until the seventh century, after which they became absorbed into the mêlée of competing polities.

The predatory nomads who moved into the Pontic steppe after the departure of the Cimmerians were known to Herodotus as Scythians. They had, he believed, come from beyond the Volga, from somewhere in Central Asia. The archaeological

NOMADS AND EMPIRES

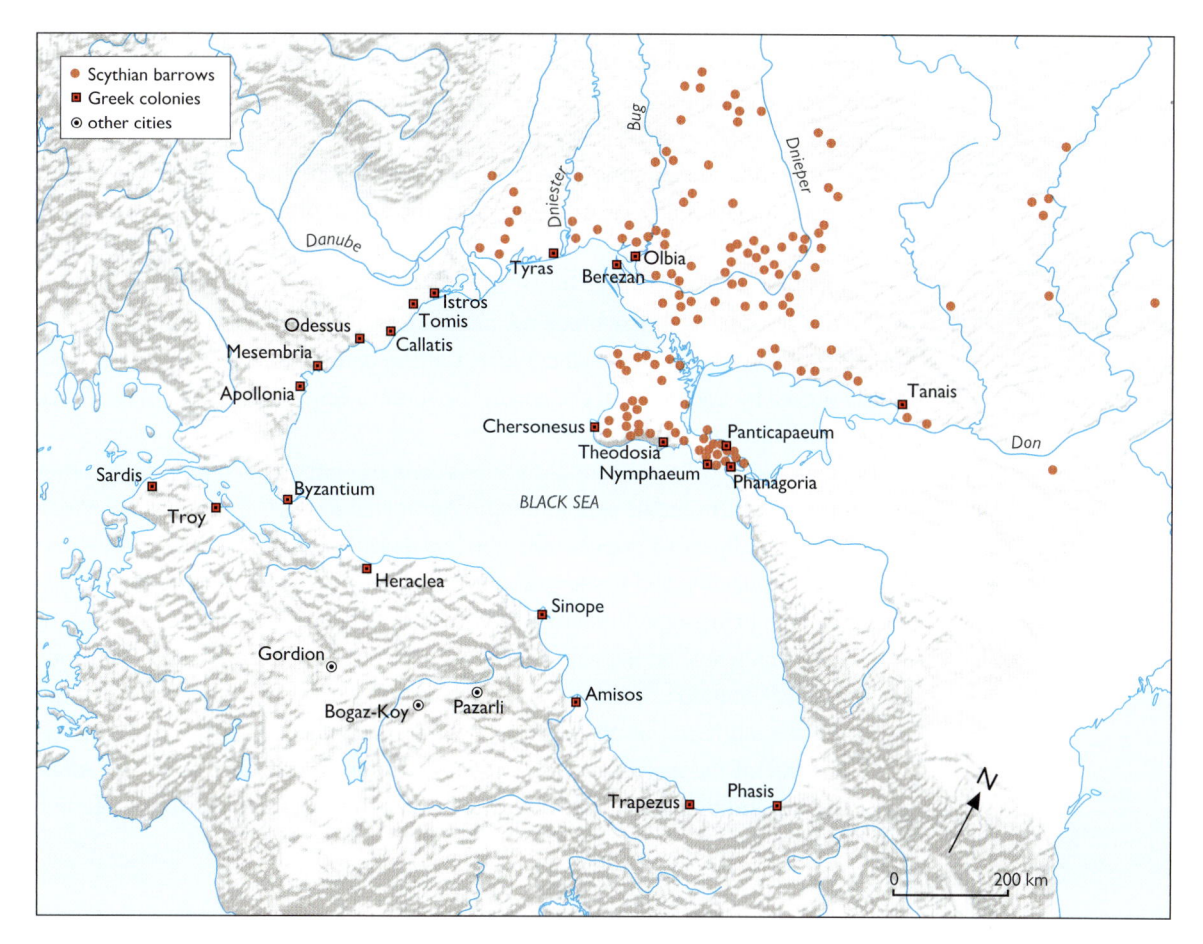

5.26 The distribution of Scythian barrows on the Pontic steppe defines the extent of Scythian territory from the seventh to the fifth century BC. The Greek colonies around the north shores of the Black Sea were centres where trade between the steppe communities and the Greek world was articulated

evidence shows that the earliest Scythian burials, dating from the mid-eighth to the fifth centuries, were scattered across the steppe between the Don and the Danube with particular concentrations in the Kuban region north of the Caucasus, the valley of the Dnieper, on the Crimean peninsula, and along the coastal steppe as far west as the lower Danube. This defined what was to remain of their homeland until the end of the third century. We shall consider the culture of the Scythians later (pp. 196–8), but here we must say more of the migratory movements that brought these nomads to their final homeland.

The settlement in the Pontic zone to the west of the Don and in the Kuban was only part of a more expansive movement which also saw some bands of migrant nomads moving down through the Caucasus into eastern Anatolia. One branch of this southerly migration, according to Herodotus (*Histories* 4.2), chose the route along the west shore of the Caspian sea, the traditional route through Azerbaijan, and set up a powerful kingdom in Asia Minor, from where they involved themselves in various conflicts in the Near East, even to the extent of threatening Egypt. They are first mentioned in the Assyrian records in 677 BC, taking part in a local rebellion in Mannai in eastern Anatolia. It was here, benefiting from the extensive pastures of the region, ideal for horse breeding, that they established their main bases. They remained involved in many local conflicts until, according to Herodotus, they were finally ousted by the Medes at the end of the seventh century and were driven back across the Caucasus to the steppe.

The archaeological record and the various contemporary texts support each other in identifying two nomadic peoples on the Pontic steppe: the Cimmerians, who may have been an indigenous population, who had developed a mobile way of life dominated by horse riding and herding, and the Scythians, an intrusive nomadic people from the east, bringing with them a distinctive elite cultural package including not only horse riding but also a highly effective form of mounted archery and a vigorous animal art originating in the eastern steppe region. The Cimmerians dominated the region in the tenth and ninth centuries, while the Scythians seem to have arrived in the middle of the eighth century. How, then, can the evidence from the Altai-Sayan region and that of the Pontic steppe be brought together in a single cohesive narrative?

Who Were the Scythians?

For much of the twentieth century the debate about the Scythians was dominated by the descriptions and opinions offered by Herodotus in his famous *Histories*, written at the end of the fifth century BC. These we shall consider in the next chapter. Herodotus thought it most likely that the Scythians had moved into the Pontic steppe region 'from Asia' and that they were one of many similar nomadic pastoralists found extending across the steppe and desert fringes eastwards towards the Altai: peoples including the Sauromatae, living at the time between the Don and the Volga, and the Massagetae, east of the Aral Sea.

The Scythians were given spectacular archaeological reality by grave goods found during the excavation of their elite burials scattered across the Pontic steppe and in the Kuban region. One aspect that particularly caught the attention of observers at the beginning of the twentieth century was the energetic animal art used in various forms of decoration. Stylistic similarities with indigenous art styles in southern

Siberia led to it being called Scytho-Siberian art, the implication being that Scythian culture was in some way influenced by events in Siberia. The discovery of elaborate nomadic burials at Pazyryk in the Altai Mountains in the 1930s and later at Arzhan in the Tuva region gave new focus to the debate, and it has become conventional in the Russian literature to describe all these cultures as Scythian and to divide the time span covered into three phases: a pre-Scythian and initial Scythian period dating from the ninth to mid-seventh century; an early Scythian period from the mid-seventh to the end of the sixth century; and a classical Scythian period covering the fifth to the third century.

The first phase, which can more conveniently be called the formative stage, includes the Tagar culture of the Altai-Sayan region and the two burials at Arzhan, which, as we have seen, are the result of local developments from the indigenous Karasuk culture. It was in this region that horse-riding nomadism developed, associated with archery and with Scytho-Siberian art styles. Since this distinctive package does not appear in the Pontic steppe until the late eighth century, a logical interpretation would be to argue that 'Scythian' culture originated in the Altai-Sayan in the ninth century and spread westwards, reaching the Pontic steppe during the next century. If this scenario is correct—and it broadly conforms to the views of Herodotus—then we have to accommodate the fact that predatory nomadism, practised by the Cimmerians, may already have been under way in the Pontic region, possibly even as early as the ninth century, before the Scythians arrived.

There is much detail still to be resolved, not least the need for a concerted programme of radiocarbon dating, but the picture that is emerging leaves little doubt that predatory nomadic pastoralism spread very quickly across the steppe from the tenth to the ninth centuries BC. Society was now far more mobile, with warrior-herders offering allegiance to powerful leaders not necessarily from their own tribes and prepared to follow them on raids extending over great distances. In this way the steppe pastoralists were swept up in a new mobility. With status determined by the success of the raid there would have been an imperative for warrior hordes to raid unrestrained, no longer bound by the need to care for flock and herds. Such forces could find gainful employment as mercenaries in the tangled conflicts of the Near East. Behind it all lay the impetus for constant movement inherent in life on the steppe.

In such an atmosphere of rapid social readjustment, with the rise of charismatic leaders fuelling a restless mobility, it is easy to see how populations could move quickly across great tracts of land. There is nothing inconsistent in supposing that segments of the Altai-Sayan community moved westwards, with some of them calling themselves Scythians, eventually settling down in the congenial Pontic region.

These large-scale predatory movements to the west were to become a feature of steppe life, culminating in the invasion of the Mongols in the thirteenth century AD.

Steppe Culture and the Western Sedentary States, 800–600 BC

Around the entire southern fringes of the nomadic zone well-established states confronted their mobile neighbours. We have already seen how, during the seventh century, Cimmerians and Scythians were active in the Near East, participating in various alliances with the competing polities. It was Scythians who, with the Medes and Babylonians, helped to destroy the Assyrian capital of Nineveh in 612 BC, bringing to an end the Assyrian empire. But such dangerous allies could not be tolerated for long, and as the power of the Medes grew, the nomads were driven back beyond the Caucasus. In the centuries to follow, the Medes and the Persians were to take a more aggressive stance against the nomadic communities of the desert-steppe of Central Asia.

Another interface where nomads confronted state polities was around the shores of the Black Sea, where in the eighth century BC the Greeks began to develop an entrepreneurial interest. The earliest formal Greek colonies were founded on the southern Anatolian shore at Sinope and Trapezus (now Trebizond) towards the middle of the eighth century at a time when the Greek cities, particularly Miletus, were sending expeditions to explore the coasts and estuaries of the Black Sea and the Sea of Azov. The seventh century saw colonial settlements established along the west coast of Thrace at Histria, just south of the Danube delta, at Berezan on a promontory or island close to the estuary of the river Bug, and on the coast of Asia Minor, where a colony was set up at Amisos between Sinope and Trapezus. Exploration also focused on the approach to the Sea of Azov. Greek pottery of the late seventh century has been found as far north as the estuary of the Don, close to where the city of Tanais was later to be founded. A new wave of settlement in the sixth century saw the foundation of Olbia, close to Berezan, and colonies on the Kerch and Taman peninsulas guarding the approach to the Sea of Azov. Further colonies filling in some of the gaps were still being set up in the later sixth century.

The motives behind the establishment of the Greek Black Sea colonies were many, ranging from personal ambition, the desire to escape from oppressive regimes at home, and the relief of population pressures by colonizing new ecological niches, to the simple commercial imperative of setting up potentially lucrative ports of trade on the interface of the vast and productive Pontic steppe hinterland. In exchange for wine and manufactured goods the entrepreneur could acquire cereals, furs, fish, and probably slaves—all much needed in the cities of the Greek homeland. The colonies were not part of a land grab by an expansionist state but commercial enclaves maintaining close trading links to their founding cities. As such they were little threat to the indigenous Scythians, and the two communities could coexist, for the most part in harmony, to the benefit of both. Over the centuries the frontier interface developed a distinctive hybrid culture.

Nomads and the Chinese States, 800–600 BC

At the other end of Eurasia the nomads confronted a very different kind of sedentary society, that of the competing polities of China during the Spring and Autumn period of the Eastern Zhou. We have already seen that by the Late Shang period, from 1200 BC, active links had been established between the elites of the Central Plains and the nomads of the Mongolian steppe, from which regions the concept of the horse-drawn chariot had been introduced together with a flow of people with the technical skills needed to build the vehicles, to train the horses, and to drive them. The popularity of the chariot throughout the period suggests that the links between the northern nomads and the states of the Central Plains were continuously maintained. Other items of steppe origin were accepted into Chinese culture at this time, including the curved knives with loop terminals to the handles decorated with animals frequently found with the chariot burials. These have their origin in the Late Bronze Age culture of the steppe region. So, too, do circular bronze mirrors with loop handles attached to the centre of the back. Mirrors of this kind originate in Andronovo culture of Central Asia and are found regularly in the Karasuk culture of the Altai-Sayan region. From here they reached Xinjiang and are also found in royal graves of the Shang period at Anyang, arriving either as gifts from the north or in the possession of members of the northern elite, who may have married into the leading Shang families. No doubt Chinese-made gifts, like the silk fabrics found in later Altai burials, were offered in return. More tangible are the Chinese cast bronze helmets that found their way into the hands of nomadic groups, some of them distributed as far as the Pontic steppe, where five were found in the Scythian burial at Kelermes. Items of this kind reflect not only the cycles of gift giving practised by the Zhou and their northern neighbours, but also the vast extent of the exchange networks now binding the entire steppe zone.

Relationships between the Shang and Zhou states of the Central Plains and central and northern Asia were managed across an arc of territory known as the Northern Zone stretching from the river Liao across the Inner Mongolian Plateau and the Ordos region, within the great bend of the Yellow River, to the upper reaches of that river. It was a zone of varied landscapes, of steppe, desert, and fertile land, support-

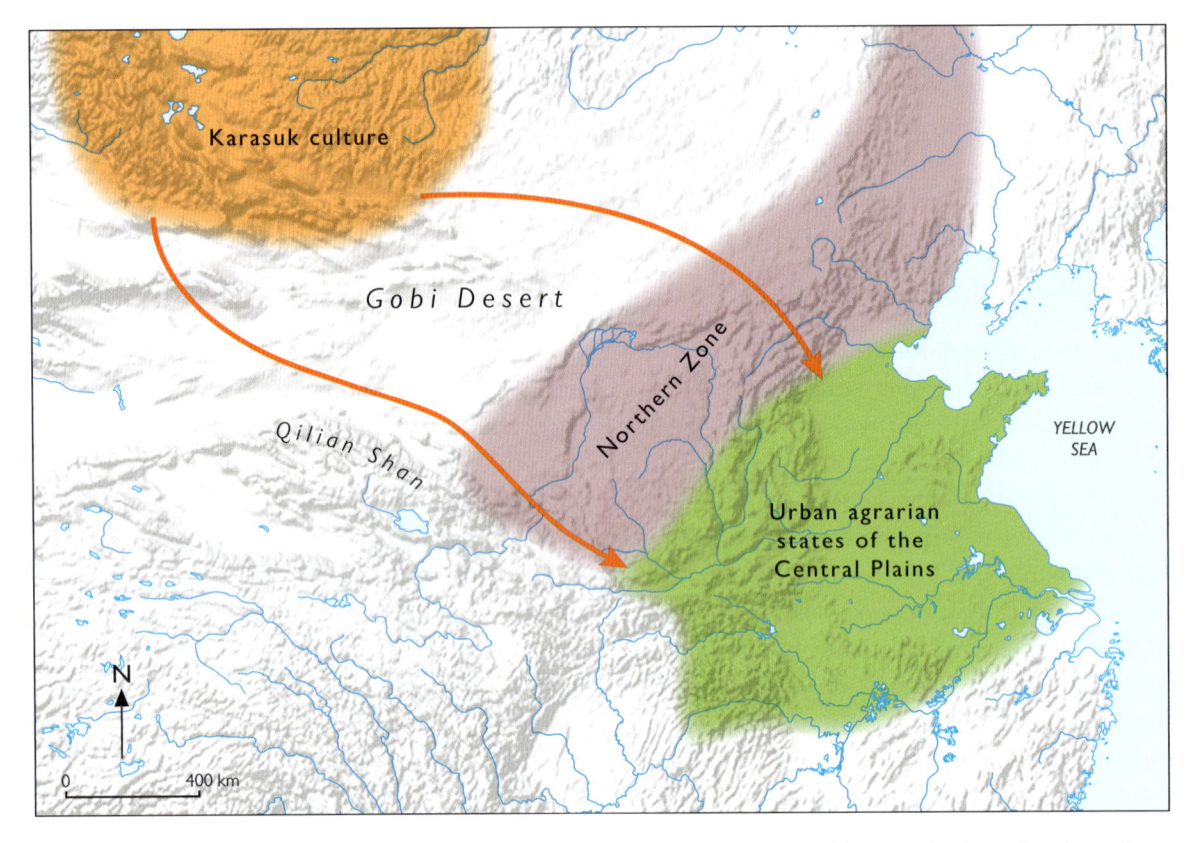

5.27 Early in the first millennium BC the horse-riding nomads of the Karasuk culture of southern Siberia and western Mongolia were in contact with the urban agrarian states of the Chinese Central Plains. Two principal routes were in use: the desert route to the south and the steppe route to the north

ing a variety of cultural groups practising differing economies, including sedentary agriculture. This zone was to serve as both a link and a filter for contacts between the Chinese states and the steppe nomads to the north-west.

Over time significant changes can be detected in the Northern Zone. By the tenth century, although composed of distinct cultural groups, the population shared a common metallurgical tradition derived from the north-west and characterized by daggers, axes, mirrors, and the beginnings of animal-style ornamentation. In the ninth century there was a move to a more pastoral economy, the increased use of horses and the prevalence of horse sacrifices, and the appearance of weapon sets including daggers, spears, arrows, shields, and helmets. Together these changes suggest the spread of a militaristic nomadic pastoralism. From the sixth century, especially in the Ordos and the region east of the Taihang Shan, the characteristics of

Scythian-style culture begin to appear: horse riding, archery, and Siberian animal art style. While the observed changes were no doubt the result of many factors, the prime cause seems to have been a change to more arid climatic conditions encouraging mounted pastoralists to move into the Northern Zone from the north-west. These movements took place over time, putting increasing pressure on the indigenous semi-nomadic populations. By the seventh century the pressures were such that the southward movement of displaced peoples began to impact on the Zhou states, initiating a new set of relationships between Zhou and non-Zhou. Arm's-length diplomatic exchange, military attack, conquest, and incorporation were all tried in different measure. The last attempt at a solution, the building of the Great Wall, was still some centuries away.

Nomads and Empires

The thousand years between 1600 and 600 BC can be simply characterized. In the Near East and in China the complex sedentary polities moved uncertainly and with much faltering towards the creation of empires. In the west, with Assyrian domination in the period 900–600 BC, this was achieved. In China progress was less assured, and the breakdown in the centralizing power in the early eighth century led to six centuries of inter-state rivalry before any degree of unity could be achieved.

On the steppe there was a spectacular transformation. Already intricate networks of connectivity had been established, linking the many different cultures across the vast region. But in the tenth and ninth centuries a totally new form of pastoral nomadism emerged, focused on warrior leaders able to command multi-ethnic contingents of mounted archers. This social phenomenon spread rapidly across the steppe, characterized by weapon sets, an animal art style, and highly distinctive belief systems most clearly manifest in elite burial rites. On present evidence the innovating centre of this development seems to have lain within the Altai-Sayan, and its impact was soon experienced as far afield as the Pontic steppe in the west and the Northern Zone of China in the east. Since raiding was an essential feature of this social system, we may fairly call it predatory nomadism. Both the Assyrians and the Eastern Zhou states experienced the impact of raiding nomads, at its height during the seventh century. The scene is now set for a long period of interaction between the nomadic and the sedentary worlds, a major theme in the narrative of the next two thousand years.

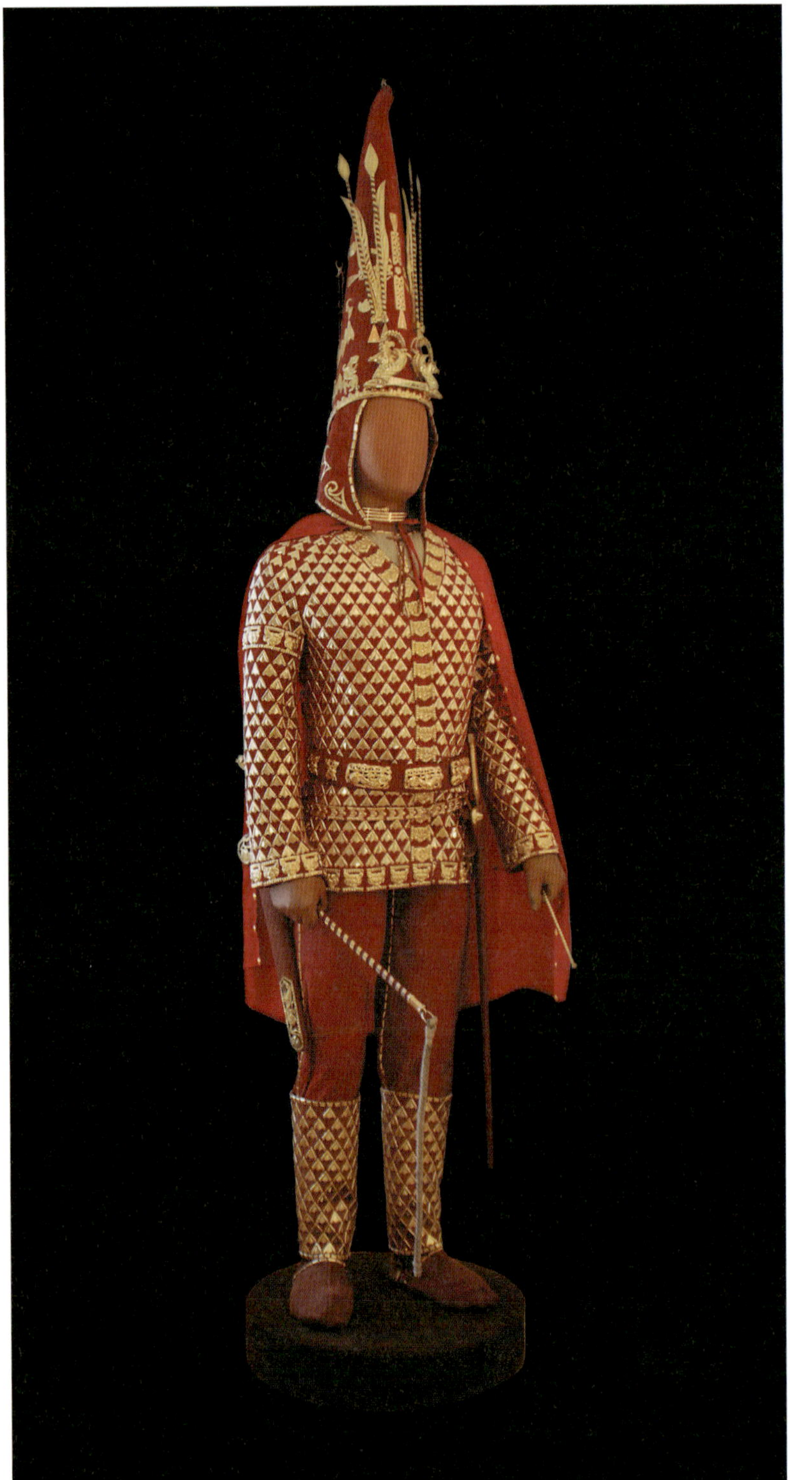

6

LEARNING FROM EACH OTHER

INTERACTION ALONG THE INTERFACE, 600–250 BC

During the three hundred and fifty years reviewed in this chapter three regions of state development, Greece and Macedonia, the Persian empire, and the Warring States of China, came into direct contact with the nomad world. The interaction varied from frontier to frontier and over time, but for all sides the contact brought lasting change.

In the west the city states of Greece consolidated their colonies around the shores of the Black Sea and established new enclaves wherever opportunity arose, but there were no aggressive land grabs. This was a settlement of consent, with the colonies articulating trade for the benefit of both the Greeks and the nomads. For several centuries the system worked reasonably well, but changes in nomadic society gradually eroded Greek influence except around the Sea of Azov, where the descendants of the Greek colonists banded together for mutual protection and developed a resilient confederacy, the kingdom of the Bosporus.

The Persian empire took a far more aggressive stance from the beginning, campaigning far to the north of the Iranian plateau across the Karakum and Kyzylkum deserts to the Syr Darya (or Jaxartes), incorporating these vast territories as provinces of the empire. But this was an unstable region, as Alexander was to find out when he installed himself as the ruler of the Persian empire. It was perhaps because of this that Alexander and his successors established new cities in the region, populating them with Greeks. When the empire began to fragment after 300 BC, the easternmost regions of Bactria and Gandhara remained outposts of Hellenism for many generations to come.

Throughout this period China was in the thrall of incessant warfare as individual states fought each other for ascendancy. The northern frontier with the nomads remained an unstable region, but by about 300 BC a series of 'long walls' built across nomad territory formed a physical boundary between the two worlds, allowing the Chinese to regulate their engagements with the northern peoples.

While these three regional scenarios were playing out, the world of the mounted nomads, stretching from Mongolia to the Great Hungarian Plain, was being driven by its own internal dynamics. The very nature of the mobile and predatory nomad society encouraged movement, often over huge distances. The intensity and range of these movements created broad cultural similarities, not only in style of burial and weapon sets, but in the intriguing animal art that encapsulated belief systems and spread across the breadth of Eurasia.

The Rise of the Persian Empire

The sack of Nineveh by the Medes and Babylonians in 612 BC brought the Assyrian empire to an end. For the next sixty years Babylonia assumed control of Mesopotamia and the Levantine coastal states, while the Medes extended their power westwards into Anatolia. While these events were in progress, a new power, that of the Persians, was growing to the south of the Zagros Mountains, south-west of the state of Elam, in the Iranian province of Fars. The Persians traced their dynastic origins back to King Achaemenes, who ruled in the seventh century, whence came the name Achaemenids, frequently used to refer to Persians.

In 559 BC Cyrus (soon to be known as Cyrus the Great) came to power, and in 550 BC he seized the moment to defeat the Median ruler, taking over the capital Ecbatana (now Hamadan) and with it the whole of the Median territory in Anatolia. Three years later, campaigning in the extreme west of Anatolia, he defeated King Croesus of Lydia and reached the Greek colonial enclaves on the Aegean coast. The next six years, 546–540 BC, were spent campaigning in the east, gaining control over the Iranian plateau. With his power base established and his army well tried, it was time to confront the state of Babylonia. The task was accomplished with little difficulty. When the city of Babylon was taken in 539, the large Jewish population, who had been exiled there by the Babylonians in 587 BC, was sent back to their homeland, thus winning Cyrus

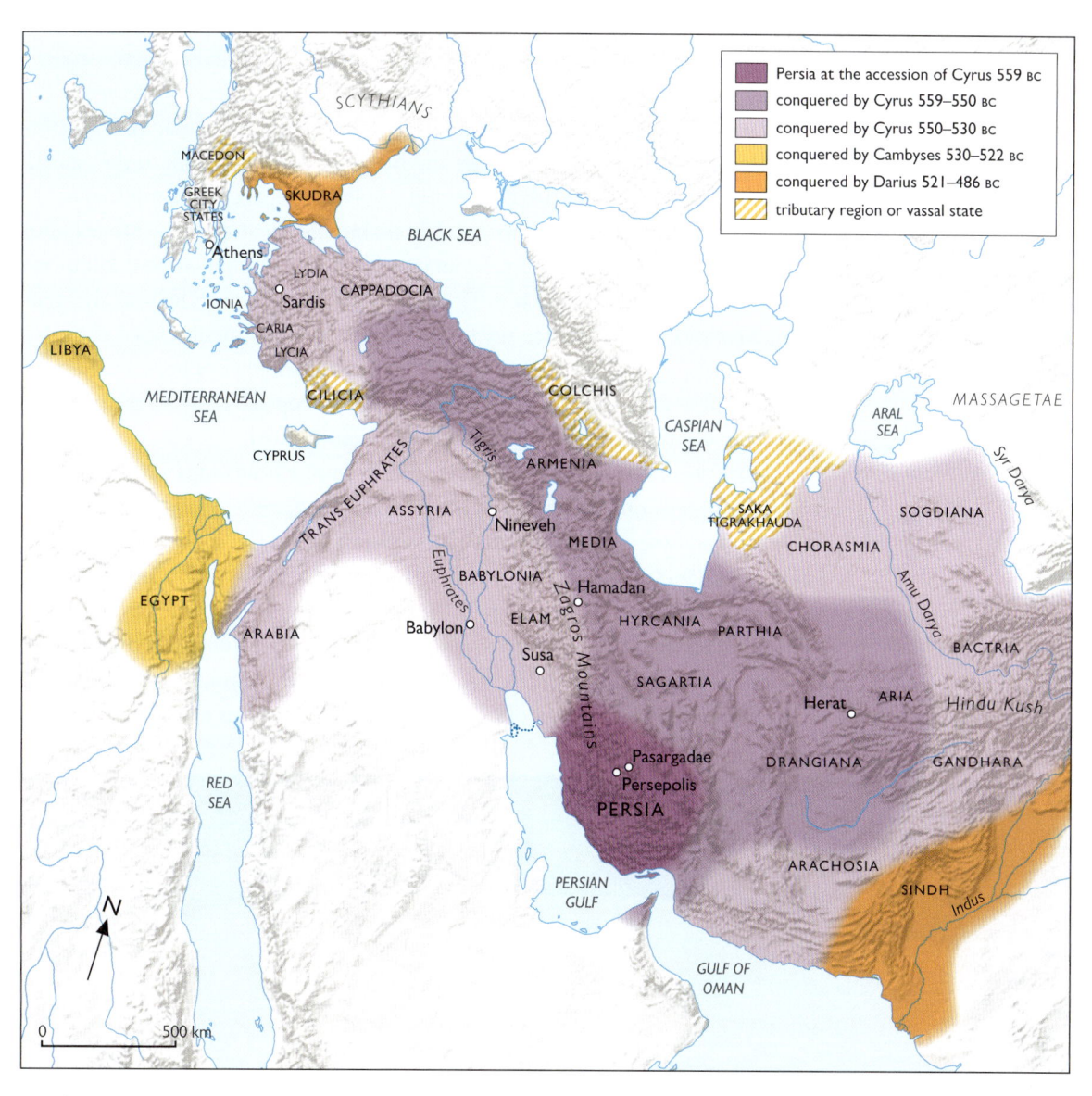

6.1 The growth of the Persian empire 559–480 BC

many friends in the Levant. The last years of his energetic reign were spent campaigning northwards from the Iranian plateau across the Kyzylkum and Karakum deserts to the Syr Darya, where, on the south bank, he established a series of forts to confront the nomadic Massagetae occupying the steppe beyond. The newly acquired land became the provinces of Margiana, Bactria, Sogdiana, and Gandhara. Between the

205

LEARNING FROM EACH OTHER

western branches of the Amu Darya (or Oxus) and the Caspian Sea he confronted another group of nomads, the Sakas, annexing some of their territory to create the Persian province of Chorasmia. It was during this campaign in 530 BC that, according to Herodotus, Cyrus died in battle and his body was taken back to the capital, Pasargadae, there to be buried in a tomb still surviving, elegant in its simplicity.

Little is known in detail about these advances into the territory of the nomads, but the Persian empire was now in direct contact with the steppe along a 1,600-kilometre frontier. However unstable the frontier zone may have been over the next two centuries, there was ample opportunity for the exchange of commodities and ideas. No doubt the steppe provided the Persians with constant supplies of horses, while the nomads absorbed into their own art styles motifs developed by Persian craftsmen. It was a creative interchange for the two very different cultures.

In a mere twenty years Cyrus had created a vast empire stretching from the Aegean coast to the edge of the Indus valley. Further conquests were to follow when in 525 BC his son Cambyses (ruled 529–522 BC) conquered Egypt. The conquest was further extended under Darius I (ruled 521–486 BC) with the addition of Libya and the establishment of a tribute relationship with Nubia to the south of Egypt, whence came gold and other luxuries in plenty. The succession of Darius following the death of Cambyses was not without problems. A contender for the throne, Gaumata, seized power in Persia, and a number of the newly conquered regions rebelled, but Darius

6.2 The Cyrus Cylinder. The cylinder, inscribed in Babylonian cuneiform, was buried in Babylon after the Persian king was captured in the city in 539 BC. It proclaims the king's grandiose titles and lists his deeds, including capturing Babylon, restoring temples, and returning deported people to their homes

6.3 Darius triumphant. This rock engraving at Bisitun, Iran, dating to 520–519 BC, shows the king with his foot on the prone body of his enemy Gaumata, who had made an unsuccessful bid for kingship. Before him are nine rebel kings roped together. The last wears a pointed helmet typical of a Saka

prevailed, recording the incident in a formidable rock relief carved on a mountainside at Bisitun (or Behistun). It shows the triumphant king stepping on the body of his rival while nine rebel kings, bound and chained by the neck, are brought before him—a vivid reminder for all to see that rebellion has its price.

Darius was also interested in extending the other boundaries of his empire. He annexed the Indus valley, campaigned against the nomad Sakas between the Caspian and Aral seas, and in 513 BC led his armies into Europe across the Hellespont, annexing much of Thrace on the west shore of the Black Sea as far north as the Danube. From this European bridgehead he could advance both north against the Scythians and south into Macedonia and to Greece beyond. In the event, his expedition against the Scythians in Europe was without tangible result since the nomads refused to engage in battle but simply melted away into the steppe, drawing his forces dangerously far from their Danube bridgehead. Eventually he gave up pursuit and returned to the Danube. Various Persian adventures against the Greeks between 499 and 478 BC initiated by Darius and his successor, Xerxes (ruled 485–465 BC), also came to nothing (see p. 212).

Darius had built upon the successes of his two predecessors and had created the greatest empire the world had ever seen. On gold and silver tablets deposited in the foundations of the great audience hall in his palace at Persepolis he could fairly claim, 'Here is the kingdom that I possess, from the Sakas who are beyond Sogdiana to the land of Kush [Nubia], from India to Sardis.' Elsewhere his inscriptions proclaimed to the world that he was 'King of Kings, King of all races, King of this great land which extends so far'.

By the early fifth century the empire had reached its natural geographical limits, bounded only by deserts, the oceans, and the steppe. After the set-back experienced in Greece, plans for further expansion into Europe were abandoned, and the empire, created in a brief fifty years, set about aggrandizing itself while coping with dynastic disputes, the periodic revolts of local governors, and the rebellions of the subject nations: successive kings were kept busy maintaining the edifice of empire. That such a vast structure could last for more than two hundred years is a measure of their success.

6.4 The Persian city of Persepolis in Iran. The large building at centre left is the Hall of a Hundred Columns. The Apadana, with its sculptured reliefs, is behind it, centre right

6.5 Part of the sculpture reliefs of the Apadana in Persepolis showing ambassadors from all over the Persian empire bringing gifts to the king. The Saka from the central Asian steppe can be distinguished by their pointed hats

An Empire of Provinces

Unlike the Assyrian empire before it, which stamped its centralizing authority on all subject peoples, moving them in great numbers at will, the Persians accepted, and indeed encouraged, diversity. Local elites were kept in power and their bureaucratic systems adopted, while local traditions and gods were respected. When Cyrus sent the exiled Jews back to their homeland, he encouraged them to rebuild the Temple of Jerusalem, an act that prompted the prophet Isaiah to proclaim that Cyrus was favoured by their god, Yahweh. Regional languages and writing systems were also adopted. Most imperial inscriptions were multilingual, though for the official business of empire Aramaic was used, written on parchment or papyrus in alphabet script. All this meant that, as far as the disparate communities were concerned, Persian rule made very little difference to their lives.

By the early fifth century the empire was divided into twenty or so provinces, or satrapies, each ruled by a governor (satrap) chosen by the king from the ranks of the Persian nobility. The satrap was rewarded with the income from a royal estate assigned to him from within the empire, but it was land which he did not own. He ruled his province with the aid of the indigenous upper class, his prime charge being to maintain peace and prosperity within his domain and to send regular tribute to the centre at Persepolis. Herodotus gives a detailed list of contributions from each of the satrapies during the reign of Darius. For the most part it was recovered in talents of silver, but there were exceptions. The Egyptians, in addition to providing 700 talents, also supplied corn to support the resident Persians. Babylonia provided an additional five hundred boy eunuchs, while the Indians, the most numerous of the nations, paid a massive sum in gold dust. A total year's tribute amounted to the equivalent of 380,000 kilograms of silver.

The annual tribute was more than just a financial arrangement, essential though that was for the maintenance of the state: it was a symbol of submission to the king. The tribute was brought to Persepolis, where it was ceremonially handed over in an act witnessed by all. The centre of the event may well have been the great audience hall, the Apadana, the outer walls of which were adorned with reliefs depicting the arrival of twenty-three delegations from the far-flung provinces, each in their traditional dress, bearing gifts. The Lydians bring a two-horse chariot, bowls, and bracelets, the Cappadocians bring a horse and folded garments, the Bactrians carry bowls and lead a Bactrian camel, while the Indians bring a donkey and various axes and jars. The symbolism is powerful: the King of Kings is paid homage by all the nations of the world, their ambassadors travelling vast distances to his court. It is also a reminder that, in addition to the annual tribute in silver, the delegations were expected to bring personal gifts for the king. When Darius built his palace at Susa, stonemasons were sent from Lydia and Egypt and brickmakers from Babylon, while rare materials poured in from all over the world: gold, lapis, carnelian, turquoise, ebony and other timbers, silver, and ivory. The power of the king to command was absolute. That said, the arrival of the delegates at Persepolis in their varied dress, speaking their many languages, would have been an act of bonding, a celebration of the multiplicity of the empire to which they all belonged under the protection of the King of Kings, selected by the god Ahuramazda from among the descendants of the founder, Achaemenes, to rule the world.

To maintain such a vast empire good communications were essential. The satrapies were all linked to the centre by a system of royal roads provided with posting stations at regular intervals. Herodotus was impressed:

> There is nothing in the world that travels faster than these Persian couriers . . . men and horses are stationed along the road, equal in number to the number of days which the journey takes—a man and a horse for each day. Nothing stops the couriers from covering their allotted stage in the quickest possible time—neither snow, rain, heat, nor darkness.
>
> (*Histories* 8.98)

The most famous of the royal roads ran from Sardis, in Lydia, close to the Aegean coast, to the capital, Susa, some 2,500 kilometres, a journey that could be covered in ninety days.

The sea played an important part in more distant trade. The empire commanded a vast maritime interface, the southern shores of the Black Sea from the Danube to the Caucasus, the eastern Mediterranean from Macedonia to Cyrenaica, the western coast of the Red Sea and the Persian Gulf and the Arabian Sea from the Tigris–Euphrates estuary to the Indus, as well as the inland seas, the Caspian and the Aral, a total shoreline of more than 9,000 kilometres. From the various Persian-controlled ports in the Mediterranean, entrepreneurs were able to access the entire Mediterranean and the Atlantic beyond, while from the Gulf and the Red Sea, the Arabian peninsula and the west coast of India were within easy reach. To facilitate transport Darius is credited with constructing a canal between the Nile and the Red Sea.

While much of the sea traffic would have been merchant vessels following traditional routes, the Persians also maintained a fleet in the east Mediterranean, referred to by one contemporary writer as a 'royal navy'. The king supplied the ships, but the crews were drawn from local seafarers like the Phoenicians and the Ionian Greeks. According to Herodotus, the fleet of triremes was already in existence by the late sixth century, and when it confronted the Greeks in the early fifth century it numbered 1,207 triremes and nearly two thousand additional vessels. The sea-battle fought at Salamis in 480 BC was a close-run engagement from which the Greeks emerged triumphant.

The creation of the Persian empire and its subsequent maintenance was dependent on the efficiency of the army. Since the army was led by the king supported by his noble attendants, the sons of the elite were subjected to intensive military training, a fact neatly encapsulated by Herodotus: 'The Persians teach their sons between the ages of five and twenty only three things: to ride a horse, use the bow, and speak the truth' (*Histories* 1.136). The Persian fighting force comprised chariots, cavalry, and infantry. As cavalry became increasingly important, chariots ceased to be a multi-purpose mobile force and instead began to be used as a close-combat weapon designed to instil fear and to break up the enemy's battle formation. The bodies of the vehicles were turned into heavily armoured turrets, while the frames were fitted with scythe-like knives to inflict maximum damage on any infantry or cavalry that got in the way. The details are described with relish by Diodorus:

> From each of [the chariots] there projected out beyond the trace horses curved knives three spans [0.7 metres] long attached to the yoke and presenting their cutting edges to

the front. At the axle housings there were two more scythes pointing straight out with their cutting edges turned to the front like the others, but longer and broader.

(Diodorus Siculus 17.53.2)

Driven at speed, even in small numbers, these fearsome machines cannot have failed to create panic and disorder among the enemy.

But the real mobile force was now the cavalry. The Medes had already adopted cavalry formations. The Persians simply continued the tradition, learning from them and from the nomad groups they encountered on the steppe frontier. The bow and the javelin were the main weapons. One late fifth-century text notes that 130 arrows were carried by each rider, together with two short throwing or thrusting spears. For protection he held a shield and wore an iron corselet and helmet. The horses also wore armour, part of which protected the thighs of the rider. Contemporary illustrations suggest that some of the styles of armour were copied from the Central Asian nomads, who habitually fought in cavalry formations.

Finally, the infantry. The foot-soldiers seem to have been organized into mixed formations of archers and shield-bearers carrying spears and short-swords. The archers were essential in the opening stages of the engagement, firing volleys of arrows into the approaching enemy, while in close combat the spear-carrying shield-bearers came into their own.

How large the Persian army was at any one time it is difficult to say, but Herodotus' statement that Xerxes led more than two and a half million men into Greece is surely a gross overestimate. The king was protected by a personal bodyguard of ten thousand lancers known as Immortals, all native-born Persians. The rest of the force, perhaps numbering as many as a few hundred thousand, was made up of soldiers drawn from the provinces, sometimes offering specialist skills, like the Libyan charioteers and the Arabian camel-drivers. To maintain the standing force required to keep order in the empire and along its borders, allotments of state land were made to groups of men who were expected to provide services when called upon. As the army became increasingly professional, this land was managed by agents to provide a steady income for the soldiers and their families. To boost numbers, mercenaries were also employed, the most famous being the ten thousand Greeks led by Xenophon in support of one of the contenders for the throne in 401 BC.

Although Greek historians present a picture of declining morale and efficiency in the Persian army and the administrative system, particularly from the time of Xerxes, their bias must be allowed for. By any standards, the Persian state remained a formidable force until the end.

The European Opposition and the Rise of Macedon

When Cyrus defeated the kingdom of Lydia in western Asia Minor in 547 BC, the annexation of the Greek cities along the Aegean shore naturally followed. What to the Persians was an act of geographical neatness was to the wider Greek world a hostile confrontation. The threat further increased when in 513 BC Darius annexed a large part of the Thracian homeland (now largely Bulgaria) and took over Greek islands and cities in the north Aegean. All that lay between the Persian empire and the Greek city states was the Aegean Sea and the territory of the Macedonians, barbarians to the Greeks, who formed a buffer between the Thracians and the north of Greece.

A rebellion of the Ionian cities against Persian rule in 499 BC refocused Darius' attention on the European issue, and once the rebellion was dealt with he decided to move against the Greek mainland. As a preliminary, Macedonia was annexed as a vassal state in 492 BC, and two years later the Persian fleet, carrying an invasion force, set out for Attica. The Greek success at the battle of Marathon in 490 BC was a significant set-back for the Persians, and their Greek adventure was left in abeyance for a decade. The expedition mounted by Xerxes in 480 BC was a more massive undertaking, with the land force crossing the Hellespont and moving through Thrace, Macedonia, and Thessaly to reach the pass of Thermopylae, and a fleet setting out from a base in Thessaly. The goal was Athens, but the ensuing sea-battle fought at Salamis in the Saronic Gulf was a disaster for the Persians. After the engagement the remnants of the Persian fleet made for the coast of Asia Minor, where at Mykale north of Miletos it was destroyed. After Salamis, Xerxes withdrew half his army, leaving the other half in Greece, where it was defeated at the battle of Plataea in 479 BC.

Although the confrontation was contained by the Greeks, working for once more or less in unison, the geographically fragmented nature of Greece and the endemic rivalries between the individual city states gave no assurance of future success. Athens grasped the problem by setting up a broad confederacy known as the Delian League in 478 BC. At first the funds of the organization were held on the neutral Aegean island of Delos, but in 454 BC they were moved to Athens, by which time the league of equals had become virtually an Athenian empire. Given its unstable nature, the league was surprisingly successful. By 475 BC the Persians had been driven out of Europe and the Bosporus opened again to Greek shipping, and in 468 BC the Ionian cities of Asia Minor were freed from Persian rule, though the formal end to hostilities was not concluded for another twenty years. There can be no doubt that it was the leadership shown by Athens that brought the Persian adventure in Europe to a halt, but had the Persian kings not been distracted by internal disruptions, history might have been very different.

Throughout the momentous events of the early fifth century Macedonia played no significant part other than being taken over briefly as a vassal by Darius and used as a staging post by Xerxes. It was a land apart, hemmed in by the Pindus Mountains and with a restricted coastline. To the south lay the Greeks and to the north the Illyrians and the Thracians. But in spite of its comparative isolation, it was a fertile territory served by the river Aliakman, and it commanded resources of gold and silver.

Isolation created a stable political system based on hereditary kingship with the king and his entourage of companions (*hetairoi*) controlling the state through autocratic rule. This was in sharp contrast to the neighbouring Greeks with their warring polities constantly at each other's throats and burdened by democracy. Elite Macedonian society was riven by intrigue and culled by frequent assassinations. It was an heroic society based on valour in warfare and skill in the hunt. A young man could only wear a belt—a mark of status—if he had killed an enemy in battle, and he was not allowed to recline at dinner unless he had killed a wild boar without using a net. It was a macho world, boisterous and dangerous, ready to be set alight by any charismatic leader who chanced his luck.

In 359 BC such a man emerged: Philip II, then aged 22. In the twenty-three years of his reign he was to transform Macedonia from a peripheral kingdom to being on the brink of world power. Like all great war leaders he moved very fast, first against his rivals, then against his neighbours. His first campaign was northwards into Paionia in the Balkans, which he conquered in 358 BC, acquiring, in the process, rich mineral resources, which funded subsequent expeditions. In 352 BC he had overrun Thessaly, and three years later he added Chalkidike and the northern shores of the Aegean to his conquests. A further thrust in 342 BC brought much of Thrace up to the Sea of Marmara and the Black Sea under his control, an event commemorated by the founding of the city of Philippopolis (modern Plovdiv) on the river Maritsa.

During this time he became increasingly involved in the incessant petty squabbles among the Greek city states to the extent that the Athenian orator Demosthenes spoke out in public about the threat posed by Macedonia. Eventually, in 340 BC, Athens tried to establish an anti-Macedonian Hellenic League, but in a decisive battle fought at Chaironeia in Boeotia in 338 BC Philip crushed the Greek opposition. He was now virtually master of all Greece except for Sparta. The stage was set for him to embark on his grand project, which he had been planning for years: the conquest of Persia. What the motives were we can only guess. No doubt there was a latent hostility towards the Persians after the devastation and death caused by Darius and Xerxes. Philip could present himself as the leader of Hellenism, taking revenge for the Greek people. But behind the political justifications lay the deep-seated dynamic driven by the imperative of perpetual warfare. The Macedonian state was a militaristic creation: heroism in battle was the driving force. Without a continuing expansive war, the social system would fall apart. Philip had been planning the attack on the Persian empire for some years, but establishing his ascendancy in Greece had to come first. After Chaironeia he was able to finalize the preparations.

By 336 BC much was in place and Philip was poised for the grand conflict in the east. But in the spring, at Aegae (now Vergina), while celebrating his daughter's wedding, as he entered the theatre packed with dignitaries from across the Greek world, he was struck down by an assassin. It was a spectacular end to a spectacular career.

The succession was rapid, his son Alexander, aged 19, quickly grabbing the reins of state. Diodorus sums up what follows: 'Alexander succeeded to the throne, first inflicting due punishment on his father's murderers and then devoting himself to the funeral of his father. He established his authority far more firmly than any did, in fact, suppose possible' (*Histories* 16.95). The tomb of Philip II can be seen today in the royal cemetery at Vergina, not far from the theatre where he died.

Alexander, bold, imaginative, and violent, acted with speed, but it took two years to deal with intrigue at home and opposition in Thrace and in Greece, where he found it necessary to crush Thebes, slaughtering six thousand and enslaving many others. His credentials established, he turned to his father's vision of the east.

Alexander: The Last King of Persia

Alexander's campaigns across the length and breadth of the Persian empire are well known and need no detailed consideration here. From 334 to 323 BC he ranged wide from the western deserts of Egypt to Punjab, and from the Central Asian steppe to the Arabian Sea. He defeated Darius III in two major battles, at Issus in north-western Syria in 333 BC and at Gaugamela on the Tigris in 331 BC, and then proceeded through Persia, destroying the great palace at Persepolis on the way. Everywhere he went he received the submission of the satrapies, replacing the governors with his own nominees but leaving the rest of the administrative structure in place. For most of the population it would have been a painless transition, hardly noticeable.

Alexander had learnt well from the example of the Persian kings. Local customs were respected and local gods revered. In Egypt he made a special journey to the distant oasis of Siwa, the sanctuary of the Egyptian god Amun, whom he proclaimed to be his father, while in Babylon he set in hand the renovation of the Temple of Marduk. No doubt his old teacher Aristotle had tutored him well in the works of Herodotus, and he remembered how Cyrus the Great had behaved in similar circumstances two centuries earlier. To the peoples he encountered he came not as a conqueror but as a new overlord, a replacement of the Persian king. His commanders were encouraged

LEARNING FROM EACH OTHER

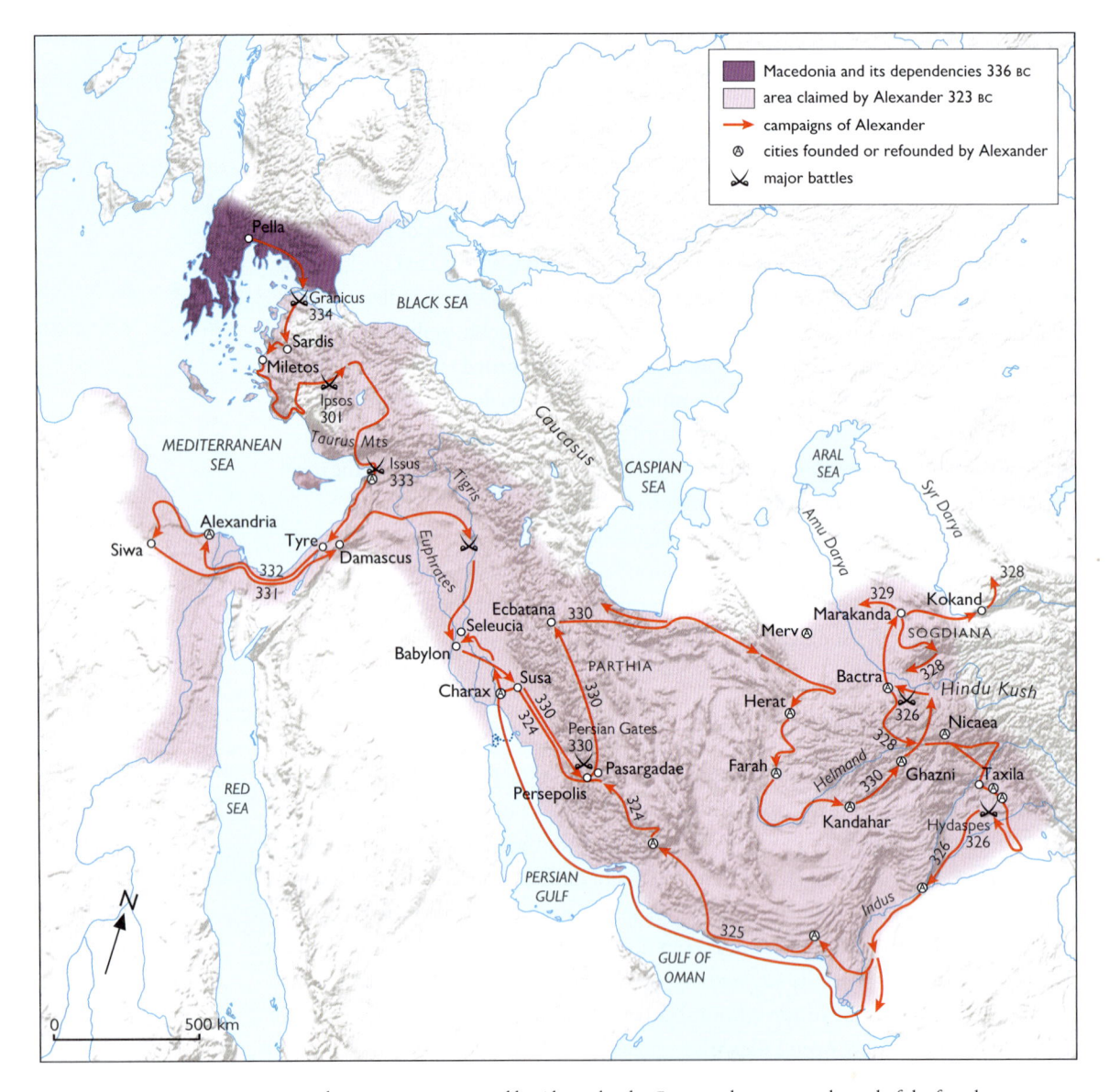

6.6 The territories conquered by Alexander the Great, as they were at the end of the fourth century BC. From his Balkan homeland Alexander assumed control of the land ruled by the Persian kings

to marry into the local elites, and he set the example himself by marrying a Sogdian princess, Roxanne. His most significant act, however, was his part in the burial of King Darius, who had been assassinated by dissident courtiers. Alexander presided over the occasion, ensuring that full ceremonial rites were observed. This was not a simple act of piety offered to a noble foe, but a calculated claim to legitimate succession. It was performed in the time-honoured manner followed by the Persian rulers before him: by this observance he was establishing his right to become the next king of Persia.

So fulsome has been the literature about Alexander that it is not easy to assess his achievements objectively. There can be no doubt that he was a charismatic leader and a skilled tactician, but he stood high upon the shoulders of others: his father, Philip, whose aspiration had been the conquest of Persia, and, more significantly, the Persian kings who had created a state system composed of self-governing units owing allegiance to a central idea. He simply took over the empire by replacing the ruling Persian elite with a Macedonian elite. He was now King of Kings, and so had begun to act before his death at Babylon at the age of 33. Perhaps the best thing he did for his reputation was to die young, before the exhilaration of marching and the battle was replaced by the dull realities of maintaining the vast edifice of empire.

6.7 The famous Alexander sarcophagus was probably made for the king of Sidon about 320 BC. The relief on one side shows Alexander at the battle of Issus wearing the lion's-head helmet of Herakles as he strikes down a Persian horseman

Hellenism in the East

With the death of Alexander in Babylon in 323 BC the huge empire he had so briefly brought under his control began to collapse into a chaos of conflicting rivalries. There were no natural successors. Alexander's heirs, his mentally challenged half-brother and his posthumous son, jointly held the Macedonian crown, but elsewhere the generals divided up the empire, becoming local warlords intent on expanding their domains. By 304 BC there were five successor kingdoms. Macedonia was ruled by Cassander and Thrace by Lysimachos. Much of Asia Minor was in the hands of Antigonos and Egypt was ruled by Ptolemy, while the rest of the old Persian empire from Mesopotamia to the Indus was controlled by Seleukos, ruling from Babylon. In that year Seleukos ceded a large part of his Indian territories to the Mauryan king Chandragupta in return for five hundred elephants, a highly desirable adjunct to warfare since horses were reported to be scared of them. In 301 BC the elephants were put to good use in a battle fought at Ipsos, which saw the end of Antigonos and the division of his lands between the allies Cassander, Lysimachos, and Seleukos. Thereafter rivalry between the main contenders was to continue unabated and boundaries were in constant flux.

Given the brevity of Alexander's personal intervention in the east and the political chaos that followed, it is surprising how deeply Hellenistic culture took root in the area. That it did so is to a large extent the result of a deliberate policy of founding cities on the Greek model and encouraging retired troops to settle in them. Many of these towns bore the name Alexandria: Alexandria in Aria (now Herat), Alexandropolis in Arachosia (now Kandahar), Alexandria in Caucasus (now Begram), and Alexandria Eschate (now Khujand in Tajikistan). These towns were concentrated in the eastern province of Bactria, which, by virtue of its remoteness, became the most Hellenized of all the eastern Persian territories. Bactria became an independent state about 250 BC. Initially its centre lay in the valley of the Amu Darya, but from the second century the state began to expand south to the Hindu Kush, reclaiming the territories of Arachosia and Paropamisadai, lost to the Mauryan empire after Alexander's death.

One of the best known of the Greek towns of Bactria is the colonial settlement established at Aï Khanum in northern Afghanistan, excavated between 1965 and 1978. The town is situated in a well-defended position at a confluence where a tributary river, the Kokcha, enters the upper Amu Darya. Here, the steep riverbanks provide good defences to the west and south, while a high plateau, occupied by the upper city and a citadel, protects the eastern approach. The lower city, facing the main river, contained a palace and a range of public buildings including temples, a gymnasium dedicated to the gods Hermes and Herakles, and a theatre seating six thousand spectators. The location is one of strategic importance, commanding routes along the river. Its proximity

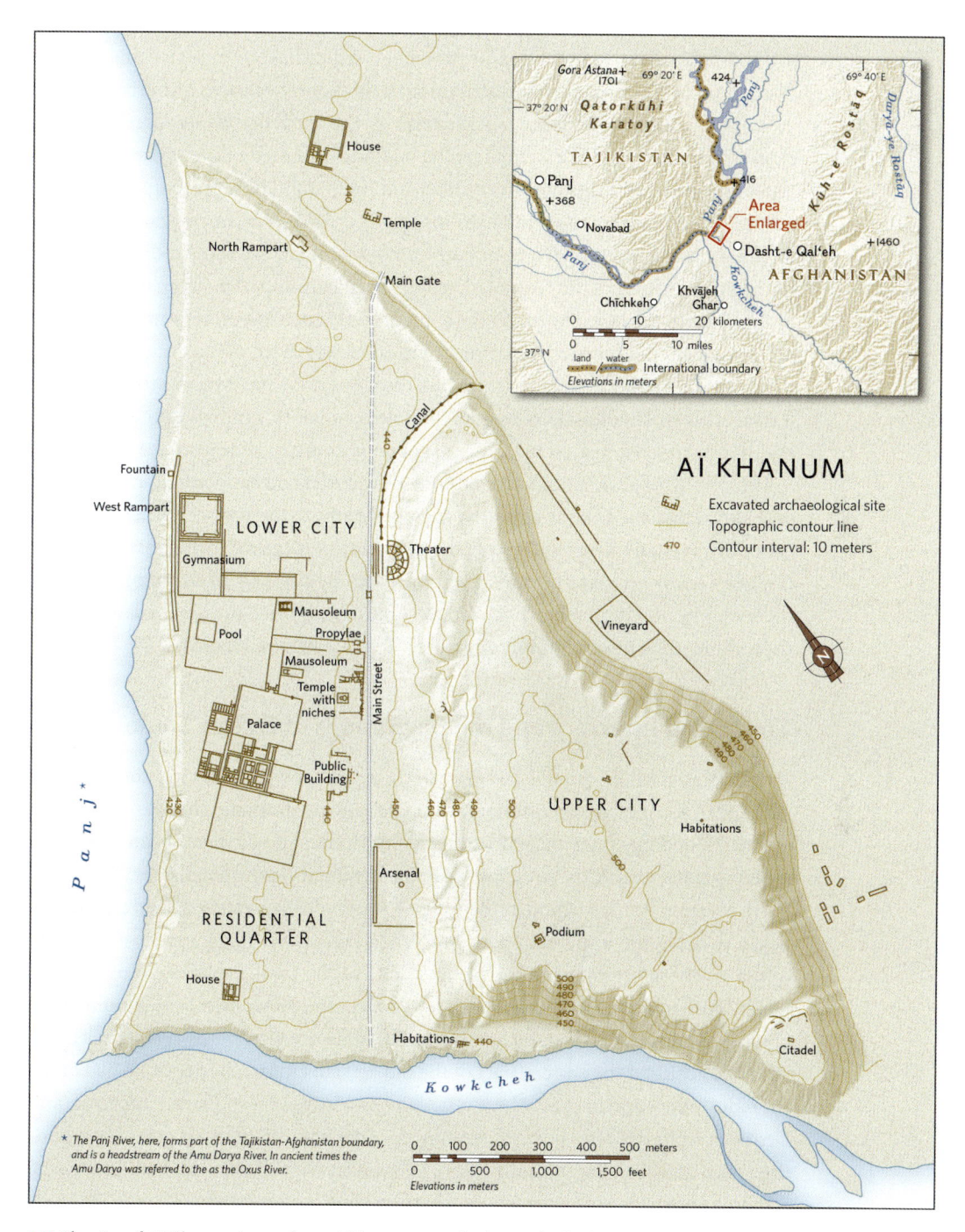

6.8 The city of Aï Khanum in northern Afghanistan was built on a high plateau commanding a river crossing on the Amu Darya (here labelled Panj). The lower city was adorned with large public buildings built in Hellenistic style

to the lapis lazuli mines in the nearby mountains would have given it an enhanced role as a control post overseeing the distribution of this hugely valuable resource.

What is astonishing about Aï Khanum is the intensity of its Greek culture, expressed not only in the essential public buildings required of every Greek city, but also in the decorative fittings, Corinthian and Ionic capitals, relief sculpture, pebble mosaics, and the terracotta antefixes for the tiled roofs. For a newly arrived Greek the urban scene would have been comfortably familiar. So, too, would have been the sight and sound of the Greek language everywhere apparent, from monumental inscriptions to scribbled notes on the contents written in ink on ceramic containers. Most poignant is a funerary monument inscribed with a list of maxims copied from the shrine of Apollo at Delphi, reminding the viewer of what it means to be a Greek. It ends with 'In childhood, learn good manners; in youth, control your passions; in middle age, practise justice; in old age, be of good counsel; in death, have no regrets.'

The colony of Aï Khanum was not one of the Alexandrian foundations but was probably established about 300 BC by Seleukos on a site already occupied by the residence of a Persian satrap. Its life was short. It was first attacked by northern nomads, probably Sakas, in 145/4 BC, and again in 130 BC by nomads of different origin. In these remote northern regions the Greek summer was brief, the dream dissolving in the turbulence of new migratory pressures. To these we shall return.

The Indian Interface and the Beginnings of Ocean Trade

As the Macedonian generals were scrabbling for power following the death of Alexander, the Indian subcontinent was experiencing dramatic changes. A country of small kingdoms interspersed with tribal territories, it had never been ruled by a unifying force until Chandragupta Maurya, a military commander serving in the north-western border region at the time of Alexander's advance, seized power and began to bring the disparate polities together. During his reign (321–293 BC) much of the northern region from the Ganges delta to the Iranian plateau and from the Hindu Kush and the Himalayas south to the Deccan plateau was brought under his control. What was particularly notable was his advance westwards against Seleukos, who had acquired the eastern part of the old Persian empire. By 311 BC he had taken the Indus valley, and in 304 BC he wrested the provinces of Gandhara, Arachosia, and Gedrosia from the Macedonians, sealing the deal with the famous gift of five hundred elephants. During this long period of contact with the Macedonian powers he acquired knowledge of Hellenistic values, heralding the beginning of a creative interaction between Indian and Greek culture.

LEARNING FROM EACH OTHER

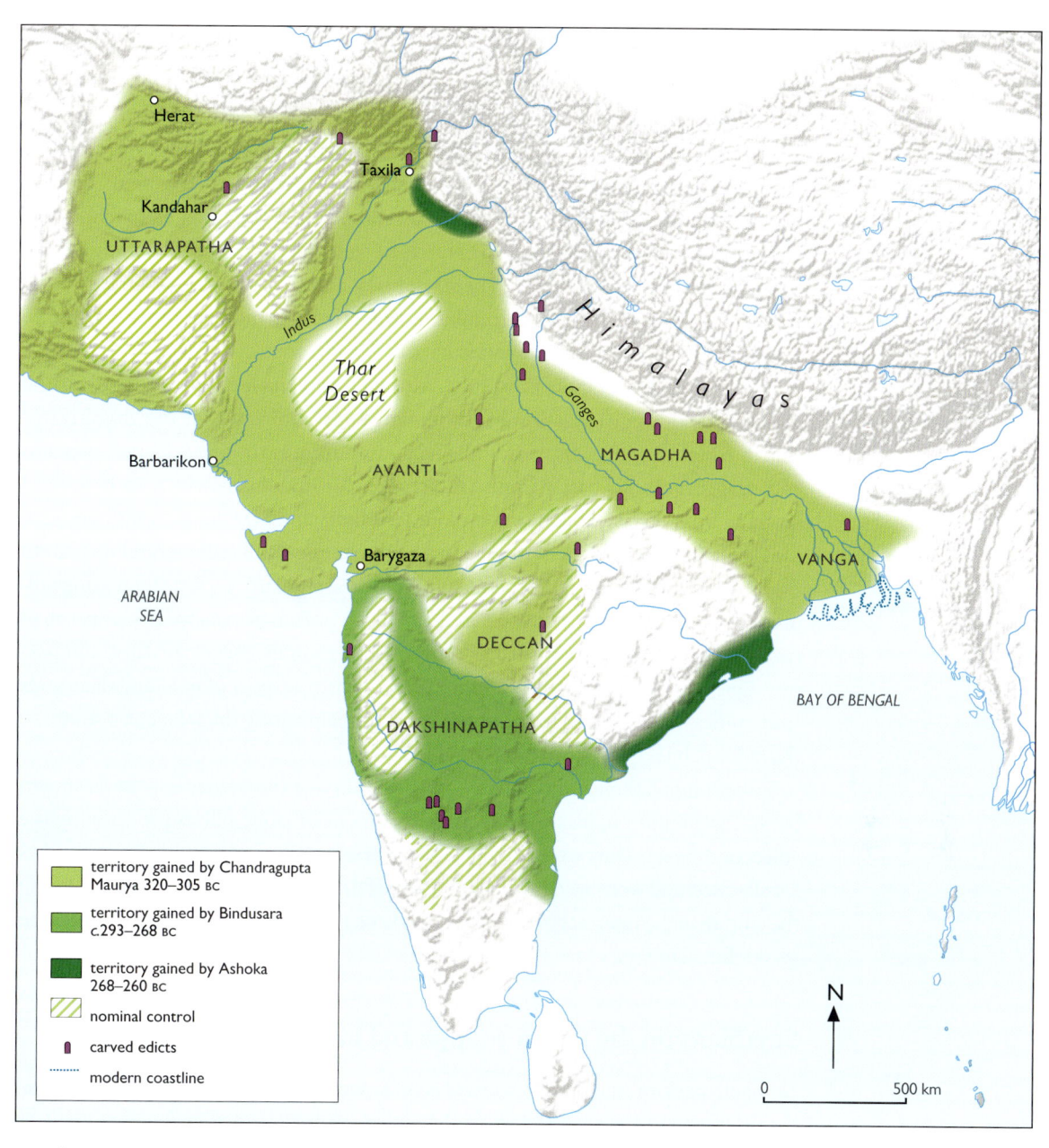

6.9 The Mauryan empire 320–260 BC

Chandragupta initiated the Mauryan dynasty, which was to last for 130 years. About 293 BC he abdicated power and became a Jain monk, leaving the empire to his son Bindusara, who was succeeded by his son Ashoka in 268 BC. By this time the reach of the empire extended across much of the subcontinent except for some unconquered inland tribes, the southern tip of the peninsula, and the island of Sri Lanka.

Ashoka, who ruled until 233 BC, was a remarkable leader. Having extended his empire through the customary use of force, he suddenly converted to Buddhism and espoused non-violence (*ahimsa*). The strict penal code of the previous era was moderated, and he set out to rule through the strength of his moral authority alone, an aspiration unusual among those who have led empires.

Under the Mauryas, India prospered. Attempts were made to increase agricultural productivity through irrigation and by moving populations to bring under-cultivated land into better use. Towns were built and communication improved. Trade was also encouraged, growing partly from Ashoka's zeal for Buddhism, which set in motion far-flung missionary expeditions, to southern India and Sri Lanka, to Indonesia, to the Hellenized states of western Asia, and to the steppe nomads in Central Asia. Both the east and west coasts of the peninsula were now regularly used by increasing volumes of shipping, engaged in local journeys from port to port as well as longer-haul trips carrying commodities such as semi-precious stones, metals, textiles, and pottery. One text of the mid-third century records the transport of gold and diamonds from mines in the Deccan to the north, most probably using the west coast routes to the Indus delta region.

Something of the extant power and the quality of the Mauryan state is shown by the distribution of inscriptions carved on rocks or stone pillars proclaiming the edicts of Ashoka. They were sited in city centres, at crossroads, and at frontier posts for all to see, and were based on the pious belief that the king had the duty of ordering the empire in the interests of his subjects, whose rights and responsibilities had to be set out for all to see.

Scythians on the Pontic Steppe and in Europe, 600–300 BC

Nomadic pastoralists, known to the classical world as Scythians, appeared on the Pontic steppe in the second half of the eighth century, and over the next century or so some bands moved westwards into Europe, settling in Transylvania and the Great Hungarian Plain. The earliest arrivals chose to settle in three areas: in the forest-steppe zone between the Donets and the Dniester, at the mouth of the Don, and in the Kuban valley. This last group could have been (or could have been enhanced by) the Scythian mercenary warrior bands driven out of Asia Minor by the Assyrians.

The situation was probably very fluid in the early years, with much mobility, before territories were claimed and a semblance of stability established, but even so, new groups may have continued to arrive from the east.

In the middle of the fifth century, between 470 and 430 BC, there was a phase of unrest as the nomadic population grew, as the result of both natural population growth and the arrival of new groups from the Caucasus or the eastern Eurasian steppe, recognizable from their different style of material culture. A new aggressiveness, leading to outbreaks of warfare, may have caused the decline evident in agricultural production in the vicinity of some Greek colonies, particularly in the lower Bug and Dniester regions. But it was not only the colonies that came under pressure. There was a marked decline in production along the edge of the forest-steppe zone where the original Scythian groups had settled. It was a period of social and economic turmoil as rival nomad groups fought to gain territory and prestige.

By the 430s a new order seems to have been established. This is reflected in the appearance of large cemeteries, which themselves are a claim to ownership and a statement of group identity. Elite burials now began to appear, proclaiming the status not only of the individual but also of his lineage. Out of the fifth-century turmoil, then, emerged a more stable system with well-established nomadic hierarchies able to maintain a degree of control over a subservient sedentary population sufficiently productive to meet the needs of the elite. In the new period of comparative peace the Greek settlers began once again to work extensive agricultural territories along the Black Sea littoral, and new settlements were established, like Chersonesos on the southern tip of the Crimean peninsula, soon to be surrounded by a rigorously ordered agricultural landscape scattered with small farmsteads. The nomadic elites could now begin to develop a symbiotic relationship with the settlers.

Something of the variety among the different nomadic groups is evident in an account of the region written by Herodotus. He visited the colony of Olbia on the estuary of the Bug towards the middle of the fifth century, where he gathered information from local people and no doubt made observations of his own, carefully reporting what he had learnt in book 4 of his *Histories*. With all the qualifications one might reasonably have in using material of this kind, his lively presentation of the Scythians is, for the most part, a convincing portrayal of the mixed economies of the Pontic steppe communities at a time of change. He was, above all, aware of the ethnic variety among the people he calls Scythians, recognizing different groups with their own tribal names and, sometimes, different languages. Between the Dnieper and the Donets were the 'Royal Scythians', the 'bravest of the Scythian tribe, who look upon other tribes as their slaves'. Further to the north-west, living on the open, treeless steppe, were the 'wandering Scythians who neither plough nor sow', while in the

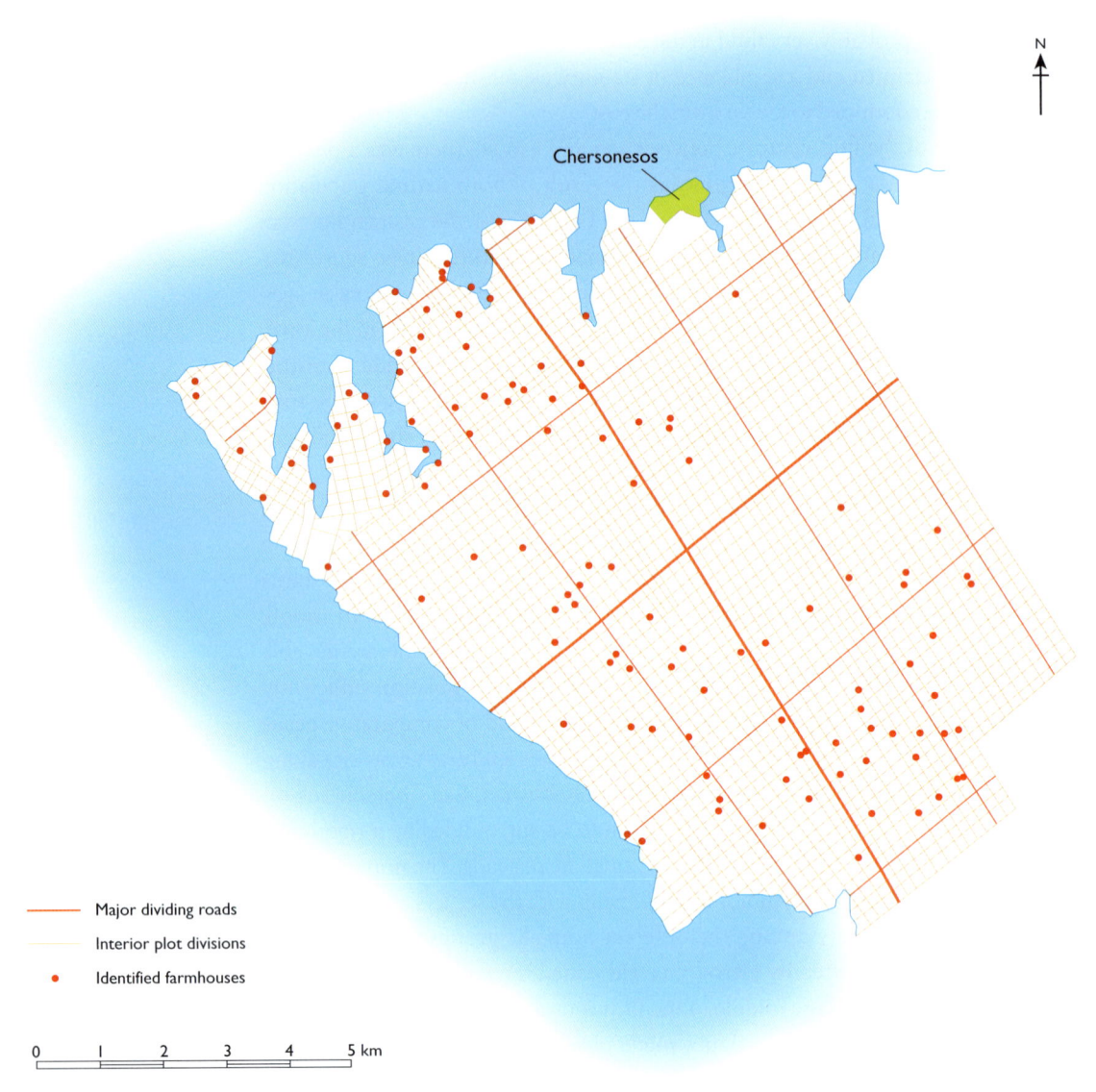

6.10 The territory (*chora*) belonging to the Greek city of Chersonesos, near modern Sevastopol on the Crimean peninsula. The land was divided into regular plots contained within a grid of roads. Many of the farmhouses of the rural population have been identified

forest-steppe west of the Dnieper he describes two groups of more sedentary peoples, one who 'sow and eat grain, also onions, garlic, lentils and millet' and another who trade their grain, some of it no doubt contributing to the shipments sent from the colonies to the Greek mainland. He was also aware of the acculturation taking place around the Greek enclaves, referring to the people who lived closest to Olbia as Graeco-Scythians. Such a blending of population must have been common along the Black Sea littoral. It is also apparent in the region of the Don delta, where in the fourth century at a Scythian settlement at Elizavetovka archaeologists have identified a special zone set aside for Greek traders.

In one particular passage clearly based on close personal observation (either his own or an informant's), Herodotus gives a meticulous account of Scythian elite burial practices. The entire *rite de passage* is described from the moment of death and the preparation of the body for display to the final offerings which completed the process. It is a masterpiece of precise and practised anthropological reporting.

> Here, when the king dies, they dig a grave, which is square in shape, and of great size. When it is ready, they take the king's corpse, and, having opened the belly and cleaned out the inside, fill the cavity with a preparation of chopped cypress, frankincense, parsley-seed, and anise-seed, after which they sew up the opening, enclose the body in wax, and, placing it on a wagon, carry it about through all the different tribes. On this procession each tribe, when it receives the corpse, imitates the example which is first set by the Royal Scythians; every man chops off a piece of his ear, crops his hair close, and makes a cut all round his arm, lacerates his forehead and his nose, and thrusts an arrow through his left hand. Then they who have the care of the corpse carry it with them to another of the tribes which are under the Scythian rule, followed by those whom they first visited. On completing the circuit of all the tribes under their sway, they find themselves in the country of the Gerrhi, who are the most remote of all, and so they come to the tombs of the kings. There the body of the dead king is laid in the grave prepared for it, stretched upon a mattress; spears are fixed in the ground on either side of the corpse, and beams stretched across above it to form a roof, which is covered with a thatching of osier twigs. In the open space around the body of the king they bury one of his concubines, first killing her by strangling, and also his cup-bearer, his cook, his groom, his attendant, his messenger, and some of his horses. They also bury the pick of all his other possessions, and some golden cups ... After this they set to work, and raise a vast mound above the grave, all of them vying with each other and seeking to make it as tall as possible.
>
> When a year is gone by, further ceremonies take place. Fifty of the best of the late king's attendants are taken, all native Scythians—for as bought slaves are unknown in the country, the Scythian kings choose any of their subjects that they like, to wait on them—fifty of those are taken and strangled, with fifty of the most beautiful horses. When they are dead, their bowels are taken out, and the cavity cleaned, filled full of chaff, and straight away sewn up again. This done, a number of posts are driven into the ground, in sets of two pairs each, and on every pair half the rim of a wheel is placed archwise; then strong stakes are run lengthways through the bodies of the horses and they are hoisted up so that the wheel rim in front supports the shoulders of the horse, while that behind sustains the belly and quarters while both pairs of legs hang free. They put reins and bridles on the horses, draw them forward and tie them to ropes. They then hoist every one of the strangled youths onto his horse, after driving a second stake through his

body along the course of the spine to the neck. The lower end of this projects from the body, and is fixed into a socket in the stake that runs lengthwise through the horse. The fifty riders are thus ranged in a circle round the tomb, and so left.

(Herodotus, *Histories* 4.71–2)

The validity of the account is amply borne out by details of burial practice brought to light in the excavations of kurgans across the Pontic steppe, from the rich early burial at Kostromskaya in the Caucasus to the later fourth-century burial at Chertomlyk in the Dnieper valley, where the king was buried with quantities of gold finery, made by Greek craftsmen, beneath a kurgan that survived to 9 metres in height. Many of the same rituals are evident in the burial excavated at Arzhan in the Tuva region of Siberia, dating to the ninth or eighth century (pp. 189–92), reinforcing the suggestion that Scythian culture originated in this eastern region before spreading westwards.

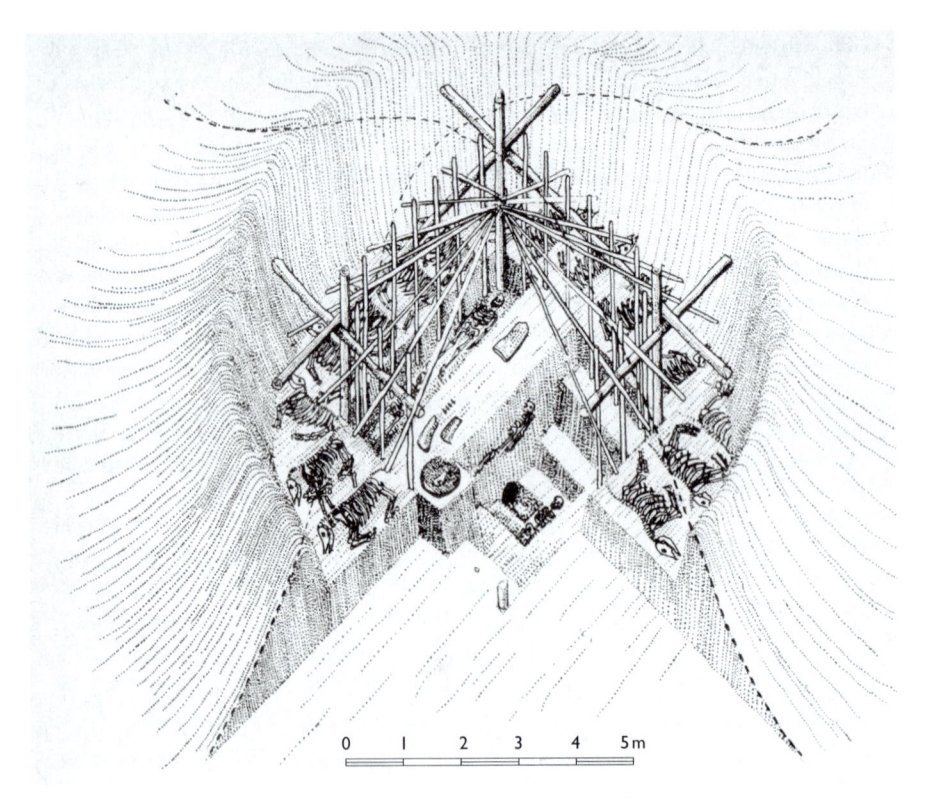

6.11 The great Scythian burial at Kostromskaya in the Kuban region of southern Russia. Excavations showed a succession of human burials within the burial chamber in which the Scythian king was buried, with sacrificed horses placed around the outside deposited before the final mound was heaped up. The ritual involved was similar to that described by Herodotus

LEARNING FROM EACH OTHER

While the Greek colonies soon developed into self-sustaining communities supported by farms established in their territory (*chora*), they were above all trading centres managing exchanges between the Scythian nomads and the Greek world. From the steppe hinterland would have come three principal exports: grain, furs, and slaves; to which could be added the ample fish from coastal waters. In return the Greeks provided wine, oil, and consumer durables such as pottery.

Perhaps the most remarkable products resulting from the interaction between Greek and nomad were highly elaborate craft works in gold, and sometimes silver, made for the elite Scythian market and known to us now largely from grave finds. These items, while incorporating scenes from nomad life and mythology, are the

6.12 Gold pectoral from a Scythian grave at Tolstaya Mogila dating to the second half of the fourth century BC. The upper register shows scenes from the daily life of pastoralists. The lower register shows beasts, some mythical, in conflict

work of Greek craft schools active in the colonial towns. One of the most spectacular of the products is the great gold pectoral from the fourth-century kurgan of Tolstaya Mogila near Ordzhonikidze in Ukraine. In the upper register are scenes from everyday life: two Scythians sew a shirt cut from a sheepskin, animals suckle their young, and a ewe is milked. The second register contrasts this idyllic scene with the savagery of the untamed world where lions and winged griffins prey on horses, deer, and pigs. Predatory scenes of this kind are a common theme in Scythian art and can be traced back to Siberian origins. Similar scenes of predation occur on a gold scabbard found in the same tomb. Another set of spirited daily scenes is shown on a gold beaker from the Kul'-Oba kurgan on the Kerch peninsula of the eastern Crimea. Nomads are shown in various stages of engagement: two sit at repose in conversation, while one strings his reflex bow. Two other pairs appear in caring relationships, one bandaging his partner's leg, another pulling a friend's tooth. These scenes of intimate life are depicted in intricate detail, providing a rare vision of nomadic clothing and hairstyles as well as behaviour in daily life.

These items and many more made in Greek workshops for the Scythian elite are redolent of the relationship between the two different worlds. The Greeks were work-

6.13 Gold drinking vessel from a burial at Kul'-Oba, Kerch, on the Crimean peninsula, fourth century BC. The vessel, of Greek workmanship, depicts scenes from nomadic life and provides vivid detail of nomadic dress

LEARNING FROM EACH OTHER

ing for clients whose requirements and culture they respected. They used their skills of craftsmanship but seldom imposed their ideology.

The foundation of the colony at Berezan in the seventh century, followed by Olbia, established nearby in the sixth century, focused the early trading ventures on the Bug–Dnieper estuary. But by the fourth century the area had become a backwater, with Olbia declining to little more than a local port. Meanwhile, the Cimmerian Bosporus—the Strait of Kerch between the Back Sea and the Sea of Azov—had become the vital focus of commercial activity. About 480 BC thirty of the cities in the region came together under the leadership of Panticapaeum (now Kerch) to form an alliance that become known as the Bosporan kingdom. By the end of the fifth century the kingdom had expanded to include all the Greek establishments around the Sea of Azov as far north as Tanais at the mouth of the Don, a mysteriously remote place regarded by the Greeks as marking the limit of the civilized world. It was in the cities of the Bosporan kingdom that Scythians mixed with Greeks, producing the mêlée of values and beliefs that inspired the gold- and silversmiths to create their highly distinctive art style, one of great humanity and originality.

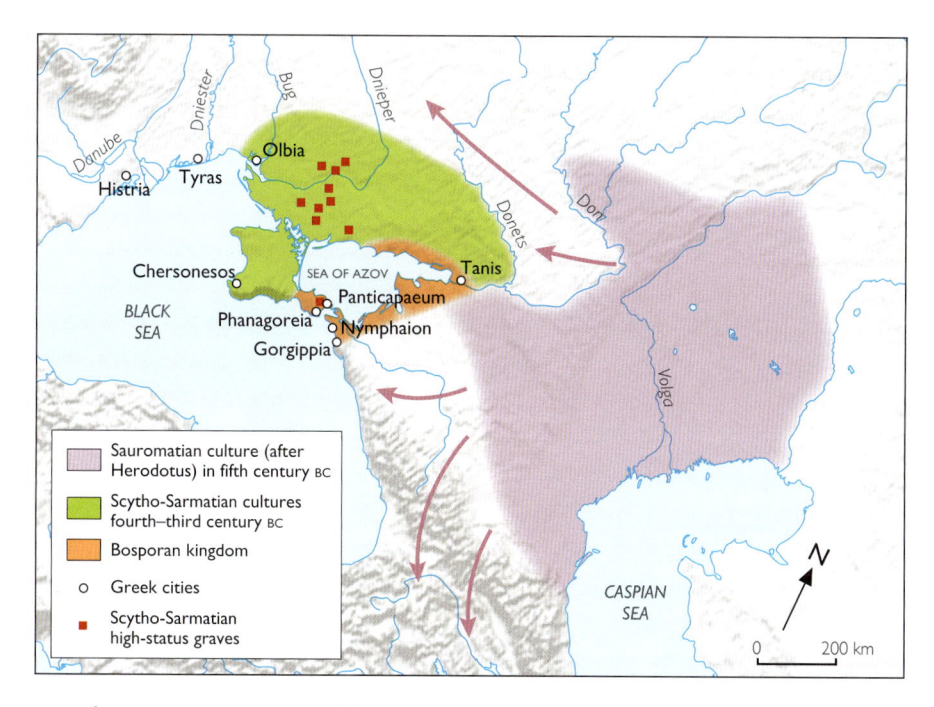

6.14 The Pontic-Caspian steppe and forest-steppe region in the fourth–third century BC at the time of the Sarmatian expansion. The Bosporan kingdom and the Sea of Azov still maintained aspects of its Greek identity, but it was fast coming under the influence of the Sarmatians

Scythians in Europe

The momentum with which the Scythian communities swept into the Pontic steppe carried some groups much further westwards into Europe, crossing the Carpathian Mountains into Transylvania and further west still, into the Great Hungarian Plain, where, several centuries before, the migrating Cimmerians had settled.

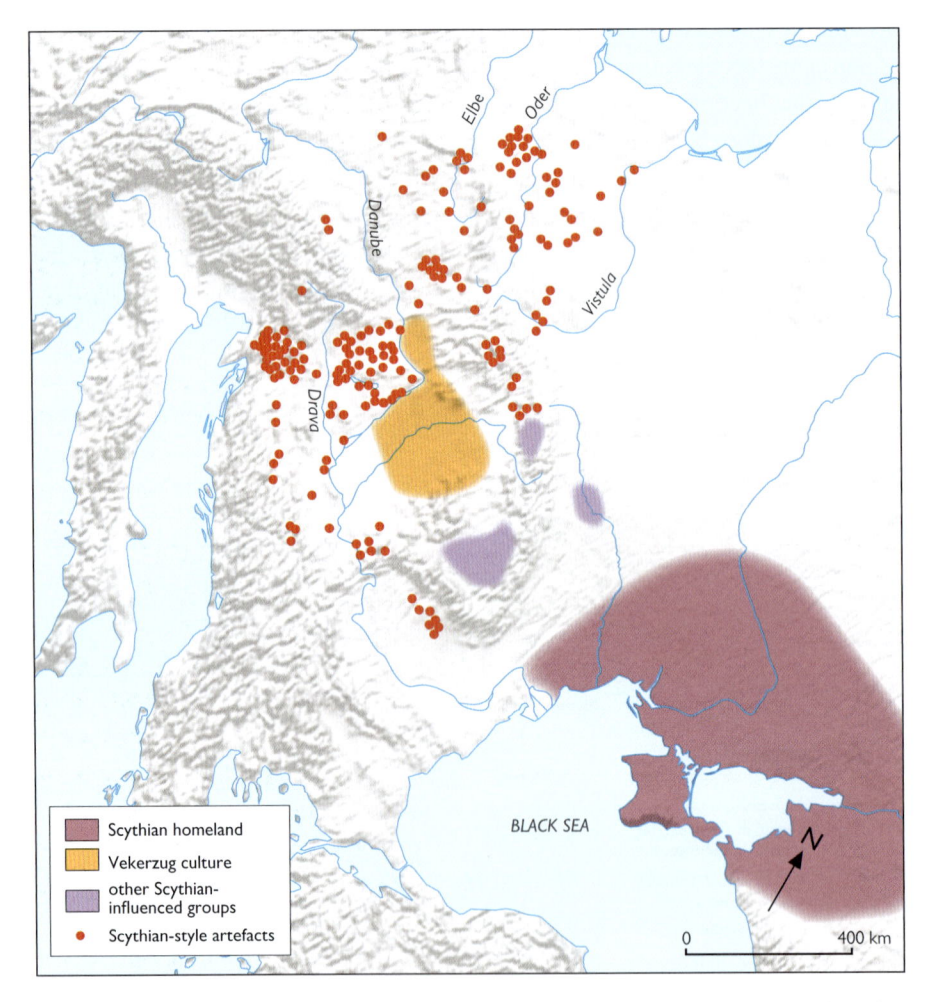

6.15 Under constant pressure from nomad groups to the east, the Scythians of the Pontic steppe looked to Europe. Groups of migrant Scythians settled in Transylvania and in the Great Hungarian Plain (Vekerzug culture), where a steppe landscape, similar to their homeland, offered a congenial environment. The distribution of Scythian-style objects (mainly horse-gear and arrowheads) across central Europe indicates areas of raiding and trade

The Scythian settlement in the Great Hungarian Plain, known archaeologically as the Vekerzug culture, began in the late seventh or early sixth century, but contacts were maintained with the east, and small-scale inflows of people may have continued to augment the original settlements. The new enclaves are recognizable though the highly distinctive horse-gear that they introduced together with trilobate arrowheads, short-swords, and scale-armour. But seldom are there ostentatious burials like those of the Pontic region. One of the richest, from the cemetery of Ártánd, contained two bronze vessels, a Greek bronze vessel (hydria) from Sparta and a handled cauldron from the west, in addition to personal ornaments and trappings for a single horse. The Scythians who had penetrated into the heart of Europe were poor relations, largely out of reach of the Pontic craft skills. That said, the discovery of two fine gold appliqués of deer in the classic Scythian animal style, both probably shield mounts, implies the presence of some men of status in the west. Perhaps they were the leaders of the pioneer wave.

Beyond the area of Scythian settlement, items of Scythian-style metalwork, mainly horse-gear and trilobite arrowheads, are found widely distributed throughout the middle regions of Europe. Many of the finds probably represent trade in horses and weaponry, but some may have resulted from the activities of raiding parties or mercenaries. One group of objects found at Witaszkowo in Poland, however, may be from the burial of a rich warrior once resplendent with gold ornamented armour and jewellery comparable with the best Pontic work. It is tempting to think that this was the burial of a member of the Scythian elite who had led his entourage to the far west and died on foreign soil. However, it could equally well be that of a local chief who had acquired these strangely exotic items by trade and used them to enhance his status.

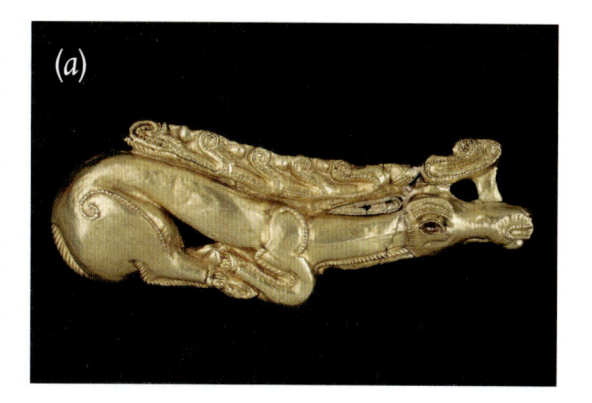

6.16 Gold stag ornaments of the Scythian period, seventh–fourth century BC, from (*a*) Tápiószentmárton, Hungary; (*b*) Kostromskaya, Kuban region of the Caucasus; (*c*) Kul'-Oba, near Kerch, in the Crimea. These plaques may have been mounted on shields

Nomads of the Caspian and Kazakh Steppe and Beyond

Herodotus' knowledge of the steppe peoples living beyond the Pontic region was limited. He understood that to the north of the Don was the land of the Sauromatae, who spoke 'the language of Scythians but never spoke it correctly'. Their territory extended 'northwards a distance of fifteen days' journey' across 'a country which is entirely bare of trees' (*Histories* 4.21). The women here were particularly warlike. They hunted with their menfolk or on their own, wearing the same dress as the men. He develops the point further by recording that 'their marriage law lays it down that no girl shall wed until she has killed a man in battle' (*Histories* 1.116–17). As a consequence, some women die unmarried at an advanced age. In presenting this topos, Herodotus is setting out to distinguish the Sauromatae from the Scythians. It is debatable how stark the differences really were, but the archaeological evidence does suggest that, among the Sauromatae, women could be buried with weapons in a style similar to men. The extent of the territory of the Sauromatae is not well defined, but there is a broad similarity in material culture stretching across the Caspian steppe from the valley of the Volga to that of the river Ural.

The Sauromatae (by this time also called Sarmatians) seem to have moved into Scythian territory in the Pontic steppe about 300 BC, causing widespread social disruption. The royal kurgans and clan burial-grounds of the old Scythian elite disappear, and by the 260s most of the unfortified Greek settlements had been destroyed. The new burial-grounds that emerged reflected the warlike nature of the incomers. It was under Sarmatian pressure that many of the Scythians moved westwards to Dobruja, the steppe region south of the lower Danube, which became known as Little Scythia. Later the Sarmatians were to continue their westward move, some of them reaching the Great Hungarian Plain in the second century AD (pp. 181–5). The change in name from Sauromatae to Sarmatians is a construct of the historical record. Archaeologists tend to regard the whole development from the sixth century BC to the second century AD as essentially one cultural complex, called for convenience Sarmatian, though it is recognized that over time there was significant cultural change as Sarmatian tribes located to new territories.

Beyond the Sarmatians the classical world was dependent on hearsay, the only source being a poem quoted by Herodotus written in the seventh century BC by Aristeas of Proconnesus, who claimed to have made a journey eastwards across the steppe 'as far as the Issedonians. Above them dwelt the Arimaspians, men with one eye; still further, the gold-guarding griffins; and beyond these, the Hyperboreans . . .'. Herodotus adds the interesting observation that there was constant population pressure, one tribe invading the territory of the next; thus, 'the Arimaspians drove the Issedonians from this country, while the Issedonians dispossessed the Scyths' (*Histories* 4.13).

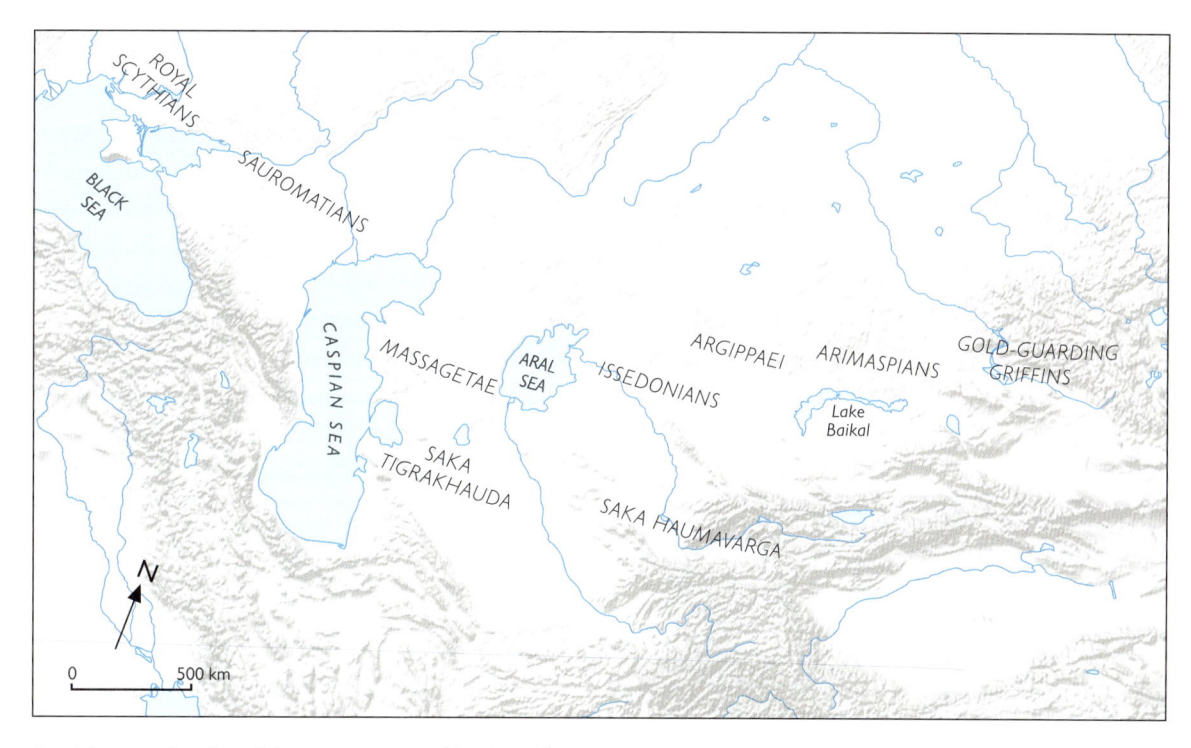

6.17 The nomadic tribes of the steppe mentioned by classical writers

The Issedonians, visited by Aristeas, probably occupied the Kazakh steppe westwards from the river Ural up to the river Irtysh. To the east were the Argippaei, described by Herodotus as having flat noses and large chins, suggesting that they may have been of Mongolian origin. They lived 'at the foot of lofty mountains', a reference most likely to the Altai. Beyond them, Herodotus admits, 'no one can speak with certainty'. Knowledge tails off into myths about 'men with goats' feet' and 'gold-guarding griffins' who lived in the 'lofty and inaccessible' mountains. These would be the people of the Altai-Sayan region, an area of ample gold resources. It may not be irrelevant that the griffin is a frequent motif in the art of the Pazyryk culture in the Altai.

South of the Kazakh steppe between the Caspian Sea and the foothills of the Pamir nomadic peoples occupied the steppe and desert fringes and, in particular, the large deltaic expanses of the Amu Darya and Syr Darya, where the rivers approach the Aral Sea. These people were generally known as Sakas, which is the Persian equivalent to Scythians, but there were many different groups. The most powerful at this time were the Massagetae, who occupied much of the territory east of the Aral Sea between the two rivers. Herodotus tells us that they were much like the Scythians in their dress and way of life, and their children lived in wagons drawn by oxen. They lived mainly on milk, fish, and sheep, but there was much variety in lifestyle. Those occupying the marshy deltas of the Syr Darya bred cattle, horses, and camels, and cultivated irrigated land, but others, living in the drier regions, were entirely nomadic. What impressed the Persians was their warlike nature. They were strong and valiant opponents, fighting both on foot and on horseback with bows, javelins, and battle-axes, resplendent in light body armour decorated with gold. The bridles and cheek-pieces of the horses were similarly decorated, while the horses wore breast-plates. By the end of the fourth century BC the Massagetae were famed for their heavily armed cavalry, the cataphracts, regarded with awe by their opponents.

The Massagetae shared many beliefs and practices with other nomadic groups. Social organization may have been matriarchal, with women afforded status, and it seems that ritual cannibalism may have been practised. Herodotus records that the elderly were sacrificed and their flesh boiled and eaten by all their kinsfolk together with that of sacrificed cattle. It is not clear how widespread the practice was, but it may have been restricted only to the elite, representing the symbolic transference of power from one generation to the next. The discovery of human bone fragments in the debris of funeral feasts of the Sarmatians of the southern Urals provides some supporting evidence.

Other Saka tribes lived to the east of the Caspian Sea. The Persians mention two groups in particular: the Saka Haumavarga (the 'hauma-drinking Sakas'), and the Saka Tigrakhauda (the 'pointed-hatted Sakas'). It was the king of the latter group, King Skuka, who is depicted, complete with his tall, pointed hat, as one of the captives in chains before Darius on the famous Bisitun relief. A Saka grave found at Issyk, south of Lake Balkhash, dating to the fifth century, was evidently that of a member of the elite. He wore a tunic sewn with thousands of gold plaques looking like scale-armour. His long- and short-swords were gilded and hung in decorated sheaths from a belt embellished with gold animal figures, and he wore a gold neck torc and finger-rings. Most remarkable was his tall, pointed hat, which was elaborately decorated with appliqué golden animals, to which were attached featherlike projections sprouting miniature spears.

6.18 A reconstruction of the dress of a Saka chieftain based on archaeological remains found in a tomb at Issyk in southern Kazakhstan, fourth–third century BC

Here, in all his bizarre glory, was a Saka warrior conforming in every detail to the description provided by Herodotus' informant.

The Saka tribes occupying the Central Asian zone were confronted by the might of the Persian empire and, as we have seen, Cyrus was killed when campaigning against them. At its most expansive the empire had incorporated Saka Tigrakhauda into the province of Chorasmia, east of the Caspian, and much of the region between the Amu Darya and Syr Darya. The nomads, now within the Persian sphere, inevitably absorbed elements of Achaemenid culture. They acquired Persian manufactured items, and local craftsmen assimilated Persian motifs into the nomadic repertoire. One of the most spectacular examples of this is the Oxus Treasure, a collection of gold and silver artefacts found together in a hoard at Takht-i Kuwad in the upper Amu Darya and dating to the fifth or fourth century BC. While some of the items, like the model of a two-horse chariot and a silver statue of robed figures, are likely to have been Persian productions, others, like a pair of griffin-headed armlets and an embossed gold plaque depicting a fabulous winged creature with the body of a deer and the head of a horned lion, are firmly within the tradition of Scytho-Siberian art. Items of Achaemenid type are found even further afield in nomad territory. A

6.19 Model chariot made in gold from the Oxus treasure found in Central Asia. It is probably Persian in origin and dates to the fifth–fourth century BC

rich nomad burial from Filippovka in the southern Ural region produced a golden amphora and a silver rython (drinking cup), both of Achaemenid manufacture, found alongside a remarkable set of stylized golden stags, so clearly local products. The famous burials at Pazyryk in the Altai Mountains (to be considered in the next section) were accompanied by imported Persian fabrics. These valuable and exotic items found in the graves of the nomads may well have been diplomatic gifts carried north by Persian ambassadors interested in establishing good relations with their steppe neighbours.

The cultural interfaces between the Greek world and the Pontic steppe and between the Persians and Central Asia were very different. The Greeks were content to remain in their coastal zone, providing craft products for the nomad market, taking back into Greek culture little of the vitality of Scythian animal art. In Central Asia the territorial ambitions of the Persian state produced a far more fluid situation. Not only did the Sakas embrace Achaemenid stylistic ideas, but the Persian craftsmen readily adopted elements of Saka animal art. Yet these interactions and borrowings went far beyond decorative styles. The Sakas had much to teach the Persians in the art of mounted warfare, and the lessons were well learnt. The zone of interaction was a place of energy and innovation. It was here that another powerful people, the Parthians, were soon to emerge.

The Nomads of the Altai-Sayan

The frozen burials found at Pazyryk in the High Altai are rightly famous. So rich and varied are the finds that they would require much space to do them justice. Here we can select only a few themes relevant to our general discussions.

The Pazyryk cemetery, composed of some twenty-five kurgans, lies at a height of 1,600 metres. The five largest kurgans, producing the richest finds, are clearly the burials of the elite. The dating of the cemetery has been much debated, largely using art-historical comparisons, and various dates between the fifth and third centuries have been suggested, but recent analysis of a series of radiocarbon assessments suggests that the earliest of the rich graves, tomb 2, dates to the first decades of the third century and the latest, tomb 5, to the third quarter of the third century. This is confirmed by dendrological studies, which show that the two graves were separated by fifty years or so. What makes the Pazyryk graves so important is the survival of a wide range of organic material: wood, furs, fabrics, including carpets, tapestries, feltwork, and silks, and even human flesh, skin, and hair. This remarkable survival is the result of the ground beneath the kurgan remaining frozen throughout the year, thus preventing bacterial decay.

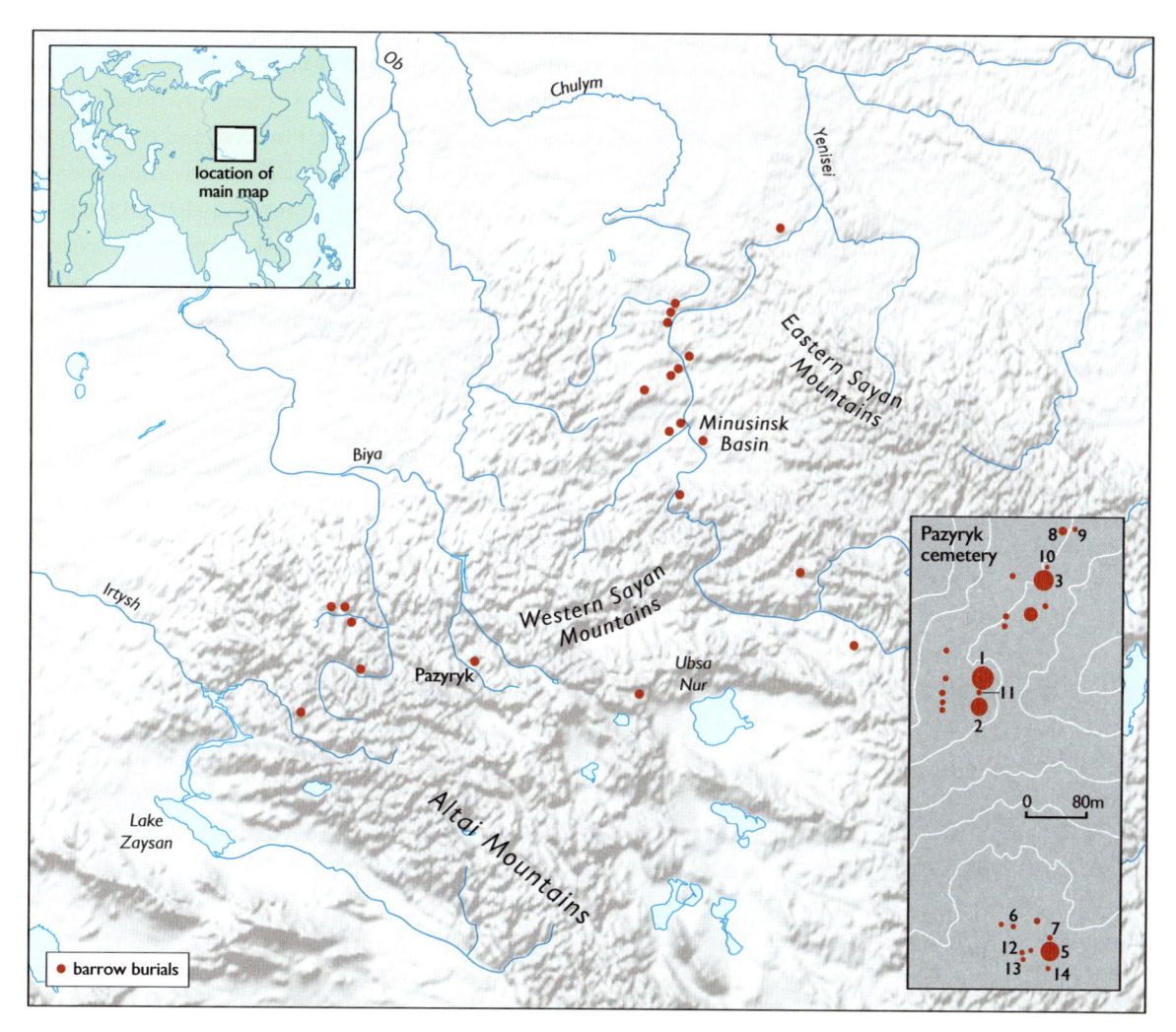

6.20 Barrow burials (kurgans) from the later first millennium BC in the Altai-Sayan region. The inset map shows the barrow cemetery of Pazyryk

Each tomb consisted of a timber-lined pit in which the burial and grave goods had been placed, sealed by a roof of logs, above which a kurgan of soil and boulders had been heaped. Tomb 2 was one of the most elaborately furnished. Two bodies were recovered: a female of European type and a man, about 60 years old, who had the physical characteristics of a Mongolian. Both had had their organs removed and the body packed with vegetable material before being sewn up. The man appears to have been killed by axe blows to the head and had been scalped. He had been extensively tattooed early in life, with elaborate animal-style designs, including a leaping stag.

LEARNING FROM EACH OTHER

Among the offerings recovered from the tomb were wooden tables, a drum, a stringed instrument, and clothing, including a squirrel-fur coat and two pairs of fur boots, one of leopard skin. There was also a bronze cauldron filled with large stones and charred seeds of hemp. This was from the final purification process of the kind that Herodotus reports among the Pontic Scythians. He describes how the cauldron was set up in a small felt tent and the hemp seeds were thrown onto hot stones, emitting a vapour, hashish, which the occupants inhaled, howling all the time with delight. Herodotus confesses some bewilderment at the practice.

Tomb 5 was also richly furnished. The grave goods included a dismantled four-wheeled ceremonial cart with wheels 2 metres in diameter, a 4-metre-square pile carpet of Persian origin, a felt wall hanging, and a Chinese silk textile with embroidered birds. With the vehicle were buried nine horses complete with their saddles and bridles. Two of the horses, perhaps those that drew the vehicle, wore headdresses, one in the form of a stag, the other a griffin. The horses were of a sturdy breed probably from Central Asia and had been stall-fed with grain in contrast to the smaller local breeds left to feed in the pastures.

While the fabrics are remarkable in their variety and their vividness, it is the wood carvings, invariably of animals real and mythical, and the cut-out leather silhouettes that astonish. Here we see Scytho-Siberian animal art of the kind that would have pervaded the life of the people irrespective of status. It is a reminder of how intimately the life of the nomad was bound up with the animal world.

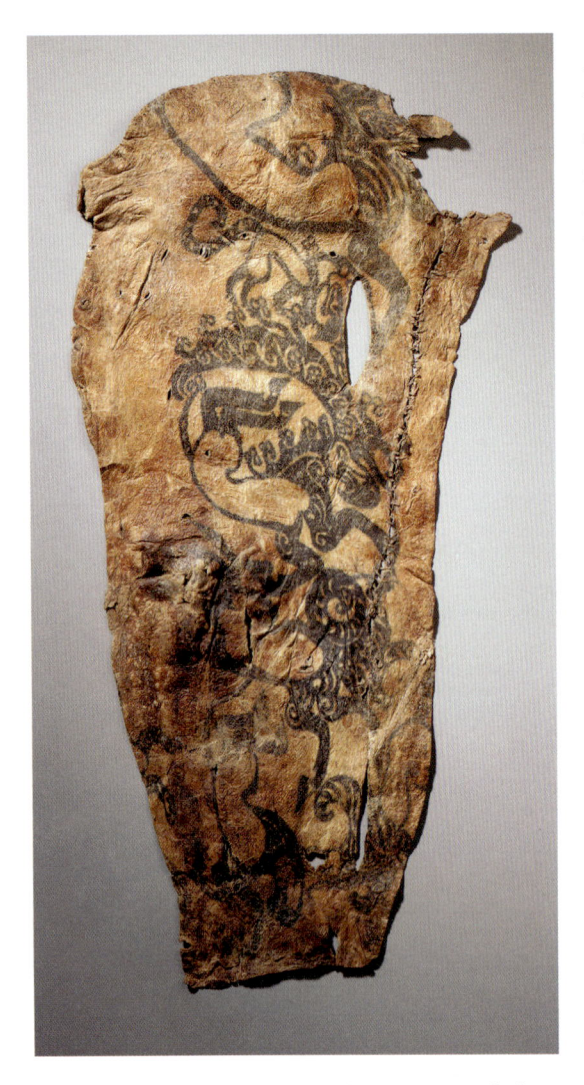

6.21 The tombs at Pazyryk in the Altai Mountains of Siberia have produced a spectacular array of well-preserved organic materials including the skin of the right arm of the man buried in barrow 2 tattooed with a spirited rendering of galloping beasts, third century BC

6.22 (*Opposite*) The cemetery of Pazyryk in the Altai Mountains. The section is of barrow 2: it shows the layer of permafrost, protected by the barrow mound, which has been responsible for the remarkable preservation of the organic materials in the burial. The plan is of the grave pit of barrow 5. The body of the deceased was in the log coffin with his partner. His large funerary vehicle was dismantled and laid just outside. The cemetery dates to the third century BC

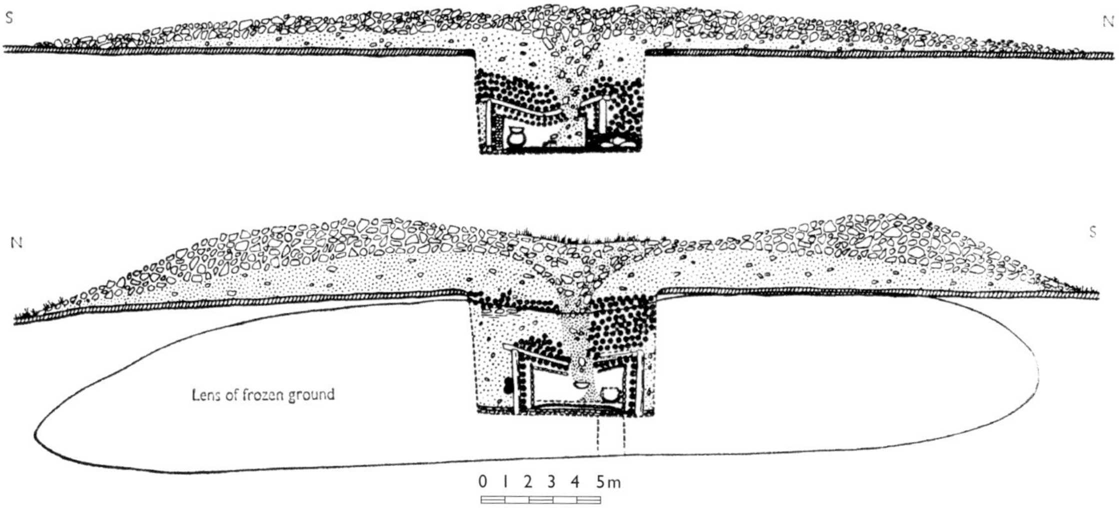
S
N
N
S
Lens of frozen ground
0 1 2 3 4 5m

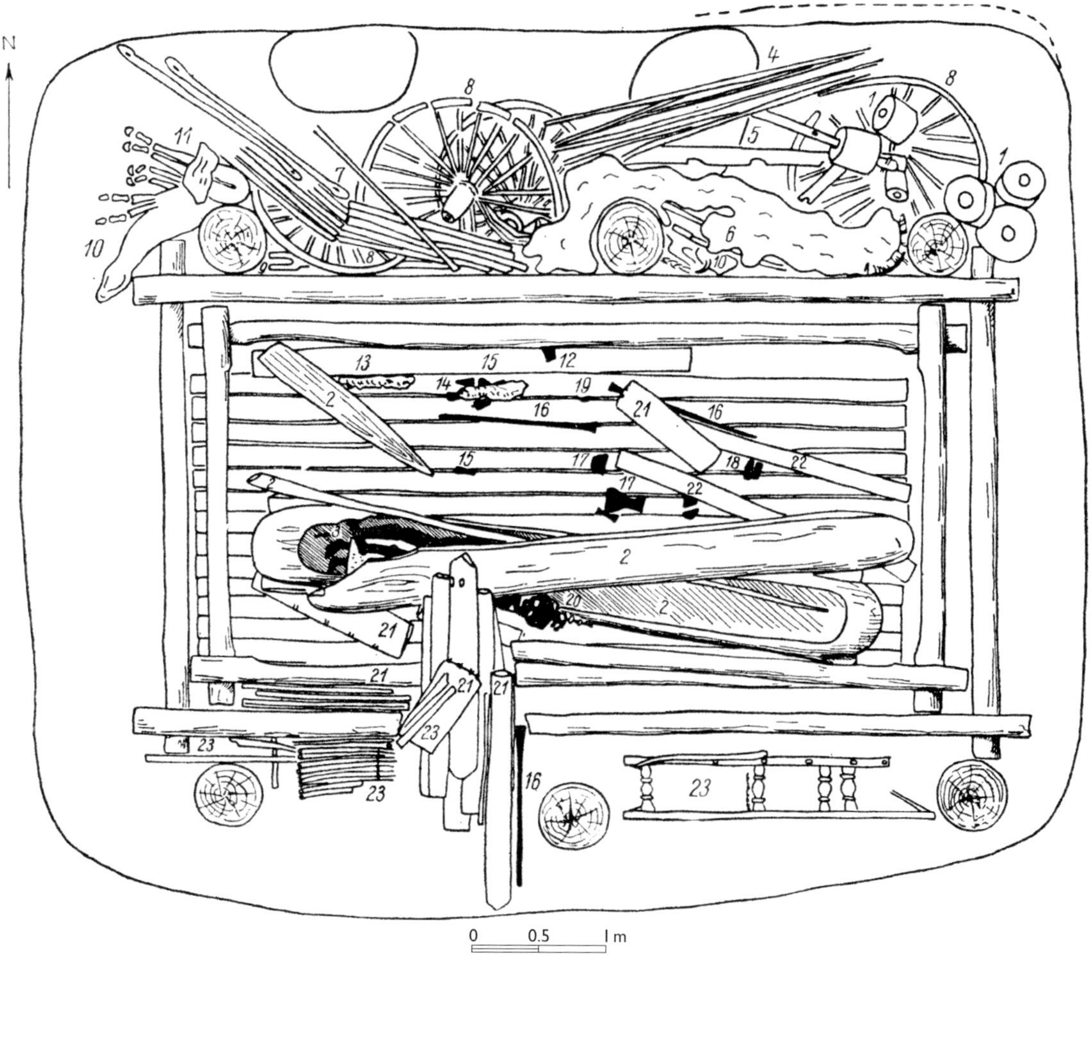
N
0 0.5 1 m

LEARNING FROM EACH OTHER

6.23 Among the exotic goods available to the chieftains of the Altai Mountains was this embroidered silk cloth of Chinese origin found at Pazyryk in barrow 5

6.24 The carriage found dismantled in barrow 5 at Pazyryk (Figure 6.22) is reconstructed here. It resembles the carriages with large wheels of the kind found in the burial pits around the tomb of the first emperor, Qin Shi Huangdi, near Xi'an, dating to 210 BC. The Pazyryk carriage is also of the third century and may have been imported from China

LEARNING FROM EACH OTHER

6.25 This elaborate head-gear worn by one of the horses is in barrow 1 at Pazyryk. It might have been sight of this kind of ritual finery that caused one incredulous observer to write of the distant 'gold-guarding griffins'—a phrase which Herodotus recorded

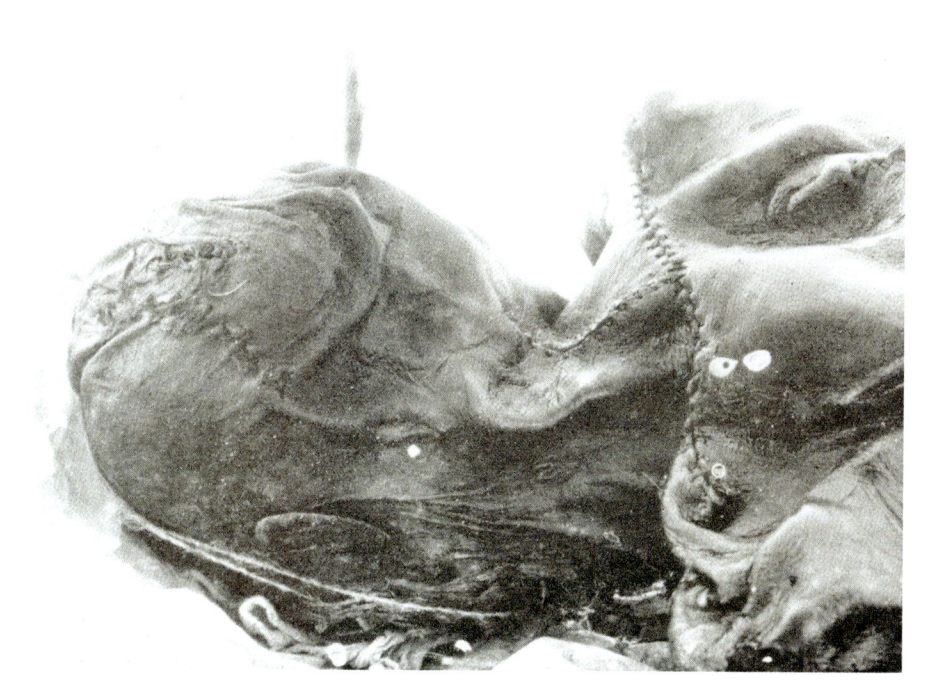

6.26 Detail of the female body from barrow 5 at Pazyryk. The body had been cut open to remove the organs and carefully sewn up again

6.27 Tree coffin from barrow 5 at Pazyryk soon after excavation still containing its male occupant. The coffin had originally also contained a female body but she had been dragged out by tomb robbers

The Altai communities lay at a nodal point in the networks of connectivity that threaded through Eurasia, and the finds from the royal tombs are a reflection of this. From the Persian world came pile carpets and tapestries; from the deserts and steppe of Central Asia came the leopard furs, the sturdy horses, and coriander seed; from India came a mirror of tin and cotton fabrics; and from China came a bronze helmet, lacquer-work bowls, and silk embroidery. It is even possible that the ceremonial cart, with massive wheels, was a product of China. How all these exotics came to be in the hands of the Altai elite in the third century is a matter of speculation. Some may have come through down-the-line trade in exchange for local products like furs and gold. Others may have been diplomatic gifts from distant rulers keen to develop trading relationships with nomad leaders commanding the trans-Eurasian routes. It may even be that some of the exotic goods travelled as dowries with brides sent to strengthen agreements or treaties. Whatever the mechanism, these exotics point to the growing interconnectedness of central and eastern Eurasia.

The Altai-Sayan nomads are a people without a name, beyond the reach of the contemporary historians. It may be, however, that they were the 'gold-guarding griffins' of Herodotus. Think of the effect that a man riding a horse that was wearing a griffin headdress like that from tomb 5 of Pazyryk might have had on an unsuspecting observer.

The Tian Shan and the Taklamakan Desert

The long ridge of the Tian Shan range, running eastwards from the Pamir along the north side of the Tarim basin, formed a formidable barrier to communication between the Saka communities of the south-eastern Kazakh steppe (the Semirech'ye region) and the people occupying the northern fringe of the Taklamakan desert. But in the middle region of the range a series of valleys, particularly that of the river Ili, which flows westwards into Lake Balkhash, provides routes through the barrier, and it is here, on the northern side of the mountain range, that concentrations of population have been identified. Further to the east another concentration of sites stretches along the northern foothills of the mountains facing the Dzungarian Depression. These settlements command a major east–west route from the Kazakh steppe to Mongolia and to the Gansu Corridor. To the south of the main ridge of the Tian Shan the well-watered foothills overlooking the Taklamakan provide favourable conditions for settlements, which tend to occur where there are constant water resources and where natural routes converge. Other settlements cluster around oases along the southern rim of the Taklamakan.

Altogether over sixty sites, mostly cemeteries, have been identified, some of them, where unusually dry conditions prevail, yielding exceptionally well-preserved organic materials. The comparative isolation of some of the settlement clusters has allowed archaeologists to define twelve distinct cultural groups, of which the largest, in the Ili valley, is known as the Tiemulike culture. The material remains are comparatively sparse and dates are few, but there appears to be a considerable continuity of occupation from the second millennium until about 300 BC.

In spite of the diversity of culture among these highly dispersed groups, all seem to have had contacts with nomadic peoples to the north and west and there may well have been some exchanges of population over time. The Tiemulike culture has yielded a range of artefacts of Saka type, including bronze trays and cauldrons similar to material found in the Saka sites of the Semirech'ye region, and it may be that this archaeologically defined culture should be regarded simply as an extension of the Sakas. Indeed, a Chinese text, the *Hanshu* ('History of the Han Dynasty') records that the Sakas were active in the region from the seventh to the second centuries BC.

Saka-related material is also found along the southern side of the Tian Shan, showing that Saka influences were now passing through the mountain ridge into the Tarim basin. Finds include bronze-footed trays, cauldrons, mirrors, and distinctive horse-gear, all of which could have come from the Semirech'ye–Ili region. One site, the cemetery of Alagou, produced a number of gold plaque attachments, some of them depicting fabulous beasts with their hindquarters turned through 180 degrees. These are very similar to items from Altai-Sayan sites and show that north–south contacts were being maintained across or around the Dzungarian Depression. Another interesting link between Alagou and Pazyryk is the occurrence in both cemeteries of lacquer wares and silk from the Chinese Central Plains. It was probably through communities like Alagou, commanding a major route through the central part of the Tian Shan, that trade between China and the Altai was articulated. In the second half of the first millennium BC Chinese goods became increasingly common around the northern fringes of the Talakaman, and the discovery of etched carnelian beads at some of the sites shows that trading links had also been established with India, a point further stressed by the Indian mirror and cotton fabric found at Pazyryk.

It is difficult to say to what extent these disparate cultural groups regarded themselves as sharing an ethnic identity, but by the second century BC the Chinese sources record the presence of a tribe called the Yuezhi, who occupied the arid grasslands at the eastern end of the Tarim basin. It was through the Yuezhi that the Chinese acquired nephrite jade from Khotan and the rare white jade found as pebbles in the river Yarkand at the western end of the basin. During the Warring States period the Yuezhi were known as the suppliers of fine horses. By virtue of their location at the east end of the Tarim basin, close to the Gansu Corridor, which provided the most convenient route to China, the Yuezhi were able to serve as middlemen between the Chinese states and the various desert fringe communities to the west and the nomads of the north. When, early in the second century, they were attacked by the nomadic Xiongnu coming from Mongolia, they fled westwards, first to the Ili valley and thence to Central Asia, their migration evidently following the trade-route which, for a while, they had been able to command.

Standing back from the detail it is interesting to see how, during the first millennium BC, the Tarim basin had begun to assume a central position in the patterns of connectivity that were then developing. Although the Taklamakan desert and the surrounding mountains were significant barriers, the desert fringes, comparatively well watered from the mountains, were conducive to settlement and supported a series of oasis settlements along the two east–west routes lying to the north and south of the desert. Both routes eventually reached passes leading through the Pamir to the Ferghana valley, while the northern route offered further opportunities, with links through the Tian Shan to the Ili river valley and to the Dzungarian Depression, from where it was possible to reach the Altai communities and the nomadic groups of the eastern Kazakh steppe. Along these networks goods and peoples moved, and the Tarim basin became something of a melting pot of cultures, with Sakas coming in from the north and Mongolian settlers from the east. While the oases provided conditions where crops could be grown, there were large areas, particularly in the east, where a more nomadic lifestyle would have been the norm: it was here that the Yuezhi emerged as a distinct ethnic group. Over the years the Chinese will have begun to learn of the west through traders' tales. They were soon to take a more active interest in the area, invigorating the east–west traffic along routes that much later came to be referred to as the Silk Road.

The Chinese States and the Northern Nomads

In China the long period of conflict that characterized the Eastern Zhou is divided into two: the Spring and Autumn period (770–481 BC) and the Warring States period (480–221 BC). In the early stages, as the core states of the Central Plains exhausted themselves, the non-Zhou peoples of the periphery began to increase their involvement until, in the mêlée of alliance and conflict, the differences between Zhou and non-Zhou became blurred, with the Qin in the west and the Chu in the south becoming part of Zhou China.

The conflict continued during the Warring States period. By 300 BC eleven states were engaged in continuous warfare, but by 256 BC, when the last of the titular Zhou kings had been deposed, the numbers had been reduced to seven, the rest having been destroyed or absorbed. Finally, by 221 BC only one state, Qin, remained. Its leader, Ying Zheng, had united the whole of China and took for himself the title Qin Shihuangdi ('the First August and Divine Emperor of Qin').

The Spring and Autumn period and the Warring States period were a time of continuous conflict, often on a massive and brutal scale, but it was also a time of dramatic social, technological, and cultural change. It was almost as if the state of endemic warfare drove human inventiveness. Cities grew in number and size as commercialization burgeoned, encouraged by better communication. Agriculture intensified to feed the growing populations, and there were rapid advances in technology and manufacturing. Some of the major cities numbered their inhabitants in hundreds of thousands, and for the well-to-do life was good. Linzi, capital of Qi, was so wealthy that its inhabitants had the leisure to 'play the flute, strum the harp, pluck the zither, or stroke the lyre'. Its streets were so crowded that 'the carriages rub rims, and its populace so great that people rub shoulders'.

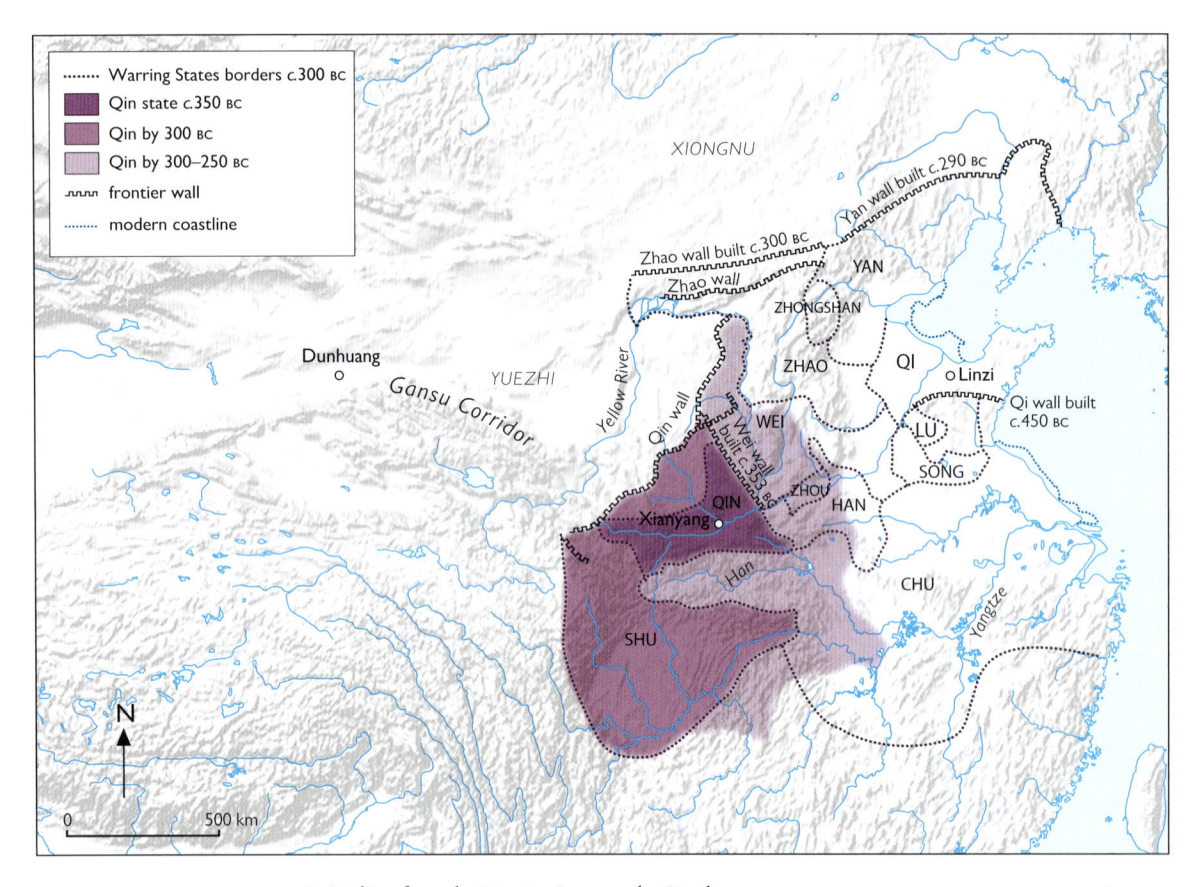

6.28 China from the Warring States to the Qin dynasty

Agricultural productivity was now on a prodigious scale, not least to provide for the rapidly growing population. New irrigation systems, ox-drawn ploughs, and the development of iron tools, replacing bronze, facilitated production, but there was also a move towards intensification. One contemporary writer, commenting on agriculture in the state of Wei, noted that 'all the land between the cottages in the fields and the galleried houses is farmed. Not a foot is turned to pasture or grazing.'

In technology invention abounded. Although meteoric iron had been known since the Shang period, by the sixth century BC ironsmiths had learnt to cast iron, a process requiring much higher temperatures. Iron was now widely used for all tools and weapons. In warfare the invention of the crossbow, with a range of up to 800 metres, greatly added to the efficiency of the fighting force, while to facilitate commerce, now practised on a grand scale, many of the states developed their own bronze coinage in the shape of spades, knives, and cowrie-shells. The energy and inventiveness of the period was remarkable.

The pace of political and social change was such that the old aristocracies could no longer cope with the increasing complexity of the workload. This led to the creation of new bureaucratic systems, the bureaucrats being drawn from the intellectual class. The result was that the intellectual elite grew in numbers and in influence, and schools of thought began to develop led by men such as Mengzi (Mencius) and Kongfuzi (Confucius), who were responsible for developing Taoism and Confucianism. That five hundred years of incessant and brutal war should bring about great advances in technology and administration is little surprise, but that the period should see the emergence of schools of philosophy debating such abstract concepts as humanism and individualism raises interesting, if uncomfortable, questions about how the human mind is stimulated.

Many improvements were made to military tactics and equipment during the Warring States period, but none more far-reaching than the adoption of regular cavalry. Cavalry had long been used by the nomads of the north, and those northern states in conflict with the nomads will have learnt of its advantages, particularly in hilly regions, where chariots could not effectively be deployed. Yet there was a reluctance among the Chinese to adopt anything quite so barbaric. Indeed, the issue was openly debated in 307 BC when the far-sighted ruler Wuling, of the state of Zhao, tried to persuade his conservative advisers that the Zhao should develop their own cavalry units. The king's arguments were direct: cavalry was needed not only to overcome the northern nomads but to protect the borders against the aggression of neighbouring states; where there was a military problem it was prudent to choose the appropriate force to deal with it. His opponents used the argument typical of dynamic conservatives throughout time: change is dangerous. To adopt the custom and clothing (trousers) of 'northern foreigners' would upset the ordinary people of the state and their allies. 'If the garment is outlandish, the intentions become disordered; when custom is flouted, people become rebellious.' To this Wuling's response was: 'a talent for following the ways of yesterday is not sufficient to improve the world of today'. His arguments won, and mounted archers fighting in close formation thereafter became a powerful part of Chinese armies.

To the north of the warring Chinese states were agro-pastoral communities like the Rong and the Di, and beyond them groups that were fully nomadic, dependent on their livestock and upon trade with their southern neighbours. These peoples, renowned for their horse riding and their archery skills, were referred to by the Chinese as the Hu—a name more likely to be a general description of people sharing a nomadic life style than the ethnonym of a single people. The development of nomadic pastoralism was well under way in this region by the seventh century BC. By the fifth century the disparate groups, speaking different languages and spread over a wide territory, were beginning to feature large in the Chinese consciousness.

Nomadic pastoralists needed to trade to provide themselves with the commodities that their highly specific lifestyles could not. In consequence, regular trading relationships were set up between the nomads and the Chinese, with the agro-pastoral Rong and Di probably serving as middlemen. There is good documentary evidence that the Zhou states received horses, furs, and probably cattle and sheep from the Hu in return for precious gifts of gold, silk, and women as brides. That coinage produced by the states reached the northern nomads suggests that the trade may have been more than simple bartering and probably involved quite complex market exchanges.

During the period of the Warring States some of the northern states began to erect linear boundaries known as 'long walls' (*changcheng*) to define their territories. Wall building had begun in the Central Plains but was soon to extend to the northern regions, where, in the late fourth and early third century, three states were involved in constructing linear boundaries: the Qin created a boundary running from the upper reaches of the Wei in a north-easterly direction to the eastern part of the Yellow River loop; the Zhao built two successive barriers 50–100 kilometres apart across the steppe to the north of the Yellow River; while the Yan added a similar boundary, roughly continuing the line of the northern Zhao wall, stretching eastwards to the sea. After the unification of China under the Qin the original Qin boundary was extended north and west to the Yellow River, incorporating the Ordos region.

The long walls, built of puddled earth and stones, were up to 5 metres wide at the base and 3–4 metres high. They were usually built facing downslope and incorporated natural barriers where possible. Some of the lengths were strengthened with a fronting ditch, and forts, watchtowers, and beacon emplacements were added at intervals where necessary. The function of the long walls has been much debated, the main question hinging on whether they were primarily intended to be defensive or offensive. On the whole the evidence favours the latter. The boundaries are not sited along the ecological boundaries between pasture and arable land but are often well to the north of this divide so as to include large tracts of pasture. In other words, the walls were designed to formalize a land grab on the part of the northern states. The new territories thus gained, together with the native populations who inhabited them, provided much-needed new resources, notably extensive horse-breeding pastures and skilled people to train the horses and to swell the ranks of the cavalry archers.

6.29 The defensive wall built in the Qin period (221–210 BC) to protect the northern parts of the empire from nomad attack, seen here at Guyang, Inner Mongolia. It was built of rammed earth

The long walls also, of course, performed a defensive function. Nomad movements to the north could be observed and, if necessary, checked, while trading interactions between the two sides could be carefully controlled at the guarded crossings. For the nomads to the north, whose livelihood had depended on easy access to the agro-pastoralists and the luxuries offered by the states, the restrictions were unwelcome and caused widespread social tensions, exacerbating changes already in progress: the disparate Hu lineages were now coming together in larger confederations. At the end of the fourth century we hear of a new political entity among the nomads, the Xiongnu, who were soon to become a formidable enemy of China, a centralized power amassed on the Mongolian steppe ready to strike at any time.

States and Nomads: Three Hundred and Fifty Years of Interaction

The pastoral communities of the steppe came into contact with developed states along three very different interfaces: the Black Sea littoral, the Central Asian desert-steppe, and the steppe land of northern China. On each the interactions were different. Along the Greek maritime interface a symbiosis developed, unstable at times but for the most part maintained for mutual benefit. The Central Asian interface was quite different. Here the Persians and their Macedonian successors were expansionist, intent on acquiring new territory. China was different again in that the Chinese states were content with minimal territorial gain so long as a stable, fixed frontier could be sustained.

Different though the attitudes were, all three regions shared one characteristic: the frontiers were always permeable enough to allow exchange to take place between the confronting worlds. The steppe nomads could supply horses, furs, livestock, and sometimes grain, while in return the southern states could offer manufactured consumer durables. Each was dependent on the other. Horses were essential to maintain the cavalries needed by the states, who were habitually plagued by internal warfare, while the nomad elites were now dependent on a regular supply of prestige goods to maintain their social systems: thus it was that Chinese, Indian, and Persian commodities reached the remote Altai.

By the third century regular networks of exchange had come into being between the southern states and their northern nomad neighbours. It was a prelude to the growth of the lateral east–west networks that were soon to develop, creating the intricate cross-continent connectivity popularly referred to as the Silk Road.

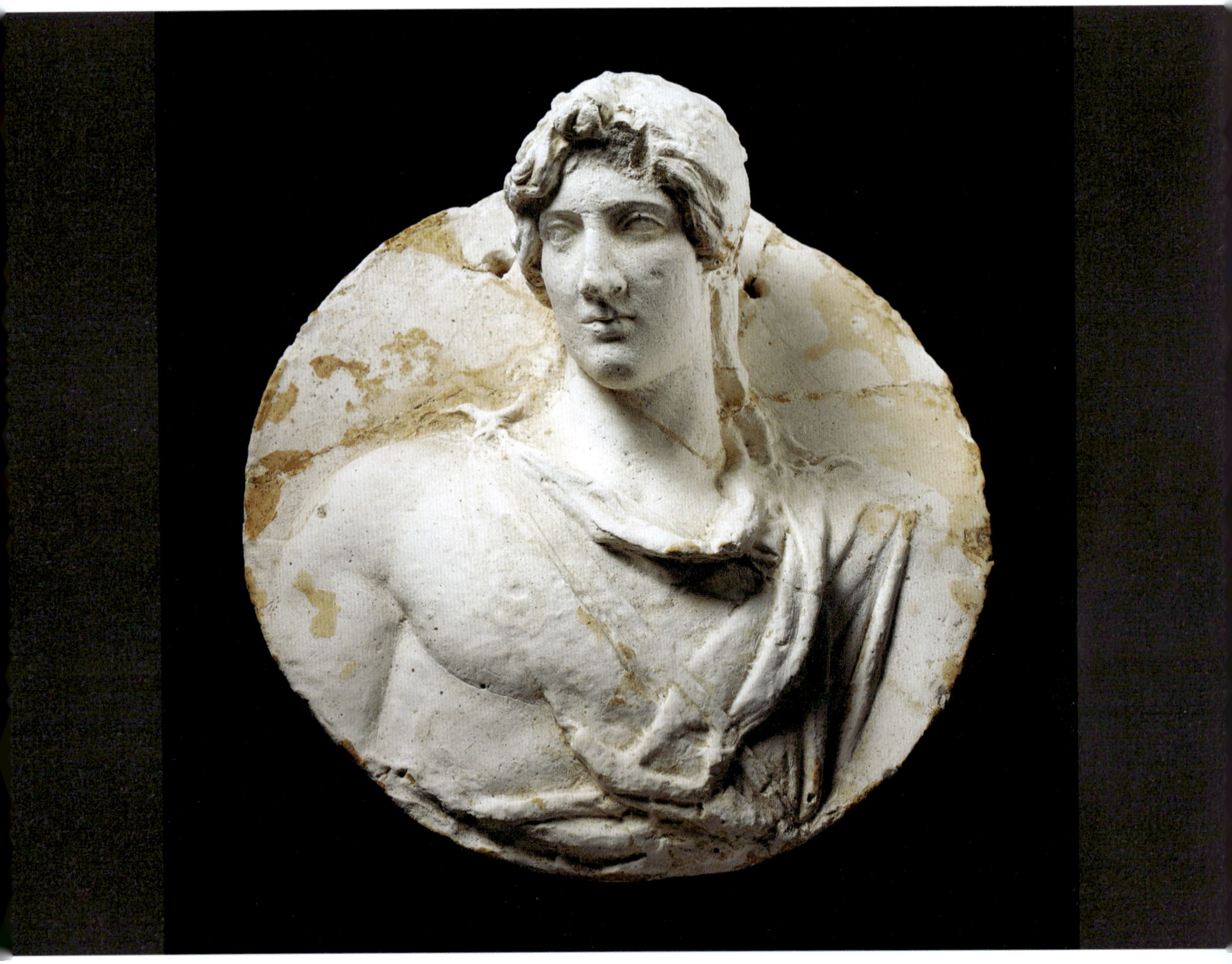

7

THE CONTINENT CONNECTED,
250 BC—AD 250

THERE is a pleasing symmetry about the period 250 BC–AD 250. Within a few decades at the end of the third century BC three empires were born. In Europe the First Punic War, fought out on Sicily between the Carthaginians and the Romans, ended with Roman victory in 241 BC and the annexation of Sicily, Rome's first overseas acquisition and the beginning of its empire. In the Middle East, about 240 BC, the Parni moved from their homeland south-east of the Caspian Sea to Parthia on the Iranian plateau, initiating the Parthian empire. And in China, in 221 BC, the Qin army overcame the last of the warring states to unite China under the First Emperor, Ying Zheng, creating stability for the Han dynasty soon to follow. The three empires lasted for about the same length of time. In AD 220 the Han empire, weakened by corruption, came to an end; in AD 224 the last of the Parthian kings was defeated by one of his vassals, and it was in the first half of the third century that the western Roman empire began its painfully protracted decline.

The three big players in world history—Rome, Parthia, and China—tend to dominate the narrative, but the Eurasian nomads had their own important part to play. In the east, the nomads of Mongolia, the Xiongnu, were instrumental in forcing the Han to extend their influence westwards across the Tarim basin and through the Pamir to the desert-steppe of Central Asia. Pressure from the Xiongnu also drove other nomad groups to migrate, resulting in a series of southerly nomadic movements into Bactria, and beyond into Gandhara in north-western India, where the mix of populations, indigenous Bactrians and Indians with a heavy overlay of Hellenism, and the nomadic incursion gave rise to the wonderfully eclectic culture of the Kushans.

The Kushan empire occupied a central position between Parthia and China: it also commanded the Indus valley route, which provided access from the Indian Ocean across the Hindu Kush to Central Asia and through the Karakoram Mountains to the Tarim basin. It was along the latter route that Buddhism was transmitted to the Chinese world from its home in the Ganges valley.

Eurasia was fast becoming connected. The western adventure of the Han opened up the routes around the two edges of the Taklamakan desert to passes through the Pamir leading to the Ferghana valley and to the Central Asian desert-steppe and thus to Parthia. It was not long before the consumer market that drove the Roman empire began to crave eastern luxuries like Chinese silk. Ensuring the supply required the establishment of understandings with the Parthians, but it also encouraged the more adventurous to develop sea-routes via the Red Sea to the Indian Ocean and thus to the Indian subcontinent, circumventing the Parthian middlemen and at the same time developing entirely new markets trading in spices, particularly pepper.

The rapidity with which the transcontinental and ocean routes were opened up was astonishing. At the beginning of the period a few Chinese goods was reaching the nomads of the Altai, while a trickle of carnelian beads and sea-shells were being carried from India across the Karakorams to the oasis settlements of the Tarim basin. By the first century AD Chinese silk was in great demand in Rome, the Chinese could wonder at the quality of Roman glassware, and the emperor Claudius could take Indian elephants to Britain to terrify the Britons and their horses. Eurasia had very suddenly shrunk. The empires were consuming commodities on an unprecedented scale, the more exotic the better, and a growing cohort of entrepreneurs was hard at work supplying and encouraging the demand. So it was that the dendritic pattern of caravan routes later known as the Silk Road came into use, linking the Central Plains of China with the ports of the eastern Mediterranean.

The Hellenistic Legacy: Bactria and Gandhara

The eastern extremity of the empire acquired by Alexander from the Persians was a difficult territory to manage since it comprised two quite distinct regions divided by the Hindu Kush. To the north lay Bactria and Sogdiana, roughly separated by the Amu Darya, while to the south, in the upper reaches of the Indus valley, lay Gandhara. In both areas Alexander and his immediate successors had encouraged Greeks to settle in new towns or towns laid out afresh in the Greek style (pp. 218–20). It was a deliberate attempt to stabilize a region at the limits of the 'civilized' world, and as a policy

THE CONTINENT CONNECTED

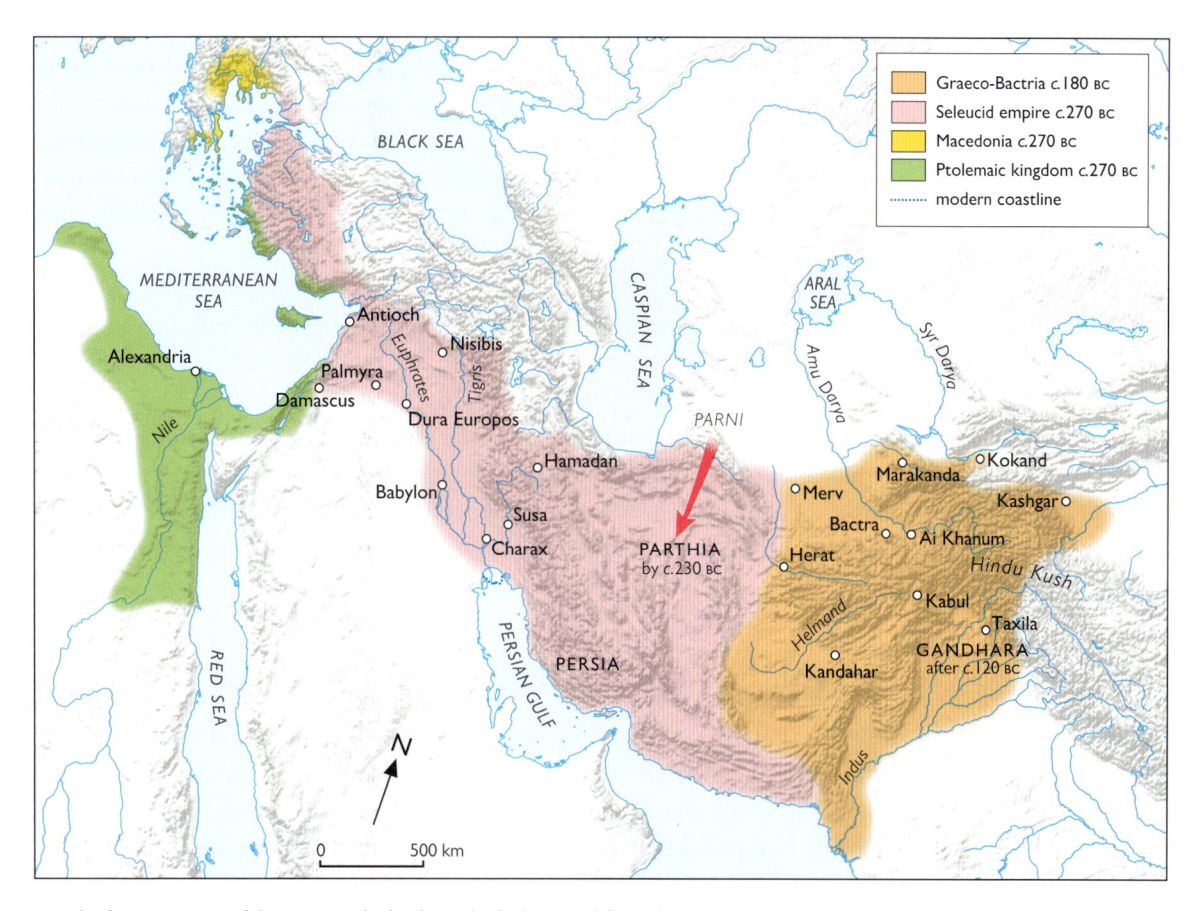

7.1 The fragmentation of the empire which Alexander had wrested from the Persian kings began on his death. By about 270 BC some semblance of stability had emerged. The eastern territories Bactria and Gandhara retained much of their Greek culture, which had been deliberately encouraged by Alexander and his immediate successors

it succeeded to a remarkable degree. Hellenistic culture became deeply rooted and continued to maintain its own distinctive characteristics through the next centuries of political change.

In the aftermath of Alexander's death, Gandhara, together with the provinces of Aria and Arachosia, south of the Hindu Kush, were absorbed into the empire of Mauryan India. Half a century later, about 250 BC, the governor of Bactria rebelled against the Seleucids and established an independent kingdom. Subsequent peace treaties between Bactria and the Seleucids stressed the need for the two states to work together in the interests of mutual security. As the historian Polybius noted, 'there were indeed vast hordes of nomads threatening them both, who would be bound to drag the country down into barbarism if they were allowed to enter it'.

255

About 180 BC the Bactrians moved south through the Hindu Kush and took control of Aria, Gandhara, and much of Punjab. They also extended their dominion northwards into Sogdiana, taking over the important oasis trading centre of Marakanda (Samarkand). But Bactrian power was short-lived. Parthians encroached upon eastern Bactria, while Gandhara and Punjab became an independent Indo-Greek kingdom ruled from Taxila. The Graeco-Bactrian state finally came to an end between 126 and 120 BC as attacks from the north, by the Saka nomads, increased. The Indo-Greek state remained independent and, under its king Meander (ruled 180–160 BC), embraced Buddhism. The iconography associated with the new belief system was soon interpreted through the eyes of artists brought up to respect Hellenistic ideals, resulting in the remarkable Gandhara style, incorporating elements of Hellenistic, Persian, and Indian traditions. Gandharan art is in harmony with itself, but reflections of the contributing styles remain apparent, reminding the observer of the complex ethnic mix in this frontier zone lying between east and west. It continued to flourish through the later Kushan period into the fifth century AD.

The Parthian Empire and their Roman Neighbours

In 245 BC, about the time the Bactrians were rebelling against the Seleucid kings, the Parni, a nomadic tribe who occupied a territory on the south-east side of the Caspian Sea, decided to ride south to the Iranian plateau to establish themselves in the region of Parthia. It was an opportunist move, making good use of the political confusion of the time, but the possibility remains that the Parni may have been responding to pressure from other nomadic groups to the north. Once established in their new homeland, they began to expand their hold on territory while notionally acknowledging the supremacy of the Seleucid king Antiochus III. All this changed when Antiochus died and the Parthians, as they were now called, began a new policy of expansion led by their king Mithridates I (ruled 171–138 BC). First Bactria was conquered, and then a campaign was launched against the west, taking, in turn, Media, Assyria, Babylonia, and Elam. The new overlords were, in effect, reconstituting the western part of the old Persian empire.

The ruling elite were comparatively few in number and were content to take over existing systems of government and the administrative classes, who were largely Greek in origin. Local languages were accepted and independence tolerated even to the degree of allowing local leaders to strike their own coinage and maintain their own fighting forces. It was empire with a light touch and goes some way to explaining why, after the initial period of expansion, little attempt was made to move beyond the confines of Iran and Mesopotamia.

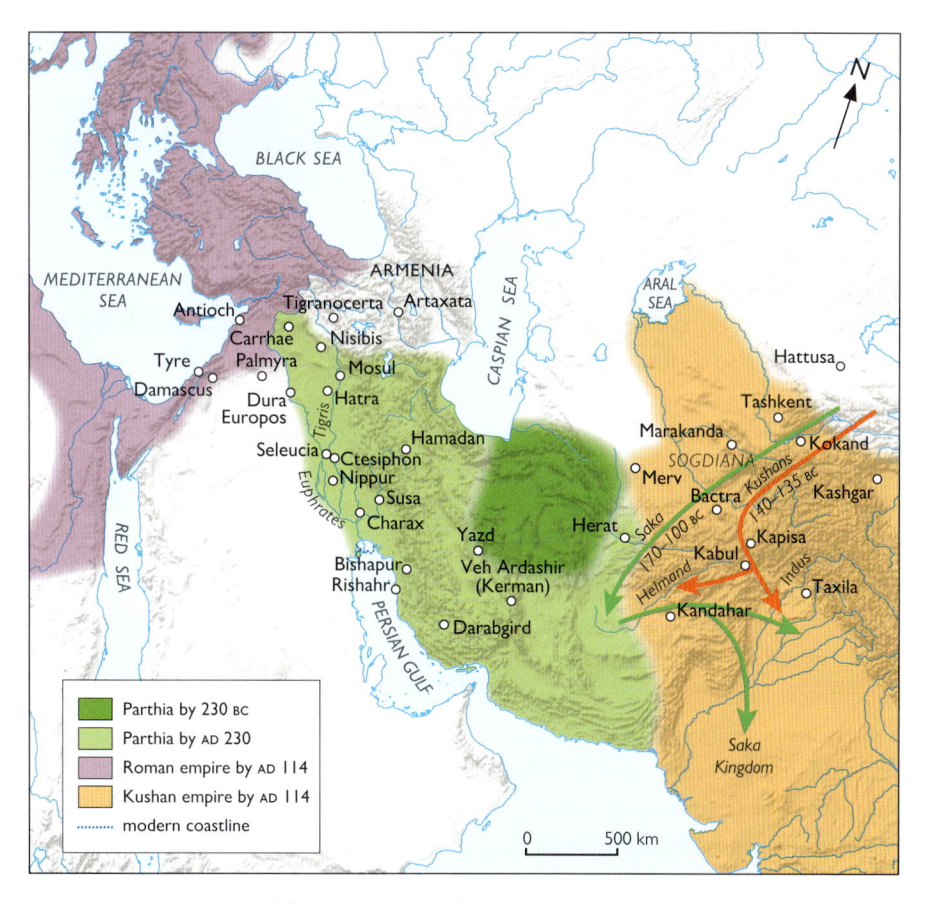

7.2 The growing strength of the Parthians in the late third and second centuries BC created a unified empire embracing the Iranian plateau and Mesopotamia. Meanwhile, in the west the Roman empire grew. An unstable frontier between the two powers ran from the south-east corner of the Black Sea to the Syrian desert

Parthia was constrained on all sides. To the east was a large territory still ruled by the Bactrian kings. In the second century BC hordes of nomads, among them Sakas and Yuezhi, migrated into the region. Some were employed as mercenaries, but others wanted land and settled on the Iranian plateau in the region that came to be known as Sakastan (Sistan). We shall consider the broader context of these events later (pp. 275–7). To the west the Arabian and Syrian deserts formed a natural barrier, but Asia Minor was something of a no man's land. It was here that the Parthians faced first the successor states of the old Persian, and later Macedonian, empire and, from the first century BC, the expanding Roman empire. It was to be, for centuries, a zone of conflict. For the most part the Euphrates formed the border, but for brief periods in the second century BC Parthian control extended as far as the Mediterranean and incorporated parts of Egypt, the Levant, and Cilicia in southern Anatolia. After about 90 BC the eastern edge of the Syrian desert became the natural limit of empire, with Dura Europos on the Euphrates serving as a garrison city controlling the two main caravan routes to the west, a northerly route along the river and across northern Syria to the Mediterranean port of Antioch, and a southerly route crossing the desert to Palmyra and thence to Damascus, reaching the Mediterranean at Tyre. These routes provided the principal overland links from the east, through Parthia, to the Roman world in times when the two states were not actively engaged in fighting each other. Parthia also controlled the maritime routes in the Persian Gulf leading to India, and on its northern border it could access the various caravan trails that crossed the deserts and desert-steppe of Central Asia. In short, it occupied a central position on the exchange networks crossing Eurasia and was able to gain considerable benefit from the exponential increase in the volume of trade that began in the first century BC.

The Parthian empire maintained no campaigning army but was so organized that a fighting force could be amassed quickly when need arose. The frontiers, meanwhile, were fully garrisoned. Central to the success of the Parthian army were the cataphracts: heavily armoured cavalry with the horse as well as the rider protected by scale-armour. They were armed with a long lance and a bow and, fighting in brigades, flung themselves at the enemy with devastating effect. The cost of the equipment meant that the cataphracts generally came from the elite, equivalent to the knight in medieval England. The army also included light brigades, cavalry with little armour using the short composite bow. They were faster and could manoeuvre more easily and were famed for the way in which they could turn in the saddle and fire arrows back at their pursuers. This became known as the Parthian shot, but it was really a technique developed by the steppe nomads centuries earlier.

The principal military objective of the Parthian kings was to secure their western border against the growing power of Rome. In the first half of the first century BC conflict centred on the political position of Armenia in eastern Asia Minor. Trouble came to a head when the Roman proconsul of Syria, Marcus Licinius Crassus, invaded Parthia in 53 BC with an army seven legions strong. The Parthian force that met him included a thousand cataphracts and nine thousand mounted archers. The result was a devastating defeat for the Romans. The conflict continued, spreading to Syria and the Levant, but was finally brought to an end in 20 BC through negotiations that saw the return of the captured legionary standards to Rome and the release of surviving Roman prisoners. The whole episode had been a massive humiliation for Rome. The uneasy peace that followed was riven with intrigues but lasted until AD 58, when war broke out again over the position of Armenia. It was resolved by political compro-

7.3 Parthian cataphract, a heavily armoured cavalry man riding an equally heavily armoured horse. The original sketch was inscribed on a tile found at the Parthian capital of Dura Europos on the Euphrates

mise five years later, but the situation remained unstable and in AD 114 the Roman emperor Trajan led his army into Armenia, annexing it for the Roman empire. This was the preparatory stage of his grand scheme to conquer Parthia.

In spring AD 116 Trajan set out for Antioch using the northern caravan route to the Euphrates and then marched down the river valley, capturing Dura Europos, Ctesiphon, Seleucia, and the port of Charax (in the kingdom of Characene) at the head of the Persian Gulf, where, it is said, he looked longingly at the ships in the harbour, saying that if he were still young he would have sailed against the Indians. While this may have been a myth invented by historians, Trajan may have seen himself as something of a latter-day Alexander. Returning through Babylon later that autumn, he stopped to make a sacrifice in the house in which Alexander had died more than four centuries before. Later in the year Trajan captured Susa, but returning along the Tigris valley he found the Babylonian settlements in revolt. He reached Antioch early in 117 but died suddenly in August before the next expedition was ready to leave. His successor, Hadrian, whose prime concern was to stabilize the frontiers of the empire, immediately abandoned the eastern campaigns.

Why had Trajan embarked upon the costly and dangerous eastern adventure? Opportunism spurred on by personal ambition no doubt played an important part, but there was also a strong economic incentive. Trade with the east was burgeoning as the Roman consumer market demanded ever-increasing quantities of exotic commodities. Prices were high, not least because of the substantial customs dues charged by the Parthians on transhipment. By controlling Parthia, Rome not only could bring down prices at home but could generate additional income by taxing trade. That Trajan was already fixing the dues to be paid on camels and horses crossing the Mesopotamian rivers while he was in Babylon shows that the economic imperative was never far from his thoughts.

For more than forty years following Trajan's death the Euphrates was accepted as the border between Rome and Parthia, but in AD 161 the Armenian problem flared up once more, initiating a new phase of warfare which saw the Romans active again in Mesopotamia in a conflict that was to last until AD 166. During this time Seleucia was burnt to the ground, Ctesiphon was captured, and the Roman armies thrust into Media. In the end, only minor territorial gains were made. A more dramatic consequence was that Roman soldiers returning to the west carried a plague that was to devastate the empire.

Roman aggression in the Euphrates valley was renewed in AD 197 but with no lasting effect, and after further abortive attempts to gain territorial advantage a settlement was finally drawn up about AD 212, with the Romans agreeing to make a substantial cash payment to their old enemy.

The endemic hostilities between Rome and Parthia spanning more than three centuries were to no one's advantage and for the most part the Parthians were able to maintain their western frontier, with Armenia and the desert acting as buffers between the two empires. In spite of episodes of all-out warfare, trade flourished and caravan cities like Palmyra, Aleppo, and Damascus grew rich on the proceeds.

While the Parthians and Romans were directly confronting each other on the western frontier, on the north-eastern frontier a very different cultural engagement was beginning to develop. Long-established trade-routes led from Parthia northwards via the oasis cities of Sogdiana to Ferghana, and thence through the Pamir to the Tarim basin. By the second half of the second century BC the Chinese were beginning to take a direct interest in these routes and in the people through whose territories they passed. In 138 BC the Han emperor Wu sent a member of his staff, Zhang Qian, on an expedition to the Western Regions. The prime purpose was to seek alliances against the Xiongnu (pp. 270–1). After many adventures Zhang reached Ferghana and then journeyed south to Sogdiana and Bactria, where he gathered information about Parthia, Mesopotamia, and north-western India. In the markets he visited in Bactria he was surprised to find bamboo and cloth made in the Chinese province of Sichuan—a reminder of the huge reach of the exchange networks. Zhang's report to the emperor inspired a flurry of further activity. More embassies were sent to the west, the largest numbering many hundreds, and up to ten parties could be sent out in a single year. A Chinese account of one mission dispatched about 100 BC records:

> When the Han envoy first visited the Kingdom of Anxi (Parthia) the King of Anxi despatched a party of 20,000 horsemen to meet them on the eastern border of the Kingdom . . . When the Han envoys set out to return to China, the king of Anxi sent envoys of his own to accompany them . . . The Emperor was delighted.
>
> (*Shiji* 123, trans. B. Watson)

Clearly, the opening up of the trade-routes was to everyone's advantage. But the curiosity of the Chinese extended beyond Central Asia and Parthia. At the end of the first century AD the Chinese general Ban Chao, having finally taken control of the Western Regions (including the Tarim basin), began to develop an interest in the lands further to the west beyond the Pamir. In AD 97 he sent an embassy led by Gan Ying to explore. Gan penetrated as far as Charax, a major port linking the Indian Ocean shipping routes to the caravan routes across the desert. There he enquired about the best way to get to the Mediterranean, only to be told by the local traders that it required a two-year sea journey around the Arabian peninsula exposing the traveller to many horrors and dangers en route. By giving this partial misinformation the local entrepreneurs were presumably attempting to protect their own trading monopolies. Gan Ying decided against the onward journey and returned to China after having gathered as much second-hand information about the Roman worlds as he could from other travellers.

There is little evidence that Roman entrepreneurs explored the overland routes to China. This is hardly surprising given the state of war that often existed between Rome and the Parthians, but during the interludes of peace a Macedonian merchant, Maes Titianus, travelled from the Mediterranean as far as the Pamir in the late first or early second century AD. The text mentioning his exploits adds that, although he did not himself go to China, he 'sent others there'. Later, a Chinese text records that during the reign of the emperor Huan, about AD 166, 'The King of the Da-Qin

[Roman empire], Antun [Marcus Aurelius], sent envoys who offered ivory, rhinoceros horns, and tortoise-shells from the border of Annam: this was the first time they communicated with us.' The Chinese were unimpressed, adding: 'Their tribute contained no precious stones whatever and makes us suspect that the messengers kept them back.' A more likely explanation is that this was a private trading enterprise and not an official imperial embassy. The goods that they chose to take suggests that they travelled by sea, amassing their cargo somewhere in southern Asia. That this was the first mission to reach China indicates that long-haul journeys by land or sea were exceedingly rare.

Trade between China and Parthia, opened up by the Han embassy in 100 BC, flourished. Among the many commodities that passed along the caravan routes, silk was probably the most profitable, but Chinese pearls, another high-value, low-bulk product, will have found a ready market. Other items mentioned are iron from India, together with high-quality leather and spices. In return the Chinese received glassware from Roman Syria, while the Han emperors were sent presents of exotic animals, including lions and Persian gazelles. With a flow of suitable gifts keeping the kings and emperors happy, it was in the interest of the states to hold communications open and well protected. The result was that the multitude of small traders working the routes thrived and grew rich.

The Roman Empire: A Consumer State

At the end of the First Punic War (264–241 BC) Rome, until that time a small state confined to the Italian peninsula, acquired its first overseas territory, Sicily. Soon to follow were the islands of Sardinia and Corsica. The Second Punic War (218–202 BC) left Rome in control of a large tract of south-eastern Iberia, and with the destruction of Carthage in 146 BC, at the end of the Third Punic War, Rome had acquired the most prosperous and fertile part of the North African coast. In the same year Rome destroyed Corinth and inherited Greece. The destruction of Carthage and Corinth, the two great maritime powers of the day, left Rome in control of the Mediterranean. Other territorial acquisitions followed, usually as the result of military conquest, until by AD 106, with the submission of Dacia and the annexation of Arabia, the empire had reached the limits of its ecological niche. It occupied two ecozones: the Mediterranean and temperate Europe. To the south lay only desert, to the north the forest and steppe zones; to the west was the Atlantic Ocean. It was only in the east that there was no natural limit, and it was here, as we have seen, that Rome and Parthia laboriously contested the broad frontier zone extending between the Caucasus and the Euphrates.

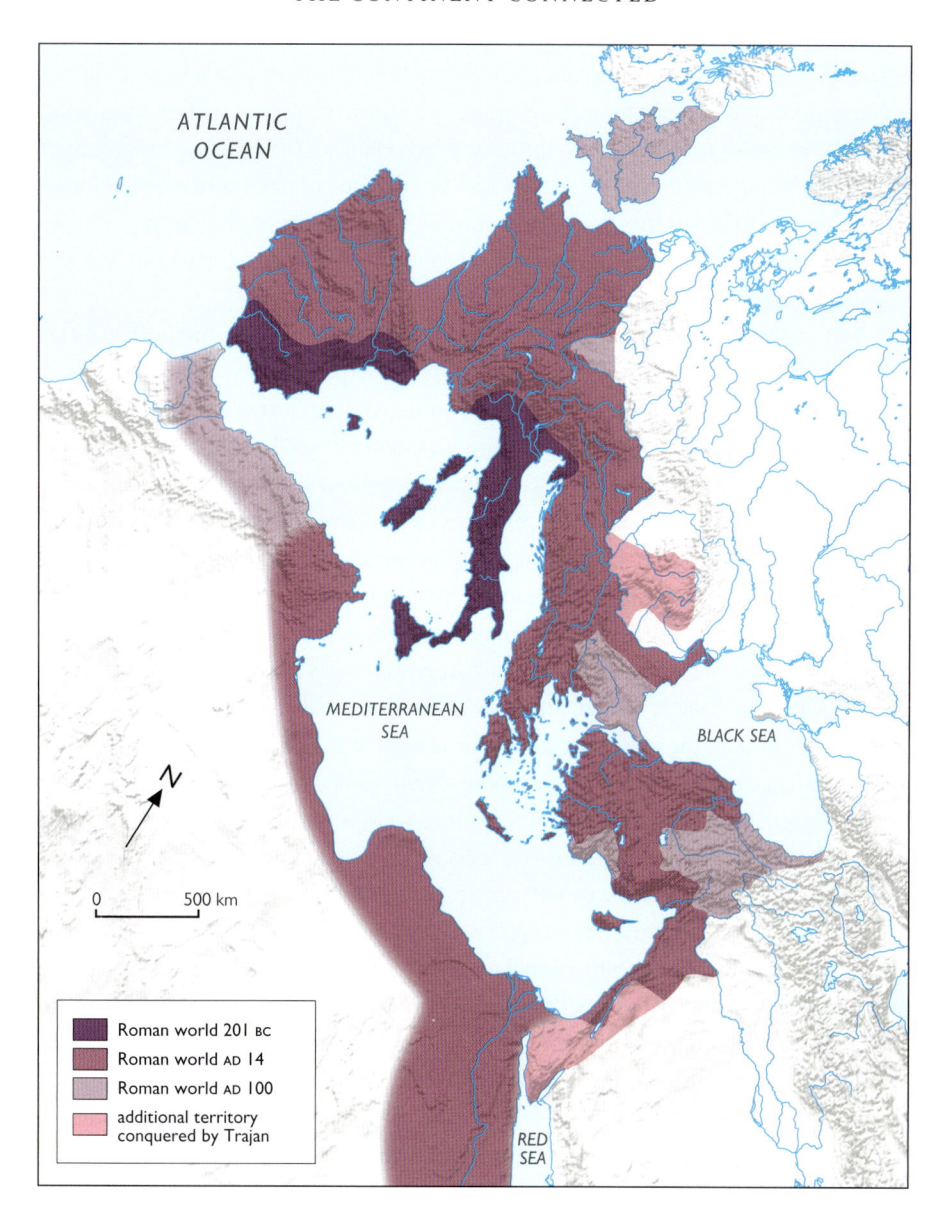

7.4 The annexation of Sicily following the end of the First Punic War in 241 BC was the first step in the growth of the Roman empire. By the early second century AD the empire extended from the Syrian desert to the Atlantic and from the North African desert to the forests of northern Europe

Trajan was the last of the emperors to expand significantly the borders of empire. He was driven by ambition but also by economic necessity: the empire was in financial crisis. His conquest of Dacia was motivated by the desire to acquire the rich silver deposits of the region. The annexation of Arabia gave Rome greater control of trade via the Red Sea, cutting out the Nabataean middleman, while his campaigns in Mesopotamia and Assyria were designed to be the first stage in further expansion along the lucrative trade-routes to the east. When Hadrian (ruled AD 117–38) came to power following Trajan's sudden death, he brought the policy of continuous expansion to an end. The limits of empire had to be made secure with firm boundaries properly garrisoned, and the economy of the empire had to be reformed to become self-sustaining.

It was a significant moment in the history of Rome. Until now the policy, so far as it was ever formulated, was one of continuous expansion. Around a decaying, highly consuming core were added new productive peripheries able to sustain the centre. Each province added to the empire was heavily taxed, siphoning off its surplus wealth. Some of the revenue was fed back to support the provincial administration and frontier defences, while the rest went to fund the non-productive centre. All the time that new resources could be drawn into the boundaries of empire the system more or less worked, but once expansion stopped, crisis loomed.

Hadrian appreciated that the natural limits had been reached and the empire had now to be made self-sustaining. His practical response was to encourage greater productivity. In Greece, Macedonia, and Asia Minor he increased the number of small landowners, and on the under-used imperial estates in Africa he brought in new tenants to cultivate olives and fruit trees, giving them the right to pass on their holdings to their families. Elsewhere the imperial mines were leased out to private entrepreneurs. The provinces were the key to economic reform, and here he encouraged investment, particularly in the urban infrastructure. It was a far-sighted initiative and for a while it worked. But the devastation of the plague brought back from the east in AD 166 and the incursion of northern barbarians disrupted the system and the provinces progressively failed to meet their financial targets. In the political anarchy of the third century the situation only got worse, and it required the draconian reforms of Diocletian to stabilize the economy, but then only for a short time.

Many contemporary Roman observers were well aware that rampant consumerism was the greatest threat to the economy. Early in the first century AD the emperor Tiberius, not a man noted for his modest tastes, bewailed the flow of gold from the empire to pay for 'articles that flatter the vanity of women; jewels and those little objects of luxury which drain away the riches of the empire. In exchange for trifles, our money is sent to foreign lands and even to our enemies.' A little later Pliny the Elder joined the cry for moderation. The importation of eastern luxuries like tortoiseshell, frankincense, and silk, he claimed, weakened Rome. He was particularly upset by silk, so immodestly worn by Roman women, 'so manifold is the labour employed and so distant the region of the globe drawn upon, to enable the Roman matron to flaunt transparent raiment in public'. Pliny the Younger calculated that the annual burden on the Roman state to pay for these luxuries was 55 million sesterces paid to India and 45 million to Arabia and Seres (Central Asia and China). Figures of this kind give some idea of the volume of trade with the east. The problem was that, apart from glass and a few other manufactured goods like pottery and wine, the empire had to pay for its eastern luxuries with the gold and silver it could ill afford to allow to flow out of its economic system. Short of curbing demand, the only way to deal with the problem was to take firm command of the points of entry and to try to control throughput by means of tolls and taxes. This was what Trajan was attempting to do in the east.

The two prime zones of entry were the Red Sea and the various crossings on the Euphrates. In AD 106 Trajan annexed Arabia, that is, the land south and west of Judaea, including the east bank of the river Jordan, the Sinai peninsula, and the Gulf of Aqaba. By taking over this territory Rome now had control of the entire northern end of the Red Sea and in particular the port of Aila (Aqaba), a point of transhipment and a major route node. Here vessels coming from the Indian Ocean would unload cargo for overland carriage to the Mediterranean port of Gaza or for transport northwards to Syria. Aila was also the terminal port on the caravan route along the eastern side of the Red Sea from the tip of the Arabian peninsula, the route bringing frankincense and myrrh as well as Indian Ocean goods offloaded at Eudaimon Arabia (Aden) or Muza at the tip of the peninsula.

By annexing the province of Arabia, the Romans also took control of the two cities of Petra and Bostra, which served as the terminal markets on the trans-desert caravan routes originating at Ctesiphon and Babylon. It was by way of this network that commodities arriving through the Persian Gulf port of Charax were carried to the Mediterranean. Trajan's acquisition of Arabia was an astute move. It gave the empire a much firmer command of eastern trade, at the same time mitigating the challenge which the Ethiopian kingdom of Aksum was beginning to make against Rome's monopoly of Red Sea traffic.

We have already seen that Trajan's strategy also included the conquest of Mesopotamia and Assyria and of Parthian territory to the east. Nothing came of it and the Euphrates remained the effective boundary between the two states, but Rome's involvement in the affairs of the kingdom of Armenia meant that it could exercise a degree of control over the routes between the Caspian Sea and the Black Sea. The potential of this network was not, however, developed at this time. With the Parthian frontier always in contention, and the Parthians able to demand huge customs dues, it was inevitable that Roman trade with the East would focus on the maritime routes via the Red Sea.

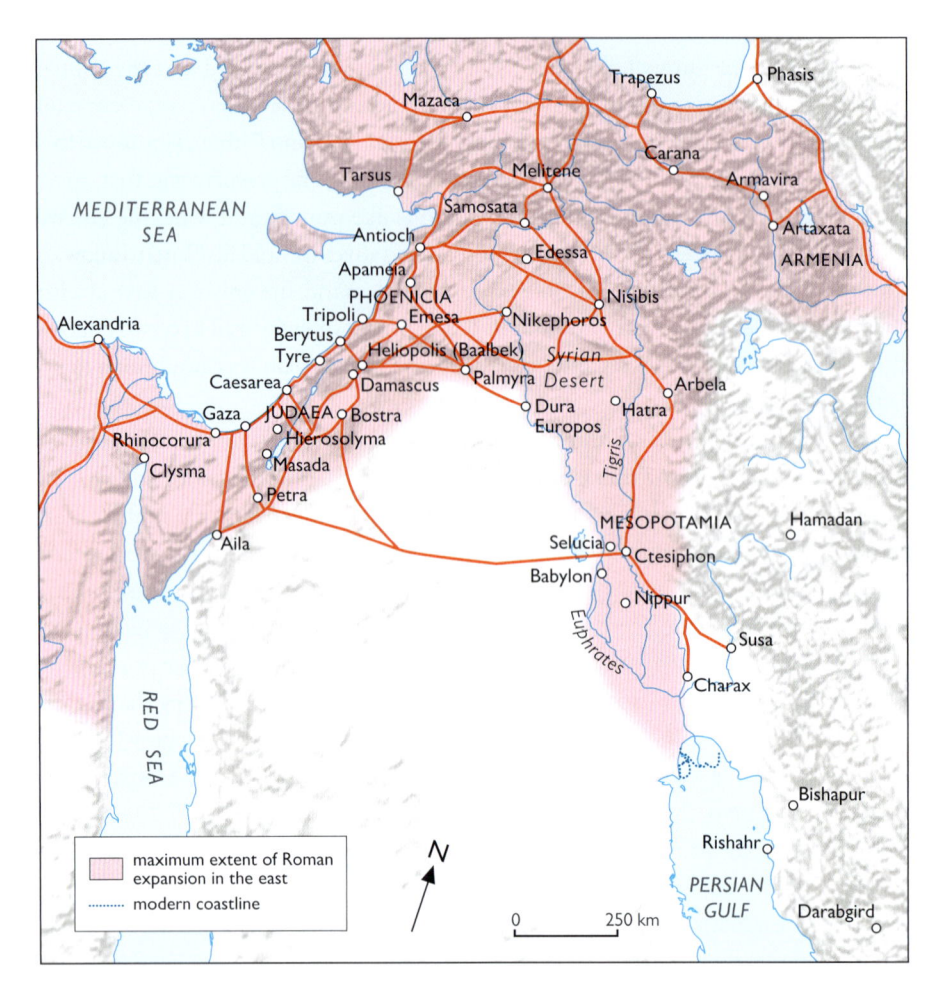

7.5 The interface between the Roman and Byzantine empires and the Parthians, and their successors the Sasanians, was a zone of almost continuous conflict between the competing powers from the second to the seventh century AD

China and her Northern Neighbours

In 221 BC, after half a millennium of inter-state warfare, the Qin, under their leader Ying Zheng, finally triumphed, bringing the factions together and allowing Ying Zheng to proclaim himself Qin Shihuangdi, 'First August and Divine Emperor of Qin'. During his short reign (221–210 BC) the northern frontier with the nomads was extended and consolidated, and further territories were added in the south, reaching as far as Vietnam. A new administrative structure was put in place to manage the vast empire and a huge bureaucracy was set up to support it, creating a system that remained little changed until the early twentieth century. Some flavour of the lavish scale on which the First Emperor was thinking is reflected in the arrangements made for his own famous burial guarded by the more than six thousand 'terracotta warriors'.

The funerary arrangements of the First Emperor are remarkable for many reasons. They reflect the grandiose vision that the emperor had of himself, the affluence of the state, and his ability to coerce the enormous labour force needed to accomplish the task. But more than that, it hints at something new. The sudden acceptance of the full-size modelling of humans and horses and the techniques of hollow bronze casting used in the manufacture of water birds had no antecedents in China but were well known at the time in the west in Bactria, Gandhara, and beyond. It seems not at all unlikely that western ideas and possibly even western craftsmen were now being introduced into the elite culture of China.

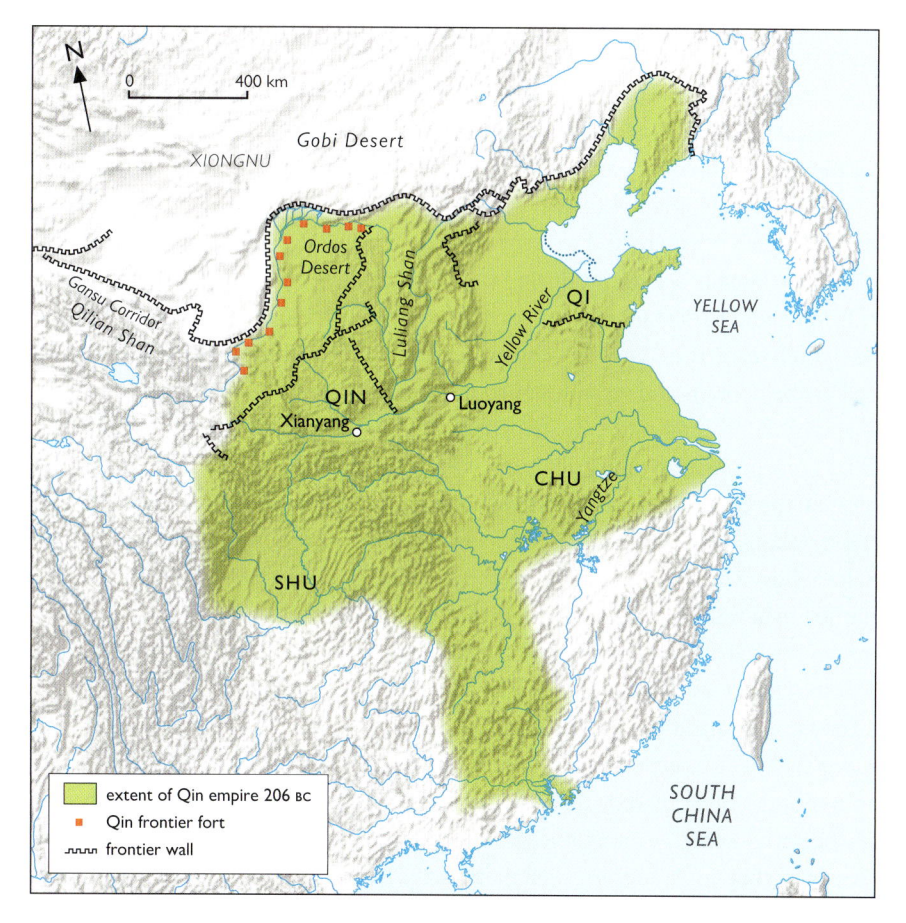

7.6 In 221 BC the Qin emperor Shihuangdi succeeded in unifying China after a long period of conflict between warring factions. Extensive fortifications were built to protect the northern frontier from nomad raiders, who became united under the Xiongnu

The death of the First Emperor was followed by civil war, but in 206 BC China was again united by one of the rebel leaders, Liu Bang of Han, initiating the Han dynasty, which was to last until AD 220. The dynasty is divided into two periods separated by a short interregnum: the Western (or Former) Han (206 BC–AD 9), whose capital was at Chang'an (now Xi'an), and the Eastern (or Later) Han (AD 25–220), who ruled from Luoyang. The administrative system, built upon that set in place by the Qin, divided the unwieldy empire into two unequal parts. The eastern two-thirds was subdivided into ten semi-autonomous kingdoms, while the western third was organized into thirteen commanderies under the direct control of the central government. The system took with it certain risks, not least of usurpation, but for the most part it served to maintain a degree of coherence across the huge and varied territory.

The Han dynasty was a period of great cultural advance in China in all fields of study: literature, philosophy, mathematics, astronomy, navigation, medicine, and engineering. It was also a time when the writing of official histories developed under state sponsorship. Thus it was that Sima Qian (145–80 BC) completed the massive *Shiji* ('Historical Records'), an invaluable source for the early Han period covering not only internal state affairs but also relations with the nomadic Xiongnu, who lived beyond China's northern and western borders.

We have already seen how, during the Warring States period, a series of frontier walls were built to demarcate lines considered by the various states to be the boundaries of their territories. The lines chosen were usually well within the land habitually used by the nomads and were designed both as a means of limiting nomadic mobility and of controlling trade. By incorporating nomad territory they created a wide buffer zone protecting the agricultural communities of the south. After unification in 221 BC the Qin consolidated some lengths of wall and advanced across the Ordos region, taking in huge swaths of nomadic territory in order to extend the frontier to the Yellow River along its western and northern courses. The new boundary was guarded by a number of forts. The extension and formalization of the Great Wall frontier created a new reality with which the nomads to the north now had to contend: the effect was to unite them under the leadership of the Xiongnu.

The Xiongnu are first mentioned in the fourth century BC, when they were numbered among the Hu—the general name used by the Chinese for the northern barbarians. By the end of the third century they had become the dominant force. In all probability they began as a small tribe or lineage who gradually established their authority over other nomadic people and gave their name to the larger confederation, in the same way as the name and authority of royal Scyths was imposed on other nomadic groups in the Pontic steppe. The building of linear boundaries across their traditional pastureland would have caused social upset among the nomads. The problems were further

THE CONTINENT CONNECTED

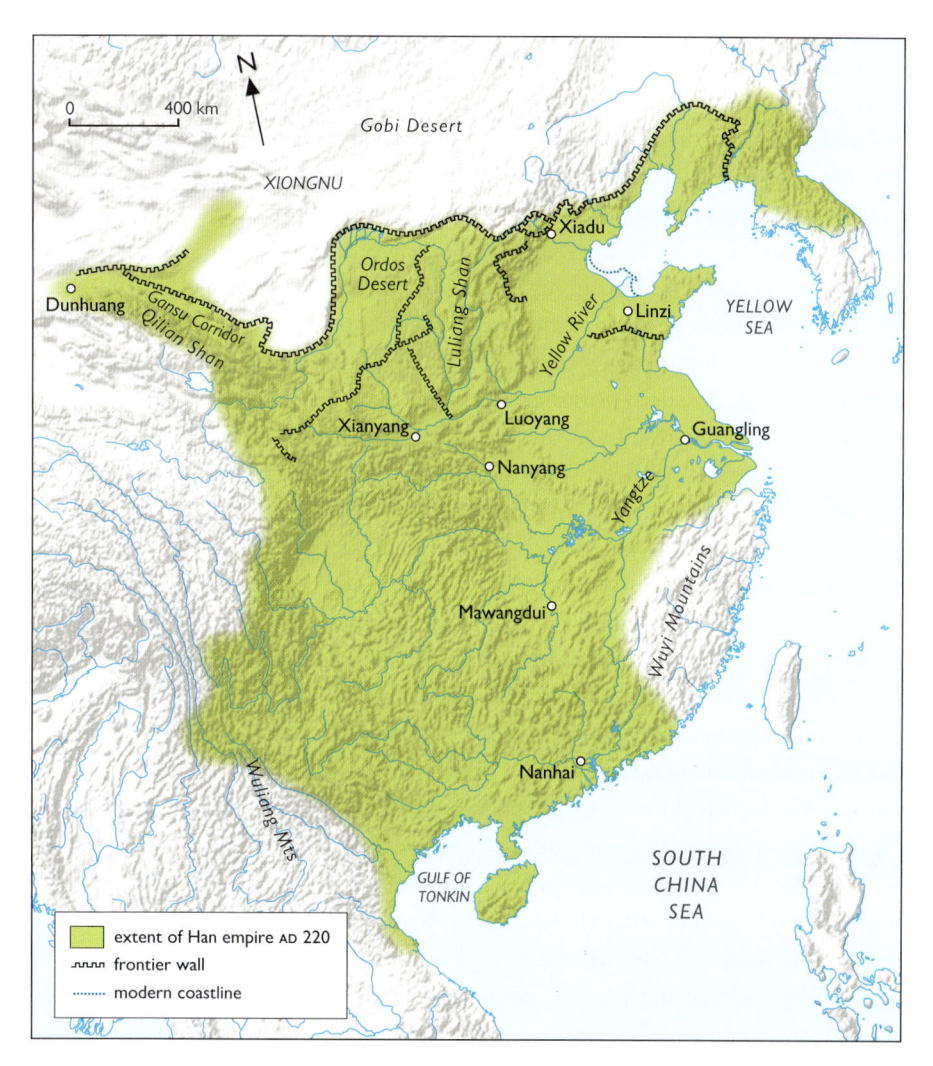

7.7 Built upon the achievements of Shihuangdi, the Han empire was established in 202 BC. By AD 220 it covered a huge area and had expanded westwards along the Gansu Corridor

exacerbated when, in 215 BC, the Qin annexed the Ordos, a huge area of fertile steppe essential to the livelihood of the nomadic inhabitants. In the social turmoil that ensued, one man, Modu, emerged as supreme leader of the Xiongnu. His power rested partly on his charismatic leadership and partly on the loyal bodyguard he had accumulated around himself. But power once achieved had to be maintained, and crucial to this was the continued support of the entourage. These were men who had dedicated themselves to their leader and were the new elite. They expected rewards and they expected to enhance their status through further action. Such pressures led to a militarization of society. Modu moved to establish his supremacy by bringing other clans into subordinate positions and extracting tribute from them. By the end of his reign (d. 174 BC) he had extended Xiongnu authority over Mongolia, Manchuria, and the Tarim basin. He was now a super-tribal leader, seen to be endowed with sacral power.

Tribute from subordinate clans enabled Modu to redistribute wealth to his growing band of followers, but the resources available on the steppe were limited in range: much that was desirable was only available from the sedentary agricultural communities of China through trade, tribute, or raid. When the Chinese authorities, concerned about the flow of iron weapons from China to the nomads, began to exercise a trade embargo, the social infrastructure supporting the Xiongnu elite came under threat. The inevitable result was that cross-border raiding increased, and in 200 BC the Han suffered a serious defeat when attempting to contain the nomadic incursions.

Confronted by the new reality of Xiongnu power, the Chinese were forced to negotiate a treaty, known as the *heqin*, which was agreed in 198 BC, recognizing the two sides as equals. The borders were reopened for trading, and the Han agreed to send a yearly tribute of silk, cloth, grain, and foodstuffs to the Xiongnu. The list is interesting in that it underlines the importance of food from the agrarian areas of the south as necessary supplements to the nomadic diet. The word *heqin* means 'peace through kinship relations', and an essential element of it was to establish marriage alliances between the ruling houses of the two states. To the Chinese mind this had particular advantages. If the emperor sent his eldest daughter to Modu to become his wife, their male offspring, Modu's son, would be the emperor's grandson, which would make him subservient to the emperor so that the Xiongnu would become subjects of the Han. The Xiongnu response was to propose that Modu married the dowager empress, which would have reversed the situation. The other Chinese ploy was to try to corrupt the Xiongnu elite with lavish gifts, believing that these would upset native systems of patronage and thus weaken the ruling tribe. The Han's acceptance of the *heqin* was, at least in part, a realization that they were militarily inferior to the Xiongnu, who, by extending their dominion over their nomadic neighbours, had greatly increased the size of their fighting force.

The appeasement policy worked poorly in practice. The Xiongnu demanded additional tribute and continued to raid the Han regions, while the Han's only response was to strengthen the frontier garrisons. The Han were the losers, yet the policy continued in place for sixty years.

The accession of Emperor Wu in 140 BC marked the beginning of a change to a more aggressive stance. The argument was succinctly put by an experienced border official: 'When the Han conclude a peace agreement with the Xiongnu, usually after a few years the Xiongnu violate the treaty. It would be better to reject their promises and send soldiers to attack them.' The issue was extensively debated in 135 and 134 BC, and in 133 BC the policy of appeasement was replaced by a new military initiative. The first major campaign, fought in 129 BC, saw a major thrust into Xiongnu territory as far as the nomads' religious centre at Longcheng. This was matched by a Xiongnu counter-offensive the next year. And so the confrontation continued over the following years, with increasing Han successes. By 119 BC Emperor Wu's first strategic objectives had been met. New territories had been taken and settled by large numbers of Chinese, the northern border had been strengthened and secured, and tribute was no longer paid. More to the point, the Han showed that they could now defeat the Xiongnu in battle. It was time for a new strategy: the annihilation of the Xiongnu as an effective political force.

By 110 BC, after several successful Chinese campaigns, the Xiongnu had been forced out of the region between the Yellow River and the Gobi desert and had retreated to the northern steppe and forests. In the newly conquered regions the Han established fourteen new border commanderies and were now sending expeditions westwards deep into the Tarim basin. We shall consider the commercial significance of these western campaigns later.

To maintain their power the Xiongnu needed a continuous flow of commodities, particularly foodstuffs, hitherto available through trade and tribute from the Chinese in the south and from the oasis communities of the Tarim basin to the west. After 133 BC the flow from the south ceased altogether, leaving the Xiongnu even more dependent on the west. By cutting off these supplies by the advance into the Tarim region the Han were isolating the nomads and forcing them back on their own resources. The social system of prestige gift giving which supported the warrior elite could no longer be sustained, with the result that the hitherto centralized confederacy of the Xiongnu collapsed. In 51 BC the Xiongnu leader accepted the superiority of the Han empire. The Xiongnu were now at last vassals of the Chinese state.

One of the more intriguing aspects of the long confrontation between the Han and the Xiongnu is the anthropological detail with which the nomads were described in the contemporary Chinese history the *Shiji*, compiled by Sima Qian. What the historian presents is a carefully observed account of nomad life:

> Most of their domestic animals are horses, cows, sheep and they also have rare animals such as camels, donkeys, mules, hinnies and other equines ... They move about according to the available water and pasture and have no walled towns or fixed residences nor any agricultural activities, but each of them has a portion of land.
>
> (*Shiji* 10.2879, trans. B. Watson)

Children were trained from an early age to use a bow and to ride. The youngest children rode sheep and shot birds and mice. 'Thus as adults they are strong enough to bend a bow and all can serve as cavalry soldiers. In battle they will advance when all is going well and will rapidly retreat if under pressure.' 'They do not regard running away as something shameful; they only care about profit and know nothing of propriety and righteousness.' They retained all the booty they could carry, and captured enemies became slaves. 'Therefore in battle each man pursues his own gain.'

The maintenance of the lineage was of prime importance so that when 'a father, son or brother dies they take [the widow] as their own'. In this way 'the ancestral clan is always preserved'. The elite were given elaborate burials: 'They use inner and outer coffins, gold and silver, clothes and fur coats: however, they do not erect earthen mounds or plant trees, nor do they use mourning garments. When a ruler dies, his ministers and concubines are sacrificed in numbers that can reach several tens or even hundreds of people' (*Shiji* 110.2892, trans. B. Watson). The historian has managed to piece together a balanced picture of a nomadic people relatively free of critical judgements. For his readers it provided a convenient topos of the nomads as 'the other': different from us in many ways yet people with whom we must engage. To begin with, that engagement attempted to treat the nomads as, at least nominally, equals, but when, after sixty years, the policy failed, there was nothing for it but to regard them as a threat to be annihilated.

The Han Campaigns in the Western Zone

The Gansu Corridor—the narrow tract of land between the Qilian Mountains and the Gobi desert which provided access between China and the Tarim basin—was occupied by the Han armies in 121 BC. It was a decisive step in the Han campaign to cut off the Xiongnu from the resources of the west.

The advance had been preceded by exploration and diplomacy. Soon after he came to power, Emperor Wu (ruled 140–87 BC) sent his envoy Zhang Qian to the west to persuade the Yuezhi, now living in the Ferghana valley, to join the Chinese against the Xiongnu, who some years earlier had driven the Yuezhi out of their homeland at the eastern end of the Tarim basin. Zhang's mission was somewhat delayed by his capture by the Xiongnu and his detention for ten years. When he eventually reached the Yuezhi, he found them unwilling to engage in the conflict. However, he made good use of his journey, visiting a number of the peoples of Central Asia (p. 261). On his return to China about 126 BC he had much new intelligence to impart, not only about Parthia and the far west, but also about the oasis towns of the Tarim basin strung out along the caravan routes that made their way around the northern and southern fringes of the Taklamakan desert. This region was of immediate interest to the Chinese, and Zhang's report may have been the impetus for the annexation of the Gansu Corridor and the

THE CONTINENT CONNECTED

town of Dunhuang, which commanded the western end of the corridor and from where the northern and southern circum-desert routes could be directly accessed.

As the Han army moved into alien territory, they attempted to set up peaceful relationships with the natives, but they also established small garrisons of troops stationed at intervals to control the flow of traffic and to protect travellers. At several of these locations hoards of documents have been found, usually written on bamboo or wood, preserved by the arid conditions of the desert. Some of the collections are considerable. At Xuanquan, not far from Dunhuang, thirty-five thousand documents have been recorded, about two thousand of them dating from between 111 BC and AD 107. Xuanquan was a small posting station where officials engaged on public business were able to change horses. Many of the documents found in the site's rubbish dump reflect the everyday activities of the station, from overseeing the passports of those travelling through, to posting notices of new imperial edicts. There were even records of expenditure on meals for the official guests. The documents provide an incomparable record, not only of daily life, but of the diplomatic and commercial traffic now on the move (pp. 287–9).

The political situation in the Tarim basin was complex as each of the small oasis settlements acted as an independent principality and was free to negotiate with the Xiongnu or the Han, and sometimes both. The town of Loulan on the northern route, for example, had tried to maintain good relationships with both sides since the Han first became involved in the region in 108 BC, but in 77 BC the king of Loulan let it be known that he now favoured the Xiongnu. The Han responded by having him killed

7.8 The expansion of the Han empire along the Gansu Corridor as far west as Dunhuang and Anxi by AD 8 meant that the Han could now control the trade-routes to the west around the Tarim Depression. The entire region was soon to become a Han protectorate

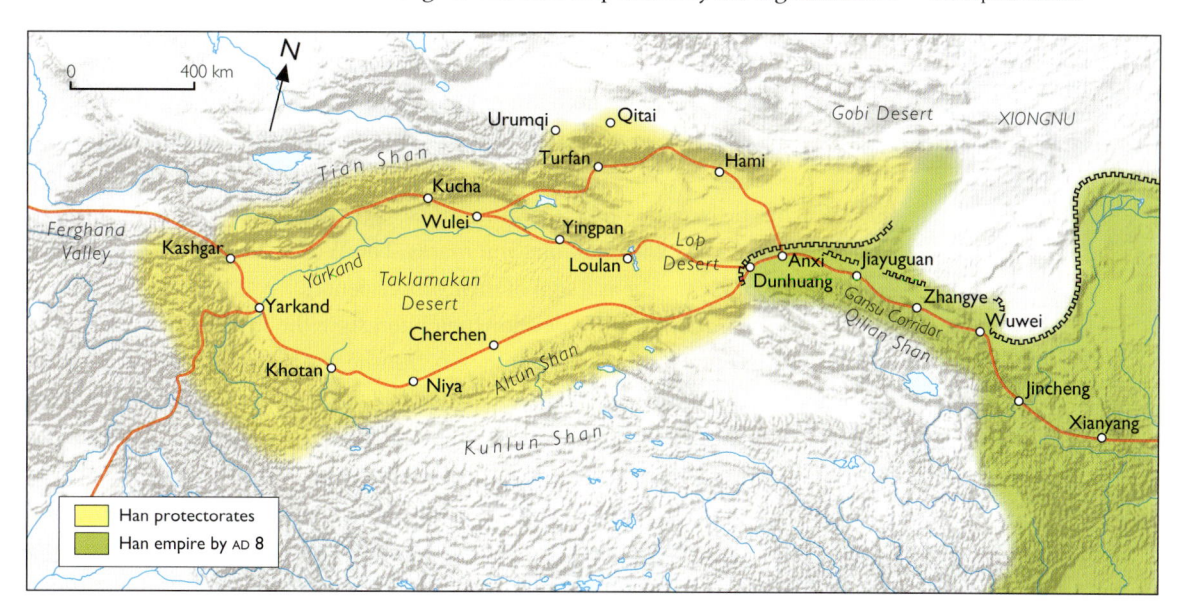

273

and staging a military takeover. A new capital was then built at Endere, which became the base of the Chinese administration for five centuries. The Xiongnu's interest in the northern part of the Tarim basin was strategic since it provided direct access to the nomadic Wusun in Dzungaria. By establishing themselves at Loulan the Han were better able to engage with the Wusun and, through bribery, persuade them not to offer support to the Xiongnu. It was, as the historian put it, 'like cutting off the right arm of the Xiongnu'.

Zhang Qian made a second journey to the west in 116 BC, this time to the region north of the Tian Shan, exploring routes to the north and west, and in 101 BC the Han armies, using the intelligence he brought back, moved through the mountain passes into the Ferghana valley, thus procuring direct access to the magnificent long-legged horses of the region, the 'heavenly horses' that the oracle had predicted would come from the north-west. The emperor Wu's policy, to take military control of the Western Regions, may have been driven by the military expedient of cutting off the Xiongnu from supplies of goods and manpower, but he was not slow to recognize the enormous commercial potential of the region.

Access to the Ferghana horses was a prime attraction. In 102 BC the emperor himself led a military campaign of some sixty thousand men and thirty thousand horses to Ferghana, besieging the capital and gaining a huge haul for the famous 'blood-sweating' horses. Thereafter Ferghana continued to supply the Han court with stallions and mares. The Wusan also agreed to send the emperor two horses a year as a sign of their subservience.

7.9 Three wooden strips inscribed in ink in Chinese characters representing an almanac for the year 59 BC. Collected by Aurel Stein during his second expedition to Dunhuang, Xinjiang, China, 1906–8

The Han empire continued to develop their interests in the Tarim basin throughout the first century BC and the first century AD, but the Xiongnu remained a constant threat and were not finally expelled until General Ban Chao was sent to the region in the early 70s of the first century AD and, by diplomacy and military force, finally established full Chinese control by AD 94. As protector-general of the Western Regions, he was in charge of fifty states, all of which recognized their subservience to the Han. Trade was now flourishing along the northern and southern routes, and ambassadors were being sent to explore Central Asia and the west. The Silk Road, as it was much

274

7.10 The famous 'flying horse' from Wuwei in Kansu, China, dates to the Han dynasty. It is probably modelled on one of the heavenly horses from Ferghana and represents the Han ideal of a horse

later to be called, was now fully operational, and the Tarim basin, once an inward-looking backwater, had become a vibrant part of the trans-Eurasian trading network.

Migrating Nomads

The various nomad groups living in the steppe and arid grasslands of Central Asia were now being mentioned by name in the Western and Chinese sources, allowing a broad narrative of the major movements to be put together within a reasonably tight chronological framework. Apart from the Xiongnu, we can identify the Yuezhi and Wusun, who were living west of the Yellow River and south of the Gobi desert during the time of the Warring States period, and the Sakas, who occupied the well-watered grasslands between the Aral Sea and the Pamir, in the upper reaches of the Syr Darya and Amu Darya and the Ferghana valley. During the early part of the Han dynasty the growing power of the Xiongnu put pressure on the Yuezhi and the Wusun, forcing them to migrate to the west. This had a knock-on effect across the entire Central Asian steppe.

THE CONTINENT CONNECTED

Between 176 and 160 BC the Yuezhi were driven westwards into the northern part of the Tarim basin and through the Tian Shan to take refuge in the valley of the river Ili. The Wusun, also under pressure from the Xiongnu and moving in the same direction, came into conflict with the Yuezhi. As the Wusun took over the Ili valley and the region of Issyk Kul, the Yuezhi were forced to move on into the Ferghana valley. Later, about 135 BC, some of them progressed southwards into eastern Bactria, where they settled down and adopted the sedentary culture of the indigenous inhabitants while maintaining their social system as a confederation of five powerful clans.

Meanwhile the Sakas, who had been ousted from Ferghana by the Yuezhi, also moved southwards but into western Bactria, some settling south of the Hindu Kush in the lower reaches of the Helmand river valley in the region later known as Sakastan. Others moved on into India in the period 110–80 BC, establishing kingdoms in Gandhara in the north, and to the east of the lower Indus valley, an area that the second-century AD geographer Ptolemy recognized as Indo-Scythia. The

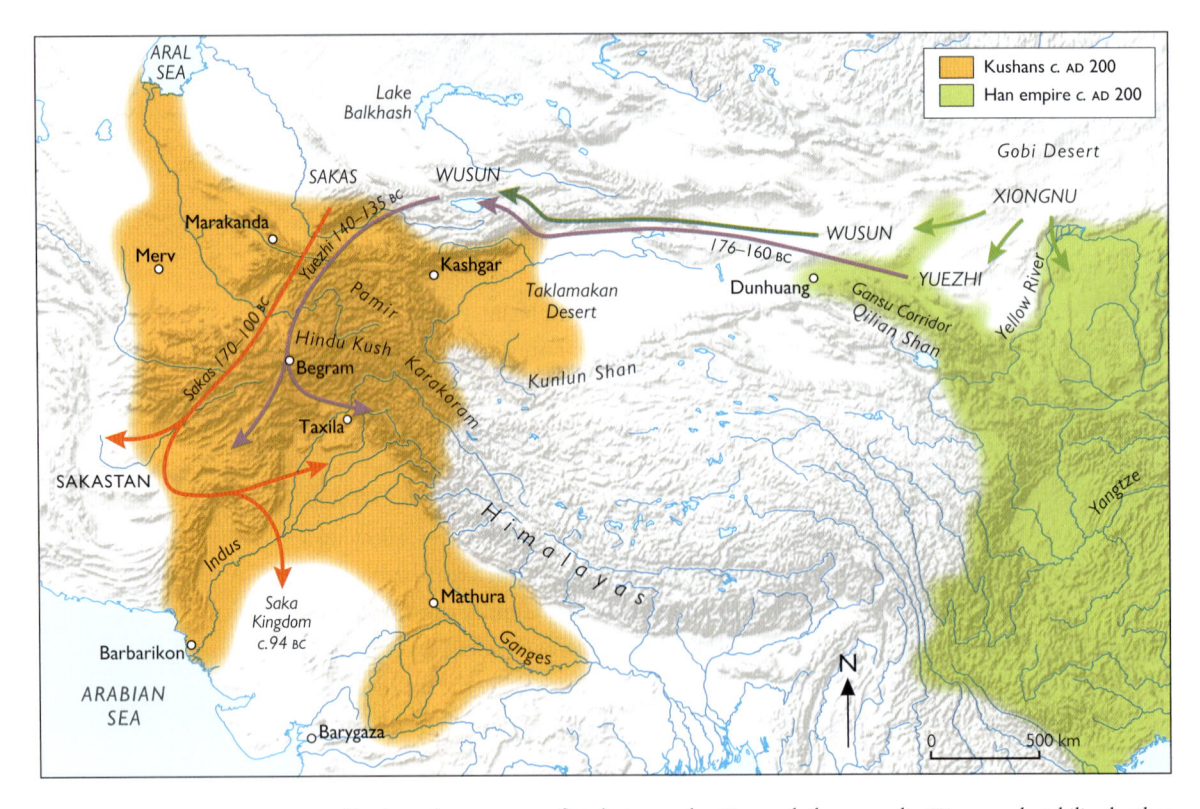

7.11 The long-drawn-out conflict between the Han and the nomadic Xiongnu destabilized other nomadic tribes between the Gobi and Taklamakan deserts, forcing them to move westwards into western Central Asia, where some settled to create the Kushan empire

passage of the nomads on their southward journey can be traced in an episode of destruction identified at the Greek city of Aï Khanum in the Amu Darya valley. To complete the outline of the story, in the late first or early second century AD one of the Yuezhi clans, the Kushans, pushed south into northern India, there to establish the Kushan empire.

There is no doubt that during the period 200 BC–AD 100 the nomads of Central Asia were involved in complex migratory movements. The sources allow us to sketch this only in outline, but the general trends are clear. The emergence of the great confederation of the Xiongnu in Mongolia drove the nomadic tribes living along its western border to move westwards into Central Asia, setting up further reverberations, which were deflected southwards into the Indus valley by the ability of the Parthians to stand firm against further westward advance. To the north, nomadic communities in the Kazakh steppe were less able to resist the pressure, setting in motion a general westerly flow of Sarmatian tribes across the Pontic steppe and into the Danubian region and the Great Hungarian Plain (pp. 281–5). Thus, the pebble thrown into the water by the Han dynasty's aggressive moves against its northern neighbour the Xiongnu set up ripples throughout the steppe which were to be felt as far afield as Europe and India.

The Kushan Empire

The Yuezhi arrived in Bactria about 135 BC as a confederation of five ethnically related clan groups and soon adopted the settled lifestyle of the native population. In the middle of the first century AD Kujula Kadphises, the ruler of one of the clans, the Kushans (Guishuang in the Chinese texts), set himself up as king over all the other clans and began to expand his territorial rule into Indo-Parthia, the Kabul region, and the upper reaches of the Indus valley. Subsequent rulers made further territorial gains until, in the middle of the second century AD, the Kushan empire, with its centre in Gandhara, extended from the Syr Darya to the mouth of the Indus, and from its boundary with the Parthian empire eastwards to include much of northern India to the mid-Ganges valley. It was ruled from two capitals, Purushapura (now Peshawar) in north-west Pakistan and Mathura in northern India, while the ruling family had a palace at Begram in Afghanistan.

The geographical centrality of the empire explains its wealth and the variety of its culture. It bordered Parthia, the steppe, and China: it commanded the whole of the Indian subcontinent and through its port (known as Barbarikon to western sailors) close to the mouth of the Indus it was in direct contact by sea with the Roman world. The empire was the inheritor of a richly varied culture, indigenous Indian overlaid by

Persian and Greek with a strong nomadic component. Its eclectic culture is nicely reflected in its gold coinage, copied from Roman models. The coins bear images of Greek, Roman, Persian, Hindu, and Buddhist deities and are inscribed with a script adapted from Greek.

Direct contacts with China were established through the embassy of Zhang Qian in the 120s BC. For the most part relations were diplomatic and commercial, but in 86 AD the Kushan king sent a military force of some seventy thousand cavalry through the high mountain passes into the Tarim basin to avenge the insult of the Chinese refusal to send him a princess as a bride. The expedition ended in disaster and the Kushans were compelled to pay tribute to the Han emperor. Later, in the early second century, another military force was sent, which successfully subdued the towns of Khotan, Yarkand, and Kashgar, then under Chinese domination. The distances were too great for the Kushans to maintain control for long and the Tarim territories were soon given up, though the trade-routes remained open.

After the death of King Vasudeva I in 225 AD the Kushan empire began to fragment, partly as a result of internal dissension and partly because of encroachments by the Sasanid dynasty, which had come to power in Persia following the collapse of the Parthians. By the middle of the century much of the western part of the Kushan empire had passed under Sasanian control.

For two centuries the Kushan empire had been a hub in the trade network that criss-crossed Eurasia, allowing the Indian subcontinent to become fully integrated into the system. A crucial factor driving the opening up of these routes and the intensification of trade was the growing demand coming from the Roman world, a consumer market increasingly avid for eastern luxury goods. The endemic hostility between Rome and Parthia forced the Roman entrepreneurs to find ways to outflank Parthia by developing maritime routes via the Red Sea and the Indian Ocean. In addition to providing easy access to the Indian subcontinent, the sea also enabled traders to explore mar-

7.12 A gold coin of the Kushan king Kanishka I (c. AD 127–50). The king, wearing baggy trousers, is on the obverse. The reverse depicts Helios, the Greek god of the sun, reflecting the strong Greek influence that still survived during the Kushan period

kets, like Barbarikon and Barygaza, linked to the overland routes along the Indus and through Gandhara to the Karakoram passes and to the Tarim basin and China. In this way the Romans could access the markets of the east without having to go through Parthia and Bactria.

A mid-first-century AD text, *Periplus of the Erythraean Sea*, provides an insight into the goods in transit through the ports. Among the long list of exports sent from the Mediterranean and Red Sea worlds were clothing, printed fabrics, gemstones, coral, frankincense, copper, glassware, silverware, fine wine, Roman gold and silver coins, slave musicians, and 'pretty females' for sale as concubines. Products being brought to the Indian ports from inland for export included various drugs and aromatic resins, turquoise, lapis lazuli, onyx, agate, ivory, cotton cloth, and Chinese silk.

Something of the reality of this international trade is shown by the contents of two sealed store-rooms found by archaeologists in a building thought to be the summer palace of the Kushan kings at Kapisa near Begram. The doors of the rooms had been bricked up and carefully plastered over. Inside the astonished archaeologists found piles of goods dating to the first or early second century AD, including 180 Roman glass vessels, mostly of Egyptian origin, bronze tableware, carved and polished stone vessels from Egypt, ostrich eggs worked to be wine pourers, quantities of furniture of Indian origin decorated with carved and painted ivory and bone plaques, and hundreds of painted lacquer bowls from China. There were also fifty or so plaster casts used for manufacturing metal vessels decorated with scenes from Roman mythology. No doubt there were other goods such as fabrics and plant materials that have not survived. It is tempting to see this great cache of luxury goods as diplomatic gifts accumulated by a Kushan king, brought to him by ambassadors coming from India, China, and the Red Sea, material redolent of his status but surplus to his immediate needs.

7.13 Ivory carving of a woman from the sealed store-room at Begram, Afghanistan, dating to the first century AD. She resembles the Indian river goddess Ganga, and was most likely made in India

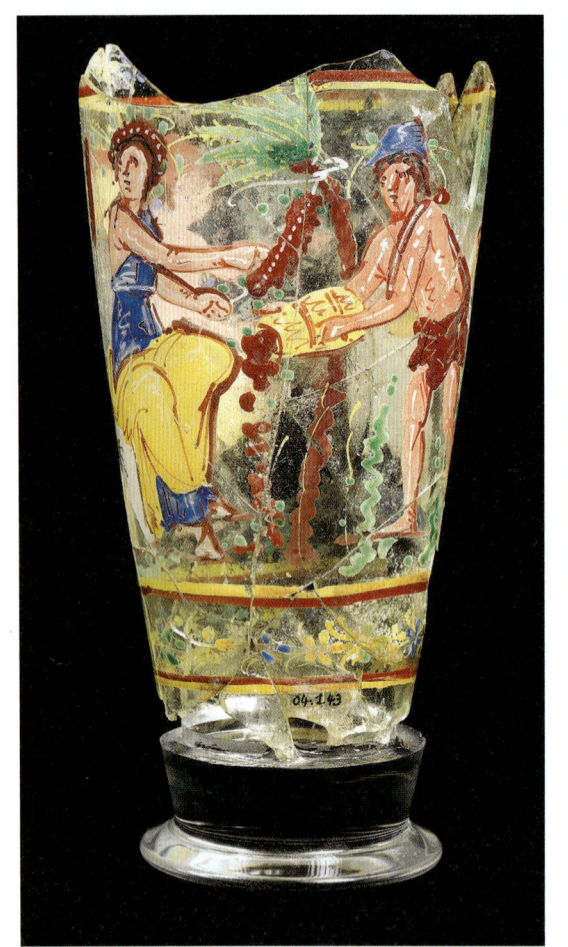

THE CONTINENT CONNECTED

7.14 (*Left*) Painted glass beaker from the sealed store-room at Begram, Afghanistan, dating to the first century AD. The vessel was probably imported from Syria. The scene depicts a date harvest

7.15 (*Above*) Plaster cast in classical style of a young man from the sealed store-room at Begram, Afghanistan, dating from the first century AD

Another revealing archaeological find comes from Tillya Tepe in north-western Afghanistan. Here, in the late first century AD, a male was buried surrounded by the graves of five or six females elaborately dressed in clothing adorned with appliqué gold and wearing intricate golden diadems. Their jewellery is a mixture of Graeco-Bactrian items, some possibly heirlooms, and figured pieces made in the style of nomad art depicting animals and inset with turquoise. The sheer quantity of gold buried with the dead is a reflection of their exalted status and is highly reminiscent of the nomad burial tradition of the Kazakh steppe. The Tillya Tepe burials must represent the elite of a nomad clan, presumably the chief and his wives. The small cemetery is a reminder that within the Kushan empire traditional nomadic culture still existed alongside a more settled way of life, and that the different ethnic groups could all share in the remarkable wealth of the region.

7.16 The 'Dragon Master', a gold pendant inset with turquoise, lapis lazuli, garnet, carnelian, and pearls, from a tomb at Tillya Tepe in northern Afghanistan, first century AD. The piece reflects the styles of steppe art present in the cultural mix of the Kushan empire

7.17 Crown made in fine gold sheet from a tomb at Tillya Tepe in northern Afghanistan, first century AD

Sarmatians: The Pontic Steppe and Beyond

About 300 BC the nomadic Sarmatian tribes (or Sauromatae-Sarmatians) began to move westwards across the river Don into territory occupied by the Scythians, gradually taking over control of the Pontic steppe until the Scythians were reduced to two small enclaves, the Crimean peninsula and Dobruja at the mouth of the Danube. It was a complex and long-drawn-out process involving a number of tribes whose names and locations, which change over time, are recorded by classical writers. The most frequently mentioned are Aorsi, Siraki, Roxolani, Iazyges, and Alani. Initially the Sarmatians had occupied the arid steppe and semi-desert regions stretching from the southern Ural steppe to the Don, where agriculture was difficult, forcing the tribes to follow a nomadic lifestyle, but the move west into a far more fertile ecozone brought them into contact with communities practising agriculture and with the Greek cities of the Black Sea coast, creating conditions for social change as the immigrant nomads adapted to their new environments.

Classical writers like Diodorus Siculus presented the arrival of the Sarmatians as a major historical event, stressing how they plundered much of Scythia, exterminating the Scythian population. The archaeological records offer some support to this scenario. Scythian defensive works are found at this time along the lower Dnieper, and new styles of burial rite appear; yet the reality was probably more nuanced, with the new clans driving out the old Scythian elites and establishing their authority over the indigenous populations while adopting much of the local culture. The arrival of Sarmatian clans in the Pontic steppe, and later in Europe as far west as the Great Hungarian Plain, took place over some four centuries, during which time successive waves surged west, causing much disruption. It was the old story that we have encountered many times before of a constant flow of populations from east to west ending up in favoured parts of eastern Europe. The attractions of the west—its welcoming ecology and opportunity for lucrative raiding—must have been one reason for the movement. Another was the effects of the protracted conflict between the Han and the Xiongnu, which ended up driving displaced nomadic groups into Central Asia, where they put pressure on the indigenous Sakas, who in turn pressured their immediate neighbours the Sarmatians.

The classical texts give some indication where the different Sarmatian tribes lived and how they moved over time. The region between the rivers Ural and Don was the territory of the Aorsi, who may have been one of the tribes visited by the Chinese ambassador Zhang Qian about 125 BC, when they were reported to have been a mighty people who could mount a force of a hundred thousand archers. Strabo, writing at the end of the first century BC, mentions the region as crossed by major trade-routes between India (presumably through Bactria) and the Iranian plateau via the Caucasus. To the south of them on the steppe, from the valley of the Kuban to the Caucasus Mountains, were the Siraki, a comparatively small tribe who, in the early first century BC, were twenty thousand horsemen strong. They developed a close relationship with their neighbours the Bosporan kingdom, and as a consequence became Hellenized. They are last mentioned in an inscription of AD 193, which records their defeat in a confrontation with the Bosporans.

The Bosporan kingdom, which came into being about 480 BC, when the cities around the Sea of Azov banded together under the leadership of Panticapaeum (modern Kerch), remained an enclave of Mediterranean civilization closely linked by trade to the classical world, though through generations of intermarriage it had become virtually a Sarmatian state. Strabo, writing of the commodities passing through Tanis at the mouth of the Don, lists the main exports of the region as slaves, hides, and 'other such things as nomads possess', while the ships brought to the port clothing, wine, and 'things belonging to civilized life'. The Bosporan kingdom was annexed by Rome in 65 BC and continued as an outpost of empire in this remote, and often hostile, region until it succumbed to attacks by the Goths in the late third century AD.

7.18 A marble stele commemorating Diodotus Tryphon found in the Greek city of Tanis at the mouth of the Don in the kingdom of Bosporus. He is dressed in scale armour typical of a Sarmatian cavalry man

In the second century BC the Roxolani, one of the Sarmatian tribes, destroyed the Scythian royal capital at Kamianka on the lower Dnieper, forcing the tribal leaders to retreat to the Crimean peninsula to establish a new capital at Neapolis, a well-fortified commercial and political centre strongly influenced by Greek architectural traditions. An uneasy relationship between the new settlement and the leading Greek colony of Chersonesos, near modern Sevastopol, culminated, in 110–109 BC, in a Scythian attempt to seize the city. The Greeks called in help from the kingdom of Pontus in Asia Minor, with the result that the Scythians were defeated and Neapolis taken. After the Roman annexation of the kingdom of Bosporos in 65 BC all the Greek cities in the Crimea came under Roman authority and a garrison was stationed in Chersonesos, the city remaining under Roman protection until the end of the third century AD.

The long-term mobility of the Sarmatian tribes is nicely demonstrated by the history of the Iazyges and Roxolani in the period from the second century BC to the second century AD. The Iazyges originally lived between the Don and the Dnieper north of the Sea of Azov, with the Roxolani located to the west of them on the lower Volga. In the second century BC the Roxolani, under pressure from their eastern neighbours the Aorsi, moved westwards across the Don, forcing the Iazyges to migrate westwards to the steppe of the lower Dniester, where they came up against indigenous agriculturalists, the Bastarnae (possibly of Celtic origin) and the native Getae, forcing them to turn southwards, following the Black Sea littoral to the Danube delta. To the south of the Danube lay territory under the control of the Romans. The strengthening of Roman power in the region and the creation of a fortified frontier zone along the lower Danube made any hope of further movement to the south unrealistic, but the Iazyges were frequently involved in raids into Roman territory, working in concert with their neighbours the Dacians, who occupied much of modern Romania. Raids were recorded in AD 6 and 16, but soon after AD 20 the Iazyges moved on again, this time travelling west through the Carpathians into the Great Hungarian Plain, where they established themselves on the steppe to the east of the middle Danube, confronting the Romans across the Danube frontier. To begin with, relations between the Iazyges and the Romans were friendly and the Iazyges provided auxiliary cavalry units for the Roman army fighting the Dacians, but when Trajan's armies eventually conquered Dacia in AD 101 and made it a Roman province, the Iazyges found themselves almost surrounded by the Romans to the east, south, and west. It was an untenable position.

Towards the beginning of a long conflict which became known as the Marcomannic Wars (AD 166–80) the Iazyges broke out, crossing the Danube, and raided the province of Pannonia (now in western Hungary). But the might of the Roman army prevailed and they were defeated, allowing the emperor Marcus Aurelius to award himself the honorific title 'Sarmaticus'. As part of the settlement in AD 175 the Iazyges were required to contribute eight thousand cavalrymen to Rome to serve as auxiliaries. Of these, 5,500 were sent to Britain. One detachment was based at Ribchester, near Lancaster, and the discovery of the tombstone of a Sarmatian soldier shows that others were based at Chester. The Sarmatians had finally reached the western extremity of Europe.

The Roxolani, who had put pressure on the Iazyges, lived for some time north of the Sea of Azov. They were described by Strabo at the beginning of the first century AD as being wagon dwellers who led a transhumant existence, spending their summers close to the sea, hunting deer and wild boar in the marshes, and their winters on the more northerly steppe, where they could hunt asses and roe deer. They were warlike but only lightly armed. Throughout the first century BC it was they who were the nomads involved in the affairs of the Bosporan kingdom and the Crimean Scythians.

In the middle of the first century BC the Aorsi, occupying the land to the east of the Don, came under pressure from the Alani to the east, forcing them to cross into the territory of the Roxolani, some of whom moved westwards, much as the Iazyges had done, and ended up in the plain of Wallachia on the northern side of the lower Danube. From here they raided the Roman province to the south and later became involved in Trajan's wars in Dacia. Some were taken as captives to Rome in AD 104 to appear in Trajan's triumph and were later depicted on Trajan's column riding armoured horses. The surviving population continued to live in the lower Danube region as vassals of Rome well into the third century.

The last of the nomadic group to be considered in this chapter, the Alani, appeared on the steppe north of the Caspian Sea in the middle of the first century BC, forcing the Aorsi to migrate to the west of the river Don, and in AD 68 Alani are recorded close to the Sea of Azov causing the inhabitants of Tanis to refortify their city walls. Since further advance west of the Don was blocked by the Aorsi, the Alani moved south against the Siraki, between the Black Sea and the Caspian Sea, taking control of the territory as far as the Caucasus. In AD 73–4 they moved against Parthia, presumably along the east shore of the Caspian, but achieved nothing. Fifty years later they attacked Roman territory in northern Asia Minor, but again without much effect. It was only later, in the late fourth and fifth centuries, that they were to have a devastating impact on Europe.

This sketch of the Sarmatian story has, of necessity, been brief and rather breathless, but at best it gives an impression of the mobility and cohesion of the Sarmatian clans over some four centuries when they came into the vision of the literate classical world. Over such a long period of time, and living in a number of different ecological zones, their lifestyle will have changed both socially and economically, and yet they retained their traditional names and the essence of their ethnicity. They were essentially nomadic peoples whose elites commanded entourages of warriors always fighting from horseback, and it was as expert cavalry that the Romans recognized them. Even those exiled from the Great Hungarian Plain in the late second century to serve out their lives as auxiliaries in Roman forts on the Atlantic coasts of distant Britannia had the comfort of remaining with their horses.

The Overland Connections

By the first century AD Eurasia was interconnected by an intricate network of trade-routes that allowed commodities, belief systems, and technologies to flow with comparative freedom. It would, in theory, have been possible to travel from the Han capital of Luoyang on the Yellow River to Rome in the central Mediterranean never deviating from well-used routes. Yet few, if any, would have made such a journey. While commodities travelled over vast distances, the people who carried them made much shorter journeys, restricting themselves to familiar routes between markets they knew

7.19 The Trajan column erected in the forum of Rome in the early second century AD depicts scenes from the Dacian Wars. Here heavily armoured Sarmatian cavalry (probably Roxolani) are shown fleeing from the Roman cavalry

well and where they were known. A bolt of silk would have changed hands many times on its journey from China to Rome. For long-distance down-the-line trade of this kind to flourish there had to be safe caravan stops at convenient intervals along the roads and some assurance that the local authorities were able to provide a degree of security for goods and personnel. If one route became dangerous, another could be found.

Most of the networks had been in existence for hundreds or thousands of years, their individual strands determined by geography. Westward from the Central Plains of China the obvious route lay through the 800-kilometre-long Gansu Corridor, constrained by mountains and the desert. Going forward there was the choice of flanking the Taklamakan desert around the north or south sides before converging on Kashgar, where a decision had to be made on which of the passes through the Pamir should be taken. Once through the mountains and faced with Central Asia, the desert oases of Marakanda, Bukhara, Merv, and Khiva offered places to pause en route to the west. And so the journey proceeded, geography and the political situation of the time determining the way forward. In the third and second millennium commodities were already on the move, often travelling over considerable distances: lapis lazuli from northern Afghanistan was used extensively in Mesopotamia, while jade from Khotan in the Tarim basin was enjoyed by the elites in China's Central Plains. By the third and second centuries the networks had coalesced, and even remote communities like those in the Altai were able to draw on lacquer-work and silks from China and carpets from the Iranian plateau.

The globalization of the network had many causes. Perhaps the most immediate was the dramatic rise in the demand for consumer goods and raw materials by the Roman and Parthian states and, to a lesser extent, by the Han dynasty in China. A no less important factor was the imperative felt by the Chinese to control the Tarim basin. The Zhang Qian embassy to Central Asia was motivated by the desire to seek allies against the Xiongnu and to prevent them from gaining support from the west. Thus, the primary reason for these western adventures was military: that they opened up the east–west trade-routes was a secondary consequence. Small quantities of Chinese goods had already reached northern Afghanistan, as Zhang Qian saw for himself, but it was the Chinese military presence in the Tarim basin that created conditions favourable for the entrepreneurs to develop this crucial link in the east–west network.

The arid conditions in the Tarim basin have preserved thousands of documents, providing a vivid picture of life in the oasis trading centres. Whether on wood, leather, or paper, in a multitude of languages these texts include cargo manifestos, receipts, contracts, legal disputes, and even medical prescriptions. They refer to consignments of spices, chemicals, metals, silk, saddles, and glass, showing that the trade goods were transported in comparatively small quantities and were carried over short distances of up to a few hundred kilometres before being traded on.

The largest collection of early documents comes from the Chinese garrison at Xuanquan, 60 kilometres east of Dunhuang, which, as we have seen, served both as a posting station for officials travelling on government business and as a customs post where passports were checked. All travellers carried documents specifying the itinerary they were permitted to take. Some of the travellers were delegations en route to the Han court. One, recorded in 52 BC, consisted of two envoys, ten aristocrats, and a number of followers bringing with them nine horses, thirty-one donkeys, twenty-three camels, and a cow. This seems to be about average size, but some could number more than a thousand. Another document mentions four envoys from Sogdiana who, in 39 BC, were in dispute with the Chinese officials over the price they were paid for their camels. They failed in their petition to have the price increased.

Another cache of documents, from Loulan, provides details of what garrison life was like for the Chinese officials serving in the oasis towns. The soldiers on garrison

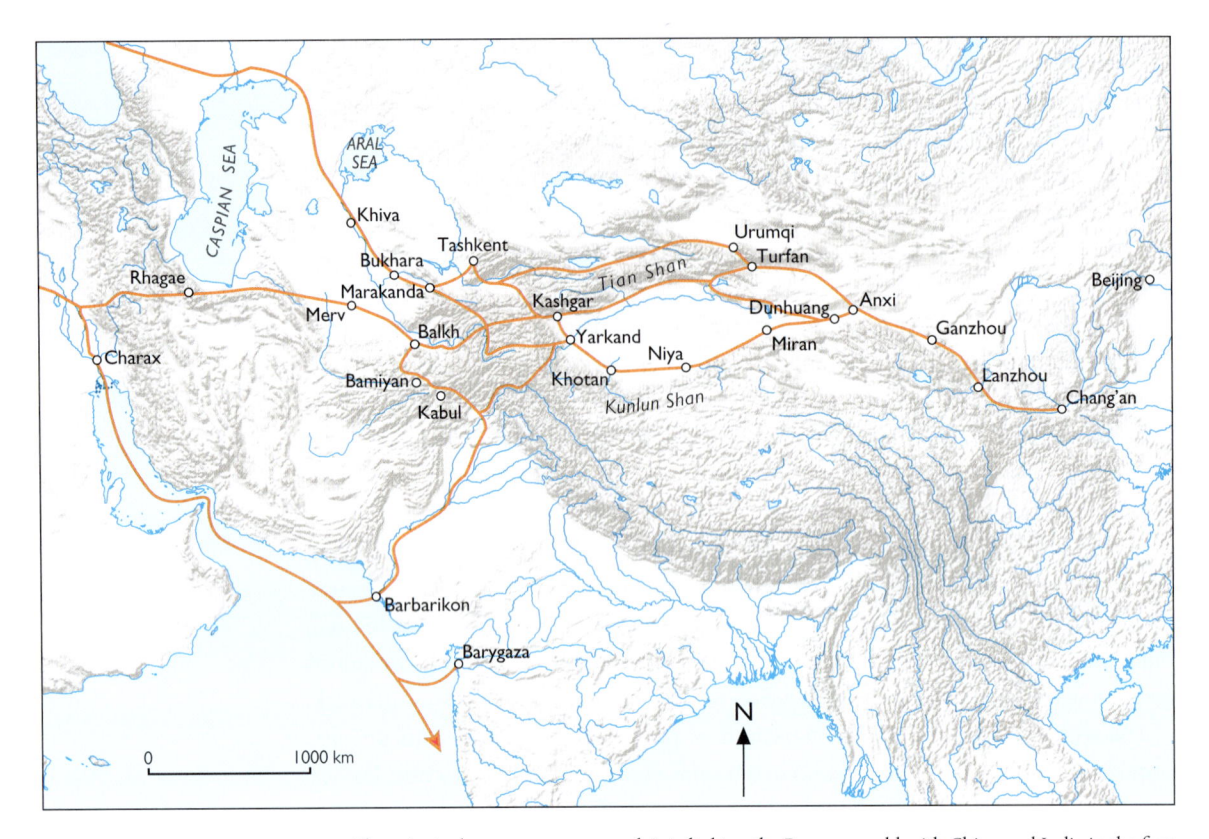

7.20 The principal routes across central Asia linking the Roman world with China and India in the first and second centuries AD

duty were expected to grow their own food, but if supplies ran short they could buy it from the locals with coins or bolts of coloured silk. The same currency was used to acquire other necessities like horses and clothing. In this way silk became an important medium of exchange, and once in the hands of the local people it could be used to obtain other goods from travellers.

What is surprising is that the abundant documentation makes little mention of merchants at work in the region in the first century BC and first and second centuries AD, though frequent delegations are noted passing to and from the Han capital carrying tribute. One possibility is that the delegates indulged in a little private enterprise on their own behalf, carrying goods to trade along the route. Once the flow had got under way, local entrepreneurs would have begun to seize upon the commercial possibilities that were being opened up by consumer demand in Rome and China.

It is difficult to quantify the volume of trade, but one dramatic visual reminder of its magnitude is the city of Palmyra on the edge of the Syrian desert. Palmyra commanded few local resources, but it funnelled the overland trade-routes from Asia and the maritime routes from the Indian Ocean by way of the Persian Gulf. It lived off the profit of trade, and in the second and third centuries AD it had grown to become a substantial city graced with grand public buildings. Its prominent citizens, most of them merchants, were buried in opulent tombs dominating the hills around. Without its command of international trade, Palmyra would have been nothing. Among the many commodities passing through the city were cloth, locally produced linen, cotton from India, fine woollen fabrics probably from Kashmir, and silk from China. One of the fragments of silk found in a local tomb depicts scenes of men harvesting grapes with a Bactrian camel nearby; it was woven using Chinese technology. In all probability it was manufactured in one of the oasis settlements of the Tarim basin, perhaps Turpan, where these scenes would have been common, using silk yarn exported from China. Had it not ended up in Palmyra, it might have graced the home of an aristocrat in Rome.

The Ocean Networks

Under the Ptolemys, who ruled Egypt from the fourth to the first centuries BC, the sea-routes down the Red Sea to the Gulf of Aden and the Arabian Sea beyond were gradually opened up for trade. To facilitate this a canal was dug from the Red Sea at Clysma (Suez) to the Nile so that goods transhipped at Clysma from sea-going vessels to smaller craft could be taken by water directly to the great Mediterranean port of Alexandria. Alternative routes were also in use from the Red Sea ports of Berenike and Myos Hormos leading overland across the eastern desert to the Nile. It was at Berenike that African elephants, desirable adjuncts for every army, were offloaded.

The Red Sea navigation was only one of a series of maritime networks in use. The ports at the southern end of the Arabian peninsula were host to vessels sailing south down the east coast of Africa and north to join the networks serving the Persian Gulf and the Makran coast to the estuary of the Indus and beyond. There is also ample evidence to show that local cabotage was in operation around the coasts of India. In other words, short- and medium-range sailings would have linked the communities around the whole of the north shore off the Indian Ocean.

By the second century BC the Red Sea ships' masters knew of the potential of the Indian Ocean. Strabo tells the story of one entrepreneur, Eudoxus of Cyzicus, who met an Indian on the Nile in the second century and decided to follow up what he had learnt from him by making an exploratory voyage to India. By this time it is highly probable that sailors were already using the monsoon weather pattern to make direct journeys from the Gulf of Aden to the subcontinent. The monsoons blew south-east from April to October and north-west from October to April. Knowing this, it is possible to make the journey out and back within a year. It was probably the Arabs from the south of the Arabian peninsula (now Yemen) who first discovered this: Arabian frankincense and myrrh were much in demand in India. It may be no coincidence that 'monsoon' comes from the Arabic word *mawsim* (literally, 'season').

Early in the first century AD a Graeco-Egyptian merchant from Alexandria collated knowledge of the Indian Ocean seaways, the art of riding the monsoons, and the ports encountered en route in the *Periplus of the Erythraean Sea*, essential as a handbook for those sailing in the Red Sea and beyond, and invaluable to archaeologists trying to piece together ancient trading networks. The author of the *Periplus* claims that he gathered the information from a sailor, Hippalus, but by this time it must all have been fairly common knowledge among sailors in the Red Sea. The annexation of Egypt by Augustus in 30 BC had provided a huge incentive to develop the trading routes. Strabo, who journeyed up the Nile in the early years of the first century AD, noted that, whereas formerly very few ships left the Red Sea port of Myos Hormos for India, now 120 vessels sailed annually.

The *Periplus* provided the essential information for the navigator. Thus:

> The port of Muza [southern Arabia], though without a harbour, offers a good roadstead for mooring because of the anchorages with sandy bottom all around ... The best time for sailing to this place is around the month of September ...

And:

> This gulf, which leads to Barygaza [on the Bay of Cambay], since it is narrow, is hard for vessels coming from seaward to manage ... At the very mouth of the gulf, there extends a rough and rock-strewn reef ... Opposite it, on the left-hand side, is a promontory ... mooring here is difficult because of the current ...

The compiler also gives copious details of the commodities traded at each port. At Muza, for example, he mentions the availability of purple cloth, Arab sleeved clothing, some interwoven with gold thread, blankets, saffron, myrrh, date wine, wheat, and alabaster.

After describing ports in the Red Sea, the east coast of Africa, Arabia, and India, the *Periplus* ends with travellers' tales of what lay beyond the known world. The last fixed point was an island to the east of the port at the mouth of the Ganges:

> Beyond this region, by now at the northernmost point, where the sea ends somewhere on the outer fringe, there is a very great inland city called Thina [China], from where silk floss, yarn, and cloth are shipped by land ... and via the Ganges river ... It is not easy to get to this Thina; for rarely do people come from it and only a few.

THE CONTINENT CONNECTED

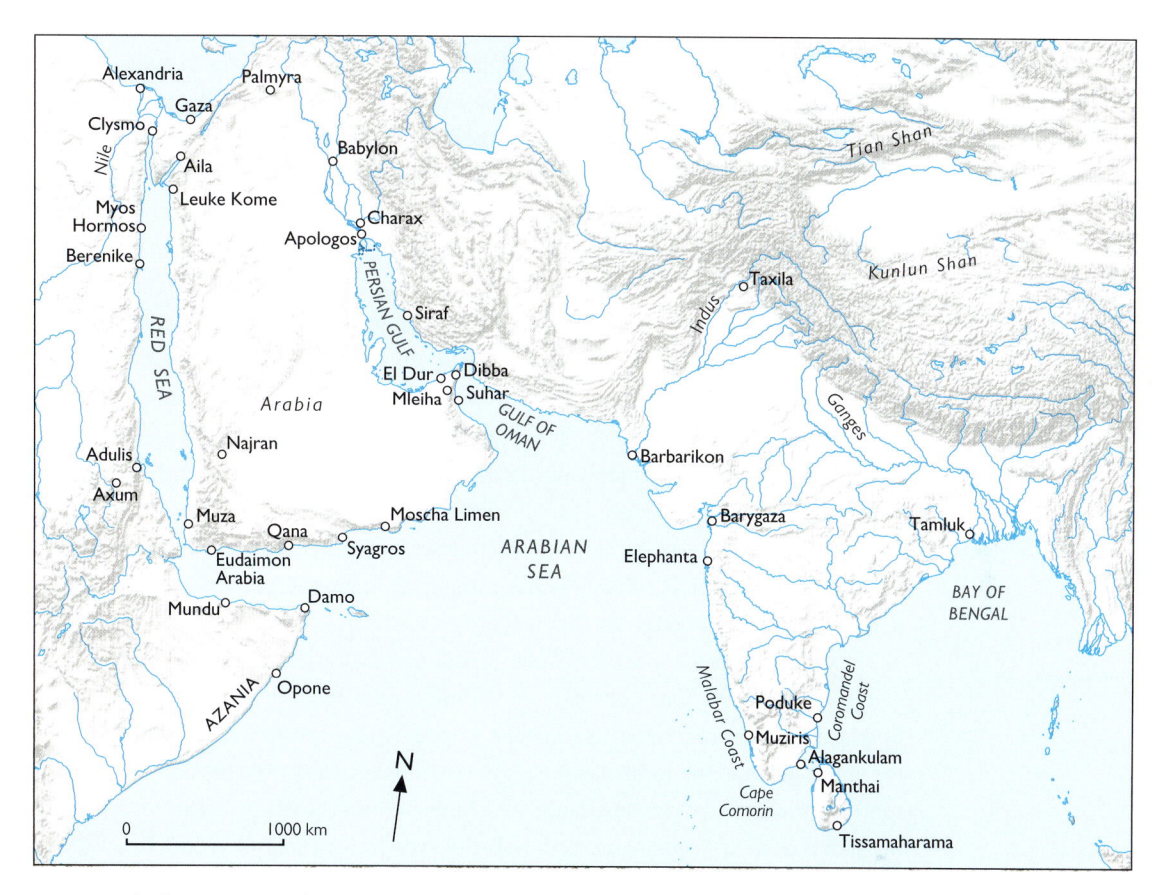

7.21 From the first century AD the sea-routes between the Roman world and India via the Red Sea and the Persian Gulf became increasingly important for trade, leading to the development of a number of thriving ports

The *Periplus* is a remarkable document reflecting on the intensity of the trade and the sheer variety of goods on the move: frankincense and myrrh from Arabia, indigo, cotton, and furs from the mouth of the Indus, ivory, carnelian, and black pepper from southern India, and high-quality pearls from Sri Lanka. Excavations at many of the ports mentioned have confirmed some of the details and added many more besides.

Much of the Red Sea traffic made for the ports of Berenike and Myos Homos on the western coast or Clysma at the head of the sea. On the east coast Leuke Kome seems to have been less involved in maritime traffic but heavily engaged in caravan trade from the south. Aila (or Aelaea) at the head of the Gulf of Aqaba served the routes into Syria or to Gaza on the Mediterranean coast. Excavations at Myos Hormos and Berenike have provided a mass of evidence of Indian Ocean trade. Actual imports found in archaeological contexts include gemstones, spices, textiles, baskets, coconuts, mung beans, rice, bamboo, and glass beads, all from southern India and Sri Lanka. One site also produced an Indian storage jar containing 7.5 kilograms of black peppercorns. But perhaps the most revealing finds were Indian teak from a ship, items of rigging, and Indian cotton sailcloth, all clearly indicating that ships made (or repaired) on the subcontinent were reaching the port. Other indications of an Indian presence were graffiti scratched on pottery in more than one of the Indian languages.

The main ports of southern Arabia were Muza, on the approach to the Bab el-Mandeb channel, and Qana on the Gulf of Aden. These were the principal stopover ports where, in addition to essential supplies, ships could take on the locally grown frankincense and myrrh as well as date wine and fabrics. The excavations at Qana uncovered a warehouse where incense had been stored. Qana was the main point of embarkation for northern and southern India, and the discovery of Indian cooking vessels suggests the presence of Indian sailors. From here it was also possible to travel down the east coast of Africa and to sail north along the coast of the Arabian peninsula to the Persian Gulf, where the maritime trade seems to have been largely in the hands of the Arabs and the Parthians.

The principal ports of northern India were Barbarikon at the mouth of the river Indus and Barygaza on the river Narmada, 30 kilometres upstream from the Bay of Cambay. Both provided direct access to the Kushan empire, Barbarikon to Gandhara and beyond to Central Asia and the Tarim basin, Barygaza to northern India and the Ganges valley. In southern India two ports were frequented: Muziris (near the village of Pattanam) on the Malabar coast and Arikamedu (modern Poduke) on the Coromandel coast. Excavations at Arikamedu have shown that the port was a fishing village before contact with the Roman world began in the late first century BC. During the contact period, at its peak from 50 BC to AD 50, large quantities of Mediterranean wine were imported together with fine Mediterranean tableware. At the port, workshops were found where the local inhabitants made glass beads and worked gemstones, ivory, and shell for export.

The picture built up from the classical sources and from excavation shows something of the complexity of the maritime networks at the height of their productivity in the first and second centuries AD. Sailors from all regions—Roman Egypt, Arabia, Parthia, and India—were involved. Indians were resident, at least for part of the year, in the Red Sea and Arabian ports, while there may have been enclaves of Roman traders established at Muziris and Arikamedu in much the same way as the East India Company had its factories at Kolkata and elsewhere in more recent times. There would also have been much flexibility in the goods carried and the ports where they were traded. Ships from Egypt laden with Mediterranean goods may have offloaded some part of the cargo at Muza or Qana to take on incense and fabrics before sailing on to India. Stopping on the return journey, some of the Indian cargoes could have

7.22 The excavation of the Red Sea port of Myos Hormos (Quseir el-Qadim), Egypt, exposed part of the harbour area and a jetty partly constructed of disused amphorae of Egyptian and Italian origin dating to the early first century AD. Amphorae were used for the transport of wine and other liquids

been exchanged for Arabian incense taken on board for the last leg of the voyage to satisfy the Roman market. There were infinite opportunities to turn a profit, and one can be sure that the experienced entrepreneurs, whatever their ethnicity, balanced all the options with a degree of finesse.

Connectivity

Sufficient has been said to show that half a millennium, from 250 BC to AD 250, saw the whole of Eurasia bound, for the first time, to become a single global system. In the early second century AD a member of the Korean elite could admire a glass vessel made in the Roman world, while soldiers stationed on Hadrian's Wall could spice their meals with Indian black pepper. Buddhism had spread from its origin in the Ganges valley to the Chinese-controlled oases of the Tarim basin, where paper, a Chinese invention of the second century BC, was beginning to appear used as wrapping for medicines. And while some descendants of the nomad tribes of the Kazakh steppe were ruling northern India, others were serving as auxiliaries on the British frontier. The world was fast becoming much smaller.

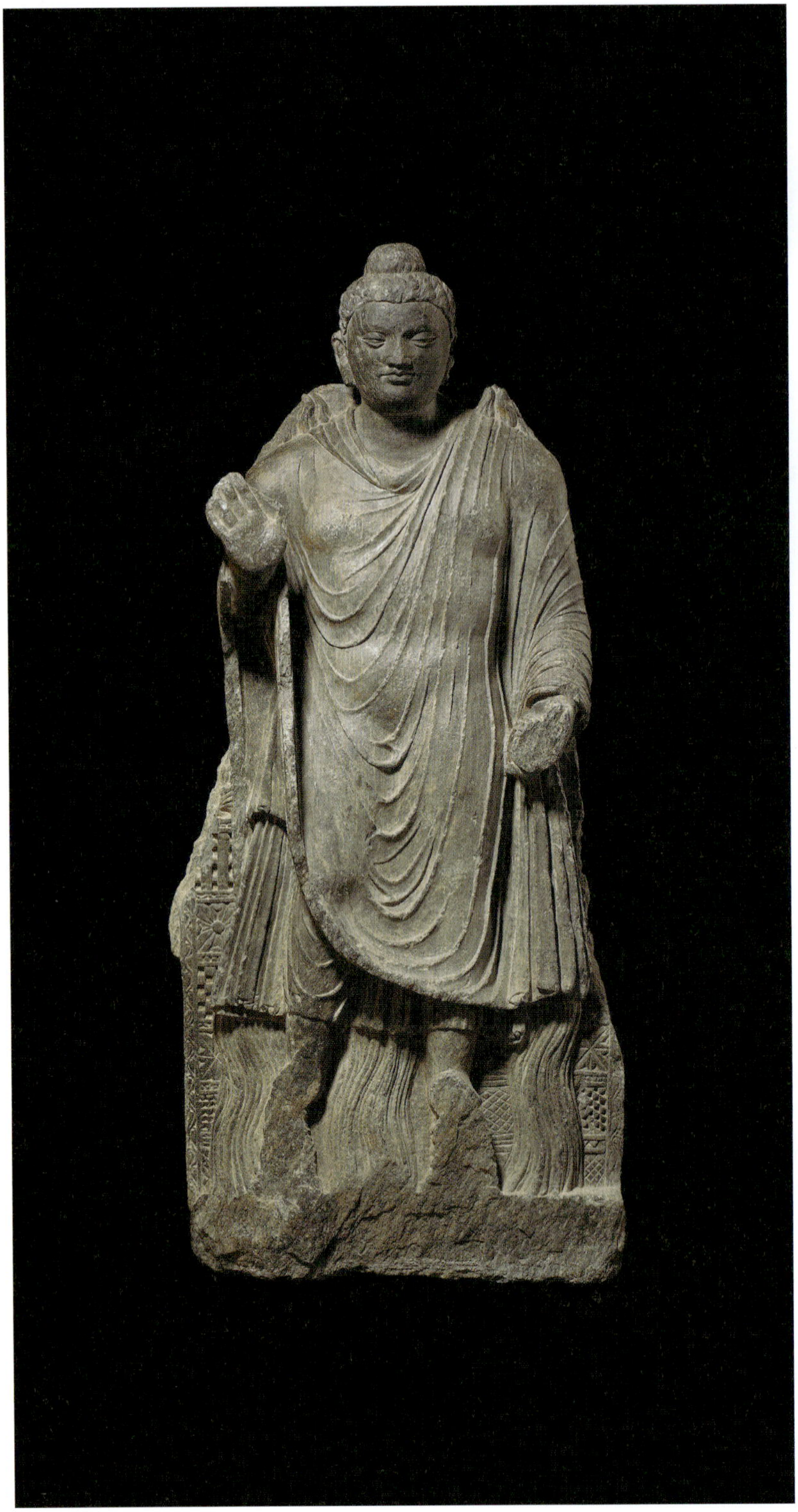

8

THE AGE OF PERPETUAL WAR, AD 250–650

'Perpetual war' may be something of an overstatement, but, given the constant internal fighting in China during the period known as the Six Dynasties (AD 220–581), the long-drawn-out decline of the western Roman empire as northern barbarians tore it apart, and the interminable warfare between the Roman world and the Sasanians along the frontier zone between the Euphrates and the Caucasus, there can be little doubt that during this brief four hundred years a significant part of Eurasian productivity was consumed by conflict. By the beginning of the seventh century the old world states were exhausted, yet, despite the carnage and the chaos, trade flourished, and with it a new cosmopolitanism, and there were major cultural advances driven by the growing power of Christianity, Buddhism, and Islam.

In the three regions with long-established settled state systems—Persia, Europe, and China—interminable regiments of kings and emperors came and went. In vying for territory, power, and wealth, they created an intricate mesh of superficial 'history' that floated on the surface of the deep social and economic adjustments taking place in the swell beneath. It is well beyond the scope of this book to offer a précis of these events—the decline and fall of the Roman empire, only one small part of the story, is far from easy to condense, as others have found—but very brief outlines of the major changes must be attempted to provide a basic chronological framework. What is of far more interest is what was going on along the interfaces between the major state systems and the broad corridors that connected them. It is on these innovative areas that we shall concentrate after having first outlined the histories of the three empires.

Complex networks of exchange had been established throughout the length of Eurasia, across the deserts and the ocean. They came into being to meet the demands of the consuming states, but by the third century AD they had developed a momentum of their own, and even while the states were busy tearing themselves and each other apart, the trading networks continued to function, protected by self-generated systems of self-preservation. From the third to the seventh centuries it was the relentless dynamics of trade that held Eurasia together.

China: The Age of Disunity, AD 220–618

The final collapse of the weakened Han dynasty in AD 220 heralded a new period of disunity in China known as the Six Dynasties. It was to last until AD 581, when the country was reunited under the Sui dynasty, a brief interlude paving the way for the more stable and longer-lasting Tang dynasty, which began in AD 618. After the abdication of the last Han emperor China split into three kingdoms, the Wei in the north, the Wu in the south, and the Shu in the west, each struggling for supremacy. The long contest between them ended in AD 280 with the Wei becoming the dominant power, its success based partly upon its agricultural productivity and partly upon its network of canals, which greatly facilitated transportation.

The northern border with the nomads continued to be a problem. Already in the Late Han it had become policy to settle nomad groups within the Great Wall. This relieved pressure on the frontier and provided a buffer against raids from the north. But the settlers themselves posed a threat: they were constantly warring among themselves and were prone to call in allies from among the free nomads to the north. In an attempt to keep things under control, and to prevent the different tribes from coalescing into larger confederations, the administrative units of the frontier region were kept small and were placed under the authority of Chinese officials. But it remained an unstable arrangement and in AD 304 two rival groups in a local conflict called upon different bands of free nomads for support. One sought help from the Xiongnu, the other from the Xianbei. Chinese troops intervened, and in the mêlée that followed more steppe nomads poured in. In AD 311 the capital of the Wei, Luoyang, was sacked by the Xiongnu and the emperor was captured, and in AD 316 Chang'an fell and another emperor was taken prisoner. In the wake of these events there was an exodus of Chinese from the northern territories to the comparative safety of the south, the remaining members of the imperial house taking up residence in Nanjing in the Yangtze valley, in the territory of the Wu. One contemporary

THE AGE OF PERPETUAL WAR

writer gave a succinct analysis of the situation saying that the success of the nomads who had settled within the frontier was due less to their natural vigour and more to the skills they had learnt from the Chinese in organization, warfare, and production.

By AD 317 a new boundary had been established between the mixed-ethnicity northern region and the Chinese south. It was roughly parallel to the river Wei–lower Yellow River, but lay 100–150 kilometres to the south. That the line marked the approximate divide between the northern wheat- and millet-producing land and the

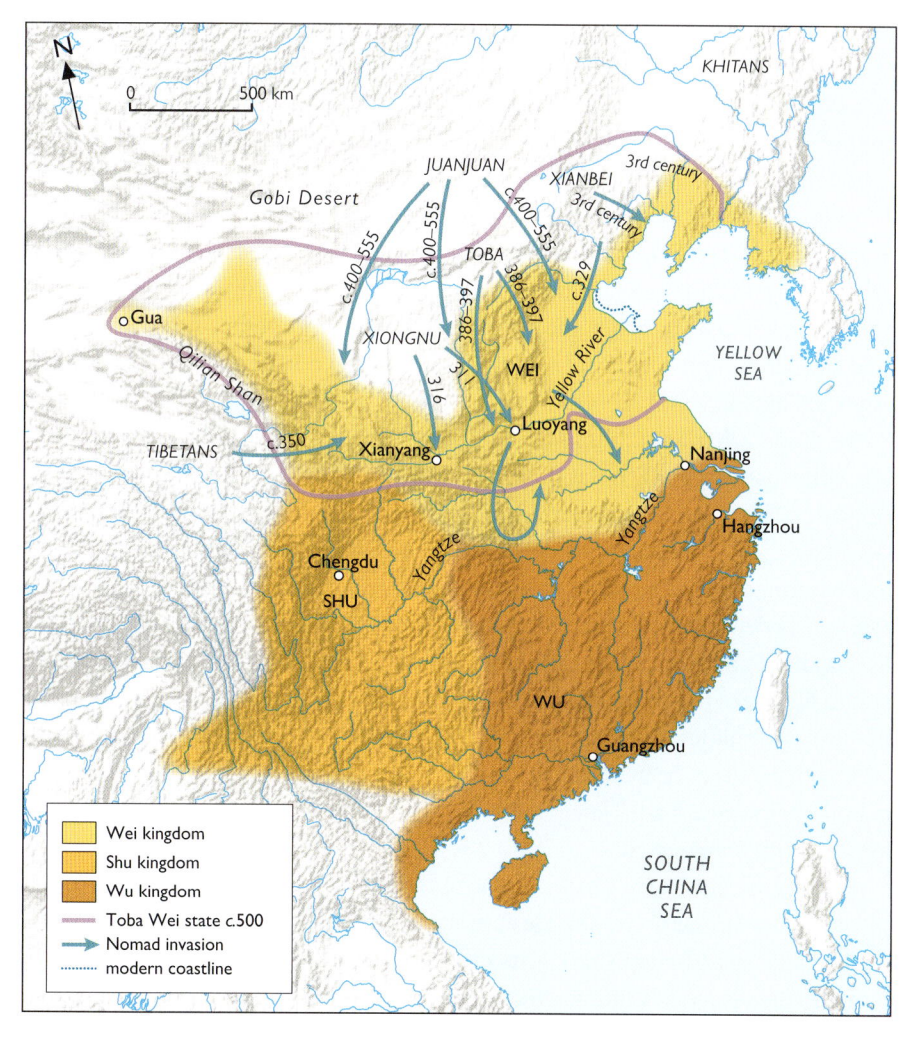

8.1 The breakdown of centralized power in China at the end of the Han dynasty in AD 220 led to political division. Nomad incursions from the north, culminating with the settlement of the Toba in northern China, divided the country into two distinct parts by c. AD 500

southern zone of irrigated rice production is no accident. The cavalry, so important to the nomad-led northern region, could not function efficiently among rice fields: it was a geography that imposed a limit to their advance south. One attempt was made in AD 383, but the northern armies were halted at a battle fought at Feishui.

The northern region, like the south, was divided into a number of kingdoms often in conflict with one another, but the infrastructure of Chinese culture was well established. The turbulent situation was to some extent stabilized by the appearance of the Toba Tatars, a branch of the semi-agricultural Xianbei living in eastern Mongolia. By AD 439 they had managed to establish themselves as overlords of the disparate northern kingdoms, initiating the Toba Wei dynasty, which lasted until AD 589. What is remarkable about the new leadership is the energy they put into embracing Chinese culture. The Toba were already used to agricultural production, and in the northern region they found a mixed population, most practising a settled economy based on agriculture. There was also a significant educated class trained in Chinese administration already at work in the individual kingdoms. The Toba leadership built on this, encouraging acceptance of Chinese culture in all its forms. The ultimate expression of this came in AD 500 when the emperor of the north prohibited the use of Tatar language, dress, and customs. From this point on the northern kingdoms were, in essence, Chinese.

The Sino-barbarian synthesis evident in the northern regions has certain parallels with what was going on at this time in western Europe as the western Roman empire collapsed under pressure from influxes of northern barbarians, mostly of German origin. The incursions destroyed the Roman centralized government, but many among the immigrant population were quick to adopt aspects of Roman culture as they developed new state structures. This is particularly true of the Visigoths, Burgundians, and Franks. The Latin language and Christianity were shared by all, and eventually one of the kingdoms, the Carolingians, made a concerted attempt to unify the disparate polities into a reinvention of the western Roman empire. While the parallels with the situation in northern China are by no means exact, it is interesting how in both regions the 'barbarians' readily absorbed the more advanced culture of the territories they conquered.

In China the final act began when one of the northern generals, Yang Jian, seized the northern throne in AD 581. He appears to have been of mixed ethnicity, part-Xianbei and part-Chinese. Once firmly established in the north, he marched south, bringing the disparate Chinese kingdoms under his authority, thus uniting China once more in AD 589. He assumed the title Sui Wendi, becoming the first emperor of the Sui dynasty, which lasted until AD 618. Sui Wendi was an energetic leader. He did much to stabilize the borders, fighting against the Mongolians in the north-east, the

Turks in the north-west, and the Tibetans in the south. The Mongolians were forced to recognize the Chinese emperor as khan, while the king of Tibet married a Chinese princess, signalling his subservience to the emperor. The Sui dynasty did not last long. Grandiose schemes, including the building of the Grand Canal and the invasion of the Korean peninsula, put massive strains on the economy and led to rebellion, but out of the unrest emerged a new dynasty, the Tang, who managed not only to maintain the unity of the country but to institute a new golden age.

Persia and the Sasanians: An Outline

The Parthians and the Romans had spent two centuries in conflict, and by the early third century AD the Parthians were drained of resources and in political disarray. Out of the squabbling polities that remained, one man, Ardashir, the ruler of the kingdom of Persia, found himself strong enough to make a bid for supreme power. In AD 224 he overthrew the last of the Parthian kings and was crowned in the capital, Ctesiphon, thus initiating a new dynasty, the Sasanians (named after his legendary ancestor Sasan). The dynasty was to last until AD 651.

Ardashir chose the title King of Kings, a direct reference to the times of Cyrus the Great, nearly eight hundred years before, when the Persians were at their most expansive. His intention, and that of his immediate successors, was to restore the grandeur of the old Achaemenid empire, and this they did. In the east a large part of the Kushan empire was conquered, including much of Gandhara, Bactria, and Sogdiana, making the Indus the eastern boundary of the empire, with the northern boundary fringing the arid deserts of Central Asia. In the north the Sasanian state faced a series of nomadic incursions, first the Hephthalites (White Huns) in the fifth century and later the Turks, who were to take control of much of Sogdiana. In the west the frontier with the Roman world, running in an arc from Babylon on the Euphrates to the centre of the Caucasus, remained a zone of perpetual tension incessantly fought over and constantly moving. Seldom were two states to expend so much blood and resources on a frontier conflict to so little lasting effect. At best, the effort did little more than maintain the status quo.

The Sasanians also looked to their maritime trading enterprises. By AD 260 much of the south shore of the Persian Gulf and the Gulf of Oman had come under Sasanian authority, ensuring that the trade with India by way of the Arabian Sea was now firmly under control. Later, in the late sixth and early seventh centuries, an attempt was made to extend Sasanian control to the Red Sea routes by making Sheba (modern Yemen) a dependency (p. 312).

THE AGE OF PERPETUAL WAR

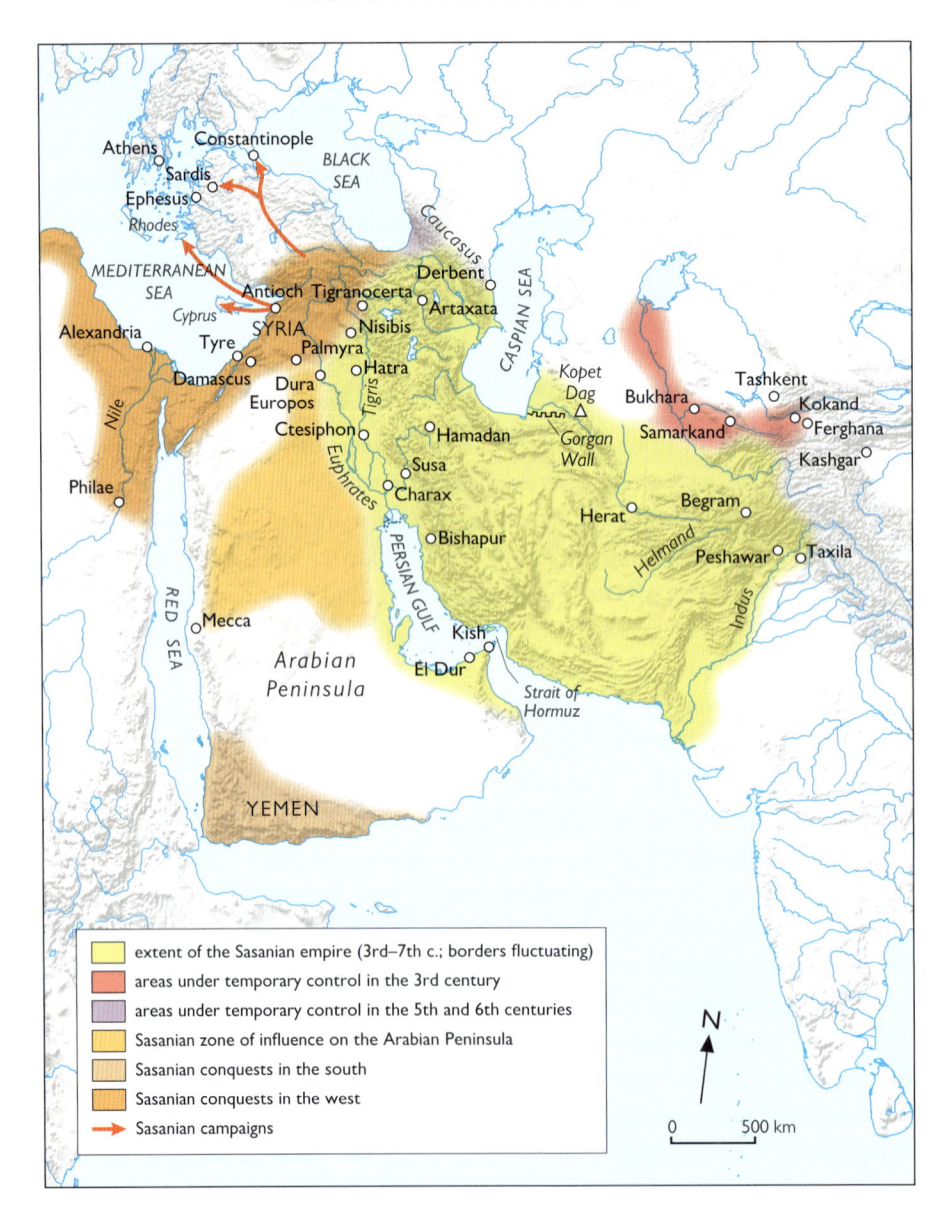

8.2 In the third century AD the Sasanian dynasty came to power, taking hold of the old Parthian empire, which they extended to include Egypt, Yemen, and Central Asia. The Sasanians were in constant conflict with Rome and Byzantium until the early seventh century AD

8.3 Rock relief at Naqsh-i Rustam, Iran. The Sasanian king Shapur I (reigned AD 240–72) sits on horseback with two defeated Roman emperors before him, Philip the Arab and Valerian. Philip sued for peace after the emperor Gordian III had been killed in battle in AD 244, and Valerian was taken prisoner in AD 260

While Parthian rule had loosely held together a confederation of disparate kingdoms, the Sasanian rulers strove for a more unified state, with the provinces kept under close centralized control. Zoroastrianism became the state religion, and society was organized within a strict class system. The new administrative structure created an equilibrium that gave the state the power to maintain a vast empire and to confront Rome. But in the end constant expenditure of resources and manpower on the western frontier drained the energy and resolve of the people, leaving the exhausted Sasanian empire to be overrun by the Arabs—a process which began in AD 634 and ended with the capitulation of the last king in AD 651.

Rome and Byzantium

Rome's northern frontier, stretching from Britain to the Black Sea, was a heavily militarized zone. It used natural boundaries like the Rhine and the Danube, but augmented them where necessary with man-made barriers such as Hadrian's Wall and the German Limes. Like the contemporary Han Great Wall in China, the fixed fron-

8.4 Silver dish with some parts gilded showing the Sasanian king Shapur II (reigned AD 309–79) stag hunting, an activity appropriate to the elite. The depiction of the hunted beast closely resembles the way stags were presented in nomad art going back to the early first millennium BC

tier was designed to control relationships with the 'barbarians' beyond. It prevented mass movements of people (settlers or raiders) from invading the empire while being sufficiently porous to allow managed trade. That, at least, was the theory, but the Marcomannic Wars of AD 166–80 showed that the frontier could not be relied on when population pressures built up against it. As part of the solution to the problem Germans and Sarmatians were brought into the empire and settled. It was the beginning of a policy that was to be increasingly used in the third and fourth centuries, totally changing the ethnic mix in the frontier provinces.

By the middle of the third century the empire was facing a crisis. The centralized power structure was in disarray, the fiscal system was failing as debt mounted, and large confederations of barbarians—Franks, Alemanni, and Goths—were threatening the stability of the northern frontier zones. Between AD 250 and AD 280

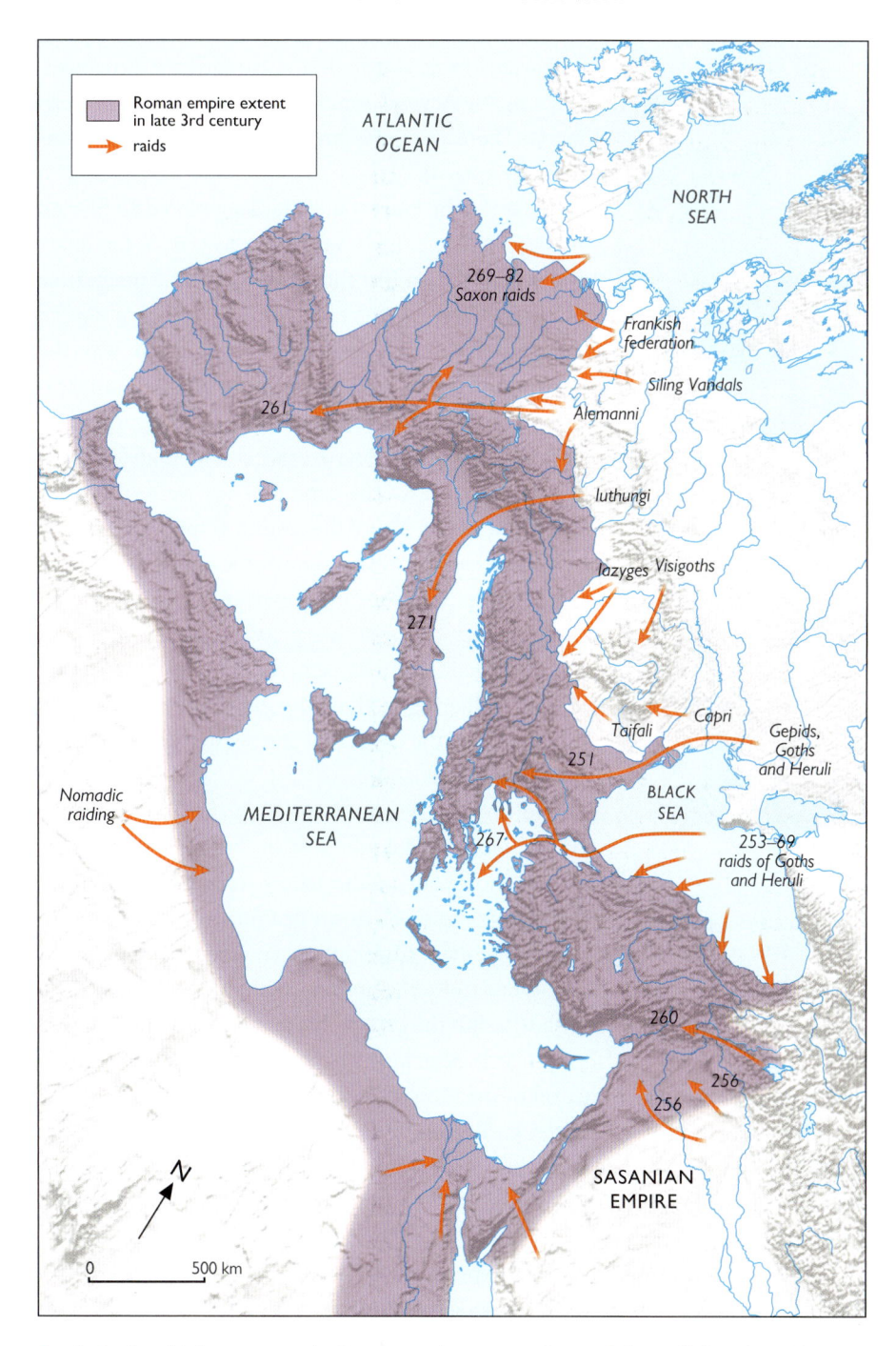

8.5 In the late third century AD the Roman empire came under attack from all directions. The most intensive attacks were from the north from across the Rhine–Danube frontier in the period AD 250–80

THE AGE OF PERPETUAL WAR

barbarians broke through and ravaged the provinces, reaching the Aegean islands, central Italy, and northern Iberia. There were also problems on the eastern frontiers (pp. 306–11).

In AD 284 the Praetorian Guard appointed an Illyrian soldier, Diocletian, as emperor. It was a fortunate choice. Diocletian had the vision to see the magnitude of the problem and the energy to act on it. Among the many wide-ranging reforms he introduced was the splitting of the empire into two separate administrative parts ruled by Augusti of equal rank supported by Caesars, who would take over when the Augusti retired after twenty years. The capital of the western empire was Rome, while that of the eastern empire was soon to become Byzantium. The logic of the divide was simply that the empire had become too large for any single man to administer, but underlying it was the realization that the west Mediterranean-centred world, Latin-speaking and still adhering to the old gods, was culturally very different from the Greek-speaking east, with its growing interest in Christianity.

The divided system, known as the Tetrarchy (the rule of four), worked for a while, but after the abdication of Diocletian and his fellow ruler Maximian in AD 305 it began to break down in a mire of rivalries out of which one man, Constantine, emerged supreme in AD 324. Once more the empire was united under a single authority, but the geographical logic of the two-centred empire was clear. More to the point, Constantine immediately grasped the importance of the position of Byzantium, commanding as it does the east–west land route between Europe and Asia and the north–south maritime route between the Black Sea and the Mediterranean. In AD 330 Byzantium became the new capital of the empire, New Rome, or Constantinople, and so it was to remain for over a thousand years.

The rise of Constantinople at the expense of Rome was rapid, the more so after the emperor Theodosius I (ruled AD 379–95) made Constantinople his imperial residence. While the eastern empire, comprising the Balkans, Asia Minor, the Levant,

8.6 The system of tetrarchy, introduced by Diocletian to give stability to the unwieldy empire, is neatly characterized by the red porphyry carving of the Tetrarchs dating to about AD 300. It was taken from Constantinople to Venice following the Fourth Crusade. The partners grasp each other in a friendly gesture but keep their hands on their swords

304

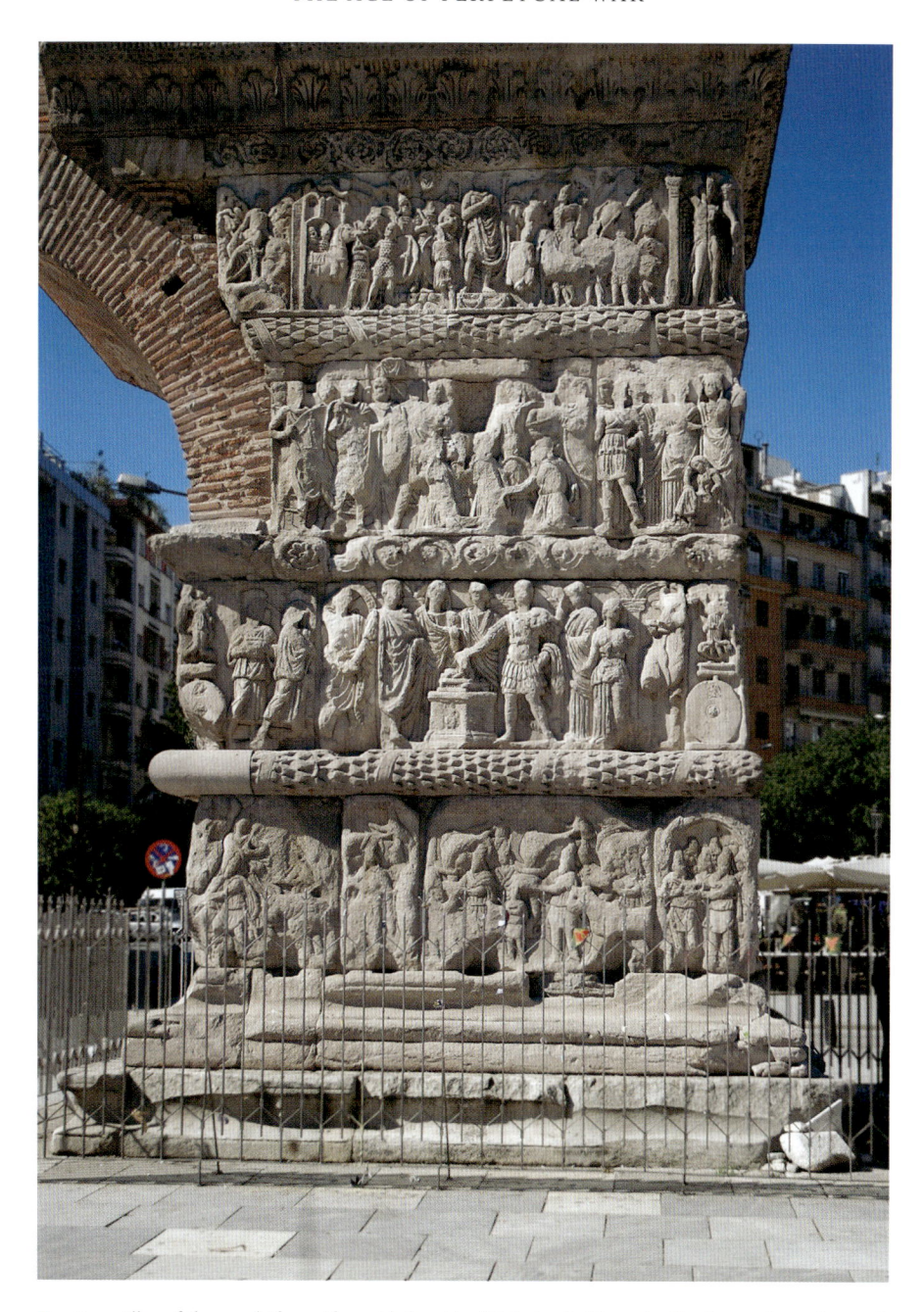

8.7 One pillar of the quadrifrons (four-sided arch) of Galerius in Thessalonika, in northern Greece. It was built in AD 299 and dedicated in AD 303 to celebrate the victory of Galerius, one of the Tetrarchs, over the Sasanians and the capture of Ctesiphon in AD 298

Egypt, and Cyrenaica, flourished, the west began to collapse under incessant attacks from the northern barbarians, north European confederations augmented by immigrant nomads like the Alans. The Roman policy had long been to invite barbarians into the empire. They were to serve in the army and to settle land close to the frontier abandoned by Roman provincials, the hope being that their presence would hinder further incursions. The result was that the northern provinces became heavily Germanized and, after the middle of the fourth century, floods of new immigrants arrived to raid and to settle. The end of the Roman west is formally marked by the deposing of the last emperor in AD 467. By this time Visigoths, Burgundians, and Franks had taken over the western provinces and were settling into the old Roman infrastructure, creating hybrid cultures firmly rooted in Roman values. The situation was not unlike that in northern China.

Meanwhile, the eastern empire, now properly called the Byzantine empire, maintained its integrity and grew in strength. But there was nostalgia for the world that had been, and under Justinian, who became emperor in AD 527, a determined attempt was made to win back the west. After thirty years this vastly expensive aspiration had partially succeeded with the reconquest of most of the Mediterranean lands, but the enterprise had been a financial disaster. When Justinian died in AD 565, his successor, Justin II, 'found the treasury burdened with many debts and reduced to utter exhaustion'.

The western reconquests were not to last. Much of northern Italy was lost by AD 572 and other losses followed. Byzantium simply did not have sufficient resources to hold onto the west while protecting its frontier on the Danube against Avars and Slavs and fighting a succession of campaigns on its eastern frontier against the Sasanians. Yet by AD 630 the Avars had been defeated in the Balkans and a favourable settlement had been reached with the Sasanians. Byzantium was now in a position to begin the long process of rebuilding its shaken infrastructure, but at this very moment a new threat was fast gathering in the Arabian peninsula.

Interactions: Rome and the Sasanian Empire

The Arabian and Syrian deserts provided a convenient buffer zone between the two empires, but from the upper Euphrates to the Black Sea there was no natural

8.8 (*Opposite*) In the middle of the sixth century AD, during the reign of Justinian, the much-reduced Byzantine empire made strenuous attempts to regain the Mediterranean territories that once were ruled by Rome. The successes gained by AD 565 were short-lived and the effort crippled the Byzantine empire financially

extent of Byzantine empire at Justinian's accession
Justinian's conquests
raids
SUEVI
FRANKS
VISIGOTHS
Rhône
LOMBARDS
Milan
Lucca
Ravenna
Balearics
Corsica
Sardinia
Rome
Naples
Carthage
GEPIDS
ANTAE
SLAVS
Sicily
Siracusa
Thessalonika
AVARS
Constantinople
Athens
BLACK SEA
MEDITERRANEAN SEA
Crete
Rhodes
ALANS
Cyprus
Antioch
Carrhae
Araxes
Alexandria
Berytus
Tigris
Caesarea
Jerusalem
Euphrates
Nile
N
RED SEA
Aksum
0
500 km

boundary. Instead there lay a wedge of disputed territory 200–300 kilometres broad centred on the kingdom of Armenia. Towards the northern apex of the desert divide were two cities: Palmyra on the western limit of the Roman province of Syria, and Dura Europos 200 kilometres to the east, guarding a crossing point on the Euphrates. Dura had been captured by the Romans in AD 165 and served as an important forward military base confronting the Parthians and, after AD 224, the Sasanians. The desert oasis city of Palmyra, as we have seen, was the convergence point of caravan routes from the east and had already grown rich from the through trade to the Roman world, which it controlled. But, with the virtual collapse of stable government in Rome and the strengthening of Persian power under the Sasanian dynasty, the city's future was beginning to look uncertain. The Palmyrenes therefore began to look to their own defence.

In AD 230 the Sasanians began attacks on the northern regions of Syria. After the initial forays there was some respite, but in AD 253 a more concerted advance brought them to the gates of Antioch and three years later Dura Europos was captured. In the ensuing campaigns, in AD 260, the Roman emperor Valerian was captured. In the same year the governor of Syria, Septimius Odainat, a member of the Palmyrene aristocracy who had taken to the field against the Sasanians, defeated the Sasanian king Sapur, and, flushed with victory, assumed the title King of Kings. At this moment

8.9 The main street of Palmyra, a Roman city on the edge of the Syrian desert. It grew rich from the caravan trade which passed through it. The camel, now as then, was the main beast of burden

8.10 Ancient Palmyra, largely ruined, lies on the edge of an oasis, now a date plantation, beyond which the empty desert stretches for 300 kilometres to the river Euphrates

Rome could do nothing but ignore his claim to autonomy. But when Odainat was eventually murdered and his wife, Zenobia, assumed power, an army was sent against her. The force was weak and was defeated, encouraging Zenobia to greater ambition. First, she captured the capital of Syria, Bosra, and in AD 269 she invaded and conquered Egypt, sending shock waves through the Roman world. Flushed with success, she then began to turn her attention to Asia Minor. The situation was eventually retrieved when, in AD 272, Palmyra capitulated to a new Roman force and Zenobia was captured.

The events showed just how vulnerable Rome's eastern frontier was and demanded some display of strength. In the following decades conflict was almost continuous. Ctesiphon, the Sasanian capital, was sacked, and Armenia passed to Roman control. Renewed Sasanian aggression in AD 296 led to another major Roman offensive. Ctesiphon was again taken, and in AD 299 the Sasanians ceded large expanses of territory to Rome, but it was an uneasy peace.

Serious conflict broke out again in AD 359 when the Sasanians captured a Roman frontier post on the upper Tigris. In retaliation the Roman army made a spectacular advance on Ctesiphon, but, after a series of poor judgements and the death of the emperor Julian in battle, the Roman army was allowed to retreat, having agreed to surrender Roman-held territory. With the accession of Justinian in AD 527 a new

8.11 The city of Dura Europos dominates a crossing point on the river Euphrates in Iraq. It was founded by the Seleucids in 303 BC and remained a crucial strategic place throughout the Parthian and Sasanian periods. It was captured by the Romans in AD 165 and was abandoned after a Sasanian siege in AD 256–7

Byzantine offensive began but was brought to a temporary close when an 'eternal peace' was concluded in AD 532 requiring the Byzantines to pay 440,000 aurei to the Sasanians. The peace was short-lived, but in AD 591, in return for political support, the shah made significant territorial concessions to the empire.

The last act began in AD 602 when the Sasanians set out to retrieve the territories ceded ten years earlier and, finding the Byzantine empire in some disarray, decided to make an all-out attack on the west. By AD 610 they had reached the Euphrates and the next year overran Syria and advanced into Anatolia. In AD 614 they took Jerusalem, Alexandria fell, and two years later all of Egypt had been conquered. The shah could now claim that he had restored the Achaemenid empire. The Byzantine counter-offensive began in AD 622. The lost territory was quickly recovered, and five years later, in AD 627, the Byzantine emperor Heraclius defeated a large Persian army near Nineveh before proceeding south to Ctesiphon. The Sasanian hierarchy was now in a state of disarray and a peace treaty was finally agreed in AD 630, restoring the frontiers to the line agreed forty years earlier.

The confrontation between the Roman world and the successive dynasties of Persia had lasted for nearly seven centuries. Huge resources had been dissipated by both sides. The conflict had caused a massive loss of life and all to very little effect: the frontier had changed hardly at all. The old tug-of-war had succeeded only in exhausting both contestants. A totally new game was to begin when the Arabs, freshly united by Islam, marched into Persian territory.

Why Rome and Persia should have allowed themselves to be locked for so long into this deadly conflict is an intriguing question. It was always to be a contest between two equals—a point acknowledged by the Romans, who were careful never to refer to the Parthians or Sasanians as barbarians, a term used for their other enemies. One explanation probably lay in the fact that the frontier provided a convenient place for new leaders to demonstrate their prowess. So much 'history' had accumulated around the conflict, going back to the first century BC, that there was something macho about the eastern frontier, something irresistible: it was the place for an emperor or a shah to be seen in action. There was also the issue of trade. Persia sat astride the major overland routes from the east, and it also controlled the flow of goods by sea via the Persian Gulf. While trade was good for both parties, the Persians, if they wished, could have cut off supplies to the west. To do so would have been to destabilize the Roman economy: it was a threat that could not be allowed to happen. While the Roman world could trade freely via the Red Sea with India and beyond there was no problem, but once the Persians began to turn their attention to the southern seaway the threat to Roman well-being became serious.

The Red Sea and the Arabs

The importance of southern Arabia to Roman trade with the east has already been outlined. Not only were the ports of Yemen useful stop-over points for sailors making long-haul journeys between the Egyptian ports at the north end of the Red Sea to India, but the region was one of the few areas of the world where frankincense and myrrh were grown—highly desirable commodities in both eastern and western markets. Moreover, sailors plying the Indian Ocean routes who preferred not to face the dangerous coral reefs of the Red Sea could unload their cargoes in the south Arabian ports for sale to local merchants, who would then arrange for them to be sent by the caravan route along the eastern side of the Red Sea to Petra and thence onwards to the markets of the Roman empire.

By the early sixth century the commercial importance of southern Arabia was firmly in the consciousness of both the Byzantines and the Sasanians. It was also appreciated by the kingdom of Aksum, which lay in Ethiopia to the west of the Red Sea and had by this time become a regular participant in trade. When religious riots broke out in the Arabian cities between the Christian and Jewish communities, the Aksumites sent troops to reinforce the Christians and invited Byzantine support. Justin II responded by sending a military detachment and offered encouragement to the Aksumites and Arabs to unite to cut the Persians out of the trade network altogether. Little came of it since certain Arab leaders preferred Sasanian protection. Encouraged by this, a Sasanian military unit accompanied by a naval detachment landed at Aden about AD 570 and marched to Sana'a in support of one of the Arab contenders for power. Thereafter the Sasanians controlled the passage of shipping to and from the Red Sea. An attempt to remove them in AD 598 was countered by a new expedition, resulting in the formal annexation of southern Arabia, which remained a part of the Persian empire until the capitulation of the Sasanian army to Byzantium in Mesopotamia in AD 628.

The rivalry between the Roman–Byzantine world and that of the Sasanians from the mid-third to the early seventh century seems to have had little effect on the flow of trade with the east. For most of that time the Sasanian trade went via the Persian Gulf, while the Roman trade used the Red Sea routes. The distribution of distinctive storage amphorae found at the Indian trading centres hints that the ships' masters plying the different routes tried to keep clear of each other by favouring rival ports. After the Persians took control of the south Arabian ports in the late sixth century, it is difficult to see much change in trading patterns except that the state of Aksum, on the African side of the Red Sea, became more active and may have been increasingly used by the Byzantine merchants as a way round the Sasanian-controlled ports in Yemen, but these matters, though hinted at in the archaeological evidence, are difficult to quantify. In any event the Sasanian dominance in southern Arabia can hardly have failed to have a distorting effect on trade.

The meddling of the two great powers in the affairs of the Yemeni Arabs sparked off a nativist revolt in the 620s. Not long after, the dissidents became unified under the banner of Islam. This consequence, and the exhaustion of the Byzantines and

Sasanians after their long war of attrition, set the scene for the spectacular advance of Islam in the next three decades.

The Indus Corridor and the Spread of Buddhism

The Indus valley provided the wide corridor of interaction that linked the Indian Ocean port of Barbarikon to the inland region of Gandhara with its major cities of Peshawar and Taxila. From this northern region two convenient routes led into Central Asia, one via Kabul through the Hindu Kush to Bactria, the other across the Karakorams to the Tarim basin. Gandhara was a major crossroad and had in consequence over the centuries acquired an ethnically varied population. Until about AD 230 the region had been ruled by the Kushans, but, with the rise of the Sasanian dynasty, first Bactria and then Gandhara were lost, leaving the indigenous Guptas to take over much of the rest of northern India during the fourth century. Indo-Sasanid rule lasted until the seventh century, but the situation was further confused by an incursion of nomads, the Hephthalites, in the late fourth and fifth centuries. Dynastic shifts brought about by the influx of northern nomads changed little but simply added to the cosmopolitan nature of the population. The two stabilizing factors that created a strong sense of continuity through to the seventh century were the maintenance of a high volume of trade and the developing importance of Buddhism: the two were closely linked.

Buddhism emerged in the Ganges valley from the teachings of Siddhartha Gautama (c.563–c.483 BC), who became known as the Buddha, or 'Awakened One', but the belief remained of only local significance until it was taken up and championed by the Mauryan emperor Ashoka about 260 BC. Under his encouragement missionaries spread throughout India and Sri Lanka and along the trade-routes into Central Asia, where the religion became firmly established by the first century BC. By the first century AD Buddhism has spread through the Tarim basin to China, and about AD 400 Indian seafarers were introducing it to South East Asia. The spread of Buddhism went hand in hand with the rapid development of trade under the Kushans in the first century BC and the first and second centuries AD, and, once established in far-flung parts, the momentum continued.

In the absence of Buddhist scripts, until the first century BC the faith had to be taught by word of mouth, creating a situation in which divergent interpretations could easily emerge. There were two main schools: the Theravada ('Doctrine of the Elders') and the Mahayana ('Great Vehicle'). The Theravada adhered strictly to the original canon of teachings. Life was full of suffering, which was fuelled by desire.

THE AGE OF PERPETUAL WAR

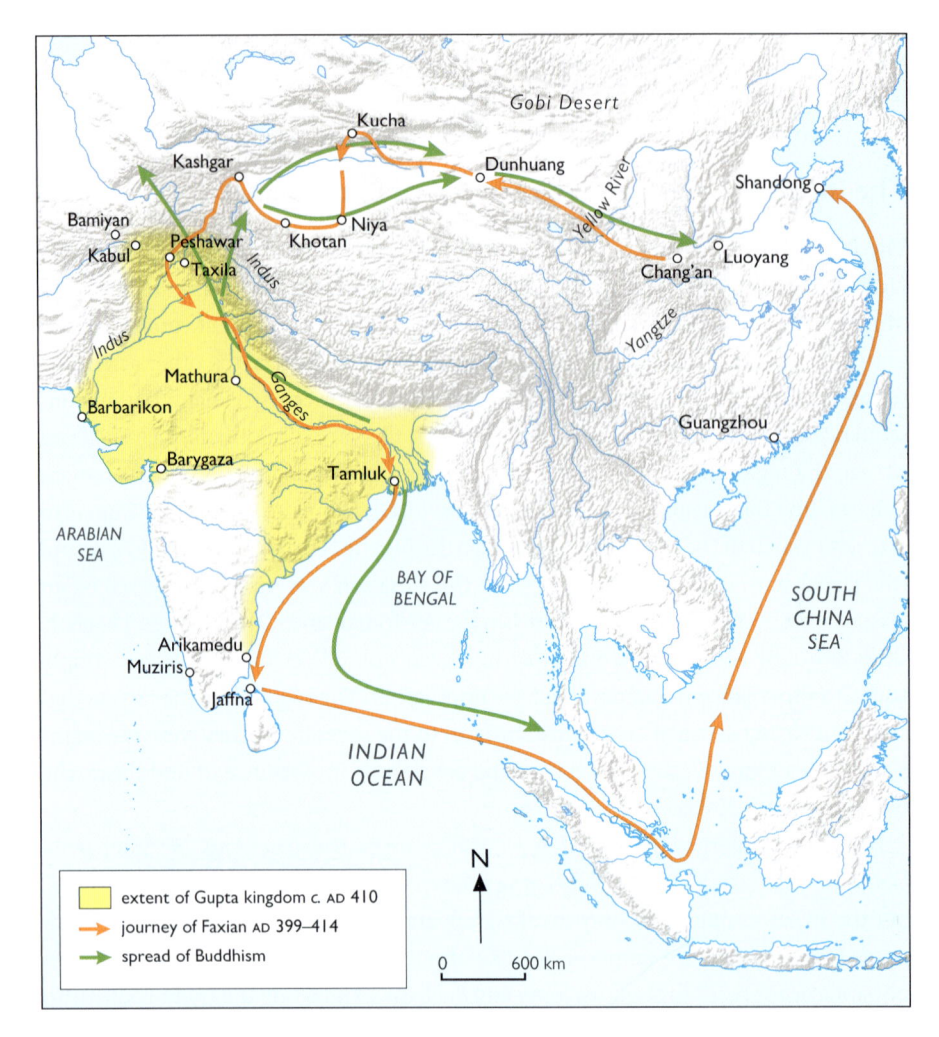

8.12 Buddhism, originating in the valley of the Ganges, spread along the trade-routes, north into Central Asia, and around the Taklamakan desert to China, and also by sea, through the Malacca Strait to the coastal ports of China. These routes were embraced by the Chinese Buddhist scholar Faxiang, who went in search of Buddhist documents in the early fifth century AD

One had therefore to remove suffering by removing desire, thus reaching the state of nirvana (nothingness). It was a personal journey and there was no need to seek the intervention of the supernatural. Without reaching the state of nirvana one would be reborn, and the cycle of desire and suffering would begin again.

The Buddha and his followers were itinerants who preached and begged for food. Initially this worked without significant difficulties, but as the number of disciples— the sangha (gathering)—increased, finding communities rich enough to be able to

THE AGE OF PERPETUAL WAR

8.13 Fire Buddha found near Kabul, Afghanistan. The figure is dressed in Hellenistic-style clothing, reflecting the strong Greek influence to which the region was exposed following the conquest of Alexander the Great. Second–third century AD

feed the multitude became difficult. The answer was to encourage the lay followers to become merchants and to work hard to generate profits, which could be used to provide for the sangha. By doing this the merchants would bring great honour to the urban communities in which they lived. Thus, Buddhism and trade became inextricably bound in a web of interdependency driven by the dynamic that the more the community could provide for the sangha, the greater was its reputation and the more it would attract trade. This led to the monumentalizing of the religion with stupas—buildings containing relics of the Buddha—and with statues of the Buddha, giving a more tangible focus for those who felt the need to believe that the Buddha was a god.

Buddhism in its pure form was an austere religion that offered only a journey to nothingness. The cosmopolitan flow of traders coming from many different cultural and religious backgrounds wanted something easier to comprehend with more tangible rewards. It was in response to this that the Mahayana school developed: it was altogether more liberal and more eclectic. By making appropriate donations to Buddhist establishments a believer could 'buy' himself a journey across the sea of suffering in the 'great vehicle' (*mahayana*) aided by a host of bodhisattvas, superhuman beings serving as intermediaries. These were conceived of as people who had reached the state of nirvana but had chosen to stay to help others. They were individuals with particular strengths who could be worshipped and were able to accommodate in their own paradises those who had not yet reached nirvana. For many, one suspects, the belief of being reborn into a paradise would have been more attractive than the option of the extinction of the self.

It was a belief system easily comprehended by traders whose life was spent in accumulating material wealth: by giving a tithe to the Buddhists they could buy a comfortable salvation. So it was that the Buddhist establishments grew rich. Large permanent monasteries were built with elaborate stupas, and colossal statues of the Buddha became a familiar sight. Gifts of gold and silver, fabrics including silk, precious stones, and incense, all accumulated in the monasteries, giving a sense of colourful opulence and well-being and providing patronage for craftsmen whose skills could further add to the grandeur of the buildings. The caves along the caravan routes, used by travelling monks and traders alike, became formalized as monasteries, and many of them were greatly extended to accommodate the growing religious communities. The increase in the number and size of monasteries along the caravan routes provided ever greater security for traders, who could now make their journeys knowing that they would find hospitality and safe havens along the way.

From the second to the seventh centuries AD, as the trade-routes flourished, so the Buddhist infrastructure became grander and ever more present. One of the finest expressions of this was the monastery of Bamiyan in the Hindu Kush in Afghanistan,

8.14 The monastic site of Dunhuang, Gansu, China. The caves hollowed out of the cliff face served as Buddhist shrines. In all there were some four hundred, many of them elaborately painted. The first was created in the fourth century AD, but the site continued as a Buddhist sanctuary and pilgrim centre for a thousand years

where an approaching traveller could spot from miles away the two great statues carved into the cliff side sometime in the fourth or fifth centuries, one 37 metres high, the other 55 metres high. A Chinese traveller in the early seventh century described the great Buddha as 'splendid with golden colour and decorated with gems'. It served as a welcoming sign to pilgrims and travellers for fifteen hundred years until, in 2001, it was reduced to rubble by the Taliban. Five colossal statues of the Buddha were also found at the eastern end of the trans-Asian route at the Chinese capital of Yungang created under the auspices of the Xianbei, the Mongolian nomads who had taken over the northern part of China in the fifth century. The Bamiyan and Yungang Buddhas are a forceful reminder not only of the affluence of Buddhism, but also of its embeddedness in disparate cultures across a vast tract of territory.

While traders using the caravan routes were usually involved in comparatively short journeys, the Buddhist pilgrims often spent much longer on the road, par-

8.15 The Bamiyan valley in Afghanistan. In the cliff overlooking the valley a colossal statue of Buddha, 55 metres high, dominated the landscape. The statue, and another nearby, were destroyed by the Taliban in 2001

ticularly after the middle of the third century AD. One such was Faxian, a Chinese Buddhist, who set out from Chang'an (Xi'an) in AD 399 to visit the holy places and to collect Buddhist texts so as to improve the translation used in China. His journey took him along the Gansu Corridor around the north side of the Tarim basin to Kucha and then across the desert to Niya. He comments on the aching loneliness of the journey and the difficulty of finding the route, marked only by dried dung and the bleached bones of those who had died on the way. He then took the southern route through Khotan to Kashgar and from there crossed through the Karakorams to Peshawar, a fearsome journey following narrow tracks cut in the face of the sheer cliffs so steep that 'the eye becomes confused and the foot finds no resting place'. Once in India he spent six years travelling down the Ganges visiting the holy sites associated with the Buddha's life and collecting manuscripts as he went.

His onward journey by sea is even more revealing of the connectedness of the world. From the mouth of the Ganges he took a two-week voyage to Sri Lanka, where he visited the famous jade Buddha, more than 6 metres high, and spent two years among the vibrant community of monks, scholars, and merchants before deciding to return home by sea. The first leg of the return journey, on a large merchant ship

8.16 Coffin from Niya, Xinjiang province, China, one of the settlements on the southern Silk Road, dating to the third or fourth century AD. A man with knife wounds to the neck was buried with his wife, the bodies wrapped in thirty-seven silks. Some of the silks bear the Chinese characters for 'king' and 'lord', suggesting that they were gifts from the Chinese elite to local leaders

carrying two hundred people, took him through the Strait of Malacca, when a violent storm drove them to land, probably on Sumatra. After a stay of five months he boarded another large merchant ship bound for Guangzhou, a journey reckoned to take fifty days. In the event storms and overcast skies drove them off course in the South China Sea and they eventually made land on the Shandong peninsula, 1,600 kilometres further north than their planned landing.

After fifteen years away Faxian was content to return home to spend the rest of his life writing an account of his travels and translating and editing the texts he had collected. The accounts that he gives of the sea-voyages provide a tantalizing insight into the maritime systems at work at the time and the massive scale of the enterprises then under way in Indonesian and Chinese waters. In the ports at the mouth of the Ganges and on Sri Lanka he could well have found himself in the company of Roman ships' masters who had set out from the Red Sea ports of Egypt, and heard the stories of their very different worlds.

At the beginning of the seventh century we learn of another Chinese traveller, Xuanzang, who also set out to collect Buddhist manuscripts. He was already a famous Buddhist scholar when he left China in AD 629. It was a time when long-distance journeys were forbidden by the Chinese authorities, but for him the lure of new knowledge overcame the difficulties of travelling without an official pass. He chose to take the northern route around the Tarim basin crossing the Tian Shan to Issyk Kul.

In the mountains he encountered blizzards so severe that fourteen of his fellow travellers died. Having reached the lowlands he travelled on via Tashkent and Samarkand (Marakanda) before crossing the Hindu Kush to Taxila, from where he set off down the Ganges. Travelling clockwise around India on a journey that took twelve or thirteen years he collected 520 cases of documents, which were carried on an elephant supplied by a sympathetic local king. His return journey took him via Balkh across the Pamir mountain range to Kashgar and then along the southern route around the Tarim basin back to Chang'an, where he was welcomed home by a vast crowd. The magnitude of the journey and the perils faced were considerable, yet the well-established route, the security and hospitality of the Buddhist monasteries along the way, and the reverence bestowed on a scholar, all helped to make it possible.

Travelling around the Tarim Basin

Between Dunhuang at the western extremity of the Gansu Corridor and Kashgar at the foot of the Pamir there were two principal caravan routes around the Taklamakan desert, one looping south in the shadow of the Altun Shan and the Kunlun Shan, the other going north along the southern foothills of the Tian Shan. Each was served by a number of oasis towns spaced at intervals of about a day's journey. The river Tarim, flowing across the northern part of the desert, and the river Khotan, which flows through the desert to join it, provided other possible routes for those prepared to brave the rivers in the months when they were unfrozen and free from dangerous ice floes. Most travellers preferred to take the caravan routes, where they could be assured of food, rest for the night, and the opportunity to engage in some small-scale exchanges.

Many of the oasis towns had origins going back to the first millennium BC or even earlier, but growth came as the flow of travellers and traders began to increase in the first century BC, and many of them grew to accommodate the large number of traders, pilgrims, and envoys who were constantly passing through. For the most part, the local population was engaged wholly or largely in farming. Grain was a valuable commodity, and in some towns the farmers were allowed to pay their taxes in grain, which could then be sold on by the local authorities. Others paid taxes in silver coins. By the third century most towns could boast a Buddhist monastery, many of which were large and flourishing. There were also centres set aside for craft production of varying kinds. A description, in AD 384, of the city of Kucha on the northern route gives some idea of urban life.

> The city wall had three overlapping enclosures and was equal in area to Chang'an [the one-time Chinese capital]. The pagodas and temples inside numbered in the thousands. The palace of the Bai kings were imposing and lovely like the residence of the gods. The

8.17 The northern part of the Taklamakan desert, south of Aksu, in a sandstorm. The fairly high ground-water in this area allows the growth of some trees, though the sand is constantly moving

> non-Chinese of the city lived luxurious and rich lives. Their homes had stores of grape wine verging on a thousand piculs [200 litres] that did not spoil even in ten years.
>
> (Li Fang, *Taiping yulan* 125.604)

Kucha was a particularly affluent city and was required to pay a very large tribute to China. Its products were listed as fine carpets, felt wall hangings, copper, iron, lead, and ammonium chloride (used principally in dyeing), deerskins, fine horses, cattle, and powders for make-up. From the nearby mountains a foul-smelling ointment-like substance oozed out of the ground. This was petroleum. It was claimed to have exceptional healing and regenerative powers.

Kucha was well sited at a point where the northern road was joined by a track that led northwards through the Tian Shan to the steppe beyond. In the period of political instability following the collapse of the Han dynasty, travelling was difficult and usually took the form of large caravans that could afford to pay for guards, but after the Sui dynasty had re-established order, small caravans were able to travel again in comparative safety. A collection of official travel passes written on skins or poplar wood in the period AD 641–4 shows that most caravans were of fewer than ten people, though a few were larger, with one comprising as many as forty individuals. They were accompanied by donkeys, horses, and cattle, the donkeys presumably carrying belongings and items for trading.

THE AGE OF PERPETUAL WAR

During the Han dynasty many of the oasis towns accepted a Chinese garrison, but thereafter, until the Tang conquest in AD 640, the official nature of the Chinese presence seems to have become far less clear, though some towns had quite large Chinese populations. Other ethnic groups were present in large numbers, particularly Sogdians, originating from the region between the Amu Darya and the Syr Darya, who were heavily involved in trade (pp. 323–6). Many of the towns along the southern route were settled by immigrants from Gandhara, who came in small waves from north-western India through the Karakoram passes after about AD 200 and took up residence in towns like Niya and Loulan, which were then part of the Kroraina kingdom, where they intermarried and became assimilated in the local populations. They brought with them the Kharoshthi script, which was widely used throughout the kingdom until it was replaced by Brahmi about AD 400.

8.18 Chinese burial figures often depict foreigners (barbarians) like this military attendant on an armoured horse dating to the early sixth century AD. The facial characteristics and dress distinguish them from the Chinese

At its peak the Kroraina kingdom incorporated most of the towns of the southern route east of its rival, the kingdom of Khotan. The king received tribute from the towns and villages in his domain, and when they were unable to pay in silver they did so in local products like sacks, baskets, cloth, cattle, sheep, wine, and grain. Silk was also used in some transactions, but that depended on the arrival of merchants from China. Envoys making diplomatic visits also brought fine silks for the rulers. In AD 40 the Kroraina kingdom formally submitted to the authority of the Toba Wei, but it was now a period of great turbulence and insecurity, when some towns were deserted. The conditions were so unsettled that by the fifth century the southern route had been largely abandoned in favour of the northern route.

With the shift to the northern route towns like Kucha and Turfan began to flourish. Turfan was the principal city in the state of Gaochang. It had a mixed population of the local Jushi people together with large numbers of Chinese and Sogdians, reflecting the fact that after AD 500 it was one of the most important trading cities on the direct route between China and Sogdiana at a time when the Chinese elites were welcoming Persian goods, particularly fine silverwork. This link with the west is manifest in a large number of Sasanian silver coins found at Turfan. The commercial importance of Turfan and its comparative proximity to China made it a prime target when, in AD 640, the Tang armies turned their attention to conquering the Tarim basin.

The oasis towns around the Taklamakan desert are of particular fascination, not least because the desert conditions have preserved thousands of written documents offering a vivid picture of the people and of their daily lives. What emerges from these texts, written in a variety of languages, is the cosmopolitan nature of the oasis communities and the mobility of populations. Waves of refugees and settlers added to the ethnic mix, while traders, envoys, and pilgrims passed through. There were raids by nomads, and invading armies occasionally brought about changes in the hierarchy. All this generated a creative turbulence, but one mitigated by the calm stability of the Buddhist monasteries. A kind of unstable equilibrium prevailed. Here the sedentary states of China, Persia, and India interacted with each other and with the nomad world of the steppe, while the oasis settlers patiently tended their fields and their animals, waiting for the arrival of the next caravan. It was a region like no other in the world.

Sogdian Middlemen

The large tract of land between the Amu Darya and the Syr Darya, which flowed from the Pamir into the Aral Sea, divides roughly into two zones. To the west lies the Kyzylkum desert, but moving eastwards the land merges into arid steppe, which

8.19 The gaunt mud-brick ruins of the Silk Road town of Jiaohe in the Turfan Depression on the northern side of the Taklamakan desert. The town was founded in the Han period (second century AD) and flourished until it was finally abandoned in the fourteenth century

eventually gives way to the foothills of the Pamir. The steppe region is watered by the river Zeravshan, which originally flowed into the Amu Darya. Along the river are a number of oasis settlements, the best known of which are Samarkand, Bukhara, and Qarshi. The region was known as Sogdiana, at least from the sixth century BC. It occupied a central position in relation to the natural communication routes: to the south through Bactria lie Gandhara and Persia; to the east are the mountain passes leading to the Tarim basin; to the north is the open steppe; while to the west it is possible to reach the Caspian Sea and, beyond it, Europe.

Sogdiana was always something of a border territory, open to cultural influences and migrating populations coming from without and, periodically, being brought under the authority of the ruling dynasties of Persia. Those able to control the oasis towns could command the through passage of a huge volume of trade. It is hardly surprising, therefore, that the Sogdians became merchant middlemen throughout much of Central Asia. The fifth to eight centuries AD were a golden age, and cities like Samarkand and Bukhara grew to be among the greatest merchant centres of Eurasia.

8.20 Painted stone panel from the tomb of a Sogdian chief who was buried at Xi'an in AD 579. The swirling dance performed by the central figure was popular among Sogdian traders along the Silk Road

The documents found at the caravan cities around the Tarim basin refer to large communities of Sogdians resident in the settlements. One of the collections of documents from Turfan, dating to about AD 600, records the tax charged in silver coins on trade goods sold. Of the forty-eight merchants named, forty-one are Sogdians, suggesting that the Sogdian community dominated the merchant class at least by this date. An earlier set of documents, from Loulan dating to about AD 330, records Sogdian merchants dealing with the resident Chinese authorities. One document mentions a large quantity of grain and silver coins; another records the exchange of 319 animals for 4,326 bolts of coloured silk. This would seem to suggest that the Sogdians were providing bulk food for the Chinese garrisons. It may have been to service the military in the region that they were first drawn to the Tarim basin.

Large influxes of Sogdians into the oasis cities will inevitably have led to tensions with the local populations and other ethnic communities. The Sogdians in their homeland were Zoroastrians worshipping at the fire altar and excarnating their dead, but away from home they soon began to adopt local customs. In the late sixth and early seventh centuries the Sogdians living in the Chinese capital at Chang'an were regularly being buried according to Chinese custom. But even so, they were perceived as 'other'. Xuanzang gives the Chinese view of the Sogdians: 'Their customs are slippery and tricky, and they frequently cheat and deceive, greatly desiring wealth, and fathers and sons alike seek profit.' A later Tang account says that when a son is born they put honey in his mouth to sweet-talk customers and put glue on his hands, the better to grasp the coins. 'They are good at trading, love profit and go abroad at the age of twenty. They are everywhere profit is to be found.' These are the classic stereotypes suffered by traders throughout the world, but the point is well made that Sogdians were everywhere.

Most of the evidence we have shows them to have been active along the route between Samarkand and Chang'an, particularly along the northern route, but they are also attested on inscriptions carved on rocks along the passes leading to the Indus valley in the fourth century. They were present in the court of the Sasanian king two centuries later attempting to open up a market for Chinese silk in Persia. The mission failed because the Sasanian king was intent on protecting the monopoly of the Persian silk producers. On this occasion the Sogdians seem to have been trying to trade silk obtained from the Turks, who at this time were living in the steppe region to the north. Having failed with the Persians, they persuaded the Turks to let them act as middlemen with the Byzantine empire, and in AD 571 the emperor received a Sogdian mission in Constantinople.

The Sogdians were, then, an enterprising people who, by the seventh century, were involved as merchants across the whole of Asia from Chang'an to Constantinople: their language was widely spoken throughout the network. As specialist merchants they were apolitical, able to ride out the vicissitudes of history that saw different foreign dynasties rule their homeland. Trade brought wealth, and wealth could be taxed. For this reason it was in everyone's interest that the systems should be left intact and the Sogdians be allowed to get on with what they were good at. It was under the Tang dynasty that the Sogdian merchants reached the peak of their affluence and cities like Samarkand and Bukhara rose to spectacular heights of grandeur.

Enter the Hephthalites, the Avars, and the Turks

In the early fifth century a new nomadic confederation appeared in Central Asia: the Hephthalites, or White Huns. Their ethnicity and origin has been much debated, but with little firm consensus. Most likely they came ultimately from Dzungaria or southern Siberia, and they may have been forced to move westwards as a result of population pressure or by being driven out of their homeland by nomadic tribes coming from Mongolia. They first appear about AD 420 to the west of the Pamir and proceed, like their nomadic predecessors the Kushans (a branch of the Yuezhi) and the Sakas before them, to move southwards into Persia and through the Hindu Kush into India, settling and establishing a degree of control in both areas over the next 150 years.

They were briefly described by the sixth-century Byzantine writer Procopius:

> The Hephthalites are of the stock of the Huns in fact as well as name; however, they do not mingle with any of the Huns known to us, for they occupy a land neither adjoining nor even very near to them, but their territory lies immediately to the north of Persia … They are the only ones among the Huns who have white bodies and whose countenances are not ugly. They are not nomads like other Hunnic peoples but for a long period they have been established in a goodly land.
>
> (Procopius, *Secret History* 1.3)

The text is interesting in distinguishing the Hephthalites from the rest of the Huns, who were attacking Europe at about this time. They were geographically distant, they led a more settled way of life, and they were physically different. Procopius was implying that they were not Mongoloid. That said, the migrating waves of the Huns who attacked Europe and the Hephthalites might both have been driven by the social turbulence emanating from Mongolia, the same pressures perhaps that drove a branch of the Xianbei into northern China in AD 439, initiating the dynasty of the Toba Wei.

The Hephthalites began a series of attacks on the Sasanian empire in AD 420 but were driven back in AD 427 after an overwhelming defeat. Further attacks followed in AD 454, and later in the decade they became embroiled in a power struggle in the Sasanian royal house. Hostilities began again in AD 464 and continued intermittently until the early years of the sixth century. It was during this period that the Sasanians built a massive frontier defence, the Gorgan Wall, running eastwards from the south-east corner of the Caspian Sea. It consisted of a brick-built wall with forward-projecting bastions fronted by a water-filled ditch and strengthened at intervals by military garrisons. A defensive work on this scale was clearly intended to provide protection against a threat

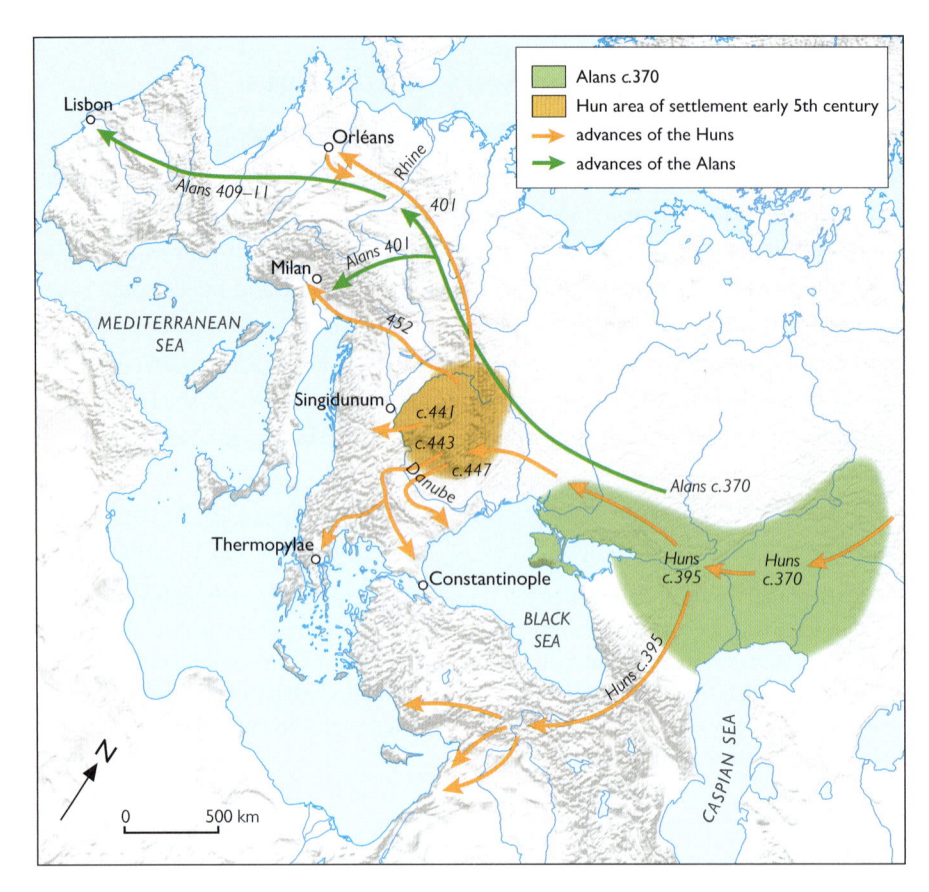

8.21 The advance of nomadic horsemen into Europe added to the folk movements that destroyed the Roman west. The Alans crossed the Danube in AD 401, forced west by the Huns, who had established themselves in the Pontic steppe. In the mid-fifth century the Huns penetrated deep into Europe

coming from across the steppe. Its sheer size, involving a huge input of energy and resources, shows that the threat was considered to be serious and long-term.

While the conflict with the Sasanian empire was progressing, the Hephthalites extended their control of other lands. Between AD 465 and 470 they conquered Gandhara, and then, between AD 473 and 479, they took control of Sogdiana before moving across the Pamir to conquer Kashgar and Khotan in the Tarim basin. Later, beginning in AD 493, they marched through Dzungaria and crossed the Tian Shan to take Turfan and other prominent cities on the northern Tarim basin route.

By the early decades of the sixth century the Hephthalites controlled a large area of Central Asia and northern India, but their hold was essentially light of touch. Apart from displaying some hostility towards Buddhism, existing systems were largely unaltered. Trade continued as before, the only significant difference being that the ethnic mix had been further enhanced and taxes were paid to a different elite. After the middle of the sixth century the Hephthalites began to lose control, first in the north, when a new wave of nomads, the Turks, began to take over, and then in India, where Hephthalite rule was finally overthrown by local intervention in AD 570.

The Hephthalite interlude has many similarities to the episodes of Saka and Kushan domination: it is almost as though history was repeating itself. But perhaps a better way to see it is as a continuous process of population drift from the southern Siberian–Mongolian region, which, once past the Tian Shan–Pamir massif, flowed westwards and southwards across the open steppe until it impinged upon the enclosing rim of settled states. For much of the time the flow passed unnoticed. It was only on those few occasions when the pace of movement intensified that it impacted upon recorded history.

While these events were unfolding in western Central Asia, new confederations were arising in the east, to the north of the Great Wall of China. The fifth century saw the ascendancy of the Avars, a ruling power said by the Chinese annals to have been descended from slaves. The leading clan acknowledged their subservience to the Wei by sending annual tributes of horses, furs, and cattle, an act that allowed them to develop trading relations with the Chinese. In this way they were able to acquire luxury goods with which to establish their superiority over their fellows. Their leader was soon in a position to take the title of khan (emperor) and was recognized as overlord of all the nomadic peoples between the Gobi desert and Lake Baikal as far eastwards as Manchuria.

8.22 Hunnic cauldron of cast copper from Hőgyész in southwest Hungary, dating to the late fourth or early fifth century. Cauldrons of this general type were found with burials of the Xiongnu, who may have been distant ancestors of the Huns

To the west of the Asian Avars, in Dzungaria and the Altai, a new confederation was crystallizing out. The details are obscure but it would seem that nomads from Gansu and the north-eastern Tarim had migrated northwards in the fifth century to the Altai region, merging there with the local Turkic speakers to create a dominant leadership calling themselves Turks. At first they were subservient to the Avars, providing them with iron, but as their power grew the Turkic leader requested an Avar princess as a bride (in AD 551), an act by which he was claiming equal status with the

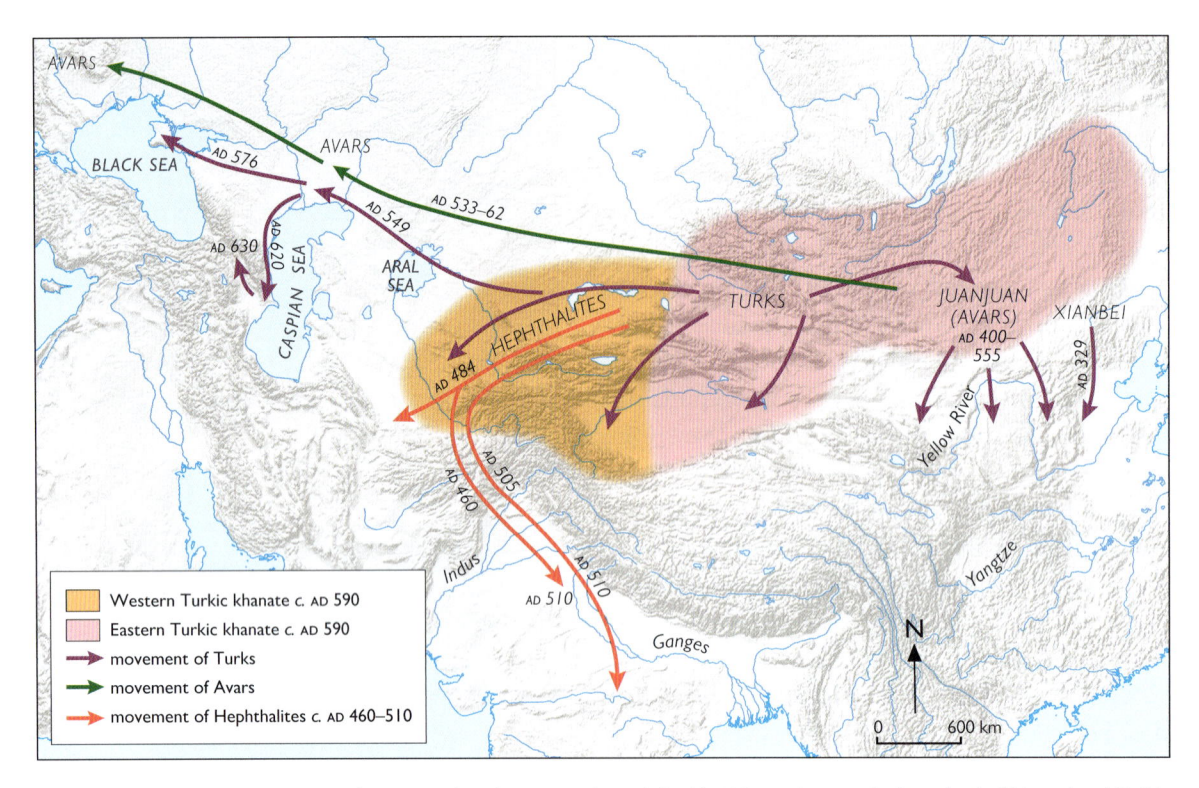

8.23 The region of modern Mongolia and the Altai Mountains was the homeland of Mongol and Turkic peoples who migrated south into China, west into Central Asia and India, and across the Pontic-Caspian steppe into Europe in the fifth and sixth centuries AD

Avar leadership. The request was refused, with derisory insults being traded. In angry response the Turks sent in an army, totally destroying the Avar empire and driving the remnants westwards. Their successors finally ended up in Europe (pp. 337–8).

The triumphant Turks now expanded their influence east, west, and south until their empire extended from Manchuria to the Black Sea. At first the huge khanate was ruled by a single man, but in AD 584 it was split into two, an eastern khanate and a western khanate, along a line running approximately through the Pamir.

The eastern khanate at first established good relations with the Chinese, acquiring Chinese brides and copious supplies of silk in exchange for horses and keeping the peace. The Chinese policy was, as always, to try to maintain equable relations with their neighbours while exploiting their political differences, but with the rise of the Tang dynasty a more robust position was taken, leading to open warfare and, in AD 630, the capture of the Turkic khan. With this the centralized power of the eastern khanate collapsed, and successive rulers were forced to acknowledge the Tang as overlords.

THE AGE OF PERPETUAL WAR

The western khanate took on a more expansive stance. In AD 549 they had reached the Volga, pushing their old enemy the Avars before them, driving them eventually to settle in the Great Hungarian Plain. About AD 557 they entered into an alliance with the Sasanians against the Hephthalites and within six years had taken control of Sogdiana and the Tarim basin. From this new homeland in Central Asia the broader political situation will have become apparent to them. A fight to the death was now under way between Persia and the Byzantines: the Turks could look on or become involved.

The decision seems finally to have been taken in AD 568 when a Turkic embassy heavily staffed by Sogdians went to Constantinople to negotiate an alliance with the Byzantine emperor against the Sasanians and to open up direct trading relationships offering to supply iron and Chinese silk. The Turks also wanted the Byzantines to take a much tougher line against their old enemies the Avars, who were now occupying land just beyond the frontier of the empire in Hungary. After the initial meeting a Byzantine ambassador was sent to the khan in Central Asia. A contemporary account records the ambassador's astonishment at the grandeur of the nomadic court, with its silken tents and the khan's golden throne mounted on two wheels so that it could

8.24 Turkic grave marker for a cemetery at Bayan Olgi, Mongolia, sixth–eighth century AD

331

be pulled by horses when the court was on the move. Among the other finery was a golden couch supported by four golden peacocks. Sixty years later another visitor, the Chinese Buddhist scholar Xuanzang, was equally impressed by the grandeur of the Turkic court. The officers were dressed in fine brocade and the troops wore furs, while the officials all wore embroidered silk, the khan himself resplendent in green satin. Xuanzang was offered a splendid feast of mutton and chicken accompanied by wine, while musicians played for the company. This was not what he had expected of 'the ruler of a wandering horde'.

There was some reluctance on the part of the Byzantines to be drawn into a costly conflict with the Sasanians, but in a show of strength in the 580s the Turks crossed the Amu Darya and drove deeply into Sasanian territory. They had, however, overestimated their strength and were soundly beaten in a pitched battle fought at Herat.

Meanwhile the Turks had been expanding their influence westwards across the steppe, and in AD 576 they had crossed the Cimmerian Bosporus to take control of the Crimea. The Kazakh steppe and much of the Pontic steppe was now under their authority. When the final conflict was being played out between the Byzantines and the Sasanians in the late 620s, the Turks launched a massive attack on Transcaucasia, taking Debent and Tbilisi, and in AD 630 marched into Armenia. But these campaigns

8.25 Turkic burial at Shoroon Bumbagar, Mongolia, seventh century AD. The burial mound is here partially excavated, showing the entrance ramp and the door leading to the burial chamber

8.26 Model cavalry and infantry soldiers from the Turkic burial at Shoroon Bumbagar, Mongolia, seventh century AD

were costly and brought no real advantages. In the aftermath there was internal dissent within the Turkic army, culminating in the murder of the khan. In the turmoil that followed, the Chinese chose the moment to invade Central Asia (pp. 349–53).

The Turkic domination of the vast Eurasian steppe had been comparatively brief—a mere eighty years—but it had a profound effect on the region. The new elite allowed the existing social system to remain largely intact, knowing that Sogdian diplomacy and commercial experience could work very much to their benefit if left unhindered. The Sogdian towns continued to flourish, but there was an influx of Turks into the region, which added to the already rich cultural and ethnic mix, so much so that the region was still commonly called Turkistan into the last century, and one part of it is today the state of Turkmenistan. The other effect of the Turkic migration was to nudge the existing steppe community to move further to the west into Europe.

The movements of nomadic groups across Central Asia were part of a general swell of mobility that washed into the European peninsula, there to merge with the folk wanderings of Germanic peoples bearing down on the crumbling Roman empire. The thrust west was deflected by the remaining strength of the Byzantine enclave but was constrained by the geography of Europe. Confronted by the Atlantic, the more far-reaching of the mobile bands had little option but to cross the Strait of Gibraltar and flow back eastwards along the North African coast, where their energy was finally dissipated. Amid the mêlée of movement three nomadic confederations emerging from the east are known by name: the Alans, the Huns, and the Avars.

The Alans

The Alans were a Sarmatian people originating in Central Asia. The Chinese sources suggest that they lived close to the Aral Sea, a view to some extent borne out by the late Roman historian Ammianus Marcellinus, who believed them to have been descended from the Massagetae. In the first century they had extended their influence westwards to the river Don and the Sea of Azov. By the middle of the fourth century Ostrogoths moved to the Pontic steppe from northern Europe, concentrating their settlement on the Crimea, where they were near neighbours of the Alans. It was at this point that the Huns began to push rapidly through the region, totally disrupting systems and alliances that had maintained the equilibrium of the area for many generations. Some of the Alans joined the Huns on their western rampage, others moved off to the west to join the Germanic groups, but many will have chosen to stay in their steppe homeland as vassals of the Huns.

The clans who moved deep into northern Europe appear in the Roman sources, alongside German bands, as fearsome barbarians intent on overrunning the western empire. In AD 401 Alans and Vandals crossed the Danube frontier and raided deep into Roman territory. A few years later, in AD 406, together with Vandals and Suevi, they crossed the frozen Rhine and rampaged through Gaul. Two years later they had moved into Iberia, finally settling in the south-west of the peninsula, thus becoming the first of the steppe nomads to reach the westerly extremity of Eurasia under their own volition. In AD 418 they were routed by the Visigoths and the remnants fled to Galicia in the north-western corner of Iberia, there to merge with the Vandals already in residence. The story of the Alans is a reminder of both the mobility and the flexibility of the marauding and migrating peoples of the time. While they could maintain a level of ethnic identity through the leadership of a dominant clan, the composition of the horde must have changed significantly over time as some chose to stay where they were, breaking away from the horde, and different groups of different ethnicity joined. The Alans who eventually ended up in Galicia in AD 448 would have been very different from their ancestors who, fifty years earlier, had ridden the Pontic steppe.

The Huns

The Huns, who about AD 370 had attacked the Alans in their steppe homeland, came from further east, but from exactly where is unclear. In AD 150 there were Huns active in the Caucasus and before that, at the end of the first century AD, the Roman historian Tacitus notes the presence of Hunnoi near the Caspian; beyond that their origins are obscure. Some scholars have long believed that the Huns originated as an offshoot of the Xiongnu since the names have the same origin. The fact that their predominant racial type was Mongoloid does indeed add support to the view that they may have come from far in the east, possibly from Mongolia, but, even if this is so, it is likely that the horde that eventually broke into Europe in the late fourth century was a confederacy of nomads of many different ethnic origins who had come together under the leadership of the Hun clans somewhere in the Altai–Dzungaria–southern Siberia region. It may have been in this same melting pot that the Hephthalites also originated.

Sometime around AD 370 the Huns moved west through the territory of the Alans in the Don–Dnieper region, attacking the Ostrogoths, then settled on the Black Sea, forcing the latter to flee south across the Danube into the comparative protection of Roman Europe. The first confrontation of Huns (in confederation with Goths and Alans) and the Roman armies took place at Adrianople in the Balkans in AD 378. At this engagement the Romans were defeated, but the following year the barbarian army was soundly beaten, and in the aftermath some of the Huns moved to the province of Pannonia to serve as frontier troops (*foederati*) in Roman employ. There matters rested for a generation.

The next onslaught began in AD 395 when the Huns began a major offensive against the Roman world initiating a confrontation that was to last on and off for nearly sixty years. It was the Hunnic presence and manoeuvring north of the Rhine–Danube frontier that forced German tribes and the Alans to move out of their way and to break through the frontier in the first decade of the fifth century. At first Huns engaged with the sedentary states on a number of fronts. Some crossed the Caucasus to attack Cappadocia and Syria, others crossed the lower Danube into the eastern Roman empire, while some groups were active in the west serving as allies of the western Roman armies. This spread of effort probably reflects the looseness of the Hunnic confederacy at this stage.

The largest force concentrated its efforts on extracting the maximum amount of wealth from the eastern Roman empire by plundering the provinces of Moesia and Thrace and threatening Constantinople. Like so many steppe nomads before them, they decided to settle in the Great Hungarian Plain sometime between AD 410 and

420. Meanwhile, in AD 409 the western Roman empire made a treaty with the Huns, employing ten thousand of them to fight against Germans who had invaded Italy. Three years later they employed a mercenary force six times as large to fight off barbarians trying to settle in Gaul. This east–west divide may have led to the splitting of the Hunnic command between two kings of equal status sometime before AD 430. Dual leadership was to continue until AD 445, when one man, Attila, became powerful enough to take over sole command.

In the east an uneasy equilibrium developed between the nomads and the eastern Roman empire. Treaties were agreed, with the Romans paying huge tributes in return for peace. The treaty of AD 435 required them to pay 700 pounds of gold annually to the Huns, the treaty of AD 443 increased the quantity to 21,000 pounds, and so the escalation continued. It is estimated that, over the period AD 420–50, 10 tonnes of gold were sent by the empire to the nomads. As part of any treaty the Huns were anxious that the frontier was kept open for trade to support the growing need for prestige goods by which the social hierarchy was maintained. Since all the incoming goods were under the control of the king, only he was able to distribute favours down the chain to his immediate subordinates and they to theirs. So long as the supply of prestige items continued to flow, social stability would prevail. Some of the imports will have come as diplomatic gifts, but much would have been bought from the Roman frontier traders using the gold received as tribute. In this way gold was returned to the Roman economy. The system had an equilibrium, but it was very unstable.

Such a system could only have developed after the Huns came into a direct relationship with the Roman world about AD 420. Until then the confederacy was loose-knit and difficult to control, but once the luxury goods started to flow, strong leaders could assert their power over ever-increasing numbers of followers and could create a protective elite about themselves. Such followers were called 'picked men' and 'close associates' and could include non-Huns. Each of the picked men commanded a large force of horsemen and was assigned tracts of land from which he could collect tribute, particularly food. The power of a king like Attila was judged by the number of his followers, which, in turn, was based on his powers to reward.

Frontier trade would see low-value goods like Roman linen, grain, and weapons exchanged for horses, meat, furs, and slaves. But luxury goods like silk, Indian pearls, gold and silver vessels, Indian pepper, dates, and wine would mostly have been acquired from the empire by other methods: gift, tribute, or plunder. Simply put, the emergence of Attila as the commander of a huge nomadic confederacy was totally dependent upon his ability to maintain a largely parasitic relationship with the Roman world. This required him constantly to demonstrate his powers, both to the Romans and to his own followers.

In AD 447, taking advantage of riots, famine, and plague in the eastern empire, Attila launched a major attack through Dacia, Illyria, Thrace, Moesia, and Scythia, reaching as far south as Greece. As one Roman writer observed rather overdramatically, 'Attila ground almost the entire empire to dust.' During the negotiations that followed, the Romans attempted, unsuccessfully, to have Attila assassinated.

It was at this point that Attila turned his attention to the western Roman empire, where the Huns were considered to be allies of the west: indeed, Attila held an official position in the western Roman army as master of soldiers. In a fascinating incident, highly reminiscent of the relationship between nomads and the Chinese state, Attila claimed his right to marry Honoria, sister of the western emperor Valentinian III, and thus to receive half of the western empire. In AD 451, in support of his claim, and ostensibly as a friend of Rome, he marched to Gaul with a mixed army of Huns and Germans. The Romans decided to resist, and in the resulting battle, fought on the Catalaunian Plains, won the day. It was a devastating defeat for Attila, who, in the aftermath, contemplated suicide but for some reason was allowed to retreat. The next year he moved into the Po valley intent on attacking Rome, but famine, plague, and superstition forced him to retire. In AD 453 he decided to make another attack on the eastern empire, but before he could set out he died, either from the excesses of a good life or by assassination. His behaviour in the last three years of his life was certainly erratic. It may have been that the social pressure for ever-greater achievements drove him on. His failures in Gaul and Italy will have been a massive blow to his prestige. In such circumstances assassination would have been a real threat.

After the death of Attila the eastern Roman empire grabbed the opportunity. Uprisings were encouraged in the lands held by the Huns, causing the nomadic social system rapidly to fragment. The Romans also made the astute move of closing the borders to trade so that the Hunnic elite would be deprived of prestige goods, further undermining the authority of the would-be leaders. Within a generation the Huns were no longer a significant force in Europe.

The Avars Again

The incursion of the Huns into Europe was followed by that of the Avars, who had been driven westwards by the Turks. In the mid-sixth century they were living in the Volga region, where the Turks caught up with them and forced them to move once more. By AD 568 they had reached the Carpathian basin, occupying both the Great Hungarian Plain and the old Roman province of Pannonia (now western Hungary). By this time the ethnicity of the migrants had become very mixed, but they still retained their tribal name and were ruled by a khan. In their new homeland they began to make demands on the Byzantines, extracting considerable quantities of silver in return for non-aggression treaties. Their demands greatly increased over time and, while the Byzantine army was away fighting in the east, the Avars began to expand their hold on the Balkan peninsula.

Matters finally came to a head when, after first unsuccessfully attempting to take Constantinople on their own, the Avars returned in AD 626 with a huge army including Huns, Gepids, and Bulgars and, with the support of the Persians, made a final attempt on the city. The Byzantines held out and managed to destroy the Persian fleet. Demoralized, the khan's great army withdrew and dispersed. Although the Avars remained a force to be reckoned with, the advance of the Slavs, Bulgars, and Franks eventually brought them to their knees.

Byzantium, the rump of the Roman empire, had managed to hold out as a bulwark of European civilization against the successive waves of migrants from the steppe. The ferocity of the nomads had posed a far more serious threat to the old order than the Germanic tribes of northern Europe and the Sasanian dynasty of Persia, but for two centuries Byzantium had stood firm against the onslaught.

The Arab Awakening

The kingdoms of the southern end of the Arabian peninsula had long been involved in the trading systems that linked the Roman world to the Indian Ocean networks, but during the sixth century direct interference in Arab affairs by the Aksumites, the Byzantines, and the Sasanians increased political awareness among the Arab leaders, making them more conscious of their central place in the changing geopolitical situation. Beyond the developed coastal strip with its major international ports lay a desert inhabited by nomadic tribes breeding camels and sheep and leading a far simpler existence. Here warfare between the tribes was endemic, but it was a warfare based on personal competition between individuals and the upholding of honour: it was the stuff of poetry that could be recited at evening gatherings around the campfire to entertain and inspire and to strengthen tribal loyalty.

While much of the trade between the southern Arabian ports and the Mediterranean world went by sea, the sea journey was not without its dangers and a significant volume of the trade was sent by land along the western side of the peninsula to Aila (Aqaba) and thence to Egypt, Syria, or the Mediterranean ports. Midway along the caravan route was the desert town of Mecca. In the late sixth and early seventh centuries it was dominated by the Quraish clan, who were merchants but also had religious responsibilities for the shrine of the spirits housed in a building called the Kaaba. Once a year the surrounding tribes made a pilgrimage to the shrine at

Mecca. The occasion served both as a religious ceremony in which the spirits could be honoured and also as a great fair where goods could be bought and sold, social alliances enacted, and where the merchants of Mecca could grow rich on the proceedings.

In 570 AD the wife of one of the Quraish gave birth to a son, Muhammad. Muhammad's early life was not easy. Custom required that he was brought up by a foster-mother in the desert for the first six years of his life. Not long after he returned to his family in Mecca his birth mother died and he was looked after by successive relations, all involved in trade. At the age of 25 he was put in charge of a caravan to Syria belonging to a rich widow of the Quraish family. He carried out the task successfully and soon after, at her request, he married her.

Now relieved from the burden of having to earn a living, Muhammad devoted himself to meditation, often in the desert, and on one such occasion, in AD 610, he had a vision which convinced him that he was chosen by God to be prophet to the Arabs. The message he transmitted was clear: there was only one God and Muhammad was his prophet; he had been sent to restore the religion of Abraham, which had been perverted by the Israelites; and the spirit worship of the past must be swept away. The revelations he received, he said, were the Word of God, and his task was to recite it to followers so that it could be recorded in writing for posterity. After his death these texts were collected together to become the Koran. The new way of life was to be called Islam ('surrender to God'), and those who accepted it were Muslims ('surrendered ones').

The new teachings met opposition, not least from those who had most to gain from perpetuating the annual pilgrimage to the shrine of the spirits. In 622 Muhammad and his followers fled Mecca for the oasis town of Medina, 400 kilometres to the north, and there established the new religion. But by now the message had changed. God, said Muhammad, had told him that the Muslims must fight the unbelievers. In this belief lay the motivation for the Arab conquests that were soon to have such a dramatic impact upon most of the civilized world.

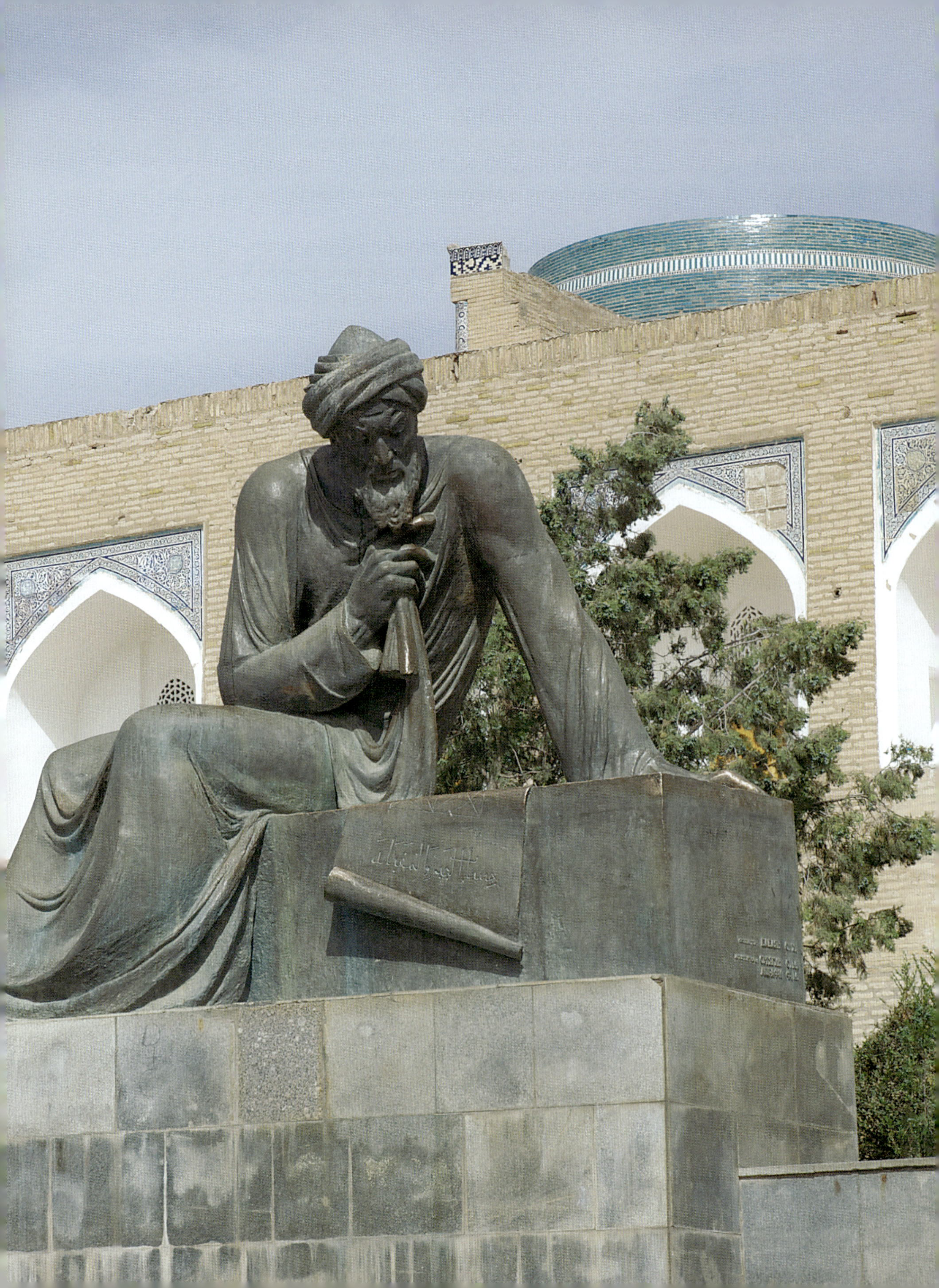

9

THE BEGINNING OF A NEW WORLD ORDER,
AD 650–840

In 1965 a bulldozer constructing a new road across the site at Afrasiab, the ancient core of Samarkand, long abandoned after the city had migrated further to the south, uncovered the upper part of a palatial building dating to the seventh century. The archaeological excavations that followed exposed a large central hall decorated with an astonishing series of painted scenes redolent of the cosmopolitan high life of elite society in one of the greatest trading cities of the time. The building was quite possibly the palace of the Sogdian king Varkhuman, who is known from Chinese chronicles to have sent an embassy to the Tang emperor in 605 asking for Chinese citizenship. The context for this remarkable request was the imminent threat to the freedom of Sogdiana posed by the advancing Arab armies. Varkhuman was clearly desperate to build a firm alliance with the Chinese, who were fast developing their trading interests in Central Asia. In the event the emperor recognized him as governor of Sogdiana.

The painted hall, now beautifully displayed in the Afrasiab Museum, was decorated to impress visitors to the palace. The west wall, which faces the entrance, probably once had a large figure of the king-god up high in the centre, but this upper zone had been destroyed. Below are ambassadors who have come from far and wide to pay homage. Two, identified by the texts of their speeches recorded in the painting, came from neighbouring kingdoms, one from Chach (Tashkent), the other from Chaghanian, a kingdom south of Samarkand. Others, wearing black caps, are from China: they bring

THE BEGINNING OF A NEW WORLD ORDER

9.1 The Hall of the Ambassadors found in an excavation of Afrasiab (Samarkand), Uzbekistan, is thought to be the reception hall of the palace of King Varkhuman dating to the later seventh century AD. Its walls are elaborately painted with scenes designed to impress visitors with the king's political power. This scene is part of a procession making its way towards a mausoleum

gifts of silk fabric, thread, and silkworm cocoons. Two others, with feathered caps, are probably Koreans. The scene also includes Turkic soldiers with long pigtails, who were most likely in the service of the royal house. This wall, facing the grand entrance, was intended to proclaim the power of the king both regionally and internationally.

The wall to the left (the southern wall) shows the king riding in procession led by his queen carried in a palanquin on a white elephant. The group, which includes two Zoroastrian dignitaries on camels, a priest, and four geese for sacrifice, is travelling towards a mausoleum and may best be interpreted as a Zoroastrian ceremony, possibly the festival of Nouruz. It is balanced on the right-hand (northern) wall by a spirited scene of a leopard hunt featuring the Chinese emperor on horseback about to make a kill, while two boats, one carrying Chinese ladies grouped around the empress, approach across a lake or a river. The whole ensemble is carefully contrived to impress the visitor with the king's power and piety. People of all nations pay tribute to him, he shows reverence for the dynastic cult, and he and his consort are shown as equals to his would-be allies, the emperor and empress of China. It was a bravura attempt to claim powerful friends and influence, but came to nothing.

When the first Arab attack on Samarkand took place in 671, King Varkhuman was no more, and the city seems to have been without a ruler. Ten years later an Arab governor was briefly installed in the region, and in 712 Samarkand was finally conquered by the Arab general Qutayba ibn Muslim: the old order was at an end.

The Afrasiab palace, with its exuberant painted reception hall, marks a significant moment. The Sogdians, under the benign control of the western Turkic khanate, were the great traders of Central Asia: they dominated the trade-routes crossing the Tarim basin to China. The Chinese were now extending their influence even further westwards, while the Turks, growing increasingly rich on managing the burgeoning trade, were establishing commercial and diplomatic links with the Byzantine empire by way of the steppe route to the north of the Aral and Caspian seas, thus providing a secure trans-Eurasian connection circumventing Sasanid Persia. A new world order was beginning to be established, but it was not to be: the desert Arabs, energized and inspired by the Prophet Muhammad, were now on the move.

The Arab Advance, AD 632–750

During the last two years of his life Muhammad had brought a degree of unity to Arabia by persuading the disparate and highly individualistic desert tribes to embrace the Muslim religion. But after his death in 632, with no successor appointed, inter-tribal rivalries led to a period of outright warfare known as the wars of *riddah* (apostasy). The question of succession hinged around two basic questions: whether the Muslim community (*ummah*) should have one leader or whether each tribe should have its own leader (imam), and, if there was to be one leader, should he be a kinsman of the Prophet or one of his close followers? In the end an old and trusted friend of Muhammad, Abu Bakr, was appointed caliph (*khalifa*) to lead the *ummah*, which he did with wisdom and clemency, bringing the spate of tribal warfare to an end in the summer of AD 633. But the problem remained. How was a naturally warlike cluster of competing tribes, occupying an extreme and resource-poor environment, who had developed a social system based on raiding and feats of valour, to be kept under control when the Prophet had expressly forbidden Muslims to fight each other? The only answer was to encourage the tribal leaders to turn their aggression on their non-Muslim neighbours, unleashing a fury of incessant warfare.

And so the conquest began, partly as the result of individual initiatives and partly with encouragement from the new caliph, Umar ibn al-Khattab (ruled 634–44). By turning the energies of the young males outwards from their desert homeland, with its highly restricted holding capacity, harmony could be maintained in the centre while along the fringes there were new lands and riches for the taking. The desert offered two interfaces with sedentary states. To the east the valley of the Euphrates marked the eastern limit of the Persian empire, now under the Sasanian dynasty, while to the west lay the eastern provinces of the Roman empire, now part of the Byzantine empire, extending from Syria to Egypt. As we have seen, by the early decades of the seventh century, the Sasanians and Byzantines were exhausted after generations of unproductive warfare along their common frontier. As both contestants, now in a state of uneasy truce, were licking their wounds, the Arab onslaught struck with unexpected ferocity. Neither of the old rival states was fit to resist.

Under the caliph Abu Bakr the whole of the Arabian peninsula had been unified. Now, in the brief decade of Umar's caliphate, a huge swath of territory from the Iranian plateau to Cyrenaica was brought under Arab control. The rapidity of the conquest was astonishing. In the west Damascus was first entered in triumph in 635, and after a brief retreat the conquest of the whole of Syria was completed in 636. Jerusalem was taken in the winter of 637–8 and Egypt fell in 641. In the east the Sasanian power collapsed after the battle of Qadisiyah in 637. Ctesiphon was captured the following year and Arab rule extended to the Zagros Mountains.

The initial conquests were driven by demographical and social factors, encouraged by the attractions of plunder and the lure of new commercial opportunities: in no sense was this a religious jihad designed to impose Islam. The capture of Damascus in 635 is particularly informative. Since the town surrendered, there was no looting or killing. All non-Muslim inhabitants became *dhimmis* (protected subjects) and were required to pay an annual poll tax of 1 dinar. The cathedral was divided into halves, one part for the Christians, the other for the Muslims. In all the conquered territories there was little desire to convert the new subjects to Islam. Indeed, there was a reluctance to do so, not least because all Muslims, whatever their ethnic background, would have to be accepted as part of the *ummah* and thus afforded a range of privileges. Early caliphs like Umar were strict in segregating Muslim Arabs from the subject peoples. With the exception of Damascus, they were not allowed to live in the conquered towns but were restricted to newly built garrison towns placed at strategic locations. Nor was land redistributed among the conquerors but was left in the hands of the original owners, who had to pay tax to Medina. Such regulations left existing

THE BEGINNING OF A NEW WORLD ORDER

9.2 The initial advance of Islam across the Arabian peninsula was rapid, and further advances east, to engulf the Sasanian empire, and west along the North African coast were accomplished within half a century. By the early eighth century Islam had reached the shores of the Atlantic

social, cultural, and commercial infrastructures largely intact and were deliberately designed to preserve the simplicity of the Arab Muslim lifestyle laid down by the Prophet. But so great had been the changes over this first decade that unrest among the Arab soldiers was inevitable: their simple desert existence had been transformed into that of soldiers exiled to a distant frontier. Moreover, they had been introduced to the luxuries and benefits that could accrue to those with a sedentary life.

9.3 The Great Umayyad Mosque in the centre of Damascus was begun in AD 708 on the site of an earlier Christian cathedral. It took some years to build and employed architects, building workers, and mosaicists brought in from Constantinople. The green and gold mosaics were created by the Byzantine craftsmen working alongside local Syrians

In November 644 Umar was stabbed to death at Medina and Uthman ibn Affan of the Umayyad family was elected caliph. Under Uthman the stunning pace of conquest was maintained. Along the North African coast the Arab armies thrust forward to Tripoli, while in the east they ousted the Byzantines from eastern Anatolia, pushing north to the Caucasus, and continued to spread eastwards, absorbing much of the old Persian empire up to the Amu Darya. In the Mediterranean their fleet took the commercially important island of Cyprus from the Byzantines. The military advance had absorbed much of the frantic energy of the time, but discontent seethed below the surface.

In 656 a group of Arab soldiers mutinied in Egypt and, having returned to Medina, assassinated the 82-year-old Uthman, setting up in his stead the Prophet's cousin Ali ibn Abi Talib as the new caliph. Ali was seen as the upholder of the rights of sol-

9.4 A graphic representation of the siege of Constantinople in AD 820 led by Thomas the Slav with an army of Arabs, Armenians, and Byzantine discontents; the siege failed. The scene comes from the chronicle of John Skylitzes, an eleventh-century Byzantine historian

diers over the conservatives, whose concern was to maintain the power of the central authority. What followed was a five-year civil war known as the *fitnah*, the 'time of temptation'. Eventually, after Ali had succumbed to an assassin in 661, his rival Muawiyah, who had been governor of Syria and was a kinsman of Uthman, became caliph, the first of the Umayyad dynasty. He chose Damascus to be his capital.

The rule of the Umayyads, from 661 to 750, spanned a period of far-reaching change in the Muslim world. Another period of bitter civil war (the second *fitnah*), together with continued territorial expansion in both the east and the west, led to inevitable changes in the nature of Muslim society as a people who had been desert nomads learnt to come to terms with the complexity of empire. The new Muslim empire, the largest the world had ever seen, needed firm and assured leadership and an efficient administrative system. The first of the Umayyad caliphs, Muawiyah, upheld many of the old values, but even he realized the need to create a secure succession with power passing from father to son in the manner of other empires. The administration was also changing. In the early years the educated non-Muslims (*dhimmis*) in the conquered territories were given the top administrative posts, but with time these went increasingly to Arabs who had learnt the relevant skills. The effects were twofold: a Muslim court life began to develop, and the *dhimmis*, now increasingly excluded from lucrative positions, discovered the desire to convert to Islam. At first this was discouraged, but in the early eighth century Caliph Umar began to welcome converts, though one of the effects of the new policy was drastically to reduce income from the poll tax which *dhimmis* had to pay. Gradually, the rules that had carefully separated the Arab Muslims from the conquered people in whose territory their garrisons were located broke down. Arabic became widely spoken, replacing Persian in the east, and the exclusivity of the garrison towns diminished as workers and merchants, both non-Muslim and converts, moved in. The Arab empire had now begun to function like any other.

These changes were taking place against another bout of civil war fought among Muslims of different allegiances. The biggest divide opened up between those who believed that legitimacy lay with the Prophet's cousin Ali ibn Abi Talib and those who were content that the succession should pass between the Prophet's closest followers. The first group, the Party of Ali (the Shiah-i Ali), became known as the Shia, while the remainder came to be called Sunni, from *sunna*, meaning 'the lawful', those who tried to follow closely the ways of Muhammad. The divide is all too evident in the world today. One incident, in the second *fitnah*, helps to explain the bitterness of the split. In 680 the inhabitants of the garrison town of Kufa in Iraq, who were Shiah-i Ali, acclaimed Ali's second son, Husain, as caliph. Husain and his family and a small group of followers set out from Medina for Kufa to join their supporters, but at Karbala, not far from Kufa, they were surrounded by Umayyad troops and massacred. The civil war was to continue for another twelve years until some semblance of peace at least was restored, but the massacre of Karbala has never been forgotten.

After the turmoil of the second *fitnah* energies were once more directed to new conquests. In North Africa the general Uqba ibn Nafi made a lightning dash across the Maghrib in 682–3, reaching Agadir on the Atlantic coast, but was killed on the way back. Later expeditions were more successful. In 698 Carthage was taken and destroyed, and within a few years the Berbers of Algeria and Morocco came to terms and embraced Islam. In April 711 a force of twelve thousand men crossed the Strait of Gibraltar and began the systematic conquest of Iberia, reaching the north coast by 713 and taking the Mediterranean coast as far as the Rhône delta by the end of the following year. Raiding north along the Rhône valley, they reached Sens in 725, and a final onslaught through Bordeaux brought them to Poitiers, where the Arabs were soundly beaten by the Frankish army in 732. But western Europe made poor pickings, and the Arab forces were thereafter content to remain in Iberia, where mineral resources were more abundant and the climate more acceptable.

Through the century or so of the Arab advance the Byzantine empire was struggling for existence as the result of both internal dissension and external attack. The Mediterranean lands from Syria to Cyrenaica fell quickly to the Arabs, and Cyprus was to follow, but much of Anatolia held firm, with an uneasy frontier developing from the north-eastern corner of the Mediterranean to the Caucasus, backed by the ridge of the Taurus Mountains. Two concerted Arab attacks were made on Constantinople, a long siege from 670 to 677 and another, briefer attempt in 716–17. Both failed as the empire gradually recovered its strength.

In the east the advance was renewed. A new thrust took the Arab armies to the valley of the Indus: Multan was taken in 713 and the territories of Sindh and Tukharistan came under Arab control. Further north the Amu Darya was crossed in 706 and the important towns picked off one by one: Paykend (just south of Bukhara on the Amu Darya) in 706, Bukhara in 709, Samarkand in 712, Chach in 713, and Khujand in 715. Raids reached as far east as Kashgar, and it was from here that an embassy was sent to the Chinese court demanding the submission of the emperor. It was a warning: the Arab leaders would have been well aware of the growing Chinese interest in Transoxiana (now Uzbekistan). The commander, who one may suppose entered the palace at Afrasiab in Samarkand in 712 and saw the vivid murals, can have had little doubt of the close relationship the local rulers were building with their Chinese allies.

But at this point the advance stalled as further inhibiting dissension gripped the Arab leadership. In 717 troops were withdrawn, and for the next thirty years local rebellions against Muslim governors and incursions by Turkic armies brought chaos to Central Asia. By the mid-eighth century the region was exhausted. The Chinese grasped the moment and in 751 sent an army through the Tian Shan with the intention of capturing Chach from the north. On the river Talas they were met by a Muslim army of equal strength. It was a crucial engagement. Both sides claimed victory, but in the aftermath the Chinese retreated to the Tarim basin, while the Muslims made no further attempt to extend their power eastwards. The battle of Talas was one of the most decisive in the history of Eurasia.

The Tang Empire

From the moment of its establishment in 618 until the rebellion led by An Lushan in 755 Tang dynasty China was in expansive mode. What gave the state its great strength was the solidity of the bureaucracy that underpinned it—a bureaucracy based on a rigorous examination system that allowed the most able of the educated elite class to rise to the top. A strong bureaucracy shifted power from the military to civil society and provided the bedrock stability to ensure that the comings and goings of emperors and empresses of varying abilities had little or no effect upon the steady running of the system. Another factor of great importance to the stability of the state was the

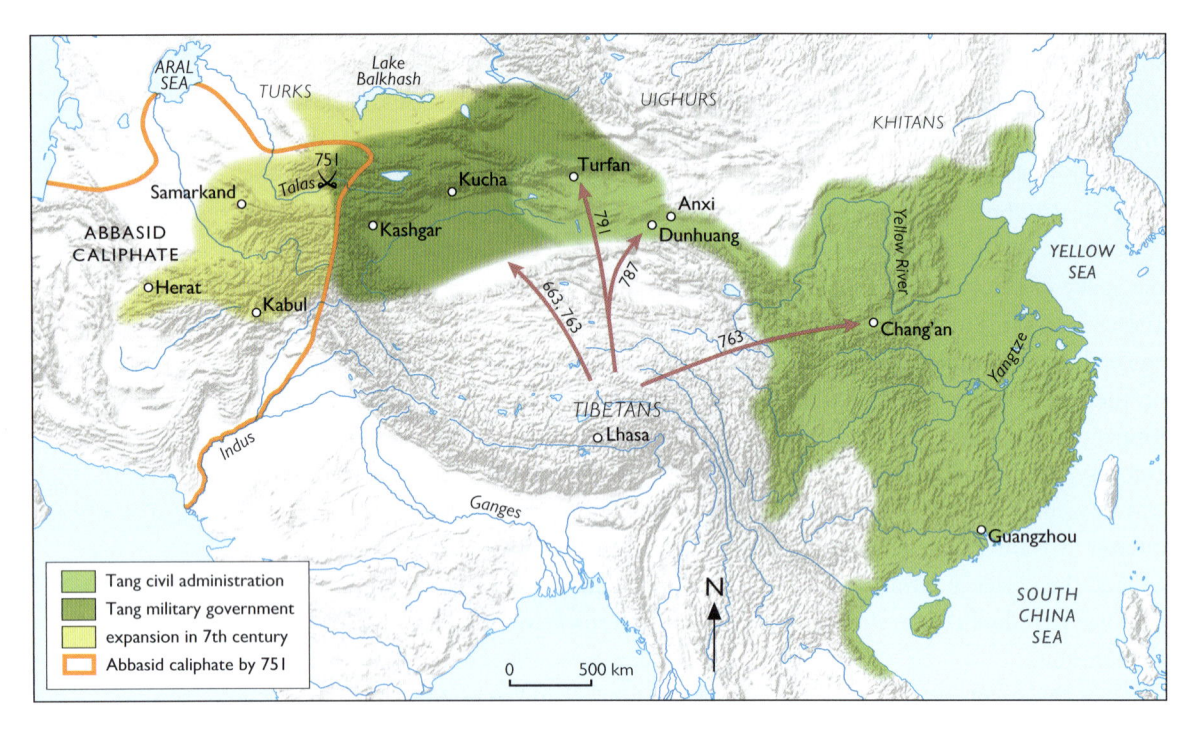

9.5 The rise of the Tang empire in China in the period AD 618–907 coincided with the expansion of Islam in the west. The Tang rulers took firm control of the trade-routes around the Taklamakan desert and the steppe to the north, and established a protectorate in western Central Asia

maintenance of an increasing supply of grain to feed the civilian population and the armies, and its efficient distribution by the system of canals, particularly the Grand Canal, begun in the early seventh century to join the north of the country to the south.

In these times of relative stability and plenty the population increased. A census taken in 754 showed that there were over nine million families living within the empire, suggesting a population in the order of fifty-three million, all paying taxes. There were probably several million others, some constantly on the move to avoid tax, and others, like the landless labourers, who were exempt from taxation. The Tang empire was the most populated of the world and its capital city, Chang'an (Xi'an), one of the largest.

The first century or so of the Tang dynasty saw China at its most expansive. The Gansu Corridor had already been taken within the empire at the beginning of the seventh century, and Turfan was garrisoned with Chinese soldiers after its capture in 640. By the middle of the century the Tarim basin had been absorbed to become the Anxi protectorate, and a wide area of Turkic territory north of the Tian Shan, extending north to the Altai and west to Lake Balkhash, had become the Kunling and Mengchi protectorates. In 659 Chinese influence was spreading even further west through Central Asia to include a huge swath of territory from Chach and Samarkand in the north to Herat and Kabul in the south. This was the context for the palace at Afrasiab in Samarkand. As we have seen, the Chinese histories record that the Sogdian king Varkhuman had been given the title governor by the Chinese emperor Gaozong. Thirty years or so earlier another Sogdian king had asked for diplomatic alliance, but the emperor had refused, saying that Samarkand was too far away to send troops if called for. The change of attitude in only a generation is interesting. Emperor Gaozong was far more of an expansionist than his predecessors. It was during his reign that, in addition to Central Asia, much of Korea and Manchuria was taken over to become the protectorate of Koguryo. But he had overextended the aspiration of empire: the state simply could not sustain its hold on such a vast territory. Sogdiana was given up by 669 and Koguryo in 676.

The administration of the newly annexed territories is well exemplified by the town of Turfan on the north edge of the Tarim basin, which was taken by the Tang army in 640 and for which a considerable body of documentation has survived, preserved by the arid conditions. Turfan became a prefecture like the three hundred or so others that made up the empire. As such, it was subject to the redistribution of land based on household registers updated every three years. Each household was entitled to 1.2 hectares of land to be held permanently and 4.8 hectares of farming land redistributed on a three-year cycle (though scarcity of land in the oasis meant that only a percentage of the legal allowance could be given). In return they were taxed in grain, cloth, and labour dues. Frontier towns like Hami, Turfan, Beiting, and Kucha were each garrisoned with a force probably numbering several thousand, though by no means all the soldiers were Chinese. The upkeep of so large a force was colossal. Records showed that in the 730s and 740s the garrisons of four frontier posts cost nine hundred thousand bolts of silk each year to maintain. There was no way in which such a level of expenditure could be met by local taxes. Indeed, in 742 local taxes accounted for only 9 per cent of the cost of the five-thousand-strong garrisons at Turfan. The cost to the Tang state for keeping the desert-edge routes open and secure was therefore enormous. The silk paid to the troops would have been exchanged with local producers for food and other necessities, and in this way would have entered the trading network, much of it eventually reaching the west. Thus, the Tang state was subsidizing trade to an unsustainable degree. It may be that the new military advance westwards into Sogdiana was an attempt to take a firmer control of the trade network in the hope of reducing the cost of garrisoning the Tarim oasis towns.

9.6 A bolt of white, plain-weave silk (broken into two), excavated at Loulan, Xinjiang, China, and collected by Sir Aurel Stein, third–fourth century AD. Bolts of this kind were used as currency

In any event, the set-back on the river Talas in 751 marked a turning point in the fortunes of the Tang dynasty. In the same year another Chinese army was beaten in the south at Dali when it attempted to intervene in the Thai kingdom of Nanzhao. It was also at about this time that the Khitans, a nomadic tribe living beyond the frontier to the south of the Gobi desert, began seriously to threaten the stability of the northern provinces. The Khitans had been causing trouble for some time, and as early as 744 a Chinese army, led by An Lushan, achieved a victory against them, but thereafter he seems to have had little success. An Lushan, the child of a Sogdian–Turkic marriage, started life as a horse-dealer but rose rapidly in the ranks of the Chinese army. In 755, in charge of the strategic province of Hebei, he proclaimed himself emperor and, building on general disquiet arising from the excesses of the Tang court, led a rebellion which was to last for eight years. Although the Tang dynasty survived, the economic infrastructure of the country had been greatly weakened and the unity of the state had been shaken. Strong central rule had broken down, and instead the country was divided into some forty semi-independent governments under military control. To help put down the revolt the Tang leaders had called in the help of Uighur

9.7 One of six reliefs of horses by Li Yanben (d. AD 673) which adorned the tomb of the emperor Tang Taizong at Xi'an. The horses were the emperor's favourites and probably came from Ferghana

mercenaries, tribesmen of Turkic origin who at this time occupied the Altai region. The Uighurs were to become a regular support for the Tang in the north.

China's western provinces shared a long mountainous frontier with the huge upland plateau of Tibet: the Qilian Mountains flanked the narrow Gansu Corridor while the Kunlun Mountains separated the Tarim basin from the plateau. The growing power of the Tibetan kings began to confront the Chinese. The first aggressive encounters, in the 630s, were patched up by the dispatch of a Chinese princess to be the bride of the son or brother of the Tibetan emperor, but the expansion of the Tang armies in the Tarim basin in the 640s brought them into territory considered by the Tibetans to be within their orbit. The disputes were to simmer on for more than a century until, by 753, the Tang had taken control of all the Tarim basin and were beginning to turn their attention to the Tibetan plateau. It was at this point that the An Lushan uprising broke out in China, but, with Tibet also in the throes of rebellion, direct confrontation between the two powers came temporarily to a halt.

The Tibetan empire was quick to recover, and in 763 a force managed to penetrate deep into China and even occupied the capital, Chang'an, for a few days. Thereafter the Tibetans made attempts to take control of the Tarim basin and the Gansu Corridor, culminating in the battle of Tingzhou, to the north of Turfan, in 791, where the Tang army and their Uighur allies were defeated. Turfan was taken the next year and remained under Tibetan control until it was captured by the Uighurs in 803. Hostilities between the Tibetans on one side and the Chinese and Uighurs on the other dragged on until 821–2 when all three peoples finally agreed a peace. Continued warfare was simply not sustainable. The Uighurs and the Chinese symbolized their alliance by the marriage of a Chinese princess to the Uighur kaghan; peace between the Tibetans and the Chinese was affirmed in a bilingual inscription erected in Lhasa, the Tibetan capital.

The Chinese had now lost control of the routes through the Gansu Corridor and the Tarim basin, and with it their entire western territory. With these traditional routes to the western markets closed, a more northern passage through Uighur territory began to come into more regular use, while the shipping lanes to India and beyond were given a new importance (pp. 365–9).

Byzantium: The Dark Age, AD 628–780

The long, exhausting slog of almost constant warfare between the Byzantine empire and the Persians eventually ground to a halt in 628 when the two protagonists finally agreed to return to the frontier negotiated nearly forty years earlier. The east Mediterranean provinces were now back in Byzantine hands, and on 21 March 630 the emperor Heraclius restored the True Cross to Jerusalem. Eight years later, in the winter of 637–8, the Arab armies marched into the city; it took a further three years for Egypt to fall. The Byzantine world was simply too weak to resist the Arab onslaught. The completion of the great mosque, the Dome of the Rock, in the centre of Jerusalem in AD 691 symbolized the supremacy of Islam and its intention to stay.

With the loss of Syria, Palestine, and Egypt, as well as Mesopotamia and Armenia, the eastern border of the empire lay roughly along the line of the Taurus Mountains running across eastern Anatolia from the Mediterranean to the Black Sea. The Arab intention was clearly to press on through Anatolia and to take Constantinople. They realized at an early stage that success depended not only on the strength of their land army but on their ability to mount attacks from the sea. By as early as 654 they had developed a powerful fleet, no doubt employing the skills of shipwrights living in the newly conquered ports of the Levant, and were already using it to loot the islands of Cyprus, Rhodes, and Crete.

THE BEGINNING OF A NEW WORLD ORDER

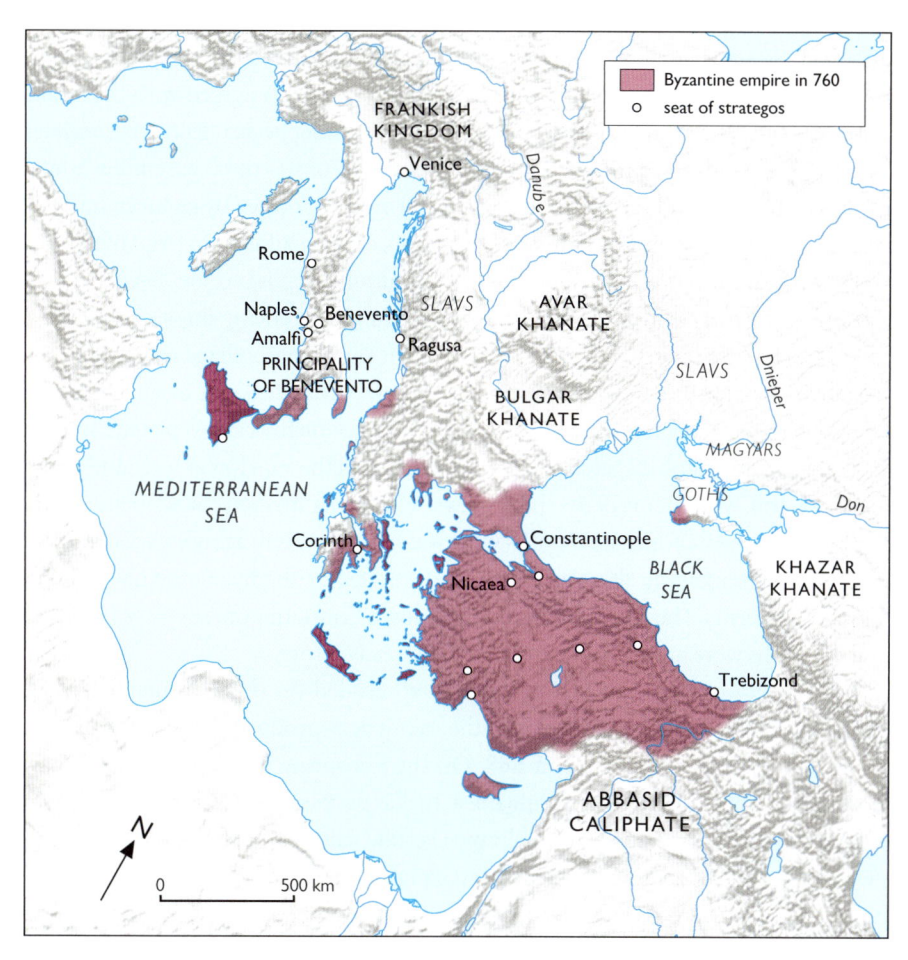

9.8 The Byzantine empire in AD 780 confronted the Muslim Abbasid caliphate in the east and pastoralists from the steppe who had established themselves around the northern shores of the Black Sea and along part of the northern frontier

In 670 the Arab maritime campaigns began in earnest with an attack on Constantinople. The siege of the capital lasted through the winter of 670–1 but was abandoned in the spring. The force returned again in 674 and this time settled in for a longer stay. It was under this duress that the Byzantines perfected a new weapon masterminded by a refugee from Syria. It involved the rapid discharge of a naphtha-based chemical from nozzles attached to ships. When fired, the chemical would float on the surface of the sea burning fiercely. Greek fire, as it became known, was used with spectacular success against the besieging Arab fleet in 677, and the few vessels that escaped the onslaught were wrecked in a storm as they made their retreat. Elsewhere the Arab mariners were more successful. Rhodes was captured in 672 and Sicily suffered several attacks. But on the land front the Byzantine armies managed to recapture Cilicia and to re-establish a protectorate in Armenia. In 685 a truce was agreed with the Arabs, but it was short-lived and hostilities along the land frontier began again six years later.

In 716 the Arabs once more attempted to besiege Constantinople, sending a huge army, said to be a hundred and twenty thousand men, supported by eighteen hundred ships. The army took up positions across the neck of the peninsula in front of the land walls, while the ships were deployed at sea to cut off supplies to the defenders. The Byzantines turned again to the use of Greek fire against the enemy ships, causing great losses and forcing them to stay in port. With their ships immobilized and their foraging parties harried by a Bulgar force allied to the emperor, the Arabs began to suffer, a deprivation made much worse by a long, bitter winter, which greatly depleted the force. In spring 718 the caliph dispatched reinforcements, but the land forces were ambushed and driven off, while many of the ships' crews, who were Christian conscripts, deserted to the emperor. After thirteen months what was left of the Arab army escaped through Anatolia; the remaining ships were mostly destroyed by the Byzantine navy or succumbed to storms. The two attempts to bring down Constantinople by siege had failed and the Arabs were never again to mount such an adventure.

The Byzantine empire was, however, being eroded on other fronts. The Arab successes in North Africa robbed it of the rich wheat-producing regions of Tunisia after the final loss of Carthage in 698. On the European frontier inroads of Slavs from north central Europe and Bulgars, a Turkic people driven from the steppe by Khazars to take up residence in the lower Danube valley, proved to be troublesome neighbours. The Byzantines made modest gains in the Balkans, mostly against Slavs, but the Bulgars were more resistant. At first, they were accepted and new borders were agreed. They proved to be useful allies against the Arabs, but by the mid-eighth century their raids on Byzantine territory had begun again, provoking successive emperors to mount large-scale campaigns between 759 and 774. The Bulgars were contained but remained an ever-present threat.

The success of the Byzantine empire in its struggle against external threats is made more remarkable when seen in the context of the incessant internal power struggle. Emperors came and went with startling rapidity, some assassinated, others mutilated: blinding and insult nose slashing became occupational hazards. In one twenty-two-year period, just before the Arab siege of 717, there had been seven violent revolutions and a civil war. And yet the empire survived. What gave it its extraordinary resilience was partly the strength of its deeply rooted administrative system and partly its geographical position. By the mid-seventh century the territory was divided into a number of administrative units known as *themes*, each with its own military detachment under its own commander, *strategos*. The soldiers were

9.9 Byzantine marines using Greek fire against an enemy vessel. Greek fire was developed in the seventh century and was used to good effect by Constantinople against Arab fleets attacking the city. From a miniature in the chronicle of John Skylitzes

allotted land and thus had a real incentive to protect their home district. The land grants were large enough to support the soldiers' families as well as tenants and hired hands. In this way at least some of the financial burden of the army was met by their own labour. The military domination of the *themes* also led to a shrinking of the civil service, which saved further costs. While the system had many advantages, not least in providing a degree of stability spread across the empire and making it difficult for any one commander to assume control of the whole army, there was understandable reluctance among the sedentary forces to respond to the emperor's demands if this meant fighting far from home. The problem was to some extent countered by the creation of six regiments (*tagmata*) stationed in and around the capital. Although they, too, were landholders, they were trained to be a mobile force capable of being deployed quickly either as a field army or in defence of the emperor and the city.

The other great strength of the Byzantine empire was its unique geographical position sitting astride the crossroads linking Asia with Europe and the Mediterranean with the Black Sea. While there can be little doubt that the volume of trade overall diminished and the number of coins in circulation fell, the large and moderately affluent urban pop-

9.10 The rolling uplands to the west of Aleppo in Syria were intensively developed by farming communities in the Byzantine period living in small towns. While the towns have long been abandoned, the buildings are still remarkably well preserved

ulations still required a basic range of commodities as well as luxuries when they could afford them. One marketing innovation of this period was the provision of provincial warehouses run by *kommerkiarioi*. Their function seems to have been to supply arms and equipment for soldiers to buy using the produce of their farms. The goods brought in from the countryside could then be sold on into the regional market system.

At the elite level two of the most sought-after products were silk and purple dye made from murex, a mollusc found in the eastern Mediterranean. Silken garments, particularly those dyed purple, were the prerogative of the elite and were used extensively in court and ecclesiastical vestments throughout the Roman empire, both east and west. As early as the sixth century, the emperor Justinian had made silk production in the Byzantine empire a state monopoly. There were huge profits to be made, not least in meeting the demands of the western Church. Silks and the rare purple could also be used as diplomatic gifts. In 705 Justinian II rewarded the Bulgar khan with gifts of silk cloth and purple leather for helping him to regain the throne. That he also licensed him to trade in controlled Byzantine goods is a fair indication that trade was still an essential underpinning for the fragile Byzantine state.

That said, there can be no doubt that the empire suffered a dramatic economic contraction during the seventh and eight centuries, and the population declined significantly, partly as the result of a declining birth rate in times of stress and partly from repeated outbreaks of plague, which had begun in the sixth century and returned many times until the middle of the eighth century. The declining population and economic downturn were responsible for many changes. Once-great towns like

THE BEGINNING OF A NEW WORLD ORDER

Ephesus, Corinth, and Athens shrank to a half or quarter of their original size, but nonetheless urban life continued. There were also social changes. The old senatorial class, once so dominant in Roman life, died out, to be replaced by new men whose power was based on the productivity of their land and who built their careers in the military world. Stark distinctions in personal wealth began to level out and, with the decline in the size of the cities, the urban poor all but disappeared.

Taking a broad view of empires one might have expected the Byzantine world to fall apart in the turmoil of the sixth and seventh centuries, much as the western Roman

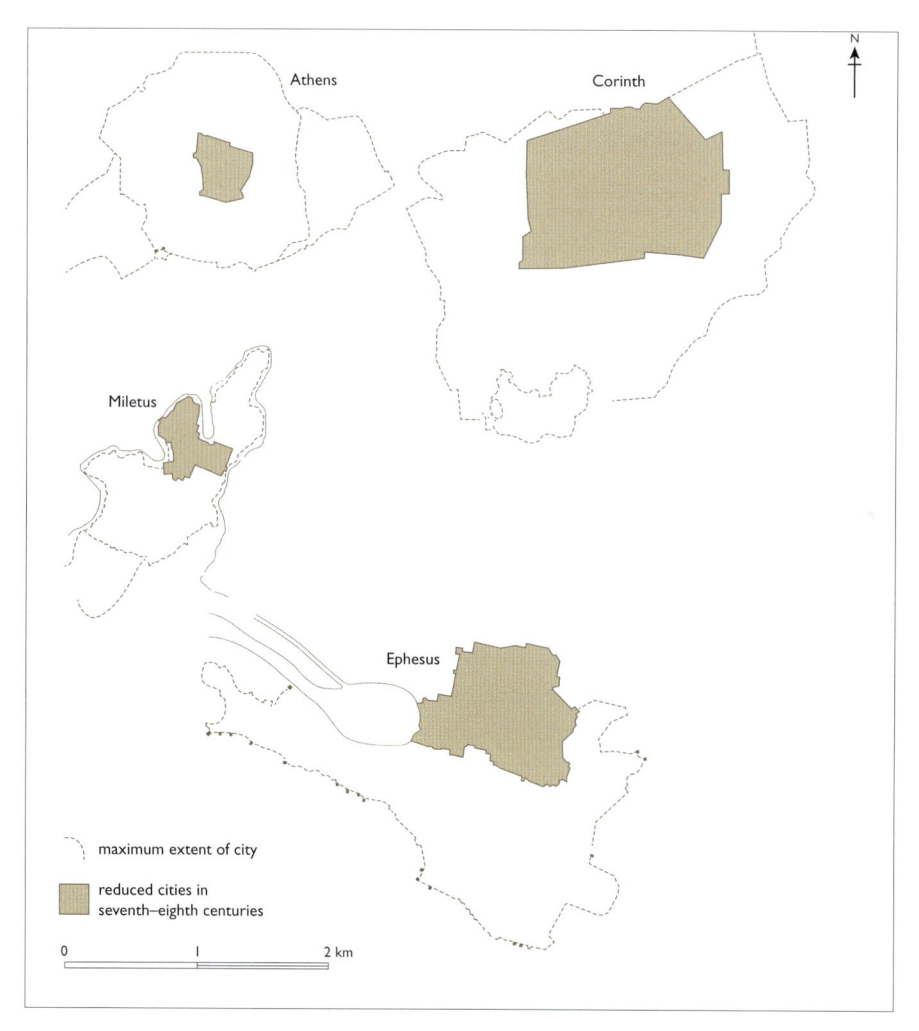

9.11 In the seventh and eighth centuries AD many of the long-established towns of the Byzantine empire had become much reduced in size, with new defences built on a restricted circuit around the main administrative buildings

empire and the Persian empire had fragmented, but miraculously it kept going, its deep roots sustaining the delicate organism through two centuries of hibernation, with all systems reduced while it gathered strength to flourish again.

The Abbasid Empire

By the beginning of the eighth century Damascus was the centre of a vast empire stretching from the Atlantic to the borders of India and China, but therein lay the problem: it was too large to manage. Already there were serious financial difficulties brought about, in part, by the Prophet's ruling that only non-Muslims should pay a poll tax. Throughout the time when conversions to Islam were limited, poll tax provided a significant income for the state, but now that large numbers of non-Arabs found it convenient to accept the faith, tax income fell drastically. In response, the concession was removed and non-Arab converts (*mawalis*) were required to continue to pay the poll tax. Inevitably the sense of alienation grew. Another source of tension lay in the deep divisions that existed within Arab society, some continuing traditional family feuds, others growing from the Shia–Sunni divide. There were also other religious differences developing with the appearance of sects like the extreme Kharijites of North Africa.

Early threats to the stability of the Umayyad state began in the west in the early 740s with a rebellion among the recently converted Berbers of the Maghrib leading to an Arab–Berber civil war, which spread to Iberia. But a more serious threat flared up in the heart of the empire when, in June 747, Persian Muslims in Kufa rebelled and marched to Merv, one of the greatest commercial cities of Central Asia, where the rebellion blossomed. In the turmoil that ensued Abu al-Abbas was proclaimed caliph, the first of the Abbasid dynasty. In 750, at a crucial battle fought on the river Zab south of Mosul, the Umayyad armies were defeated.

The differences between the Umayyads and the Abbasids were profound. In spite of the huge geographical extent of the Umayyad empire, it was focused on the Mediterranean, with its capital at Damascus within the old Roman world. The Abbasids were a product of the old Persian world. Their original capital was at Kufa, not far from the Sasanian capital, Ctesiphon, and in 763 they moved up-river to found a new capital at Baghdad, at a point where a canal joined the Tigris and Euphrates and where a convenient overland route to Persia began. Whereas the Umayyads were largely Arabs rooted in Roman urban culture, the Abbasids were a multi-ethnic Muslim state with a strong Persian component. The Umayyad caliphs still tried to respect the values taught by the Prophet, values of simplicity and accessibility; the Abbasid caliphs isolated themselves in well-protected palaces and adopted a more

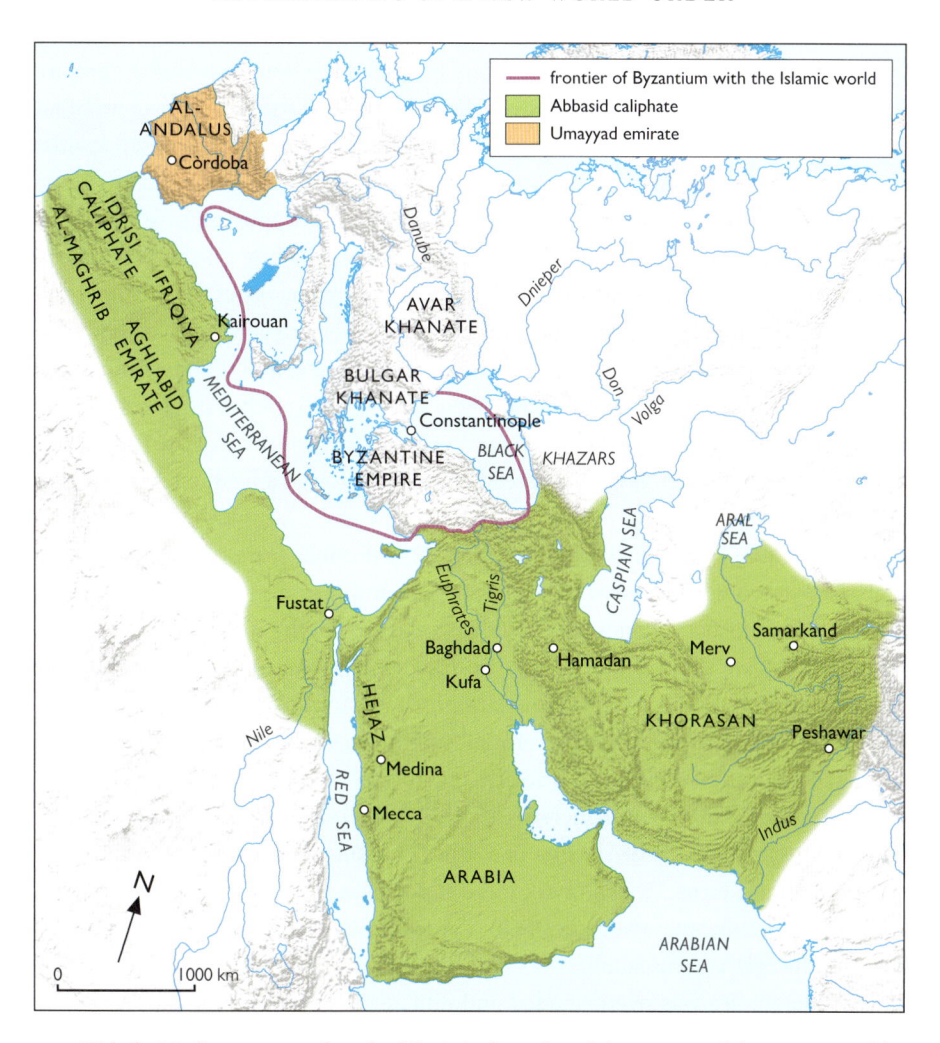

9.12 With the Muslim conquest of much of Iberia in the early eighth century, and the expansion of the Abbasid caliphate, the Byzantine empire was fast becoming surrounded by hostile neighbours to the east, south, and west

sumptuous lifestyle far more appropriate to an oriental potentate. With the loss of influence by the great Arab families, who had hitherto kept the excesses of the caliphs in check, constraints on excess and delusions of grandeur had been removed. The sheer complexity of the Muslim empire also drove change. A large and intricate civil service arose, with many of the officials appointed from among the class of freed men who owed a deep allegiance to their patrons, often the caliph's family. This bureaucracy was under the control of a chief minister (vizir), thus freeing the caliph from the day-to-day administration of the empire.

The Abbasid dynasty showed little desire to extend the boundaries of the empire except in Central Asia, where successive caliphs consolidated their hold over the great trading cities of Transoxiana, and except for the occasional show of strength against the Byzantine emperors. In 782 the Muslim army advanced through the passes of the Taurus Mountains and reached the shores of the Bosporus opposite Constantinople. There was little the Byzantine emperor could do except to buy off the Muslims by agreeing to pay a substantial annual tribute, presumably the result the Muslims had desired. The tribute continued to be paid until 805, when the newly elected emperor wrote to the caliph, Harun al-Rashid, demanding the return of all the tribute paid over the previous twenty-three years. The caliph replied with a brief note scribbled on the back of the emperor's letter: 'From Harun, the Prince of the Faithful, to Nikephoros, the Roman dog. I have read your letter, son of a heathen mother. You will see, not hear, my reply.'

The army that Harun dispatched was met some distance from Constantinople by ambassadors from Nikephoros offering apologies and agreeing to continue payment. With honour satisfied and annual tribute assured, the caliph's force withdrew. These events show, if anything, a reluctance to be drawn into a long and costly conflict with the Byzantine empire. The city of Constantinople was too strong, and there was little advantage to be had from minor territorial gains in Anatolia. The payment of tribute was a recognition of Muslim superiority, and, more to the point, it allowed the two states to continue to engage in lucrative trade. But it was an unstable situation, and in 830 the Muslims undertook the first of a series of annual attacks on Byzantine territory across the Taurus. The nature of these attacks suggests that they were more the result of border disputes than a desire for renewed conquest. Campaigning ended in 833 with the death of the caliph.

That the empire was overextended and difficult to control became apparent to the Abbasids soon after they came to power. In 755 a revolt broke out in Africa, and Kairouan was sacked. Although the situation was partially restored six years later, Africa festered with rebellions, and in the Atlas Mountains Berbers set up a number of independent Kharijite states. Rebellion also spread to al-Andalus in southern Iberia. By 800 the Abbasids had realized that the western territories were a lost cause and responsibility for Africa was handed over to Ibrahim ibn al-Aghlab, who agreed to keep the region under some kind of control. Thereafter he and his successors ruled Africa as a separate state with little reference to the Abbasid centre. The western extremity of the old empire was too distant and too troublesome for the orientalized Abbasids to bother about.

The death of Harun in 809 exposed another fracture line in the edifice. He had realized that the empire had developed two centres, one focused on Baghdad, the

9.13 In the great Arab surge along the North African coast in the seventh century AD a city was founded at Kairouan, Tunisia, by Uqba ibn Nafi about AD 670. The Great Mosque of Sidi Uqba, built at this time, incorporated more than four hundred columns taken from Carthage. Its present form dates from the ninth century

other in Khorasan, embracing the eastern part of the Iranian plateau and the caravan cities of Central Asia. He made it known that his first son, al-Amin, was his heir and was to succeed him, but that his second son, al-Ma'mun, was to become governor of Khorasan and was to govern without interference. It was a destabilizing decision. On Harun's death Ma'mun made a claim for the caliphate and eventually took Baghdad in 813, but, recognizing the new reality of the political geography, he made his commander the governor of Khorasan, allowing the governor's son to succeed him. Thereafter Khorasan became increasingly independent.

At its height, from the mid-seventh to mid-eighth century the Abbasid empire was a hothouse for the development of culture. It was the direct inheritor of Mesopotamian and Persian learning and, by virtue of its central position, it had easy access to the works of the classical Greek and Roman writers as well as Indian and Chinese wisdom. In the sciences and mathematics Muslim scholars excelled. A major advance was the concept of zero, most likely learnt from the Chinese. Arabic numerals replaced the cumbersome Roman, and the hundreds, tens, and units system was developed. There were major advances in plane and spherical trigonometry. One scholar, al-Khorezmi (c.787–850), a native of the oasis town of Khiva, wrote a book entitled *Al-Jebr* ('Algebra'), and his name, Latinized as Algorism, gives us today's 'algorithm'.

In Baghdad an institute called the House of Wisdom was opened to translate foreign works, including the great philosophers Aristotle and Plato, and the medical works of Hippocrates and Galen. Within a short space of time there was an explosion of knowledge, encouraging new research and the development of specialist schools of medicine, astronomy, mathematics, and natural science. The spread of knowledge was greatly facilitated by the introduction of papermaking into Central Asia from China. Paper was quick and cheap to make and was far more accessible and flexible than papyrus and parchment. Translations and new works could be produced in multiple copies for distribution. It was from these eastern centres, by way of the Muslim cities of Andalusia, that old and new scientific knowledge began to penetrate to the wilds of western Europe.

The outpouring of scholarship under the Abbasids was astonishing. It owes much to the relatively stable political situation at home and the lack of ruinously expensive wars of conquest, allowing society's surplus to be reinvested both to improve the urban infrastructure and to fund the arts and sciences. But it is also a reflection of the ethos of the times. The Abbasid empire sat astride the route nodes of Eurasia. Trade flourished, and with it came a flood of knowledge engendering a new curiosity. There were also men in power with a deep interest in culture who had the leisure and resources to pursue it. It was a brief golden age.

9.14 Modern statue of the famous mathematician al-Khorezmi (AD 787–850) at his home town of Khiva, now in Uzbekistan. Al-Khorezmi was the author of *Al-Jebr* ('Algebra') and the word 'algorithm' is derived from his name

Muslim Ocean Trade

The initial Arab expansion brought the two approaches to the Indian Ocean, the Red Sea and the Persian Gulf, directly under Muslim control. Of the two it was the Persian Gulf that seems to have been the most intensively used. It provided a safer entry than the Red Sea, with its dangerous sandbanks and reefs, and, more to the point, by leading directly to the mouth of the Tigris it gave easy access to the capital, Baghdad, only 450 kilometres up-river. As the Abbasid caliph al-Mansur said in the mid-eighth century, 'this is the Tigris; there is no obstacle between us and China; everything on the sea can come to us on it'. In the late ninth century another Muslim observer wrote that Baghdad was the harbour of the world, receiving not only river traffic from the port of Basra at the head of the Gulf, but caravans from Syria, Egypt, and northern Africa in the west, from Armenia in the north, and from Isfahan and Khorasan in the east. Basra, the main port of entry at the mouth of the Tigris, was founded about 638, early in the conquest, to protect the Arab garrison from attack by Oman and allies of Persia. It soon became a major commercial centre, though the larger ships were often unloaded at nearby Ubulla. As Muslim trade developed, so a string of ports

THE BEGINNING OF A NEW WORLD ORDER

grew up along the north shore of the Gulf, notably Siraf, Kish, and Hormuz. Of these, Siraf became a massive commercial entrepôt favoured by the large ocean-going ships coming in from the Indian Ocean and beyond. It had good overland links to the cities of Persia and Khorasan, and the approach was much safer than trying to navigate the delta system leading to Basra. Goods could be transhipped at Siraf to smaller vessels better designed to navigate the approach to Basra. Another attraction of ports located towards the south end of the Gulf was that they provided convenient anchorages for vessels waiting for weather systems to change before venturing onto the open ocean.

Red Sea traffic also continued, with Aden, on the Bab el-Mandeb, providing the first and last port of call between the Red Sea and the ocean. Halfway along the Red Sea, Jiddah, the port of Mecca, served much the same purpose as Siraf as a transhipment base to smaller vessels and as a port to serve the caravan routes. On the Egyptian shore the port of Aydhab was a convenient place to offload cargo bound for the Nile and the fort city of Fustat (Cairo).

9.15 The main trading centres for Indian Ocean trade in the seventh to ninth centuries AD

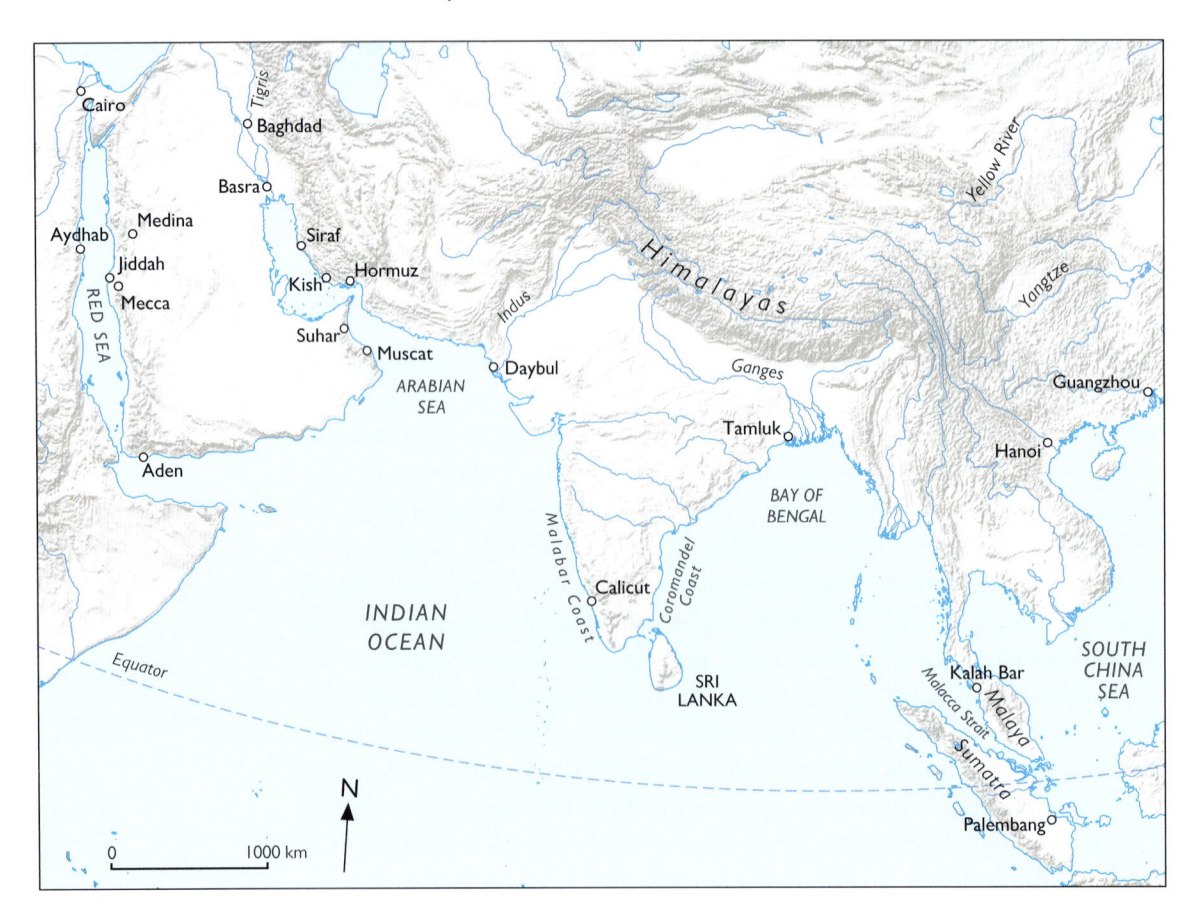

9.16 A fresco from Ajanta, north-east of Mumbai. It shows an Indian ship of about AD 600 with three square-rigged sails set aft, a fore and aft sprit-sail, and a jib-sail over the bow

By the late seventh and early eighth centuries, while many of the Muslim vessels leaving the Red Sea and Persian Gulf traded with the Malabar coast off India sailing for ports like Calicut, and some went further, to Sri Lanka and the Coromandel coast on the Bay of Bengal, a significant number were now making the onward journey to South East Asia and China. The journey was not without its hazards, but one famous Muslim sea-captain, Buzurg ibn Shahriyar, is said to have made the journey seven times. Texts of the mid-ninth century give details of the route. Having left Siraf, vessels would first call at Muscat or Suhar on the south coast of the Gulf of Oman before entering the ocean. Thereafter some ships' masters would choose to go via the port of Daybul, close to the mouth of the Indus, while others would go straight across the Arabian Sea to the Malabar coast. From here the onward journey would take them around the southern tip of Sri Lanka to Kalah Bar on the Malaccan Strait. The final leg of the voyage led up the coast of Indo-China, via Hanoi, to Guangzhou (Khanfu), part-way up the estuary of the Pearl River. A few of the more adventurous sailed on to ports further up the coast of China. The voyage from Basra to Guangzhou took about five months.

Guangzhou was a major commercial entrepôt with a large resident Middle Eastern population. Some indication of its size is given by an Arab account of an attack on the city by a Chinese rebel leader in 878 when, it is claimed, a hundred and twenty thousand Muslims, Christians, Jews, and Zoroastrians were killed. While the number may be exaggerated, it indicates a sizeable foreign population, most of whom would have been engaged in commerce and shipping. One Arabic account of China, written in 851, describes how cargoes coming from the Persian Gulf were impounded by the Chinese authorities on landing so that 30 per cent import tax could be collected. Among the goods offloaded at Guangzhou were ivory, frankincense, cast copper, and tortoise-shells. In return the traders could acquire for export gold, silver, pearls, and of course silk, and other 'rich stuff in great abundance'. Another export of some interest was an 'excellent kind of cohesive green clay' for pottery manufacture, its particular property being that it made translucent vessels. This was porcelain, which Chinese potters were beginning to perfect at this time, and would have been of considerable interest to the burgeoning ceramics industry in the Arab cities.

The rebel attack on Guangzhou in 878 and the ensuing slaughter, heralding a period of unrest in China, cannot have failed to have a devastating effect on sea-trade with the Middle East. In the aftermath the Persians, who seem hitherto to have been the principal carriers along the entire route, withdrew from the South China Sea, preferring now to meet Chinese shippers at Kalah Bar on the Malay peninsula, there to exchange their cargoes.

While the Persians were the principal shippers on the China route from the seventh to mid-ninth century, the flow of different nationalities along the seaways must have been considerable, the cargo ships providing passage for travellers from the Muslim world, India, Indonesia, and China wishing to make short-haul journeys. One such was the Chinese Buddhist monk Yijing, who in 671 set out from Chang'an on a journey to India in search of Buddhist texts. He chose to go by sea, probably because the overland route was considered to be more dangerous. Embarking from the Chinese port of Yangzhou, he took a local boat to Guangzhou, where he joined a Persian ship bound for Palembang on the island of Sumatra. After a stay on Sumatra he joined another boat, which sailed directly to Tamluk in the Ganges estuary near modern Kolkata. After a time he returned to Palembang, where he intended to make further studies, but his work was interrupted when, in 689, he boarded a boat to hand over a letter for dispatch to Guangzhou and the boat set sail with him aboard, refusing to return. Stranded in Guangzhou, he was obliged to wait for a passage back to Palembang. Yijing later made a record of monks he encountered while travelling in India. Of the fifty-six he listed, forty-seven were

Chinese, eight were Korean, and one was a Sogdian. Thirty of them used the sea-route. Clearly there was no lack of speedy vessels sailing the South China Sea.

It is impossible to provide reliable statistics for the volume of trade between China and the Muslim world but it must have been considerable, increasing dramatically over the period from the early seventh to the mid-ninth century as navigational skills improved and knowledge of the seaways became more widely shared among the maritime community. Unrest in the Tarim basin in the late eighth century will have been another factor encouraging travellers and traders to favour the sea-route. From the anecdotal scraps of documentary evidence which survive and the increasingly rich archaeological data, it is clear that the seaways of the Indian Ocean were alive with shipping, and the ports along the way were thriving multicultural enclaves where many different religions were practised and through which knowledge was transmitted with great rapidity, together, one suspects, with a constant flow of skilled craftsmen. Something of the connectivity of the time is reflected in the fact that there was a large Muslim Persian trading community resident in Guangzhou, and Chinese workers were taking part in building the Abbasid capital at Baghdad.

The Rise of the Far West

The flood of barbarians, mostly of Germanic origin, into western Europe in the fifth century had totally disrupted the infrastructure of the Roman empire, which had disintegrated into a number of small polities ruled by the successors of the invading forces. But this was far from a breakdown of civilization. It so often happens when a simple warrior society conquers a people with a higher level of development that the invaders soon adopt many aspects of the culture of those whose territories they have won. So it was in western Europe, where Burgundians, Franks, and Visigoths, among others, settled down as masters among the Romanized peoples of Gaul and Iberia, creating vigorous new kingdoms that embraced much of the culture they had found but instilling it with a new energy and coherence. Over time these peoples came to see themselves as the successors of the Romans. They spoke the Romance languages derived from Latin; they adopted Christianity and showed allegiance to the pope in Rome. The new 'Roman' west, if we may so call it, was very different from the rump of the old Roman world which had survived the period of turmoil as the Byzantine empire. The two were now separated by a wedge of tribes, Slavs, Avars, and later Bulgars, who owed nothing to Roman culture. The divide encouraged the east and west to develop along their own distinctive trajectories.

Among the western polities the Franks, who had originally migrated from east of the Rhine into Roman Gaul between the Rhine and the Seine, began to assume leadership, and by the mid-fifth century they were ruled by the Merovingian dynasty. Succession was complicated by the fact that they adopted the Germanic tradition of dividing the kingdom between the male heirs, causing dissent and fragmentation. Real power was wielded by senior court officials known as 'mayors of the palace'. In 687 one of the mayors, Peppin II, took over the running of almost the entire empire, and his successors Charles Martel (ruled 714–41) and Peppin III (ruled 741–68) continued his strong and effective rule. When, in 751, Peppin III made an alliance with the pope (who was being threatened by the Lombards), the pope agreed that Peppin should depose the last of the ineffective Merovingian monarchs and assume the kingship of the Franks. This marks the beginning of the Carolingian dynasty.

On Peppin's death the kingdom was divided between his two sons but was reunited by one of them, Charlemagne, in 771 when his brother died. Charlemagne was an able ruler whose energies were focused on enlarging the empire by military conquest. Campaigns against the Saxons, Bavarians, Bretons, and Lombards greatly extended the territories under Carolingian control. In north-western Iberia he was less successful against the Umayyad caliphate, but in central Europe he destroyed the power of the Avar empire, contesting land as far north and east as the Danube. In the thirty years of his reign he doubled the size of the territory under Frankish control. With the exception of Britain and Iberia, Europe west of the Elbe was now united under a single king. Charlemagne had succeeded in re-creating the western Roman empire.

'King of the Franks and the Lombards' was no longer an appropriate title for a man who had brought western Europe together, so Charlemagne arranged for Pope Leo III to crown him *imperator et legatus* in Rome on Christmas Day 800. The symbolism was clear for all to see: Charlemagne was claiming to be emperor of the restored Roman empire in the west, successor to the Caesars. Such a claim immediately brought him into conflict with the Byzantine emperors, who regarded themselves as the legitimate heirs of Rome. The issue was to divide the two powers for the next twelve years until a compromise was reached which allowed Charlemagne to style himself as emperor, so long as the word 'Roman' was not used. The empire that Charlemagne had drawn together transformed western Europe, creating a degree of stability that the region had not known for five centuries. It was a time of economic prosperity and of cultural renaissance. With peace, productivity and trade increased. Markets were developed on rivers and estuaries within easy reach of the English Channel and the North Sea—places like Rouen, Quentovic, Domburg, and Dorestad—to trade with the British Isles, while the ports of Ribe and Hedeby on the Danish peninsula facilitated exchange with the Baltic zone, which was fast becoming a significant player in long-distance trade. Two major trade-routes connected the North Sea–Baltic interface with the Mediterranean, one using the river Seine and the Rhône-Saône, giving access to

THE BEGINNING OF A NEW WORLD ORDER

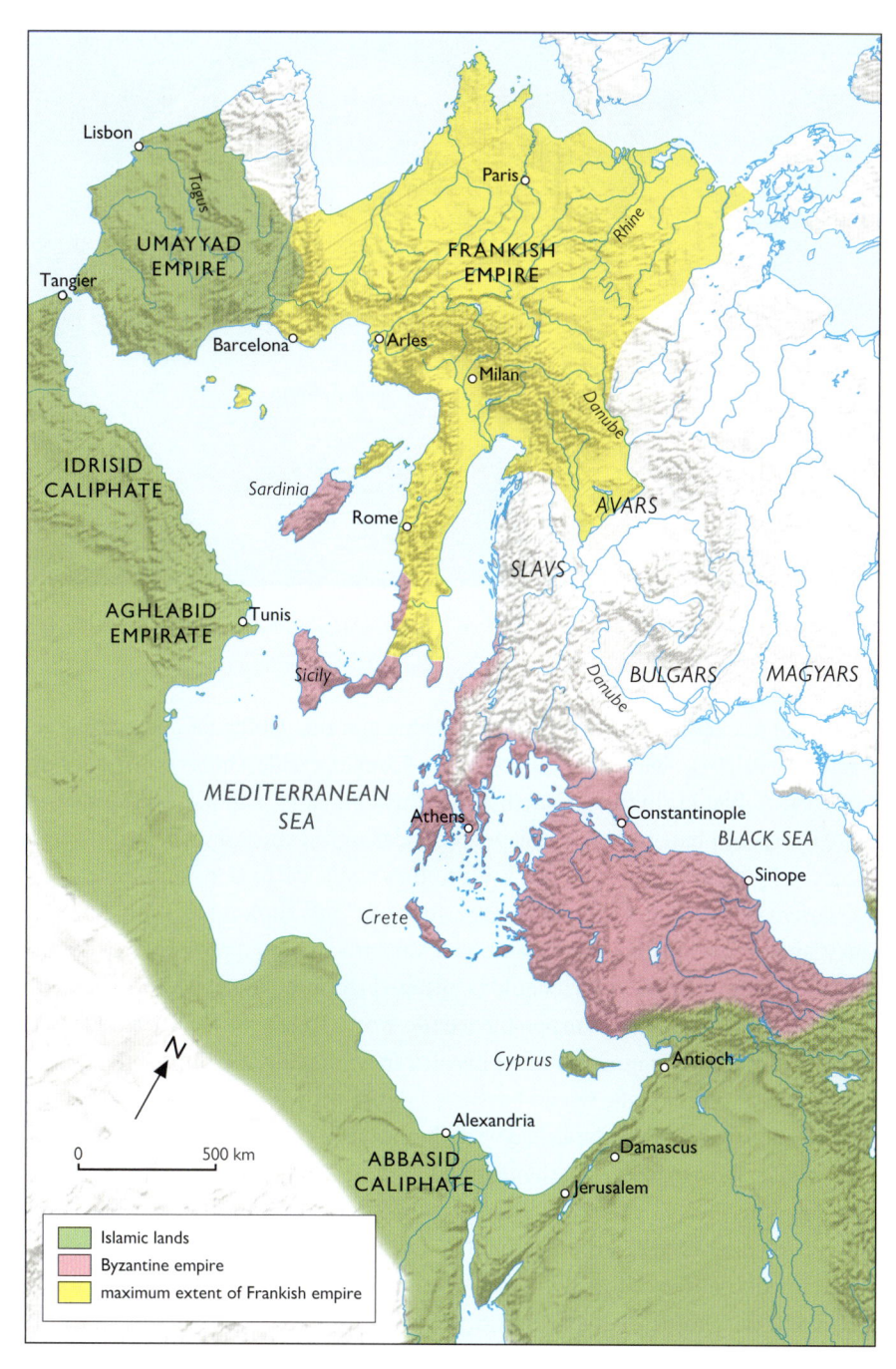

9.17 The expansion and consolidation of the Frankish empire under Charlemagne in the early ninth century AD created a new power block in the west strong enough to face further Muslim advance. The Carolingian empire now rivalled Byzantium for leadership of the Christian world

9.18 Gold coin of King Offa of Mercia (ruled AD 757–96) minted in the style of an Arabic dinar to facilitate trade with the Arab world

the port of Marseille, the other using the Rhine and the Alpine passes to reach the head of the Adriatic, with Venice as its outlet. From Marseille, ships could trade with Rome, the Aghlabid emirate in North Africa through Tunis, and more distantly with the Abbasid caliphate by way of the ports of Alexandria and Antioch. From Venice, already a significant regional power by 730, ships could sail to Constantinople.

Charlemagne was content to engage in trade and diplomacy with both his Christian and his Muslim neighbours. The Muslims offered a receptive market for slaves, ample supplies of which could be gleaned from raiding expeditions into the Slavonic lands of northern Europe (hence the word 'slave'). To facilitate trade with the Muslims, Charlemagne modified his currency, making it compatible with the dirham. Much of this trade would have been direct with Tunis and Sousse, but that good relations were also established with the Abbasid caliphate is evident from the gift of an elephant made to Charlemagne by Harum al-Rashid, dispatched on a boat from Egypt to Pisa. It is likely that the principality of Benevento in southern Italy, which had come under Carolingian influence in the early ninth century, served as an intermediary in exchanges with the Muslim world through its ports, including Naples and Salerno. The large quantities of gold and silver demanded from the principality by the Carolingians may have been trade dues.

Charlemagne was recognized as the protector of the Church of the Holy Sepulchre at Jerusalem and, indeed, made significant benefactions to it. To the Byzantines, unable to be of much influence in the Holy Land, this was a matter of concern—another example of how Charlemagne was staking a claim to be defender of the Christian Church. His close relationship with the pope, his direct leadership of the German Church, and his many acts of piety in supporting Christian scholars and missionaries were seen as a direct challenge to Byzantine authority. Yet the two empires maintained good diplomatic relations. They were sufficiently separated geographically to exclude territorial disputes, and they needed each other as trading partners.

Charlemagne died in 814 and was succeeded by his only surviving son, Louis the Pious, on whose death in 843 the empire was divided between Louis's three sons, Charles, Luther, and Louis. Further divisions and readjustments followed until, by the last decade of the ninth century, the basis had been laid for the emergence of France, Germany, and Italy as separate entities.

The energy and vision of men like Charlemagne had given western Europe time to catch up. Though comparatively poor in comparison with the Byzantine empire and the Abbasid caliphate, the Franks were now serious players on the world stage. They, too, could receive the silks and other luxuries that were the privilege of the elite.

The Steppe Corridor

While the sedentary states of the south, the Tang Chinese, the Umayyads and Abbasid Muslims, and the Byzantines, were constantly readjusting themselves to the traumas of revolution and internal struggles for power and managing their inter-state frontier relationships, the *longue durée* rhythm of life on the steppe continued to be governed by the familiar domino effect of relentless pressure from the east driving a flow of population to the west. Already, by the beginning of the seventh century, Turkic peoples had spread as far west as Sogdiana with the Amu Darya as their westernmost border. They were divided into two confederations, an eastern Turkic khanate and a western Turkic khanate, the border running roughly across Dzungaria. This was the situation when the Chinese and, slightly later, the Muslim Arabs began taking an active, and aggressive, interest in Sogdiana.

The Turkic khanates were a complex amalgam of many Turkic-speaking peoples loosely bound by shifting alliances. One early confederation, mentioned by the Chinese sources, were the Tiele, a group of nine separate peoples who emerged to the north of China after the break-up of the Xiongnu, occupying a territory to the south of Lake Baikal around the river Yenisei. One tribe of the Tiele were the Uighurs, first mentioned in the fifth century, who had rebelled against the Göktürk elite and, in the mid-seventh century, established their own khanate in Mongolia with their capital at Ordu-Baliq (Khar Balgas) in the Orkhon valley. As we have seen (p. 354), the Uighurs became allies of the Tang in their conflicts with the Tibetans in the Tarim basin and the Gansu Corridor until a general peace was concluded about 820.

Climatic changes, recorded in Chinese sources in the 830s, may have been the cause of social disruption on the steppe. At any event, in 840 disagreements among the Uighur elite encouraged the Kyrgyz, their traditional enemies living in the Yenisei valley, to move west to attack them. The Uighurs were unprepared: their capital was taken and those who survived were driven off and scattered. The country was left largely abandoned, to be gradually colonized by Mongolic speakers who moved in from the east.

The majority of Uighurs moved south to the steppe just north of the Ordos bend of the Yellow River in the expectation of Chinese help. In the stand-off that followed in 843, the Chinese offered the refugees some material assistance, but when it became clear that the Uighurs would not formally submit to Tang authority, the Chinese army moved in and slaughtered them. The sight of the gers (felt tents) of nomad refugees spanning the horizon on their border had sent a wave of panic through the Chinese soul: it was a reminder of the horror of the Xiongnu a few centuries earlier, and they reacted in fear. The event stirred up a paranoia aimed at all foreigners, which lead to widespread religious persecution. One outcome was the closing of Buddhist monasteries and the confiscation of their assets. It was a dark episode in the declining decades of the Tang era.

Other Uighur refugees, following the defeat by the Kyrgyz in 840, moved west. Some settled in Gansu; others made for the Tarim basin, where a few decades earlier they had fought on the side of the Chinese. In the west of the region they established the small kingdom of Kucha on the northern edge of the Tarim basin, with Gaochang as their capital.

The Kyrgyz were also a Turkic tribe. They lived on the Yenisei river valley in the southern part of the Minusinsk Depression, the heart of modern Tuva, occupying a crucial position between the eastern and western steppe. The Muslims with whom they came into contact were not impressed: 'these people have the nature of wild beasts . . . they are lawless and merciless . . . [and] are on hostile terms with all the people living around them'. One outcome of the Kyrgyz's aggressive stance to their neighbours was that they always had an ample supply of captives who could be sold as slaves to the Muslims. From their forest-edge location they could also supply furs, timber, and musk to the trade-routes to the south.

Other Turkic tribes displaced by the Uighur rise to power in the mid-seventh century were the Qarluqs, who settled in south-eastern Kazakhstan in the mid-eighth century and took over leadership of the region. To the south of them, on the Syr Darya, were the Oghuz, who appeared in the region in the 770s, forcing the Pechenegs, who lived there, to migrate to the Pontic steppe.

Another Turkic people once belonging to the Tiele confederation and driven from their homeland in Mongolia and southern Siberia after the fall of the Xiongnu were the Khazars. They had migrated westwards across the steppe, driving the Avars before them, and arrived in the Caspian region as early as the fourth century. They are mentioned by the Byzantine writer Priscus in 463 as a people of the west Eurasian steppe. In the mid-sixth century they forced the Avars out of the Volga region (the Avars eventually settling in the Carpathian basin) and set up the nucleus of their khanate between the Caspian and the Black Sea to include the valleys of the Volga and the Don. By the mid-ninth century they had extended their power to control the zone between the Dnieper and the Aral Sea. Another dislocation caused by their expansion was the expulsion of the Bulgars, a nomadic people who had established themselves on the Pontic steppe to the east of the Sea of Azov in the early seventh century. In 679, in a fight for supremacy, the Bulgars were forced to move on. One group went north to settle in the middle Volga valley, another group moved westwards into Europe, settling between the Dniester and the lower Danube. Later they were to cross the Danube to occupy territory on the edge of the Byzantine empire in what is now Bulgaria.

The Khazars chose to settle in what was fast becoming one of the major crossroads of Eurasia, where the caravans coming from the east along the valleys of the Syr Darya and the Amu Darya converged to go northwards around the Caspian Sea en route to the Black Sea and thence to the Byzantine world and the European markets. It was in Khazar territory that the steppe corridor met the great river routes to the north, the Dnieper, Don, and Volga, along which commercial contact with the Baltic world was already fast developing.

The Khazars were confronted with the two great powers, the Muslim state and the Byzantine empire, the first separated by the Caucasus, the second by the Black Sea. They established alliances with the Byzantines. In 695 the emperor Justinian II, who had been exiled to the Crimea, escaped to the Khazars, and on his return to power in 705 married the sister of the khan. Later, to cement a new alliance with the Khazars against the Muslims, another marriage was arranged between the emperor's son and the khan's daughter.

The Byzantines were at arm's length and therefore less of a threat, but with the Umayyads, then in a conquering mood, the Khazars shared a frontier along the Caucasus. Conflict broke out in 652 when the Arabs began to advance. They were defeated, but in the first half of the eighth century there were frequent outbreaks of hostility, culminating in an all-out war between 762 and 764. After the demise of the Umayyads, lack of territorial ambition among their successors, the Abbasids, meant that friendly and profitable commercial relations could develop between the two peoples.

THE BEGINNING OF A NEW WORLD ORDER

The Khazar khanate soon became the middlemen in the burgeoning trade that developed between the Muslim world and the Varangian Rus of the forest zone and with the Baltic states beyond. To facilitate the exchange processes the Khazars issued their own coinage compatible with the Arab dirham. The commodities exported to the south through Khazar territory were typical of the steppe and forest zones: wool, furs, honey, fish, and cereals, especially millet, to which were added the all-important

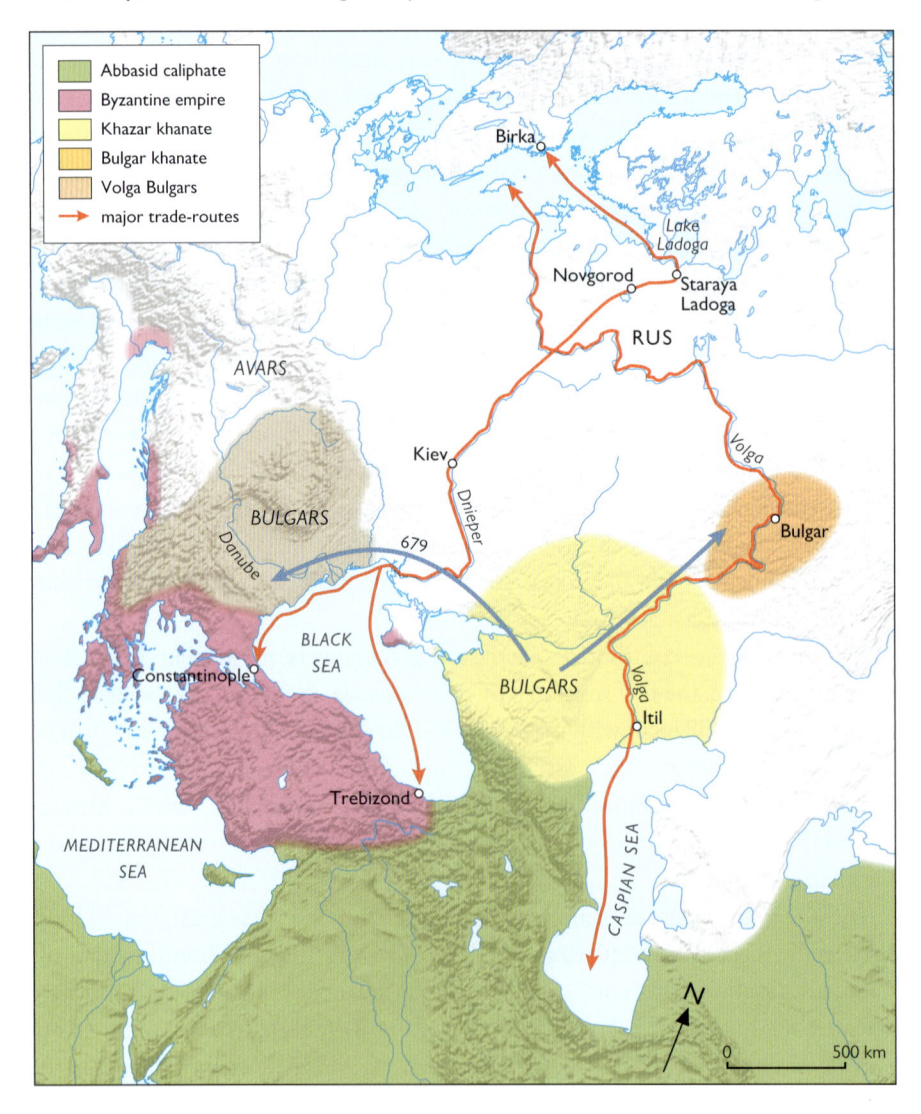

9.19 The nomadic Khazars, who had established themselves over a large tract of the Pontic-Caspian steppe, commanded the trade-routes between the Byzantine empire, the Abbasid caliphate, the steppe, and the disparate communities of northern Europe

slaves, some captured by the Rus in raids against the Slavs, others by the Khazars in the periodic campaigns against their Turkic neighbours. Turkic slaves were particularly valued for their fighting and riding skills and were much in demand as specialist troops in the Abbasid armies.

To complete the story we must look briefly at the nomads who penetrated the European peninsula. The Avars, as we have seen, were driven westwards by the advance of the Khazars. By the mid-sixth century they had crossed the Carpathians and had established themselves in Pannonia and the Great Hungarian Plain, from where they began to raid their neighbours. In 626 a massive Avar force pillaged its way across the Balkans to Constantinople, which they unsuccessfully besieged. From the seventh century until the end of the eighth century the Avar khanate remained a strong and successful enclave in the heart of Europe, but in 791 Charlemagne led a Frankish army deep into their territory, causing the polity to fragment. The plunder which he proudly carried away included much that the Avars had gathered as booty from the Byzantine empire over 160 years before. The Byzantine emperor was not best pleased.

Finally, there were the Bulgars from the Pontic steppe who had been driven into Europe in AD 679 by the Khazar advance and ended up in the valley of the lower Danube. Had it not been for the Avars already occupying the Carpathian basin it is likely that they would have followed all their predecessors from the steppe and ended up on the steppe land of the Great Hungarian Plain. As it was, they had to be content to settle down as close neighbours of the Byzantine empire, with whom they eventually developed an uneasy kind of equilibrium which from time to time gave way to outright hostility. Proximity to Byzantium toughened the emerging Bulgar state, which combined the ferocity of the horse-riding steppe Bulgars with the stability of its indigenous Slavonic population, who were agriculturalists, to create a powerful polity. The conversion of Khan Boris to Christianity about 865 initiated a new stage in Bulgar–Byzantine relations.

Enter the Scandinavians

The establishment of the stable Khazar khanate in the Pontic steppe around the middle of the seventh century opened up entirely new opportunities for trade. Over time agricultural villages and rural communities specializing in craft production grew up within Khazar trading territory, rooting the hitherto nomadic peoples to the land. At the estuary of the Volga the trading town of Itil developed as the capital of the khanate, providing a crucial route node where the trans-steppe caravan trails joined the great river corridor. It also served as a port for ships sailing the Caspian Sea to Gorgan on the southern shore, where the caravan route leading to Baghdad began.

The stability of the khanate over the next three hundred years encouraged the development of trade by river northwards across the European forests to the Baltic Sea. For Scandinavians wishing to trade with the Muslim world and the Byzantine empire there were several routes on offer. Most traders would begin by sailing up the Gulf of Finland and make the portage to Lake Ladoga, where the port town of Staraya Ladoga provided access to the river Volkhov. From the upper reaches of the river alternative routes opened up. One required an overland portage to the river systems of the upper Volga and thence to the Caspian. This meant passing through the trading town of Bulgar, in the territory of the Volga Bulgars, an important junction where one of the trans-steppe caravan routes terminated. Other river routes, using the Don and the Dnieper, led to the Black Sea, giving access to Byzantine port cities such as Trebizond and Constantinople.

The trans-forest routes encouraged traders and entrepreneurs, mostly Scandinavians and Slavs, to congregate at the fast-growing trading ports along the rivers. These multi-ethnic populations soon became known as Rus, a word which may have derived from 'Ruotsi', the West Finnish name for Sweden. Another name used to describe the peoples of the forested zone was 'Varangian', but this tends to refer specifically to more warlike groups who later became famous as the fearsome bodyguards of the Byzantine emperors. Out of these complex processes of ethnogenesis the Russian state was to emerge.

The Baltic and the forest zone provided a range of products much in demand in the Byzantine and Muslim world: furs, wax, honey, walrus ivory, amber, strong steel swords, and of course slaves. In return the Scandinavian world received huge quantities of silver in the form of coins, which were used in exchange, melted down to make ingots, or crafted into items of enhanced value. About a thousand hoards, amounting to over two hundred thousand coins, are at present known in Scandinavia and European Russia. The earliest hoards date to the 780s. In the beginning, supply was modest and somewhat erratic, and during the ninth century there was a decline due partly to increased warfare in the Muslim caliphate and partly to the exhaustion of some of the mines supplying the Muslim state. But after about 900 new supplies came on stream and there was a marked increase in the quantity of silver being exported to the north. Other exotic imports reaching Scandinavia include Chinese silk like that found in a grave close to the Swedish trading port of Birka. Other fabrics, such as the red taffeta enlivened with appliqué bands of yellow silk found at Lund, are likely to have been made in the Byzantine world. Occasional exotics like the statue of Buddha from Helgö hint at the reach of the entrepreneurs.

There can be little doubt that the burgeoning trade between the Baltic and the east, beginning after the middle of the eighth century, was a factor in the stable economic system developed by the Khazars in the Pontic steppe, but this was, in turn, only possible because the Abbasids to the south were content to develop their state without making territorial claims on their neighbours' land. The competitive urge was now channelled into trade.

Retrospect: A Changing World Order

The restless century from about 649 to about 740, which saw the astonishing advances of the Arabs and the Tang Chinese at their most expansive, ended in a period of continent-wide revolution. In the eastern steppe the Uighurs overthrew their Turkic masters, in Central Asia Muslim merchants set up the Abbasid caliphate in rebellion against the Umayyads, and in China An Lushan led a successful uprising against the Tang leadership. Meanwhile, in the west constant rebellion gripped the Byzantine empire, and on the Atlantic extremity the Carolingian dynasty was busy establishing itself as masters of the Frankish kingdom. It was as though revolution had gripped all the peoples of Eurasia, spreading across the continent like a forest fire.

Some historians, impressed by the near-synchronicity of the revolutions, have looked for a common cause. One thought-provoking suggestion is that some at least of the ferment may have been orchestrated by Sogdian merchants anxious to strengthen their hold on the Central Asian trading networks. The Abbasid revolution was begun in Merv, one of the greatest trading cities of the region, by commercial entrepreneurs, while the revolution against the Tang was led by a man of Sogdian–Turkic parentage. The possibility of collusion is intriguing but difficult to prove. That rebellion was in the air in the middle of the eighth century from the Atlantic to the South China Sea is not in doubt; its extent, however, may have been little more than a factor in the fast-growing connectivity binding Eurasia and allowing news of events to travel fast and far, stimulating discontent.

Out of the turmoil of the 740s and 750s emerged a new early medieval world order that was to last for a century until about 840, when a series of disruptive events plunged the continent into economic uncertainty. Charlemagne's empire was dismantled and shared between his grandsons, the Abbasid empire began to fragment, the power of the Uighurs was smashed, and huge numbers were slaughtered by the Tang rulers, whose paranoia against anything foreign exacerbated the state's decline. Only the Byzantine empire managed to retain its strength and to grow, further boosting trans-European trade with the Scandinavians. It was from these fast-growing polities around the remote Baltic that vigorous entrepreneurs, traders and raiders alike, were to develop a will and an energy to change the face of western Europe.

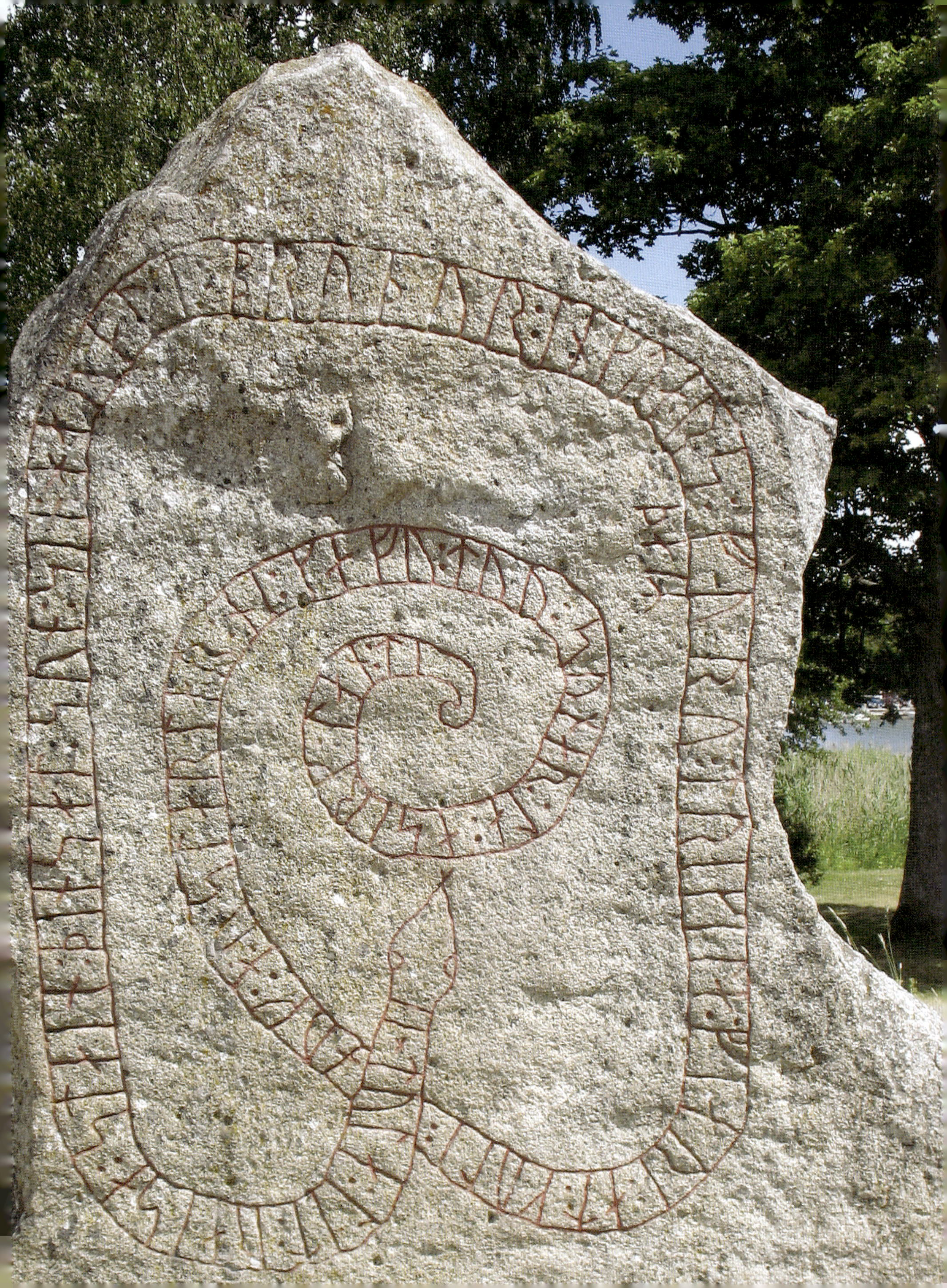

10

THE DISINTEGRATION OF EMPIRES, AD 840–1150

In the high Middle Ages, the period covered by this chapter, the great empires of the early Middle Ages fragmented: the Tang and Abbasid empires in the ninth century, and the Byzantine empire, after a brief period of growth, in the eleventh century. What emerged was a confusing number of polities always jostling for power but too small, or too transient, to become dominant for long. If there is one overriding mood to this period, it is of a tense, unstable equilibrium constraining the powers and holding them in a web of interdependence. Another significant characteristic of the times was a blurring of the boundaries between the pastoral and agricultural societies. States spanning the divide developed mixed economies, while migrant groups of steppe nomads, finding themselves among agriculturalists, willingly embraced the indigenous economies. Clear-cut social, economic, and religious divides were now becoming a thing of the past.

China: Collapse, Reunification, and Division

After the middle of the ninth century the centralizing power of the Tang rulers weakened and peasant rebellions broke out, the most serious in 859, 868, and 874–84. The last, led by Huang Chao, saw the destruction of the port of Guangzhou in 878 when an estimated hundred and twenty thousand people, mostly foreign merchants, were slaughtered. In 881 the rebels reached the capital, Chang'an, and sacked the city. The government forces drove the rebels away, before themselves looting what remained. Something of the one-time grandeur of the Tang capital is captured in the poet Wei Zhuang's lament describing the desolation of the place after the attack:

> Chang'an lies in mournful stillness: what does it now contain?
> Ruined markets and desolate streets, in which ears of wheat are sprouting.
> Fuel-gatherers have hacked down every flowering plant in the Apricot Gardens,
> Builders of barricades have destroyed the willows along the Imperial Canal.
> All the gaily coloured chariots with their ornamented wheels are scattered and gone.
> Of the stately mansions with their vermilion gates fewer than half remain.
> The Hanyuan Hall is the haunt of foxes and hares.
> The approach to the Flower-Calyx Belvedere is a mass of brambles and thorns.
> All the pomp and magnificence of the older days are buried and passed away;
> Only a dreary waste meets the eye; the old familiar objects are no more.
> The Inner Treasury is burnt down, its tapestries and embroideries a heap of ashes;
> All along the Street of Heaven one treads on the bones of state officials.

After a brief revival the royal household was sent away by the now all-powerful generals, and in 907 the last of the Tang emperors was killed. Much of the infrastructure of government had already collapsed, and what remained fragmented as the warlords fought for power.

In the half-century or so that followed, known as the Five Dynasties (907–60), China was divided between north and south. In the north, five successive military dictatorships maintained the semblance of empire but had to cede considerable tracts of territory lying to the south of the Great Wall to the Khitans, northern nomads of Mongolian origin. Meanwhile, the southern part of the old empire was divided into ten independent kingdoms.

Eventually, in 960, a military coup in the north brought Song Taizu to power. He was proclaimed emperor, the first of the Northern Song dynasty (960–1127), and within the next nine years the ten kingdoms of the south were absorbed into the new empire by diplomacy and coercion. Thus, with the exception of the Khitan-held territory of the north-east, the unified empire had been restored, with a new capital established at Kaifeng.

The Khitans were one of the many nomadic tribes of Mongolia who had once made up the Xianbei confederation. They had grown in strength on the north-eastern border of China, and in 916, under the leadership of the Liao dynasty (916–1125), had expanded first into northern China and a little later into the eastern steppe and southern Manchuria. Once the Song had established themselves, they attempted to drive the Khitans out of north-eastern China but, after a long and unsuccessful war, were forced in 1004 to agree not only to allow them to remain but to pay them a sub-

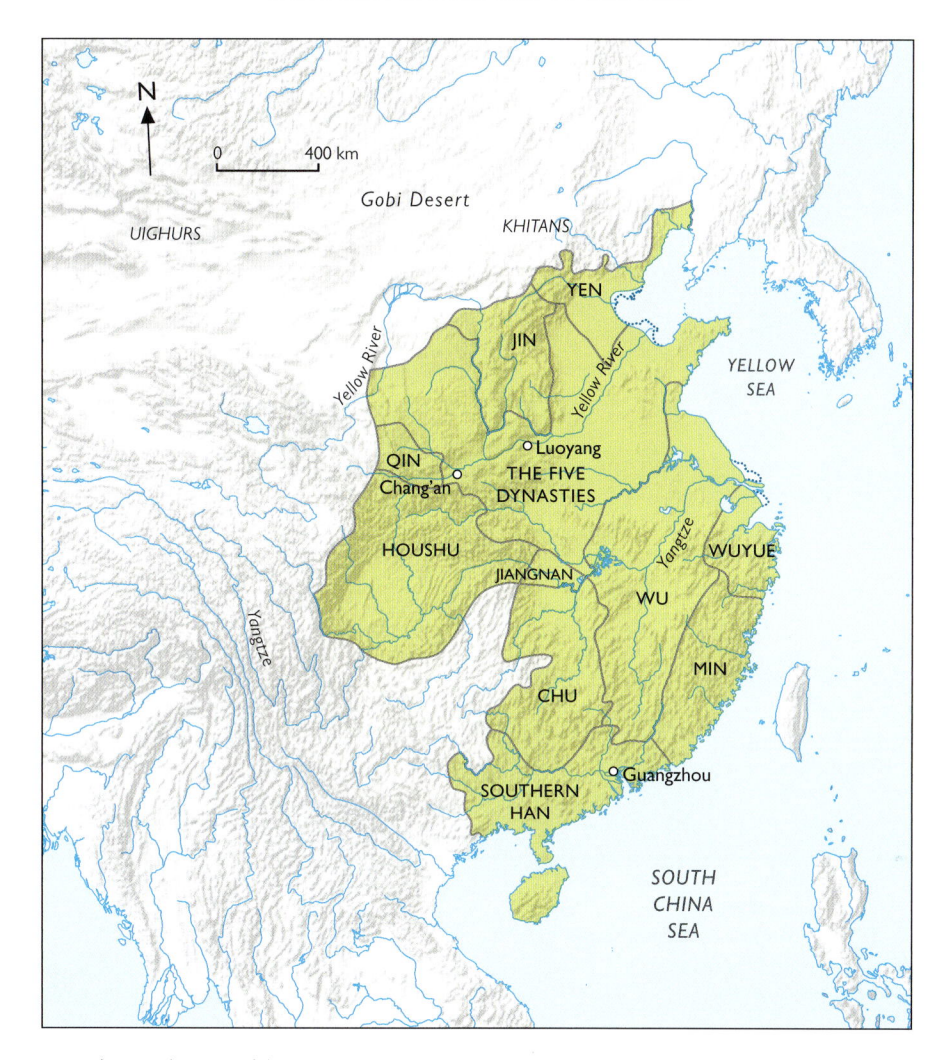

10.1 China at the time of the Five Dynasties (AD 907–60)

stantial annual tribute in tea, silk, and silver. In doing this the Song were accepting the reality of coexisting with powerful horse-riding neighbours, much as the Han had done a thousand years before when they adopted their *heqin* policy towards the predecessors of the Khitans, the Xiongnu.

The Khitans divided their Liao kingdom into five regions, each with its own administrative centre. In the south the city of Yanjing (Beijing) became the centre of the agricultural zone, but in the steppe region to the north they still followed their traditional nomadic lifestyle. While a strong conservative element strove to maintain the old ways, the Khitans soon adopted Chinese administrative systems and became

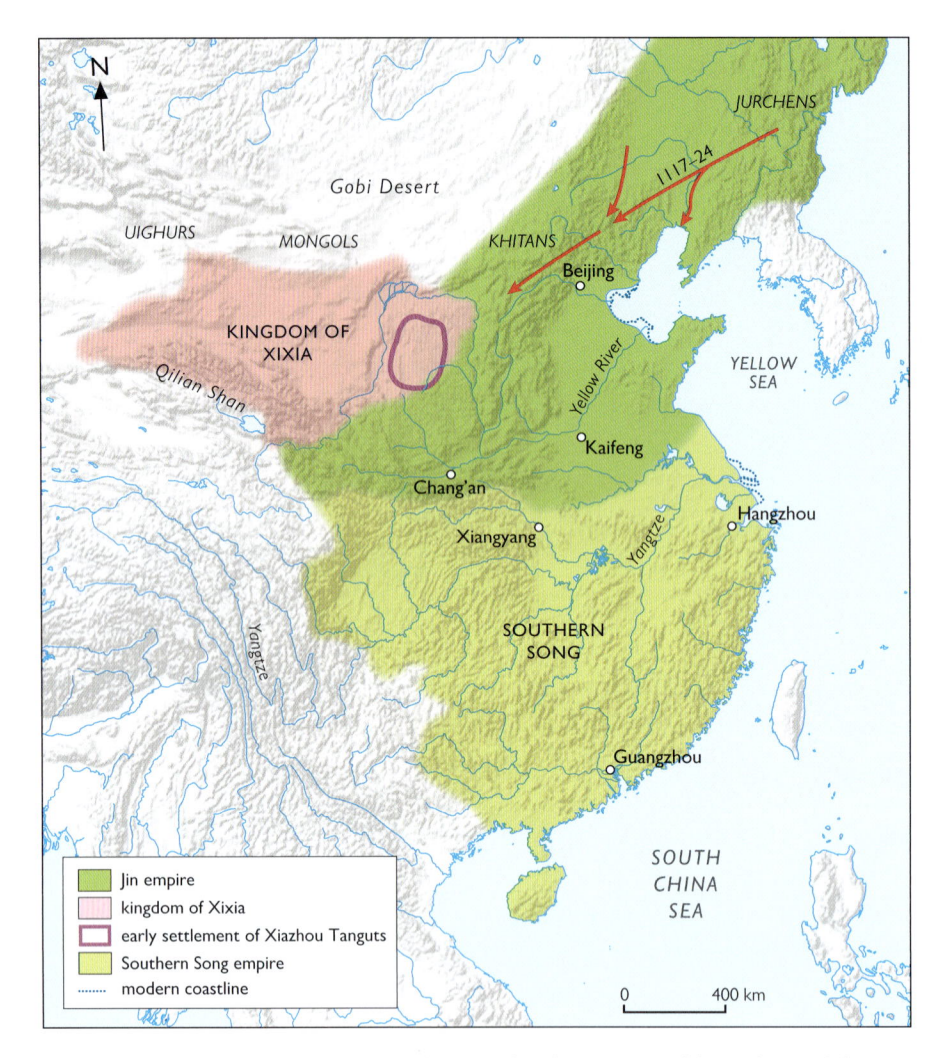

10.2 China at the time of the Southern Song dynasty, when the Jin empire of the Jurchens and the Xixia kingdom of the Tanguts occupied much of the north of the country

increasingly sinicized, growing close to the Northern Song and living in harmony with them.

The Song were confronted on their north-western border by another powerful polity, the kingdom of the Xixia, occupying the Gansu Corridor and the desert area to the north. The kingdom was founded by the Xiazhou Tanguts, a Tibetan-speaking people who had migrated from north-eastern Tibet and settled in the eastern Ordos region in the great bend of the Yellow River during the Tang period. In the early eleventh century they began to expand their power to the south-west, into their old

Tibetan homeland, and westwards along the trade-routes leading to the Tarim basin.

By virtue of their control of the Gansu Corridor and their general hostility to the Song, the Xixia blocked Song China from trade with Central Asia along the old Silk Road. At the same time, the Khitans to the north-east controlled access to the steppe routes leading via Dzungaria to the west. The result was twofold: the Song began to turn in upon themselves and developed their own highly distinctive culture, and they began to lose the aggressive imperialism that had characterized the Tang period. This is nowhere better expressed than in their painting and pottery, which now relied for their inspiration on nature. The change of mood is perfectly captured in the contrast between the flamboyant forms and glazes of Tang ceramics and the gentle flower forms and subdued colours that gave pleasure to the Song potter and his clients. This isolationism was to some extent mitigated by the activities of merchant entrepreneurs in the southern coastal ports, who grew rich on maintaining the supply of luxury goods from Indonesia, the Indian Ocean, and the Near East, reminding the Song of the wider world (pp. 387–8).

10.3 Foliate Jun Yao dish from the Northern Song region dating to the twelfth century AD. The form and colour of the vessel reflects a love of the natural world that characterizes the art of the Song potter and the taste of his patrons

To the east of the Liao kingdom of the Khitans, in eastern Manchuria, lived the Jurchens, a nomadic community who for some while were vassals of the Khitans. Taking advantage of the growing weakness of the Liao rulers, the Jurchens stopped paying annual tribute. When a Khitan army was sent against them, they retaliated in force, soundly beating their overlords, and in 1115 proclaimed themselves the empire of the Jin. With their new-found strength they set about conquering Khitan territory in southern Manchuria. The Song saw this as an opportunity to recapture Chinese territory held by the Khitan Liao dynasty. In 1123 they entered into a treaty with the Jurchens by the terms of which the Song were allowed to reclaim part of their lost land in return for an annual payment. The treaty held for two years, but in 1125 the Jurchens, having completed the conquest of the Liao kingdom, now turned their aggressive attention on the Song, proceeding south across the Yellow River to besiege the Song capital at Kaifeng. A peace was eventually negotiated, in return for which the Song had to cede territory and pay a vast annual tribute in silver and silk. Not long after, the Song reneged on some of the terms and the Jurchens attacked again, in 1127 sacking Kaifeng and capturing the emperor and other members of the court. The remnant of the Song administration fled further south to establish the new capital of what now became the Southern Song dynasty at Hangzhou. Another treaty, signed in 1142, agreed a border between the Jin state and the Southern Song, coinciding in part with the Huai valley. China was again divided between a nomad-ruled north and a Han-dominated south, much as it had been six hundred years before when, following the collapse of the Han dynasty, the nomadic Toba rode into the north to establish the Toba Wei dynasty.

The revival of this boundary is interesting. It coincides roughly with a natural environmental division between the dry loess-covered north, where wheat and millet were grown, and the much wetter south, which produced rice. The northern ecological zone offered good fighting country for nomadic horsemen in contrast to the wetter rice-growing territory of central and southern China, which was impossible terrain for cavalry warfare—an intriguing example of the recurring influence of geography on politics.

The defeat of the Liao dynasty by the Jurchens was by no means the end of the Khitans. Out of the chaos emerged a new leader, Yelü Dashi, who led his followers northwards into the steppe; there, with Chinese and Mongol contingents, he regrouped his followers to create an efficient fighting force, proclaiming himself Gür Khan ('Universal Ruler'). In 1131 he moved westwards into the northern part of the Tarim basin and later into Dzungaria, establishing his authority over first the Uighurs and then the Karakhanids. Having taken control of Kashgar, Khotan, and Kirghiz, he attacked and defeated the Western Karakhanid ruler in 1137, and in 1141, at the battle of Qatwan near Samarkand, he defeated the Seljuk Turks, bringing Transoxiana (now Uzbekistan) into his domain. In a decade he had created a new empire, known as the Kara Khitai ('Black Khitans'), stretching from western Mongolia almost to the Aral Sea. In this he was repeating the now familiar pattern of the advance of peoples of Mongol and Turkic origin from a homeland in Mongolia and southern Siberia westwards into Central Asia and sometimes beyond. Again we see geography influencing the course of history. Peoples of the steppe region of Mongolia and Manchuria were hemmed in on three sides: by the forest to the north, the sea to the east, and the Chinese agriculturalists to the south. Under demographic and social pressure, their only route for expansion or escape was westwards through the Tarim basin and Dzungaria into Central Asia.

With the Southern Song now firmly established in central and southern China, many of the Han population living in the north chose to move to the south, enhancing the Chinese character of their culture, sustained by the productivity of the rice-growing economy. The dynasty soon became strong enough to resist any further Jin intervention, but since it no longer displayed imperialist aspirations, productivity could now be used to enhance the lifestyle and culture of the people. Under the Song emperors education was revitalized, and philosophy, science, and the arts developed apace, bringing the country into the early stages of an industrial revolution. For the Chinese it was another golden age.

The strong nomadic kingdoms that developed along the northern and western borders of the Song empire effectively cut off the overland trade-routes with the west, leaving the Song to rely increasingly on the sea as a means of communication with the wider world, the source of foreign commodities so much in demand by the elite. Until the late ninth century ships from the Muslim states, mostly with Persian ships' masters, regularly visited the international port of Guangzhou, but the slaughter of the population by rebels in 878 and the constant unrest thereafter seems to have made Muslim sailors increasingly reluctant to journey much beyond the Malay archipelago. By the early tenth century a Muslim traveller noted the importance of the port at Kalah Bar on the Malay peninsula, where ships from Siraf and Oman met those from China. Heavily planked, multi-deck junks were plying the South China Sea from the Late Tang period. By the mid-twelfth century, according to the Arab writer al-Idrisi, they were sailing the Indian Ocean, taking their cargoes of iron, swords, silk, velvet, and porcelain to the Indus valley ports, to the Euphrates, and to Aden. The transport of iron and porcelain, both weighty commodities, is a reminder that sea-going vessels of this nature needed ballast of a kind that could be sold on along with the luxury goods. The ballast carried by the Muslim ships making for the east included dates, wine, and building materials.

10.4 Ceramic model of a Chinese junk from the Eastern Han dynasty (AD 25–220) found at Xianlielu, Guangzhou, Guangdong province. These robust sea-going vessels have a long ancestry, but with the increase in maritime trade in the Song period they came to dominate the eastern Asian seaways

The rising volume of sea-borne traffic during the Song period saw the authorities begin to exercise greater control. At the end of the tenth century an imperial edict was passed forbidding the inspectors of shipping, the governor, and other officials from buying goods from foreign merchants; the effect was to introduce a state monopoly and thus to control prices. A little later we hear of special inspectors stationed at the main ports of Guangzhou and Quanzhou to facilitate the activities of foreign merchants and to deal with their complaints. The development of ports all along the south China coast and the increasing complexity of the administrative systems put in place to deal with maritime matters leave little doubt that overseas trade had expanded to considerable proportions under the Song. In 1132 the first permanent navy was instituted, a further indication of the growing importance of the sea.

The Fragmentation of the Muslim Empire

Many factors led to the disintegration of the huge empire created by the explosive Arab conquests of the seventh and early eighth centuries. First and foremost were its sheer size and geographical diversity: it was simply too unwieldy to manage. We have already seen how, by 840, much of the west had been lost to Abbasid control: Iberia broke away to become the Umayyad emirate in AD 756, the Idrisid caliphate of the Maghrib was set up in 789, and Ifriqiya (Tunisia and western Libya) became an independent Aghlabid emirate in 800: others were to follow, and by 900 the Abbasid caliphate was reduced to little more than Mesopotamia and Hejaz on the eastern Red Sea coast. But there were other factors at work. Religious divides, most particularly the Shi'ite–Sunni conflict, played an important part in the fragmentation, but so, too, did the numerous other factions that emerged, as well as the growing divide between conservatives and moderates. There was also a widespread discontent between the Arab Muslims and the other ethnic groups newly converted to Islam but taxed and treated differently. In much of Persia and Central Asia the converts made up a high percentage of the population. Given the depth of the divisions, political disintegration was inevitable.

Even with the loss of the Iberian and North African territories the Abbasid caliphate maintained its hold, reaching the peak of its power under Harun al-Rashid (ruled 786–809), but the civil wars that broke out after his death as his sons fought for power exacerbated the endemic disintegration. The most serious loss was of Egypt, Palestine, and Syria, which became the Tulunid emirate in 868 (through briefly recovered by the Abbasids between 905 and 972). Much of Arabia, apart from Hejaz, was lost in 899 to the Qarmatians, whose power base lay on the southern shore of the Persian Gulf. Meanwhile, in the east, in Persia and Central Asia, native rulers set up the independent Saffarid and Samanid emirates after 875. The Sunni Samanids even-

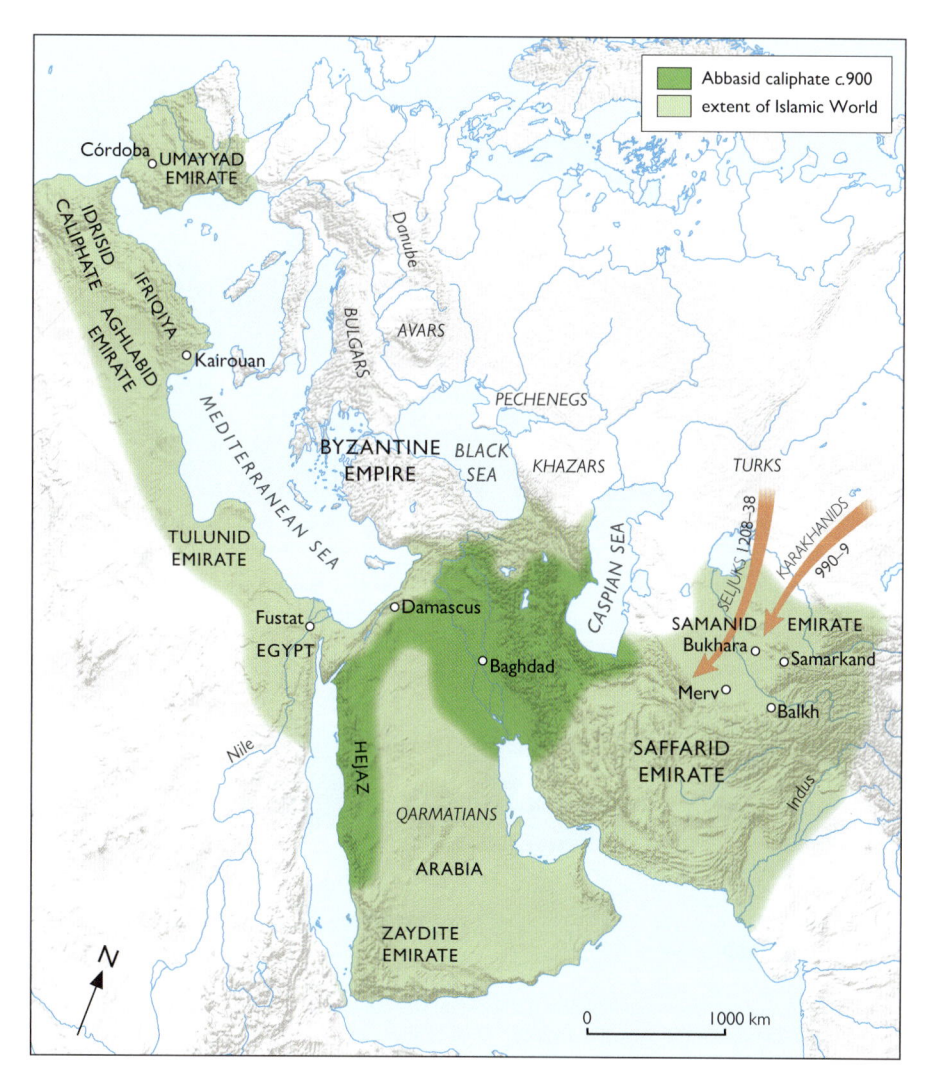

10.5 The fragmentation of the Muslim world between the tenth and the late twelfth centuries AD at the time of the Turkic advance

tually annexed the territories of the Shi'ite Saffarids in 908, creating a powerful emirate bounded by the Pamir, the Caspian Sea, the Iranian plateau, and the steppe.

The Samanid dynasty oversaw a period of peace and prosperity in Central Asia, particularly in the first half of the tenth century. The economy remained strong, benefiting both from a revival of international trade and from the exploitation of deposits of silver, gold, and jade in the Ferghana and Zeravshan valleys. Economic prosperity allowed the rulers to invest in ambitious building programmes: mosques,

10.6 The Samanid mausoleum in Bukhara (Uzbekistan) was built between AD 892 and 943 as the resting place for the founder of the Samanid dynasty, Ismail Samani, and his relatives. Its intricate brickwork marks the beginning of a new style in building

caravanserais, palaces, and forts now graced the major towns. It was also a time when scholarship in the arts and the sciences developed apace under the patronage of the elite, and Muslim missionaries were hard at work among the Turkic tribes. But after the middle of the tenth century the system began to come under strain from rivalries in the ruling household and from confrontation between two rival schools of Islam: the Sunnis and the Shia Ismailis. The 990s saw the appearance of new Turkic armies entering the region from the north, a process culminating in an invasion by the Karakhanids (p. 394), whose capture of Bukhara in 999 brought the Samanid kingdom to an end.

THE DISINTEGRATION OF EMPIRES

In the meantime, in the heart of the Muslim world, after a brief recovery in the early years of the tenth century, the Abbasid dynasty declined into insignificance, though the caliph remained as the spiritual leader. By the year 1000 a new dynasty, the Fatimids, had taken control of Ifriqiya, Egypt, Palestine, and much of Syria. Meanwhile, in the heartlands of Mesopotamia and western Persia, the Buwayhids, a tribal confederation from the southern shore of the Caspian Sea, assumed control, having captured the Abbasid capital, Baghdad, in 945.

In the early decades of the eleventh century Turkic tribes, many of them already Muslim, were moving in to take control of Central Asia. The conquest of Khorasan by the Seljuks in 1038–40 marks the effective end of Arab Muslim rule in the Near East.

While it is true that the period from 840 to 1040 saw the political fragmentation of the Arab world, it was more a time of transition than of collapse. In spite of the change of dynasties and the constant readjustment of frontiers, Muslim beliefs and culture bound the disparate regions together and the Abbasid caliph, though shorn of most other authority, was still acknowledged as the supreme leader of the community (*ummah*). More to the point, the energy of the Muslim world was soon to be reinvigorated by Turkic peoples recently converted to Islam. For many, the Seljuk capture of Baghdad in 1055 was the beginning of a new era, when the Middle East and Central Asia were once again reunited under a single dynasty.

10.7 The Kalon Minaret in Bukhara was built by the Karakhanid ruler Arslan Khan in AD 1127 in the elaborate brick style introduced by the Samanids; it is 47 metres tall. Chinggis Khan was so impressed that he left the building standing when he destroyed the city

The two centuries before the arrival of the Seljuks saw major developments in Muslim culture focused on the fast-developing urban centres. Samarkand, Bukhara, Baghdad, Damascus, Fustat (Cairo), Kairouan, and Córdoba all became great centres of learning, where some of the most innovative scholars of the world studied and taught. The importance attached to learning was matched by an enthusiasm for building madrasahs, where the young could be schooled in the Islamic sciences. The vibrant Muslim culture which, four hundred years after the Prophet's death, now spread across the face of Eurasia, across some 7,000 kilometres, was very different from the austere, tightly focused desert culture of its founding fathers. It had evolved and diversified, enriched by the contributions of a myriad different peoples, and

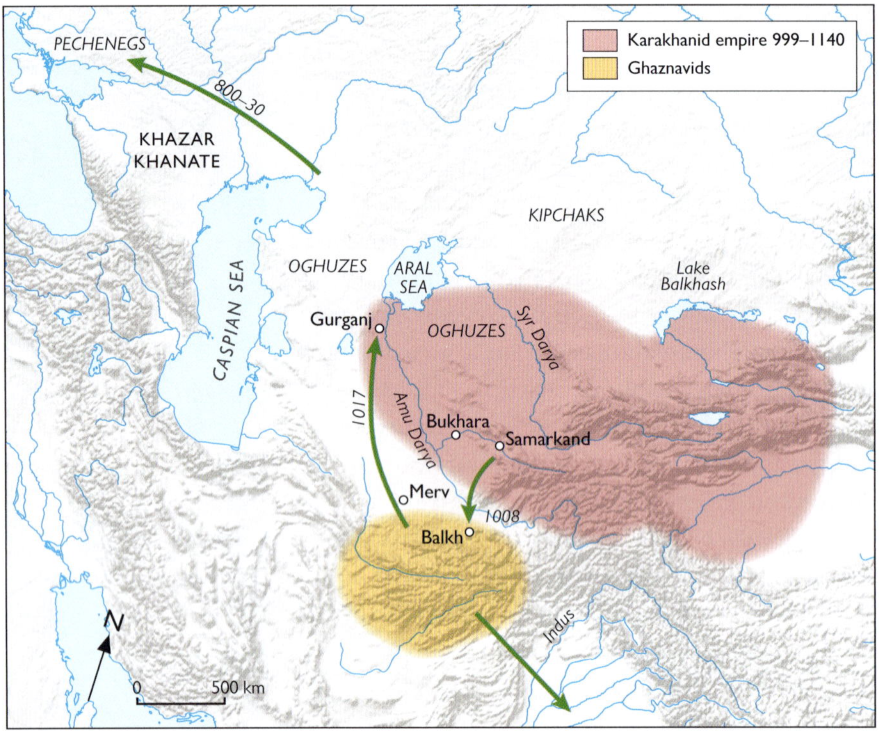
Karakhanid empire 999–1140
Ghaznavids
PECHENEGS
800–30
KHAZAR KHANATE
KIPCHAKS
OGHUZES
ARAL SEA
CASPIAN SEA
Lake Balkhash
Gurganj
OGHUZES
Syr Darya
1017
Amu Darya
Bukhara
Samarkand
Merv
1008
Balkh
Indus
N
0
500 km

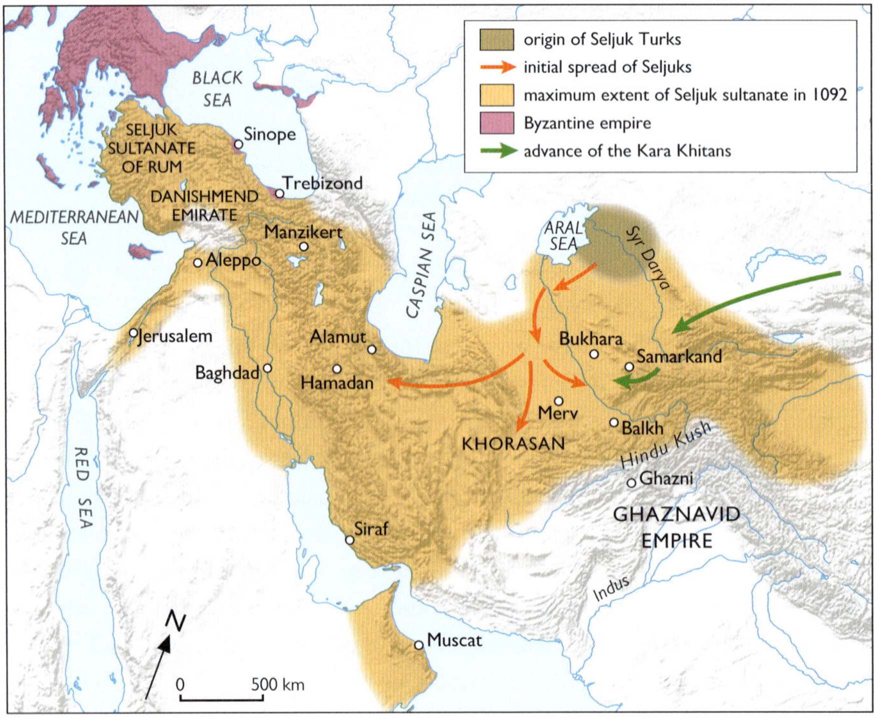
origin of Seljuk Turks
initial spread of Seljuks
maximum extent of Seljuk sultanate in 1092
Byzantine empire
advance of the Kara Khitans
BLACK SEA
SELJUK SULTANATE OF RUM
Sinope
Trebizond
DANISHMEND EMIRATE
MEDITERRANEAN SEA
Manzikert
CASPIAN SEA
ARAL SEA
Syr Darya
Aleppo
Jerusalem
Alamut
Bukhara
Samarkand
Baghdad
Hamadan
Merv
Balkh
KHORASAN
Hindu Kush
Ghazni
RED SEA
GHAZNAVID EMPIRE
Siraf
Indus
Muscat
N
0
500 km

10.8 (*Opposite top*) The Turkic tribes of Central Asia in the tenth to twelfth centuries

10.9 (*Opposite bottom*) The origin and spread of the Seljuk Turks by the end of the eleventh century

had developed a dense tissue of subtle complexities born of the creative thought of generations of scholars. Although the Muslim world had fragmented politically, its enriched culture created a coherent web from the Atlantic to the Indus.

Turks on the Move

Between the third and eighth centuries successive waves of Turkic-speaking nomads moved westwards from their homeland in southern Siberia and western Mongolia. By the early sixth century they had reached Central Asia in sufficient numbers to assume control of the trading cities of Sogdiana, forming the western Turkic khanate, which remained in power until the Arab conquest of the mid-seventh century. From the conquest to the end of the Samanid dynasty (999) the Turkic component of the population of Muslim Central Asia remained strong. Turks were renowned for their ability as cavalry fighters and formed a significant part of the Muslim armies. The Turkic communities living north of the Muslim-held territory around the Aral Sea and spreading into the steppe were an important source of these fighters. In this area constant conflicts, caused by tribal rivalries and the flow of new people from the east, generated a supply of slaves that could be sold to the Muslims for service in the army. Unsettled conditions also encouraged fighting men to offer themselves as mercenaries and at the same time forced entire communities to seek new lands in the west.

One of the tribes, driven westwards by pressure from stronger neighbours, were the Pechenegs. In the late eighth century they lived in Central Asia but were forced out by the stronger Oghuzes, who dominated the marginal lands between desert and steppe to the east and west of the Aral Sea. Eventually, by the early ninth century, the Pechenegs had established themselves in the Pontic steppe between the Sea of Azov and the river Dnieper in the region between the Khazar khanate and the Magyars. Constant pressure from the more powerful Khazars forced them further westwards, driving the Magyars to settle in the Carpathian basin, thus allowing them to extend their territory westwards to the river Siret. They now occupied a crucial position between the Khazars, the Rus, the Byzantines, and the Bulgars, with all of whom they fought at one time or another. After some successes against the Kievan Rus they were eventually defeated in a series of battles by the Byzantines and their allies between 1091 and 1122 and their territory was taken over by another Turkic tribe, the Cuman-Kipchaks, who had recently arrived on the scene and had allied themselves with the Byzantines.

THE DISINTEGRATION OF EMPIRES

Meanwhile, in Central Asia the descendants of the early Turkic empires were regrouping to the north of the Tian Shan, and by the tenth century they had firmly established themselves as far west as the Aral Sea, forming the tribal confederation of the Karakhanids. By the late ninth century they were strong enough to begin to attack the Samanid state to the south and, after the capture of Bukhara in 999, Karakhanid rule was established as far west as the valley of the Amu Darya. Though politically unstable from the beginning, the state was to hold together until about 1140. It was during this time that Turkic communities began to absorb the values and aspirations of Muslim culture to create a new Muslim Turkic identity. The fusion took place in that hothouse of cultural interaction between the valleys of the Amu Darya and Syr Darya where, over the millennia, Eurasian cultures had melded with such innovative results. The region was a great route node and as such could not fail to attract creative energies from far and wide.

While the Karakhanids were extending their control over Transoxiana, a Turkic mercenary, Mahmud of Ghazni (a city south of the Hindu Kush in what is now Afghanistan), was busy setting up a rebel state to the south. The Ghaznavids, as they became known, defeated the Samanids at Merv and in 997 declared independence. They then proceeded to extend their area of control eastwards into northern India as far as the upper Ganges. Mahmud was a militant Muslim and regarded the conquest as a holy war against the Hindus and their religious beliefs. He also campaigned eastwards, annexing much of north-western Iran and extending his influence almost to Baghdad. Proximity to the Karakhanid state to the north brought them into conflict. A Karakhanid campaign into Ghaznavid territory lost a major engagement at Balkh in 1008, and in 1017 the Ghaznavids captured Gurganj, the capital of Khwarezm, in the delta area of the Amu Darya, which had been a Karakhanid preserve. The two states maintained a hostile stand-off until the 1030s, when both were threatened and drastically weakened by a new external force, the Seljuks.

Enter the Seljuks

The Seljuks were a Turkic clan led by a local chieftain, Seljuk, who had broken away from the Oghuz confederacy and settled his people on the lower Syr Darya to the east of the Aral Sea in the ninth century. By the tenth century they were a powerful regional polity with regular contact with the Samanids, from whom they accepted Islam. In the middle of the tenth century they expanded southwards, first along the Aral Sea to the estuary of the Amu Darya (the region of Khwarezm) and then to Khorasan, taking the city of Merv. After some initial set-backs they captured the

Ghaznavid capital of Ghazna in 1037. This event is generally taken to mark the beginning of the Seljuk empire. In 1040 the Seljuks defeated the Ghaznavids in a major battle, forcing their leader to flee for India. For the next few years they proceeded first to establish themselves in Transoxiana, at the expense of the Karakhanids, and in Khorasan, and then to make a rapid and spectacular advance to the west, taking Hamadan on the east flanks of the Zagros Mountains and reaching Mosul on the Tigris in 1042. In 1055, at the request of the Abbasid caliph, they entered Baghdad, wresting it from the Buwayhids. The caliph's invitation was prompted by his belief that he would be better treated by the Sunni Seljuks than by the Shi'ite Buwayhids.

After a pause the westward thrust continued. In 1064 the Seljuk armies moved into northern Syria, taking Aleppo. From there attacks were made on Byzantine territory in eastern Anatolia, culminating in the battle of Manzikert north of Lake Van, where the Byzantines were decisively beaten. The way was now open for the conquest of the rest of Anatolia, which proceeded apace. Apart from Lesser Armenia and enclaves around the Black Sea ports of Trebizond and Sinope, the whole of Asia Minor was overrun, the Seljuks referring to conquered Byzantine territory as Rum (Rome). Advances were also made through Syria and Palestine. By 1092 the Seljuk sultanate had reached its maximum extent, stretching from the Mediterranean to the Pamir and from the Persian Gulf to the edge of the steppe.

On the death of Malik Shah in 1092 the sultanate was divided between his brother and his four sons, with the inevitable consequence that dissent broke out, leading to civil war, and the empire began to fragment into a dozen separate polities. This weakness was quickly seized upon by the Byzantines, who orchestrated the First Crusade (1095–9), an attempt to use the west European powers to reconquer the Holy Land and in the process to reinstate Byzantine territories (pp. 399–403).

In the east the Karakhanids and what remained of the Ghaznavids acknowledged their subservience to the Seljuks, but the situation was very unstable and in the early twelfth century the Seljuk sultan moved his capital to Merv to be within easy reach of potential trouble. It was at this stage that an entirely new power, the Kara Khitans, who had been driven from their homeland on the Mongolian steppe (p. 386), began to move west through the Dzungarian Corridor, defeating the Karakhanids first at Balasagun in 1134 and then at Khujand in the Ferghana valley in 1137. At Samarkand in 1141 they confronted and defeated the Seljuk armies. The Karakhanids now became vassals of the Kara Khitans, while the prestige of the Seljuk sultanate began to decline rapidly and finally collapsed in 1194, leaving only the sultanate of Rum in Anatolia as the rump of the Seljuk empire.

The Seljuk phenomenon was fairly short-lived. In 160 years they had gone from being a minor regional polity occupying the eastern shores of the Aral Sea to becoming a world power controlling a territory almost comparable in size to the Persian empire a millennium and a half earlier. The creation of the Seljuk empire was due to the energies of three generations of sultans exploiting the opportunities offered by the fast-disintegrating Muslim empire. The energy of the new men, combined with the exhaustion of the fragmented Abbasid and Byzantine world, made the task comparatively easy. But people who were nomads at heart and whose tradition of social organization was to assign territory to family members who regarded themselves as autonomous were not able to control a straggling empire for long. Their great contribution was to bring together three disparate elements: the vigour of a nomadic lifestyle, the deep-seated inheritance of Persian culture and language, and the Islamic religion. The process had started before them, but it was they who finally wove the threads together, creating a distinctive culture quite different from that of the Arab-speaking Muslims, whose focus had, by the tenth century, shifted westwards to Cairo under the protection of the Fatimid caliphate.

The Resilient Byzantines

Until the mid-ninth century the Byzantine empire had continued to be eroded on all sides. The Arab expansion had removed from its sway Syria, Palestine, Egypt, and North Africa and the islands of Cyprus, Crete, and Sicily. The Lombards made advances in Italy, while the Bulgars took land and caused upset throughout much of the Balkans. The empire now was reduced to Anatolia west of the Taurus Mountains and the fringe of countries around the west side of the Aegean from Thrace to the Peloponnese. But although the empire was beleaguered on all sides, a remarkable tenacity held the core together throughout the two centuries of crisis. By the mid-ninth century the fragmentation of the Muslim world and the gradual weakening of Bulgarian power enabled a succession of emperors to push forward the frontiers once more until, by 1025, much of the old empire in Asia Minor and eastern Europe had been restored.

In Europe the Bulgars, who had established themselves south of the Danube, posed the greatest threat. Although now settled, they retained the ethos of their nomadic past, making them fearsome opponents. The death of the Byzantine emperor while campaigning against them near Sofia in 811 was a reminder of the threat posed by the Bulgar army, only three days' march from the capital.

The conversion of the Bulgar khan to Christianity about 865 gave the Bulgar state a new coherence and an increasingly powerful voice in the episodes of inter-state diplomacy that were interspersed with periods of aggression. After a forty-year peace in the mid-tenth century the Byzantines began a concerted campaign to reduce the Bulgars to subservience, calling in the Magyars, Pechenegs, and the Rus to assist. The final stages were completed by Boris II (reigned 976–1025), who earned for his efforts the sobriquet 'the Bulgar-Slayer'. By the time of his death the Bulgars, along with the Serbs and the Croats, had been brought within the empire. The northern border now followed the Danube and the river Drava, allowing the old overland route between the Aegean and the Adriatic, the Via Egnatia, an axis of great commercial value, to be restored.

In the east the frontier was pushed forward by about 200 kilometres by concerted military efforts between 931 and 968 designed to pick off the small Muslim states along the border. Much of Armenia was recaptured, and the north Syrian coastal zone was recovered inland to the Orontes, bringing Antioch back within the empire. The islands of Cyprus and Crete were also regained. The comparative ease with which these territories were retaken was due largely to the fragmented nature of the Abbasid caliphate. In the west the disintegration of the Carolingian empire meant that only the Byzantines were powerful enough to resist the advance of the North African Arabs in Italy.

The boundaries of the empire in 1025 put Constantinople once more in the geographical centre, with the European territories balancing those in Asia. Although a few small additions were made in the next thirty years, the empire had reached a new equilibrium. That it was able to remain united and strong was largely due to the regional infrastructure of *themes*—districts with locally recruited soldiers who were settled on state land in return for paying tax and being prepared to provide military service when required. It had served the empire well, but after the death of Basil II in 1025 successive emperors, fearful of the growing power of the military, let the system lapse, with disastrous results.

Threats came from three directions: steppe nomads from the north, Seljuks from the east, and Normans from the west. In the north the Pechenegs, who had now extended their territory to the Danube, began to raid the empire in 1033, and raids intensified as they came under increasing pressure from new waves of nomads pushing in from the east. It was the old story, and the Byzantine response followed traditional lines, combining outright attacks, diplomacy, and attempts to stir up internal discontent among their attackers. One tactic, successfully used at the time of Attila, was to create special trading centres along the frontier zone to make available commodities such as agricultural products and manufactured goods, which the nomads were avid to obtain. But still the pressures grew, and in 1091 a Pecheneg force reached Constantinople. The Byzantine response was to enlist the help of the Cuman-Kipchaks—nomads who had recently arrived on the steppe from the east and who were prepared to fight the Pechenegs to gain more territory. The strategy worked at first, but, once the Pechenegs had been crushed, the Cuman-Kipchaks began to raid the empire. They were eventually beaten back, and in 1092 the Danube was restored as the frontier, with its trading centres once more in operation to satisfy the needs of the nomads, who were now persuaded that regular trade was preferable to the vagaries of the raid. The Danube frontier was to remain stable for almost a hundred years.

The eastern frontier was a more serious problem. Here the full force of the Seljuk onslaught was felt, encouraged by the authority of the Abbasid caliph. It began with the battle of Manzikert in Armenia in 1071. The Byzantine force was defeated and the emperor taken prisoner. This unleashed civil war among the contending Byzantine factions, which opened the way for a rapid Seljuk advance through the heart of Anatolia. Within twenty years the Seljuks had reached the Aegean coast and were establishing themselves in the principal cities like Nicaea and Smyrna. The collapse of Anatolia, apart from the northern coast, was a devastating blow for the empire, not least because it had been one of the most productive agricultural areas and one of the most prolific regions for raising military levies. The fight-back began in 1094 and, with the help of the armies of the First Crusade, which arrived two years later, Alexios I Komnenos (reigned 1081–1118) managed to regain much of the west of Asia Minor, with the southern coastal zone being reconquered by about 1140, but leaving the uplands of east central Anatolia, the sultanate of Rum, still in the hands of the Seljuks.

The arrival of the Crusaders in 1096–7, albeit at the request of the Byzantine emperor, marked a significant escalation in the interference of the west European states in the affairs of the empire. In Italy the conflict between the Latin Church and Byzantium had already taken a new turn in 1059 when the pope brought in a Norman adventurer, Robert Guiscard, to rule Apulia. The Normans were the descendants of Vikings who had been allowed to settle in the Seine valley and had intermarried with the local Frankish elite, and were still behaving like freebooters keen to make territorial and financial gain wherever they could. By 1071 Guiscard had taken over the last of the Byzantine enclaves in southern Italy and was later to acquire the whole of Sicily. In 1081, with the blessing of the pope, he invaded the Balkans and for a while posed a major threat to the empire until his death in an epidemic. The Byzantine emperors had an ambivalent attitude to the Normans, believing that they could be treated like any other mercenary troops and would respond to payment rather than remain loyal to any particular cause. They were a new force and were there to be used. It was this belief that encouraged the Byzantine leadership to petition the pope in 1095 to send a western army, the First Crusade, to help to confront the Muslim threat.

The continued survival of the Byzantine empire over the three hundred years from the mid-ninth to the mid-twelfth centuries in the face of continued external threats is remarkable. The energy of its expansion up to the middle of the eleventh century, and its defence of its frontiers against onslaughts on all sides after that, can only have been achieved with a stable socio-economic system deeply rooted in tradition and able to withstand the frisson of excitement caused by the coming and going of emperors. It was a state in balance with itself that could cope with the pressure of pagan nomads on its northern frontiers and the fractious Muslim polities riven by religious differences to the east. Far more dangerous enemies were its co-religionists in the west, who were now casting covetous eyes on the riches of the old empire.

A Migration from the West: The Crusades

Having dealt with the various threats along the European frontiers of the empire, the emperor Alexios I Komnenos turned his attention to the situation in Asia Minor, where the Seljuks were now well entrenched. Although the Byzantine army was strong, Alexios felt the need for reinforcements. Well aware that the Seljuk presence was posing a serious hindrance to the passage of Christian pilgrims coming from Europe to visit the holy places in Jerusalem, he called on the pope, Urban II, to send help. The pope took up the challenge and in November 1095 called a council to assemble at Clermont in France. The rumour that this was to be a momentous occasion spread, and three hundred clerics turned up together with hundreds of laymen—so many that the meeting had to be held in a field outside the city. The pope rose to the occasion, giving a rousing speech stressing the menace posed by the barbarian Turks who were even now advancing through Christian lands. He talked of the desecration of shrines and the ill treatment of pilgrims. Christendom should rise up, rich and poor alike, and march to free the east—it was the Will of God.

His brilliant oratory was met with a tumultuous response. News spread rapidly across Europe, and people of all classes clamoured to join the Crusade. Why this should be raises interesting questions. No doubt the pope's assurance that those who died in battle would have their sins absolved offered some comfort, but there must have been more to it than that. The root cause probably lay in demography. Populations had been expanding rapidly across western Europe as large-scale warfare died down and the political situation stabilized. As numbers grew, so pressures on all levels of society intensified. For the poor, trying to gain a living on land which they did not own, life became wretched and their lords more demanding. For the elite, young men of fighting age, the opportunities were few and the social system

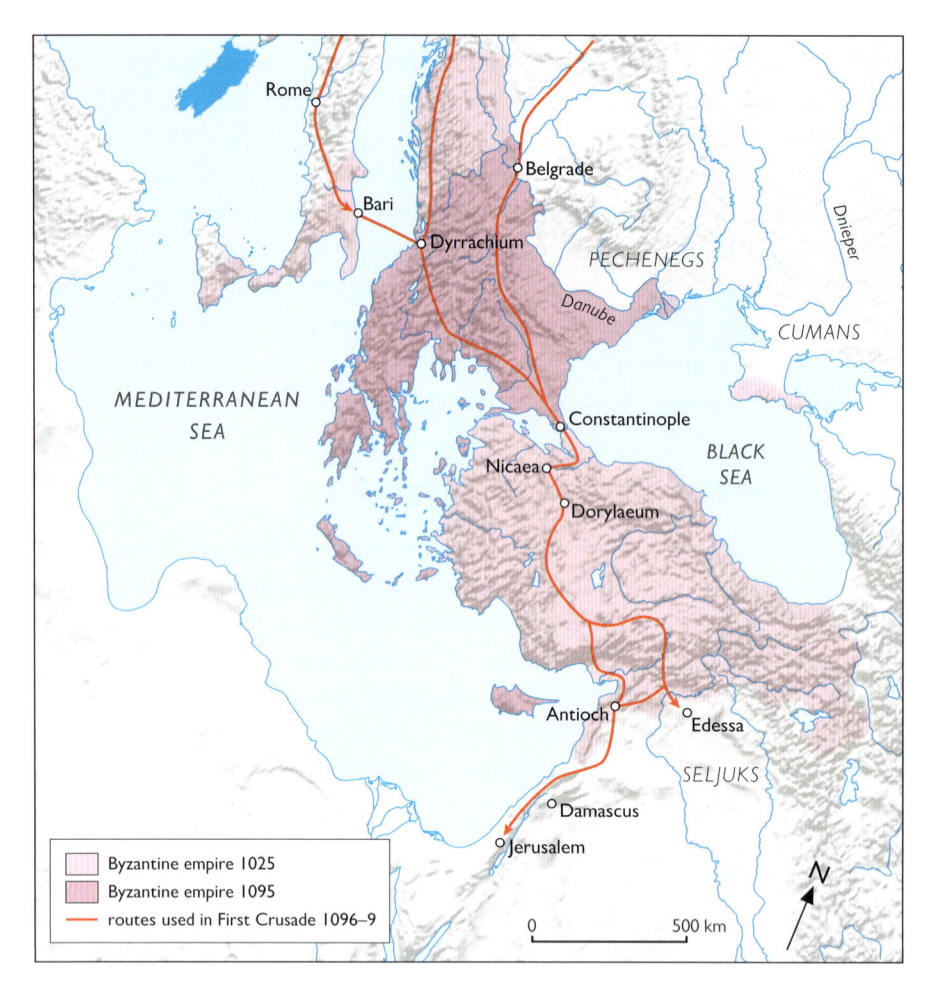

10.10 The Byzantine world in the eleventh century and the First Crusade, AD 1096–9

restrictive. These were the classic tensions that arise when populations begin to exceed the holding capacity of the land. In such circumstances migration is one of the options, offering the prospect of an exciting and less restricted life in a new ecological niche. The pope's call had come at an opportune moment for Europe's discontented masses. Throughout the continent community leaders would have welcomed the opportunity to send their surplus peasant population away and to encourage their young elite males to find a cause in a distant land where they could expend their surplus energies and not cause trouble at home. To what extent the pope understood the social tensions that were rising in the west and engineered the Crusades to siphon off the potentially explosive energy it is difficult to say, but one contemporary observer

10.11 Pope Urban arriving in France to attend the Council of Clairmont. From *Roman de Godfroi de Bouillon*

recorded the pope as saying, 'In this land you can scarcely feed the inhabitants. That is why you use up its goods and excite endless wars among yourselves.' The implication is that he was keenly aware of the evils of an unsustainable population.

The date set for the start of the Crusade was after the harvest in the summer of 1096. The Crusaders set out from various parts of western Europe, and the plan was to converge on Constantinople. Some were bands of peasants under charismatic leaders like Peter the Hermit; others were cohorts of knights and their followers. Different routes were taken. Peter's band travelled along the middle Danube and across Hungary to the Byzantine frontier post at Belgrade before crossing the Balkans to Constantinople. The duke of Lower Lorraine followed much the same route. Raymond of Toulouse marched through the Alps and down the coast of the Adriatic, while groups of knights from Blois, Normandy, and Flanders chose to travel through Italy and make the crossing from Bari to Dyrrachium and then take the famous Via Egnatia through Thessalonika to Constantinople. The movement of so many people, all needing to be fed, caused widespread disruption as rowdy elements got out of hand

and local people moved to defend their property. The Byzantine authorities, who had the responsibility of feeding the Crusaders once they had reached the empire, looked on aghast as thousands of people began to swarm towards Constantinople. A modest assessment by Princess Anna Komnene that 'all the West and all the barbarian tribes from beyond the Adriatic as far as the Pillars of Hercules were moving in a body through Europe towards Asia bringing whole families with them' was a careful understatement belying the horror the Byzantines must all have felt. In the event, the potentially explosive situation was well handled and the Crusader forces were quickly transhipped to the Asian shore to begin the reconquest.

The opening stages met with disaster when the ill-led peasant army, pillaging in the countryside around the well-fortified Seljuk capital at Nicaea, was cut to pieces by the Turkic armies. The elite Crusader armies arrived a little later. Having crossed to Asia early in 1097, they joined what remained of the peasant force. The first object, to take Nicaea, was achieved after a long siege. Then the long march through Anatolia began, the Crusaders winning a decisive battle at Dorylaeum. The rest of the march was unopposed but hindered by the scorched-earth policy the Seljuks had adopted. On reaching Cilicia, the force divided. One army, led by Baldwin of Boulogne, went eastwards across the Euphrates, taking the town of Edessa, there carving out a polity which became known as the state of Edessa.

Meanwhile, the rest of the army marched on Antioch and besieged the great city. The siege was long and hard, lasting eight months, and ended in the slaughter of most of the inhabitants. By now, dissension among the Crusaders was weakening their effectiveness as a fighting force, but leaving the knight Bohemond with his supporters as prince of Antioch, the rest made their way to Jerusalem. The city was finally taken in 1099 after a long siege and another horrendous massacre. The Holy Land was now in the hands of the Latin knights divided into four Crusader states: the county of Edessa, the principality of Antioch, the county of Tripoli, and the kingdom of Jerusalem.

The situation was not to last for long. In 1144 the Muslims retook the county of Edessa, prompting the Second Crusade in 1147–9, which came to nothing after the Crusader forces were attacked and dispersed by the Seljuks as they attempted to cross Anatolia. Meanwhile, the Muslims were gathering their strength, intent on ousting the invaders altogether.

The Crusades were a fascinating interlude in Eurasian history. The motives of those taking part have been much debated. At best they were complex and disparate. The emperor Alexios I, hoping for a contingent of manageable Frankish mercenaries to be used in driving the Turkic armies out of Anatolia, must have been shocked at what he had unleashed. At some early stage he must have judged it to be unwise to try to lead so many arrogant aristocrats and instead managed to extract an oath of allegiance from all but one. It was of little use, and in the event the leaders jealously held onto the territories they had conquered. He had, however, achieved his aim in regaining much of Anatolia. And what of Pope Urban's motives? He may genuinely have believed, as some have argued, that he saw this to be a way of bringing the Latin and Byzantine churches closer together. If so, it was a resounding failure, as subsequent events were to show. But as a safety valve designed to relieve social tension in western Europe it was a success and did much to create a new spirit of unity. And the participants? No doubt the usual conflicting mêlée of human emotion—genuine religious fervour, desperation, rebellion, and self-interest—were stirred into the dangerous mix.

The Crusades were a relatively minor happening. But in the greater scheme of things they can be seen as the beginning of the Franks' engagement in geopolitics on a truly continental stage.

The Rus and the Scandinavian Entrepreneurs

By the middle of the ninth century Scandinavian entrepreneurs had been trading with, and through, Russia for over a century, and many had settled down and integrated with the indigenous Slavonic population. A late eleventh-century document, the *Russian Primary Chronicle*, compiled by monks in Kiev, provides a narrative account of the origin of the Rus state. It records how, after an initial attempt by a group of Varangians (Scandinavians) to extract tribute from the Finns and Slavs of north-western Russia had failed, the Finns and Slavs invited another group of Varangians, the Rus, to rule them. Under the leadership of Riurik the Rus, based at Novgorod, began to take control, and it was from there that some of his followers moved south to establish themselves at Kiev, which at the time was an outpost of the Khazars. These events took place in the 860s–880s, and it was from Novgorod and Kiev that the Rus expanded their control over European Russia from the borders of Poland to the Volga.

Kiev, sited on the river Dnieper within easy reach of the Black Sea and Constantinople, provided a convenient base from which the Rus could engage with the Byzantine world. Raids began in the 880s, interspersed with attempts to establish trading relations with the Byzantine capital. It was an uneasy relationship, but by the middle of the tenth century the volume of trade had greatly increased, with the Rus ships setting out each year with cargoes of slaves, furs, wax, and honey for the Byzantine markets. A treaty agreed between the Rus and the Byzantines in 945 included the condition that the Kievan rulers should supply the Byzantines

10.12 A runic inscription scratched on a marble balcony rail in the Hagia Sophia in Istanbul. It reads 'Halfdan', who was evidently a Scandinavian visitor to the Byzantine capital. He may have been a member of the Varangian guard

with Scandinavian mercenaries on request, some to fight in the various conflicts in which the Byzantines were engaged, others to serve in the famous Varangian guard to protect the emperor. One of these Scandinavian mercenaries, Halfdan, took time off from his duties to scratch his name in runic script on a marble balustrade in the church of Hagia Sofia, where it can still be seen today.

The site of Kiev was well chosen. It lay on a major river route leading from the heart of Russia to the Black Sea and close to the interface between forest and forest-steppe, able to benefit from the resources of both and from the traditional steppe route that led east to the flourishing trading centres of the Khazars.

While the Rus rulers in Kiev were developing their uneasy relationships with the Byzantines, other Scandinavian entrepreneurs were continuing to trade with the east via the trading city of Bulgar and the Volga. After the initial phase of exploration the volume of trade declined, but by the beginning of the tenth century it had picked up again largely because of the rise of the Samanid state in Central Asia, which had become a prime trading partner. A dramatic indication of the greatly increased volume of trade is that 80 per cent of the hoards of dirhams found in Europe date to between 900 and 1030. The rise of the Samanids caused the trade-route to be readjusted. In the ninth century much of the trade had come from the Iranian plateau via the Caspian Sea to the Khazar trading port of Itil at the mouth of the Volga. The centre of Samanid power lay in Central Asia, in Transoxiana and Khwarezm, making the most convenient route to the north-west the steppe corridor leading to the Volga or direct to the city of Bulgar. It was here that the Scandinavian and Muslim merchants could meet to enact their exchanges.

The volume of the eastern trade peaked in the 940s and 950s, but around 965 the flow of silver from the Muslim world rapidly declined as the Central Asian mines became exhausted. The Scandinavians, still avid for silver, had to look elsewhere, particularly to Britain and Ireland, where there was plenty of silver to be had for the price of a raid and the spilling of a little blood.

The meeting of the Scandinavians and the Muslims in the trading cities on the Volga brought two very different worlds face to face. Something of the wonder of these engagements is captured in the account written by the Muslim traveller Ibn Fadlan in 922 at the port of Itil:

> I have seen the Rus as they come here on their merchant journeys and encamp on the Volga. I have never seen more perfect physical specimens, tall as date palms, blond and ruddy; they wear neither tunics nor caftans, but the men wear a garment that covers one side of the body and leaves a hand free. Each man has an axe, a sword, and a knife, and keeps each by him at all times... Each woman wears on either breast a box of iron, silver, copper, or gold... each box has a ring from which hangs a knife. The women wear neck-rings of gold and silver... Their most prized ornaments are green glass beads.

He adds: 'they are the filthiest of God's creatures'.

We know nothing of the Scandinavian perception of the Muslim traders but Ibn Fadlan records a prayer attributed to the Rus: 'I wish that you will send me a merchant with many dinars and dirhams, who will buy from me whatever I wish and will not dispute anything I say.'

Within less than a hundred years of this encounter regular Scandinavian trade with the east was at an end, but this did not stop the occasional adventurer setting out to explore for himself the possibilities of a quick profit. One such was a Swede, Ingvar the Widefarer, who sailed with a small fleet from central Sweden in 1036. His exact route is unclear, but he reached the Caspian Sea using the great rivers, either going via the Black Sea or following the Volga route. Somewhere in Central Asia in 1041 the expedition ended in disaster, but miraculously a few survivors managed to return home to tell the story. The relatives of those who had died erected a series of memorial stones, thirty of which survive, around Lake Mälaren. One was put up by Ingvar's mother to commemorate his brother Harald. Others mention ships' captains, navigators, and steersmen.

The story, incomplete though it is, is a vivid reminder of the difficulties of travel over these vast distances, journeying by boat along rivers and across lakes, and having to make long overland portages through the forests to get from one river system to another or to avoid rapids. No doubt there were tangible profits to be made, but for many the excitement of the journey and the honour of having made it would be reward enough.

10.13 One of the Ingvar rune stones from Gripsholm, Södermanland, Sweden. It commemorates the death of a ship's captain who died during the expedition to the Caspian Sea led by Ingvar in AD 1036–41

Between the Kievan Rus and the Byzantine Empire

At various points in this chapter and the last we have briefly considered the various nomadic groups, largely of Turkic origin, who at different times occupied the Pontic steppe, many of whom were driven westwards into the westernmost extremity of the steppe in the Carpathian basin. The constant presence of an unstable nomadic population on the northern fringes of the empire posed problems for the Byzantines, but through diplomacy, trade agreements, and shows of military strength some kind of equilibrium was maintained. The mobility of the nomadic groups and the constant pressures they were under from new peoples pushing in from the east kept the situation fluid. Those who were closest to the Danube frontier could either move on westwards through the Carpathians to the Great Hungarian Plain or cross the river into the Byzantine domain. Over and above this *longue durée* reality was the desire of the nomads for a symbiotic relationship with their sedentary neighbours. The nomadic societies required grain and other commodities, particularly luxury goods, that they could not themselves produce in sufficient quantity to meet their social needs. The goods could be taken by raiding, but could also be acquired by regular trade to everyone's advantage. There was also another kind of symbiosis. The surplus warlike energy of nomadic societies under pressure could be organized into mercenary contingents, always much in demand by the Byzantines, who were constantly short of military manpower. Given the social pressures and the competing aspirations, relations between the empire and the nomads were often fast-changing.

We have already seen how the westward movement of the Khazars drove the Avars before them. By the mid-sixth century the Avars were in the Volga region, but they were forced to move on, eventually ending up in the Carpathian basin about 680, where they established a strong and successful khanate, which lasted until 791 when they came under attack from the Frankish armies led by Charlemagne. The Bulgars, who lived east of the Sea of Azov, were also forced out of their home by the Khazars, settling first to the north of the lower Danube and, in 679, crossing into Byzantine territory to the south of the river. The reason for this dangerous move was presumably because the Avars were already making for the traditional nomad territory in the Great Hungarian Plain, leaving the Bulgars with little choice. The Bulgars later extended their influence in the Balkans, but by the eleventh century their khanate had been absorbed by the expanding Byzantine empire. While these migrations were taking place, the Khazars were busy establishing themselves between the Caspian and the Black Sea, settling into the landscape and growing rich by facilitating trade. They gave stability to the region throughout the next few centuries.

By the late eighth century new nomadic tribes were moving into the west. The Pechenegs, pushed out of Central Asia, took over the Pontic steppe on the flank of the Khazar khanate between the Sea of Azov and the Dnieper. A little later, in the early ninth century, a new tribal confederation, the Magyars, appeared on the scene. They may have originated in the Dzungaria–Altai region, migrating across the Kazakh steppe and crossing the Volga to settle first in the region of the upper Don before moving on to take control of the steppe between the Dnieper and the Carpathians to the west of the Pechenegs. This was a crucial position between the Kievan Rus, the Khazars, the Bulgars, and the Byzantines. Throughout the ninth century the Magyars acted as middlemen between their powerful neighbours, at one stage, in the war of 894–6, siding with the Byzantines against the Bulgars. The Bulgars retaliated by persuading one of their neighbouring tribes to attack the Magyars. With the situation

THE DISINTEGRATION OF EMPIRES

becoming increasingly difficult, the entire Magyar confederacy, some half a million people, decided to move through the Carpathian Mountains to take up residence in the safety of the Carpathian basin, settling at the beginning of the tenth century on either side of the Danube in the Great Hungarian Plain and Transdanubia, a territory that had previously been the homeland of the Avars.

For the next fifty years, until the middle of the tenth century, mounted Magyar forces raided widely into western Europe, reaching Italy, Provence, Burgundy, Bavaria, and Saxony. It was the first time since the Huns that western Europe had faced the terror of nomadic horsemen, but the raids were finally brought to an end in 955 when a united German force destroyed the Magyar army at the battle of Lechfeld near Augsburg. A few raids continued into the Balkans, but by 970 the force had been

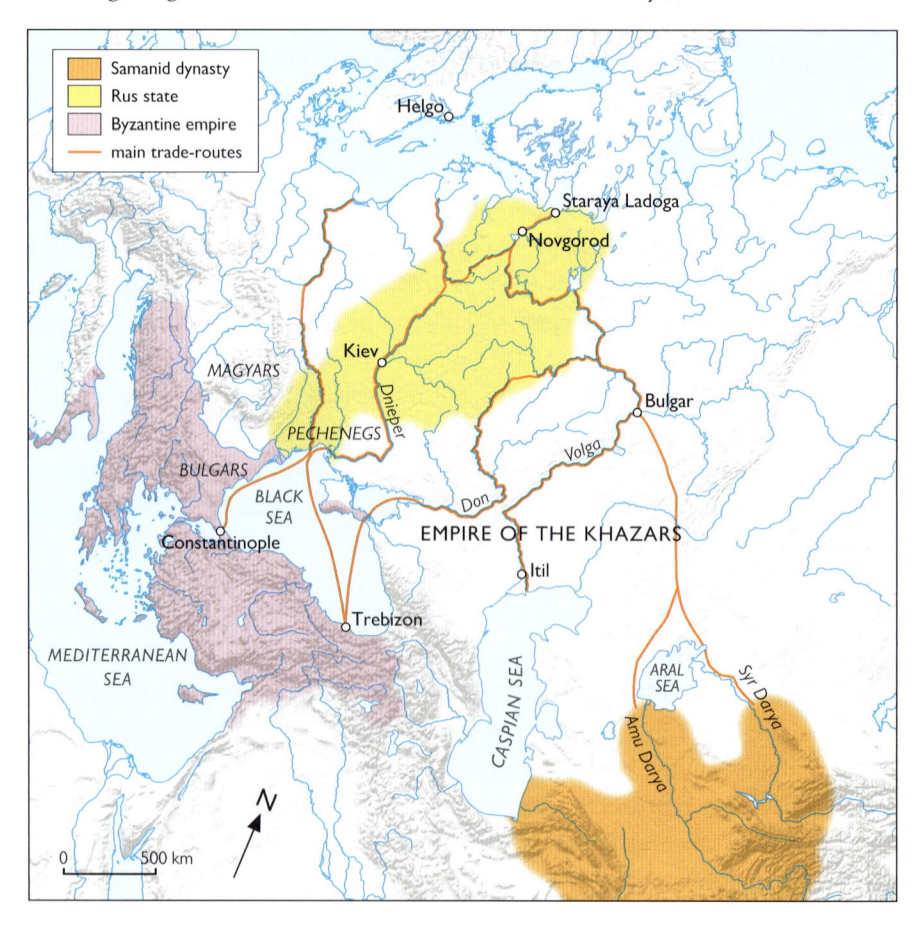

10.14 The Rus state, which arose in north-eastern Europe, served as a major trading partner with both the Byzantine empire and the area of Central Asia ruled by the Samanid dynasty. It provided access to the products of the forest zone and the Baltic beyond

spent. Magyar society was changing fast and in the year 1000 their leader, Stephen, was crowned king of a new peaceful, sedentary Christian state.

Connectivity in its Many Forms

The constant westward flow of nomads, the clash of armies and ideologies, and the hugely damaging internecine struggles within the ruling elites created the narrative history of the age, but below these surface eddies the deep rhythms of life continued. People raised food to feed their families, and those who were able traded with others to obtain resources for themselves and to turn a profit. Beneath the bluster of aggression the simple connectivities that bound communities continued. Two remarkable caches of documents, one sealed in a cave at Dunhuang on the Silk Road, the other recovered from a synagogue in Fustat (Cairo), throw an intriguing light on the contrasting patterns of connectivity at work in the tenth and eleventh centuries.

The oasis town of Dunhuang commanded the way between the caravan routes around the Taklamakan desert and the Gansu Corridor giving access to China. The tenth century had been troubled times for the Tarim region, and the fall of the Buddhist kingdom in Khotan in 1006 to the Muslim Karakhanids may have been the event that drove the Buddhist monks of Dunhuang to seal off the library in their cave monastery. The latest document in the collection dates to 1002. The cave was rediscovered about 1900 by a former soldier, and was visited by the traveller-antiquarian Sir Aurel Stein in 1907, after which the remarkable cache of documents, long protected there, was introduced to the world.

Among the documents recovered a number, dealing with the inventories of the monastery and with the passage of embassies and traders, give glimpses of the movement of goods along the caravan routes and the availability of exotic products from abroad. The monastery received gifts from those passing through, made in recompense for hospitality and in piety to the Buddha. Among the goods listed in the inventories are textiles, metalware, incense, and precious stones. Much was of relatively local origin, but mention of Iranian brocade and Merv silk hint at long-distance contact. Another item, possibly of Iranian origin, was listed as a silver censer with silver lions. Other foreign-sourced products included lapis lazuli, agate, amber, coral, and pearls. Materials such as these reflect the movement of the traders and pilgrims, whose links stretched to distant parts along the trading networks. But these treasures were few, and were probably accumulated over a long period of time. The bulk of the everyday trade seems to have been in local goods.

One set of documents gives a fascinating insight into a failed embassy involving seven princes who set out for China in the mid-tenth century. They carried with them

360 kilograms of locally sourced jade, together with horses and leather tack, camels, falcons, yak tails, textiles, furs, medicines, herbs, minerals, fragrances, amber, coral, and slaves. While they must have acquired the amber and coral through trade, everything else could have been gathered relatively locally. In the event the mission failed, and cargo was dispersed to local purchasers as the envoys attempted to raise funds to pay for their return home.

Other documents from the library refer to trading at a more basic level. One collection is a series of reports from a merchant who went from village to village buying up woven cloth from different families. On one trip he acquired a hundred pieces of white cloth and nineteen pieces of red wool-based fabric suitable for making warm clothing. On another trip he managed to find four dyed pieces and twenty-one undyed. Another text written in Uighur mentions silk, woollen cloth, cotton, slaves, sheep, lacquer cups, combs, casseroles, knives, pickaxes, embroidery, and dried fruits, all local products, together with musk and pearls, which must have come from outside the region.

While it could be argued that the surviving documents do not give a fair reflection of the trading system in the ninth and tenth centuries, taking the evidence as it stands one is bound to conclude that trade was now low-level and largely local. Only state-sponsored delegations carried goods in quantity, and, even then, foreign products from outside the region were rare. This sector of the trading networks linking China to the west had suffered from the political uncertainties of the time: its connectivity was restricted, and such trade as there was served the needs of local communities looking after their own limited interests.

The contrast with the picture built up from the documents recovered from Fustat, dating mainly from the eleventh to the mid-thirteenth century, could not be greater. The collection consists of the letters, contracts, invoices, price lists, and suchlike resulting from the activities of generations of Jewish merchants from the tenth to the nineteenth century. It had accumulated in the store-rooms of a synagogue and came to light in 1896.

Fustat was the primary city of the Fatimid dynasty, which now controlled most of North Africa and Egypt and, for a while, Palestine and Syria. One contemporary writer describes it as 'the treasure-house of the West and the emporium of the East', saying that it far eclipsed Baghdad. The cache of documents certainly bears this out. Fustat articulated trade between the Indian Ocean and the Mediterranean. The documents mention a network of Jewish merchants around the Mediterranean, in Andalusia, Sicily, and Tunisia, who were in contact with other networks in the port of Aden and on the Malabar coast of India. One merchant is mentioned as being resident in India in 1097–8, while another had lived in India from about 1132 to 1149, where he owned a foundry. It was the merchants resident in Fustat who managed the contracts between the two far-flung networks. Close family ties and reliance on friends and partners were crucial to the success of these potentially hazardous ventures. One institution that developed at this time was the *karim*, an annual convoy of ships organized for mutual security. One can imagine the anxiety of the merchants waiting for the safe arrival of their precious cargoes.

There can be no doubt, from the Fustat archive, that after about the year 1000 trade between the Indian Ocean and the Mediterranean was organized on a massive scale and the quantity of goods arriving from the Indian Ocean by sea must have been enormous. These would have included luxury products from China, transhipped in the ports of the Malay peninsula, increasing in quantity as China's sea-borne trade was expanded under the Song dynasty. Trade with the East African coast also developed at this time, reaching as far south as the ports of Kilwa and Manda. At Kilwa there is archaeological evidence of ocean trade as early as the ninth century, and at Manda, Islamic and Chinese pottery of the ninth and tenth centuries has been found.

It is impossible to quantify the changing volumes of long-distance trade passing through the different networks, but standing back from all the detail it does seem that the ocean routes were beginning to take over from the overland networks after the mid-eighth century. The turmoil caused by nomadic migrations and the clashes between the Tibetans and the Chinese must have made the old Silk Road unsafe. At the same time, the growing confidence of seamen, the skills of shipbuilders, and the institutionalization of trade by the port authorities would have made ocean travel a far more attractive and profitable option.

A More Distant Perspective

Amid the clash of arrogant elites, the relentless westerly flow of population, and the frenetic bustle of traders, other developments of great moment were under way. In Song China, enclosed and inward-looking, the beginning of an industrial revolution was in progress. Coal was being exploited, water power was being developed to drive textile machines, and wood-block printing was perfected together with movable type. This last, in conjunction with the now widespread use of paper, facilitated the multiple-copy printing of books and paper money. Gunpowder, first developed in the Tang period, was now being used to fire missiles from early forms of iron guns, to power rockets, and to be packed into thick ceramic containers to make lethal bombs. At the same time medicine was developing fast, human bodies were being dissected, and major progress was being made in pharmacy. The burgeoning pharmaceutical industry became so extensive that a government agency, the Imperial Drugs Office, was set up in 1076 to ensure that patients got a fair deal.

The frantic pace of change in industry and science was matched by innovation in painting, literature, and pottery-making, which were seen by many contemporaries to be a way of compensating for hectic daily life. One artist, Guo Xi (1020–90), in his book *Advice on Landscape Painting*, accepts that it is natural for humans to seek solace in the forests, streams, and hills, but duty requires them to remain in the busy world. The purpose of the artist is to provide them with landscape paintings to offer peace in the home when they return from work.

Meanwhile, in the Muslim cities of Central Asia, a quite separate intellectual life was thriving, with major advances in mathematics, astronomy, and medicine continuing to build on the stunning discoveries of scholars like al-Khwarizmi, whose famous treatise on mathematics was introduced to a stunned west European world through its translation, *The Compendious Book on Calculation by Completion and Balancing*. Many of the works of Central Asian scholars were now reaching the west through contacts with the Muslim communities in Iberia. Once in circulation the translations inspired western scholars to new heights of scientific endeavour. But the decline in overland trading contacts between China and the west at this time ensured that the traditions of scientific and artistic endeavour in the far east and the far west developed in their own distinctive ways, largely in ignorance of each other.

One final reflection needs to be made on this crucial period, 840–1150. It was now that the old divisions between pastoralists and sedentary agriculturalists were beginning to break down along all the interfaces across which they had once confronted each other: the north China steppe, Central Asia, and the Pontic steppe. New waves of pastoralists met earlier nomads who had already settled down to take up agrarian practices and to form states. They soon followed suit. In this way urbanism crept gradually northwards into the steppe.

بر مسجد نخار را		
نه در بندان دام و دانه ستم	شمار است تا بان جهانده ام	ان سای شما مسید هیج پنا
جو باد خزان آمد نوبر آمدن	بزد ندمذ عزان من آمدم	هر دو جهان تان من جان جا
سوتم پیکارکی خشک	با نام ازکدره یوم	نشتکار ره را روز با باشد سیا
نبرید برید نب با ب سل	آن روز بر دشت نابد سا	بریزند جوزر باکی رو ید
اگر مسجد ار خانقه شد	پیکارا آنش با افروخت	زر در برد سیم برسرش پر

11

THE STEPPE TRIUMPHANT,
AD 1150–1300

THE Orkhon valley, in the centre of the Mongolian steppe, was the ancestral home of successive nomadic confederations who had grown strong here in the lush, protected landscape and had spread out to rule great tracts of eastern Asia and beyond. It was the homeland of the Xiongnu, and during the period of the Turkic empire, in the sixth to eighth centuries, it was a major centre of power, as the rich funerary monuments of the valley vividly display. From 750 to 840 the Uighurs had their capital here at Ordu-Baliq (Khar Balgas), and during the tenth and eleventh centuries it lay within the fortified northern borders of the Khitan empire.

The Orkhon rises in the Khangai Mountains of Mongolia and flows northwards to Lake Baikal in Siberia. In its upper reaches the Orkhon is a stream constricted to a narrow flood-plain by the flanking hills and mountains, but at Harhorin (ancient Karakorum) the river suddenly opens onto a wide plain, well watered and fertile. Upstream the lush, hilly pastures provide ideal grazing for horses, with sheep and goats roaming the upper slopes, while the plain, suitably irrigated, could produce grain in abundance. It was a favoured landscape and Karakorum commanded the full range of resources. It was here that Chinggis Khan began to consolidate the Mongol empire in 1220, but it was his successors who formalized the camp, converting it into a city with a defensive wall enclosing a square kilometre. Karakorum served as the

11.1 The upper reaches of the Orkhon valley in the central Mongolian steppe. The fertile, well-watered valley was the centre for Turkic, Uighur, and Mongol cultures

Mongol capital until 1256 when Qubilai Khan moved the centre to Xanadu and later to Dadu (Khanbaliq, Beijing). The city continued as a regional centre until its destruction by Ming troops in 1380. Karakorum undoubtedly had many natural advantages, but its choice as the rallying point of the Mongols by Chinggis and his immediate successors lay in the belief that the Orkhon valley was the spiritual home of the eastern steppe nomads—a landscape steeped in the memory of the ancestors, from whom legitimacy and strength could flow.

The Rise of the Mongols in Eastern Asia

By the middle of the twelfth century the geopolitical situation in eastern Asia had settled down. The Khitans, who had dominated Mongolia and much of northern China (as the Liao dynasty), had been driven westwards by the Jurchens from Manchuria, who had established themselves as the Jin dynasty in north China south of the Gobi desert. Their western neighbours the Xixia (of Tibetan origin) occupied the crucial Gansu Corridor and the routes to the west through the Tarim basin. The Xixia and the Jin together formed a wide buffer zone, heavily influenced by Chinese culture, between the fully sedentary Song empire to the south and the nomadic tribes of Mongolia to the north occupying the Gobi and the broad steppe zone beyond.

The many different tribes living on the Mongolian steppe in the early twelfth century spoke the Turkic and Mongolian languages. Though tribal loyalty gave them a sense of discrete identity, the practice of exogamy meant that there was much interchange between groups. The Mongols were but one, and by no means the most powerful, of a dozen or so different tribes known by name. Inter-tribal rivalries led to conflicts, and inter-clan disputes could be no less murderous. The Mongols and their eastern neighbours the Tatars were avowed enemies. Chinggis Khan, as he later became known, was the son of a leader of a lesser Mongol clan who chose to name his boy Temüchin after a Tatar enemy he had recently killed. Temüchin was 9 years old when his father was murdered by the Tatars, and the family were turned away to look after themselves. By his ability to lead raids and his charismatic leadership, Temüchin soon acquired a following of like-minded young warriors who were prepared to give up their own tribal allegiances to join him as his comrades (*nökers*). Later they were to become his imperial guard and his trusted generals. With his increasing success in raiding, his following grew until he was strong enough to negotiate with other tribal leaders, building obligations through marriage and through military partnerships. Eventually he was recognized as leader of the Mongols. He then set about bringing other tribes under his command. In 1206, at the age of about 40, he had succeeded in unifying Mongolia, and in a great meeting (*quriltai*) he was formally recognized as the supreme khan of all the tribes, an achievement confirmed in his assumed title Chinggis Khan ('Universal Ruler').

Chinggis's power was based on his command of a highly efficient cavalry army under his absolute control. All adult males below the age of 60 could be required to serve, leaving the daily tasks of looking after the flocks and herds to the women, children, and the elderly. The men were natural riders, brought up in the saddle and trained to hunt: to be called up to fight required little adjustment. Estimates of the size of the fighting force under Chinggis's direct command vary, but suggestions of

11.2 Gigantic stainless steel statue of Chinggis Khan opened in 2008 on the banks of the river Tuul to the east of Ulan Bator, Mongolia. Since gaining independence from the Soviet Union, the Mongolian nation has reinstated Chinggis Khan as a symbol of their nationhood. There is a viewing platform large enough to hold ten people on the horse's head

about 105,000 men in 1206 seem reasonable and are supported by another estimate of 129,000 at the time of his death in 1227. Given that each rider probably took with him at least five horses, the horde on the move was considerable. Even so, these are conservative figures when compared to those quoted for the Mongol armies of conquest fighting in Central Asia.

Like other eastern steppe nomad armies before, the Mongol army was organized in units of ten, a hundred, a thousand, and ten thousand. Men brought into the force after armed resistance were dispersed among the units, but the coherence of tribes who were regarded as friendly was usually retained. The overall effect was that old tribal loyalties gave way to loyalty to the units of ten thousand (*tümen*) or to one of the smaller units. In addition to the main fighting force there was also an elite imperial guard (*keshig*) of about ten thousand recruited from among the original group of followers reinforced with men selected from the tribal nobilities. This had the effect of binding the tribal elites directly to the person of the khan while enabling him to keep a close eye on their loyalty.

In the beginning the fighting forces were composed largely of lightly armed cavalry carrying short recurved bows, but there were also detachments of more heavily armed mounted lancers. Such a varied force was well suited to engagements with other nomadic horsemen, but, once the Mongol armies had moved out of their familiar steppe environment and were confronting sedentary communities protecting themselves in fortified cities amid irrigated agricultural land, new skills had to be acquired through the expedient of employing foreign experts in siege warfare and detachments of infantry. The Mongol war-leaders were quick to learn and to adapt to the demands of their ever-expanding world.

11.3 Mongolian hunter with his stocky steppe horse depicted in a Chinese miniature. Constant practice as hunters using the bow from horseback was good training for fighting as cavalry

In uniting the tribes of Mongolia, Chinggis had created a huge army held together by expectations of conquest. With unification complete, he faced a turning point. To reduce or disband the force would have led to disintegration into squabbling polities and a loss of everything that had been achieved. The only way forward was further conquest, directed, in the first instance, against the Sino-Mongolian borderlands to the east and south, home to the empires of the Jin and the Xixia, to be followed by a direct assault on Song China beyond. This had been the traditional response of the great nomadic confederations over the last fifteen hundred years.

In 1209 the Xixia were attacked and rapidly agreed to submit to the Mongol leaders. This brought the all-important Gansu Corridor under Mongol control, opening up the way to the west via the oasis routes around the Tarim basin. It also facilitated attacks on the Jin and the Song. Two years later the invasion of the Jin began, and in 1215 the north Jin capital at Dadu (Beijing) was destroyed and several other towns taken. Confronted by sedentary urbanized northern China for the first time, Chinggis's instinct was to follow the advice of the Mongol leaders, who said that the country was useless and he should exterminate all the Chinese and turn the land back to pasture for their animals to graze. An alternative view, however, was offered by a newly arrived scholar-official, Yelü Chuchi, a member of the Khitan aristocracy who had served in the Jin court and had been summoned by Chinggis in

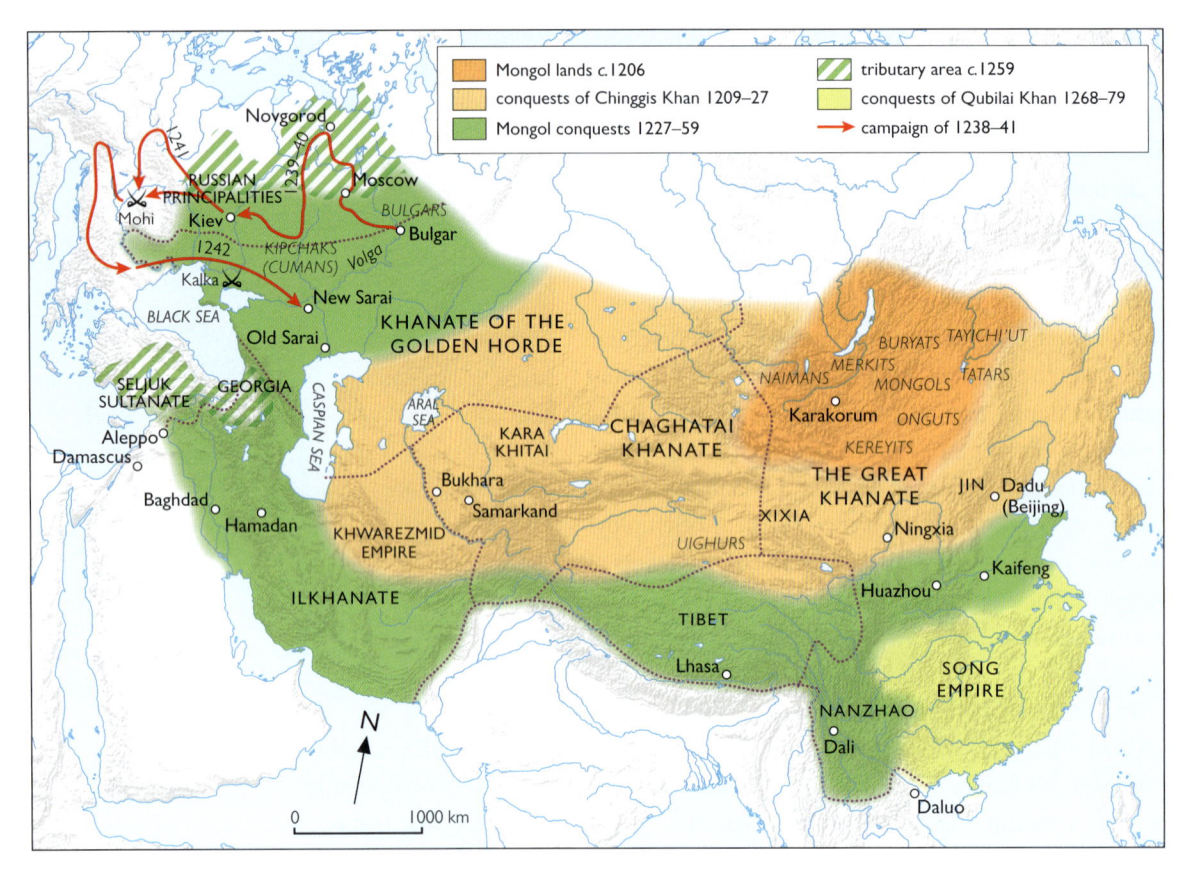

11.4 The empire of the Mongols as it developed during the thirteenth century AD

1218. His advice was persuasive. Since Chinggis had conquered the world, he could have anything he wanted. It would be sensible to tax land and trade, and to make profits on wine, salt, and iron and the produce of mountains and marshes. In this way the revenue in a single year would amount to half a million ounces of silver, eighty thousand rolls of silk, and 400,000 *piculs* of grain. Chinggis saw the sense of the argument. In facing this new and alien world he was willing to learn from those who understood it. It was this willingness to adapt rapidly to new environments and situations that gave Chinggis the facility to conquer at great speed and to hold vast territories.

In 1218 Chinggis called a temporary pause on the southern advance into China and turned his attention to the west. While this decision may have been driven by events, it has plausibly been suggested that it was part of a deliberate policy: the perceived need to settle the situation in the steppe and the deserts before proceeding with the conquest of the sedentary state of China. Chinggis will have been aware of the mistakes of the past when confederations of nomads from the eastern steppe had flung themselves eagerly at the Chinese state only to leave a dangerous vacuum in their home territories, from which new confederacies could emerge to challenge them. Chinggis made his base resolutely in the heart of Mongolia and, having taken control of the Xixia and the Jin territories on his southern and eastern border, now turned his attention to the west. Song China could wait.

The Conquest of Central Asia

In Central Asia the disintegration of the Seljuk empire in the mid-twelfth century created a volatile situation in which the hitherto insignificant state of Khwarezm rose suddenly to power. Khwarezm occupied the fertile delta area where the Amu Darya fed into the Aral Sea and Lake Saryqamysh. Its two principal towns, Khiva and Gurganj, lay on the caravan route leading from Bukhara and Samarkand around the northern shores of the Caspian Sea to the Volga and beyond. It was a small and prosperous polity with few pretensions to leadership until the middle of the twelfth century when, in a series of rebellions against the Seljuks between 1138 and 1148, it began to expand its borders to take in new territories around the Aral Sea and between the Aral and Caspian seas. Once under way the spread of the power of Khwarezm continued. Bukhara and Samarkand were taken under control in 1158, and ten years later campaigns were mounted to the south across Khorasan and into the Iranian plateau. In the period 1200–20 Khorasan was finally conquered, and expansion to the north and east absorbed the territory up to the Syr Darya and the Ferghana valley. By 1217 the shah of Khwarezm was strong enough to send an army against the caliph in Baghdad. Although the expedition ended in disaster, such were his successes in Central Asia that the shah felt he could proclaim himself a second Alexander the Great. The creation of the Khwarezmid empire spanning the mid-twelfth to the early thirteenth century corresponded with the Mongol expansion under Chinggis Khan.

Having extended his power across the territories of the Jin and Xixia and received the submission of the Uighurs in the Tarim basin, Chinggis now turned his attention to the Kara Khitai in the west, the remnant of whose empire had been taken over by Küchlüg of the Naiman tribe, who were the traditional enemies of Chinggis's Mongols. Clearly, if there was to be peace and stability on the steppe, as a prelude to the conquest of China, Küchlüg and his power base had to be destroyed. Of no less relevance was the fact that the Kara Khitai controlled the steppe trade-routes leading to the riches of the west. In 1218 Chinggis sent one of his generals into Central

Asia. Küchlüg was hunted down and killed, and the territory of the Kara Khitai was brought within the Mongol domain. The Mongols were now neighbours of the Khwarezmid empire.

How Chinggis perceived the Khwarezmids is not clear, though by referring to the shah as his 'son' he implies that he considered them to be subservient, and so to be absorbed into the Mongol realm when the time was right. In the event, a diplomatic incident brought matters to a head.

Chinggis was eager to encourage trade with the west, and to do this he ensured that the traditional overland trade-routes were well guarded for the safety of travellers. Three merchants from Bukhara took advantage of the improved conditions to transport a range of exotic goods, including gold-embroidered fabrics and silks, to the Mongol court. Chinggis was impressed and, having bought the goods, decided to send back with the original entrepreneurs a massive trade delegation of 450 Muslim merchants provided with gold and silver ingots. They carried with them a letter to the shah of Khwarezm from Chinggis: 'Merchants from your country have come among us and we have sent them back to you in the manner that you shall hear. And we have likewise dispatched to your country in their company a group of merchants in order that they may acquire the wondrous wares of those regions...'. However, when the trade mission reached the Khwarezm frontier city of Otrar on the Syr Darya, the governor of the city had them detained and killed and their goods confiscated on the grounds that they were spies. This would not have been unlikely since merchants had long been a source of intelligence, but the incident was ill-judged and could not go unchallenged. Ambassadors were sent to the shah demanding recompense and that the governor be surrendered. The shah responded by killing one of the ambassadors and humiliating the others. This was just one of the flawed judgements that he was to make.

The Mongol response was devastating. In 1219 Chinggis launched a three-pronged attack on Central Asia. In response the shah, instead of trying to meet the armies in the field, dispersed his troops to guard each of the major cities and eventually fled to an island in the Caspian, where he died. This left the Mongol armies to pick off the cities of Central Asia one at a time, often with a level of violence unprecedented since the time of the Assyrians. A detailed description of the capture of Samarkand in 1220 written by the historian Ata-Malik Juvaini (c.1226–1283) gives some idea of the processes involved. The first imperative was to slaughter the shah's military forces. Then the Islamic religious leaders and other scholars were gathered together and given special protection. Thirty thousand craftsmen were identified and distributed among Chinggis's sons and kinsmen, while a similar number of young men were dragooned

THE STEPPE TRIUMPHANT

into a military levy to serve with the Mongols. The rest of the population, those who were allowed to return to the city, were required to pay a substantial ransom. It was clearly in the interest of the Mongol conquerors that the cities should continue to function as trading centres. It was equally in their interests that scholars, craftsmen, and able administrators should be absorbed into the greater Mongol empire to

11.5 (*Left*) Persian miniature from the Shahanshahnama (fourteenth century) showing Chinggis Khan addressing an audience of the city elite from the pulpit of the Kalon Mosque in Bukhara. After explaining that he had been sent by God to punish them, Chinggis sacked the city and killed most of its leaders

11.6 (*Below*) The Mongol army shown besieging a town using a catapult. They readily adopted siege engines, using the expertise of conquered people, when they confronted urban-based enemies. From a manuscript of Rashid al-Din

423

serve the insatiable demands of the Mongol elite for luxury goods and to provide the administrative infrastructure for the fast-expanding empire. Muslim bureaucrats and intellectuals were much in demand and could reach the highest positions. The historian Juvaini is a case in point. He was a native of Khorasan whose grandfather had served the shah. As a young man Juvaini served in the khan's court at Karakorum and later went on to become governor of Baghdad under Mongol rule. Without the varied skills of the Central Asian urban elites the Mongol empire would have been unable to function.

The conquest of the Khwarezmid empire was accomplished in 1220, stunning the local inhabitants with its speed and brutality. Chinggis dealt effectively with Transoxiana, leaving his son Tolui to rampage through Khorasan with even greater savagery in the following years. Whether he intended to incorporate Central Asia as part of the empire is unclear, but the appointment of Mongol viceroys suggests that he planned to maintain a firm hold on the newly conquered land.

The task completed, Chinggis set off south on a limited reconnaissance mission, passing through Kabul to the Indus valley before leaving for Mongolia in 1223. A second force of some twenty thousand riders under the command of General Subetei went off to explore the west. Having travelled around the south end of the Caspian Sea they passed through Georgia, sacking Tbilisi on the way, and crossed the Caucasus into the more familiar surroundings of the Pontic steppe. In 1223 the expeditionary force defeated the Slavonic princes of Kiev at the battle of the river Kalka (now Kalchyk) in the valley of the Dnieper. After this they explored the Crimea and travelled up-river towards Kiev. From there a swing eastwards through the forest-steppe brought them to the territory of the Volga Bulgars. Having followed the river southwards, they reached the north shores of the Caspian before crossing the Kazakh steppe on their way back to Mongolia. It had been a monumental journey of reconnaissance, paving the way for the campaign of conquest that was to begin thirteen years later.

When Chinggis reached Mongolia in 1223, he found that the Xixia, who had refused to send troops to support the western campaign, were now building an alliance with the Jin, threatening to destabilize his southern front. This was potentially dangerous, and in 1226 he mounted a furious campaign, tearing through their territory and winning several battles, which culminated in the destruction of the Xixian capital, Ningxia, on the Yellow River, and the annihilation of the imperial family. Soon afterwards Chinggis died, perhaps in battle. His body was carried back to his Mongolian homeland for burial.

Contemporary observers leave little doubt that the destruction and loss of life wrought by Chinggis was on a monumental scale, particularly in Khorasan. One contemporary estimate of the death toll at the sack of Herat put it at 1.6 million; another suggested that it was as high as 2.4 million. While the figures may be exaggerated, there was universal agreement among contemporary observers that death and destruction were meted out on a vast scale, a disaster exacerbated by the removal of skilled men to serve elsewhere in the empire. Although the cities of Central Asia were eventually to recover and thrive as the trade network was re-established, the after-effects of the onslaught lasted for several generations.

After Chinggis

On the death of Chinggis in 1227, the empire was divided among his sons, largely in accordance with Mongol practice, and the apportionments were confirmed in an assembly (*qurultai*) held two years later. Ögedei, his third son, became Great Khan, as Chinggis had decreed before his death. It was normal for the eldest son to inherit territories furthest from home. These would have fallen to Jochi, but he had predeceased his father so his son Batu took over a huge swath of territory from the Kazakhh steppe to eastern Europe—as far west as the hoof of a Mongol horse had trodden. This later became known as the khanate of the Golden Horde. Chinggis's second son, Chaghatai, assumed control of Central Asia as far west as the Amu Darya, while the youngest son, Tolui, inherited the original Mongol homeland.

Under Ögedei's khanate (1229–41) the empire grew: large tracts of Persia were added, Russia and parts of eastern Europe were brought into the realms of the Golden Horde, and the Jin empire was totally absorbed.

Later successions, following the death of Ögedei, were less orderly as family rivalries took their toll. Ögedei's son **Güyük** became Great Khan in 1246 but died two years later. He was succeeded by Möngke (1251–9), the eldest son of Chinggis's youngest son, Tolui, and in time he was succeeded by his brother Qubilai (1260–94). Meanwhile, in the other khanates power struggles continued as rival factions of the family competed with each other. Yet by the end of Möngke's reign in 1259 the Mongol empire had grown to be the largest the world had ever seen, stretching from the Pacific to the border of Hungary and Poland and from the northern forests and taiga of Asia to the Persian Gulf, the Himalayas, and the jungles of Myanmar and Annam (now central Vietnam). Only Song China held out, and that was soon to be brought under Mongol rule, when Qubilai turned his attention to its conquest in 1268. By 1279 the Mongol empire had reached its limits, less than a hundred years after Temüchin had begun to build his small band of followers in the heart of the Mongolian steppe.

11.7 The Mongol city of Karakorum in the Orkhon valley of central Mongolia. The site, used by Chinggis Khan, was established as a permanent settlement under Ögedei Khan. It was destroyed during the Ming period when the Buddhist monastery of Erdene Zuu was built on the site of the khan's palace

THE STEPPE TRIUMPHANT

11.8 Modern Karakorum lies partially over the site of the Mongol town, its economy based now, as then, on the fertile Orkhon valley, which spreads before it. The white enclosure wall of the Erdene Zuu monastery can be seen at the top right

The Conquest of China

By the time of the death of Chinggis Khan a great swath of northern and western China held by the Xixia and the Jin had been brought under Mongol control, but it was a partial conquest left on hold as affairs in Central Asia required urgent attention. On his return to the east, the question of China had once more become pressing. In 1226 the Mongol army moved again into the territory of Xixia, and, as we have seen, the capital, Ningxia, was laid waste. The next year a campaign was mounted against the Jin city of Huazhou, but the death of Chinggis brought the advance to a temporary halt.

Once confirmed in power, Ögedei turned his attention to the south, beginning by setting up an alliance with the Southern Song. Further campaigns against the Jin saw their capital at Kaifeng fall in 1232, finally breaking the rule of the Jurchens: many fled back to their homeland in Manchuria, but others joined the Mongol army. When it became clear that the Mongols intended to hold onto their Chinese conquests, the Song attacked them, provoking Ögedei to declare war on the emperor. It was a bold decision. The population of China amounted to about a hundred million, while that of Mongolia was barely one million, of which the fighting force would have numbered between a hundred and a hundred and fifty thousand. To be effective in all the fields of conflict throughout Eurasia the Mongols had to rely on forces recruited from the many other nationalities. In taking on Song China they were also pitting themselves against an urban-based state, much of whose territory was divided into irrigated arable plots, making cavalry warfare very difficult. In the event, it was to take forty-five years before the Song were conquered, largely because events in the west were once again to take precedence.

Once Möngke had been confirmed as Great Khan in 1251, he turned his attention to the Southern Song, who were now strong enough to put up a stout resistance. The Mongol strategy was to surround them first by pushing down through south-western China in 1253, overrunning the territory of Nanzhao (Yunnan province) and then sweeping through Annam to take Daluo (Hanoi) on the South China Sea in 1257. With the Song encircled, the scene was set for the final kill, but at the crucial moment Möngke died. His brother Qubilai, who was leading the forces against China, immediately called an assembly in the field, which declared him to be the new Great Khan—an unconstitutional act which unleashed civil war among the Mongol elite and saved the Song for another decade.

Eventually, in 1268, Qubilai was able to return to the conquest of the Song. The capital, Hangzhou, was taken in 1276, and by 1279 the rest of the empire was fully under Mongol control. Qubilai had already (in 1272) proclaimed himself to be emperor of united China, the first ruler of the Yuan dynasty. In choosing the dynastic name Yuan ('the Origin'), he was playing to ideological beliefs deeply rooted in the Chinese psyche: he was also claiming the Mandate of Heaven, which all Chinese would understand. Though his territorial ambitions were not satisfied by the acquisition of China, the conquest marked the maximum extent of the Mongol empire. Subsequent campaigns, to Japan in 1281, Champa (southern Vietnam and Cambodia) in 1281, Annam in 1285, Myanmar in 1287, and Java in 1292, met with little success: the oceans and the jungles were alien territory to the Mongols.

In 1272 Qubilai moved his capital to Dadu ('New-Built Great City'), siting it in two massive enclosures already begun in 1266. They were described in meticulous detail

Dadu

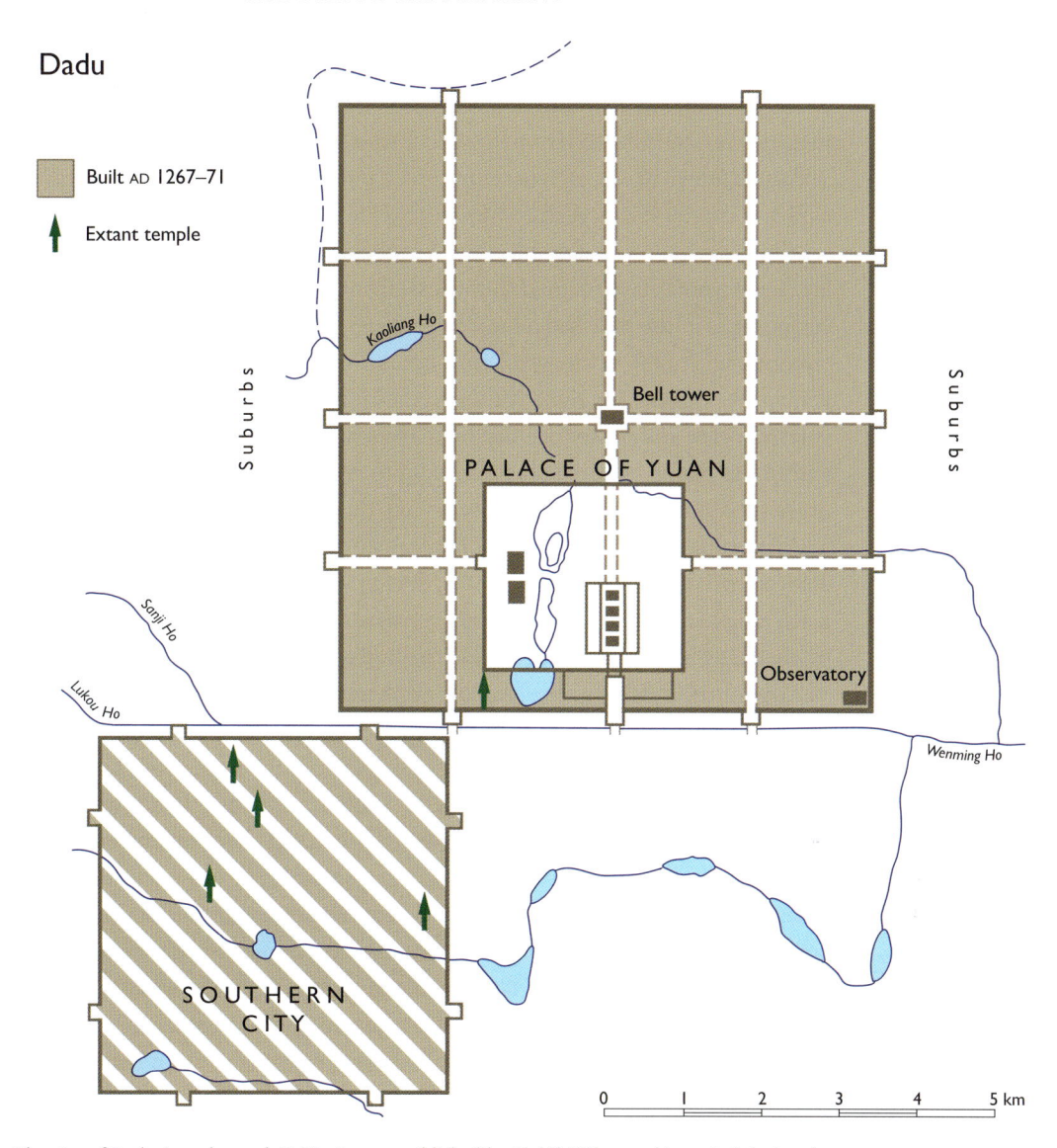

- Built AD 1267–71
- ↑ Extant temple

11.9 The city of Dadu (now beneath Beijing) was established by Qubilai Khan as his capital during the Yuan dynasty

by Marco Polo. The southern enclosure of Dadu housed the Chinese. According to Marco Polo, it was laid out on a rigorous grid system: its buildings were 'handsome, with corresponding courts and gardens ... The whole interior of the city is disposed in squares, so as to resemble a chess board, and planned out with a degree of precision and beauty impossible to describe.' The northern enclosure was Kambala ('City of the Sovereign'). It, too, was laid out on a classical Chinese grid system with a massive palace enclosure in its southern part, complete with lakes and gardens and groves of mature trees transplanted from the wild forests. Amid all this Chinese splendour it is said that Qubilai had a patch of steppe grassland planted to remind him of his homeland. It was a significant gesture. Many of his Mongol kin would have been appalled to see the Great Khan abandon his nomad roots to embrace the luxuries of a sedentary life. They would have pointed to the lessons of history, which showed how northern nomads in the past had all too easily been seduced by the novelties of Chinese culture, the city life of an agriculture-based society sapping their restless energies. Perhaps the critics were right. Although the long reign of Qubilai was a time of comparative peace and prosperity, his Yuan dynasty, the Mongol rule of China, was over within less than a hundred years, brought to an end by Chinese rebels in 1368, who drove the Mongols from the country, paving the way for the Ming dynasty.

China, united under its Mongol rulers after three hundred years of division, enjoyed half a century or so of peace, during which its culture flourished. Writers had a far greater freedom to express themselves than before, and landscape painters reached new heights of achievement. The traditions of the north and south of China were reunited, creating a reinvigorated excitement. Symbolic of this was the creation of a new Grand Canal, nearly 1,800 kilometres long, joining Beijing with Hangzhou in the south and making the transport of surplus rice from the south both rapid and inexpensive. That said, the Mongol system of government was heavy-handed and relied on a rigorous class system. The most privileged class was the Mongols: they were followed by immigrants, usually skilled specialists from Central and western Asia. Below them were the former subjects of the Jin empire, and at the bottom, the Song Chinese. It was hardly a system to endear itself to the subservient population. Yet for fifty years Yuan China flourished and visitors from the west were overawed by the sophistication and opulence of its culture. It was stories of Qubilai's court, brought back by Marco Polo, that inspired generations of western entrepreneurs to try to make the journey to share in the splendours of 'Cathay', travelling by land and later by sea.

The end, when it came, was rapid. Struggles for power among the Mongolian elites gave rise to factional fighting among local Mongol warlords. The troubles were further exacerbated by environmental disasters and the outbreak of a devastating plague. Large-scale revolts followed, and the dynasty was toppled. One of the first things that the new Chinese Ming dynasty was to do was to re-engineer the old northern frontier walls to create the Great Wall of China, a symbolic and functional border designed to ensure that henceforth the northern nomads were kept firmly in their steppe homeland.

The Mongols in the Middle East

Chinggis's campaigns against the Khwarezmid empire of Central Asia had brought the cities of Transoxiana under Mongol control. On his death much of this territory passed to his second son, Chaghatai, together with the lands of the Kara Khitai extending westwards into the Tarim basin and northwards across the steppe to Lake Balkhash. For a while the Amu Darya served as the southern border.

Following the accession of Möngke as Great Khan in 1251, a new forward policy was set in train both in China and in the Middle East. The Great Khan's brother Hülegü was appointed to the command of the latter. His first task was the destruction of the Nizari branch of the Ismailis, whose power centre lay in the Alborz Mountains on the south shore of the Caspian Sea. They were a radical Muslim sect whose speciality was killing their opponents by stealth, usually by stabbing. Those who perfected the art were known as Assassins, a name possibly derived from the word 'hashish'. The Nizaris were both a power and a menace, but in 1256, three years after leaving Mongolia, Hülegü received their surrender and proceeded virtually to annihilate them.

The way was now clear to push west, through Hamadan to Baghdad, where in 1258 the caliph was invited to submit. The city resisted for a while, but eventually the caliph surrendered. Baghdad was looted, two hundred thousand or more of its inhabitants were killed, and the caliph executed, bringing to an end the Abbasid caliphate. The act was applauded by Christians and Shi'ites alike. The Mongol dominance had now reached the Euphrates, which provided, as it had done for previous empires, a convenient western frontier behind which to consolidate and from which to probe the west.

In 1260 Hülegü marched into Syria, taking Aleppo and Damascus, to confront the Mamluks, an elite of emancipated white slaves who had by now taken control of Egypt and Palestine, but the death of the Great Khan Möngke in 1259 had caused much uncertainty, and Hülegü felt it necessary to return to Persia leaving only a small force in Syria, which was soon defeated by the Mamluks near the Sea of Galilee. Although the Mongols raided Syria on subsequent occasions, the Euphrates marked the effective limit of their territory: Syria presented an ecology wholly alien to steppe nomads.

It is quite possible that when Möngke commissioned his brother Hülegü to conquer the Near East, he was tacitly agreeing to him setting himself up as ruler of a new khanate. The territory west of the Amu Darya soon became known as the Ilkhanate (subservient khanate), but Hülegü's authority went unchallenged by the central authorities. He and his successors were to rule the Ilkhanate—in reality a reincarnation of the old Persian empire—from 1259 until 1335, when, on the death of the last khan, central government broke down. By this time the Mongol elite had embraced Islam and had intermarried with the indigenous population. The vigour of the nomads had been dissipated.

The Thrust into Peninsular Europe

The expeditionary force of some twenty thousand Mongol horsemen led by General Subetei that had explored the eastern approaches to Europe in 1221–3 following the defeat of the Khwarezmians provided the Mongols with a first glimpse of the lush Pontic steppe then occupied by Cuman-Kipchaks, a nomadic people not unlike themselves. The fertile western steppe was immediately attractive. Further to the north, in the forest-steppe and the forest zone beyond, they learnt of the rich trading cities of Kiev and Bulgar commanding the great river routes to the north. On the river Kalka they met and defeated the Slavonic armies of the princes of Kiev. The brief reconnaissance was enough to show that here was a world worth conquering.

For the indigenous population the sudden appearance of these wild horsemen was a shock. As the Novgorod chronicler recorded in 1224, 'The same year for our sins, unknown tribes came, whom no one exactly knows, who they are, nor whence they came out, nor what their language is, nor of what race they are, nor what their faith is; but they call them Tartars . . . God alone knows who they are' (*The Chronicle of Novgorod*, trans. R. Michell and N. Forbes). After the unnerving confrontation a brief normality returned, but the Mongols were now a presence on the fringes of Europe. The vast region west and north of the Caspian Sea was put under the control of Batu, grandson of Chinggis, who began to consolidate his authority on the steppe by leading an offensive against the Bulgars of the middle Volga region.

In 1235, after the Jin had been finally conquered, the Great Khan Ögedei ordered a new offensive in the west. The combined force moved first against Bulgar, which was taken in 1237, and then northwards through the Russian principalities, which all collapsed in the face of the onslaught with the exception of Novogorod, where the onset of spring made campaigning difficult for the invaders. The Mongol army, claimed to be six hundred thousand strong, now turned south to Kiev, which fell late in 1240. The massive force ascribed to the Mongols may well have been enhanced by other tribes throwing in their lot with the invaders. The nomadic Cuman-Kipchaks, who lived in the Pontic steppe, were certainly one. Confronted by the Mongols, many of the Cuman-Kipchak clans decided to join them, while others chose to migrate to the Great Hungarian Plain to seek sanctuary but were murdered by the Hungarians.

Meanwhile, in the spring of 1241, the attack on Europe began, with the invading army divided into two forces. One marched into Poland and east Germany, defeating an army of Poles and Teutonic knights at the battle of Legnica. The second, larger force invaded Hungary, decisively defeating the defending army at Mohi (now Muhi) on the Great Hungarian Plain, where, in the familiar steppe landscape, the Mongols began to build a homeland. From here further expeditions were mounted against the west, but with winter closing in, the Mongol forces returned to the Hungarian steppe to rest before a new spring campaign could begin.

Whatever plans there may have been for a spring offensive, all was thrown into disarray when news arrived that the Great Khan Ögedei had died in Mongolia. In the political uncertainty of the moment, Batu judged it safer to move to the Pontic steppe, where he could be ready, if required, to defend his territory. Not only was the Pontic steppe more central to his interests, but its unlimited grassland could support a much larger mounted force than the restricted steppe of Hungary.

Thereafter, the Golden Horde, as it became known in the west, began to focus on the Pontic-Caspian steppe with its capital at Old Sarai on the lower Volga. Its control of the Russian principalities was administered through Mongol agents and a compliant local Russian elite: the constricting forests and rivers of the north were never a comfortable environment for nomads used to the freedom of the open grassland. Nor did western Europe offer much attraction. After the initial exploration in 1241 subsequent khans showed little interest in it apart from some limited involvement in the 1290s. Again, the reason is probably that the Mongols regarded it as an alien land with little to offer that could not be acquired by trade.

The relationship of the Golden Horde to their cousins the Ilkhanate was complex. They shared a long land boundary marked by the Caucasus and the deserts of Central Asia, and it was probably the desire of the Golden Horde to gain control of the caravan routes through northern Persia and Azerbaijan that led to the outbreak of hostility between the two khanates in 1261–2. Tensions were made worse when the khans of the Golden Horde began to ship captives via the Byzantine world to the Mamluk sultanate in Egypt to serve in the Mamluk armies engaged against the Ilkhanate in Palestine and Syria. The open clash between the two khanates marks the beginning of the break-up of the Mongol empire.

The Ilkhanate was to collapse within a few generations, but the Golden Horde was much more resilient. Whereas the Ilkhanate Mongols lived in the territory of an advanced urban society and were soon assimilated, the Golden Horde inhabited the steppe, where their nomadic way of life and their social systems could continue uncorrupted. The indigenous tribes already occupying the steppe when they arrived shared a similar lifestyle and came ultimately from much the same homeland. The

Golden Horde retained its identity and remained a recognizable component of the south Russian population until the late eighteenth century. Even the deportation of the Crimean Tatars by Stalin at the end of the Second World War has not totally removed the Mongolian presence from the current gene pool.

The Mongols in Retrospect

The sudden rise of the Mongol empire was, by any standards, a remarkable phenomenon. How was it that a steppe nomad tribe could, in the space of a mere eighty years, conquer the greater part of Eurasia? There were many factors involved. Foremost was the nature of social organization on the eastern steppe. Tribal allegiances had become weakened by long-drawn-out conflicts, and new power groups were emerging in the latter part of the twelfth century—confederations based on personal loyalties to those who could and would lead. Total obedience was expected at all levels in the chain of command. In such a system charismatic leaders like Chinggis could acquire large followings irrespective of tribal affiliations, and could wield absolute power. Yet the number of active fighters under his command was not large, seldom exceeding a hundred and forty thousand, but all had grown up in a nomadic lifestyle: they were trained from youth in the art of hunting in groups, and they belonged to a pastoral society that could maintain itself even though the adult menfolk were away from home for long periods of time.

Once set in train, the system gained momentum: the entourage looked to its leaders for success and for ever-increasing returns, and so the scope of their activities had to grow. At first, Chinggis did little more than had nomad leaders before him. He challenged the agricultural and semi-agricultural polities on his southern periphery and chased opponents westwards through Dzungaria onto the Central Asian steppe: so it had always been. But the urban world he found in Central Asia was in a state of decline. The states were fast disintegrating, leaving the cities to look after themselves. In three years of violent and bloody assault he suddenly became master of Central Asia and, rather uncertainly, had to put in place a loose system to control it. Reconnaissance expeditions showed him what lay beyond.

The death of Chinggis in 1227 posed a potential crisis, but by following nomad tradition, which entailed leaving discrete blocks of territory to his sons, he propagated the empire, transplanting the Mongol system into distant parts of the world, where the imperative to lead and to grow took root with a fresh energy. Firm control from the centre set new goals for the peripheries, requiring them to expand. In 1235 the Great Khan Ögedei initiated the advance into Europe, and when Möngke became Great Khan in 1251 he set one brother, Qubilai, the task of conquering Song China and the other, Hülegü, the challenge of taking over the Middle East. While these initiatives would undoubtedly expand the empire and bring benefits, behind them probably lay the need to keep the elite in gainful and demanding engagement well away from the centre of power in Mongolia.

But the empire had reached beyond the boundaries of its ecological niche. In China, Qubilai and his successors relaxed into the comforts of the Chinese sedentary lifestyle, while the Ilkhanate of the Middle East was subsumed into the indigenous cultural inheritance. The Golden Horde, in its wisdom, kept out of peninsular Europe and left the Russian principalities of the forest zone on a loose rein, preferring to remain firmly based in the familiar steppe. The Chaghatai khanate likewise remained within the steppe, mountain-steppe, and desert zone, where its nomadic lifestyle could be maintained. While the Golden Horde and the Chaghatai khanate survived, the urban-based Ilkhanate and the Yuan dynasty quickly collapsed.

The successes and failures of the Mongol empire were undoubtedly conditioned by the environmental niches in which its various manifestations were planted, but another factor can be discerned. The Mongol empire was very much a three-generation phenomenon. The founder, his sons, and grandsons were the builders, but after that familial coherence broke down and rivalries became destructive.

Yet, that said, a disparate band of nomad horsemen coming together on the Mongolian steppe had, in the thirteenth century, gone on to create the largest empire the world had ever seen.

The Latin Advance and the Death Struggles of Byzantium

The First Crusade, called by Pope Urban II in 1095, caught the mood of the time, and for nearly two hundred years, in eight separate Crusades, young men of fighting age made for the east, encouraged by the idea that they were fighting for Christianity and for the freedom of the Holy Land. The territories in the Levant, which they had wrested from the Muslims in the First Crusade, were precariously held at great cost for a few generations, but by 1291 the fall of Acre to the Mamluks marked the end of the adventure.

For all the sound and fury that the Crusades have generated in literature and in history books, the whole episode would have warranted little more than a footnote to the history of Eurasia were it not for the Fourth Crusade, which began to gather at Venice in 1202.

The background to this momentous event starts a little earlier, in 1189, when the army of the Third Crusade, led by the German emperor Frederick Barbarossa, moved into Byzantine territory expecting support but was met with outright opposition by

11.10 The walls of Constantinople were begun by Constantine the Great, but the massive land defences seen here were the work of Theodosius, built in the fifth century AD. The city's defences stood firm against all attacks until the Crusaders broke through in AD 1204

the Byzantine emperor. In response the Crusaders besieged Philippopolis (Plovdiv) and campaigned through Thrace, capturing the city of Adrianople (Edirne) before amassing a fleet outside the walls of Constantinople. The Byzantines had little option but to relent and to agree to provide transport and food for the Crusaders. It was a telling incident. On the one hand, the Byzantines were showing irritation at being expected to support successive Latin adventures in the Holy Land which were of little advantage to them; on the other, it was a reminder to the west that the Byzantine empire was ripe for the picking.

The opportunity came in 1202. While the army of what was to become the Fourth Crusade was gathering at Venice awaiting transhipment by the Venetian fleet to the east, Alexios Angelos, a scion of the Byzantine royal house, fled to the German court seeking help for his father, who had been deposed. Other political intrigues were also at work. Venice, under its octogenarian doge Enrico Dandolo, was engaged in a struggle with other Italian states for control of the Mediterranean maritime trade-routes, and the Venetian offer to transport the Crusaders, for which they intended to charge a huge amount, was part of a carefully crafted strategy to gain credit, gold, and possibly territory at the expense of their rivals. When it became clear that the Crusaders could not afford the Venetian price, Alexios offered to pay 800,000 pieces of gold if they helped to reinstate him in Constantinople. The doge, for his part, asked the Crusaders to make a detour via the Adriatic port city of Zara (Zadar), which they were required to capture and give to Venice. Thus, the Crusaders who enrolled to fight the Muslims were being used as pawns in the power struggle of Christian polities.

Having taken Zara for the doge, the Crusaders arrived at Constantinople in July 1203 and Alexios was installed as co-emperor with his father. It soon became clear that the promise of gold to pay the Venetians could not be met by the city, and after months of rioting and the assassination of Alexios, the new emperor to emerge from the chaos, Alexios V, simply refused to pay. The Crusaders, led by the doge, now had the excuse they had been waiting for, and in April 1204 they stormed the city and overcame its defences. Pillage, rape, and destruction lasted for several days. They then set about installing a Latin emperor and dividing the Byzantine empire among the conquerors, with the greater part going to Venice. Those of the Byzantine elite who had managed to flee retained some of the territory of the old empire, carving out principalities for themselves. The three largest were the despotate of Epirus, the empire of Nicaea, and the empire of Trebizond.

The sack of Constantinople by the Christians, after the city had stood firm against all comers for a thousand years, was a devastating blow: it was the end of the old order, a weakening of the political geography of the world which, two and a half centuries later, was to allow the Muslim Ottoman Turks to pour into eastern Europe. But at the time the western world rejoiced at the short-term gains that were to be had. Nothing more clearly sums up the mood of the time than the gloating delight of one of the knights present:

> Of holy relics I need only say that it contained more than all of Christendom combined; there is no estimating the quantity of gold, silver, rich stuffs and other valuable things—the production of all the climates of the world. It is the belief of me, Geoffrey de Villehardouin, marshal of Champagne, that the plunder of this city exceeded all that had been witnessed since the creation of the world.

The wealth of the great city, its holy relics and its huge array of art treasures accumulated from across the ancient world, was now dispersed throughout the Christian west, with Venice taking the greater share. The holy relics were particularly valued since they encouraged pilgrimage, and pilgrims brought great wealth to the

Byzantine states
Islamic states
Venetian territory
Crusader territory
Fourth Crusade
Venice
Zara
Dyrrachium
DESPOTATE OF EPIRUS
KINGDOM OF THESSALONIKA
LATIN EMPIRE
Constantinople
PRINCIPALITY OF ACHAEA
BLACK SEA
Nicaea
Sinope
EMPIRE OF NICAEA
Crete
SELJUK SULTANATE OF RUM
Trebizond
MONGOL ILKHANATE
MEDITERRANEAN SEA
COUNTY OF EDESSA
Antioch
Edessa
PRINCIPALITY OF ANTIOCH
Tripoli
COUNTY OF TRIPOLI
Acre
FATIMID CALIPHATE
Cairo
Jerusalem
KINGDOM OF JERUSALEM
N
0
200 km

11.11 (*Opposite*) The Fourth Crusade in AD 1204 saw the western Christian states turn on the eastern Christian empire of Byzantium, substantially dismantling it

shrines where the relics were displayed. Venice, poised for greatness, saw the fallen Constantinople as a source not only of monetary wealth but also of fine building materials—columns and marble inlay—and the stuff of cultural heritage like the bronze horses of the great quadriga taken from the emperor's pavilion at the head of the hippodrome. These icons of power have since graced St Mark's Square in Venice, apart from an appearance in Paris when, briefly, they were appropriated by Napoleon.

The trauma of the sack of Constantinople echoed throughout the eastern Mediterranean for generations. The sense of loss, of the end of time, is nicely captured by the lament of the contemporary historian Niketas Choniates: 'Oh city, city, eye of all cities, subject of narratives all over the world, supporter of churches, leader

11.12 The bronze horses which now grace St Mark's Basilica in Venice were once part of a quadriga set up in the circus of Constantinople. They were transported to Venice as part of the loot brought back from the Fourth Crusade

of faith and guider of orthodoxy, protector of education, abode of all good, thou has drunk to the dregs the cup of the anger of the Lord . . .'. Venice emerged triumphant. In Constantinople the doge took the most salubrious quarter for the Venetian entrepreneurs and presided over the dismemberment of the Byzantine empire between the Crusader elites. He was not interested in the inland areas, but encouraged the Frankish barons to share them out, creating a confusion of feudal fiefdoms. Instead he demanded for Venice strings of islands and well-fortified coastal locations along the sea-routes that were to be so crucial for his fast-developing maritime empire. So long as he could keep the seaways open for Venice and restrict the trade of his rivals, he was satisfied. So it was that Crete and Euboea became Venetian territory, the Cyclades were offered to any Venetian noble who could take and hold them, and a series of fortified ports was positioned along the sea-lanes leading from Venice to Constantinople and the eastern Mediterranean. At the end of the dismemberment of the Byzantine empire the doge, Dandolo, could add to his titles 'Lord of a Quarter and Half-Quarter of the Roman Empire'.

The birth of the Venetian empire of the sea marked a significant shift in European history. Several Italian city states—Genoa, Pisa, and Amalfi—were attempting to create maritime empires in the Mediterranean, and now Venice had triumphed over them all. It was, in fact, the beginning of the process later to be more fully developed by the Atlantic states, notably the Portuguese, Spanish, English, and Dutch, driven by curiosity and commercial imperative, that saw the command of the oceans create an entirely new kind of connectivity.

Although it was not long before the Byzantine elite, exiled in the empire of Nicaea, ousted the Latin dynasty and returned Constantinople to Byzantine rule (in 1261), the empire was now only a pale reflection of its former self and quite unable to defend the approaches to Europe when the Ottoman Turks advanced on the west two centuries later.

The Holy Land: A Side-Show

The huge investment of toil and blood lavished by the west European states in an attempt to maintain a presence in the Levant came to nothing. It was an episode of Eurasian history blown out of all proportion by Christian chroniclers. The initial influx of Crusaders who set out in 1096 established a foothold, creating four separate states, but two centuries later, in 1291, the capture of Acre and the fall of Jerusalem to the Muslim Mamluk sultanate brought the dream to an end. It had begun as a response to population pressures in the west, the new challenge in new lands providing a safety valve, much as Greek colonization in the eighth to the sixth century BC

11.13 The Krak des Chevaliers in Syria is a supreme example of a Crusader castle built and extended during the twelfth century. Its massive strength reflects the difficulty experienced by the Christians in maintaining their tenuous hold on the Holy Land and the huge input of resources which this entailed

had siphoned off the surplus population from the Greek city states, alleviating demographic pressures. But in the end it failed because the flow of immigrants from western Europe was not sufficient to sustain the necessary infrastructure of the new settlements. Those who set out with such enthusiasm found themselves in a hostile environment very different from the green fields of France and England. In simple biological terms, they had chosen an ecological niche for which they were ill-prepared: this, together with the hostility of the indigenous population, encouraged many of those who survived to return home. The few who stayed were forced to create massive fortifications to protect themselves, an activity which dissipated the limited resources they controlled.

One factor that might have played to the Crusaders' advantage was the arrival of the Mongols in Syria in 1260. At first the Christians showed an interest in this new potential ally. The ruler of Antioch and Tripoli joined forces with them (for which he was excommunicated), and the Christians were present when the Mongols entered Damascus, but when, later, the Mamluk sultan sought assistance against the Mongols, the Christians in Acre decided to allow the Islamic forces safe passage through Christian-held land and even supported them with supplies. It was this ambivalence towards the Mongols that deprived the Crusader states of a potential opportunity to beat the Mamluks once and for all. In the event the Mongols were defeated by the Mamluks at the battle of Ain Jalut in Galilee. In a subsequent letter written by Hülegü to Louis IX, king of France, the Mongol leader explained that he had had to withdraw his army from Syria because of the lack of available grazing for his horses. The Mongol cavalry could only be effective where grassland was abundant: once more the ecology of the Levant offered a real constraint to the trajectory of history.

Travellers from the West

The rise of the Mongols in Central Asia and their appearance in eastern Europe and the Near East brought the new power into the consciousness of the European world and reignited a curiosity about the people of the Far East. The immediate concern of the western leaders was to learn of the intentions of the Mongols and to establish diplomatic relations with them. The king of Hungary had sent a friar to make contact with the Mongols in the 1230s, with little effect, but the incursion into Europe by Batu in 1241 had refocused minds, and in 1245 Pope Innocent IV dispatched three embassies headed by members of the mendicant orders. Only one, that led by the Franciscan John of Plano Carpini, managed to reach the Great Khan, Möngke, in Mongolia. The message he brought back was clear: the pope and the other European leaders were required to make haste to the court of the Great Khan to offer their submission. An ambassador sent by Louis IX in 1248 returned with a similar demand. Not deterred, Louis sent another Franciscan friar, William of Rubruck, to Mongolia in 1253–5 as a missionary, not as an ambassador, to gather intelligence. William reached Karakorum and had several meetings with the Great Khan, recording in his book *Itinerarium* a detailed description of his journey, the Mongol court, and of his many religious debates. His outward journey had taken him across the Black Sea to the Crimea and then across the Pontic steppe through the Cuman-Kipchak khanates to Old Sarai on the Volga. Once around the north side of the Caspian and the Aral seas, he made his way across the Kazakh steppe and the Altai Mountains and thence to Karakorum. His return journey took a more northerly route to Old Sarai and then south along the western shore of the Caspian Sea, eventually crossing Anatolia to reach the Crusader states of the Levant. Both the outward and the return journeys were carefully planned to miss the Central Asian and Tarim basin routes, which at this time were probably regarded as dangerous.

William's *Itinerarium* gives a detailed account of Mongol life and of the cosmopolitan nature of the capital, Karakorum, where Muslim and Chinese craftsmen jostled for custom. He met a French silversmith, a woman from Lorraine who cooked dinner for him at Easter, several Germans, and the nephew of an English bishop. The city was surrounded by an earthen wall and was provided with four gates, outside each of which was a specialized market, one for grain, one for sheep and goats, one for oxen and carts, and one for horses. Within the walls, beside the Muslim and Chinese quarters and 'twelve idol temples', two mosques, and a Christian church, there were palaces for the court officials and the great number of ambassadors, and the palace of the khan. William was particularly impressed by the bustling nature of the place and its energetic religious life, encouraging lively debates. The picture he took back to the west on his return in 1255 was very much at odds with the initial impression of the 'barbarian Tatars' gleaned from encounters with the Mongols who had attacked Europe thirty years earlier.

About ten years after William of Rubruck made his observations of the merchant colony in Karakorum, two Venetian merchants, Niccolò and Maffeo Polo, were en route to the east. From their base in Constantinople they usually traded with the Crimea, but in 1260, perhaps sensing that political changes were in the air, they extended their activities to Central Asia. At Bukhara they were persuaded by an envoy to make the trip to China to meet the Great Khan, Qubilai, who had recently moved his capital to Dadu (Beijing). In 1266 they arrived at the court and were welcomed by the khan, who was eager to learn about the west and its Christian religion. Before they left for home he provided the brothers with letters for the pope requesting that he send a hundred learned teachers and oil from the lamp in the Church of the Holy Sepulchre. They eventually arrived back in Venice two years later and in 1271 were ready to set out again, this time accompanied by Niccolò's 17-year-old son Marco. Instead of a hundred scholars, the pope was able to provide only two Christian monks, both of whom fled the expedition at the earliest opportunity.

The party sailed from Venice, landing at Acre (still at that time in Crusader hands), and travelled overland to Tabriz near the Caspian Sea, then through Persia to the Gulf port of Hormuz, expecting to find a vessel to take them to China, but all that was on offer was what he described as 'wretched affairs . . . only stitched together with twine made from the husk of the Indian nut'. Having abandoned the idea of a sea-voyage, they travelled inland through Herat and Balkh, crossing the Pamir to reach the Tarim basin, taking the southern route through Khotan to Dunhuang, where they spent a year. Eventually they crossed the Gobi desert to China, reaching the khan's summer palace at Xanadu in May 1275, where they were welcomed by Qubilai.

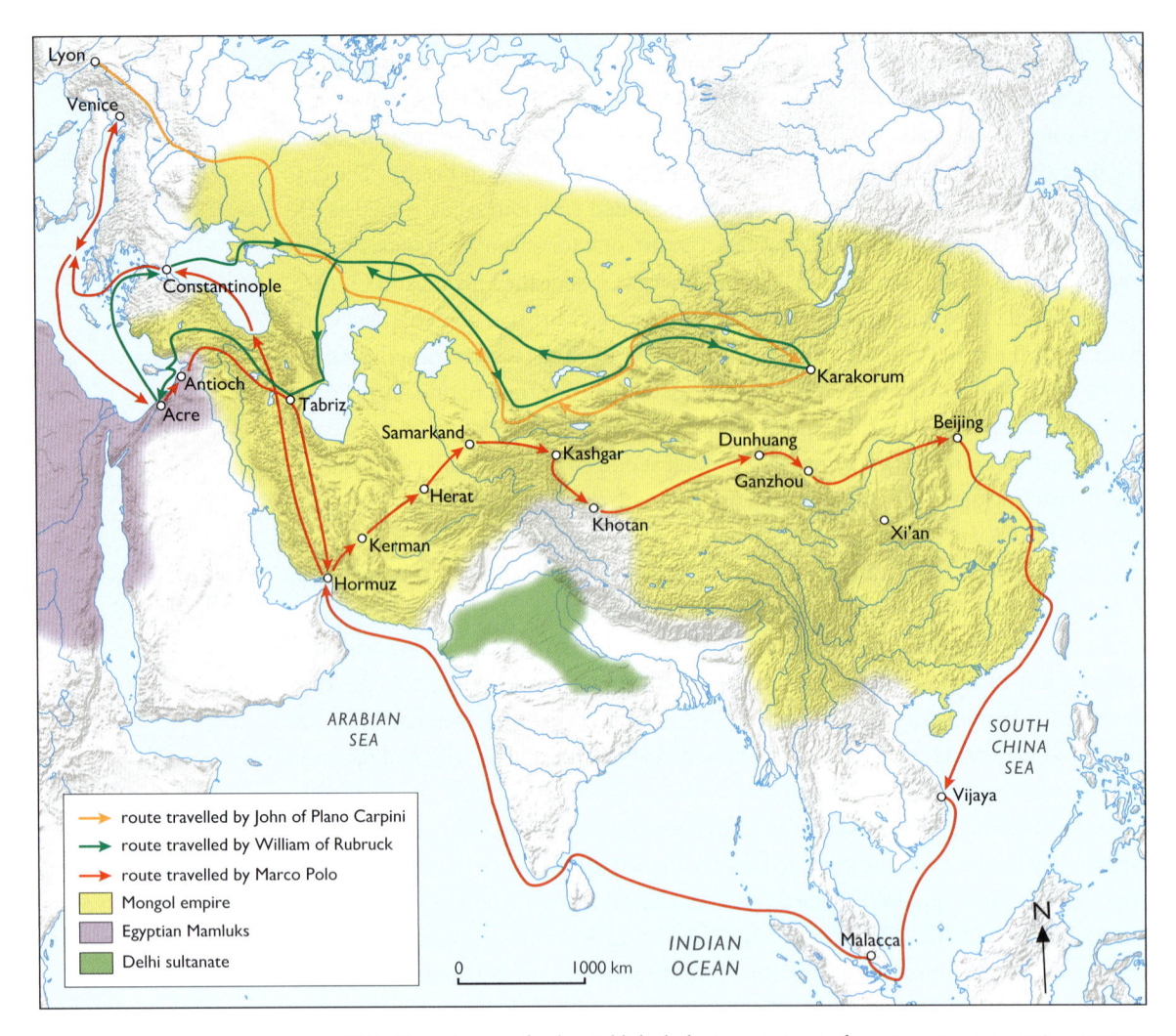

11.14 With Mongol power firmly established, the trans-Asian trade-routes were once again comparatively safe for traders. In the thirteenth century many western travellers set out for the Mongol court, some returning to write about their travels

Marco's linguistic and administrative skills made him popular with the khan, who employed him in an administrative capacity that required him to travel extensively through China as far south as Burma. After years in service to the khan, the family were eventually allowed to leave in 1292 as part of an official naval expedition comprising fourteen junks that were engaged to accompany a Mongol princess on her journey to Persia, where she was to marry the local khan. The journey took them through the Strait of Malacca, across the Indian Ocean to the southern tip of India,

444

and then up the west coast of India to Hormuz. It lasted two years, and Marco claimed that, of those who set out, six hundred died en route. From Hormuz the Polo family crossed Persia and Anatolia, eventually reaching Trebizond, and then travelled by sea via Constantinople to Venice, where they arrived in 1295.

Three years later, following his capture during a war between Venice and Genoa, Marco Polo found himself locked in a Genoese prison in the company of a writer of romances, Rustichello da Pisa, to whom he dictated his story. It was Rustichello's fertile imagination and skills as a writer that have given us the extraordinary and intriguing *Livres des merveilles du monde*, Marco Polo's famous *Travels*. The *Travels* gives a brief description of his journeys to and from the court of Qubilai together with detailed accounts of people and places supposedly seen by him in the course of his seventeen years away from home. From the moment of its publication the *Travels* was criticized, incredulous observers regarding the books as largely fabrications embroidered around scraps of information readily available at the time. But modern opinion now accepts the general narrative as largely accurate and the descriptions as having a reasonable basis in observations made by Polo himself or information collected by him during his journeys. Seen in the context of the records made by William of Rubruck and others, there is no reason to doubt that

11.15 Mongolian passport of the thirteenth century, guaranteeing the holder a safe passage throughout the Mongol empire

western travellers frequently visited the Mongol courts and that they were generally welcomed by the khan. Marco Polo's stunning revelations may have come as a shock to Venetian society, but by the late thirteenth century the number of travellers making the long overland or ocean journey to Mongolia and China had greatly increased. The exploits of Marco Polo stand out simply because his imprisonment by the Genoese provided him with the time and a willing chronicler to commit them to the written word. Suddenly the sheer magnitude and diversity of Eurasia was presented in a single text vivid with surprising detail: it is little wonder that many were unconvinced. For those prepared to accept the work at face value, the entire continent, from the Mediterranean to Japan and from Siberia to Zanzibar, had at last begun to come into sharp focus.

11.16 One of the observations reported by Marco Polo was that the Chinese used paper money. His detractors regarded this as fantasy, but paper banknotes were indeed in circulation. This example, dating to the reign of Yuan Zhiyuan (ruled AD 1264–9), was found in Tibet

The Ocean Passage

When the Polo family were planning their return journey to the east, their intention was to go by sea, buying passage on a ship sailing from the Persian port of Hormuz: they were only diverted to make the land crossing by the lack of an available seaworthy craft. Their return journey from China to Hormuz was on a flotilla of fourteen vessels, 'each having four masts and being capable of being navigated with nine sails'. Four or five of them had crews of at least two hundred and fifty men. These ships are likely to have been junks, a type of vessel already perfected during the Song dynasty. In his *Lingwai daida* ('Information on What Is Beyond the Passes'), Zhou Qufei, writing in 1178, describes the junks:

> The ships that sail in the southern sea and south of it are like houses. When their sails are spread they are like great clouds in the sky. Their rudders are several tens of feet long. A single ship carries several hundred men and has in the stores a year's supply of grain. Pigs are fed and wine fermented on board... A great ship with heavy cargo has nothing to fear from high seas, but rather in shallow water it will come to grief.

Chinese shipbuilding technology was now well advanced. The vessels were held together with iron nails and had double hulls with watertight bulkheads. They were waterproofed with a compound of lime and tung oil, and each carried lifeboats, several iron anchors, and stabilizing floats for use in heavy seas. The magnetic compass, known by this time, made open-sea sailing a safe possibility. Marco Polo's return journey shows that Chinese ships were now regularly sailing to India, and some were reaching as far west as the Persian Gulf.

His detailed descriptions of ports in the Indian Ocean give an impression of burgeoning maritime trade. Merchant ships from Aden carrying great numbers of Arab horses to India and the islands were charging high prices and making substantial profits, the island of Java 'abounds with rich commodities' such as pepper, nutmegs, and cloves, 'which occasions it to be visited by many ships laden with merchandise, and along the east coast of Africa, Madagascar, and Zanzibar are good sources of red sandalwood, ambergris, and elephant ivory which are eagerly acquired by merchants from various parts of the world in exchange for brocades and silks'. And so the astute merchant Marco Polo goes on to detail the endless trading opportunities presented to those prepared to face the uncertainties of the ocean. His enthusiastic description leaves little doubt that the seas of China and the Indian Ocean were now open for

THE STEPPE TRIUMPHANT

الفران ثم ورنبعد لناطير لأنها وخارف جلها وكبواها بسم الله مجراها ومرساها ثم نفى نفس المعرّبين أو عباد الله لكن منى وقال أما أنا

11.17 An Indian ship pictured on an Arab manuscript of AD 1238. The vessel has a stern-mounted rudder and was strongly built to cope with the monsoon winds of the Indian Ocean

business. For many the ocean routes were quicker and safer, and offered a greater variety of commodities, than the long treks across the deserts and the steppe. The ocean was fast becoming the favoured highway. It was the realization of this fact by the maritime states of Atlantic Europe in the fifteenth century that was to change the world for ever.

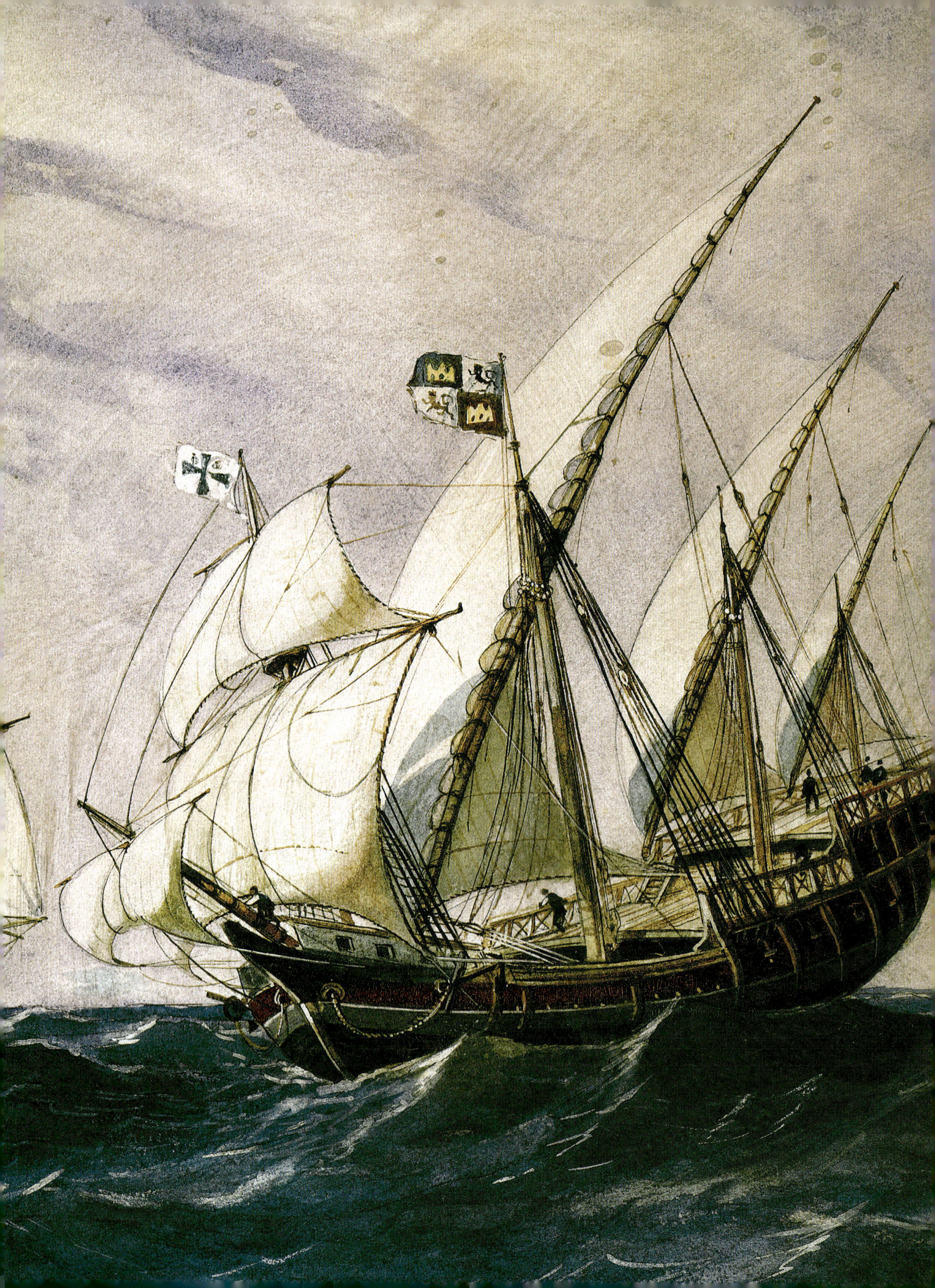

12

LOOKING BACK, LOOKING FORWARDS

THE year AD 1300 is a convenient point at which to close this narrative. In so many ways it marks the end of the old world and the beginning of the modern age, but before we can look forwards to what is to follow, it will be helpful to summarize, in the very broadest terms, the great sweep of Eurasian history explored in this book. One immediate impression is that many patterns can be traced recurring over time. This raises the much-loved question of whether history repeats itself. History does not repeat itself: the patterns we are seeing in the rise and fall of empires and the episodic migration of nomadic peoples are the result of the interplay of geography and the behaviour of humans as conditioned by their genetic make-up. This may sound like geographical determinism at its most naive, but the issue was nicely nuanced by the French historian Fernand Braudel, who reminded us that 'history is made not by geographical features, but by the men who control or discover them'. Put another way, history is the result of the interaction between human agency and the constraints and opportunities imposed by geography. Let us begin, then, by reviewing the 'big geography' of Eurasia.

Eurasia is divided into a series of roughly parallel ecological zones determined largely by latitude, ranging from the tropical forests of the south to the tundra of the north and passing through mixed temperate woodland and grassland, desert-steppe, forest-steppe, and the forest or the more open taiga, before the tundra is reached. One zone, that of mixed grassland and woodland, provided the ecological niche for settled agriculture to develop. There were two focuses, one in South East Asia, in

China, centred on the Yellow River and the Yangtze, the other in South West Asia, in the Near East, stretching from the east Mediterranean coast to the Indus valley. The two favoured niches were very different. China was far more tightly contained than the Near East. It was surrounded on three sides by tropical forests, mountains, and desert, and faced the Pacific Ocean on the fourth. The Near Eastern zone was essentially a core surrounded by not dissimilar peripheries: the Indus valley, the Nile valley, and the Mediterranean with its peninsular European hinterland. Into these peripheral ecozones sedentary agricultural modes of production soon spread, creating new bases from which complex societies—'civilizations'—could develop. The contrast between geographically constrained Chinese civilization and the manifestations of civilization that developed in the Near East and its diverse hinterlands could not have been greater.

The Sedentary States and Empires

In China, in spite of periodic inroads of nomads from the north, there was massive continuity reflected in the successive dynasties. There were periods when the north and south were under different rule, but also long periods when the whole country was unified. Capital cities may have migrated over time, and there were long bouts of civil war, but overall it is the cultural continuity that most impresses.

In the core zone of the Near East, from the Tigris and the Euphrates to the Indus valley and incorporating the vast Iranian plateau, there was also a high degree of continuity, with one dynasty following another. First Babylonians and Assyrians and then, covering a more extended territory, Persians, Macedonians, Parthians, Sasanians, Arabs, Seljuks, and finally the Mongols of the Ilkhanate. While the ethnicity of the ruling elites changed over time and the gene pool was constantly refreshed by inflows of people from beyond the borders, the culture of each generation was heavily dependent on that of its predecessors going back far in time. To some extent the Near East was constricted, hemmed in between the deserts of Syria and Arabia, northern India and Turkmenistan, and by the Arabian Sea. In this way it was not unlike China, but the difference was that immediately to the west lay a huge hinterland comprising Asia Minor, the Mediterranean, and the European peninsula, where rival civilizations could emerge. The first development lay in the east Mediterranean region, home of a succession of increasingly powerful states: Mycenaean, Greek, Macedonian, eastern Graeco-Roman, and Byzantine, all Greek-speaking and with a strong thread of cultural continuity. The aggressive interaction between the polities of the two zones—the east Mediterranean and the Near East—provided the dynamic which persisted throughout much of the period, and during this time it was the

Euphrates that was to provide the interface across which they so often confronted each other.

West of the east Mediterranean zone, a new polity developed later in the first millennium BC focused on the city of Rome. The Roman empire grew to incorporate the east Mediterranean zone and much of peninsular Europe, albeit only for a few hundred years, and with its demise left a fertile base from which the Frankish kingdom and a penumbra of other states in western Europe could emerge to positions of leadership. It was these Atlantic-facing polities that were, through the latter half of the second millennium AD, to take over leadership of an ever-expanding world.

The sharing of commodities through processes of gift exchange began in Eurasia among hunter-gatherer communities long before the development of sedentary farming, but, once communities had settled and were beginning to produce surpluses, the range and volume of goods exchanged began to increase dramatically. Their surplus foodstuffs could be used directly in exchanges or could be invested in the time of specialists employed to make craft items that might then be traded on. We have seen how, over time, the systems of exchange became increasingly complex. In the Neolithic period items of exchange were fairly restricted and favoured brightly coloured stones like lapis lazuli, turquoise, carnelian, and jade, which could be used for personal decoration as an outward and visible sign of the wearer's ability to command exotic goods. Later, with the discovery of metal technology, the demand for copper, tin, gold, and silver became universal, and those favoured locations where the ores naturally occurred became integral to complex networks of exchange.

And so connectivity developed: the dendritic networks threaded through Eurasia, binding the disparate communities and allowing knowledge to flow. Given the inquisitive nature of humankind there can be little doubt that individuals made journeys of exploration following the trade-routes to acquire esoteric knowledge as well as rare materials and outlandish artefacts with which to impress their contemporaries at home. We have glimpses of this in the journeys of men like Xuanzang, who spent twelve or thirteen years in India visiting Buddhist sites and collecting manuscripts, and returned to Xi'an, in AD 645, to a hero's welcome. Later, in 1295, Marco Polo arrived back in his native Venice after spending many years in the service of Qubilai in China. The story of his adventures and of the strange lands he visited brought him both fame and notoriety in his lifetime. These are two of the later adventurers about whom we happen to know through the written sources. How many more must there have been in the more distant past drawn into the depths of unknown Eurasia by their insatiable curiosity?

With the birth of empire, trade and travelling began to take on a different guise. While individual entrepreneurs continued to arrange the movement of goods, encouraged by the demands of an ever-growing consumer market, emperors and their like began to require tribute from subsidiary states, essentially as a public demonstration and reaffirmation of their overlordship. Such expectations increased productivity in the satellite polities and allowed huge accumulations of resources to be built up in the dominant states, resources which could be invested in grandiose construction programmes or dissipated in wars of conquest and the endemic internal conflicts which tended to tear the states apart. During the time of the Persian empire the inflow of tribute came in the form of raw materials and manufactured goods. Later, the Roman empire monetized the tributes owed to it and required the provinces to pay their dues in gold coin.

Diplomatic relations between dominant polities also required goods to change hands as gifts sent by rulers under the protection of ambassadors to their peers in distant states. It is tempting to believe that the Persian carpets and Chinese embroideries found in the graves of the Pazyryk chieftains commanding the passes through the Altai Mountains were diplomatic gifts sent to encourage those who controlled this crucial region to foster obligations of friendship and to facilitate the passage of trade goods. Later many gifts were being sent to Chinese and Byzantine emperors to ease diplomatic relations.

Whatever the form of the tribute, whether sent under coercion or in the expectation of establishing good relations with distant elites, the overall effect was to drive production and to increase greatly the movement of commodities. Put another way, it was the sedentary agricultural societies in their increasingly complex political guises that drove commercial mobility, creating a tight network of interconnecting routes. By the first century BC the networks had joined up to such an extent that the Roman world and China were embraced in a single system.

The Nomads of the Steppe

Throughout this book stress has been placed on the importance of the steppe corridor as a highly distinctive environment favourable to pastoral nomads that encouraged the movement of people. While at a general level this is true, the reality is a little more complex. The steppe is in fact a palimpsest of micro-environments dominated by grassland. Its river valleys, of which there are many, provided well-watered meadows and woodland, while the mountains that in places intruded themselves supported zones of forest giving way to alpine pastures. These variations in ecology provided the opportunity for communities to adapt their economic strategies. Where river valleys prevailed, the rich meadows offered favourable spaces for base camps which might, in certain circumstances, be occupied by a sector of the community throughout the year. They were places where fodder could be grown and stored for the flocks and herds when they returned from their summer grazing. Mountains, on the other hand, could encourage vertical pastoralism when all or part of the community moved to the mountain pastures in summer and returned to the lower altitudes for winter. Over the more open steppe, like that of Kazakhstan, the annual movements, quite often over long distances, were north–south, conditioned largely by latitude, which determined the best winter and summer pastures.

The great swath of steppe, some 9,000 kilometres of it stretching from the Great Hungarian Plain to Manchuria, varied from east to west, the variation being the result in part of differences in relief and in part of the effects on the more westerly regions of the oceanic climate coming in from the Atlantic. Thus, the low-lying Great Hungarian Plain with its mild climate was a far more congenial environment than the uplands of Mongolia, much of it above 1,500 metres, where winter temperatures could plummet to −40°. The environmental gradient was one of the factors that encouraged the periodic movements of populations from east to west, particularly at times of climatic stress.

The nature of nomadic pastoralism has been widely debated, and it is well recognized from the ethnographic literature that it may take many forms, from transhumance, where one sector of the community moves away with the animals for a few months, returning later to the home base, to full nomadic pastoralism, involving the movement of the entire community, which may or may not reoccupy old campsites on a cyclical basis. Full nomadic pastoralism presupposes the existence of wheeled vehicles to carry the family and its possessions from one pasture to the next. The appearance of wheeled vehicles on the Pontic steppe in the early third millennium BC in the Yamnaya culture is usually taken to signal the beginning of full nomadism in the steppe zone.

The origin of pastoralism is another hotly debated topic. There is, however, a broad consensus that pastoralism is an adaptation of mixed-farming regimes, and it is clear from the archaeological record that domesticated animals—sheep, goats, and cattle—spread from the fully farming communities of eastern Europe eastwards across the Pontic steppe beginning in the fifth millennium. Some of the recipient foraging communities of the steppe also adopted cereal growing, but seldom on a significant scale. Over much of the steppe zone it was easier for the mobile foragers, many of whom relied heavily on fishing to support their hunting and gathering, to adapt to caring for domesticated animals than it was for them to change their lifestyles to become sedentary and tied to cycles of crop growing. But not all foragers were passive receivers of ideas from the west. The horse hunters of the Botai region of Kazakhstan learnt to domesticate the more docile of their prey so that they could

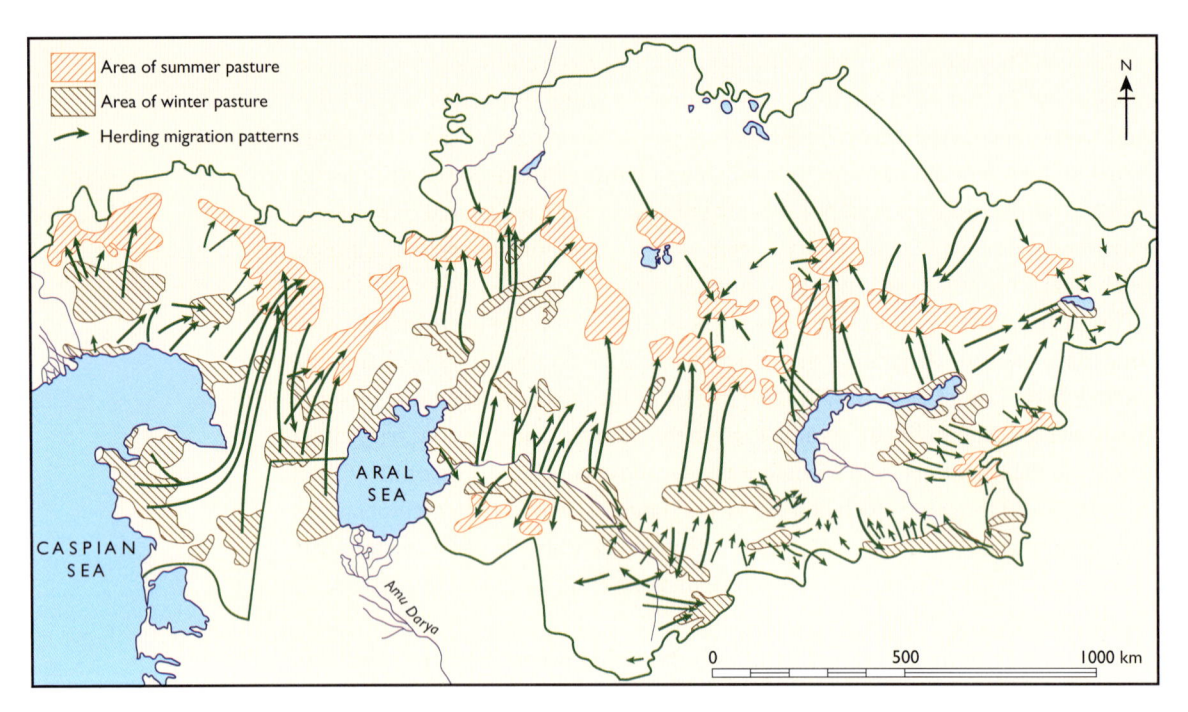

12.1 Transhumance routes used in Kazakhstan in recent times. Herds were moved from their winter pastures, some of them travelling considerable distances to upland summer pastures

be ridden to facilitate the hunting of the wilder beasts. This enabled the herds to be better managed and led to the full domestication of the horse and its use, not only for riding but for meat and milk, and also for traction. Elsewhere, probably on the southern edge of the Karakum desert or the foothills of the Kopet Dag mountains, wild Bactrian camels were being domesticated as beasts of burden and also for their milk and fine neck wool. The different environments that made up the steppe and the desert steppe were utilized in different ways by the pastoralists who inhabited them. The flocks and herds they chose to husband and the regimes of mobility required to manage them were constrained by the demands of the environment. This, in turn, influenced social structure. Communities whose livelihood depended on flocks of sheep and goats and herds of cattle could move around in family or extended family groups, while those who ran large herds of semi-wild horses would need to work together in larger groups. Others, reliant on valley meadows for forage, may have developed a more sedentary aspect. Across the length and breadth of the steppe, with its great variety of micro-environments, many different socio-economic systems must have been at work. All that archaeology can, at present, provide is a glimpse of that variety.

12.2 Bactrian camels in the Gobi desert in southern Mongolia. The fine neck wool of the beast, which is beginning to grow well on the seated specimen, is favoured for making high-quality carpets

Against the background of regional mobility must be seen broader flows of people and ideas. Knowledge of crop cultivation and the domestication of sheep, goats, and cattle spread eastwards from eastern Europe in the early fifth millennium BC to be followed by the technology of copper metallurgy. By the early fourth millennium pastoralism and copper working were well established as far east as the southern Urals, and by 3500 BC these skills were being practised by communities in the Altai-Sayan region, known archaeologically as the Afanasievo culture. The evidence currently available suggests that the phenomenon was probably the result of the migration of significant numbers of people from the Ural region across 2,000 kilometres of steppe to the Altai. It was from the Altai-Sayan region that knowledge of pastoralism and copper working spread to the Tarim basin and to Mongolia.

In parallel with the west-to-east flow of ideas and skills it is possible to detect the beginning of migratory patterns which saw nomads move westwards across the steppe. The earliest manifestation is the appearance of horse-riding nomads in the Danube delta region at the end of the fifth millennium (the Suvorovo culture). This was followed about 2800 BC by a more extensive movement of pastoral nomads (the Yamnaya culture) from the Pontic steppe into Europe as far west as the steppe region of the Great Hungarian Plain. The Yamnaya incursion was the first of a long succession of migrations of steppe communities into the Carpathian basin culminating with the Mongol invasion in the thirteenth century AD. The near-continuous flow of people into the westernmost extremity of the steppe over a period of five thousand years is one of the most persistent and remarkable features of Eurasian history. At a simplistic level it could be explained as a demographic issue: a constant rise in population in the eastern steppe zone of the Altai-Sayan–Mongolia region spilling over into the neighbouring regions of China, Central Asia, and the western steppe. In China and Central Asia the nomads came up against sedentary societies with whom they eventually merged, but in the western steppe they met nomadic pastoralists like themselves, setting them in motion like a row of falling dominoes. A succession of climatic changes may have encouraged, and will sometimes have forced, migration. There was also the fact that the western steppe provided a more congenial and productive environment than the eastern region.

While these factors were, in all probability, the prime movers behind the westerly flow of populations, evolving social systems also had an impact. The most significant change took place in the early first millennium BC with the emergence, in the Altai-Sayan region, of powerful nomadic elites who were able to attract large bands of followers. These groups seem to have been able to remain dissociated from the daily routine of productivity, giving them freedom to roam at will. The maintenance of such bands depended upon the prowess of the leader, reflected in his ability to organize successful raids and to satisfy the expectations of his followers. For such a system to survive, ever-increasing territories were needed to sustain the persistent imperative to raid. Once established, this kind of predatory nomadism gave an entirely new impetus to the mobility inherent in pastoral societies.

What created the conditions for predatory nomadism to emerge is very difficult to say, and in all probability it was a combination of factors, but population growth and climatic shifts provided the underlying pressure for change. The rise of the sedentary states to the south and the development of trading networks introduced a new distorting presence since it began to bring the nomadic pastoralists into extended systems of exchange. As the demand for their produce—trained horses, furs, gold, and copper—grew, so, too, did their access to manufactured goods from the south. The availability of an increasing range of exotics created expectations and demands which could be met only by increasing the quantity of locally sourced commodities to be used in exchange. Their acquisition through raids empowered the successful nomad leader, giving him the means to gain access to the desired exotic goods to distribute to his followers. In other words, the growth of consumer markets in the sedentary states fed the acquisitive nature of the steppe nomads, exacerbating the process that led to the development of predatory nomadism. The importance of access to southern markets is well demonstrated by the pressure that the Huns, the Xiongnu, and the Khitans put on their southern neighbours to keep open the trade-routes. Easy access to southern goods was a precondition in negotiations designed to reduce hostilities.

Predatory nomadism first becomes apparent in Scythian-Saka cultures from the ninth to the eighth century BC, where it is known largely through archaeological evidence, but thereafter successive waves of warrior nomads of Turkic and Mongol origin poured out of the eastern steppe to impact upon literate societies, where their actions and behaviours were recorded, creating the topos of the marauding barbarian nomad. As the texts make abundantly clear, charismatic leaders like Modu of the Xiongnu, Attila the Hun, and the Mongol Chinggis Khan were able to command huge armies of followers for brief periods. But inherent in the system was an instability that inevitably led to collapse.

Between Steppe and Sown

The unstable equilibrium that developed between the pastoral nomads and the sedentary farming states saw the two worlds often in conflict, but each needed the other. The dependence of the nomads on southern luxury goods to maintain their social systems has been stressed, but they were also dependent on supplies of grain and other such necessities, and, indeed, it could be argued that, without access to imported grain, pastoral nomadism could not have worked. Some, like certain groups of Scythians living on the Pontic steppe, produced their own grain, sometimes sufficient for export, and many of the later nomadic groups who came into contact with Europe took up agriculture, but over a large swath of the steppe grain production, if practised at all, was of minimal significance. A number of the nomadic leaders who had come into contact with China openly rejected the idea of becoming agriculturalists, arguing, quite correctly, that to do so would be to undermine the military strength of their people.

The sedentary states, in turn, looked to the nomads for a range of raw materials and also for constant supplies of fine riding horses. The extremes to which the Tang emperor went to acquire the famous flying horses from Ferghana speaks to their value in the eyes of the Chinese elite. The north was also a source of manpower. Supplies of slaves could always find a market, but so, too, could people of skill. Nomadic horse trainers must have been in constant demand in China, especially during the Shang

12.3 Horse figure in glazed earthenware, Tang dynasty, from a burial at Luoyang, Henan, China, dating to AD 695–725. The horse is meant to represent one of the 'heavenly horses' from Ferghana

and Zhou dynasties, and throughout the later first millennium AD Turkic fighting men were avidly sought after to serve in the state armies of Persia and southern Central Asia. The nomads also facilitated trade, notably that which followed the steppe route from Mongolia via Dzungaria to the Kazakh steppe and thence to the Central Asian and European markets. In the sixth century AD Turkic intermediaries offered their services in opening up direct trade between China and Constantinople, and in the eleventh century the Khazars in the Pontic steppe acted as middlemen between the Muslims of Central Asia, the Byzantine world, and the Scandinavians.

The interaction of Turkic and Mongol peoples and agrarian communities along the interfaces with China, Central Asia, and the Black Sea led to a blurring between the pastoral nomadic way of life and the agricultural tradition which intensified after the middle of the first millennium AD. By the thirteenth century the descendants of Chinggis Khan ruling Persia and China were content to encourage the sedentary economy of their subjects but were still mindful of their nomadic past. Their way of maintaining a precarious hold on their traditional inheritance was to ensure that their own people held most of the positions of power.

Crossing Thresholds

To stand back from the detail of Eurasian history spanning the period from the ninth millennium BC to AD 1300 and attempt to identify the most significant transitions when society crossed a threshold to a new state of complexity is a difficult task, not least because the stage is vast and the evidence, particularly in the earlier millennia, is often thin and at best ill-focused. Yet, in order to understand the past rather than simply to narrate the story, it is necessary to try to distinguish those events or developments that forced change on a continent-wide scale.

Most archaeologists would agree that the transition from foraging to food production was of fundamental importance to humanity. Indeed, when these issues were considered in the twentieth century, the archaeologist Gordon Childe referred to the transition as the 'Neolithic revolution'. That the change was dramatic is not in doubt, but the evidence now available suggests that the processes were more long-drawn-out than the word 'revolution' would allow. During the period of climatic readjustment spanning the cold spell of the Young Dryas and the amelioration that followed, food-producing strategies in Eurasia developed independently in two quite separate regions: in the Near East and in China. In the Near East, in the Fertile Crescent and on the hilly flanks, the process began soon after 10,000 BC and the Neolithic way of life was fully established by 6000 BC, but by that time agricultural production had begun to spread to Baluchistan and the Indus valley, the Nile valley, and to the Aegean, and by 5000 BC much of Europe had adopted food-producing strategies. The speed of advance is astonishing. In China, in the valleys of the Yellow River and the Yangtze, plant cultivation and annual husbandry began a little later, between 9000 and 8000 BC, and by 6000 BC had spread to much of China, but geographical constraints—deserts to the north, mountains to the east, and tropical forest to the south—hindered further advances much beyond the region of origin.

The establishment of stable food-producing regimes in the two regions totally changed the pace and trajectory of development. An assured food supply and the need to become sedentary to protect the growing crops quickly led to the development of settled societies, which grew in size and social complexity as populations increased. The generation of food surpluses allowed craft and other specialisms to be maintained, and it was not long before state systems began to emerge.

The two ecozones providing ideal conditions for the early domestication of plants and animals soon became the centres of successive empires. In the Near East the core soon extended, encompassing the Iranian plateau and adjacent lands bounded by the Euphrates, the Amu Darya, the Indus, and the sea. This extended area can most conveniently be called the Persian core. The Chinese core remained mostly within its original limits, bounded by natural barriers. Over time these two dynamic cores, irrespective of the ethnicities of those who ruled them, created a massive demand for manpower and raw materials, energizing the networks of connectivity throughout Eurasia. In the eighth century BC, with the expansion of Greek and Phoenician colonial enterprises, the European peninsula was gradually drawn in to become a new sedentary core. The rivalries between this European core and the original Persian core soon came to dominate the history of western Eurasia. In summary, then, the development of food-producing strategies was the first significant threshold in Eurasian development: it set the scene for much that was to follow.

The second threshold was the domestication of the horse. The natural home of horses in the wild was the open grassland of the steppe, and it was probably somewhere on the Pontic-Caspian steppe that the horse was first domesticated in the second half of the fifth millennium. Familiarity with the beasts would have come from hunting them. It was eventually found that docile animals selected for domestication could be ridden, greatly facilitating the hunting of the wild herds and the management of the domesticated stock. The close symbiotic relationship that developed between man and horse was to have a dramatic impact on humankind throughout the world. There is nothing in human history to compare with it: two animals working in concert, creating a force far more effective than the sum of the parts.

While there is still much debate about the origins of horseback riding, most would now agree that by the fourth millennium BC horses were being regularly ridden on the western steppe. The impact was considerable. A single man on horseback with a good dog or two could run large flocks and herds over considerable areas, extending the livestock numbers that a single family or group of families could manage. Horse riders were also better able to protect flocks and herds from predators, both animal and human: and, for those with the initiative, the horse also greatly facilitated raiding.

On the steppe horse riding changed the nature of pastoralism. Not only could the herder manage increased numbers of animals over greater distances, but riding facilitated the mobility of the entire community and encouraged the development of the type of pastoral nomadism that became the prime economic mode across the steppe zone and was eventually to lead to the emergence of predatory nomadism.

The third threshold is a little more difficult to define, but embraces the initial stages in the developing interaction between the pastoralists of the steppe zone and the sedentary states to the south. It began on a limited scale with trading across the Caucasus in the latter part of the fourth millennium BC, but intensified in the first half of the second millennium, when extensive networks developed throughout Central Asia, linking the Kazakh steppe with the Persian core region. One of the products of the steppe zone, much in demand in the south, was trained riding horses and horses specifically taught to pull chariots. The chariot seems to have been invented in the region of the southern Urals about 2100 BC, quite possibly as an elite plaything for use in competitive events and hunting, but it could also have been used more aggressively against rivals when need arose.

Chariots soon appeared in the southern states of the Near East in the eighteenth century, in eastern Europe in the seventeenth century, and in China in the thirteenth century. In the initial stages this would have meant the export of the range of expertise needed to create a functioning chariot ensemble, but alongside these machines other commodities would have been exchanged, including copper, furs, and other products of the forest zone such as wax and honey, in return for which the steppe communities received exotic coloured stones and quite possibly elaborate woven fabrics.

Exchange between the steppe and the Near Eastern states required the development of a network of trade-routes across the Kyzylkum and Karakum deserts. Links with China at this time were via the Tarim basin and the Gansu Corridor, and may well have involved the movement of people from the Altai-Sayan region to the Tarim basin, where they settled at the oases around the Taklamakan desert. It was only later, about 1500 BC, that exchanges between the Mongolian steppe and China intensified.

The development of regular trade-routes linking the steppe and the southern sedentary states in the early centuries of the second millennium was a crucial stage in the emergence of more global systems of exchange. The new connectivity also facilitated the transfer of knowledge and technology. The chariots have already been mentioned. Another transfer of some significance was the introduction of copper-smelting technology to China, initiating the spectacular rise of Chinese bronze casting, which reached a peak of achievement in the Shang dynasty. The movement of people and ideas between the steppe and sedentary states at the time was the beginning of a process that was to lead to the interconnectedness of Eurasia.

The fourth threshold was the emergence of predatory nomadism on the steppe in the century or two after 1000 BC, characterized by distinctive elite burials. It has been suggested that it developed from pastoral nomadism as the result of increasing access to luxury items from the south which gave rise to an elite able to build large personal followings by the manipulation of prestige goods and, in doing so, to demonstrate their personal prowess.

The earliest archaeological manifestation of this kind of social system appears in the Altai-Sayan region in the eighth century BC and seems to have spread westwards, taking root in the Pontic steppe by the seventh century. It may have been about this time, or soon after, that the system reached Mongolia. Archaeologically it is often referred to as the Scythian-Saka culture because the phenomenon of elite burial spans the territories known from historical sources to have been occupied by peoples who were identified by these names. In addition to rich burial goods, the Scythian-Saka culture is also characterized by the burial of horses, often in extravagant numbers, the presence of weapons including bows and arrows, and a highly distinctive animal art style. While there is still some debate about where the practice of predatory nomadism originated, a strong case can be made for the Altai-Sayan region, where the earliest manifestations have been identified and where the animal art style seems to have had its origins. What this means in terms of movements of population it is difficult to say. It could be argued that it was only social values that were transmitted, together with the cultural symbols of elite status (the animal art), but it is more likely that folk movement was involved. Herodotus believed that the Scythians moved into the Pontic steppe 'from Asia', and, from what we know of the behaviour of later groups of predatory nomads on the steppe, large-scale migration from the east to the west soon became the norm.

There can be no doubt that the development of predatory nomadism in the early centuries of the first millennium BC created an entirely new situation in Eurasia. It initiated a long period of successive folk movements that were to grow exponentially in the first millennium AD.

The fifth threshold saw the final establishment of long-distance trading networks threading across Eurasia, linking the continent from east to west. The impetus came partly from the Chinese and partly from the Romans. Under the Han dynasty the Gansu Corridor was incorporated into the empire (in the late second century BC), opening the way for the Chinese to establish their dominance in the Tarim basin and thus to open up routes into Central Asia and beyond. A little later Roman ships operating from the Red Sea began to move out into the Indian Ocean, linking up with maritime traders based in India, who in turn were in regular contact with ships sailing the Strait of Malacca to the South China Sea. While it was the two empires that forced the development of the long-distance trade through the deserts and across the ocean, it was a host of middlemen of different ethnicities, working sections of the route, that created the essential links. Many of the routes had long been in use, but the economic imperatives of the two empires at the opposite ends of Eurasia are what forged them into a single system.

The sixth and final threshold really grows from the fourth, the emergence of predatory nomadism. For the first six hundred years or so nomadic migrations seem to have been on a fairly limited scale, involving movements of people across the steppe and desert-steppe between the Altai Mountains and the Black Sea. But in the second century BC a new dynamic appears to take over, with people of Turkic and Mongol origin from southern Siberia, Mongolia, and Manchuria periodically bursting out of their homelands and thrusting deep into China, India, Central Asia, and Europe. Unlike the Scythian-Sakas before them, who restricted their activities largely to the steppe and desert-steppe, the Turkic and Mongol peoples were prepared to range wide and to take on the sedentary states. The migrations increased in magnitude over time, culminating with the audacious conquests of the Mongols in the thirteenth century AD.

To reduce the entire history of Eurasia to six thresholds of advance is, of course, oversimplistic, but the scheme has the advantage of focusing on the major transitions that created the fertile ground in which new energies could grow, maturing in a new thrust forward. All were interlinked. Thus, the development of sedentary food-producing economies introduced the concepts of animal husbandry to steppe foragers and led to the domestication of the horse. Later the sedentary civilizations' need for raw materials generated systems of north–south connectivity. Connectivity was given a new impetus, this time advancing east–west mobility, when the Han dynasty and the Roman empire coincidentally became more entrepreneurial. In a separate trajectory, once the horse had been domesticated and pastoral nomadism had developed, the ground was laid

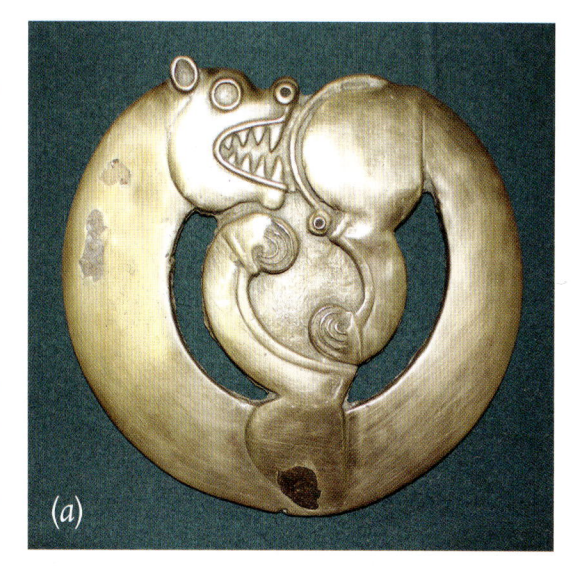

12.4 Two bridal decorations depicting a feline coiled in a distinctive position. (a) This object in bronze comes from the burial of Arzhan 1, Tuva, southern Siberia, and dates to about 800 BC. (b) This example in gold was recovered from somewhere in Siberia and dates from the seventh or sixth century

for the emergence of the constrained predatory nomadism of the Scythian-Sakas and later for the unconstrained migrations and conquests of the Turkic and Mongol peoples. The causal interlinking is, of course, infinitely more complex than the bare skeleton outlined here, as anyone who has read the previous eleven chapters will recognize, but the advantage of attempting to tease out the essential threads is that it reminds us that history is much more than 'just one **** thing after another'.

Thereafter

The fourteenth century was a time of massive change and reorientation throughout Eurasia. East–west connectivity had allowed many of the technological advances made in China to reach the west: paper, printing using movable type, the horse-collar (which allowed horses to be harnessed more efficiently for traction), gunpowder, the magnetic compass, the fixed stern-rudder, and many others. All in their different ways made an impact on European society, initiating advances that were to change the course of history.

The most devastating was gunpowder, which was perfected in China during the Song dynasty. It was first used in grenades and bombs launched by catapults and featured in the equipment of Chinese military engineers employed by the Mongols in their assaults on Central Asian cities. In 1259 we hear of a Chinese gun made from a bamboo tube which fired pellets. The first mention of gunpowder in Britain was by Roger Bacon in 1267. Since Bacon was in close contact with William of Rubruck, it is not impossible that it was William who brought knowledge of gunpowder to Britain following his visit to the Mongolian capital of Karakorum, but by that time gunpowder had already been used against eastern European cities by the advancing Mongols. The Europeans learnt fast, and by the fourteenth century the advantages of gunpowder were being widely exploited by the armies of Europe.

Another introduction, credited to the Mongols, was bubonic plague, the Black Death. The plague was caused by the bacillus *Yersinia pestis*, carried by rodents and transmitted to humans by their fleas. The bacillus was endemic to the Siberian, Mongolian, and Manchurian steppe, where the burrows of rodents provided the ideal micro-environment for its survival even during hard winters. The indigenous inhabitants of these regions had probably developed immunity to the disease or ways of avoiding exposure, but it was transmitted widely throughout Eurasia by the movement of the Mongol hordes. The bacillus-carrying fleas could find favourable environments in the fur clothing of the horsemen and could easily transfer to new host rodents wherever the horses rested. To distant human populations without natural immunity, contact could be devastating.

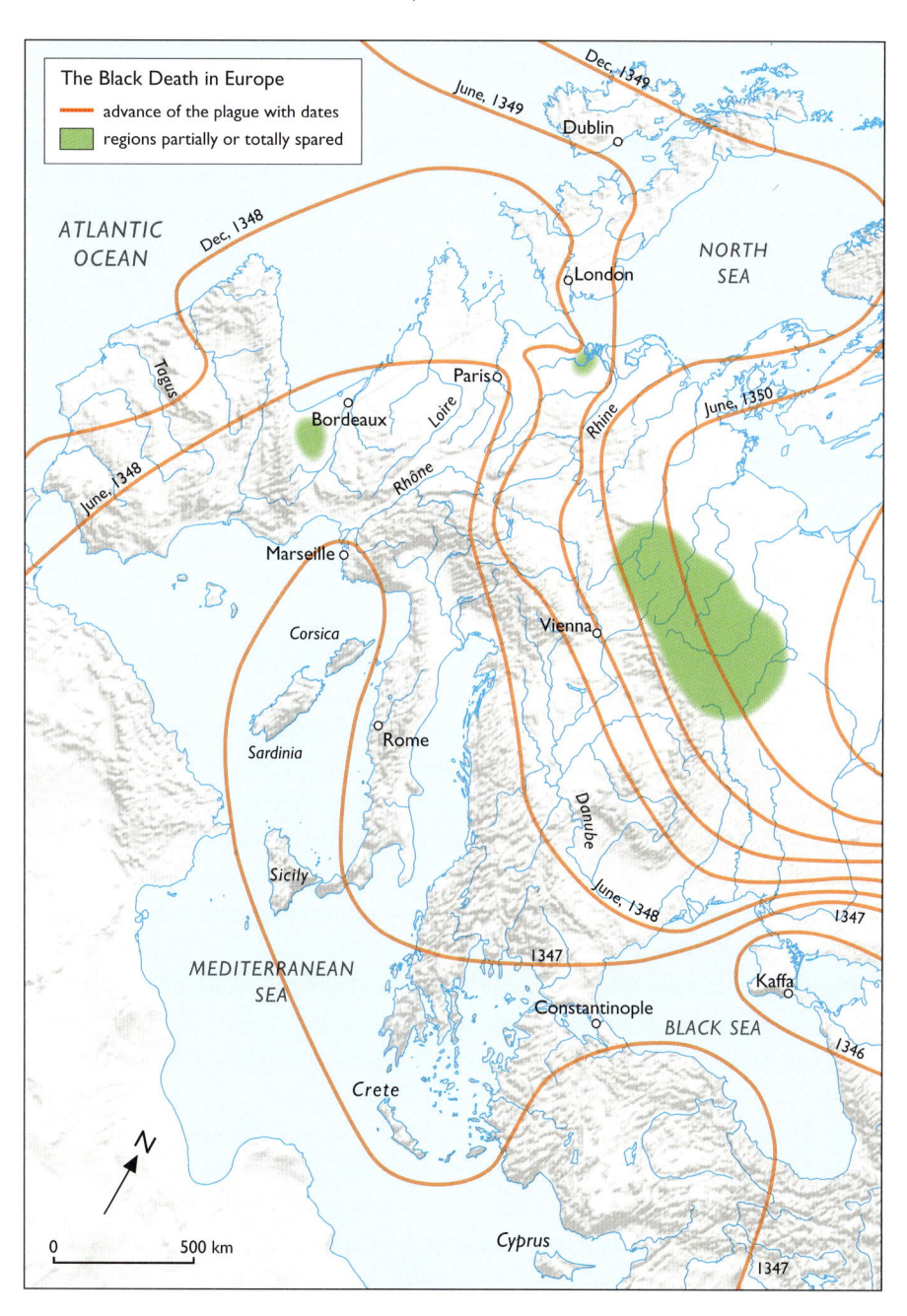

12.5 The spread of the Black Death through Europe in the fourteenth century

In China plague, together with massively damaging floods, fuelled the unrest that led to the overthrow of the Mongol Yuan dynasty and its replacement by the Chinese Ming dynasty in 1368. The first recorded outbreak of plague in 1331 had only a local effect, but it returned in 1353–4, ravaging the population, and after this initial impact recurred at frequent intervals. It is estimated that under Mongol rule the population of China was halved: plague was a significant factor in this massive decline.

In Europe bubonic plague is first recorded in 1346 in the Crimea, appearing among the Mongol army besieging the trading city of Kaffa (now Feodosia). Within four years it had spread across practically the whole of Europe, carried in the first instance by Mediterranean shipping and then passing along the inland trade-routes that embraced the peninsula. The rodent host responsible for the rapid march of the plague in Europe was the black rat. Mortality rates varied from place to place. A few localities were spared but most succumbed, and in some the whole population was wiped out. Overall it is estimated that in the first four years about a third of the population died through plague, and recurring outbreaks continued their devastation, though with lessening severity.

The effects on Europe were considerable. The exponential rise in population which had been causing considerable social stress over the previous centuries went into sudden reverse, releasing pressure on land and in some regions creating real shortages of manpower. The plague created a pause, a time for reflection, when values and beliefs could be reassessed and the traditional teachings of the Church re-examined. The economic impact called for widespread readjustments both locally and regionally. A shock of this magnitude deflected many of the trajectories and imperatives that had driven society: the way had been opened for change and people began to glimpse new horizons.

In all probability the plague bacillus had spread from its eastern niche along the routes threading the steppe used by Mongol armies and by traders alike, taking hold in the caravanserais and giving rise to sporadic outbreaks of disease. This was probably one of the prime causes for the diminution of trade along the steppe network. Trade across the deserts of Central Asia also dropped away in the political unrest that gripped the area. As the fourteenth century advanced, the markets of the west were increasingly deprived of eastern goods.

By about 1400 Europe had recovered from the Black Death and the demand for luxuries from the east, especially spices and gold, had revived, but, with the old caravan routes now far less active and the Ottoman Turks gaining power in the east Mediterranean, the maritime states of the far west began to look to the Atlantic Ocean as a gateway to the east. About the same time the Chinese intensified their exploration of the sea-routes to the west. The oceans were about to become the new highways.

12.6 Comparison between Christopher Columbus' *Santa Maria* and Zeng He's junk

The Chinese adventure was comparatively short-lived. In 1402 the Ming emperor commissioned Zheng He to embark on a series of naval expeditions to 'the western oceans'. Shipbuilding in China was far more advanced than in the west. Huge ocean-going junks with up to nine masts were now in operation, steered by mounted stern-rudders and made safe from accidental ruptures by a system of internal watertight bulkheads. These vessels, at 1,500 tons, were five times the size of the ships used by Vasco da Gama to sail around the Cape of Good Hope sixty years later. Navigational aids were also advanced. Charts of the sea were now available, and the magnetic compass had been regularly in use since the tenth century.

In 1405 Zheng He left the mouth of the Yangtze with an armada of sixty-three junks carrying twenty-eight thousand men and a vast cargo of trade goods including silk, lacquer-work, and porcelain. It was the first of seven voyages between 1405 and his death in 1433, the most distant reaching the coasts of East Africa, where, famously, the sultan of Malindi offered him a giraffe as a gift for the emperor. His remarkable achievements were not to be followed up. His death coincided with a stark change of attitude in the Ming court: China had once more become inward-looking, and the

12.7 Several African giraffes were presented to the Ming court and were kept in a menagerie in the palace grounds along with other exotic animals. This particular beast was presented on 20 September 1414. It was a gift from the sultan of Bengal, who received in return silks, other textiles, and porcelain

12.8 A Portuguese caravel of the fifteenth century with three lateen sails, enabling it to sail close to the wind. Painting by Rafael Monléon, AD 1885

oceans and the lands beyond were now regarded with indifference as the new isolationism took hold. And so China was to remain apart from the rest of the world until its awakening in the twentieth century.

The maritime states of the Far West could not have been more different. Advances in shipbuilding saw the sturdiness of the square-rigged cob combined with the sleekness of Arab caravels with their lateen sails allowing vessels to steer much closer to the wind. It was the Portuguese who spearheaded these improvements to facilitate their exploration of the coast of West Africa. By 1419 they had reached Madeira and two years later had got to Cape Non on the African coast in southern Morocco, beyond which, it was widely believed, it was not safe to pass. But the enthusiasm for exploration had grown, and a year after the death of Zheng He, Portuguese ships were forcing a passage further south, reaching Sierra Leone by 1460. The equator was crossed in 1483, and five years later the Cape of Good Hope was rounded and the sea-route to the east lay open. It was left to Vasco da Gama to make the great leap forward. In July 1497 he sailed from Lisbon to India, where he took on board a cargo of pepper and cinnamon, arriving home in triumph in September 1499.

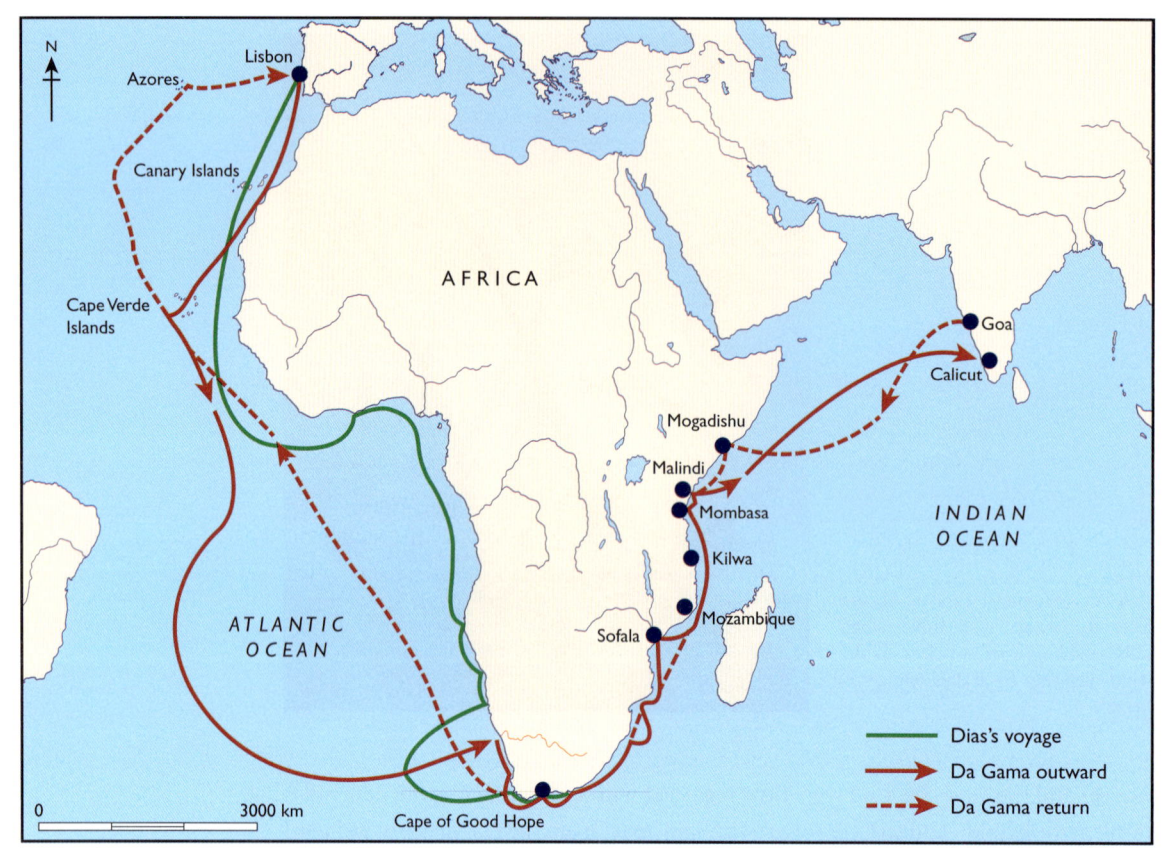

12.9 The routes used by the early Portuguese explorers at the end of the fifteenth century to cope with the wind systems inhibiting their progress around the Cape of Good Hope to reach the Indian Ocean

A few years earlier, in 1492, an enterprising Genoese sailor, Christopher Columbus, had persuaded the Spanish royal house to sponsor his quest to reach China and India by sailing west along the latitude across the Atlantic. That this could be done was first put forward by Eratosthenes in the third century BC. What neither man knew was that the continent of America lay in the way.

The maritime enterprise of the Portuguese and the Spanish, later followed by the British, the French, and the Dutch, was to open up the world, incorporating Eurasia into an entirely new world system. The oceans had at last triumphed.

A GUIDE TO FURTHER READING

It is no easy task to make a selection of reading to accompany this book simply because the many narratives that make up the story have fascinated writers over the years and have generated a huge literature. None more so than the adventures of the wandering warlords who have slaughtered their way across the continent—men like Alexander, Attila, and Chinggis Khan—about whom biographies descend annually. While many are largely repetitious, often there are new insights to be added. And then there is the archaeological literature, much of it tucked away in highly specialist tomes, conference proceedings, and journals. The amount of entirely new material, from excavations, field surveys, and scientific analyses, grows exponentially by the day.

To make the selection offered here I have followed several guidelines, the most important of which is to choose works that I have found useful, reliable, and up to date, and which have good bibliographies of their own, leading the reader to a wider literature. For the larger subjects I have usually offered more than one text, especially in those cases where there are alternative views or approaches. For the more distant prehistory it is less easy to find syntheses, and here it has been necessary to resort to excavation reports, published conference papers, and journal articles. I have tried to resist the temptation to bore down too deeply into the literature, but the fascination of the debates can, I hope, be appreciated from what is offered. Those wishing to follow the arguments in detail will be able to use the bibliographies in the cited works. For the most part I have chosen texts in English published in the last twenty years, but it is difficult to resist classic accounts published earlier, especially where they have not been bettered.

Papers published in journals are seldom readily available to those without access to university libraries, but for the reader wanting to keep up with current research I can recommend two that are not difficult to find. The journal *Antiquity*, published in Britain since 1927 and now appearing six times a year, presents current archaeo-

A GUIDE TO FURTHER READING

logical research from around the world and has, over the last twenty-five years or so, published a constant stream of high-quality new research on Eurasian topics. The second is the *Silk Road*, published annually in America by the Silk Road Foundation since 2003. It offers authoritative short reports on new excavations and other studies, together with notes of conferences and exhibitions around the world and reviews of relevant books. The volumes are available electronically and can be downloaded without charge. The reader who wants to build on his or her knowledge of the subjects covered in this book and to be involved in the fast-changing picture cannot do better than to follow these two journals.

To keep within acceptable limits much has had to be left out of the suggested reading which follows. I can only hope that what is offered here encourages the reader to begin to delve more deeply.

Chapter 1 The Land and the People

This chapter is about the nature of humanity, climate change, and the geography of Eurasia—each a vast subject in its own right—but the topics are dealt with briefly to introduce readers to some of the themes that recur throughout the book and which will therefore be more fully referenced in later chapters. Here we shall concern ourselves with useful introductory readings. The geography of the vast Eurasian continent is unlikely to be familiar to many readers, and most of us will find a good atlas to be a useful companion. Many maps are also available. Two that I have found helpful are the *Globetrotter Travel Map: Asia* (2008) and *The Ancient Silk Road* (Odyssey Maps, 2011). There are also the invaluable online applications, Google Earth and Bing, which no archaeologist, traveller, or general reader should be without. They enable us to explore the vastness of the landscapes and to zoom into detail to examine the location and siting of individual settlements.

Eurasia has generated a huge volume of travel literature including a number of works by the great pioneers Sven Hedin, Sir Aurel Stein, and Albert von Le Coq, written at the beginning of the twentieth century. An excellent introduction to the work of these early explorers is to be found in P. Hopkirk, *Foreign Devils on the Silk Road* (London, 1980). This book, and the same author's *The Great Game* (London, 1990), which deals with the scrabble for territorial power in Central Asia in the nineteenth century, together offer brilliant evocations of landscape and the way it has constrained human action. They provide an excellent introduction to the narrative we explore in this volume.

Historical atlases are a useful adjunct. Two can be strongly recommended: J. Haywood, *The Cassell Atlas of World History* (London, 1997), and P. Bahn, *The Atlas of*

World Archaeology (London, 2000). In both the detail is fine-grained and the scholarship immaculate. Two, more regional, studies are also extremely helpful: C. Blunden and M. Elvin, *Cultural Atlas of China* (Oxford, 1983), explains the varied nature of the Chinese landscape, while R. Abazov, *The Palgrave Concise Historical Atlas of Central Asia* (New York, 2008), is invaluable in making spatial sense of the complex comings and goings in Central Asia.

For the physical geographical background to the huge region we are considering there are a variety of sources. M. Shahgedanova, *Physical Geography of Northern Eurasia* (Oxford, 2003), is a substantial study. A shorter and more regional account can be found in R. Taaffe, 'The Geographic Setting', in D. Sinor (ed.), *The Cambridge History of Early Inner Asia* (Cambridge, 1990), 19–40.

It is widely believed that one of the prime causes of population movement, particularly in the steppe region, was climate change. The dramatic impact of successive severe winters on nomadic communities is presented in a contemporary study, S. Begsuren et al., 'Livestock Responses to Droughts and Severe Winter Weather in the Gobi Three Beauty National Park, Mongolia', *Journal of Arid Environments*, 59 (2004), 785–96. It shows how susceptible nomadic societies are to even short-lived weather events. The impact of climate change on past Eurasian societies is investigated in a number of detailed papers in E. M. Scott, A. Y. Alekseev, and G. Zaitseva (eds.), *Impact of the Environment on Human Migration in Eurasia* (Dordrecht, 2004). Other studies include G. I. Zaitseva et al., 'Chronology and Possible Links between Climatic and Cultural Change during the First Millennium BC in Southern Siberia and Central Asia', *Radiocarbon*, 46/1 (2004), 259–76, and R. van Geel et al., 'Climate Change and the Expansion of the Scythian Culture after 850 BC: A Hypothesis', *Journal of Archaeological Science*, 31 (2004), 1735–42. The possibility that the Mongol invasions may in some way have been related to the onset of cooler conditions is discussed by G. Jenkins in 'A Note on Climate Cycles and the Rise of Cinggis Khan', *Central Asiatic Journal*, 18/4 (1974), 217–26. More recently, work on tree-rings in Mongolia has shown that the rise of Mongol power coincided with a period of increased rainfall between 1211 and 1230, when grass will have flourished and carried greater numbers of livestock. The evidence for this is presented in M. Hvistendahl, 'Roots of Empire', *Science*, 337 (2012), 1596–9. Other specific instances of climate change influencing social change are considered in later chapters and will be referenced then.

The inquisitive nature of the human animal encouraging both the acquisition of rare commodities and a seeking after new knowledge is a recurring theme in this book. These issues are brilliantly explained from an anthropological perspective in three books by M. Helms: *Ulysses' Sail* (Princeton, 1988); *Craft and the Kingly Ideal: Art, Trade and Power* (Austin, Tex., 1993); and *Access to Origins: Affines, Ancestors and Aristocrats*

(Austin, Tex., 1998). A useful collection of papers relevant to these debates in the context of Eurasia is to be found in F. Hiebert and N. di Cosmo (eds.), *Between Lapis and Jade: Ancient Cultures of Central Asia, Archaeology and Anthropology of Eurasia*, 34/4 (1996), 1–104. Issues surrounding the questions of recognizing exchange in archaeological contexts are thoughtfully explored in I. L. Goode, 'When East Met West: Interpretive Problems in Assessing East–West Contact and Exchange in Antiquity', in A. V. G. Betts and F. Kidd (eds.), *New Directions in Silk Road Archaeology* (Berlin, 2010); in Andrew Sherratt's stimulating essay 'The Trans-Eurasian Exchange: The Prehistory of Chinese Relations with the West', in V. H. Mair (ed.), *Contact and Exchange in the Ancience World* (Honolulu, 2006), 30–61; and in V. H. Mair and J. Hickman (eds.), *Reconfiguring the Silk Road: New Research on East–West Exchange in Antiquity* (Pennsylvania, 2014).

Another general theme of importance to the human story is demography. I still find one of the first books I read on the subject, E. A. Wrigley, *Population and History* (New York, 1969), to be the clearest exposition of the principal issues. More detail is given in F. Hassan, *Demographic Archaeology* (London, 1981), and A. Chamberlin, *Demography in Archaeology* (Cambridge, 2006). The all-important issue of holding capacity is nicely explored in E. Zebrow, *Prehistoric Carrying Capacity: A Model* (Menlo Park, Calif., 1975).

The two core areas of Eurasia where sedentary societies first developed—South West Asia (the Near East) and East Asia (China)—are introduced in this chapter. Much will be said of both in subsequent chapters, but here, by way of introduction, the physical nature of the regions is considered. There are several helpful works. For South West Asia, T. Watkins's chapter 'From Foragers to Complex Societies in Southwest Asia', in C. Scarre (ed.), *The Human Past* (London, 2005), 200–33, carefully sets out the scene with an emphasis on the changing environment. A more detailed treatment appears in G. Barker, *The Agricultural Revolution in Prehistory: Why Did Foragers Become Farmers?* (Oxford, 2006). The background for East Asia is well introduced in broad perspective in Blunden and Elvin, *Cultural Atlas of China*, 14–46. For a more archaeological treatment stressing the changing environment over time, see L. Liu and X. Chen, *The Archaeology of China* (Cambridge, 2012), ch. 2.

Finally, there is the issue of nomadism and the mobility of populations across the Eurasian steppe—a theme that runs through this book. It is a vast topic with a literature of comparable size, some of which will be cited later, but a few general works can be mentioned here by way of introduction. Foremost is A. Khazanov's classic *Nomads and the Outside World*, 2nd edn (Madison, 1983), which is essential reading. A series of useful chapters, some of direct relevance to our theme, are to be found in A. Bell-Fialkoff (ed.), *The Role of Migration in the History of the Eurasian Steppe: Sedentary Civilization vs. 'Barbarian' and Nomad* (Basingstoke, 2000). For a very specific but thought-provoking archaeological study of Central Asian pastoral nomadism in the Bronze Age, see M. Frachetti, *Pastoralist Landscapes and Social Interaction in Bronze Age Eurasia* (Berkeley, 2008), which offers a clear demonstration of the complexity of the issue. The same author has raised the interesting possibility that the great swath of mountains from the Hindu Kush to the Altai may have served as a 'mountain corridor' along which the domesticated animals may have been introduced, in M. Frachetti, 'Bronze Age Pastoralism and Differentiated Landscapes along the Inner Asian Mountain Corridor', in S. A. Abraham et al. (eds.), *Connections and Complexity: New Approaches to the Archaeology of South Asia* (Walnut Creek, Calif., 2013), 279–98. The relationship of nomadic and sedentary societies features large in our book. Specific texts will be quoted where appropriate, but to get a taste of the issues the work of O. Lattimore, now a little out of date, has much to offer, in particular his classics *Inner Asian Frontiers of China* (Boston, 1962) and *Studies in Frontier History: Collected Papers, 1928–1958* (Oxford, 1962). Finally, the story of the steppe communities has recently been outlined in C. Baumer's beautifully illustrated *The History of Central Asia: The Age of the Steppe Warriors* (London, 2012).

Chapter 2 The Domestication of Eurasia, 10,000–5000 BC

A number of books offer a broad overview of the origin of agriculture on a worldwide basis. Among the more recent are P. Bellwood, *First Farmers: The Origins of Agricultural Societies* (Oxford, 2005), and G. Barker, *The Agricultural Revolutions in Prehistory: Why Did Foragers Become Farmers?* (Oxford, 2006). More specific to Eurasia are D. Zohary and M. Hopf, *Domestication of Plants in the Old World*, 3rd edn (Oxford, 2000), and a collection of very useful papers edited by D. R. Harris, *The Origins and Spread of Agriculture and Pastoralism in Eurasia* (London, 1996). The most up-to-date synthesis of the evidence for Central Asia is in D. R. Harris, *Origins of Agriculture in Western Central Asia* (Philadelphia, 2010).

A very readable overview of the transition to agriculture in South West Asia is provided by T. Watkins's essay 'From Foragers to Complex Societies in Southwest Asia', in C. Scarre (ed.), *The Human Past* (London, 2005), 200–33. The same author returns to the subject in a stimulating paper, 'New Light on Neolithic Revolution in South-West Asia', *Antiquity*, 84 (2010), 621–34. For an extended treatment, see J. Cauvin, *The Birth of the Gods and the Origins of Agriculture*, trans. T. Watkins (Cambridge, 2007). A useful collection of papers dealing with social and cultural issues arising from the transition to farming in the Near East is brought together in I. Kuijt (ed.), *Life in Neolithic Farming Communities: Social Organization, Identity and Differentiation* (New York, 2000). Specific studies of hunter-gatherer communities in the Levant include O. Bar-Yosef and F. R.

Valla (eds.), *The Natufian Culture in the Levant* (Ann Arbor, 1991), and D. O. Henry, *From Foraging to Agriculture: The Levant at the End of the Ice Age* (Philadelphia, 1989).

Detailed considerations of some of the specific Near Eastern sites mentioned in this chapter are to be found in the following: A. M. T. Moore, G. C. Hillman, and A. J. Legge, *Village on the Euphrates: The Excavation of Abu Hureyra* (Oxford, 2001); O. Dietrich, 'The Role of Cult and Feasting in the Emergence of Neolithic Communities: New Evidence from Göbekli Tepe, South-Eastern Turkey', *Antiquity*, 86 (2012), 674–95; J. Mellaart, *Çatal Hüyük: A Neolithic Town in Anatolia* (London, 1967); I. Hodder (ed.), *On the Surface: Çatalhöyük, 1993–1995* (Cambridge, 1996); I. Hodder, *Çatalhöyük: The Leopard's Tale* (London, 2006); G. O. Rollefson, ''Ain Ghazal (Jordan): Ritual and Ceremony III', *Paléorient*, 24 (1998), 43–58; G. O. Rollefson, 'The Aceramic Neolithic of Southern Levant: The View from 'Ain Ghazal', in O. Aurenche, M.-C. Cauvin, and P. Sanlaville (eds.), *Préhistoire du Levant: processus des changements culturels* (Paris, 1990), pt 2, pp. 138–43.

The establishment of farming regimes in the Nile valley is helpfully summed up by S. Henrickx and P. Vermeersch in their chapter 'Prehistory: From the Palaeolithic to the Badarian Culture', in I. Shaw (ed.), *The Oxford History of Ancient Egypt* (Oxford, 2000), 17–43. The most up-to-date synthesis of the evidence from Central Asia is in D. R. Harris, *Origins of Agriculture in Western Central Asia* (Philadelphia, 2010). The transition to a Neolithic lifestyle on the Iranian plateau has received little attention in the west until recently, but much of the current work has been very usefully brought together in a volume edited by R. Matthews and H. F. Nashli, *The Neolithisation of Iran: The Formation of New Societies* (Oxford, 2013). The important early Neolithic site of Mehrgarh in Baluchistan is described in C. Jarriage et al., *Mehrgarh: Field Reports, 1974–1985, from Neolithic Times to the Indus Civilization* (Karachi, 1995). The evidence for early boats and sea-borne trade from the Persian Gulf is presented by R. A. Carter in his chapter 'The Social and Environmental Context of Neolithic Seafaring in the Persian Gulf', in A. Anderson, J. H. Barrett, and K. V. Boyle (eds.), *The Global Origins and Development of Seafaring* (Cambridge, 2010). For an introduction to the Indus civilization, see J. M. Kenoyer, *Ancient Cities of the Indus Valley Civilization* (Karachi, 1998). An earlier, but data-rich, text is B. and F. R. Allchin, *The Rise of Civilization in India and Pakistan* (Cambridge, 1982). Evidence for the spread of farming practices from the Iranian plateau into Central Asia is conveniently summed up in D. Harris and C. Gosden, 'The Beginnings of Agriculture in Western Central Asia', in D. Harris (ed.), *The Origins and Spread of Agriculture and Pastoralism in Eurasia* (London, 1996), 370–89. The excavations at Jeitun are published in D. R. Harris (ed.), *Excavations at Jeitun* (Philadelphia, 2010).

The spread of farming regimes to Europe has produced a huge and rapidly growing literature. The bare essentials of the story are summarized in B. Cunliffe, *Europe between the Oceans* (London, 2008). The essential textbooks are A. Whittle, *Europe in the*

Neolithic: The Creations of New Worlds (Cambridge, 1996), and T. D. Price (ed.), *Europe's First Farmers* (Cambridge, 2000). The interface between Europe's developing Neolithic communities and the Pontic-Caspian steppe is attractively introduced in a catalogue edited by D. Anthony, *The Lost World of Old Europe: The Danube Valley, 5000–3500 BC* (Princeton, 2010), comprising a number of thoughtful essays as well as an array of striking photographs of artefacts. D. Anthony gives a far more detailed assessment of the archaeological evidence for the impact of sedentary farming on the Pontic-Caspian steppe foragers and the development of pastoralism in his important book *The Horse, the Wheel and Language* (Princeton, 2007), ch. 8. The work is fully referenced to the relevant Russian sources, making much of this primary source material, little known in the west, readily available. A series of detailed papers on the Neolithic of the Pontic-Caspian steppe (in English) are to be found in K. Boyle, C. Renfrew, and M. Levine (eds.), *Ancient Interactions: East and West in Eurasia* (Cambridge, 2002).

The origin of agriculture in East Asia has been energetically studied in the last two decades. A comprehensive overview of the situation by C. Higham is presented in 'East Asian Agriculture and its Impact', in C. Scarre (ed.), *The Human Past* (London, 2005), 234–63. The evidence from China is comprehensively treated in L. Liu and X. Chen, *The Archaeology of China: From the Late Palaeolithic to the Early Bronze Age* (Cambridge, 2012), with a full bibliography. The volume makes available a mass of data hitherto published only in Chinese. The genetic evidence suggesting that rice may have been cultivated first in the Pearl River valley is published in X. Huang et al., 'A Map of Rice Genome Variation Reveals the Origin of Cultivated Rice', *Nature*, 490/7421 (25 Oct. 2012), 497–501. The earliest evidence for millet cultivation is summarized in H. Lu et al., 'Earliest Domestication of Common Millet (*Panicum miliaceum*) in East Asia Extended to 10,000 Years Ago', *Proceedings of the National Academy of Sciences of the United States of America*, 106/18 (5 May 2009), 7367–72. Papers presenting interesting aspects of early cultivation in China include X. Liu, H. V. Hunt, and M. K. Jones, 'River Valleys and Foothills: Changing Archaeological Perceptions of North China's Earliest Farms', *Antiquity*, 83 (2009), 82–95, and Z. Chi, 'The Emergence of Agriculture in Southern China', *Antiquity*, 84 (2010), 11–25.

The question of the early transmission of crops from one end of Eurasia to the other has been the subject of much recent discussion raising questions of the mechanisms of transmission and the routes. The principal contributions are M. Jones, 'Between Fertile Crescents: Minor Grain Crops and Agricultural Origins', in M. Jones (ed.), *Traces of Ancestry: Studies in Honour of Colin Renfrew* (Cambridge, 2004), 127–35; M. Frachetti et al., 'Earliest Direct Evidence for Broomcorn Millet and Wheat in the Central Eurasian Steppe Region', *Antiquity*, 84 (2010), 933–1010; M. Jones et al., 'Food Globalization in Prehistory', *World Archaeology*, 43/4 (2011), 665–75; and N. Boivin, D. Fuller, and A.

Crowther, 'Old World Globalization and the Columbian Exchange: Comparison and Contrast', *World Archaeology*, 44/3 (2012), 452–69. The complexities of the issues are clearly brought out in an exhaustive study of the early use of millet across the region in E. Lightfoot, 'Why Move Starchy Cereals? A Review of the Isotopic Evidence for Prehistoric Millet Consumption across Eurasia', *World Archaeology*, 45/4 (2013), 574–63. The most recent contribution to the debate, G. Motuzaite-Matuzeviciute et al., 'The Early Chronology of Broomcorn Millet (*Panicum miliaceum*) in Europe', *Antiquity*, 87 (2013), 1073–85, fails to find any evidence of cultivated millet in Europe before the mid-second millennium. The origins of domesticated animals in China is subject to active investigation. The best summary of the present state of research is in L. Liu and X. Chen, *The Archaeology of China: From the Late Paleolithic to the Early Bronze Age* (Cambridge, 2012), 96–122.

Chapter 3 Horses and Copper: The Centrality of the Steppe, 5000–3000 BC

The archaeology of the Pontic-Caspian steppe in the period from 5000 to 3000 BC is dealt with in considerable detail in chapters 9–14 of D. Anthony, *The Horse, the Wheel and Language* (Princeton, 2007), with extensive reference to the primary literature. It combines narrative with detail in a way that makes it easy to read while providing the specialist with a thorough summary of the supporting evidence. Another excellent and thought-provoking account is P. L. Kohl, *The Making of Bronze Age Eurasia* (Cambridge, 2007), which is particularly strong on the processes of interaction between regions. A third useful source for the archaeology of the Black Sea region in this period is M. Ivanova, *The Black Sea and the Early Civilization of Europe, the Near East and Asia* (Cambridge, 2013). The book concentrates on the littoral zone around the Black Sea and deals thoroughly with the Kuban valley and its links with Near Eastern developments.

The varied nature of the steppe environment and the way in which human societies have used it is a recurring theme in M. Frachetti, *Pastoral Landscapes and Social Interaction in Bronze Age Eurasia* (Berkeley, 2008), esp. ch. 3. Climate change features large in discussion of steppe ecology. On the Piora Oscillation, see C. A. Perry and K. J. Hsu, 'Geophysical, Archaeological and Historical Evidence Support a Solar-Output Model for Climate Change', *Proceedings of the National Academy of Sciences*, 7/23 (2000), 12433–8. For the broader background and the impact of climate change on the Pontic-Caspian steppe, C. V. Kremenetski, O. A. Chichagova, and N. I. Shishlina, 'Palaeoecological Evidence for Holocene Vegetation, Climate and Land-Use Change in the Low Don Basin and Kalmuk Area, Southern Russia', *Vegetation History and Archaeobotany*, 8 (1999), 233–46.

Some of the questions surrounding the origins of woolly sheep are considered in S. Bökönyi, 'Horses and Sheep in East Europe', in S. N. Skomal and E. C. Polomé (eds.), *Proto-Indo-European: The Archaeology of a Linguistic Problem* (Washington, 1987), 136–44. The impact of long wool fibre on the Near Eastern economy is discussed in J. McCorriston, 'The Fiber Revolution: Textile Intensification, Alienation and Social Stratification in Ancient Mesopotamia', *Current Anthropology*, 38 (1007), 517–49. Recent genetic work on the domestication of sheep is outlined in S. Hiendleder et al., 'Molecular Analysis of Wild and Domestic Sheep Questions Current Nomenclature and Provides Evidence for Domestication for Two Different Subspecies', *Proceedings of the Royal Society of London*, 269 (2002), 893–904. The archaeological evidence is brought together in D. Harris (ed.), *The Origins and Spread of Agriculture and Pastoralism in Eurasia* (London, 1996).

The question of the early domestication of the horse has been extensively debated. The major issues are conveniently summarized (with full references) in Anthony, *The Horse, the Wheel and Language*, ch. 10. Some contrary views were presented by M. Levine in 'The Origins of Horse Husbandry on the Eurasian Steppe', in M. Levine et al. (eds.), *Late Prehistoric Exploitation of the Eurasian Steppe* (Cambridge, 1999), 5–58, and in 'Exploring the Criteria for Early Horse Domestication', in M. Jones (ed.), *Traces of Ancestry: Studies in Honour of Colin Renfrew* (Cambridge, 2004), 115–26. The evidence is considered afresh in S. L. Olsen, 'Early Horse Domestication: Weighing the Evidence', in S. L. Olsen et al. (eds.), *Horses and Humans: The Evolution of the Equine–Human Relationship* (Oxford, 2006), 81–113. Other relevant papers include S. L. Olsen, 'The Exploitation of Horses at Botai, Kazakhstan', in M. Levine, C. Renfrew, and K. Boyle (eds.), *Prehistoric Steppe Adaptation and the Horse* (Cambridge, 2003), 83–103; R. Bendrey, 'New Methods for the Identification of Evidence for Bitting on Horse Remains from Archaeological Sites', *Journal of Archaeological Science*, 34 (2007), 1036–50; N. Benecke and A. von den Driesch, 'Horse Exploitation in the Kazakh Steppes during the Eneolithic and Bronze Age', in Levine et al. (eds.), *Prehistoric Steppe Adaptation and the Horse*, 69–82; and A. Outram et al., 'The Earliest Horse Harnessing and Milking', *Science*, 323 (2009), 1332–5. The implications of these studies are taken into consideration in a comprehensive overview, D. Anthony and D. Brown, 'The Secondary Products Revolution, Horse-Riding and Mounted Warfare', *Journal of World Prehistory*, 24 (2011), 131–60. For the contribution of genetics to the debate, see V. Warmuth et al., 'Reconstructing the Origin and Spread of Horse Domestication in the Eurasian Steppe', *Proceedings of the National Academy of Sciences*, 109/21 (2012), 8202–6, and A. Ludwig et al., 'Coat Color Variation at the Beginning of Horse Domestication', *Science*, 324 (2009), 485. Aspects of the use of the horse in the daily life and burial customs of steppe communities are considered in A. K. Outram et al., 'Horses for the Dead: Funerary Foodways in Bronze

Age Kazakhstan', *Antiquity*, 85 (2011), 116–28, and M. Frachetti and N. Benecke, 'From Sheep to (Some) Horses: 4500 Years of Herd Structure at the Pastoralist Settlement of Begash (South-Eastern Kazakhstan)', *Antiquity*, 83 (2009), 1023–37. The important site of Khvalynsk on the Volga is usefully summarized in Anthony, *The Horse, the Wheel and Language*, 182–6. The horse deposits at Botai are introduced in Anthony, *The Horse, the Wheel and Language*, 216–20.

The steppe interface with Europe in the later fifth and fourth millennia is well covered in a number of papers in K. Boyle, C. Renfrew, and M. Levine (eds.), *Ancient Interactions: East and West in Eurasia* (Cambridge, 2002); in P. L. Kohl, *The Making of Bronze Age Eurasia* (Cambridge, 2007), ch. 2; and, from a European viewpoint, in A. Whittle, *Europe in the Neolithic* (Cambridge, 1996). The catalogue edited by D. Anthony, *The Lost World of Old Europe: The Danube Valley, 5000–3500 BC* (Princeton, 2010), contains much that is relevant with a thorough, up-to-date bibliography. These works have much to say about the Cucuteni-Tripolye culture and about the abandonment of tells in Europe. On this last issue, see also Y. Boyadzhiev, 'Synchronization of the Stages of the Cucuteni Culture with the Eneolithic Cultures of the Territory of Bulgaria according to C14 dates', in J. Chapman et al. (eds.), *Cucuteni* (Piatra Neamt, 2005), 65–74, and E. Marinova, 'The New Pollen Core Lake Durankulak-3: The Vegetation History and Human Impact in North-Eastern Bulgaria', in S. Tonkov (ed.), *Aspects of Palynology and Paleontology* (Sofia, 203), 279–88.

The Uruk period and the Uruk expansion is summed up in M. Van De Mieroop, *A History of the Ancient Near East, ca.3000–323 BC*, 2nd edn (Oxford, 2011), ch. 2. The classic work on the subject is G. Algaze, *The Uruk Expansion: The Dynamics of Expansion of Early Mesopotamian Civilization* (Chicago, 1993). The impact of the expansion in the Caucasus and to the north features in Anthony, *The Horse, the Wheel and Language*, and P. L. Kohl, *The Making of Bronze Age Eurasia* (Cambridge, 2007), *passim*.

The most convenient introductions to the significance of the Maikop culture are P. Kohl, 'The Maikop Singularity', in B. Hanks and K. Linduff (eds.), *Social Complexity in Prehistoric Eurasia* (Cambridge, 2009), 91–103, which references the primary Russian literature, and Anthony, *The Horse, the Wheel and Language*, 287–99.

The question of the first wheeled vehicles has generated a mass of literature. A good place to begin is S. Piggott, *The Earliest Wheeled Transport: From the Atlantic Coast to the Caspian Sea* (London, 1983). The subject of the origin and spread of wheeled transport is considered in more detail in the classic study M. Littauer and J. Crouwel, *Wheeled Vehicles and Ridden Animals in the Ancient Near East* (London, 1979), and is updated in two papers: J. A. Bakker et al., 'The Earliest Evidence for Wheeled Vehicles in Europe and the Near East', *Antiquity*, 73 (1999), 778–90, and J. Oates, 'A Note on the Early Evidence for Horse and the Riding of Equids in Western Asia', in Levine et al. (eds.), *Prehistoric*

Steppe Adaptation and the Horse, 115–25. More recently the evidence has been summed up in Anthony, *The Horse, the Wheel and Language*, 65–75, which work deals extensively with the importance of wheeled vehicles to steppe communities *passim*, especially in chapter 13, where the Yamnaya culture is considered in some detail, summarizing the Russian literature.

The Afanasievo culture and its origins have been widely discussed in the specialist literature. Significant contributions include E. Kuzmina, 'Cultural Connections of the Tarim Basin People and Pastoralists of the Asian Steppes in the Bronze Age', in V. Mair (ed.), *The Bronze Age Peoples of Eastern Central Asia* (Philadelphia, 1998), 63–98, and in J. Mallory and V. Mair, *The Tarim Mummies: Ancient China and the Mystery of the Earliest Peoples from the West* (London, 2000). While the broadly accepted view is that the Afanasievo culture was created by Yamnaya migrants from the west, the radiocarbon dates are problematical. Samples taken from charcoal suggest that it may pre-date the Yamnaya culture. See J. Görsdorf, H. Parzinger, and A. Nagler, '14C Dating of the Siberian Steppe Zone from Bronze Age to Scythian Time', in E. M. Scott, A. Y. Alekseev, and G. Zaitseva (eds.), *Impact of the Environment on Human Migration in Eurasia* (Dordrecht, 2004), 83–90; but a more recent study using bone samples presented in S. Svyatko et al., 'New Radiocarbon Dates and a Review of the Chronology of Prehistoric Populations from the Minusinsk Basin, Southern Siberia, Russia', *Radiocarbon*, 51 (2009), 243–373, suggests a later chronology. The question of the origins of the Afanasievo pastoral regime is opened up in an interesting way by M. Franchetti in his chapter 'Bronze Age Pastoralism and Differentiated Landscapes along the Inner Asian Mountain Corridor', in S. A. Abraham et al. (eds.), *Connections and Complexity: New Approaches to the Archaeology of South Asia* (Walnut Creek, Calif., 2013), 279–98. The question of the impact of steppe communities on the Caucasus and Transcaucasus is thoroughly dealt with in P. L. Kohl, *The Making of Bronze Age Eurasia* (Cambridge, 2007), ch. 3.

The origins and development of metallurgy is considered in a wide-ranging review paper, B. W. Roberts, C. P. Thornton, and V. C. Pigott, 'Development of Metallurgy in Eurasia', *Antiquity*, 83 (2009), 1012–22. The classic work on the Carpatho-Balkan Metallurgical Province is in E. Chernykh, *Ancient Metallurgy in the U.S.S.R.: The Early Metal Age* (Cambridge, 1992). An updated assessment by the same author is given in his paper 'Formation of the Eurasian Steppe Belt Cultures: Viewed through the Lens of Archaeometallurgy and Radiocarbon Dating', in Hanks and Linduff (eds.), *Social Complexity in Prehistoric Eurasia*, 115–45. The excavation of the early copper mines in Bulgaria is reported in E. Chernyk, 'Aibunar: A Balkan Copper Mine of the Fourth Millennium BC', *Proceedings of the Prehistoric Society*, 44 (1978), 203–18. Another accessible overview of the origins of copper metallurgy is E. Pernicka and D. Anthony, 'The

Invention of Copper Metallurgy and the Copper Age of Old Europe', in Anthony (ed.), *Lost World of Old Europe*, 163–77. The same edited volume contains a very useful summary of the famous Varna cemetery by V. Slavchev, 'The Varna Eneolithic Cemetery in the Context of the Late Copper Age in the East Balkans', 193–210. A fuller description of the cemetery is given in T. Ivanov and M. Avramova, *Varna Necropolis: The Dawn of European Civilization* (Sofia, 2000).

Chapter 4 The Opening of the Eurasian Steppe, 2500–1600 BC

A small group of books, already referred to, provides essential reading for this chapter: D. Anthony, *The Horse, the Wheel and Language* (Princeton, 2007); B. Hanks and K. Linduff (eds.), *Social Complexity in Prehistoric Eurasia* (Cambridge, 2009); P. L. Kohl, *The Making of Bronze Age Eurasia* (Cambridge, 2007); K. Boyle, C. Renfrew, and M. Levine (eds.), *Ancient Interactions: East and West in Eurasia* (Cambridge, 2002); and V. Mair (ed.), *The Bronze Age and Early Iron Age Peoples of Eastern Central Asia* (Philadelphia, 1998). To these should be added M. Frachetti, *Pastoral Landscapes and Social Interaction in Bronze Age Eurasia* (Berkeley, 2008), which provides a good introduction to Bronze Age pastoralism in the steppe region of Central Asia, and E. E. Kuzmina, *The Prehistory of the Silk Road* (Philadelphia, 2008), an extended essay offering a broad overview by the doyenne of Eurasian prehistory, including an up-to-date thirty-five-page bibliography.

Turning now to the more specific themes covered in this chapter, the Mesopotamian background history is thoroughly presented in M. Van De Mieroop, *A History of the Ancient Near East, ca.3000–323 BC*, 2nd edn (Oxford, 2007). The Akkadian kingdom is given detailed treatment in M. Liverani (ed.), *Akkad, the First World Empire* (Padua, 1993), while for the Ur III economy, see P. Steinkeller, 'The Administrative and Economic Organization of the Ur III State: Core and Periphery', in M. Gibson and R. Briggs (eds.), *The Organization of Power and Bureaucracy in the Ancient Near East* (Chicago, 1987), 19–41.

For Iran, the British Museum guide J. Curtis, *Ancient Persia*, 2nd edn (London, 2000), offers a helpful introduction. For a more specific study of one of the states, see D. Potts, *The Archaeology of Elam: Formation and Transformation of an Ancient Iranian State* (Cambridge, 1999). The relationship of the Iranian plateau to the development of settlements in southern Central Asia is discussed in F. Hiebert, 'Central Asians on the Iranian Plateau: A Model for Indo-Iranian Expansionism', in V. Mair (ed.), *Bronze Age and Early Iron Age Peoples of Eastern Central Asia* (Philadelphia, 1998), 148–61, and F. Hiebert and C. Lamberg-Karlovsky, 'Central Asia and the Indo-Iranian Borderlands', *Iran*, 39 (1992), 1–15. A useful introduction to the Indus civilization is J. Kenoyer, *Ancient Cities of the Indus Valley Civilization* (Karachi, 1998). The classic work, now slightly dated, is B. and R. Allchin, *The Rise of Civilization in India and Pakistan* (Cambridge, 1982). A more recent view is provided in G. Possehl, *The Indus Civilization: A Contemporary Perspective* (Walnut Creek, Calif., 2002).

The desert cities in western Central Asia (the BMAC) are thoughtfully introduced in P. Kohl, *The Making of Bronze Age Eurasia* (Cambridge, 2007), ch. 5. An older, but nonetheless very useful, introduction to the BMAC is in a special section in the journal *Antiquity*, 68 (1994), 353–427, entitled 'The Oxus Civilization: The Bronze Age of Central Asia', compiled by C. Lamberg-Karlovsky and comprising papers by seven authors. Two important site reports are V. Sarianidi, *Margush: Ancient Oriental Kingdom in the Old Delta of the Murghab River* (Ashgabat, 2002), and, by the same author, *Gonardepe, Türkmenistan: City of the Kings and Gods* (Ashgabat, 2005).

The Sintashta culture, with its fortified villages and chariot burials, has generated much interest. The subject is well introduced in Anthony, *The Horse, the Wheel and Language*; P. Kohl, *The Making of Bronze Age Eurasia* (Cambridge, 2007); and L. Koryakova and A. Epimakhov, *The Urals and Western Siberia in the Bronze and Iron Ages* (Cambridge, 2007). Further detail is provided in the two volumes edited by K. Jones-Bley and D. Zdanovich, *Complex Societies in Central Eurasia from the 3rd to the 1st Millennium BC* (Washington, 2002). Other papers offering specific insights are B. and D. Zdanovich, 'The "Country of Towns" of Southern Trans-Urals and Some Aspects of Steppe Assimilation in the Bronze Age', in Boyle et al. (eds.), *Ancient Interactions: East and West in Eurasia*, 249–63; D. Anthony, 'The Sintashta Genesis: The Roles of Climate Change, Warfare and Long Distance Trade', in Hanks and Linduff (eds.), *Social Complexity in Prehistoric Eurasia*, 47–73; K. Jones-Bley, 'The Sintashta "Chariots"', in J. Davis-Kimball et al. (eds.), *Kurgans, Ritual Sites, and Settlements: Eurasian Bronze and Iron Age* (Oxford, 2000), 135–40; and B. Hanks, 'Late Prehistoric Mining, Metallurgy, and Social Organization in North Central Eurasia', in Hanks and Linduff (eds.), *Social Complexity in Prehistoric Eurasia*, 146–67. F. Hiebert, 'Bronze Age Interactions between the Eurasian Steppe and Central Asia', in Boyle et al. (eds.), *Ancient Interactions: East and West in Eurasia*, 237–48, presents the evidence for north–south contacts across the western Central Asian deserts.

The Andronovo phenomenon features large in the literature, and the exact meaning of the archaeological construct has been much debated. Useful introductions to the subject placing the development of the concept in its historical context are to be found in B. Hanks, *Pastoralist Landscapes and Social Interaction in Bronze Age* (Berkeley, 2008), ch. 2, and L. Koryakova and A. Epimakhov, *The Urals and Western Siberia in the Bronze and Iron Ages* (Cambridge, 2007), 123–36. Some aspects of the Andronovo culture, together with contemporary developments in the Srubnaya culture and the Seima-Turbino horizon, are considered in Anthony, *The Horse, the Wheel and Language*, ch. 16. The evidence for Andronovo involvement in tin mining in the Zeravshan valley is presented in N. Boroffka et al., 'Bronze Age Tin from Central Asia: Preliminary Notes', in Boyle et al. (eds.), *Ancient Interactions: East and West in Eurasia*, 135–59. The economy of the Srubnaya culture is discussed in K. Bunyatyan, 'Correlations between Agriculture and Pastoralism in the Northern Pontic Steppe Area during the Bronze Age', in M. Levine, C. Renfrew, and K. Boyle (eds.), *Prehistoric Steppe Adaptation and the Horse* (Cambridge, 2003), 269–86. The puzzling Seima-Turbino horizon of bronze working is described in detail in E. N. Chernykh, *Ancient Metallurgy in the U.S.S.R.* (Cambridge, 1992), 215–35, and considered again by the same writer in 'Formation of the Eurasian Steppe Belt Cultures', in Hanks and Linduff (eds.), *Social Complexity in Prehistoric Eurasia*, 115–45.

The origins and relationships of the communities living within the Tarim basin are fully discussed in a very accessible book, J. Mallory and V. Mair, *The Tarim Mummies* (London, 2000), with extensive references to earlier literature. The subject is also explored in several papers, J. Mei and C. Shell, 'The Existence of Andronovo Cultural Influence in Xinjiang during the Second Millennium BC', *Antiquity*, 73 (1999), 570–8, and the same authors' 'Metallurgy in Bronze Age Xinjiang and its Cultural Context', in K. Linduff (ed.), *Metallurgy in Ancient Eastern Eurasia from the Urals to the Yellow River* (Lewiston, Ky, 2004), 173–88. A more extended treatment of the archaeological evidence for the transmission of copper mining technology is given in J. Mei, *Copper and Bronze Metallurgy in Later Prehistoric Xinjiang* (Oxford, 2000); E. Kuzmina, 'Cultural Connections of the Tarim Basin People and Pastoralists of the Asian Steppe in the Bronze Age', and T. Shui, 'On the Relationship between the Tarim and Fergana Basins in the Bronze Age', both in V. Mair (ed.), *The Bronze Age and Early Iron Age Peoples of Eastern Central Asia* (Philadelphia, 1998), 63–93, 162–8. The physical anthropology of the Tarim population is discussed in K. Han, 'The Physical Anthropology of the Ancient Populations of the Tarim Basin and Surrounding Areas', in the same volume, 558–68. Recent genetic work, beginning to throw new light on the question of origins, is offered in C. Thornton and T. Schurr, 'Genes, Language and Culture: An Example from the Tarim Basin', *Oxford Journal of Archaeology*, 23 (2004), 83–106, and Li Chunxiang et al., 'Evidence that a West–East Admixed Population Lived in the Tarim Basin as Early as the Early Bronze Age', *B.M.C. Biology*, 8 (2010), 1–12.

The archaeology of the Gansu Corridor and north-west China is fully discussed in L. Liu and X. Chen, *The Archaeology of China* (Cambridge, 2012), ch. 9, while cultural interactions along the Gansu Corridor are explored in S. Li, 'The Interaction between Northwest China and Central Asia during the Second Millennium BC: An Archaeological Perspective', in Boyle et al. (eds.), *Ancient Interactions: East and West in Eurasia*, 171–82.

Chapter 5 Nomads and Empires: The First Confrontations, 1600–600 BC

The historical background for the developments in the Near East between 1500–600 BC is given in some detail in M. Van De Mieroop, *A History of the Ancient Near East, ca.3000–323 BC*, 2nd edn (Oxford, 2007), chs. 7–13. For an excellent visual presentation in map form, see M. Roaf, *Cultural Atlas of Mesopotamia and the Ancient Near East* (Oxford, 1990). Useful works dealing with aspects of the archaeological data include R. Matthews, *The Archaeology of Mesopotamia: Theories and Approaches* (London, 2003); S. Pollock, *Ancient Mesopotamia* (Cambridge, 1999); D. Potts, *Mesopotamian Civilization: The Material Foundations* (London, 1997); and N. Postgate, *Early Mesopotamia: Society and Economy at the Dawn of History* (London, 1992). An invaluable work of reference is E. Meyers (ed.), *The Oxford Encyclopedia of Archaeology in the Near East* (Oxford, 1997). The extremely important shipwreck of Uluburun is the subject of a number of specialist works. A good overview (with reference to earlier works) is in C. Pulak, 'The Uluburun Shipwreck', in S. Swiny, R. L. Hohlfelder, and H. W. Swiny (eds.), *Res Maritimae: Cyprus and the Eastern Mediterranean from Prehistory to Late Antiquity* (Atlanta, 1997), 233–62.

The collapse of urban systems at the end of the second millennium and the question of 'sea raiders' is the subject of N. Sanders's wide-ranging book *The Sea Peoples: Warriors of the Ancient Mediterranean* (London, 1978). More specific studies include L. Stager, 'The Impact of the Sea People in Canaan, 1185–1050 BCE', in T. Levy (ed.), *The Archaeology of Society in the Holy Land* (Leicester, 1995), 332–48; and M. Liverani, 'The Collapse of the Near Eastern Regional System at the End of the Bronze Age: The Case of Syria', in M. Rowlands, M. Larsen, and K. Kristiansen (eds.), *Centre and Periphery in the Ancient World* (Cambridge, 1987), 66–73. The literature on maritime systems in the Mediterranean in the early first millennium BC is massive. I have offered an overview of some of the major systems in *Europe between the Oceans, 9000 BC–AD 1000* (London, 2008), chs. 8 and 9, with extensive suggestions for further reading, pp. 491–5, but a reader wanting to study the Mediterranean as a system in fine detail cannot do better than to consult C. Broodbank, *The Making of the Middle Sea: A History of the Mediterranean from the Beginning to the Emergence of the Classical World* (London, 2013). Other standard works, though now a little out of date, include D. Harden, *The Phoenicians* (London, 1980); M. Aubet, *The Phoenicians and the West* (Cambridge, 1993); and J. Boardman, *The Greeks Overseas* (London, 1980). A useful collection of essays is offered in G. Tsetskhladze and F. De Angelis, *The Archaeology of Greek Colonization* (Oxford, 1994). More specific studies of importance to the theme of maritime interactions in the Mediterranean are M. Aubet, *Commerce and Colonization in the Ancient Near East* (Cambridge, 2013); T. Tartaron, *Maritime Networks in the Mycenaean World* (Cambridge, 2013); and L. Steel,

Materiality and Consumption in the Bronze Age Mediterranean (London, 2013). For the Red Sea and the Persian Gulf, see D. Potts, *The Arabian Gulf in Antiquity* (Oxford, 1991).

The Medes and Persians are attractively introduced in J. Curtis, *Ancient Persia*, 2nd edn (London, 2000). Debate about the origin of the Persians usually focuses around the question of the origin and spread of the Indo-European language. Interesting new material is presented in R. Bouckaert et al., 'Mapping the Origins and Expansion of the Indo-European Language Family', *Science*, 337 (2012), 957–60, while a genetic approach is offered in V. Grugni et al., 'Ancient Migratory Events in the Middle East: New Clues from the Y-Chromosome Variation of Modern Iranians', *PLOS ONE*, 7/7 (2012), 1–14, <http://www.plosone.org/article/info%3Adoi%2F10.1371%2Fjournal.pone.0041252>, accessed 1 Oct. 2014.

Among the great many books available on Chinese history I have found two to be particularly helpful in setting the broad scene: C. Blunden and M. Elvin, *Cultural Atlas of China* (Oxford, 1983), and M. Rossabi, *A History of China* (Oxford, 2014). The classic work on the Shang dynasty is K. Chang, *Shang Civilization* (New Haven, 1980). The archaeological background for the period is laid out in detail in L. Liu and X. Chen, *The Archaeology of China: From the Late Palaeolithic to the Early Bronze Age* (Cambridge, 2012), chs. 8–10. The same authors' earlier book *State Formation in Early China* (London, 2003) is a thought-provoking essay. One of the most spectacular aspects of recent Chinese archaeology has been the discovery and highly skilled excavation of chariot burials of the Shang and Zhou periods. Much of the data has been published in Chinese, but a recent work, H. Wu, *Chariots in Early China: Origins, Cultural Interaction, and Identity* (Oxford, 2013), brings together all the relevant detail in the context of a fascinating discussion about the origin and transmission of chariot technology from the steppe to China. The volume has a thorough bibliography referencing all the significant primary sources.

The Altai-Sayan region is of crucial importance since it sits astride the steppe corridor and is therefore a major route node between the steppe cultures of Central and western Asia and those of Mongolia and the Central Plains of China. It has long been known for the famous Pazyryk burials, but more recent work has shown the region to be the origin of many aspects of Scytho-Siberian culture. There are as yet no syntheses available, but a number of accounts of current and ongoing research are published. Two important papers detail the cultural sequence in the Minusinsk basin: S. Legrand, 'The Emergence of the Karasuk Culture', *Antiquity*, 80 (2006), 843–59, and N. Bokovenko, 'The Emergence of the Tagar Culture', *Antiquity*, 80 (2006), 860–79. Absolute dates for the Karasuk and Tagar cultures have now been confirmed by a series of radiocarbon dates published in S. V. Svyatko et al., 'New Radiocarbon Dates and a Review of the Chronology of Prehistoric Populations from the Minusinsk Basin,

Southern Siberia, Russia', *Radiocarbon*, 51 (2009), 243–73. One of the most important series of excavations was that undertaken at the cemetery of Arzhan, where two spectacular burials were discovered. The details are published in M. Grjaznov, *Der grosskurgan von Arzan in Tuva, Südsiberen* (Munich, 1984), and K. Čugunor, *Der skythenzeitliche fürstenkurgan Aržhan 2 in Tuva* (Mainz, 2010). The deer stones of Mongolia are discussed in W. W. Fitzhugh, 'The Mongolian Deer Stone–Khirigsuur Complex: Dating and Organization of a Late Bronze Age Menagerie', in J. Bemmann et al. (eds.), *Current Archaeological Research in Mongolia* (Bonn, 2009), 183–99, and the same author's 'Stone Shamans and Flying Deer in Northern Mongolia: Deer Goddess of Siberia or Chimera of the Steppe?', *Arctic Anthropology*, 46 (2009), 72–88. The question of the relationship of deer stones to the Khirigsuur mounds is considered in J.-L. Houle, 'Socially Integrative Facilities and the Emergence of Societal Complexity on the Mongolian Steppe', in B. Hanks and K. Linduff (eds.), *Social Complexity in Prehistoric Eurasia* (Cambridge, 2009), 358–77, and W. W. Fitzhugh, 'Pre-Scythian Ceremonialism, Deer Stone Art, and Cultural Intensification in Northern Mongolia', in the same volume, 378–412.

The Cimmerians on the Pontic steppe are discussed in I. Lebedynsky, *Les Cimmériens: les premiers nomades des steppes européennes, IXe–VIIe siècles av. J.-C.* (Paris, 2004); J. Chochorowski, *Ekspansja Kimmeryjska na tereny Europy Środkowej* (Kraków, 1993); and S. Makhortykh, 'The North Black Sea Steppes in the Cimmerian Epoch', in E. Scott, A. Y. Alekseev, and G. Zaitseva (eds.), *Impact of the Environment on Human Migration in Eurasia* (Dordrecht, 2003), 35–44. The movements of Cimmerian and Scythian into Asia Minor based on texts are outlined in E. D. Philips, 'The Scythian Domination in Western Asia: Its Record in History, Scripture and Archaeology', *World Archaeology*, 4/2 (1972), 129–38. For the Mezőcsát culture in Hungary, see E. Patek, 'Präskythische gräberfelder in Ostungarn', in B. Chropovsky (ed.), *Symposium zu Problemen der jüngeren Hallstattzeit in Mitteleuropa* (Bratislava, 1974), 337–62. A nuanced view of the Cimmerians in the west is offered in C. Metzner-Nebelsick, 'Early Iron Age Pastoral Nomadism in the Great Hungarian Plains: Migration or Assimilation? The Thraco-Cimmerian Problem Revisited', in J. Davis-Kimball et al. (eds.), *Kurgans, Ritual Sites, and Settlements: Eurasian Bronze and Iron Age* (Oxford, 2000), 160–84.

The Scythians will be more fully considered in the next chapter; here we consider the question of the origins of the characteristic Scytho-Siberian art and conclude that it lies in the Altai-Sayan region. Much of the argument is based on chronology and is therefore dependent upon radiocarbon dating. Crucial to the debate are four papers: M. Hall, 'Towards an Absolute Chronology for the Iron Age of Inner Asia', *Antiquity*, 71 (1997), 863–74; A. Alekseev et al., 'A Chronology of the Scythian Antiquities of Eurasia Based on New Archaeological and 14C Data', *Radiocarbon*, 43 (2001), 1085–1107; A. Alekseev et al., 'Some Problems in the Study of the Chronology of the Ancient Nomadic Cultures in Eurasia (9th–3rd Centuries BC)', *Geochronometria*, 21 (2002), 143–50; and Svyatko et al., 'New Radiocarbon Dates and a Review of Chronology of Prehistoric Populations from the Minusinsk Basin, Southern Siberia, Russia', *Radiocarbon*, 51 (2009), 243–73.

Finally, the relationship between the nomadic pastoralists and the sedentary Chinese states is a matter of ongoing debate. The standard work offering a masterly review of the history of interaction is N. Di Cosmo, *Ancient China and its Enemies: The Rise of Nomadic Power in East Asian History* (Cambridge, 2002). More specific archaeological studies include S. Li, 'The Interaction between Northwest China and Central Asia during the Second Millennium BC: An Archaeological Perspective', in K. Boyle, C. Renfrew, and M. Levine (eds.), *Ancient Interactions: East and West in Eurasia* (Cambridge, 2002), 171–82; G. Sheleach, 'Violence on the Frontiers?', in Hanks and Linduff (eds.), *Social Complexity in Prehistoric Eurasia*, 241–71; K. Rubinson, 'Helmets and Mirrors: Markers of Social Transformation', in J. Aruz, A. Farkas, and E. V. Fino (eds.), *The Golden Deer of Eurasia: Perspectives on the Steppe Nomads of the Ancient World* (New York, 2006), 32–9; J. Mei, 'Early Metallurgy and Socio-cultural Complexity: Archaeological Discoveries in Northwest China', in Hanks and Linduff (eds.), *Social Complexity in Prehistoric Eurasia*, 215–32; and the same author's 'Cultural Interactions between China and Central Asia during the Bronze Age', *Proceedings of the British Academy*, 21 (2003), 1–39.

Chapter 6 Learning from Each Other: Interacting along the Interface, 600–250 BC

The Persian empire has generated a substantial literature. M. Van De Mieroop, *A History of the Ancient Near East, ca.3000–323 BC*, 2nd edn (Oxford, 2007), ch. 15, provides a succinct summary of the essential history. More extensive treatments are to be found in J. Cook, *The Persian Empire* (London, 1983); P. Briant, *From Cyrus to Alexander: A History of the Persian Empire* (Winona, Minn., 2002); L. Allen, *The Persian Empire: A History* (London, 2005); and T. Holland, *Persian Fire* (London, 2005). Specific themes are addressed in A. Kuhrt, 'The Achaemenid Persian Empire, c.550–330 BCE', in S. E. Alcock et al. (eds.), *Empires: Perspectives from Archaeology and History* (Cambridge, 2001), 93–123. Artefacts and architecture are dealt with in a beautifully illustrated catalogue with supporting essays by J. Curtis and N. Tallis (eds.), *Forgotten Empire: The World of Ancient Persia* (London, 2005).

European opposition to the Persian advance to the west is covered in the above books. The subject is also considered in T. Harrison (ed.), *Greeks and Barbarians* (Edinburgh, 2002), and more specifically in G. Cawkwell, *The Greek Wars: The Failure of Persia* (Oxford, 2005). The rise of Macedonia is fully charted in N. G. L. Hammond and

G. T. Griffith's seminal work *A History of Macedonia*, i, *Historical Geography and Prehistory* (Oxford, 1972), which is essential reading. The life of Philip of Macedon is explored in G. Cawkwell, *Philip of Macedon* (London, 1978), and in N. G. L. Hammond's book of the same title (London, 1994), while the astonishing discovery of the royal graves at Vergina, one of which is the tomb of Philip, is described by the excavator M. Andronikos in his *Vergina: The Royal Tombs and the Ancient City* (Athens, 1984). A catalogue with supporting essays for an exhibition of finds from the more recent excavations at the Macedonian capital of Vergina, providing a wealth of archaeological evidence about this remarkable site, is A. Kottaridi and S. Walker, *Hercules to Alexander the Great: Treasures from the Royal Capital of Macedon, a Hellenic Kingdom in the Age of Democracy* (Oxford, 2011). The life of Alexander has been the subject of a plethora of books, good, bad, and indifferent. If only one were to be chosen, it must be R. Lane Fox, *Alexander the Great* (London, 1973, rev. with updates, 2004). The Greek city of Aï Khanum, now in Afghanistan, is discussed in P. Bernard, 'The Greek Colony at Ai Khanum and Hellenism in Central Asia', in F. Hiebert and P. Cambon (eds.), *Afghanistan, Crossroads of the Ancient World* (London, 2011), 81–129 (including an illustrated catalogue of finds from the site); and in G. Lecuyot, 'Ai Khanum Reconsidered', *Proceedings of the British Academy*, 133 (2007), 155–62. The subsequent history of the empire which Alexander had inherited after his death is the story of a complex struggle for power well documented in F. W. Walbank, *The Hellenistic World* (Cambridge, Mass., 1992).

For the Mauryan empire, F. Allchin, 'The Mauryan State and Empire', in F. Allchin (ed.), *The Archaeology of Early Historic South Asia* (Cambridge, 1995), 187–221, is a comprehensive source. The life of King Ashoka and his many achievements are fully treated in R. Thapar, *Asoka and the Decline of the Mauryas* (Oxford, 1961).

Until comparatively recently discussions of the Scythians have been restricted to the Pontic steppe nomads known to Herodotus, but with the discoveries at Arzhan the view is developing that many, if not most, of the nomad groups of the first millennium stretching from the Altai-Sayan region to the Pontic steppe can be regarded as sharing the same basic culture, which is now often referred to as Scythian. There is, therefore, some confusion about the use of the term. The best introduction to the Pontic steppe Scythians is R. Rolle, *The World of the Scythians* (London, 1989). An earlier general work, T. Talbot Rice, *The Scythians* (London, 1957), is still well worth reading. There are several spectacularly illustrated catalogues of Scythian art including M. Artamonov, *Treasures from Scythian Tombs in the Hermitage Museum, Leningrad* (London, 1969); the Metropolitan Museum of Art (New York) catalogue *From the Lands of the Scythians* (New York, 1975); and E. D. Reeder (ed.), *L'Or des rois scythes* (Paris, 2001). The evidence for the Scythians' penetration of Europe is conveniently summed up in A. Pydyn, *Exchange and Cultural Interactions: A Study of Long Distance Trade and Cross-cultural*

Contact in the Late Bronze Age and Early Iron Age in Central and Eastern Europe (Oxford, 1999). Other relevant papers included K. Marcenko and Y. Vinogradov, 'The Scythians in the Black Sea Region', *Antiquity*, 63 (1989), 803–13, and a number of individual papers in J. Davis-Kimball, V. A. Bashilov, and L. T. Yablonsky (eds.), *Nomads of the Eurasian Steppes in the Early Iron Age* (Berkeley, 1995). Essential to a study of the Scythians is Herodotus, *Histories*. Commentaries and critiques of Herodotus can be found in F. Hartog, *The Mirror of Herodotus* (Berkeley, 1988), and J. Gould, *Herodotus* (London, 1989). Well worth consulting is the seminal early work E. Minns, *Scythians and Greeks* (Cambridge, 1913). For a major recent study of the Scythian–Greek interaction, see C. Meyer, *Greco-Scythian Art and the Birth of Eurasia* (Oxford, 2013).

Nomadic horse-riding groups (which may or may not be referred to as Scythian or Saka) on the Caspian and Kazakh steppe are discussed in a variety of lively papers in two very well-illustrated exhibition catalogues: J. Aruz, A. Farkas, and E. V. Fino (eds.), *The Golden Deer of Eurasia: Perspectives on the Steppe Nomads of the Ancient World* (New York, 2006), and S. Stark et al. (eds.) *Nomads and Networks: The Ancient Art and Culture of Kazakhstan* (Princeton, 2012). Both are to be thoroughly recommended for the range of the contributions and the illustrations of material which are new and otherwise largely inaccessible. A broad discussion of some of the current issues in nomad archaeology is offered in B. K. Hanks, 'The Eurasian Steppe "Nomadic World" of the First Millennium BC: Inherent Problems with the Study of Iron Age Nomadic Groups', in K. Boyle, C. Renfrew, and M. Levine (eds.), *Ancient Interactions: East and West in Eurasia* (Cambridge, 2002), 183–97. The remarkable Saka burial from Issyk is fully published in K. A. Akishev, *Issyk Mound: The Art of Saka in Kazakhstan* (Moscow, 1978). The intriguing Oxus Treasure is nicely summarized in J. Curtis, *The Oxus Treasure* (London, 2012).

The best-known cemetery from the Altai-Sayan region is that excavated, largely in the early part of the twentieth century, at Pazyryk. The results were presented to western audiences in a highly accessible form in S. I. Rudenko, *Frozen Tombs of Siberia: The Pazyryk Burials of Iron Age Horsemen* (London, 1970). An exhibition of selected material held at the British Museum in London was accompanied by an illustrated catalogue containing several useful essays, *Frozen Tombs: The Culture and Art of the Ancient Tribes of Siberia* (London, 1978). More recent discoveries are reported in H. Parzinger, V. Molodin, and D. Tseveendorzh, 'New Discoveries in the Mongolian Altai: The Warrior Grave of the Pazyryk Culture at Olon-Güüriin-Gol 10', in J. Bemmann et al. (eds.), *Current Archaeological Research in Mongolia* (Bonn, 2009), 203–20. The chronology of the Pazyryk cemetery has been carefully reassessed in P. Mallory et al., 'The Date of Pazyryk', in Boyle et al. (eds.), *Ancient Interactions: East and West in Eurasia*, 199–213. It had long been recognized that the Pazyryk graves contained materials from Persia and China. That Indian finds were also included is a more recent observation.

The issue of exchange networks is considered in S. Stark, 'Nomads and Networks: Elites and their Connections to the Outside World', in S. Stark et al. (eds.), *Nomads and Networks: The Ancient Art and Culture of Kazakhstan* (Princeton, 2012), 107–38. Contemporary developments in the Tarim basin are well summarized in J. Mei and C. Shell, 'The Iron Age Cultures of Xinjiang and their Steppe Connections', in Boyle et al. (eds.), *Ancient Interactions: East and West in Eurasia*, 213–34.

The history of China in this period is encapsulated in M. Rossabi, *A History of China* (Oxford, 2014), ch. 2, while the relationship of the agrarian states to the northern nomads is fully discussed in N. Di Cosmo, *Ancient China and its Enemies* (Cambridge, 2002), 70–90.

Chapter 7 The Continent Connected, 250 BC–AD 250

The Hellenistic legacy in Bactria and Gandhara is thoroughly dealt with in W. W. Tarn, *The Greeks in Bactria and India*, 2nd edn (Cambridge, 1966), while the artistic legacy is specifically covered in J. Boardman, *The Diffusion of Classical Art in Antiquity* (Princeton, 1994). The broad region from the Iranian plateau to the Indus valley, in this period and later into the sixth century AD, is conveniently summarized in E. Errington and V. S. Curtis, *From Persepolis to the Punjab: Exploring Ancient Afghanistan and Pakistan* (London, 2007), ch. 3, which brings together contemporary records with numismatic studies to create a narrative history of the period. The Parthians have generated an extensive literature. The most accessible text is M. A. R. Colledge, *The Parthians* (London, 1967). The standard historical account is E. Yarshater, *Cambridge History of Iran*, iii/1 (Cambridge, 1983), but a wide-ranging collection of essays edited by V. S. Curtis and S. Stewart (eds.), *The Age of the Parthians*, ii, *The Idea of Iran* (London, 2007), is to be thoroughly recommended. The relationship between Rome and Parthia is additionally treated in R. M. Sheldon, *Rome's Wars in Parthia: Blood in the Sand* (London, 2010); D. L. Kennedy, 'Parthia and Rome: Eastern Perspectives', in D. L. Kennedy (ed.), *The Roman Army in the East* (Ann Arbor, 1996), 67–90; and C. S. Lightfoot, 'Trajan's Parthian Wars and the Fourth Century Perspective', *Journal of Roman Studies*, 80 (1990), 115–26.

The principal contemporary texts on early contacts between China and the west are presented in A. F. P. Hulsewé and M. A. N. Loewe, *China in Central Asia: The Early Stage, 125 BC–AD 23. An Annotated Translation of Chapters 61 and 96 of 'The History of the Former Han Dynasty'* (Leiden, 1979). Another invaluable source is B. Watson's translation of Sima Qian, *Records of the Grand Historian* (Columbia, Ohio, 1993). The subject is fully discussed in J. E. Hill, *Through the Jade Gate to Rome: A Study of Silk Routes during the Later Han Dynasty, First to Second Centuries CE* (Charleston, SC, 2009), and in J. Thorley,

'The Silk Trade between China and the Roman Empire at its Height, *circa* AD 90–130', *Greece and Rome*, 18 (1971), 71–80.

The nature of the Roman economy has generated a vast literature. Two general works help to set the scene: W. Scheidel, I. Morris, and Richard Saller (eds.), *The Cambridge Economic History of the Greco-Roman World* (Cambridge, 2007), and A. K. Bowman and A. Wilson (eds.), *Quantifying the Roman Economy: Methods and Problems* (Oxford, 2009). The standard works on Roman trade with the east are E. H. Warmington, *The Commerce between the Roman World and India*, 2nd edn (London, 1979); J. I. Miller, *The Spice Trade of the Roman Empire, 29 BC to AD 641* (Oxford, 1969); and G. K. Young, *Rome's Eastern Trade, International Commerce and Imperial Policy, 31 BC–AD 305* (London, 2001). Other works will be mentioned at the end of this section in connection with the ocean networks.

The development of China in the Qin and Han dynasties is summarized in M. Rossabi, *A History of China* (Oxford, 2014), ch. 3, and is presented in more detail in M. Lewis, *Early Chinese Empires: Qin and Han History* (Cambridge, Mass., 2007). The Han expansion to the west and its economic significance is fully treated in Yu Ying-Shih, *Trade and Expansion in Han China* (Berkeley, 1969), while documents reflecting trade found along the Silk Road are discussed in V. Hansen, *The Silk Road: A New History* (Oxford, 2012). The complex relationship of the Chinese states and the Xiongnu are carefully analysed in N. Di Cosmo, *Ancient China and its Enemies: The Rise of Nomadic Power in East Asian History* (Cambridge, 2002), chs. 5 and 6, and T. Barfield, *The Perilous Frontier: Nomadic Empires and China, 221 BC to AD 1757* (Oxford, 1989).

The migrations of the Yuezhi are given detailed treatment in C. G. R. Benjamin, *The Yuezhi: Origin, Migration and the Conquest of Northern Bactria* (Turnhout, 2007), and X. Liu, 'Migration and Settlement of the Yuezhi-Kushan: Interaction and Interdependence of Nomadic and Sedentary Societies', *Journal of World History*, 12 (2001), 261–92. The remarkable discovery of the store-room at Kapisa near Begram is described, and a selection of the finds illustrated in P. Cambon, 'Bagram: Alexandria of the Caucasus, Capital of the Kushan Empire', in F. Heibert and P. Cambon (eds.), *Afghanistan: Crossroads of the Ancient World* (London, 2011), 145–209. The grave goods from the cemetery at Tillya Tepe are discussed and illustrated in V. I. Sarianidi, 'Ancient Bactria's Golden Hoard', in the same volume, 211–93.

The most comprehensive and accessible works on the Sarmatians are T. Sulimirski, *The Sarmatians* (London, 1970), and J. Harmatta, *Studies in the History and Language of the Sarmatians* (Szeged, 1970). A series of papers in J. Davis-Kimball, V. A. Bashilov, and L. T. Yablonsky (eds.), *Nomads of the Eurasian Steppe in the Early Iron Age* (Berkeley, 1995), 83–188, deal in considerable detail with the material culture of Sarmatian tribes living on the Pontic-Caspian steppe. For a perceptive review article examining the development of the conceptual framework for understanding the Sarmatians, see V. Mordvintseva, 'The Sarmatians: The Creation of Archaeological Evidence', *Oxford Journal of Archaeology*, 32 (2013), 203–19; it is essential reading, showing how our understanding has changed over time. The relationship of the Sarmatian tribes the Iazyges and Roxolani with Roman frontier provinces in the middle Danube is discussed in A. Mócsy, *Pannonia and Upper Moesia* (London, 1974). For the Alans, the most comprehensive source is B. S. Bachrach, *A History of the Alans in the West: From their First Appearance in the Sources of Classical Antiquity through the Early Middle Ages* (Minneapolis, 1973). For the later history of the Bosporan kingdom, T. Bekker-Nielsen, *Rome and the Black Sea Region: Domination, Romanization and Resistance* (Aarhus, 2006), provides an excellent overview of the broader context.

The caravan routes across Central Asia, which began, in this period, to serve as networks for the transmission of goods between east and west, are commonly referred to as the Silk Road. It is a romantic conception that has spawned a great deal of writing and continues to fascinate, not least because of the superb preservation of organic materials in the arid desert conditions along the route, including large quantities of texts. A reader wishing to learn of the swashbuckling pioneers who opened up the archaeology of the region can do no better than to read P. Hopkirk, *Foreign Devils of the Silk Road: The Search for the Lost Treasures of Central Asia* (London, 1980). An excellent review of the surviving texts in their historical context is presented in V. Hansen, *The Silk Road: A New History* (Oxford, 2013), containing copious references to the original sources. Another invaluable work is a broad overview, X. Liu, *The Silk Road in World History* (Oxford, 2010), which puts the development of the trade networks into a wider historical context. The journal the *Silk Road* (the Silk Road Foundation), available free online, is an invaluable source for short papers on current research. The famous Buddhist cave shrines at Mogao are described and brilliantly illustrated in Fan Jinshi, *The Caves of Dunhuang* (Hong Kong, 2010).

Any study of the ocean networks must begin with L. Casson, *The Periplus Maris Erythraei: Text with Introduction with Translation and Commentary* (Princeton, 1989). The archaeology of the ocean trade is well explained in an increasingly large number of works including F. De Romanis and A. Tchernia (eds.), *Crossings: Early Mediterranean Contacts with India* (New Delhi, 2005); E. H. Seland, *Ports and Political Power in the Periplus: Complex Societies and Maritime Trade on the Indian Ocean in the First Century* AD (Oxford, 2010); R. Tomber, *Indo-Roman Trade: From Pots to Pepper* (London, 2008); L. Blue and S. Abraham (eds.), *Migration, Trade and People*, pt 1, *Indian Ocean Commerce and the Archaeology of Western India* (London, 2009); M. P. Fitzpatrick, 'Provincializing Rome: The Indian Ocean Trade Network and Roman Imperialism', *Journal of World History*, 22/1 (2011), 27–54; and the classic early study J. I. Miller, *The Spice Trade of the Roman Empire, 29* BC–

AD 641 (Oxford, 1969). An interesting discussion of the different routes from the Red Sea and Persian Gulf to the Mediterranean and their relative merits can be found in E. H. Seland, 'The Persian Gulf or the Red Sea? Two Axes in Ancient Indian Ocean Trade, Where To Go and Why', *World Archaeology*, 43/3 (2011), 395–409. For reports on the excavation of port sites, see D. P. S. Peacock and L. Blue, *Myos Hormos—Quseir al-Qadim: Roman and Islamic Ports on the Red Sea* (Oxford, 2006); W. Z. Wendrich, R. S. Tomber, and S. E. Sidebotham, 'Berenike Crossroads: The Integration of Information', *Journal of the Economic and Social History of the Orient*, 46 (2003), 46–87; S. E. Sidebotham, *Berenike and the Ancient Maritime Spice Route* (Berkeley, 2011); and V. Begley (ed.), *The Ancient Port of Arikamedu: New Excavations and Researches, 1989–1992* (Paris, 2004).

The wider implications of Indian Ocean trade are well brought out in two papers: I. W. Ardika and P. Bellwood, 'Sembiran: The Beginnings of Indian Contact with Bali', *Antiquity*, 65 (1991), 221–32, and D. Q. Fuller et al., 'Across the Indian Ocean: The Prehistoric Movement of Plants and Animals', *Antiquity*, 85 (2011), 544–58. Both are strongly recommended to any reader who wants to explore the subject beyond the limits set by this book.

Chapter 8 The Age of Perpetual War, AD 250–650

Sasanian history is thoroughly treated in R. Ghirshman, *Iran: Parthians and Sasanians* (London, 1962); G. Herrmann, *The Iranian Revival* (Oxford, 1977); and J. Wiesehöfer, *Ancient Persia from 550 BC to 650 AD* (London, 1996). For Sasanian sites and monuments, see S. A. Matheson, *Persia: An Archaeological Guide* (London, 1976), and, for the art, P. O. Harper, *The Royal Hunter: Art of the Sasanian Empire* (New York, 1978). The Byzantine world can best be approached through two very readable texts: A. Cameron, *The Byzantines* (Oxford, 2002), and C. Mango (ed.), *The Oxford History of Byzantium* (Oxford, 2002). Two extremely useful works of reference are J. Haldon, *The Palgrave Atlas of Byzantine History* (Basingstoke, 2005), and A. Kazhdan (ed.), *The Oxford Dictionary of Byzantium*, 3 vols. (New York, 1990). The times and achievement of Diocletian are fully considered in S. Williams, *Diocletian and the Roman Recovery* (London, 1985), while the general background to the last centuries of the Roman empire is explored in S. Mitchell, *A History of the Later Roman Empire, AD 284–641* (Oxford, 2007). The art and architecture of the city of Constantinople is presented with superb illustrations and a comprehensive historical narrative in S. Yerasimos, *Constantinople: Istanbul's Historical Heritage* (Paris, 2000).

The background history of China in the period covered in this chapter is outlined in M. Rossabi, *A History of China* (Oxford, 2014), chs. 4 and 5. For a more detailed treatment, see A. Dien, *Six Dynasties Civilization* (New Haven, 2007), and J. C. Y. Watt et al., *Dawn of a Golden Age, 200–750 AD* (New York, 2004). Certain similarities between the

A GUIDE TO FURTHER READING

Roman and Chinese empires are touched on very briefly in the chapter. These themes are explored in a series of chapters in W. Scheidel (ed.), *Rome and China: Comparative Perspectives on Ancient World Empires* (Oxford, 2009). The long-drawn-out conflict between the Roman and Sasanian empires is discussed in detail in M. H. Dodgeon and S. N. C. Lieu (eds.), *The Roman Eastern Frontier and the Persian Wars*, pt 1, *AD 226–363: A Documentary History* (London, 2002), and G. Greatrex and S. N. C. Lieu's second volume of the same work, pt 2, *363–630: A Narrative Sourcebook*, published at the same time. An interesting approach to the conflict from the Sasanian point of view will be found in J. Howard-Johnson, 'The Sasanians' Strategic Dilemma', in H. Börm and J. Wiesehöfer (eds.), *Commutatio et Contentio: Studies in the Late Roman, Sasanian and Early Islamic Near East* (Düsseldorf, 2010), 37–70. The city of Dura-Europos on the Euphrates is best approached from M. I. Rostovtzeff, *Dura-Europos and its Art* (Oxford, 1938), and C. Hopkins, *The Discovery of Dura-Europa* (New Haven, 1979). S. James, 'Stratagems, Combat and "Chemical Warfare" in the Siege Mines of Dura-Europos', *American Journal of Archeology*, 115 (2011), 89–101, adds reality to the conflict. Palmyra is well introduced in I. Browning, *Palmyra* (London, 1979), and is considered in its broader context in B. Isaac, *The Limits of Empire: The Roman Army in the East* (Oxford, 2000). The fascinating story of Queen Zenobia is told in R. Stoneman, *Palmyra and its Empire: Zenobia's Revolt against Rome* (Ann Arbor, 1995), and R. Winsbury, *Zenobia of Palmyra: History, Myth and Neo-classical Imagination* (London, 2010). A. M. Smith, *Roman Palmyra: Identity, Community and State Formation* (Oxford, 2013), is a carefully considered account of the social dynamics of this remarkable kingdom. The conflicts between Christian and Jewish trading interests in the Red Sea in the years before the Arab ascendancy is given detailed treatment in G. W. Bowersock, *The Throne of Adulis: Red Sea Wars on the Eve of Islam* (Oxford, 2013).

Turning now to India and the importance of the rise of Buddhism to the development of trade networks, A. Agarwal, *Rise and Fall of the Imperial Guptas* (Delhi, 1989), provides a historical background. The spread of Buddhism into Central Asia and China along the trade-routes is explored in X. Liu, *The Silk Road in World History* (Oxford, 2010), and V. Hansen, *The Silk Road: A New History* (Oxford, 2012), both setting the theme within a broad context. For more detail, see X. Liu, *Ancient India and China: Trade and Religious Exchanges, AD 1–600* (Oxford, 1988), and R. C. Foltz, *Religions of the Silk Road: Premodern Patterns of Globalization* (New York, 2010). The remarkable journey of Faxiang is described in H. A. Giles, *The Travels of Fa-hsien, or, Record of the Buddhistic Kingdoms* (Cambridge, 1923). The later journey of Xuanzang (AD 629–45) is discussed in Hui-li, *The Life of Hiuen-Tsiang* (London, 1911). For the Sogdian middlemen who were so vital in organizing trade, see J. Ward's translation of E. de la Vaissière, *Sogdian Traders: A History* (Leiden, 2005).

A GUIDE TO FURTHER READING

The steppe nomads who moved westwards into Europe in the fourth and fifth centuries AD have attracted many writers. The Alans are well covered in V. Kouznetsov and I. Lebedynsky, *Les Alains: cavaliers des steppes, seigneurs du Caucase* (Paris, 1997), and B. S. Bachrach, *A History of the Alans in the West, from their First Appearance in the Sources of Classical Antiquity through to the Early Middle Ages* (Minneapolis, 1973). A very useful work of reference is A. Alemany, *Sources on the Alans: A Critical Compilation* (Leiden, 2000). The Huns are most easily approached through a classic work, E. A. Thompson, *A History of Attila and the Huns* (Oxford, 1948), later revised and reprinted as *The Huns* (Oxford, 1996). Another excellent source is I. Bóna, *Das Hunnenreich* (Stuttgart, 1991). Also to be recommended is P. Heather, 'The Huns and the End of the Roman Empire in Europe', *English Historical Review*, 110 (1995), 4–41. The same author's *The Fall of the Roman Empire: A New History of Rome and the Barbarians* (Oxford, 2007) provides the essential context against which to understand the impact of the Alans and Huns on peninsular Europe.

The Hephthalites (White Huns) are rather less well represented in the literature, but the evidence has been carefully assembled and discussed in a doctoral thesis by A. Kurbanov, *The Hephthalites: Archaeological and Historical Analysis* (Berlin, 2010). The Avars in Europe are the subject of O. Pritsak, *The Slavs and the Avars* (Spoleto, 1982). The question of the correlation of Avars with the peoples called Juanjuan by the Chinese is carefully analysed in C. Beckworth, *Empire of the Silk Road* (Princeton, 2009), 309–10 n. 18.

The rise of the Turkic peoples in Central Asia in the broader context of their time is in Beckworth, *Empire of the Silk Road*, ch. 5, and in D. Sinor, 'The Establishment and Dissolution of the Türk Empire', in D. Sinor (ed.), *The Cambridge History of Early Inner Asia* (Cambridge, 1990), 285–316. For the Turks in a longer chronological framework, see C. V. Findley, *The Turks in World History* (Oxford, 2005), and P. Golden, *An Introduction to the History of the Turkic Peoples* (Wiesbaden, 1991).

Some reading relevant to the Arab awakening will be given in the next section, but the forces influencing the emergence of the Arabs as a world power are nicely analysed in G. Fisher, *Between Empires: Arabs, Romans and Sasanians in Late Antiquity* (Oxford, 2013).

Chapter 9 The Beginning of a New World Order, AD 640–840

The seventh-century palatial building decorated with a remarkable series of paintings found at Afrasiab has been described in a volume edited by M. Compareti and E. de la Vaissière (eds.), *Royal Nawrūz in Samarkand: Acts of the Conference Held in Venice on the Pre-Islamic Afrāsyāb Painting* (Rome, 2006), and is further discussed in M. Compareti, 'Further Evidence for the Interpretation of the "Indian Scene" in the Pre-Islamic Painting at Afrasiab (Samarkand)', *Silk Road*, 4/2 (2007), 32–42. The paintings are also described and illustrated in a booklet prepared by the Samarkand State Museum of History and Art, *'Hall of Ambassadors' in the Museum on Afrasiab (Middle of the VII Century)* (Samarkand, 2002).

The Arab advance seen from an essentially military point of view is well described in J. Bagot Glubb, *A Short History of the Arab Peoples* (London, 1969). A more nuanced view of Arab history is to be found in K. Armstrong, *Islam: A Short History* (London, 2000). Another useful source is G. Hawting, *The Dynasty of Islam: The Umayyad Caliphate, AD 661–750* (London, 1986).

The history of the Tang dynasty is well summarized in M. Rossabi, *A History of China* (London, 2014), ch. 5, and is treated in far more detail in M. E. Lewis, *China's Cosmopolitan Empire: The Tang Dynasty* (Cambridge, Mass., 2009); also C. Benn, *China's Golden Age: Everyday Life in the Tang Dynasty* (Oxford, 2004). The western protectorates are given special treatment in Z. Xue, *Anxi and Beiting Protectorates: A Research on Frontier Policy in Tang Dynasty's Western Boundary* (Harbin, 1998), while the complex relationships between the Chinese states and their nomadic neighbours are explored in J. K. Skaff, *Sui-Tang China and its Turko-Mongol Neighbours* (Oxford, 2012). The broader historical context for events in Central Asia is very clearly presented in C. I. Beckwith, *Empires of the Silk Road: A History of Central Eurasia from the Bronze Age to the Present* (Princeton, 2009). The book also presents a concise account of the relationship between the growing power of the Tibetans and the Tang Chinese. For this, see also the same author's *The Tibetan Empire in Central Asia* (Princeton, 1987). Other works on the Silk Road of direct relevance to our discussion are V. Hansen, *The Silk Road: A New History* (Oxford, 2012), which is particularly strong on the documentary evidence; X. Liu, *The Silk Road in World History* (Oxford, 2010); and F. Wood, *The Silk Road* (Berkeley, 2004). The early history of the Uighurs is a hotly debated issue given the political and ethnic tensions present in modern Xinjiang, but for a balanced and scholarly account the best source in P. B. Golden, *An Introduction to the History of the Turkic Peoples: Ethnogenesis and State Formation in Medieval and Early Modern Eurasia* (Wiesbaden, 1992), ch. 6. A more detailed treatment of the historical sources is provided in C. Mackerras (ed. and trans.), *The Uighur Empire according to Tang Dynastic Histories: A Study in Sino-Uyghur Relations, 744–840* (Columbia, SC, 1972), and the same author's chapter 'The Uighurs', in D. Sinor (ed.), *The Cambridge History of Early Inner Asia* (Cambridge, 1990), 317–42. The journey to the west of the Tang general Xuanzang is described in S. H. Wriggins, *The Silk Road Journey with Xuanzang*, rev. edn (Boulder, Colo., 2003).

What has been called the dark age in Byzantine history is the subject of an essay by W. Treadgold, 'The Struggle for Survival, 641–780', in C. Mango (ed.), *The Oxford History of Byzantium* (Oxford, 2002), 129–50. For a fuller treatment, see J. Haldon, *Byzantium in the Seventh Century* (Cambridge, 1990). The economic background of the period is carefully explored in R. Lemerle, *The Agrarian History of Byzantium* (Galway, 1979), while the military situation is covered in W. Kasigi, *Byzantine Military Unrest, 471–843: An Interpretation* (Amsterdam, 1981). For an introduction to Byzantine life and society it is difficult to better A. Cameron, *The Byzantines* (Oxford, 2006).

The Abbasid empire is well covered in broad historical outline in J. Bagot Glubb, *A Short History of the Arab Peoples* (London, 1969); J. Esposito (ed.), *The Oxford History of Islam* (Oxford, 1999); and A. Hourani, *A History of the Arab Peoples* (London, 1991). F. Rosenthal, *Knowledge Triumphant: The Concept of Knowledge in Medieval Islam* (London, 1970), provides an assessment of Islamic intellectual achievement.

Excellent starting points for understanding Indian Ocean trade are K. N. Chaudhuri, *Trade and Civilization in the Indian Ocean: An Economic History from the Rise of Islam to 1750* (Cambridge, 1985), and G. F. Hourani, *Arab Seafaring in the Indian Ocean*, rev. J. Carswell (Princeton, 1995). R. Tomber, *Indo-Roman Trade: From Pots to Pepper* (London, 2008), provides a thorough summary of the material evidence for the earlier period and just overlaps with the time span of this chapter. Another work of some interest is an attractive compilation, *Oman: A Seafaring Nation*, published by the Ministry of Information and Culture, the Sultanate of Oman (1979). The travels of Yijing are summarized in V. Hansen, *The Silk Road: A New History* (Oxford, 2012), 162–5.

The rise of the west is well covered in two magisterial tomes: R. McKitterick (ed.), *The New Cambridge Medical History*, ii, *c. 700–900* (Cambridge, 1995), and M. McCormick, *Origins of European Economy: Communications and Commerce, AD 300–900* (Cambridge, 2001), both of which present a wealth of data. A more approachable introduction to some of the main themes developed in this book is R. Hodges and D. Whitehouse, *Mohammed, Charlemagne and the Rise of Europe: Archaeology and the Pirenne Thesis* (Ithaca, NY, 1983). Charlemagne and the Carolingian empire have generated a considerable literature, one of the most accessible accounts being R. Collins, *Charlemagne* (Basingstoke, 1998). Other texts to be recommended are L. Halphen, *Charlemagne and the Carolingian Empire* (Amsterdam, 1977), and R. McKitterick, *Carolingian Culture: Emulation and Innovation* (Cambridge, 1994). The campaigns of Charlemagne against the nomadic Avars are well covered in R. Collins's book *Charlemagne*, ch. 6.

The various nomadic peoples migrating to the west during the period considered by this chapter create something of a confusing picture, not least because the sources are limited (and often at variance), and the archaeological evidence is thin. By far the most balanced introduction, with extensive citations to the specialist literature and brilliantly informative endnotes, is C. I. Beckwith, *Empires of the Silk Road: A History of Central Eurasia from the Bronze Age to the Present* (Princeton, 2009). Another excellent but shorter overview is P. B. Golden, *Central Asia in World History* (Oxford, 2011). Of the individual peoples considered in this chapter, references to the Uighurs have been given earlier in this section. For the Khazars, see P. B. Golden, *Khazar Studies* (Budapest, 1980). The vicissitudes of the Avars can be followed in D. Sinor (ed.), *The Cambridge History of Early Inner Asia* (Cambridge, 1990), and their presence in Europe is specifically considered in O. Pritsak, *The Slavs and the Avars* (Spoleto, 1982). The early history and archaeology of the Bulgars is accessibly presented in D. M. Lang, *The Bulgarians: From Pagan Times to the Ottoman Conquest* (London, 1976). The various steppe peoples who settled in eastern Europe and its fringes are discussed in F. Cuta (ed.), *The Other Europe in the Middle Ages: Avars, Bulgars, Khazars and Cumans* (Leiden, 2008).

The development of the trading links between the Scandinavian world and the steppe are considered more fully in the next chapter. A good introduction is T. S. Noonan's essay 'Scandinavians in European Russia', in P. Sawyer (ed.), *The Oxford Illustrated History of the Vikings* (Oxford, 1997), 134–55. J. Graham-Campbell et al. (eds.), *Cultural Atlas of the Viking World* (Oxford, 1994), is an invaluable background source. Other more specialist works include S. Franklin and J. Shepard, *The Emergence of Rus, 750–1200* (London, 1996), and K. R. Schmidt (ed.), *Varangian Problems* (Copenhagen, 1970).

Chapter 10   The Disintegration of Empires, AD 840–1150

Essential background reading for this chapter is C. I. Beckwith's comprehensive overview *Empires of the Silk Road: A History of Central Eurasia from the Bronze Age to the Present* (Princeton, 2009), which has been recommended above. Another very useful source for the complex movements of peoples in western Central Asia is R. Abazov, *The Palgrave Concise Historical Atlas at Central Asia* (New York, 2008), which has the great advantage of clear maps supported by succinct texts.

Once more I have found that M. Rossabi's book *A History of China* (Oxford, 2014) provides a convenient overview of the period covered in this chapter in that it establishes the main competing ethnic groups and sketches their relationship. For the remarkable flowering of Song culture, two works provide an ample background: J. Chaffee, *The Thorny Gates of Learning in Sung China* (Cambridge, 1986), and A. Murck, *Poetry and Painting in Song China: The Subtle Art of Dissent* (Cambridge, Mass., 2000). For the reader wishing to explore the wonders of Song pottery, B. Gray, *Sung Porcelain and Stoneware* (London, 1984), is an excellent place to begin.

Of the various eastern nomadic tribes mentioned, the Khitans and Kara Khitai are given an extended treatment in M. Biram, *The Empire of the Qara Khitai in Eurasian History: Between China and the Islamic World* (Cambridge, 2005). The Jurchens and the Jin dynasty are discussed in H. Franke, 'The Chin Dynasty', in H. Franke and D. Twitchett (eds.), *Cambridge History of China*, vi, *Alien Regimes and Border States, 907–1368* (Cambridge, 1994), 215–320; in the same volume there is an account of the Xixia by

R. Dunnell, 'The Hsi Hsia', 154–214. The rapid development of maritime trade during the Song dynasty is well covered in K. N. Chaudhuri, *Trade and Civilization in the Indian Ocean: An Economic History from the Rise of Islam to 1750* (Cambridge, 1985).

The fragmentation of the Muslim empire is given a straightforward historical treatment in J. Bagot Glubb, *A Short History of the Arab Peoples* (London, 1969), but, for a more extended and up-to-date treatment, see J. Esposita (ed.), *The Oxford History of Islam* (Oxford, 1999), and A. Hourani, *A History of the Arab Peoples* (London, 1991). The rise of the Saffarids and Samanids is well analysed in B. Gafurov, *Central Asia: Prehistoric to Modern Time* (Delhi, 2005). The Karakhanids are given full treatment in P. B. Golden, 'The Karakhanids and Early Islam', in D. Sinor (ed.), *The Cambridge History of Early Inner Asia* (Cambridge, 1990).

The movements of the Turkic peoples across Asia is a complex issue clearly dealt with in P. B. Golden, *An Introduction to the History of the Turkic Peoples* (Wiesbaden, 1992); C. V. Findley, *The Turks in World History* (New York, 2005); and C. E. Bosworth and M. S. Asimov, *History of Civilization in Central Asia: The Age of Achievement, AD 750 to the End of the Fifteenth Century* (Paris, 2004). For the Seljuks, one of the more expansive of the Turkic tribes, see C. E. Bosworth, 'The Political and Dynastic History of the Iranian World, AD 1000–1217', in J. A. Boyle (ed.), *Cambridge History of Iran*, v, *The Saljuq and Mongol Periods* (Cambridge, 1968), 1–102.

The resilience of the Byzantine state is presented in P. Magdalino's essay 'The Medieval Empire, 780–1204', in C. Mango (ed.), *The Oxford History of Byzantium* (Oxford, 2002), 169–208, and its economic underpinning is carefully analysed in A. Harvey, *Economic Expansion in the Byzantine Empire, 900–1200* (Cambridge, 1989). Affairs in the Balkans are analysed in some detail in P. Stephenson, *Byzantium's Balkan Frontier: A Political Study of the Northern Balkans, 900–1204* (Cambridge, 2000). For a convenient survey of early Bulgarian history, D. M. Lang, *The Bulgarians: From Pagan Times to the Ottoman Conquest* (London, 1976), offers a good introduction.

The standard work on the Crusades is S. Runciman's three-volume study *History of the Crusades* (Cambridge, 1951). For an abridged but revised account of the First Crusade, with copious illustration (but without references), S. Runciman, *The First Crusade* (Cambridge, 1980), provides an excellent account that is both lively and scholarly. For more up-to-date accounts, see T. Asbridge, *The First Crusade: A New History. The Roots of Conflict between Christianity and Islam* (Oxford, 2005), and J. Riley-Smith (ed.), *The Oxford History of the Crusades* (Oxford, 1999). A useful corrective to the western perspective is A. Maalouf's popular narrative *The Crusades through Arab Eyes* (London, 1984).

The rise of Rus and the Scandinavian entrepreneurs is neatly encapsulated in T. S. Noonan's chapter 'Scandinavians in European Russia', in P. Salway (ed.), *The Oxford*

Illustrated History of the Vikings (Oxford, 1997), 134–55. The subject is more fully treated in S. Franklin and J. Shepard, *The Emergence of Rus, 750–1200* (London, 1996). Two archaeological studies address the question of trade-inspired urban development: M. A. Brisbane (ed.), *The Archaeology of Novgorod, Russia: Recent Results from the Town and its Hinterland* (Lincoln, 1992), and J. Callmer, 'The Archaeology of Kiev to the End of the Earliest Urban Phase', *Harvard Ukrainian Studies*, 11 (1987), 323–53. The role of the Khazars in articulating trade is well covered in chapters in P. B. Golden, H. Ben-Shammai, and A. Róna-Tas (eds.), *The World of the Khazars: New Perspectives* (Leiden, 2007), particularly T. S. Noonan, 'The Economy of the Khazar Khaganate', 207–44. Of the other steppe people mentioned, the origin and movements of the Magyars are described in G. Balázs and K. Szelényi, *The Magyars: The Birth of a European Nation* (Budapest, 1989), and I. Fodor, *In Search of a New Homeland: The Prehistory of the Hungarian People and the Conquest* (Gyoma, 1975).

Finally, two examples of hoards of texts reflecting on connectivity were given. The Dunhuang cave find is described in fascinating detail in V. Hansen, *The Silk Road: A New History* (Oxford, 2012), ch. 6, which brings together a large number of disparate sources. For the Fustat hoard found in a synagogue store-room, see S. D. Goitein, *A Mediterranean Society: The Jewish Communities of the Arab World as Portrayed in the Documents of the Cairo Geniza*, i (Berkeley, 1967).

Chapter 11 The Steppe Triumphant, AD 1150–1300

The Orkhon valley in Mongolia is a remarkable place, the centre for many of the nomadic confederations from the Xiongnu to the Mongols. Some flavour of the rich cultural heritage of the region is given by a small guide book, N. Urtnasan, *Orkhon Valley Cultural Landscape* (Ulaanbaatar, 2009), which has a very useful bibliography, not all of which is in Mongolian. Another useful source for urban sites in the region is J. D. Rogers, E. Ulambayar, and M. Gallon, 'Urban Centres and the Emergence of Empires in Eastern Inner Asia', *Antiquity*, 79 (2005), 801–18.

As one might expect, there are a lot of books on the Mongols. The best place to begin is with D. Morgan's highly readable *The Mongols* (Oxford, 1986). Other recommended treatments are a brilliantly illustrated and informative catalogue, W. W. Fitzhugh, M. Rossabi, and W. Honeychurch (eds.), *Genghis Khan and the Mongol Empire* (Washington, 2013); J. J. Saunders, *The History of the Mongol Conquests* (London, 1971); P. Brent, *The Mongol Empire: Genghis Khan. His Triumphs and his Legacy* (London, 1976); T. T. Allsen, *Culture and Conquest in Mongol Eurasia* (Cambridge, 2004); and E. D. Philips, *The Mongols* (London, 1969), this last giving a reasonable account of the archaeological evidence. Books dealing specifically with Chinggis Khan include P. Ratchnevsky,

Genghis Khan: His Life and Legacy (Oxford, 1992), and J. Man, *Genghis Khan: Life, Death and Resurrection* (London, 2004). For Qubilai Khan, see M. Rossabi, *Khubilai Khan: His Life and Times* (Berkeley, 1988). Much of the narrative of the life of Chinggis is based on a remarkable near-contemporary Mongolian source, *The Secret History of the Mongols*, compiled before the death of Chinggis's successor Ögedei in 1241. The text has been translated by F. W. Cleaves and published as *The Secret History of the Mongols* (Cambridge, Mass., 1982).

Mongol fighting methods are fully described in H. D. Martin, 'The Mongol Army', *Journal of the Royal Asiatic Society*, 75 (1943), 46–85. See also D. O. Morgan, 'The Mongol Armies in Persia', *Der Islam*, 56 (1979), 81–96, and the same author's 'The Mongols in Syria, 1260–1300', in P. W. Edbury (ed.), *Crusade and Settlement* (Cardiff, 1985), 231–5. The Mongolian approach to administration and government is carefully considered in J. W. Dardess, 'From Mongol Empire to Yüan Dynasty: Changing Forms of Imperial Rule in Mongolia and Central Asia', *Monumenta Serica*, 30 (1972–3), 17–65.

The city of Karakorum, first walled by Chinggis's successor Ögedei, is described in S. Kato, *The Ancient City of Kharakhorum* (Beijing, 1997). The Mongol occupation of China is discussed in a number of papers in J. D. Langlois (ed.), *China under Mongol Rule* (Princeton, 1981). The intriguing relationship between the Mongols and the Crusaders is explored in P. Jackson, 'The Crisis in the Holy Land in 1260', *English Historical Review*, 95 (1980), 481–513, and D. O. Morgan, 'The Mongols in Syria, 1260–1300', in P. W. Edbury (ed.), *Crusade and Settlement* (Cardiff, 1985), 231–5. J. J. Sanders, *Muslims and Mongols* (Christchurch, 1977), deals more widely with events in the Near East. A good source for the Ilkhans in Persia is J. A. Boyle, 'Dynastic and Political History of the Il-khans', in J. A. Boyle (ed.), *The Cambridge History of Iran* (Cambridge, 1968), 303–421. A lively account of the Mongol incursions into peninsular Europe is J. Chambers, *The Devil's Horsemen: The Mongol Invasion of Europe* (London, 1979). J. L. I. Fennell, *The Crisis in Medieval Russia, 1200–1304* (London, 1983), provides an in-depth study of the Russian principalities while D. Sinor, *Inner Asia and its Contacts with Medieval Europe* (London, 1977), broadens the picture to include the full range of interactions.

The Latin advance to the east and its engagement with the Byzantine world is introduced in two chapters in C. Mango (ed.), *The Oxford History of Byzantium* (Oxford, 2002): P. Magdalino, 'The Medieval Empire (780–1204)', 169–213, and S.W. Reinert, 'Fragmentation, 1204–1453', 248–83. More extensive treatments of the period will be found in M. Angold, *The Byzantine Empire, 1025–1204: A Political History*, 2nd edn (London, 1997), and the same author's *A Byzantine Government in Exile: Government and Society under the Laskarids of Nicaea, 1204–1261* (Oxford, 1975).

More specific studies of the west–east struggle for supremacy are to be found in P. Lock, *The Franks in the Aegean, 1204–1500* (London, 1995); D. Nicol, *Byzantium and Venice: A Study of Diplomatic and Cultural Relations* (Cambridge, 1988); and C. Brand, *Byzantium Confronts the West, 1180–1204* (Cambridge, Mass., 1968). The infamous Fourth Crusade is widely covered in the literature. See, for example, M. Angold, *The Fourth Crusade* (Harlow, 2003); G. John, *1204: The Unholy Crusade* (Oxford, 1980); and J. Phillips, *The Fourth Crusade and the Sack of Constantinople* (New York, 2004). Although Venice does not feature large in our narrative, anyone wishing to explore the origins of the Venetian republic should begin with J. M. Ferraro, *Venice: History of the Floating City* (Cambridge, 2012). The manipulating doge is given an extended treatment in T. Madden, *Enrico Dandolo and the Rise of Venice* (Baltimore, 2002). The best source for the famous horses of San Marco is the catalogue of an exhibition held at the Royal Academy, *The Horses of San Marco, Venice* (London, 1979).

The Crusader states and their demise are fully considered in P. Lock, *The Routledge Companion to the Crusades* (London, 2006), and C. Tyerman, *God's War: A New History of the Crusades* (Cambridge, Mass., 2006).

The early travellers from the west to the Mongol empire are well covered in the literature. For John of Plano Carpini, see S. Neill, *A History of Christian Missions* (Harmondsworth, 1964). John's account and that of William of Rubruck are published in translation in W. W. Rockhill, *The Journey of William of Rubruck to the Eastern Parts of the World, 1235–55, as Narrated by Himself, with Two Accounts of the Earlier Journey of John of Pian de Carpine* (London, 1900). For a more recent translation, see P. Jackson, *Missions of Friar William Rubruck: His Journey to the Court of the Great Khan Möngke, 1253–1255* (London, 1990).

Marco Polo and his travels have been the subject of much debate since the account of his travels began to be disseminated. Among the general works to be recommended are L. Olschki, *Marco Polo's Asia* (Berkeley, 1960); L. Bergreen, *Marco Polo: From Venice to Xanadu* (London, 2007); and M. Rossabi (ed.), *The Travels of Marco Polo: The Illustrated Edition* (New York, 2012). There are many editions of the *Travels*. I have used the Everyman edition, M. Komroff (trans.), *The Travels of Marco Polo* (London, 1928). The debate about the validity of the *Travels* is nicely explored in F. Wood, *Did Marco Polo Go to China?* (Boulder, Colo., 1996), and H. U. Vogel, *Marco Polo Was in China: New Evidence from Currencies, Salts and Revenues* (Leiden, 2013). The ocean routes between China and the west are explained in K. N. Chaudhuri, *Trade and Civilization in the Indian Ocean: An Economic History from the Rise of Islam to 1750* (Cambridge, 1985); P. Risso, *Merchants and Faith: Muslim Commerce and Culture in the Indian Ocean* (Boulder, Colo., 1995); and M. Pearson, *The Indian Ocean* (Abingdon, 2003), ch. 3.

A GUIDE TO FURTHER READING

Chapter 12 Looking Back, Looking Forwards

The character of the steppe has been discussed throughout this book in relation to the different peoples who inhabited it and references have been given. Two broad assessments of the steppe in general terms are K. V. Kremenetski, 'Steppe and Forest-Steppe Belt of Eurasia: Holocene Environmental History', and M. A. Bower, 'Green Grows the Steppe: How Can Grassland Ecology Increase our Understanding of Human–Plant Interactions and the Origins of Agriculture?', both in M. Levine, C. Renfrew, and K. V. Boyle (eds.), *Prehistoric Steppe Adaptation and the Horse* (Cambridge, 2003), 11–27, 29–41. M. D. Frachetti, *Pastoralist Landscapes and Social Interaction in Bronze Age Eurasia* (Berkeley, 2008), offers a detailed insight into human–steppe interactions in the Kazakh steppe.

The questions surrounding the rise of nomadism were usefully surveyed in a chapter by E. E. Kuzmina, 'Origins of Pastoralism in the Eurasian Steppes', in M. Levine, C. Renfrew, and K. Boyle (eds.), *Prehistoric Steppe Adaptation and the Horse* (Cambridge, 2003), 203–32, and were later addressed in D. Anthony, *The Horse, the Wheel and Language* (Princeton, 2007). The classic work remains A. M. Khazanov, *Nomads and the Outside World*, 2nd edn (Madison, 1994). Between steppe and sown is a theme extensively explored in P. L. Kohl, *The Making of Bronze Age Eurasia* (Cambridge, 2007).

Of the many themes all too briefly raised in the section 'Thereafter', the end of the Yuan dynasty is described in J. D. Langlois, *China under Mongol Rule* (Princeton, 1981). The origin and early history of gunpowder is classically described in J. Needham, *Science and Civilization in China*, vii, *The Gunpowder Epic* (Cambridge, 1986), and its later spread in I. A. Khan, 'Coming of Gunpowder to the Islamic World and North India: Spotlight on the Role of the Mongols', *Journal of Asian History*, 30 (1996), 41–5. The suggestion that the Black Death was spread by the Mongols is fully discussed in W. H. McNeill, *Plagues and Peoples* (Oxford, 1976), ch. 4. The maritime journeys undertaken during the early Ming dynasty are considered in L. Levathes, *When China Ruled the Seas* (New York, 1994), and F. W. Mote and D. Twitchett (eds.), *The Cambridge History of China*, vii, *The Ming Dynasty, 1368–1644* (Cambridge, 1988). For the journeys of Zheng He, see E. D. Dreyer, *Zheng He: China and the Oceans in the Early Ming, 1405–1433* (London, 2007). The vast subject of the opening up of the world by the maritime explorers of the Atlantic European states is most easily approached through J. H. Parry, *The Age of Reconnaissance, Discovery, Exploration and Settlement, 1450–1650* (London, 1963).

ILLUSTRATION SOURCES

The information for the maps in this volume was compiled by the author using a wide variety of sources. For a number, a starting point has been John Haywood's invaluable *The Cassell Atlas of World History*, i: *The Ancient and Classical Worlds* (Oxford, 1997). Where a single source has predominated, it is mentioned below. Otherwise the source is simply credited as 'author'. Unless otherwise stated, the maps were produced by Encompass Graphics Ltd.

The author and publishers wish to thank the following for their kind permission to reproduce the illustrations:

Title page image: Maggie Herdman

Chapter 1 opener: Maggie Herdman; **1.2** Author, multiple sources; drawn by A. Wilkins; **1.3 and 1.4** Author; **1.5** Roland and Sabrina Michaud/akg-images; **1.6, 1.7, 1.8, and 1.9** Author; **1.10** NASA/Science Photo Library; **1.11** Provided by the SeaWiFS Project, NASA/Goddard Space Flight Center, and ORBIMAGE; **1.12** Friedrich Schmidt/Getty Images; **1.13** Author; **1.14** Maggie Herdman; **1.15, 1.16, and 1.17** Author

Chapter 2 opener: Li Quanju/Imaginechina; **2.1** After maps by ML Design in C. Scarre (ed.) *The Human Past* (London, 2005), fig. 6.1.; redrawn by A. Wilkins; **2.2** Andrew M. T. Moore; **2.3** Israel Museum, Jerusalem/Bridgeman Images; **2.4 and 2.5** Author; **2.6 and 2.7** N. Becker © DAI; **2.8** © The Trustees of the British Museum; **2.9** Author; **2.10 a and b** Joint Kuwaiti-British Archaeological Expedition; **2.11** D. R. Harris; **2.12, 2.13, and 2.14** Author; **2.15** Li Quanju/Imaginechina; **2.16** Guoxiang Liu; **2.17** Author

ILLUSTRATION SOURCES

Chapter 3 opener: Varna Regional Museum of History; **3.1** Colin Monteath/Hedgehog House/Getty Images; **3.2** Maggie Herdman; **3.3** Photo © Asko Parpola; **3.4** Anthony and Brown, 2011 Journal of World Prehistory (2011), 24:131–160, fig. 12; **3.5** M. Videiko, 'Contours and Content of the Ghost: Trypilla Culture Proto-Cities', *Memoria Antiquitatis*, 24 (2007), fig. 4; **3.6** From S. Marinescu-Bilcu, *Tirpesti: From Prehistory to History in Eastern Romania*, British Archaeological Reports S107, (Oxford 1981), fig. 14; **3.7** Moldavia History Museum within Moldova National Museum Complex, Romania; **3.8 and 3.9** Author; **3.10** NASA; **3.11** Author; **3.12** © The Trustees of the British Museum; **3.13a** Photograph © The State Hermitage Museum/photo by Vladimir Terebenin; **3.13b** Photograph © The State Hermitage Museum/photo by Guzenzo; **3.14** Author; **3.15** After A. N. Gei, *Novotitorovskaya kul'tura* (Moscow, 2000); redrawn by A. Wilkins; **3.16** From S. Piggott, *The Earliest Wheeled Transport*, (London, 1983); **3.17** Piggott Archive, Institute of Archaeology, Oxford; **3.18** After E. N. Chernykh, *Ancient Metallurgy in USSR: The Earliest Metal Age* (Cambridge, 1992), fig. 15; **3.19** Varna Regional Museum of History

Chapter 4 opener: © The Trustees of the British Museum; **4.1** Author; **4.2** © The Trustees of the British Museum; **4.3** Author; **4.4 and 4.5** © The Trustees of the British Museum; **4.6, 4.7, and 4.8** Author; **4.9** Author, incorporating detail from P. L. Kohn *Central Asia: Palaeolithic Beginnings to the Iron Age* (Paris, 1984), 16, map 1; **4.10** After Viktor Sarianidi, 'Temples of Bronze Age Margiana: Traditions of Ritual Architecture', *Antiquity*, 68 (1994), figs. 1 and 4; redrawn by A. Wilkins; **4.11** Nadezhda A. Dubova; **4.12** After P. Kohl, *The Making of Bronze Age Eurasia* (Cambridge, 2007), fig. 5.11; redrawn by A. Wilkins; **4.13** Paris, musée du Louvre, photo © Musée du Louvre, Dist. RMN-Grand Palais/Thierry Ollivier; **4.14** Author; **4.15** After V. F. Gening, G. B. Zdanovich, and V. V. Gening, *Sintashta: Arkheologicheskie pamiatniki ariiskikh plemen Uralo-Kazakhstanskikh stepei* (Chelyabinsk, 1992), and G. B. Zdanovich (ed.), *Arkaim: Issledovaniya, Poiski, Otkrytiya* (Chelyabinsk, 1995), with modifications; redrawn by A. Wilkins; **4.16** After V. F. Gening, G. B. Zdanovich, and V. V. Gening, *Sintashta: Arkheologicheskie pamiatniki ariiskikh plemen Uralo-Kazakhstanskikh stepei* (Chelyabinsk, 1992), and N. Vinogradov, *Mogil'nik Bronzovogo Beka: Krivoe Ozero v Yushnow Zaural'e* (Chelyabinsk, 2004); redrawn by A. Wilkins; **4.17** From D. Anthony, *The Horse, the Wheel and Language* (Princeton, 2007), fig. 15.14, which is based on several Russian sources; **4.18** Dmitry Zdanovich; **4.19** After D. Anthony, *The Horse, the Wheel and Language* (Princeton, 2007), fig. 5.15; redrawn by A. Wilkins; **4.20** Author, based on D. Anthony, *The Horse, the Wheel and Language* (Princeton, 2007), fig. 16.10; **4.21** Author; **4.22** Dr Christoph Baumer; **4.23** Idelisi Abuduresule

ILLUSTRATION SOURCES

Chapter 5 opener: Vladimir Terebenin; **5.1** Author, based on J. Haywood, *The Cassell Atlas of World History*, i: *The Ancient and Classical Worlds* (Oxford, 1997), map 1.12, with additions; **5.2** Werner Forman Archive/N.J.Saunders; **5.3** ©Institute of Nautical Archaeology; **5.4** Author; **5.5** Author, based on J. Haywood, *The Cassell Atlas of World History*, i: *The Ancient and Classical Worlds* (Oxford, 1997), map 1.13, with additions; **5.6** ©The Trustees of the British Museum; **5.7** Author; **5.8** Paris, musée du Louvre, photo ©RMN-Grand Palais (musée du Louvre)/Franck Raux; **5.9** Author; **5.10** ©The Trustees of the British Museum; **5.11** ©The Trustees of the British Museum; **5.12** Author; **5.13** After L. Liu and X. Chen, *The Archaeology of China: From the Late Palaeolithic to the Early Bronze Age* (Cambridge, 2012), figs. 8.8 and 8.9; redrawn by A. Wilkins; **5.14** The Metropolitan Museum of Art/Art Resource © Photo SCALA, Florence, 2015; **5.15** After J. Haywood, *The Cassell Atlas of World History*, i: *The Ancient and Classical Worlds* (Oxford, 1997), map 1.27; **5.16** From Qiaobei Kaogudi, 'Shanxi Fushan Qiaobei Shang Zhou mu', *Guadai wenming*, 5 (Beijing, 2006), fig. 5; **5.17** After H. Wu, *Chariots in Early China* (Oxford, 2013), maps 1 and 2, simplified; **5.18** From Beijing daxue Kaoguxi and Shanxi shen Kaogu yanjiusuo, 'Tianma-Qucun yizhi Beizhao Jin hou mudi diliuci fajue', *Wenwu* 2001.8, p.4, fig. 1; **5.19a** From Zhongguo kexueyuan Kaogu yanjiusuo 1959, fig. 39; **5.19b** From Hubei sheng wenwu kaogu yanjiusuo, Xiangfan shi bowuguan, and Yicheng xian bowuguan, 'Hubei Yicheng Luogang chemakeng', *Wenwu* 1993.12, pp. 4–5, fig. 3; **5.20** Photo by Gary Lee Todd, Ph.D., Professor of History, Sias International University, Xinzheng, Henan, China; **5.21** Author, using data from D. Tseveendorj et al., *Historical and Cultural Monuments of Mongolia* [in Mongolian] (Ulaanbaatar, 1999), 68; **5.22** Hakbong Kwon/Alamy; **5.23** M. P. Gryaznov, Inst. of Material Culture, Russian Academy of Sciences, St Petersburg; **5.24** Vladimir Terebenin; **5.25, 5.26, and 5.27** Author

Chapter 6 opener: Scientific-restoration laboratory 'Ostrov Krym', Almaty; **6.1** Author; **6.2** ©The Trustees of the British Museum; **6.3** www.BibleLandPictures.com/Alamy; **6.4** akg-images/Suzanne Held; **6.5** akg-images/De Agostini Picture Lib./N. Cirani; **6.6** After J. Haywood, *The Cassell Atlas of World History*, i: *The Ancient and Classical Worlds* (Oxford, 1997), map 2.09; **6.7** The Art Archive/Alamy; **6.8** Copyright © 2008 National Geographic Society. Reprinted by arrangement with the National Geographic Society; **6.9** After J. Haywood, *The Cassell Atlas of World History*, i: *The Ancient and Classical Worlds* (Oxford, 1997), map 2.22; **6.10** G.Nikolaenko/J.Trelogan/ICA; redrawn by A. Wilkins; **6.11** Drawn by Martin E. Weaver. From E. D. Phillips *The Royal Hordes: Nomad Peoples of the Steppe* (London, 1965); **6.12** Historical Museum, Kiev, Ukraine/Photo © Boltin Picture Library/Bridgeman Images; **6.13** Photographs ©The State Hermitage Museum/photos by Vladimir Terebenin; **6.14 and 6.15** Author;

ILLUSTRATION SOURCES

6.16a Hungarian National Museum; **6.16b** Photograph ©The State Hermitage Museum/photo by Yuri Molodkovets; **6.16c** Photograph ©The State Hermitage Museum/photo by Leonard Kheifets; **6.17** Author; **6.18** Scientific-restoration laboratory 'Ostrov Krym', Almaty; **6.19** © The Trustees of the British Museum; **6.20** Author; **6.21** Photograph ©The State Hermitage Museum/photo by Vladimir Terebenin; **6.22** From S. I. Rudenko, *Frozen Tombs of Siberia* (London, 1970), figs. 4 & 15; **6.23** Photograph ©The State Hermitage Museum/photo by Leonard Kheifets; **6.24 and 6.25** Photograph ©The State Hermitage Museum/photo by Vladimir Terebenin; **6.26** S. I. Rudenko; **6.27** © RIA Novosti/Alamy; **6.28** Author; **6.29** National Museum of China, Beijing

Chapter 7 opener: Afghanistan, Kaboul, Musée national, photo © Musée Guimet, Paris, Dist. RMN-Grand Palais – ©Thierry Ollivier; **7.1 and 7.2** Author; **7.3** Yale University Art Gallery, Dura Europos Collection; **7.4, 7.5, 7.6, 7.7, and 7.8** Author; **7.9** © The British Library Board, Or.8211/26,28,29,30,31,32,35; **7.10** Bridgeman Images; **7.11** Author; **7.12** © Trustees of the British Museum; **7.13, 7.14, 7.15, 7.16, and 7.17** Afghanistan, Kaboul, Musée national, photo © Musée Guimet, Paris, Dist. RMN-Grand Palais ©Thierry Ollivier; **7.18** Photograph ©The State Hermitage Museum/photo by Leonard Kheifets; **7.19** Alinari/Topfoto; **7.20 and 7.21** Author; **7.22** David Peacock

Chapter 8 opener: National Museum of Afghanistan; **8.1** Author; **8.2** Author, using information from E. W. Sauer et al., *Persia's Imperial Power in Late Antiquity: The Great Wall of Gorgan and Frontier Landscapes of Sasanian Iran* (Oxford, 2013), end-paper; **8.3** Westend61 GmbH/Alamy; **8.4** © The Trustees of the British Museum; **8.5** Redrawn from B. Cunliffe, *Oxford Illustrated Prehistory of Europe* (Oxford, 1994), 444; **8.6** Terry Smith Images/Alamy; **8.7, 8.8, 8.9, and 8.10** Author; **8.11** Georg Gerster/Panos; **8.12** Author; **8.13** National Museum of Afghanistan; **8.14** The Author; **8.15** Bill Woodburn; **8.16** Prof. Wang Binghua; **8.17** Author; **8.18** With permission of the Royal Ontario Museum © ROM; **8.19** Author; **8.20** Cultural Relics Publishing House; **8.21** Author; **8.22** Hungarian National Museum; **8.23** Author; **8.24** Roger Arnold/Alamy; **8.25 and 8.26** A. Ochir, L. Erdenebold, S. Kharjaubai and Kh. Jantegin, Editor S. Chuluun, *Excavation Research of Tomb of Ancient Nomads Tribe* (Report on Excavation at Shoroon Bumbagar of Red Alcazar of Bayannuur Soum in Bulgan Province), The Institute of History of the Mongolian Academy of Sciences and L.N. Gumilyov Euroasian National University, Kazakhstan

ILLUSTRATION SOURCES

Chapter 9 opener: Author; **9.1** ©imageBROKER/Alamy; **9.2 and 9.3** Author; **9.4** Werner Forman Archive/Biblioteca Nacional, Madrid; **9.5** Author; **9.6** ©The Trustees of the British Museum; **9.7** Courtesy of Penn Museum image #150171; **9.8** Author, based on C. Mango (ed.), *The Oxford History of Byzantium* (Oxford, 2002), 130; **9.9** Fol. 34v from the Madrid Skylitzes (vellum), Byzantine School, (12th century)/Biblioteca Nacional, Madrid, Spain/Bridgeman Images; **9.10** Author; **9.11** W. Müller-Wiener, 'Von der Polis zum Kastron', *Gymnasium*, 93 (1986); redrawn by A. Wilkins; **9.12** Author; **9.13** ©Roger Wood/CORBIS; **9.14 and 9.15** Author; **9.16** Archaeological Survey of India; **9.17** Author; **9.18** ©The Trustees of the British Museum; **9.19** Author

Chapter 10 opener: ©Berig/Wikimedia Commons/CC-BY-SA-3.0; **10.1 and 10.2** Author, based on J. Haywood, *The Cassell Atlas of World History*, i: *The Ancient and Classical Worlds* (Oxford, 1997), map 3.21; **10.3** Sir Percival David Collection/©The Trustees of the British Museum; **10.4** National Museum of China; **10.5 and 10.6** Author; **10.7** Maggie Herdman; **10.8, 10.9, and 10.10** Author; **10.11** Bibliothèque Nationale, Paris, France/Bridgeman Images; **10.12** ©Ted Spiegel/CORBIS; **10.13** ©Berig/Wikimedia Commons/CC-BY-SA-3.0; **10.14** Author

Chapter 11 opener: British Library, London, Or 2780 f61/Bridgeman Images; **11.1 and 11.2** Author; **11.3** Paris, musée Guimet – musée national des Arts Asiatiques, photo ©RMN-Grand Palais (musée Guimet, Paris)/Thierry Ollivier; **11.4** Author; **11.5** British Library, London, Or 2780 f61/Bridgeman Images; **11.6** Ms Or 20 f.124v, with kind permission of the University of Edinburgh/Bridgeman Images; **11.7** After J. D. Rogers et al., 'Urban Centres and the Emergence of Empires in Eastern Inner Asia', *Antiquity*, 70 (2005), fig. 7; redrawn by A. Wilkins, with modifications; **11.8** Author; **11.9** From D. Morgan, *The Mongols* (Oxford, 1986), map 3; drawn by A. Wilkins; **11.10** akg-images/Gerard Degeorge; **11.11** Author; **11.12** Greg Balfour Evans/Alamy; **11.13 and 11.14** Author; **11.15** ©2014. Image copyright The Metropolitan Museum of Art/Art Resource/Scala, Florence; **11.16** National Museum of China; **11.17** Bibliothèque Nationale, Paris, France/De Agostini Picture Library/Bridgeman Images

Chapter 12 opener: Archivo Oronoz; **12.1** After M. D. Franchetti, *Pastoralist Landscapes and Social Interaction in Bronze Age Eurasia* (Berkeley, 2008), fig. 28; drawn by A. Wilkins; **12.2** The Author; **12.3** with permission of the Royal Ontario Museum ©ROM; **12.4a** National Museum of Tuva, Kyzyl; **12.4b** Photograph ©The State Hermitage Museum/photo by Vladimir Terebenin; **12.5** After W. H. McNeill, *Plagues and People* (Oxford, 1977), 167; **12.6** Drawn by Drazen Tomic after Ian Adkins. From R. Hanbury-Tenison (ed.), *The Seventy Great Journeys in History* (London, 2006); **12.7** The

ILLUSTRATION SOURCES

Philadelphia Museum of Art/Art Resource, 2015 © Photo SCALA; **12.8** Archivo Oronoz; **12.9** After R. Hanbury-Tenison (ed.), *The Seventy Great Journeys in History* (London, 2006), 93; drawn by A. Wilkins

We are also grateful to the following for their immense help in obtaining images from a wide range of sources:
Professor David Anthony, Solongo Ayush, Dorcas Brown, Prof Nadezhda Dubova, Ada Florescu, Prof Valerie Hansen, Prof Simon James, Galina Koretskaya, Gregory Porter, Axelle Russo-Heath, St John Simpson, Xiao Yang, National Museum, Beijing, Hsiao-yun Wu.

The publisher apologizes for any errors or omissions in the above list. If contacted, they will be pleased to rectify these at the earliest opportunity.

Picture research by Sandra Assersohn

INDEX

note: numbers in **bold** refer to illustrations, maps, and diagrams

Abashevo culture 131, **132**
Abbasid caliphate **350**, 360–4, **361**, **371**, 372, **376**, 379
   Byzantine tribute 362
   Byzantium, gains against 362
   culture, art and science 364, 391
   fragmentation 388–93, **389**, **390**, 397
   Mongol destruction of 431
   Muslim ocean trade 365–9, **366**, **367**
   Khazars, relations with 375–6
   Umayyads, difference from 360–1
Abu al-Abbas 360
Abu Bakr 343, 344
Abu Hureyra Epipalaeolithic settlement, Syria 40, **40**
Aceramic Noelithic, fertile crescent 38, 41, 43–7
Achaemenes, King 204, 210
Achaemenid culture 235–6
Acre, fall of (AD 1291) 435, 440
Adrianople, battle of (AD 378) 335
Aetokremnos cave, Akrotiri, Cyprus 54

Afanasievo culture **95**, 101–2, 142, 145–6, 149, 457
   copper production 108
Afghanistan, minerals and precious metals 119–20
Afrasiab palace, Samarkand 341–4, **342**, 349, 351
agate 122
Agia Varvara, Cyprus 54–5
agriculture 35–69, **39**, **42**, **44**, **49**, **57**, **60**, **62**, **68**
   animal domestication and husbandry 36, 43, 68
   beginnings of 41–8, **42**, 461–2
   Baluchistan valley, first agricultural practices 51–2
   China 246, 461, 462
   Danube valley 56–8
   East Asian homeland (8000–6000 BC) 61–6, **62**, **65**, **66**
   European peninsula 53–8, **57**, **59**
   Fertile Crescent **39**, 41–50, **41**, **42**, **44**, **49**
   Nile valley beginnings 50–1
   Pontic-Caspian steppe 56–61, **60**
   Taklamakan desert oasis towns 320
   transition from hunter-gathering 35–41

   see also barley; broomcorn/common millet (*Panicum miliaceum*); cattle; irrigation; pigs; rice; sheep; wheat
Ai Bunar copper mines, Bulgaria 105–6, **105**
Aï Khanum 218–20, **219**
Ain Ghazal, Jordan 43, 44
Ain Jalut, battle of (AD 1260) 442
Akhenaten, Pharaoh 152
Akkadians 114, 115–16, 118
   territory (*c.*2280 BC) **112**
Aksum kingdom 312
Aksumites 338
Al Mina trading enclave, Levant 168
Alagou cemetery, Tian Shan 244
al-Amin 364
Alani tribe 285, 286
Alans tribe 306, **328**, 334, 335
Alashiya, Cyprus 152, 159
Alemanni tribes 302, **303**
Aleppo, Syria 358
Alexander the Great 28, 203–4, 215–17, **217**, 218, 220, 254, 255, 259–60
   territories conquered **216**
Alexandria, Egypt 311
Alexios I Komnenos 398, 399, 402

INDEX

Alexios V 437
Alexios Angelos 436, 437
Ali ibn Abi Talib 346–7, 348
al-Idrisi 387
al-Khorezmi 364, **365**
al-Khwarizmi 412
al-Ma'mun 364
al-Mansur, Caliph 365
al-Sabiyah ceramics, Kuwait **51**
Altai mountains 8, 11, 14, 15, 31, 101, 245, 250, 329
Altai-Sayan region 197, 233, 236–43, **237**, 244, 458, 463, 464
    1600–600 BC 186–92, **187**, **189**, **190**, **192**
Amarna letters 152–4
amber, Baltic 164
Ammianus Marcellinus 334
Amorites 116–17
Amu Darya (Oxus) river 7, 19, **20**, 69, 123, **124**, 138, 218, 235, 322, 323, 324
    delta 139–40, 233–4
Amuq basin 47
An Lushan 352, 353, 379
Anatolia 8, 27, **28**, 29, 37, 194, 196, 204, 311
Andronovo culture 142–3, **143**, **144**, 145, 146, 148, 149, 185, 186, 199
animal art 204
    Scytho-Siberian 127, 188–9, 190, 196–7, 236
Anna Komnene, Princess 402
Antigonos 218
Antioch, First Crusade 402
Antiochus III 256
Anyang ('Great City of Shang') 173
Aorsi tribe 282, 284–5
Aqaba 265
Arab advance (AD 632–750) 338–9, 343–9, **345**, **355**
    Byzantium (AD 632–750) **347**, 348–9, 354–6
    defeat of fleet 677
    demanding Chinese submission 344

Indus valley 344
    and *jihad* 344
Arab-Berber civil war 360
Arabia, importance to Roman trade 311–12, 338
Arabian camel domestication 168, **169**
Arabian Sea 22
Arachosia 218, 220, 255
Aral Sea 7, 19, 88, 233
Aramaeans 160
Aramaic script 209
Ardashir, King 299
Argippaei people 233
Arimaspians 232
Aristeas of Proconnesus 232, 233
Aristotle 215, 364
Arkaim settlement 131, **133**
Armenia 309, 332
    annexed by Rome (AD 114) 259, 265, 266
Arslan Tepe 90, 91, 98
Ártánd cemetery ,Great Hungarian Plain 231
Arzawa state 152
Arzhan cemetery, Siberia 189–91, **191**, **192**, 197, 226
    burial bridal decoration **465**
Ashoka, Emperor 222, 313
Ashurbanipal, King 160
Ashurhaddon, King 194
Ashurnasirpal, King 160
Ashurnasirpal II 162, **162**
Asia Minor 213, 218, 309
ass (*Equus asinus*) 75
Assassins 431
Assyrian Empire 900–612 BC 22, 152, **153**, 157, 159, 160–4, **161**, **162**, 194, 209
    destruction 198
    kings 172
    trading networks 163–4
Ata-Malik Juvaini 422
Athens 213, 214
Attila the Hun 336–7, 398, 459
aurochs 27

Avar Empire 306, 370, 375, 377, 407, 408
    AD 250–650: 229–30, **330**, 331, 337–8
axes, shaft-hole 106
azurite 103

Babylon 89, 152, **153**, 157, 159, 198, 215, 218
    conquest by Persia 204, 210
    control of Mesopotamia 204
    sacking 117
Babylonian city states 114–17
    maritime trade 114, 115
Bacon, Roger 466
Bactria 113, 204, 205, 218, 253, 257, 261, 299, 313
    250 BC–AD 250: 254–6, **255**
Bactria Margiana Archaeological Complex (BMAC) **120**, 124–30, **125**, **126**, 138, 139
    bronze 128
    Gonur-depe royal cemetery 127, **128**, 129, **129**
    horse imagery 130
    metalsmiths 127–8
    sheep 125–7
Bactrian camel 20–1, **21**, 210, 456, **457**
Baghdad 360, 362, 364, 365, 369
    House of Wisdom 364
Balkan Mountains 8
Balkh (Bactra) 11, 28
Bal'ki, lower Dnieper 98
Baluchistan 49, 120, **121**
    first agricultural practices 51–2
Balyktyul settlement 101
Bamiyan monastery, Hindu Kush 316–17, **318**
Ban Chao 261, 274
Barbarikon port 277, 292, 313
barley 26, 41, 42–3, 51, 56
Barygaza port 292
Basra 365
Batu, Khan 425, 432, 433, 442
Bay of Bengal 22

514

Begash, Kazakhstan 67
Begram store-rooms, Afghanistan 279
   ivory carving **279**
   painted glass beaker **280**
   plaster cast **280**
Beijing, *see* Dadu
Belovode, Serbia 104
Belozerka culture 192
Berber tribes 360, 362
Berezan, Black Sea 198, 229
Bindusara, Emperor 222
Bisitun rock relief, Iran 207, **207**
Black Sea 59, 94, 203
   Greek colonization **165**, 168, **195**, 198–9, 203, 223, 224–5, 227–9, 281
blood, drinking 73
Bohemond, knight 402
Bolshoy Salbyksky burial mounds 188
Boris II 397
Bosporan kingdom 203, 229, **229**, 282, 283, 284
Botai culture **95**
   settlement, Kazakhstan 78, **79**
Botai region 455–6
Brahmi script 322
Braudel, Fernand 2, 451
bridal decorations **465**
Britain, first agriculture 58
Bronocice, Poland 98
bronze 31, 104
   ceremonial axe, Khinaman cemetery, 119, **119**
   China 463
   coinage, China 246–7
broomcorn/common millet (*Panicum miliaceum*) 62–3, 64, 65, 67
bubonic plague (Black Death) 466–8, **467**
   China **467**, 468
   and trade networks 468
Budakalász, Hungary 98

Buddha (Siddhartha Gautama) 313, 314
Buddha statues 316
   Bamiyan 317
   Fire Buddha, Kabul **315**
   jade Buddha, Sri Lanka 318
   Yungang 317
Buddhism 222, 254, 256, 295, 328
   spread of 313–20, **314**
   and trade 316
Bug river 60
Bukhara 324, 326, 421, 422
Bulgar khanate 375, **376**, 377, **408**
   relations with the Byzantines 396
   Volga **376**, 378, 424
Burgundians 298, 306
Buwayhid tribal confederation 391, 395
Buzurg ibn Shahriyar 367
Byblos 166
Byzantine Empire 304, 306, **306**, 326, 338, 344, **376**, **392**, 393, 396–9
   AD 435–40: **438**
   AD 627–780: 354–60, **355**, **357**, **358**, **371**
   administration and military 356–7
   Arab advance (AD 632–750) **347**, 348–9, 354–6
   and the Avars 338
   and the Bulgar khanate 396
   economic contraction 357–9, **359**
   and the First Crusade 398, **400**, 402
   geographical position 357–8
   Khazars, relations with 375
   Latin Church, conflict with 398
   and northern nomads 406–9, **408**
   Persia, conflict with 331, 332
   Rus, relations with 403
   Sasanians, conflict with 309–11, 312

   Seljuk Turk onslaught 398
   tribute to the Abbasids 362

Cadiz 166
Cambyses, Emperor 206
camels 17
   Bactrian 20–1, **21**, 210, 456, **457**
   domestication in Arabia 168, **169**
   dromedary 22
cannibalism 234
caravan routes 18, 101, 139, 163, **169**, 261, 262, 308, 316, 365, 375, 377
   Arabian peninsula 168–9, 265, 312, 338
   Gansu Corridor 18, **18**, 286–7, 409
   Kirghiz **12**
   Mesopotamia 258, 259, 291
   and the Mongols 433, 468
   Palmyra 260, 308, **308**
   and Red Sea ports 168, **169**, 265, 366
   Samarkand 11, 256, 324, 326, 421, 422
   Tarim Basin 320, 321, 325–6
   towns and cities 254, 260, 272, 325–6, 364
caravels, Portuguese **471**
carnelian beads 2, 93, 122, 244
Carolingian dynasty 298, 370, 372, 379, 397
Carpathian/Balkan region copper and metal production 105–7, **105**, **106**
Carpathian mountains 8, 14, 59
carriages, Pazyryk **240**
Carthage and the Carthaginians 166, 253
   destruction (146 BC) 262
Caspian Sea 17, 19, 59, 88
Caspian steppe, *see* Pontic-Caspian steppe
Cassander 218
Catacomb culture, Don-Kuban region 95, 142

INDEX

Çatalhöyük, Central Asia Minor 43, 47, 104
cataphract cavalry, Parthian 234, 258, **259**
cattle 43
   wild 50
Caucasus Mountains 8, 59, 84–8, **85**, **86–7**, **125**
cavalry:
   China 247
   nomads on the north China border 298
   Parthian 234, 258, **259**
   Persian 211–12
Celts, and population pressure 3
Central Asian deserts 2500–1600 BC 138–41
   pottery 138–9
   Sintashta–Petrovka zone 140–1
   tin mining, Zeravshan region 139, 141
   Zardchakhalif grave 139, **140**
   see also desert cities of Western Central Asia
Chaghatai khanate 425, 431, 435
Chaironeia, battle of (338 BC) 214
Chaldaeans 160
Chandragupta Maurya 218, 220
Chang'an 326, 350, 354
   sacking 381–2
chariot burials, Beizhao, Shanxi **180**, 181, **183**
chariots 31, 113, 463
   as close-combat weapon 211–12
   Shang and Zhou periods 149, 151, 179–83, **180**, **182**, **183**
   Sintashta culture **134**, 135, 136–8
   spread of technology 137–8
Charlemagne 370–3, **371**, 377, 379, 407–8
Charles Martel 370
Chekhov, Anton 16
Chenopodium (goosefoot) 186
Chersonesos settlement, Crimea 223, 224

Chertomlyk burial, Dnieper valley 226
chickpeas 41
Childe, Gordon 461
China 25, 29–31, **30**, 69, 242, 254, 330
   1700–481 BC 172–9, **174**, **178**
   800–600 BC 199–201, **200**
   600–250 BC 204, 245–9, 250
   250 BC–AD 250: 248, 253, 266–7, **267**, **269**
   AD 220–618: 295, 296–9, **297**
   AD 840–1150: 381–8, **383**, **384**
   agriculture, rise of 246, 461, 462
   Altai, trade with 242, 244
   animal domestication 68
   and the Avars 329
   bronze casting 463
   bubonic plague (Black Death) **467**, 468
   Buddhism, spread of 313, **314**
   copper metallurgy introduction 113, 148–9
   embassy mission (AD 950) 409–10
   five dynasties period (AD 907–60) 382, **383**
   Grand Canal 430
   Imperial Drugs Office 412
   invasion of Central Asia 333
   long-distance trade routes 464–5
   'long walls' 248, **249**
   Muslim ocean trade 367–9
   northern nomad neighbours 199–201, **200**, 204, 245–9, 250, 266–72, **267**, **269**, 296–8
   paper money **446**
   Persian ocean trade 368
   sedentary states and empires 452–4
   and the Sogdians 325–6
   Spring and Autumn period (770–481 BC) 172, 199, 245

   and Taklamakan oasis cities 321–2, 323
   Warring States period (480–221 BC) 172, 204, 244, 245–9, 268
   see also individual dynasties and empires
Chinese almanac 274
Chinese burial figure of a foreigner, sixth century **322**
Chinggis Khan 415–16, 417–18, **418**, 419–21, 421–5, **423**, 434, 459, 461
   death 424, 425
chlorite 119, **119**
   sources **118**
Chorasmia 206, 235
Christian/Jewish riots 312
Christianity 295, 298, 304, 369
   Europe 29
   Frankish Empire and the Roman Church 370, 373–2
Chu dynasty, China 181, 245
Cimmerians 192–4, **193**, 198, 230
   and predatory nomadic pastoralism 197
Cishan settlement, China 65
Claudius, Emperor 254
climate change 7–8
   central Asia (3300–3100 BC) 7
   and social systems 4
Colchidean Plain 88
Columbus, Christopher 472
Confucianism 247
connectivity, Eurasia 33, 293, 453, 465–6
   2500–1600 BC 111–13
   250 BC–AD 250: 253–93
   AD 840–1150: 409–11
   Central Asia/China 144–5, 147, 148–9, 242
   East Asian homeland 30–1
   intensifying 25
   maritime links from the Fertile Cresecnt 51–2

516

ocean passage (AD 1150–1300) 447–8
South West Asian 29
Tarim basin 244–5
Constantinople 326, 338, 354, 397, **436**
   Arab sieges 349, 354–5, 356
   sacked by Crusaders (AD 1204) 437–9
   siege of (AD 820) **347**
Constantine the Great, Emperor 304, 436
copper metallurgy 115, 457
   Afanasievo culture 108
   alloying process 93, 104
   arsenic/copper-antimony alloys 104, 107
   BMAC 127–8
   and bronze technology 31, 104
   Carpathian/Balkan region 105–7, **105**, **106**
   China 113, 148–9
   Iranian plateau 119–20
   Late Uruk period 90–1
   lost-wax method 104
   and pottery kilns 103
   Seima-Turbino complex 142–3
   shipments to Ur 113
   Sintashta culture 131–4, **132**
   steppe corridor (3000–2500 BC) 103–8, **105**, **106**
   steppe corridor (1800–1200 BC) 186
   Yamnaya complex 97–8, 107
Corinth, destruction of 262
cotton and cotton fabrics 93
   Indus valley 120–2
Council of Clermont (AD 1095) 399, **401**
Crete 397
   early settlements 55
Crimea 332, 334
Crimean Tatars 434
Criş site, Transdanubia 58, 59
Croats 397
Croesus, King 204
crossbow, invention of 246

Crusades 399–403
   First (AD 1095–9) 395, 398, **400**, 401–2, 435
   Second (AD 1147–9) 402
   Third (AD 1189–1192) 435–6
   Fourth (AD 1202–4) 436–40, **438**
Ctesiphon, Sasanian capital 309, 311
Cucuteni-Tripolye culture 60–1, 80–4, **81**, **82**, **84**
   mega-towns 83
   pottery 80, **83**
Cuman-Kipchaks 393–4, 397, 432, 442
cylinder seals:
   Maikup culture 93
   Uruk period 90, **93**
cylindrical container, Bactria **119**
Cyprus (Alashiya) 164, 166, 397
   Arab conquest 346, 348–9, 354
   early settlements 54–5
Cyrus Cylinder **206**
Cyrus the Great 204–6, 209, 213, 215, 235, 299

Dacia 262, 263, 284
Dadu (Beijing) 416, 419, 428–30, **429**, 443
Damascus 360
   Arab control 344
   Mosque **346**
Dandolo, Enrico 436–7, 440
Danube 14–15, 98
   delta region 84, 458
   lower 95
   spread of agriculture 56–8
Darius I 206–8, **207**, 210, 211, 213, 214
   burial 216–17
Darius III 215
deer stones, Altai-Sayan region **187**, 189, **189**
Delian League 213
Demosthenes 214
desert cities of Western Central Asia 2500–1600 BC 122–30, **123**, **124**, **125**

BMAC 124–30, **125**, **126**, **130**
deserts 13, 17–22, **18**, **19**, **20**, **21**
dhimmis (protected non-Muslim subjects) 344, 347–8
Dholavira **121**, 122
Di people 248
diamonds 222
Diaotonghuan cave, Yangtze valley 63
Dilmun **112**, 114, 170
Diocletian, Emperor 264, 304
Diodorus 211–12, 215, 281
Diodotus Tryphon **283**
DNA analysis, Tarim burials 146
Dnieper valley region 84
Dniester valley 60, 72
Dobruja (Little Scythia) 232
Dome of the Rock, Jerusalem 354
Don river delta 222, 223
Donghuishan, Gansu Corridor 148
Dongxiafeng, China 173
dromedary camel (*Camelus dromedarius*) 22
Dunhuang monastic site, Gansu 18, **317**
   documents 409–10
Dura Europos 308, **310**
Dzungarian Depression 71, 144, 243, 244, 245

East Asian homeland 29–32, **30**
   agriculture (8000–6000 BC) 61–6, **62**, **65**, **66**
   climate 31–2
   connectivity 30–1
   in the Younger Dryas 31–2
East China Sea 22, 30, 31
Egypt 152, **153**, **155**, 157, 158, 160, 215, 218, 309, 311
   Persian rule 206, 210
   trade 166
einkorn wheat 26, 41, 43, 56
Elam 115, 116–17, 118–19, 120, 128, 152, **153**, 156, 157, 159, 160
   fragmentation 130
   horse imagery 141

Elburz Mountains 8
elephants 220
   African 289
   in warfare 218
Elizavetovka settlement, Don delta 225
emmer wheat 26, 56
Epipalaeolithic period:
   Fertile Crescent 38, 41
   foragers 54
   Late 39
Equus hydruntinus 75–6
Eratosthenes 2, 472
Erdene Zuu Monastery **426**, **427**
Erlitou culture (1900–1500 BC) 148–9, 173, **174**
Euboea 166–8
Euphrates river 7, 26, 254, 308, **310**
Eurasia 4–8, **5**
   'big geography' 451–2
   fourteenth century 466
   mountain skeleton 8–11, **9**
Eurasia 1600–600 BC 151–201
   Altai-Sayan region 186–92, **187**, **189**, **190**, **192**
   China and the early states (1700–481 BC) 172–9, **174**, **178**
   Chinese chariots 179–83, **180**, **182**, **183**
   Chinese states and nomads (800–600 BC) 199–201, **200**
   collapse of the regional kingdoms (1200–900 BC) 157–60
   maritime systems in the West 164–8, **165**
   Medes and Persians on the Iranian Plateau (1400–600 BC) 170–2
   Near East great powers (1500–1200 BC) 152–7, **153**
   Pontic-Caspian steppe nomads 192–6, **193**, **195**
   Red Sea and Persian Gulf (1500–600 BC) 168–70, **169**

steppe culture and the Western sedentary states (800–600 BC) 198–9
steppe corridor (1800–1200 BC) 183–6
Eurasia 250 BC–AD 250: 253–93
   Bactria and Gandhara 254–6, **255**
   China and her northern neighbours 266–72, **267**, **269**
   Han campaigns in the western zone 272–5, **273**
   Kushan Empire **276**, 277–80
   migrating nomads 275–7, **276**
   ocean networks 298–93, **291**
   overland connections 285–9, **288**
   Parthian Empire, and their Roman neighbours 256–62, **257**, **259**
   Roman Empire 262–5, **263**, **266**
   Sarmatians: Pontic steppe and beyond 281–5
Eurasia AD 250–650: 295–340
   Alans 334
   Arab awakening 338–9
   Avars 329–30, 337–8
   China (AD 220–618) 295, 296–9, **297**
   Hephthalites (White Huns) 299, 313, 327–9, **330**, 331, 335
   Huns 327, **328**, 334, 335–7
   Indus corridor, and spread of Buddhism 313–20, **314**
   Persia and the Sasanians 295, 299–301
   Red Sea and the Arabs 311–13
   Rome and Byzantium 301–6
   Rome and the Sasanian Empire 306–11
   Sogdian middlemen 323–6
   Tarim Basin 320–3
Eurasia AD 650–840: 341–80
   Abbasid Empire 360–4, **361**, **371**
   Arab advance (AD 632–750) 338–9, 343–9, **345**, **347**, 354–6, **355**

   Byzantium (AD 627–780) 354–60, **355**, **357**, **358**, **371**
   Muslim ocean trade 365–9, **366**, **367**
   rise of the far west 369–73, **371**
   Scandinavians 377–9
   steppe corridor (AD 650–840) 373–7, **376**
   Tang Empire 349–54, **350**, **353**
Eurasia AD 840–1150: 381–406
   Byzantines 396–9, 406–9
   China: collapse, reunification and division 381–8, **383**, **384**
   connectivity 409–11
   Crusades 399–403, **400**
   Muslim Empire, fragmentation 388–93, **389**, **390**
   Pontic-Caspian steppe 406–9, **408**
   Rus and Scandinavian entrepreneurs 403–6
   Seljuk Turks 394–6
   Turks on the move 393–4
Eurasian interface interaction (state/nomad) 600–250 BC 203–50
   Central Asia 204–20, 232–6, 250
   Chinese states 204, 245–9, 250
   Greek maritime interface 203, 222–9, 250
   Greek/Pontic steppe 236
   Greeks/Scythians (Black Sea littoral) 223, 224–5, 227–9
   India 220–2
   Persia/Central Asia 235–6
   Persian Empire 203–4, 205–6, 207–8
   Tian Shan and Taklamakan desert 243–5
European Peninsula **28**, **29**, **32**
   spread of agriculture 53–8, **57**, **60**
Eynan (Ain Mallaha), Syria 40

fallow deer 55
Fars province, Iran 204
Fatimid dynasty 391, 410

Faxiang, Buddhist scholar **314**, 318–19
felt working 74
Ferghana valley 11, 145, 274
    horses 274, **275**, 459, **460**
Fertile Crescent 26–7, **28**, 32, **44**, 69
    6900–5400 BC 47–9, **49**
    beginnings of agriculture 38–41, **39**, **41**, 41–50, **42**, **44**, **49**, 461, 462
    changing environment 37–41, **39**
    Holocene period 26–7
    maritime and trading links 51–2
    Younger Dryas 37–8, **39**, 39–40, 41
    see also Mesopotamia
Filippovka burial goods, Ural region 236
Finns 403
First Punic War (262–241 BC) 253, 262
fitnah ('time of temptation'), Muslim civil war 347, 348
Five Dynasties, China (AD 907–60), 382, **383**
Flaming Cliffs, Gobi desert **18**
flax spinning and weaving 56
Flintbek, Germany 98
forest-steppe zone 16–17, 222, 223–4
    500–300 BC **229**
    Eastern Europe 59, **60**, 61
foxtail millet (*Setaria italica*) 31–2, 62–3, 64, 67
Franchthi Cave, Gulf of Argos 54
frankincense **169**, 170, 311–12
Frankish Empire and the Franks 298, 302, 306, 369–73, **371**, 377, 379, 453
    and the Christian Church in Rome 370, 372–3
    trade routes 370–2
Frederick Barbarossa, Emperor 435–6
furs 74
Fustat synagogue archive, Cairo 409, 410–11

Galen 364
galena 103
Gan Ying 261
Gandhara 204, 205, 253, 299, 313, 322, 328
    250 BC–AD 250: 254–6, **255**
    art 256
Ganges valley 122
Gansu (Hexi) Corridor 18, **18**, 31, 243, 244, 272–3, **273**, 286, 318, 417, 464
    2500–1600 BC 113, 144, 148–9
    under Mongol control 419
    and the Tang Empire 350, 354
Gaozong, Emperor 351
Gaugamela, battle of (331 BC) 215
Gaul 334, 336, 337, 369
gazelles 38
geographical determinism 7–8
Germanic tribes 302, 334, 335, 336
Ghaznavids **392**, 394, 395
gift exchange 27, 40, 74, 453
    Near East (1500–1200 BC) 154–7
Gimirrai, Cimmerian mercenaries 194
giraffes, presentation to Ming court **470**
goats 43
    BMAC complex 125–7
    domestication, Pontic-Caspian Steppe (5200–4500 BC) 74–5, **75**
Göbekli Tepe 43, **45**, **46**
Gobi desert 17–18, **18**, **21**, 31, 32, 144
Godin Tepe 117, 119
gold **116**, 206, 214, 222
    Afghanistan 119–20
    Carpathian/Balkan region 106–7
    chariot model, Oxus treasure **235**
    coinage, Kushan 278, **278**
    craft works made by Greeks for Scythians 227–8
    drinking vessel, Kul'-Oba kurgan 228, **228**

    pectoral, Tolstaya Mogila kurgan **227**, 228
    sources **118**
    stag ornaments, Scythian period **231**
Golden Horde khanate 425, 433–4, 435
Gondwanaland 4
Gonur-depe settlement 125, **126**, 139
    royal cemetery 127, **128**, 129, **129**
goosefoot (*Chenopodium*) 96
Gorgan Wall, Sasanian 327
Goths 282, 302, 335
Great Hungarian Plain 11, 14, **14**, 71, 95, 98, 102, 142, 194, 204, 230, 231, 232, 335–6, 337, 377, 455
Great Hypostyle Court, Karnak, Egypt **155**
Great Mosque, Sidi Uqba **363**
Great Temple, Medinet, Thebes 158
Great Wall of China 31, **267**, 268, **269**, 430
Greater Xing'an Mountain 15
Greece 1–2, 3, 250
    Black Sea colonization **165**, 168, **195**, 198–9, 203, 223, 224–5, 227–9, 281
    early settlements 55–6
    interaction with nomads 203
    maritime systems **165**, 166–8
    Persian hostility 207, 211, 212, 213
    Philip II 214–15
    Scythian interactions 227–9
    see also Alexander the Great; Hellenism; individual city states
Greek fire 355, 356, **357**
griffins 233
Guangzhou 367–8, 369, 388
    destruction of (AD 878) 381, 387
Guiscard, Robert 398
Gulf of Oman 24
Gumugou cemetery, Lop Desert 146–7
gunpowder 411
    introduction from China 466

INDEX

Guo Xi 412
Guptas, Northern India 313
Gutians, Zagros mountains 116
Güyük, Great Khan 425
Gyges, King 194

Hacinebi Tepe 90
Hadrian, Emperor 260, 264
Hagia Sophia, Istanbul **404**
Halafian culture **44**, 47–8
 painted pottery **48**
Halfdan, Varangian guard **404**, **404**
Hammurabi, King 117
Han Dynasty 18, 68, 253, 254, 268, 277, 282, 321, 464
 campaigns in the western zone 272–5, **273**
 campaigns against the Xiongnu 270–2
 collapse 296
 Great Wall **267**, 268, **269**
 heqin treaty 270
 Kushan, relations with 278
 overland trade routes to the Roman world 285–9, **288**
 overland trade routes to Parthia 260–2
Hanshu, Chinese text 243–4
Harun al-Rashid, caliph 362, 388
hashish 238
Hatti 152, **153**, 154, 157, 158
Hattusa 158
 archives 152–4
Hattusili III 154
Hellenism 254–6
 eastern outposts 204, 218–20
Hephthalites (White Huns) 299, 313, 327–9, **330**, 331, 335
Heraclius, Emperor 311, 354
Herat, Afghanistan 120
 Mongol destruction 425
Herodotus 192, 193, 194, 196, 206, 210, 211, 212, 215, 223–6, 232, 233–4, 238, 243, 464
Hetian, Khotan 149
Hindu Kush 8, 11, 28, 88, 218, 313

Hippalus, sailor 24
Hippocrates 364
Hittites **155**, 158
 Hattusa archives 152–4
 sacking of Babylon 117
Holocene period:
 Early 37
 Fertile Crescent 26–7
Holy Land 440–2
Homer 2, 192–3
horse (*Equus caballus*) 17, 75–80, **76**, **79**, 250
 burials 73, 77, 79, 238, **241**, **460**
 domestication 77, 465
 effects of domestication on steppe pastoralism 459–60, 462–3
 Egypt 141
 Ferghana valley 274, **275**, 459, **460**
 hunters, Botai 101
 Maikop elite 94, **94**
 milk 78
 Persian cavalry 212
 Tang dynasty **460**
 Ur 116
 Yuezhi 244
horse-gear:
 bridles, cheekpieces and bits 78–9, **79**, 187
 head gear **241**
 Massagetae 234
 Sintashta culture **135**, **140**
 Vekerzug culture 231
horse imagery:
 BMAC 130
 Ur III period 141
horse riding and training 77–80, **79**, 94, 459–60
Hu people, China 247–8, 249
Huan, Emperor 261
Huang Chao 381
huckleberry seeds 65
Hülegü, Khan 431, 435, 442
human mobility and population pressure 3–4

Huns 25, 327, **328**, 334
 cauldron **329**
 'picked men' 336
 and the Roman Empire 335–7
 see also Hephthalites (White Huns)
hunter-gatherer communities, in transition 10,000–5000 BC 35–41, **39**

Iazyges tribe 283–4
Iberia 166, 304, 334, 360, 362, 369, 370, 388, 412
 Arab conquests in 348, **361**
 Roman control 262
Ibn Fadlan 405–6
Ibrahim ibn al-Aghlab 362
Idrisid caliphate of the Maghrib 388
Ifriqiya Aghlabid emirate 388
Ili valley 243, 244, 245
Ilkhanate, Mongol 431–2, 433, 435
Immortals (Persian bodyguard) 212
Imperial Drugs Office, China 412
India 210, 242, 253–4, 299, 323
 Altai trade 242, 244
 Buddhism, spread of 313
 Hephthalite control 327, 328, 239
 Indo-Sasanid rule 313
 interface with Greek culture 220
 Mauryan Empire 220–2, **221**
 Xuanzang's journey 319–20
Indian Ocean **24**
 cyclic weather patterns 23, **24**
 seaways 290
Indian ship **448**
Indo-European language groups 170–2
Indus Corridor 254, 313
Indus river 299
Indus valley 7, 27–8, **28**, 49, 69, 114, 207, 220
 2500–1600 BC 120–2, **121**
 and Arab advance 344
 first agricultural practices 51–2
Ingvar rune stones, Grisholm 406, **406**

520

INDEX

Ingvar the Widefarer 406
Innocent IV, Pope 442
inquisitiveness and travel 1–2
Iranian Plateau 304–5
    2500–1600 BC 117–20, **118**
    1400–600 BC 170–2
    Afghanistan tin and precious metals 119–20
    trade in minerals and precious metals 119–20
Ireland, first agriculture 58
iron 164
    casting, China 246
Iron Gates, Danube river 14
irrigation 3, 36, 46, 122
    and agriculture 113
    BMAC systems 127
    canals 47
    Chinese systems 246
    Uruk period systems, 89
Islam 29, 295, 311, 312–13
    beginnings of 339
    see also Arab advance
Ismail Samani mausoleum, Bukhara **390**
Ismailis, Shia 390
    Nizari branch 431
Issedonians 232, 233
Issus, battle of (333 BC) 215
Issyk grave, Lake Balkhash 234–5
ivory 122
    Assyrian 166

jade 2, 25, 149, 287
    nephrite 244
    white 244
    workers 66
Jade Gate Pass, China 18, 31
Japan, rice cultivaton 64
javelins 212
Jebel Ash Sharqi mountains 26
Jebel Lubnān mountains 26
Jeitun, Turkmenistan 52–3, **53**
Jeremiah 194
Jerf el-Ahmar, Syria 42–3
Jericho 43, 47

Jerusalem 311, 344, 354, 372
    falls to the Mamluks 440
jet 74
Jews 204, 209
Jiaohe, Turfan Depression **324**
Jin dynasty 179, **384**, 386, 417
    Mongol invasion 419, 421, 424, 427, 428
    royal family cemetery, Beizhao, Shanxi 181, **183**
Jochi, Khan 425
John of Plano Carpini 17–18, 442, **444**
John Skylitzes 357
Jordan river 26
Julian, Emperor 309
Jun Yao foliate dish, Northern Song **385**
junks, Chinese 22–3, 447, 468–71, **469**
Eastern Han dynasty **387**
Jurassic period 4
Jurchens 385, 386, 417, 428
Justin II, Emperor 306, 312
Justinian, Emperor 306, 309–10, 358, 375
Juvaini, Ata-Malik 424

Kabul, Afghanistan 28
Kairouan, Tunisia **363**
Kalhu, Assyria 162–3
Kalka River, battle of (AD 1223) 424
Kalon Minaret, Bukhara **391**
Kanishka I **278**
kaolin 173
Kara Khitai ('Black Khitans') 386, **392**, 395, 421–2, 432
Karakhanids 390, **392**, 394, 395, 409
Karakoram Mountains 8, 11, 254, 313
Karakorum 415–16, **426**, **427**, 443, 466
Karakum ('Black Sand') desert 19, 52, 88, 203, 205
Karasuk culture 187–8, 197, 199, **200**

Karbala massacre (AD 680) 348
Kargaly copper mines, Orenburg 107, 186
karim convoy of ships 411
Kashgar 11
Kazakh steppe 15, 31, 59, 71, 80, 101–2, 131, 138, 142, 233, 243, 245, 332, 463
Kazakhstan, transhumance routes **456**
Kharijite sect 360, 362
Kharoshthi script 322
Khazar khanate 375–8, **376**, 393, 403, 405, 407, **408**, 461
    Abbasid relations 375–6
Khinaman, Iran 119, 120
Khitan tribe 352, 382–4, 385, 386, 415, 417
Khiva, Uzbekistan 17, 364, **365**
Khorasan 364, 365, 421, 424
    Seljuk conquest (AD 1038–40) 391, 395
Khorsabad, Iraq **166**
Khotan kingdom 323, 409
Khotan river 320
Khvalyn Sea 59
Khvalynsk cemetery, Volga region 61, 73, 74
Khwarezmid Empire 421, 422, 431
Khyber Pass 28
Kiev 403, 405, 432
    Mongol capture of 432
Kievan Rus 407, **408**
Kilwa, East Africa 411
Kirghiz caravan **12**
Kirthar mountains 27
Klandy tomb, Maikop culture 94
Knossos, Palace of 55
Koguryo protectorate 351
Kohl, J. G. 7, 12
Kongfuzi (Confucius) 247
Kopet Dag mountains 19, 52, 88
Koran 339
Korea 351
    rice cultivation 64
Körös site, Transdanubia 58

521

INDEX

Kostromskaya burial, Caucasus 226, **226**
Krak des Chevaliers, Syria 441
Krasnoyarsk cemetery, Afanasievo culture 102
Kroraina kingdom 322–3
Kuban valley 222
Kucha, Tarim Basin 320–1, 323
Küchlüg, ruler 421–2
Kujula Kadphises, ruler 277
Kul'-Oba kurgan 228, **228**
Kura-Araxes/Early Transcaucasian culture 88
Kushan Empire 254, 256, **279**, **280**, **281**, 299, 313
    250 BC–AD 250: **276**, 278
    AD 114: **257**
    gold coins 278, **278**
    relations with Han 278
Kyrgyz tribe 374
Kyrgyzstan 8
Kyzylkum ('Red Sand') desert 19, **21**, 88, 203, 205, 324

lacquer-work 287
lactose-tolerant mutation 73
lapis lazuli 2, 93, 115, **116**, 119, 287
    Aï Khanum mines 220
    sources **118**
Lapita people 1
Last Glacial Maximum (LGM) 4, 37, 38, 59, 61, 62, 76
Late Epipalaeolithic settlement, Zagros Mountains 41
lateen-rigged boats, Islamic 22–3
Latin language 298
Laurasia 4
Lchashen cemetery, Armenia **99**
Lechfeld, battle of (AD 955) 408
Legnica, battle of (AD 1241) 433
Leo III, Pope 370
Levant 204, 205
Li Yanben, horse relief **353**
Liao dynasty, China 382, 385, 386, 417
Libya, Persian conquest of 206

Libyans 158
Linearbandkeramik 58
    influence in Eastern Europe 59–60
Linzi, China 245
Liu Bang of Han 268
Livy 3
Lombards 370, 396
Lop dessert 18, 144
lost-wax casting techniques 104
    Seima-Turbino complex 142–3
    BMAC 127–8
Lothal, Gulf of Khambhat 122
lotus, edible 64
Louis IX 442
Louis the Pious 373
Loulan documents 287–8
Loulan silk bolts, Xinjiang **352**
Luoyang 178, **178**, 296
    Hena horse figure burial **460**
Lydia 194, 204, 210, 213
Lysimachos, ruler 218

Macedonia 203, 207, 213, **216**, 218, 250
    *c.*270 BC **255**
    rise of 214–15
Maes Titianus 261
Maffeo Polo 443
Magan trade **112**, 114–15, 170
Magyars 393, 407–9, **408**
Mahayana Buddhism 313, 316
Mahmud of Ghazni 394
Maikop culture 102
    copper production 107
Maikop elite (3700–3100 BC) 91–5, **92**, **94**
    burials 91–3, **94**
    horses 94, **94**
malachite 103, 105, 106
Malaya 22
Malik Shah 395
Mamluk sultanate 431, 433, 435, 440, 441–2
Manchuria 11, 351
Manda, East Africa 411

Manzikert, battle of (AD 1071) 395, 398
Mao Gong Ding, bronze vessel 181
Marathon, battle of (490 BC) 213
Marco Polo 11, 120, 429, 430, 443–5, **444**, 447, 454
Marcomannic Wars (AD 166–80) 284, 302
Marcus Aurelius 262, 284
Marcus Licinius Crassus 258
Margiana, oasis town 113, 205
Marhashi, Iranian plateaux 116
marine shells 122
maritime/ocean trade routes 468–72
    250 BC–AD 250: 289–93, **291**
    AD 1150–1300: 447–8
    and Babylonian city states 114, 115
    Fertile Crescent 51–2
    Greek **165**, 166–8
    Muslim 365–9, **366**, **367**
    Persian Empire 211, 368
    Phoenician networks (1000–600 BC) 164–6, **165**, **167**
    Sasanians 299
    systems in the West 164–8, **165**
Mariupol cemetery, Dnieper valley 73
Massagetae 196, 205–6, 233–4, 334
Mauryan Empire, India 220–2, **221**
mawalis (non-Arab converts) 360
Maximian, Emperor 304
Meander, King 256
Medes 170–2, 196, 198, 204, 212, 338–9
medicine 411–12
Medina 339
Mehrgarh, Pakistan 51
Meluhha, Indus valley **112**, 170
Mengzi (Mencius) 247
Merovingian dynasty 370
Mesopotamia 2900–1600 BC 2, 113–17, **116**
    Akkadia **112**, 114, 115–16, 118

Early Dynasty period (2900–2350 BC) 114–15
Third Dynasty of Ur 116–17, 118–19, 130, 141
see also Fertile Crescent
Mezőcsát culture, Hungary 194
Miletus 168, 198
millet cultivation 67, 122
  steppe corridor 67, **68**
  Yellow River valley (8000–6000 BC) 61–3, **65**, 64–6
Milos 54
Ming dynasty, China 31, 430, 468
  African giraffes **470**
  maritime exploration 469–71
Mitanni tribe 152, **153**
Mithridates I 256
Modu, leader of the Xiongnu 269–70, 459
Mohenjo-Daro 120, **121**
Möngke, Great Khan 425, 428, 431, 434, 442
Mongol Empire 7–8, 16, 22, 25, 415–16, 419, 458, 465, 466
  Abbasid caliphate, destruction of 431
  army 417–19, **419**, **423**
  bubonic plague 466–8, **467**
  Central Asia, conquest of **420**, 421–5, 442–3
  China, conquest of 425, 427–30
  Chinggis death 425
  European conquests 432–4
  Herat destruction of 425
  Ilkhanate 431–2, 433, 435
  Khwarezmid Empire, destruction of 422
  Kiev, capture of 432
  Middle East 431–2
  passport **445**
  population pressure 4
  in retrospect 434–5
  rise of 417–21, **420**
  Song China, destruction of 419, 425, 427–30, 434–5
  Syria 441–2

Mongolia 15, 31, 71, 102, 149, 189, **187**, 204, 243, 244, 245, 249, 298–9, 327
monsoon winds 23, 24, 31, 289–90
Morocco 166
Muawiyah, governor of Syria 347
Muhammad, Prophet 339, 343, 345, 360
Murghab river 123–4
Muryan India 255
Muslim art and science 412
Muslim ocean trade with China 365–9, **366**, **367**
Muslim religion 343
Muyunkum desert 19, **21**
Myanmar (Burma) 22
Mycenae 152, **153**, 159
  collapse of city states 164
  kings 156
  traders 164
Mylouthkia, Cyprus 55
Myos Hormos (Quseir el-Qadim) **293**
myrrh **169**, 170, 311–12

Nabta Playa 50
Nanjing, China 296
Natufian culture 38, 40–1
  sickle handle, Mount Carmel **41**
  trading enclave, Nile delta 168
navigational aids, maritime 469
Neolithic period:
  European peninsula 56–7
  the 'revolution' 461
  systems of exchange 453
Nestor, King 2
Netherlands, first agriculture 58
Neve David, Israel 38
Niccolò Polo 443
Niketas Choniates 439–40
Nile delta 158
Nile valley 7, 27, **28**, 49, 69
  first agricultural practices 50–1
Nimrud, Assyria:
  palace of Ashurnasirpal II **162**

sacking (612 BC) 172
Nineveh, Assyria 163
  sacking (612 BC) 160, 172, 198, 204
Niya coffin, Xinjiang province **319**
nomads of the steppe 7–8, 201, 203, 204, 454–9, **456**, **457**, 465
  Alexander the Great, and the Greeks 222–9
  Altai-Sayan 233, 236–43
  Byzantium and 406–9, **408**
  Caspian and Kazakh steppe 232–6
  Central Eastern 205–6
  China, relations with 245–9, 266–72, **267**, **269**, 296–8
  Chinese states (800–600 BC) 199–201, **200**
  Chinese states (600–250 BC) 245–9
  and farming states neighbours 407, 459–61
  Great Hungarian Plain (600–250 BC) 230–1
  horse riding and pastoralism 455–6, 459–60, 462–3
  migrating (200 BC–AD 100) 275–7, **276**
  Persia (600–250 BC) 204–12
  Pontic-Caspian steppe (1600–600 BC) 192–6, **193**, **195**
  Pontic steppe (600–250 BC) 222–9
  Tian Shan and Taklamakan desert 243–5
  predatory nomadism 458–9
  wheeled vehicles 455
  see also individual tribes and peoples; predatory nomadism
Normans 398
North Caspian Depression 59
North Sea-Baltic interface 370
Northern Song dynasty (AD 960–1127) 382–6, 385
Nouruz Zoroastrian festival 342

obsidian 27, 40, 54, 115
oceans 22–5, **24**
    and climate 5–7
    see also individual oceans and maritime networks
Offa of Mercia, and gold coin **372**
Ögedei, Great Khan 425, 428, 432, 433, 434
Olbia, Black Sea colony 198, 223, 224, 229
Oman 114
onager (*Equus hemionus*) 75
Orkhon valley, Mongolia 415–16, **416**
Orontes river 26
Ostanni, Kuban river 98
Ostrogoths 334, 335
Ottoman Turks 437, 468
ox-drawn wagons, Yamnaya complex 80, 96, 97, **97**, 98–101, **99**, **100**, 455
Oxus Treasure, Central Asia 235, **235**

painted pottery:
    Arpachiyah, Iraq **48**
    China 149
Palmyra, Syria 288–9, 308, **308, 309**
Pamir 'knot' 8, **9**
Pamir mountains 11, **12**, 17, 19, 275, 324
Pangaea 4, 6
Panlongcheng, China 173
Pannonia 337
Panticapaeum (Kerch) 229, 282
paper money, Chinese **446**
papyrus 166
Parni tribe 253, 256
Parthian Empire 25, 29, 253, 254, 277, 285
    control of trade routes 265, **266**
    overland trade routes to China 260–2
    Parthian shot 258

Roman conflict and invasions 256–62, **257, 259**, 278–9, 299, 308
    trade routes into Mesopotamia 260
Pazyryk culture 233
    cemetery, Altai 189, 197, 236–42, **237, 238, 239, 240, 241**, 244
    chieftains 454
Pearl river rice cultivation 64
Pechenegs 393, 397–8, 407, **408**
Peloponnese, early settlements 55–6
Pepkino mass grave, Sura river 137
Peppin II 370
Peppin III 370
Periplus of the Erythrean Sea, The 23–4, 290–1
Persepolis 208, **208, 209**, 210, 215
Pershin grave, Ural region 97
Persian Empire 198, 213, 323, 324, 242, 250, 454
    1400–600 BC 170–2
    AD 250–650: 295, 299–301
    Alexander's conquest of 215–17
    annual tributes 210
    army 211–12
    Byzantines, conflict with 331, 332
    Hephthalite control of 327
    infantry 212
    navy 211
    nomad interface/interaction (600–250 BC) 203–4, 205–6, 207–8
    ocean trade with China 211, 368
    and Philip II of Macedon 214–15
    provinces (satratpies) 209–12, 215
    rise of 204–9, **205**
    Rome, conflict with 311
    royal roads 210–11
Persian Gulf 22
    Muslim ocean trade 365–6
Peter the Hermit 401
Petrovsky, General 17
Philip the Arab, Emperor **301**
Philip II of Macedon 214–15, 217

Philistines 158
Phoenician maritime systems 1000–600 BC 164–6, **165, 167**
    merchants 163
    vessels **166**
pigs 43
Piora Oscillation 72, 82–3
Pithekoussai colony, Bay of Naples 168
plague (AD 166) 264
Plataea, battle of (479 BC) 213
plate tectonics 4–5, **6**, 8, **9**, 26
Plato 364
Pliny the Elder 264–5
Pliny the Younger 265
Poland 60, 98, 231, 433
Poltavka culture 96
Polybius 255
Pontic-Caspian steppe **95**, 141–2, 334, **376**, 432, 464
    1600–600 BC 192–6, **193, 195**
    470–430 BC 223
    400–300 BC **229**
    geography and topography 15, 71
    spread of agriculture 59–61, **60**
Pontic-Caspian steppe (5200–4500 BC) 72–80
    burial rituals 72–3, 73–4
    gift-exchange networks 74
    herders and farmers 59–61, **60**, 67, 72–80, 455
    horse domestication 17, 77, 462
    sheep and goats 74–5, **75**
    wool spinning and weaving 74–5
population growth:
    Aceramic Neolithic 41
    Epipalaeolithic period 38
    and human mobility 3–4
porcelain 368
Portuguese maritime exploration 471–2, **472**
pottery:
    Cardial/Impressed Ware 58
    Central Asian deserts 138–9
    Cucuteni-Tripolye culture 80, **83**

introduction of 38
painted, Arpachiyah, Iraq **48**
painted, China 149
potter's wheel invention 66
Sintashta culture 131, 139, 141
skyphoi 167–8
Yangtze valley 63
predatory nomadism 204, 466
Altai-Sayan region 190, 192, 458, 464
China (Shang and Zhou dynasties) 151, 201
emergence of 7, 151, 192, 197, 458–9, 463, 464, 465
and the Scythians 194–5, 197–8
Sytho-Siberian culture 190, 192
Priscus, Byzantine writer 375
Procopius, Byzantine writer 327
proto-cuneiform writing 91
Przewalski's horse, Hustai National Park, Mongolia **76**
Ptolemaic kingdom, c270 BC **255**
Ptolemy 218, 276
purple dye 358

Qadesh, battle of (1274 BC) 154, **155**, 157
Qadisiyah, battle of (AD 637) 344
Qana, Gulf of Aden 292
Qarluq tribe 374
Qarmatians 388
Qarshi oasis settlement 324
Qatwan, battle of (AD 1141) 386
Qi of Shandong 179
Qijia culture **144**, 148
Qilian Mountains 18
Qin dynasty, China 179, 181, **246**, 248, 253, 266–8, **267**, 269
quadrifrons of Galerius **305**
Qubilai, Great Khan 416, 425, 428–30, 434–5, 443
quernstones 43
Quraish clan 338–9
Qutayba ibn Muslim 343

Rameses II 154

Rameses III 158
Rashid al-Din **423**
Raymond of Toulouse 401
Red Sea 22, 24, 265, 289–93, 311–12
Muslim ocean trade 365, 366
and Persian Gulf (1500–600 BC) 168–70, **169**
Red Sea/Nile canal 211
Rhodes, Arab capture of 355
rice cultivation 32, 36, **68**, 69, 122
Yangtze valley (8000–6000 BC) 61, 62, **62**, 63–4
Richthofen, Ferdinand von 11
riddah wars, Muslim 343
Rift Valley 26
ritual tripod (ding), Shang dynasty **176**
Riurik the Rus 403
rock crystal 74
Roman Empire 22, 25, 29, 253, 254, 304, 453, 454
201 BC–AD 700: 262–5, **263**, **266**
AD 114: **257**
AD 250–650: 301–11
annexation of Armenia (AD 114) 259, 265, 266
Arabia and trade 311–12, 338
Bosporan kingdom annexation (65 BC) 282, 283
consumerism 264–5
Eastern Empire 304–6, 337
Huns 335–7
Iazyges conflict 284
long-distance trade routes 464–5
Marcomannic Wars (AD 166–80) 284, 302
Mesopotamian trade routes 260
and the northern 'barbarians' 295, 298, 301–4, **303**, 306, 334
overland routes to China and India (AD 100–200) 285–9, **288**
Parthia, conflict with 256–62, **257**, **259**, 278–9, 299, 308
Persia, conflict with 311

Punic Wars 253, 262
Sasanian Empire, conflict with 195, 299, 300, 306–11
Sicily, annexation of 253, 262
ships 464
splitting into eastern and western 304
Tetrarchy system 304, **304**
trade with Han China 261–2
Western Empire 253, 304, 306
Rong people 248
Roxanne, princess 216
Roxolani tribe 283–4
Rudna Glava copper mine, Serbia 105–6, **105**
Rus 378, 403–5
emergence of 378
relations with Byzantium 403
Rustichello da Pisa 445
rye 40, 41, 42–3

Sabatinovka culture 192
Saffarid emirate 389
Saka people 206, 207, **207**, 208, **209**, 220, 233–5, 236, 243–4, 245, 256, 257, 275, 276
chieftain **234**
Saka Haumavarga 234
elite burials 234–5
Saka Tigrakhauda 234, 235
Salamis, battle of (480 BC) 211, 213
Samanid emirate 389–90, **391**, 393, 394, 405, **408**
Samaria 163
Samarkand (Marakanda) 11, 256, 324, 326, 421, 422
sampans and prahus 22–3
Sardinia 56, 164, 166, 262
Sardis 194
Sargon II 163, **166**, 194
Sargon III 160
Sarmatian (Sauromatae) tribes 196, **229**, 232, 234, 281–5, **283**, **286**, 302
Sasanian Empire 278, 299–301, **300**, 306, 331, 338, 344

525

Byzantium, conflict with 309–11, 312
    dominance in southern Arabia 312
    Hephthalites, conflict with 327–8
    maritime trade 299
    Roman Empire, conflict with 195, 299, 300, 306–11
    rule in northern India 313
    silver coins 323
    silver dish **302**
Sauromatae, *see* Sarmatian tribes
Scandinavia (Varangians) 403, 404, 405
    AD 650–840 377–9
    first agriculture 58
    trade with Muslim Asia 405–6
Scythians 152, 168, **193**, 194–6, **195**, 198, 199, 207, 236, 281–2, 283, 284, 459
    elite burial practices 223, 225–6, **226**
    ethnic variety 223–5
    in Europe 230–1, **230**
    interaction with Greeks 227–9
    origins 196–8
    Pontic steppe (600–300 BC) 222–9
    population pressure 4
    and predatory nomadic pastoralism 197
    westward movement 232
Scythian-Saka cultures 459, 465, 466
    elite burials 464
Scytho-Sarmation culture **229**
Scytho-Siberian art style 127, 188–9, 190, 196–7, 236
Sea of Azov 59, 168, 198, 203, 229, 282, 334
'sea people' 159
sea travel and settlement:
    Mediterranean 11000–7000 BC 54–6
    Mediterranean 6000–5000 BC 58

seals:
    BMAC culture 128
    chariot depiction Karum Kanesh, Anatolia 137
    Maikop culture 93
    Uruk period 90, **93**
sea-shells 40
Second Punic War (218–202 BC) 262
sedentary states and empires 452–4
Seima-Turbino complex 142–3
Seleucid Empire (c270 BC) 255, **255**, 256
Seleukos 218, 220
Seljuk Turks 386, 391, **392**, 394–6, 421
    attacks on Byzantium 398
    and the First Crusade 402
    Khorasan conquest (AD 1038–40) 391, 395
Sennacherib, King 160, 163, 194
Septimius Odainat 308–9
Serbs 397
Seti I **155**
Shabwa incense burner **169**
Shahanshahnama miniature **423**
Shahdad, Iran 119, 120
Shahr-i Sokhta 119, 120
shamans, Siberia 73
Shang dynasty, China 113, 148, 149, 151, 172–8, **174**, **175**, **176**, 188, 459–60, 463
    chariots and chariot burials 149, 179–80, **180**, **181**
    and the steppe nomads (800–600 BC) 199–201, **200**
Shanidar Cave, Iraq 103
Shapur I **301**
Shapur II **302**
sheep 43
    BMAC complex 125–7
    domestication Pontic-Caspian Steppe (5200–4500 BC) 74–5, **75**
    wool 108
shell beads 74
Shia Islam:

Ismailis, 390
    Nizari branch 431
    Sunni split, and conflict 348, 360, 388, 390
Shia-i Ali 348
Shiji (Sima Qian) 268, 271–2
Shillourokambos, Cyprus 55
Shimashki people 117
Shortughai trading post 122
Shu kingdom, China 296, **297**
Siba culture **144**, 148
Sicily 56, 164, 166, 168, 396, 398, 410
    Arab conquest 355–6
    Roman annexation 253, 262
sickle, composite 40, **41**
siege warfare 419, 423
silk 254, 287, 323, 326, 358
    and Roman women 264–5
silk bolts 351, **352**
Silk Road 10, 11, **12**, 245, 250, 254, 274–5, **324**, **325**, 385, 409, 411
    settlements **319**, **324**
silver 115, 210, 214
    Afghanistan mines 120
    exports to Scandinavia 378
Sima Qian (*Shiji*) records 268, 271–2
Sintashta culture 130–8, **136**, 179
    Arkaim 131, **133**
    burial practices and rites **134**, 135–6, **136**
    chariots **134**, 135, 136–8
    copper production 131–4, **132**
    horse-gear **135**, **140**
    pottery 131, 139, 141
Sintashta-Petrovka culture 142
Sintashta–Petrovka zone 140–1
Siraki tribe 282
Sistan, Afghanistan 120
Six Dynasties period, China (AD 220–581) 295, 296–8
Skuka, King 234
slave trade 111, 114, 166, 198, 223, 227, 272, 282
    Byzantine 378, 403
    Muslim 372, 374, 376–7, 378
    Rome 336

Slavs 306, 356, 403
social mechanisms, and population pressure 3–4
Sogdiana tribes 205, 299, 323–6, 328, 331, 333, 341, 373
    chief **325**
solid-wheeled battle wagons 137
Solomon, King 170
Song dynasty, China 417, 466
    industrial revolution 411–12
    Mongol invasion 419, 425, 427–30, 434–5
    trade 411
Song dynasty, Northern (AD 960–1127) 382–6, **385**
Song dynasty, Southern **384**, 386–8
Song Taizu, Emperor 382
sorghum 50, 122
South China Sea 22, **24**, 30, 319, 368, 369, 387
South West Asian homeland 26–9, **28**
    connectivity 29
Spring and Autumn period, China (770–481 BC) 172, 199, 245
Sri Lanka, spread of Buddhism 313, 318
Srubnaya (Timber Grave) culture 142, **143**, 185–6, 192
St Mark's Basilica, Venice **439**
Starčevo, Transdanubia 58
Stein, Sir Aurel 274, 352, 409
Stephen, King 409
steppe 2500–1600 BC 111–49, **112**, **118**, **121**, **123**, **125**, **132**, **143**, **144**
    Central Asian deserts 138–41
    connectivity and trading networks 111–13
    desert cities of Western Central Asia 122–30, **123**, **124**, **125**
    Gansu Corridor 148–9
    Indus Valley 120–2, **121**
    Iranian Plateau 117–20
    Mesopotamia 113–17, **116**
    Sintashta culture 130–8, **132**, **133**, **134**, **135**, **136**, 141

Western steppe, Early Second Millennium 141–7
steppe AD 1150–1300: 415–48, **416**, **444**
    after Chinggis death 425
    Holy Land 440–2
    Latin advance 435–40, **438**
    Mongol conquest of Central Asia **420**, 421–5
    Mongol conquest of China 425, 427–30
    Mongol thrust into peninsular Europe 432–4
    Mongols in the Middle East 431–2
    Mongols in retrospect 434–5
    ocean passage 447–8
    rise of the Mongols 417–21
    travellers from the west 442–5, **444**
steppe corridor 11–17, **13**, **14**, **15**
    6000–4000 BC (Atlantic period) 70–1
    5000–2000 BC 71–109
    3000–2500 BC, copper smelting and technology 103–8, **105**, **106**
    1800–1200 BC 183–6
    800–600 BC, and the Western sedentary states 198–9
    AD 650–840: 373–7, **376**
    climatic variations 15–16
    millet cultivation 67, **68**
    nomadic tribes mentioned by classical writers **233**
    'steppe gradient' 16
    wheat cultivation 67, **68**
steppe interface with Europe, 4300–3500 BC 80–4, **81**, **82**, **83**, **84**
    mega-towns 83
    and the Piora Oscillation 82–3
Strabo 282, 284, 290
Strait of Malacca 22, 30
stupas 316
Subetei, General 424, 432

Suevi tribes 334
Sui dynasty, China 296, 298–9, 321
Sulaiman mountains 27
Sunni/Shia split, and conflict 348, 360, 388, 390
Susa 90, 91, 115, 117, 118, 210, 211
Suvorovo-Novodanilovka culture 84, **84**
Svobodnoe settlement, North Caucasus 74
Syr Darya (Jaxartes) river 19, 123, 138, 139, 203, 205, 233–4, 235, 322, 323
Syria 308, 311, 441–2
Syria-Palestine 152, 157

Tacitus 335
Tagar culture 187, 188–92, 197
    deer stones **187**, **189**, **189**
    grave goods 188, 189–90, 190–1
Taiwan Strait 22
Taizong, Emperor 353
Tajikistan 8
Takht-i Kuwad hoard 235
Taklamakan desert 2, 11, 17, 18, **18**, **19**, 21, 31, 32, 144, 243–5, 254, **321**
    and China 321–2, 323
    oasis towns 320–3, 325–6
Talas, battle of (AD 751) 349
Tal-i Iblis, Iran 104
Taliban 317, 318
Talljanky, Ukraine **81**
Tanais (Tanis) 168, **195**, 198, 229, 282, **283**, 285
Tang dynasty, China 31, 296, **297**, 299, 323, 326, 330, 341, 349–54, **350**, **353**, 379, 459
    An Lushan rebellion 352, 353
    disintegration 381–2
    and the Gansu Corridor 350, 354
    Grand Canal 350
    horse figure **460**
    silk bolts 351, **352**
    and the Tarim basin 350, 351, 352, 353, 354

Tibet, relations with 353–4
Turfan, Tarim basin 323, 325, 328, 351
Uighurs, relations with 374
Taoism 247
Tarim basin 19, 145–7, 243, 244–5, 272, 273–5, **273**, 276, 287, 289, 313, 325–6, 328, 331
   burials **145**, 146–7, **147**
   burials, DNA analysis 146
   links with China 148–9
   and the Tang Empire 350, 351, 352, 353, 354
   travel (AD 250–650) 320–3
Tatars 417
Taurus mountains 26
tectonic plates 4–5, **6**, **8**, **9**, 26
Tejen river 123–4
Telemachus 2
Tell Brak 91, 115
Temple of Jerusalem 209
temples, Uruk period 89–90, 91
   Eanna 98
Tepe Hissar 90, 171
Tepe Sialk 90
Tepe Yahya, Iran 117, 119, 120
'terracotta warriors' 267
Tertiary period 29
Tethys Ocean 4
Tetrarchy system, Roman Empire 304, **304**
Thailand, rice cultivation 64
Thar desert 27
Theodosius I 304
Theravada Buddhism 313–14
Thessaly, early settlements 55–6
Third Punic War (149–146 BC) 262
Thomas the Slav **347**
Thrace 207, 214, 215, 218, 335
Tian Shan mountains 8, 11, 17, 19, 243–5, 320, 321
Tiberius, Emperor 264
Tibet 8, 299
   cemetery, Lop desert 144, **146**–7
   relations with Tang Empire 353–4

Tiele tribe 375
Tiemulike culture 243
Tigris river 7, 26
Tillya Tepe tomb, Afghanistan 280
   'Dragon Master' **281**
   gold crown **281**
tin 115
   Afghanistan 120
   sources of **118**
   Zeravshan region mining 139, 141, 142
Tingzhou, battle of (AD 791) 354
Tirpeşti, Moldovia **82**
Toba Tartars 298
Toba Wei dynasty, China **297**, 298, 323, 327, 386
Togolok 21 **126**, 139
Tolstaya Mogila kurgan **227**, 228
Tolui, Khan 424, 425
trade 453–4
   2500–1600 BC 111–13
   AD 40–1150: 409–11
   Assyrian networks (900–612 BC) 163–4
   beginnings of ocean 222
   and Buddhism 316
   Egypt 166
   and 'exchange' 2–3
   Frankish Empire 370–2
   Han dynasty 260–2
   Iranian plateau 119–20
   long-distance networks 464–5
   Near East (1500–1200 BC) 156
   networks, and bubonic plague (Black Death) 468
   Parthia 260–2, 265, **266**
   overland routes between Roman world, India and China, (AD 100–200) 285–9, **288**
   see also caravan routes; maritime/ocean trade routes; Silk Road
Trajan, Emperor 259–60, 263, 265, 284, 285
Trajan columns **286**
Transcaucasia 88
   3000–2500 BC 102

Transylvania 230
travellers from the West (AD 1150–1300) 442–5, **444**
Trialeti wagon burial, Georgia **100**
trilobite arrowheads 231
triremes 211
Triumphant Visions of the Boundless Ocean (Ma Huan) 23
Truşeşti, Botoşani, Cucuteni vessel **83**
Tugai settlement 139
Tulunid emirate 388
Tureng Tepe 171
Turfan 323, 325, 328
   Tang administration 351
Turkmenistan 333
Turks 298–9, 299, 326, 329–34, **330**, 343
   burial, Shoroon Bumbagar **332**, **333**
   grave marker, Bayan Olgi **331**
   khanates (east and west) 330–3, 373
   on the move 393–4
Turks, Ottoman 437, 468
turquoise 93, 115, 119

Ubaid culture 48
   Early period culture **44**
   Early period ceramics **51**
   Later period **44**
Ugarit 158, **159**
Uighur tribe 373–4, 379, 415, 421
Uluburun shipwreck 156, **157**
Umar, Caliph 348
Umar ibn al-Khattab 344, 346
Umayyad caliphate 346–9, 360, 370, 388
   difference from Abbasids 360–1
   relations with the Khazars 375
Uqba ibn Nafi 348, 363
Ur 114, 115
   burial goods **116**
   copper shipments 113
Ur, Third Dynasty 116–17, 118–19
   fall of 130

horse imagery 141
Royal Tombs 115, **116**
Ural Mountains 15, 59
Urartu kingdom 194
Urban II, Pope 399, 401, **401**, 403, 435
Uruk period, late expansion 75, 89–95, **92, 93**, 102
  copper 90–1
  demise 114
  specialization 89–90
  'Standard List of Professions' 90
  trading networks 90–1, **92**, 93, **93**, 95
  writing 90
Ust'ye 131
Uthman ibn Affan 346
Uzbekistan 7, 8, 17, **20**, 349, 386

Valentinian III 337
Valerian, Emperor **301**, 308
Vandals 334
Varangian Rus 376
Varangians, *see* Scandinavians
Varkhuman, King 341–3, **342**, 351
Varna cemetery, Bulgaria **106**, 107
Vasco da Gama 469, 471
Vasudeva I 278
Vekerzug culture **230**, 231
Venice 346–7, 438, 439–40, **439**
Via Egnatia 397, 401
Vietnam, rice cultivation 64
Visigoths 298, 306, 334
Volga Bulgars **376**, 378, 424
Volga river 377–8
Volga-Ural steppe, and herding 61
Vorovskaya copper mines, upper Ural valley 134

Wadi el-Natuf 38
warfare, and population pressure 3
Warring States period, China (480–221 BC) 172, 204, 244, 245–9, 268
  and the Eastern Zhou (771–221 BC) 179, 181

water buffalo 68, 89, 120
water caltrops 64
Wei dynasty, China 296, **297**, 298, 329
Wei Zhuang 382
Wen-Amon 166
Western steppe, Early Second Millennium 141–7
  Andronovo culture 142–3, **143, 144**, 145, 146, 148, 185, 186, 199
  Zeravshan tin ore workings 142–3
wheat cultivation 29, 31, 51
  steppe corridor 67, **68**
wheeled vehicles, *see* ox-drawn wagons
wild rice (*Orryza rufipogon*) 32, 62
William of Rubruck 442–3, **444**, 445, 466
Witaszkowo, Poland 231
women:
  Massagetae 234
  Sauromatae 232
woollen fabrics 94
  Late Uruk period 91
  spinning and weaving 74–5
writing system, proto-Elamite 117
Wu, Emperor 177, 261, 270–1, **272**, 274
Wu kingdom, China 296, **297**
Wuling, King 247
Wusun people 274, 275, 276
Wuwei 'flying horse', China **275**

Xanadu 416, 443
Xenophon 212
Xerxes, Emperor 207, 212, 213, 214
Xia dynasty, China 172–3
Xianbei people 296, 298, 317, 327
Xiaohe cemetery, Xinjiang **147**
Xiashanping, Gansu Corridor 67
Xiazhou Tanguts **384**
Xinglongwa, China **66**
Xinjiang cultural groups **144**
Xintala cemetery 145

Xiongnu people 244, 249, 274, 275, **276**, 277, 296, **329**, 373, 415
  accounts in the *Shiji* history 271–2
  and the Han dynasty 253, 261, 268–72, 273, 282
  and the Huns 335
Xixia kingdom 384, **384,** 417
  Mongol invasion 419, 421, 424, 427
Xuanquan documents 263, 287
Xuanzang, Chinese monk 19, 319–20, 326, 332, 453

Yamnaya complex 3300–2800 BC 7, 16, 95–101, **95, 97, 99, 100,** 142, 185, 455, 458
  copper production 97–8, 107
  graves 96–7, **97**
  ox-drawn wagons 80, 96, 97, **97,** 98–101, **99, 100,** 455
Yan people 248
Yang Jian, Sui Wendi 298–9
Yangtze river 7, 30, 31, 32, 36, 69
  rice cultivation (8000–6000 BC) 61–4
Yanshi Shang city **175**
Yellow river 7, 15, 30, 31, 36, 69, 248
  millet cultivation (8000–6000 BC) 61–3, 64–6, **65**
Yellow Sea 22
Yelü Chuchi 419–20
Yelü Dashi 386
Yemen (Sheba) 168–70, 299, 311
Yijing, Buddhist monk 368–9
Ying Zheng (Qin Shihuangdi), Emperor 245, 253, 266
Yinxu, China 149
Younger Dryas 4, 29, 38, 50, 461
  East Asian homeland 31–2
  effects around the Mediterranean 54–5
  Fertile Crescent 37–8, 39–40, **39,** 41

529

rice cultivation 63
Yellow River region 64
Yuan dynasty, China 428–30, 435, 468
Yuezhi nomads 244, 245, 257, 275, 276
Yungang, China 317

Zagros Mountains 26, 27, 36, 37, 41, 51
Zardchakhalif grave 139, **140**
Zawi Chemi Shanidar, Iraq 41
zebu cattle 51, 68, 120
Zenobia 309
Zeravshan river 8, 139, 186, 324
Zhang Qian 261, 272, 274, 278, 282, 287
Zhao people 248
Zheng He 23, 469–71
Zhengzhou 173–4, **175**, 177, 179
    Shang city **175**
Zhou dynasty, China 151, 172, 177–9, **178**, 245, 248, 460
    chariots and chariot burials 180–3, **182**, **184**, **185**
    Eastern Zhou (771–221 BC) 172, 179, 181
    and the steppe nomads (800–600 BC) 199–201, **200**
    Western Zhou (1046–771 BC) 172, 179
Zhou Quefei 447
Zi, Shang dynasty 173
Ziwiye gold belt, Iran **171**, 172
Zoroastrianism 301, 326